*Moral and Spiritual
Cultivation
in Japanese
Neo-Confucianism*

SUNY Series in Philosophy
Robert Cummings Neville, Editor

# Moral and Spiritual Cultivation in Japanese Neo-Confucianism

*The Life and Thought of*
*KAIBARA EKKEN*
*1630–1740*

MARY EVELYN TUCKER

*State University of New York*
*Press*

The illustrations of flowers, fish, birds, and shells are taken from an undated nineteenth-century edition of Kaibara Ekken's *Yamato Honzo* (Plants of Japan) given to the author by Kimie and Tatsuhiko Watanabe of Okayama city, Japan.

Published by
State University of New York Press, Albany

For information, address the State University of New York Press,
State University Plaza, Albany, NY 12246

**Library of Congress Cataloging-in-Publication Data**

Tucker, Mary Evelyn.
    Moral and spiritual cultivation in Japanese Neo-Confucianism : the life and
thought of Kaibara Ekken, 1630–1714 / Mary Evelyn Tucker.
        p.    cm. — (SUNY series in philosophy)
    Bibliography: p.
    Includes index.
    ISBN 0-88706-889-8.    ISBN 0-88706-891-X (pbk.)
    1. Kaibara, Ekiken, 1630–1714.  I. Title.  II. Series.
B5244.K254T83   1989
199'.52—dc19                                                88-15381
                                                                CIP

10  9  8  7  6  5  4  3  2  1

To
Wm. Theodore de Bary
and
Thomas Berry
to celebrate a friendship of four decades—


*"How delightful it is when friends come from afar."*
*—Analects* 1.2

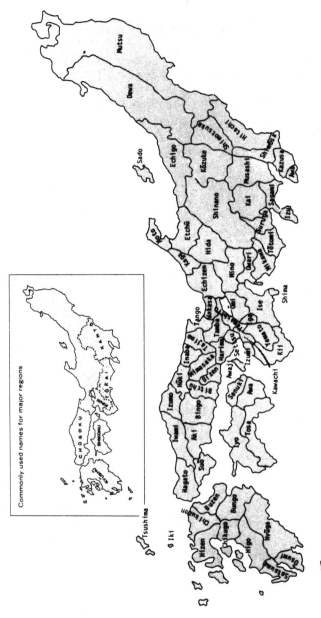

The Provinces of Tokugawa Japan. From John Whitney Hall, Nagahara Keiji, Kozo Yamamura, eds., *Japan before Tokugawa* (Princeton: Princeton University Press, 1981). NOTE: The provinces of Mutsu and Dewa were later subdivided. Reproduced by permission of Princeton University Press.

Commonly used names for major regions

# Brief Contents

# Extended Contents

# Acknowledgments

This book in many respects owes its inception to a friendship which began four decades ago when Thomas Berry met Wm. Theodore de Bary en route to China. It is these two individuals who have shaped my thinking, enlarged my horizons, and inspired my studies. On returning to the States from my first extended encounter with Japan in 1973–1974 it was Thomas Berry who gave perspective and meaning to that literally "disorienting" experience. It was he who introduced me to the richness of the Confucian tradition, and it has been his friendship which has shown me the meaning of the statement that one with a heart of compassion is "sensitive to the suffering of others." (*Mencius* 2A:6) In his articulation of a spirituality of the earth he has offered the most sustaining and the most challenging context for my own studies.

To Wm. Theodore de Bary I am especially grateful. Without his support for this project over many years it might not have come to fruition. His own distinctive insights into the Confucian tradition in East Asia have provided me with an expansive framework for interpretation. From his lectures, seminars, and writings over many years I have gained a lasting appreciation for the first lines of the *Analects*: "Is it not pleasurable to learn with a constant perseverance and application?" Moreover, his tireless commitment to scholarship, teaching, and administrative responsibilities has provided a rare model of dedication to humanistic education and to the value of collaborative efforts.

To both of these teachers I am grateful, not only for the specialized instruction they provided, but also for their breadth of understanding of the Asian world, which they consciously fostered in their students. Their interest in creating broadly trained, competent teachers for future generations lends special depth and intensity to their endeavors. In their varied roles for many as teachers, as mentors, and as friends they have no equals.

The other great friendship that nurtured this book was that of my husband, John Grim. In more ways than are nameable, it is to him that I owe its completion. Not only did he help type large sections of it in its early stages, but he patiently listened to its unfolding over many years. His equilibrium and harmony punctuated the project. More remarkably, the sincerity of his support was both "ceaseless" and "lasting." And, true to his nature, it "produced changes without motion and accomplished its ends without action." (*The Doctrine of the Mean* 26)

It was my parents who first taught me, although in different words, the implications of the *Great Learning*. Their support has been a source of constant inspiration. My father's meticulous editorial skills and patient proofreading have been invaluable at every step of the way, while my mother's bottomless reserve of encouragement has meant more than words can say. My debt to them can never be measured, but perhaps with this book ever so slightly repaid.

To others of my family and my friends I owe thanks for their understanding of dinners missed and for bearing with the distractedness such a prolonged project entails. I am grateful especially to Fanny Brett deBary for her appreciation for the difficulties of undertaking research amidst the demands of an "earthy" existence.

To those who took time from inevitably busy schedules to read through the manuscript I extend warmest appreciation. Not only was I rescued by many of them from errors of fact or judgment, but more importantly I learned the heartening lesson of scholarly support at its best—a unique blend of criticism and kindness from a variety of perspectives. To Wing-tsit Chan, Philip Yampolsky, Carol Gluck, Paul Watt, and Roger Shinn I owe many helpful initial comments. With Herman Ooms, David Dilworth, Rodney Taylor, Peter Nosco, Samuel Yamashita, and Irene Bloom I had valuable exchanges on both style and substance. The fact that I was not able to follow all of their suggestions absolves them, of course, from any responsibilities for the shortcomings of the book.

While in Japan in 1981–1982 I received invaluable materials from Professors Okada Takehiko and Inoue Tadashi of Kyushu University, both of whom have written biographies of Ekken. Professor Okada kindly gave me a manuscript copy of his Ekken biography several years before it was published, and Professor Inoue arranged for Ekken's diaries and other unpublished materials to be photocopied. Their warmth and encouragement to a fledgling researcher meant volumes to me then and now.

With regard to the translation, I benefited greatly from suggestions made by Wm. Theodore de Bary, Philip Yampolsky, Jacqueline Mueller, and Shimizu Kazuhiko. Moreover, the painstaking task of annotation in its final stages was made infinitely smoother by the skillful assistance of Ron-Guey Chu. His wide knowledge of classical Chinese sources made the search for unidentified quotations a fruitful rather than a frustrating experience.

With respect to the technical aspects of computer functioning, Ron-Guey Chu, displayed ingenious adeptness as did John Morris who kindly assisted me with the preparation and printing of the Japanese glossaries. In this area I am also indebted to the assistance of Mary Bruno and Nancy Girardi of the Secretarial Service Center at Iona College and to their staff, especially Adrianna Diello. Keiko Hosogone, Takako Murata, and Nancy Wright have been especially generous with their time and assistance. Bernadine Dawes at SUNY Press was most helpful in her painstaking efforts to bring the manuscript through the production process.

While working on this book over many years I received various grants, which I gratefully acknowledge, from the following sources: Columbia University President's Fellowship (1980–1981), Foreign Language Area Studies (1981–1982), Japan Foundation Fellowship (1982, 1983–1984), Iona College Faculty Research Grants (Summers 1985, 1986, 1987), National Endowment for the Humanities (Summer 1987), Columbia University Committee on Oriental Studies (1987–1988), the Northeast Asia Council of the Association for Asian Studies (1988), Bucknell University Faculty Grant (Summer 1989).

Whatever merit this book has is due to Kaibara Ekken himself. He was, in all respects, a pleasure to work with. Ekken is a major figure in Japanese intellectual history, and an introductory study such as this can scarcely do justice to the wide range of his scholarship and teaching. One would hope that future work in this field will help to situate Ekken and other of his contemporaries in relation to the larger field of Tokugawa intellectual and social discourse. I trust, nonetheless, that he would be surprised yet pleased to be read in another land and another culture, nearly three centuries after his death. If there is any hope in understanding other cultures in a period of history punctuated by misunderstanding of difference, it may well be through knowing the lives, work, and frequently familiar concerns of individuals such as Ekken.

# Part I

*Kaibara Ekken*

A portrait of Kaibara Ekken at age 65. It is said to have been painted by a Kyoto artist, Kano Shōren.

# 1

# Introduction

## THE TRANSMISSION OF NEO-CONFUCIANISM

Kaibara Ekken (1630–1714) was regarded by his contemporaries and by later generations as a major figure in seventeenth-century Japanese intellectual history. Well versed in the writings of the Chinese Neo-Confucians (especially Chu Hsi), he strove to transmit their spiritual essence and practical implications to the Japanese of his day. As Hsü Heng sought to demonstrate the relevance of Neo-Confucian teachings for the Mongols under Khubilai in thirteenth-century China, and as Yi T'oegye adapted the Neo-Confucianism of Chu Hsi for the Koreans in the sixteenth-century, Ekken was similarly involved in the transmission of the Way of the sages across cultural and national boundaries. Recognizing the universal elements of Neo-Confucianism, and aware of their particular application for Tokugawa society, Ekken embraced the Way with remarkable dedication. In the teachings of the Sung Neo-Confucian, Chu Hsi (1130–1200), he saw a system of personal cultivation, intellectual investigation, political organization, and cosmological orientation that provided a broad context for thought and a functional basis for action which he perceived as essential for his time.

The appeal of Neo-Confucianism to other thinkers in this period is also evident. In the seventeenth-century the Japanese, recently emerging from the devastation of the warfare and strife of the previous century, sought an interpretation of change and a means of validating human action that was distinct from the Buddhism that

3

had dominated medieval Japan. Many of the best minds of the period turned to Confucianism for a confirmation of the positive dynamics of change as the manifestation of the ceaseless creativity of heaven and earth. In contrast to the Buddhist view of the impermanence of reality and of attachment as being at the root of suffering, Neo-Confucianism's affirmation of change, and its program of harmonizing with change through self-cultivation and the investigation of things, provided a means of personal and social transformation that seemed to many to be appropriate for Tokugawa Japan. Indeed, as Tetsuo Najita has noted, for natural ontologists such as the Tokugawa Neo-Confucians, "the ceaseless activity of nature was not accidental flux as taught in Buddhism but a field of knowledge that human minds must engage in to contribute to the social good."[1] Moreover, in the vitalistic naturalism[2] of Neo-Confucian cosmology, in the deep reverence for heaven and earth as the source and sustainer of life, and in the affirmation of the sacredness of all living things, many Japanese scholars recognized these religious elements of Neo-Confucianism as having a natural affinity with their own native Shinto tradition. Indeed, conscious of this affinity, a number of Confucian thinkers, including Ekken, skillfully developed their ideas in relation to Shinto.

## THE INFLUENCE OF CHINESE AND
## KOREAN NEO-CONFUCIANISM

Japanese scholars thus took the universal elements of the Way of the sages and adapted them to their own circumstances. In so doing they were indebted to certain Neo-Confucian developments and debates in Ming China and in Yi dynasty Korea. Indeed, these Chinese and Korean developments are particularly relevant to the thought of Kaibara Ekken, which cannot be fully appreciated in isolation from the East Asian Neo-Confucian tradition. While these Chinese and Korean antecedents will not be explored in detail here, their importance must be noted at the outset as a key element in the process of Neo-Confucian assimilation that occurred in seventeenth-century Japan.

Two of the major themes in Ming and Yi Neo-Confucianism that are significant as background for understanding the concerns of many of the Tokugawa Neo-Confucians are an emphasis on the continual creativity of heaven and earth and a stress on the reality of the physical world as expressed in material force (Ch. *ch'i*, Jp. *ki*). In addition, they include the complementary interests in personal experience and practical utility, in critical rationalism and textual study, and in a deeper humanism and a broader spirituality.[3] These are all key elements in Ekken's thought, elements which signal both his awareness of developments in the larger East Asian Neo-Confucian tradition, as well as his own adaptation of these trends in Tokugawa Japan. Especially prominent in Ekken's writing, and providing a unifying dimension to it, is his profound sense of a spirit of vitalism and creativity in the natural world evoking awe and reverence from the individual. In Ekken's thought this vitalistic naturalism was expressed in four major areas, namely, metaphysics, empiricism, ethics, and spirituality:

1) Ekken's vitalism is expressed metaphysically as a naturalistic monism of *ch'i*,[4] where *li*, or principle, is seen as within, not above, *ch'i* or material force. Here Ekken is particularly influenced by Lo Ch'in-shun's (1465–1547) articulation of a naturalistic monism in *K'un-chih chi* (Knowledge Painfully Acquired) which was transmitted from China to Japan by way of Yi Yulgok (1536–1584) in Korea.[5]

2) With regard to empiricism, this sense of vitalism is further explored by Ekken in his efforts to study the principle of things in the natural world. Thus, the traditional Neo-Confucian imperative to investigate things is extended by Ekken from the moral to the physical sphere to a degree rarely matched earlier in China or Japan. While Ekken was a comprehensive scholar in his investigations and in his inclination toward practical learning (Ch. *shih hsüeh*, Jp. *jitsugaku*), late Ming and early Ch'ing thinkers were clearly engaged with similar questions. Fang I-chih (1611–1671), for example, represents the trend toward empiricism that emerged within Neo-Confucianism itself.[6]

3) In terms of ethics, the sense of vitalism is expressed by Ekken in his identification of humaneness, the creative virtue of human beings (Ch. *jen*, Jp. *jin*), with the principle of origination in the universe. Action based on humaneness is thus seen as directly related to the life-giving processes of heaven and earth. In these ideas Ekken follows both Sung and Ming Neo-Confucians such as Chang Tsai (1020–1077), Ch'eng Hao (1032–1085), and Ch'en Hsien-chang (1428–1500), who stressed the goodness of human emotions and the dynamic identification of humans with the fructifying processes of creation.

4) Finally, Ekken's vitalistic naturalism found expression spiritually in the learning of the mind-and-heart (Ch. *hsin hsüeh*, Jp. *shingaku*). This was a form of interior self-discipline that began with reverence and gratitude to heaven and earth as the source and sustainer of life. It proceeded to a recognition of personal deficiencies

and outlined a program of self-examination and reflection. The ultimate aim of this self-cultivation was to realize one's unity with
heaven and earth and all things. Clearly familiar with the earlier
expression of *hsin hsüeh* in the *Heart Classic* of Chen Te-hsiu (1178–
1235) and in later Chinese and Korean commentaries on this text,
Ekken formulated a version of self-cultivation that drew extensively
on these earlier writings while trying to make their ideas comprehensible to the Japanese.

Thus, in each of these four areas of his thought Ekken is indebted to important trends in Chinese and Korean Neo-Confucianism that embodied a naturalistic metaphysics, practical empiricism,
humanistic ethics, and disciplined spirituality. Just as the Chinese
and Korean scholars were developing options within Neo-Confucianism itself, so Ekken was working within the Chu Hsi school
as he adapted its teachings to the Japanese context.

It is essential to recognize that Ekken saw himself as part of a
long and complex tradition of Neo-Confucianism which he believed
he was transmitting and developing for his own time. Even in his
later disagreements with Chu Hsi he felt he was not breaking away
from the tradition, but rather following certain options within the
tradition already explored by Chinese and Korean scholars before
him. Because of these disagreements with Chu Hsi, Ekken has been
regarded by some as a renegade Confucian. Following this argument, Maruyama Masao and others after him have claimed that Ekken had a consciousness divided between "norm" and "nature",
namely, between a moral and empirical dichotomy.[7]

It is the aim of this work, however, to suggest that it is precisely
Ekken's interest in integrating a comprehensive program of personal cultivation, educational training, and empirical investigation
that distinguishes his thought and accounts for its particular appeal
in the Tokugawa period. For a scholar like Ekken, with such a
breadth of interests and talents, this was an arduous and all-encompassing task requiring enormous intellectual and practical efforts.
An important motivation behind his work is his ethicoreligious concerns, which will be explored throughout the work.


## THE RELIGIOUS DIMENSIONS OF NEO-CONFUCIANISM

In order to clarify the appeal of Neo-Confucianism for Ekken and to
appreciate his concerns as expressed in texts such as the *Taigiroku*
(Record of Grave Doubts) and *Yamato zokkun* (Precepts for Daily Life

in Japan), it is necessary to situate his ideas within the context of the religious aspects of Neo-Confucian thought. While the subject of Neo-Confucianism as a "religion" has been variously debated,[8] many scholars have recognized that there are "religious dimensions" to Neo-Confucian thought and practice and are working to articulate those dimensions more clearly.[9] This recent research has emphasized that Neo-Confucianism is not simply an ethical system nor only a political philosophy, although these are important aspects of it. In other words, what has often been seen as the secular or humanistic concerns of Neo-Confucians may be better understood when placed within a broad framework of the religious aspects of Neo-Confucianism.

This raises the problem of defining what we mean by religion and by related terms such as "spirituality" and "religious." Religion may be defined in its broadest sense as a means whereby humans, recognizing the limitations of phenomenal reality, undertake specific practices which aim at self-transformation and self-transcendence. This is not simply a passing or superficial enterprise but one which is all-encompassing. As Frederick Streng has suggested, religion is a "means of ultimate transformation" which allows one to live an authentic life. This perspective is particularly helpful in discussing the Confucian and Neo-Confucian tradition.[10]

For many people, however, the term religion is still closely associated with the idea of institutions, and when used in a comparative context inevitably draws on Western categories and perspectives. In the Confucian and Neo-Confucian tradition, for example, the primary concerns of Western monotheistic religions with the nature of God or with the problems of sin and salvation are rather removed. Yet to be religious in the human community has taken many forms other than Western monotheism. For this reason it is limiting and indeed distorting to use only Western categories in defining religion and religious practices.[11] Nevertheless, given the common associations of the term religion with Western traditions, I shall hold in abeyance the question of whether Neo-Confucianism taken as a whole is to be considered a religion and focus instead on some of its religious features. Wilfred Cantwell Smith has pointed to the importance of this kind of distinction by noting that "a religion" implies an institution and a set of dogmas, whereas "being religious" refers to the personal aspect of faith in relation to a community and to a larger cumulative tradition.[12]

Following in this line of thought, Tu Wei-ming has observed: "The problem of whether Neo-Confucianism is a religion should not be confused with the more significant question: what does it mean to be religious in the Neo-Confucian community?"[13] He goes on to say: "The solution to the former often depends on the particular interpretive position we choose to take on what constitutes the paradigmatic example of a religion, which may have little to do with our knowledge about Neo-Confucianism as a spiritual tradition . . ."[14] Tu Wei-ming underscores the importance of such distinctions for understanding Neo-Confucianism. He notes, "The questions of being religious is crucial for our appreciation of the 'inner dimension' of the Neo-Confucian project. For the sake of expedience, being religious in the Neo-Confucian sense can be understood as being engaged in *ultimate self-transformation as a communal act.*"[15] The implications of Tu's statement is not that self-transformation itself is communal; it is indeed a matter of individual effort. Tu points out, however, that in the Neo-Confucian context self-transformation is never intended to be an isolated or self-centered exercise, but rather one related to the larger human and natural orders and resulting in some form of social or political action.

Thus as Wilfred Cantwell Smith, Tu Wei-ming, and others have noted, religion connotes for many people particular institutions that have embodied a more immediate personal experience of the sacred. Therefore, rather than "religion," the terms "spirituality" and "religious" are used to describe various aspects of Neo-Confucian thought and practice. "Spirituality" refers to that which includes intense personal experience of the sacred, as well as the cultivation of that experience in a discipline aimed at self-transformation. It is used in conjunction with, but remains distinct from, the term "religious," which is taken to mean individual or communal expressions of spiritual experience as found in scripture, creed, practices, and institutions. Crucial to both terms is a dimension of ultimacy of commitment and depth of motivation aimed at transformation of self and society. Within this context the term "moral" means the particular ethical practices which complement spiritual experience. Both moral action and spiritual experience are cultivated through self-discipline and study.

In this work the term "moral and spiritual discipline" or "cultivation" usually refers to the learning of the mind-and-heart (Ch. *hsin hsüeh,* Jp. *shingaku*). It is sometimes used interchangeably with the term "ethicoreligious cultivation" to indicate the essentially unified aspect of this process. The more general term "Confucian spiritual discipline" indicates methods of self-cultivation practiced or encouraged by both Confucians and Neo-Confucians. The term spiritual discipline is used with the assumption that there are grounds for comparison of forms of spiritual discipline within the Confucian tradition with spiritual disciplines in other religious traditions. While Ekken's treatises (*kunmono*) are frequently referred to as moral essays, it is understood that these are not simply intended as moralizing apart from a larger religious context, namely, self-transformation motivated and sustained by a sense of reverence and gratitude toward heaven as the source and sustainer of life.

In these general terms, Neo-Confucianism can be regarded as having a religious dimension in the sense that the primary activity of Neo-Confucianism is the practice of moral and spiritual cultivation leading to self-transcendence and ultimate self-transformation for the benefit of the larger society. Followers of the Confucian path are well aware of the imperfections of human beings and the limitations of reality. Yet in their study, teaching, and practice they insist on affirming the essential perfectability of human nature and the importance of working within the social, political, and educational sphere for the transformation of both self and society. In this context, then, self-transcendence means moral and spiritual cultivation to recover the deepest wellsprings of the human spirit. It is not an escape from the self nor an obsession with the self, but a penetration into one's nature (Ch. *hsing*, Jp. *sei*) so as to activate one's humaneness (Ch. *jen*, Jp. *jin*) in relation to the larger community of life. Such activity results in the realization of one's authentic nature as connatural with the all-pervasive principle of heaven (Ch. *t'ien li*, Jp. *tenri*). This is expressed in the idea of the human as forming one body with heaven and earth and is most fully realized in the sage personality. This process is, in a profound sense, religious.

The religious aspects of Confucianism, however, are not concerned with ultimate transcendence in the same way that other traditions are. This perspective distinguishes the Confucian spiritual path, because while heaven (Ch. *t'ien*, Jp. *ten*) is regarded as a creative and sustaining principle of the universe, it is not usually seen as a personal being, as God is generally understood, although with notable exceptions, within the Western context. It is, nonetheless, a central inspiration and support for life, both past and present, both human and natural.

For the Neo-Confucian, then, knowing the will of heaven and repaying heaven for the gifts of life and nature are important religious motivations for undertaking self-cultivation. The social, polit-

ical, and educational implications of this practice are ever present
for the Neo-Confucian, and the larger goal is to form one body with
all things.

In summary, this effort at self-transformation is one that
involves:

1. religious orientation leading to
2. moral and spiritual self-cultivation
3. resulting in action in the social-political order and
4. union with heaven and earth.

All of these aim toward the realization of sagehood, which can be
seen as the ultimate goal of Neo-Confucian study and practice.

These steps were clearly present both in Kaibara Ekken's writings and in his activities. They are by no means discrete, isolated
concepts, but are interrelated and overlapping processes. Clearly for
Ekken (and for others of his contemporaries) certain aspects of Neo-
Confucianism had a compelling quality as a way of orienting human
life. This, no doubt, helped to provide a basis for his active life of
teaching, writing, and research. Although a fuller intellectual biography will be provided in chapters two and three, a brief discussion
of the appeal of Neo-Confucianism for Ekken is appropriate here.

## EKKEN AND NEO-CONFUCIANISM

Ekken had been exposed to Buddhism through his mother and stepmother, but under his brother's influence, he turned from Buddhism
to Neo-Confucianism at an early age. Recognizing the importance
of a this-worldly philosophy that addressed the need for strong
bonds of human relations in the contemporary society, Ekken avidly
embraced Neo-Confucian studies, and became increasingly inspired
by Chu Hsi's example as a dedicated teacher and writer. The particular appeal of Chu Hsi's teaching for Ekken might be seen in the
fact that throughout his life he was drawn to its two integrating
poles, namely, the investigation of things and self-cultivation.
These poles provided a structure for balancing an engagement in
worldly affairs with an attention to nourishing the inner life. Thus,
both the active commitment of Neo-Confucianism along with its
concern for interior reflection had a definite attraction for Ekken. It
is these elements that he rigorously studied, transmitted, and developed in formulating his own form of Neo-Confucianism.

His interest in the investigation of things, for example, resulted
in a practical learning and an empiricism directed toward classifying

plants, recording topography and local history, and studying farming practices. Similarly, his attention to self-cultivation led to his further articulation of the learning of the mind-and-heart along with his
detailed explication of moral and spiritual practices appropriate for
each group in the society. Underlying these concerns was a broad
interest in education that was both practical and spiritual, an interest he shared with other Neo-Confucians throughout East Asia.[16]

Philosophically, what unites his empirical and his ethicoreligious interests is a monism of *ch'i* that reflects his abiding reverence for the creative powers of heaven and earth. This vitalistic
naturalism and its implications for his ideas on investigation and
self-cultivation will be explored more fully in chapter three. It is
particularly in this area that Ekken is both a transmitter and creative
thinker in his own right. For he, perhaps more than some of his
contemporaries, recognized the varied possibilities of the Neo-
Confucian imperative to investigate things. He thus carried this
idea of investigation beyond its traditional application in examining
principle in the moral sphere to the larger area of empirical research. In so doing he significantly enlarged the scope of Neo-
Confucian concerns in the Japanese context.

Ekken, then, was both a transmitter and a transformer of Neo-
Confucianism as he received it from other Confucian scholars and
through the writings of Chinese Neo-Confucians. As a transmitter
he was primarily concerned to make Neo-Confucian ethics and
spiritual discipline more widely understood and amenable to
Tokugawa society. In this he was continuing the tradition established by Chu Hsi who hoped to foster a broad public education. To
accomplish this Chu wrote extensive public proclamations[17] and
promoted local schools and community compacts. He also wrote for
the benefit of the commoners. It is this latter task which was one of
Ekken's primary motivations for writing his ethical treatises.

As a transformer, Ekken was engaged in the interpretation and
further exploration of the larger philosophical issues which he received directly or indirectly from China and Korea. In this he was
especially influenced by certain Sung and Ming thinkers who were
wrestling with similar problems left by the Chu Hsi tradition. Some
of the most important currents of Chinese and Korean Neo-
Confucianism which appear to have also engaged Ekken are: a
spirit of vitalism and reverence based on the creativity of heaven
and earth; a monism of *ch'i* which sought to overcome dualism at
the same time that it affirmed the reality of physical things; and an
interest in empiricism manifested in both the investigation of things

and in the concern with a practical learning (Ch. *shih hsüeh*, Jp. *ji-tsugaku*). All of these elements remain underlying themes of his broad ethicoreligious concerns, and they will be more fully discussed in subsequent chapters. It was in his very effort to transmit a Neo-Confucianism which embraced moral and spiritual cultivation and empirical investigation that he brought together important elements of the tradition and developed them further. In so doing, he became not only an heir to a tradition but a dynamic transformer as well.

To understand these efforts more fully and to identify the emerging role of Neo-Confucianism in the Tokugawa period, a brief discussion of the background of his time will first be undertaken. After introducing this historical context in the opening chapter, the study examines Ekken's life in chapter two, his thought in chapter three, and his educational treaties in chapters four and five. The goal is to present a picture of Ekken's particular mode of education and self-cultivation which arose from specific philosophical and religious concerns.

This was an education emphasizing both practical learning and personal self-cultivation, not simply for the samurai class but for the benefit of various groups in the society. The essence of Ekken's educational program was the moral and spiritual discipline of the learning of the mind-and-heart which he transmitted from the Chinese and Korean Neo-Confucian sources. It is through examining this spiritual discipline that the religious aspects of Neo-Confucianism may be better understood. By understanding the dual emphasis on education and self-cultivation we may help to explain the appeal and adaptability of Neo-Confucianism to different contexts in East Asia.

# 2

# Neo-Confucianism in the Early Tokugawa Period

## ESTABLISHING THE CONTEXT

The Tokugawa period in Japanese history (1603–1868) was a time of lengthy peace and stability following a tumultuous century of war, upheaval, and disunity. It was into this peaceful age that Kaibara Ekken was born in 1630 during the reign of the third Tokugawa shogun, Iemitsu. Both the new political and social order and the increasing significance of Neo-Confucianism within it were important to Ekken's development. In particular, the growing emphasis on education and on the indigenization of Chinese Neo-Confucian teachings provide the context in which Ekken's influential role as a teacher and writer can be appreciated and his contributions as both a transmitter and transformer of Neo-Confucian thought can be better understood.

### Period of Unification

In 1620, a decade before Ekken was born, the Jesuit missionary, João Rodrigues described the results of Tokugawa unification as follows:

> Nearly everything was destroyed. All the ancient families of the lords and nobles of the kingdom were overthrown; almost all the 68 kingdoms and other smaller fiefs of individual nobles have been exchanged and given to new people who have been promoted to the nobility.

Many such people sprang from lowly stock and have risen either by force of arms or because they were the kin of *Taikō*, the lord of *Tenka*. The laws, government, culture, trade, wealth and magnificence have been restored throughout the kingdom, and buildings and populous cities have been erected in every part of the land. On account of trade and peace many people have become rich, although the ordinary folk and peasants have been impoverished by the taxes which they have been forced to pay. The lords of the provinces have become very wealthy, storing up much gold and silver. Throughout the kingdom there is a great abundance of money, new mines have been opened and the country is well supplied with everything.[1]

Here Rodrigues summarizes the early years of the seventeenth-century when Ieyasu,[2] the first Tokugawa shogun, began to consolidate his power after the battle of Sekigahara in 1600. After a century of bitter strife in the period of war in the provinces (*Sengoku jidai*), followed by the struggle for unification of Oda Nobunaga (1534–1582), Toyotomi Hideyoshi (1536–1598), and Tokugawa Ieyasu (1542–1616), Japan entered a new era of stability and prosperity, which was to last for over two hundred and fifty years.

While Ieyasu has been revered in Japan for creating the foundations of this "Pax Tokugawa," the enormous task of political organization was left to his son Hidetada (shogun from 1605–1622) and his grandson Iemitsu (shogun from 1622–1651). Under their rule the political system know as *Bakuhan* became codified, a bureaucratic administrative structure was established, and the policy of seclusion was inaugurated. These aspects of political consolidation that took place in the first half of the seventeenth-century, and their relevance to the growth of Neo-Confucianism, will be discussed in the following section.

## Political-Administrative Organization

The Bakuhan system was based on geographical and political divisions that decentralized power among the more than two hundred and sixty *han daimyo* (domain lords) while retaining final authoritative control in the shogunal government (*Bakufu*) in Edo.[3] Under this system the shogunate had superior seigneurial rights over the daimyo. This was demonstrated in the granting of fiefs by the shogun and in the presentation of cadastral registrars by the fief-holders. The moral and symbolic sanction for the Bakufu's power was derived in part from the enforced acquiescence of the Emperor, who was confined to his Kyoto palace.[4] The elaborate administrative bureaucracy established by the Bakufu was designed to maintain a delicate balance between regional autonomy and central-ized autocracy.[5]

Various Bakufu controls were maintained over the daimyo, who were first classified on the basis of their relationship to Ieyasu.[6] The system of alternate attendance (*sankin kōtai*),[7] for example, required that the daimyo travel to Edo every other year and remain in resi-dence for twelve months in their *han* mansions (*daimyo yashiki*). The expense of this obligation reduced the possiblity of military buildup and the proximity to the shogunate discouraged any treasonous plotting. To control further the daimyos' activities, their wives and children had to remain permanently in Edo, even when the daimyos returned to their local domain.

Along with their efforts to codify the *Bakuhan* system and estab-lish a civil bureaucracy was the legislation of Hidetada and Iemitsu, which inaugurated a seclusion policy (*sakoku*).[8] Under these sho-guns, seclusion edicts were promulgated forbidding any Japanese to leave the country or those abroad to return. These edicts also pro-scribed Christianity, foreign missionaries, and any books mention-ing Christianity.[9] Furthermore, all Westerners were expelled from Japan except the Dutch, who were confined to the island of Deshima in Nagasaki harbor to carry on trade. Although trade and imports were strictly regulated, recent research has indicated that Japan was not as isolated as earlier accounts have suggested.[10]

While the date of origin and the actual effects of the seclusion policy have been variously debated,[11] there is little doubt that it served to reinforce the stability and legitimation efforts of the Tokugawa government. Through this policy, foreign interference could be minimized but not completely eliminated, while economic growth could be stimulated yet theoretically monopolized. Most es-pecially, by careful manipulation of diplomatic protocol, "the bakufu was able to create the illusion of an East Asian world order that was Japanese in design and Japanese in focus."[12]

The impact of seclusion on culture and learning was also signif-icant, for it served to promote their flourishing on a wide scale. As George Elison has observed, the seclusion policy by no means im-plied stagnation:

> . . . if we take a new look at Tokugawa history we are forced to recog-nize that the Edo period was no dark age, nor the *Sakoku* policy a bane on cultural development. An equilibrium was achieved within Japan, and internal stability maintained remarkably well for a period exceed-ing two centuries . . . Japan was isolated from the rest of the world, but in the country's major cities the arts flourished and a uniquely

Japanese mode of expression was created: the townsmen's genre scene of the Tokugawa era is the golden age of Japanese culture. On another level there occurred a brilliant synthesis of East Asian thought. There was great vitality in the Tokugawa intellectual world, which the Confucian tradition dominated but did not oppress. Nor was the flow of information from Europe terminated. Scholars of the Dutch Learning maintained the contact, although some irreconcilables found their presence irksome. The Christian missionaries were excluded, but for all that Japan did not stagnate.[13]

It is significant to note the position of Neo-Confucian thinkers within the *Bakuhan* system and the relation of the growth of Neo-Confucianism to the Bakufu's policies of alternate attendance and seclusion. While there was no civil service examination system to qualify for public office as in China, various Confucian scholars (*jugakusha* or *jusha*) were employed by respective *han* daimyo as advisors and teachers. These included such prominent seventeenth-century figures as Kumazawa Banzan (1619–1691) who advised the Ikeda lord in Okayama; Yamaga Sokō (1622–1685) who served the Akō lord; and Ekken himself, who was employed by three generations of Kuroda lords in the Chikuzen domain. In a scholar such as Arai Hakuseki (1657–1725) there is also the example of a Confucian who served as an advisor to the shogun.

The influence of individual scholars in a particular domain can be seen not necessarily in direct political programs but rather through their impact on education and on the dissemination of Neo-Confucian ethicoreligious teachings. Moreover, contrary to the view that travel was severely restricted in this period, the system of alternate year attendance in Edo allowed for wide-ranging and ongoing intellectual contacts for scholars such as Ekken, who frequently accompanied their lord to Edo. It was in this way that Ekken, for example, was introduced to Hayashi Gahō, the son of Hayashi Razan, a Confucian advisor to the Bakufu. He heard Gahō lecture on various occasions during his trips to Edo. Finally, the vitality of Tokugawa intellectual life, despite the seclusion policy, was greatly stimulated by the emergence of Neo-Confucianism as a dominant force in the period. To examine further the role of Neo-Confucianism and Ekken's commitment to it, the general social and economic features of Tokugawa Japan will be considered.

## Socio-Economic Structures

The cultural flourishing which Elison describes was, in part, a result of certain social and economic factors during the Tokugawa period. In particular, the emergence of the merchant class as a dominant and prosperous presence had a decisive impact on culture and taste. To appreciate the varied audience that Ekken sought to address, one must take into account the organization of Tokugawa society, which was based on a stratification of four main groups: the samurai, the farmers, the artisans, and the merchants (shinōkōshō).[14]

A distinguishing feature of this status system was the separation of the samurai and the peasant farmers (heinō bunri), which had begun at the end of the sixteenth-century under Hideyoshi. The samurai evolved into a new class of vassals who were no longer attached to their lord solely for military purposes or to the land for agricultural purposes. The removal of the samurai from the land resulted in their gradual urbanization, whereby, living in castle towns, they were supported by income from fiefs in absentia or by stipends from the local lord. Many were forced to become masterless samurai (rōnin), who on occasion were a source of local disturbances or potential rebellion.[15] The adaptation of the samurai to civilian life is a major theme of the period, expressed by the continuing attempts of many Confucian scholars, including Ekken, to write of the complementarity of the civil and the military arts (bunbu).

The vast majority of the population, however, were peasant farmers who tilled the land and lived in rural villages.[16] During the Tokugawa period an agricultural revolution occurred because of increased reclamation of land, improved irrigation, technological developments and a growing labor force.[17] Improved agricultural methods were of great interest to Ekken, who particularly encouraged Miyazaki Yasusada's research in this area, which culminated in his important compendium on agriculture known as Nōgyō zensho.

Next on the hierarchical scale were the artisans, who were skilled in a variety of crafts from sword making and silversmithing to carpentry and masonry. Within the castle towns there were separate sections for samurai, artisans, and merchants.

Although nominally at the bottom of the status system, the merchants became a key factor in Tokugawa life. It was their role in the development of commerce and urbanization that became especially significant.[18] Osaka was the main commercial center for their activity, and it was from here that intricate networks of trade arose linking Japan from Edo to Kyushu. In addition to the growing urban centers of Edo and Osaka, the institution of the alternate year attendance system for the daimyo spawned a flourishing series of post towns along the main roads of the country.[19] These towns supplied horses and equipment as well as food and lodging to the daimyo and their retinue. Travel for the ordinary citizen was carefully restricted in form, rather than in fact. However, the practice of pilgrimages to major shrines or temples became increasingly popular and provided a legitimate reason for people to move freely between domain barriers.[20]

The economic foundation of this social order was the *kokudaka* system based on assessed agricultural productivity of land where one *koku* equaled approximately 5.1 bushels. Begun under Hideyoshi, this system involved extensive land surveys to ascertain the putative rice yield. Taxes were then levied accordingly and were collected in units of rice. The *han* daimyo and samurai sent their rice to the Osaka rice market, where it was converted into specie. The merchant class acted as the brokers in this exchange and eventually became the principal beneficiaries and sole issuers of loans. Their control of the flow of money was so pervasive that at times it forced the government to order cancellation of debts which the samurai had inevitably accumulated. Indeed, the growing indebtedness of the samurai, along with the increasing prosperity of the merchants, were developments characteristic of Tokugawa Japan.[21] Moreover, as the merchants sought entertainment with their wealth, they stimulated the rise of a popularly based literature and culture.[22] This culture was simultaneously an agent in, and a beneficiary of, the emergence of printing and the growth of education in this period.

Although learning and education were considered to be the proper funcion of the samurai class, the Confucian scholars in the Tokugawa period came from various social backgrounds and helped to spread Confucian teachings to different groups in the society.[23] Ekken is a prime example of this tendency, but other teachers were similarly inclined. Nakae Tōju (1608–1648), for example, was the son of a lower class samurai who made his living by farming. Tōju taught in the rural area of Ōmi and welcomed people of all classes to his school. Itō Jinsai (1627–1705), the son of a merchant family in Kyoto, likewise taught students of varying social backgrounds. Ishida Baigan (1685–1744), born into a peasant family and apprenticed to a Kyoto merchant, especially directed his teachings to merchants. Like Ekken, he exemplified the efforts to encourage economic developments that characterized many Confucians of this period. Other Tokugawa Confucians who came from peasant families included Shibano Ritsuzan, Hosoi Heishū, Yamada Hōkoku, and Ninomiya Sontoku. Tetsuo Najita thus refers to the *jusha* (Confucian scholars) as a "multiclass status group" who "emerged out of the interstices of the various classes."[24] Indeed, Najita claims that in the private schools they established "the intellectual evolution

among the *jusha* was relatively open and unconstrained,"[25] particularly because knowledge was not directly linked to civil service examinations and to political power.

Thus, contrary to the opinion of some scholars, Tokugawa Neo-
Confucianism was not a teaching reserved only for the samurai
class or limited in its appeal to that group alone. Rather, it spoke
across class barriers to the needs of various groups in the society
newly emerging into a peaceful era. Nor can Neo-Confucianism be
summarily dismissed as merely an ideology of the elite designed to
keep others in their place. Though some saw in it a means of but-
tressing a hierarchical order, Neo-Confucian teachings were not
simply imposed by higher authority. Instead, they developed on
many levels of the society for a variety of reasons, not the least of
which was the appeal of the teachings themselves. As Peter Nosco
has observed, Neo-Confucianism's "success in affecting change to
and response in Tokugawa discourse was due primarily to the intellectually compelling quality of Neo-Confucian thought."[26]

Tetsuo Najita has noted this as well, claiming that "the view,
advanced by the distinguished historian Tsuda Sōkichi (1873–1961),
that Tokugawa Confucianism had little bearing on the culture of
the general populace, though convincing, is also misleading." He
continues:

> The importance of Confucianism as a source from which key mediating
> concepts were drawn to grapple with specific moral issues confronting
> Tokugawa commoners is easily confirmed by the available literature of
> the period. In the case of merchants, Confucianism offered a language
> with which to conceptualize their intellectual worth in terms of univer-
> salistic definitions of 'virtue.' Thus, while Confucianism undeniably re-
> mained the preferred philosophy of the aristocracy, to view it as being
> enclosed within the boundaries of that class would be to deny that sys-
> tem of thought its adaptive and expansive abilities.[27]

Furthermore, the spread of Neo-Confucianism was facilitated by the
growth of printing, literacy, and education in this period.

## PRINTING AND POPULAR CULTURE

The Tokugawa era as a whole was distinguished by the rise of popular literature due to the adoption of inexpensive printing methods
and the gradual spread of literacy.[28] Moveable type was brought
back from Korea as a present to the Japanese Emperor in 1593 following Hideyoshi's invasion of the peninsula. Three years earlier

one of the first non-religious works was printed in movable type. This was *Setsuyōshū*, a two-volume dictionary of Japanese readings of Chinese characters.[29] At the end of the sixteenth-century the Jesuits had also started their mission press at Amakusa near Nagasaki.[30] In addition to the Bible and certain Western didactic tales like Aesop's fables, this press reproduced works of Japanese literature such as the *Heike monogatari*.

While printing was at first an avocation of the rich, commercial printing emerged with the adoption of inexpensive block printing.[31] This commercial printing flourished because of the growing interest of the samurai class in cultural and educational topics. Such interest was by no means restricted to the samurai, however, for the townspeople (*chōnin*) contributed significantly to the rise of a popularly based culture. With the emerging economic independence of the townspeople, accompanied by the availability of leisure time, there arose an appetite for stories, entertainment, and reflection which was well supplied by such prominent figures as Iharu Saikaku (1642–1693), Chikamatsu Monzaemon (1653–1725), and Matsuo Bashō (1644–1694). The Genroku period at the end of the seventeenth-century was a high point in the spread of this *chōnin* culture and serves as a further indication of the penetration of Confucian ideas into popular culture.[32]

For the Neo-Confucians the development of printing meant both a greater access to books for their own studies and a ready means for disseminating their teachings to others, whether in scholarly or popular form. While literacy was far from universal, it can be said that, relative to the past and to other countries in the same period, it was growing at a significant rate. Furthermore, the records of printing in the Tokugawa era demonstrate the continuing appeal of a writer like Ekken, whose works were being constantly reissued through the latter half of the nineteenth-century and even into the twentieth.[33]

## EDUCATION

The demand for books of all kinds increased as literacy spread, owing to the growth of schools. Until the Tokugawa period, however, education was largely restricted to the upper classes and conducted principally in temples. João Rodrigues observed at the end of the sixteenth-century:

In Japan the sons of nobles, lords, the aristocracy and gentlefolk learn to read and write. There are usually no public schools. The nobles maintain in their houses a master to teach their sons, while other children go to receive their lessons at the bonzes' monasteries; some stay at the monasteries for their studies, but others return home daily if the monastery is near their homes. These monasteries of the bonzes also serve as universities for those who study philosophy and the sciences and want to follow an ecclesiastical career. In the district of Bandō in the kingdom of Shimonotsuke, there is a university called Ashikaga, whither students flock from all over Japan in order to study all the sciences which are taught there gratis.[34]

While temple schools combined Confucian ethics with Buddhist philosophy, the curriculum of the Ashikaga academy north of Edo was Confucian. This institution, which had begun in the fifteenth-century, declined in the early Tokugawa period which saw the rise of the Hayashi school in Edo as well as the growth of local schools. In 1630 the Bakufu established a Confucian academy in Edo, later known as the *Shōheikō* (named after Confucius' birthplace). Hayashi Razan (1583–1657) was appointed director of this academy and his descendants succeeded him in this position. In addition to promoting study and lectures on the classics, the academy influenced the *han* schools by providing many of their teachers.

These *han* schools (*hankō*) were designed principally for the samurai, whose role took on new dimensions in this period of peace. Educating the samurai was considered an important means of uniting the civil and the military arts (*bunbu*). In discussing the aims of such a samurai education, Ronald Dore writes:

> The dominant view of samurai education in the Tokugawa period may be roughly summarized as follows: the means of education were provided by Chinese writings, especially the Confucian classics; its purpose was primarily to develop moral character, both as an absolute human duty and also in order the better to fulfill the samurai's function in society; a secondary purpose was to gain from the classics that knowledge of men and affairs and of the principles of government which was also necessary for the proper performance of the samurai's duties. Certain other technical vocational skills were necessary which could not be gained from classical Chinese study. Also, classical Chinese study itself brought certain legitimate fringe benefits in the form of life-enhancing aesthetic pleasures.[35]

This Confucian based education was not limited to the samurai, however. Private schools (*shijuku*) run by individual teachers were open to both samurai and commoners.[36] In addition, the temple schools (terakoya) were especially designed for the elementary education of the commoners. With the growing economic prosperity of the period, it became increasingly necessary for merchants, artisans, and farmers to acquire basic skills in reading, writing, and arithmetic. Moreover, commoners who occupied administrative positions in towns and villages needed to be able to pass down government regulations or announcements to the people at the same time that they forwarded petitions to higher government officials and drew up tax reports and family registers.[37]

In addition to the official Confucian academy and the regional school system, individual Confucian scholars became important transmitters of education and culture in this period. Sometimes they were connected with a private or a han school, as were Nakae Tōju and Kumazawa Banzan,[38] but frequently they acted as educators outside of the established institutional structures. Some served as advisors to the domain daimyo, as did Yamaga Sokō (1622–1685), or to a daimyo turned shogun, as did Arai Hakuseki (1657–1725).[39]

Some lectured or served as private tutors on the classics, either in the home, in the han castle, or in the han residence in Edo. Underlying these varied activities was a constant preoccupation with writing and scholarship that has been a hallmark of Confucian education. The public life of the scholar was nourished by his individual efforts of study and reflection. From this concern for a life of scholarship and education there emerged such prominent figures in Japanese Confucian thought as Ogyū Sorai (1666–1728), Itō Jinsai (1627–1705), and Kaibara Ekken. Japanese Confucians recognized certain limitations to their political influence owing to the hereditary system of appointing government officials, in contrast to the civil service examination system used in China. Yet this did not diminish their energies, but focused them instead on the traditional Confucian tasks of education, scholarship, and self-cultivation with remarkable vigor and commitment.

## EKKEN AS EDUCATOR

It is precisely in this area that Kaibara Ekken was a major influence on the educational concerns of his period. While it was in the eighteenth and nineteenth-centuries that institutional education flourished through the proliferation of schools, the seeds for such growth were planted in the seventeenth-century by scholars such as

Ekken. Ekken worked through more informal structures of educa-tion, for it was not until 1783 that a domain school was established in Fukuoka by a descendant of one of his disciples.[40] Ekken's activ-ities involved many of those mentioned above: he was a lecturer to the domain lord, a tutor to his heir and retainers, and a researcher for various projects commissioned by the *han*. Yet his most impor-tant contributions can be seen in his writings on education. It is his moral instructions (*kunmono*) which provided both a philosophy of education and a method for practical application that could be used not only for the samurai but for every level of the society. In these efforts Ekken carried on a tradition begun by Chu Hsi himself in encouraging popular education.

One of Ekken's preoccupations was how to make Neo-Confucian moral and spiritual practices understood by a wide num-ber of people. It is his efforts to codify and transmit a system of ethics and of spiritual discipline as the basis of a humanistic educa-tional tradition that is a distinguishing characteristic of his work. In this he was part of a larger process of the indigenization of Neo-Confucianism which took place in seventeenth-century Japan through thinkers such as Fujiwara Seika (1561–1619), Hayashi Razan (1583–1657), and Yamazaki Ansai (1618–1682). It is this process of indigenization through moral cultivation and education that is a central feature of the period and an underlying theme of Ekken's writings and teachings.

## INDIGENIZATION THROUGH THE TRANSMISSION OF ETHICS

The precise nature of the growth and impact of Confucian thought in seventeenth-century Japanese society is difficult to measure with the intervening lapse of three centuries and with the plethora of texts and commentaries written by the Japanese of the period. Among the Confucian and Neo-Confucian scholars, criticisms of one another were frequent and particular viewpoints were vigor-ously defended. In such a milieu a dispassionate observer is diffi-cult, if not impossible, to find. For this reason, Englebert Kaempfer's three-volume history of Japan is a valuable source on the period. Written by a Dutch physician between 1690 and 1692, it contains detailed descriptions of his travels to Edo and Nagasaki and records of his observations concerning religious practices, ad-ministration, and daily life. His comments on Confucius' place in

the society provide a fresh glimpse into Tokugawa Japan and a starting point for further discussion on the transmission of Confucian
ethical teachings. He writes of Confucius:

> A profound respect is shewn to his memory both in China and Japan,
> by publick as well as private Persons. Very lately the Emperor of Japan
> caus'd two Temples to be built to him in his Capital Jedo, whither he
> repair'd in Person, as soon as they were finis'd, and on this occasion
> set forth, in a handsome Speech to his Courtiers, the merits of this
> great Man, and the peculiar excellency of the maxims of Government
> laid down by him. His Picture is allow'd the most honorable Place in
> the House of Philosophers, and all Persons who apply themselves to
> studies and learning, never mention his name without particular to-
> kens of respect.[41]

What Kaempfer refers to when he speaks of "Temples" is most
probably the Yushima Seidō built in 1690 by Tsunayoshi (shogun
1680–1709) as a center of Confucian ritual. While this passage suggests that Tsunayoshi was promoting Confucian ritual and moral
teachings for the proper operation of government, it also points to
the personal respect for Confucius and his teachings among individual scholars. There were, then, various modes of transmission of
Confucian ethics both public and private.

It is also significant to note that Tsunayoshi himself was something of an exception in his official attention to Confucian learning.
His association of the Bakufu with Confucian ritual was less to promote "orthodoxy" than to encourage basic Confucian morality.
Donald Shively has elaborated on this, noting that, despite his ex-
travagances, "Tsunayoshi did more to enhance the status of Confucian studies than any other shogun."[42] As Tsunayoshi was shogun
for nearly three decades of Ekken's adult life, this clearly must have
affected the intellectual climate in which he worked. Shively asserts
that Tsunayoshi helped to spread Confucian ethics throughout the
society, and he observes that "to judge from the popular literature
of the day, these values were diffused much more widely than in
earlier decades."[43] Shively further notes the civilizing force of Confucian morality in this period:

> We should not be distracted by the modern view of the 'feudal' nature
> of Confucian ethics from recognizing the positive contribution made by
> these social values as a civilizing influence on the people of the seven-
> teenth century, who were emerging from a much ruder and more vio-
> lent age.[44]

While other scholars have agreed with this assessment,[45] the impact of Confucian morality and learning as transmitted by individual Tokugawa thinkers is a subject deserving of extensive investigation in itself. It is this personal transmission of Confucianism that is especially noteworthy and undoubtedly had a greater impact on the educational structures of pre-modern Japan than any putative Bakufu orthodoxy.

## The Bakufu and Neo-Confucianism

The relationship between Neo-Confucianism and the Bakufu is a much-debated one, often predicated on certain assumptions which have to do with the role of Neo-Confucian ethics as containing either the seeds of the modernization of Japan or antecedents to the authoritarian structures of pre-war Japan.[46] While there has been a widespread acceptance of the idea that Neo-Confucianism served as an orthodoxy upholding the Bakufu order, thus providing a rationale for its mode of wielding political power, recent scholarship indicates that this assumption is far from accurate. A notable exception to the traditionally held view of Neo-Confucianism's role in relation to the Bakufu is George Sansom, who, more than twenty years ago, wrote: "Looking at the political history from, say, 1650 to 1700, one finds little indication of an orthodox ideology approved by the Tokugawa government; and if that is a correct view, it cannot be said that the government depended upon an 'official' Confucianism for the support of its actions."[47]

More recently Herman Ooms has argued that during this period "no single tradition was privileged with exclusive Bakufu support that would have turned its teachings into an enforceable orthodoxy."[48] Thus, there was no official Bakufu ideology, but rather an illusion of one created by the Hayashi family to bolster its own political position.[49] In his extensive treatment of this subject in *Tokugawa Ideology*, Ooms states emphatically: "The trajectory of Razan's career indicates that Neo-Confucianism was never perceived by the early Tokugawa Shoguns as a tradition deserving specific support. Neo-Confucianism, in the first half of Tokugawa rule, cannot in any responsible way be spoken of as an officially espoused 'state ideology' or orthodoxy no matter how one qualifies the term."[50] Ooms believes that the samurai, in an effort to legitimize themselves as a ruling class, produced an ideology. However, he notes the samurai may not have been aware of the class bias of

their statements, for their appeal to order was "shared by other seg-
ments of the population and was thus quite legitimate."[51] Ooms
concludes that their efforts did not result in a doctrine that was
"imposed as an orthodoxy by the direct power of the 'state.' "[52]

This absence of official orthodoxy is also evident in the lack of a
civil service examination system in Japan for holding public office.
In China it was the civil service examination system which had directly and indirectly encouraged a state form of Neo-Confucian orthodoxy. Wm. Theodore de Bary notes this fact in discussing what he
calls a loose Bakufu orthodoxy in contrast to a more systematic Man-
darin orthodoxy, and observes that the former was consequently
"less pervasive in influence, less routine in its workings, and less
uniform in its effects."[53] Instead, de Bary points to the greater importance in Japan of both a philosophical orthodoxy and a broad
view of orthodoxy passed on by individual Neo-Confucian thinkers.

While there is little evidence in the early seventeenth-century
that Neo-Confucianism was directly invoked by the Bakufu as an
orthodox system of political thought, certain aspects of Neo-Confucianism's ethical and educational objectives became increasingly
significant in this period of peace and stability. The transmission of
ethics that would act as a civilizing and humanizing force was a
primary concern of both government edicts and individual treatises.
Moreover, it is precisely through this transmission of ethics that
Neo-Confucianism became adapted to the Japanese context. It was
in this period that Neo-Confucianism moved from the confines of
the Zen monasteries, where it had been transplanted from China
during the Kamakura and Muromachi periods, and into the larger
intellectual, cultural, and social milieu of Tokugawa Japan. This process of the indigenization of Neo-Confucian thought can be observed in the moral edicts, scholarly treatises, educational essays,
and popular sermons of the period. These documents are of an official, a personal, an educational, or a literary nature.[54]

On an official level, for example, the *Buke shohatto* were edicts
reissued periodically in 1615, 1635, and 1685 by the Bakufu to help
regulate the conduct of the samurai in the newly established feudal
order.[55] These *Laws of the Military Houses* were significant in attempting to introduce the samurai to a civilian role to supplement their
military role, now that peace had been established with the unification of the country. Thus, the samurai were urged to pursue learning along with the military arts. This fusion of *bun* (culture) and *bu*
(military) served as a theoretical framework for the rationale of the
samurai class in fulfilling its particular role in the society. Based in

part on Confucian moral principles and inspired by attempts of earlier shoguns and regents to regulate the warrior class,[56] these edicts had counterparts in the personal precepts of samurai to their retainers, and in the writings of individual Confucian scholars addressed to the samurai.

Having unified the country, the Tokugawa government was determined to rule not by military force alone, but also by legal and ethical restraints. The importance of their choice cannot be underestimated, for the basic Confucian ethical patterns of Tokugawa society did not disappear with the collapse of the Bakufu in the late nineteenth-century. While these codes may seem at times antiquarian to the modern reader, they were undoubtedly effective in maintaining order, discipline, and decorum. Based on mutual duties and responsibilities, these codes utilized the deep-rooted patterns of relationships built on an intricate web of loyalties.[57]

In addition to this public advocacy of ethical restraint, individual scholars and teachers acknowledged the importance of Neo-Confucian practice for Tokugawa society. Their involvement in the transmission of ethics through educational institutions, lectures, and moral treatises is a major feature of the period.

### Individual Scholars and the Way

Recognizing in the Confucian tradition certain humanistic, educational, and religious elements that were essential for the newly unified Tokugawa order, the *jugakusha* (Confucian scholars) embarked on the task of adapting Confucian teachings to the Japanese context. The process of indigenization has been described by Kate Nakai as the "naturalization of Confucianism," namely an attempt to strike a balance between accommodation and neutralization.[58] She observes:

> . . . what is most striking about the history of Confucianism in the first century of Tokugawa rule is not the increase of its ideological use. It is rather the emergence of a significant number of men who adapted the way of the sages as a personal creed. As a widespread phenomenon, this is a new development in Japanese history. Consideration of the role played by Confucianism in Tokugawa society needs to take into account the reasons why these people turned towards the Way and the outlook they brought to it.[59]

To accomplish the task of naturalization, the scholars explicated Confucian metaphysics and ethics in relation to Shinto and advocated Confucian institutions and practices in accord with specific time, place, and circumstance. Yamazaki Ansai, Kumazawa Banzan, Nakae Tōju, Yamaga Sokō, and Ekken himself are only a few of the Confucian scholars who were engaged in this intricate process of adaptation and for each of them the religious dimensions of Confucian thought were an important bridge to Shinto. As Tetsuo Najita has observed, for many of these scholars this process of adaptation was a means of giving a language and a vocabulary to an indigenous ethical system.[60]

Yet accommodation was not easily accomplished and many ambivalent attitudes remained. Richard Minear has noted that "for all Japanese Confucian scholars there existed a tension between attraction to universal values of Chinese origin on the one hand and the psychological demand to find value in Japan on the other."[61] Indeed, the strong divergent opinions of the kogakusha (Ancient Learning School) and kokugakusha (National Learning School) signal the varying directions toward which the seventeenth-century efforts at adaptation led—one back to the original texts of Confucianism and the other toward the nativist roots of the Japanese tradition before sinification had occurred. The vigor of these divergent schools reinforces the fact that the debate was far from abstract, nor was it simply directed toward political ends. The question then remains compelling as to why so many of the seventeenth-century Japanese intellectuals adopted the Way as a personal creed.

The growing appeal of Neo-Confucianism to scholars at this time is of major interest in understanding Ekken and his educational concerns. Because of the recent emergence from a lengthy period of warring factions, there was a felt need for a philosophy of life that was not primarily monastic or other-worldly oriented, as the major forms of Zen and Pure Land Buddhism were perceived to be. Instead, there was a recognition of the importance of a system of philosophy and of ethicoreligious practice that would guide human actions and order human relations amidst the demands of daily affairs. For many Tokugawa scholars Neo-Confucianism clearly had this appeal. With its broadly defined concept of the Way and its particular model of the sage personality, it provided both an overarching concept and a personalized exemplar to orient human goals and inspire human action. The major task of the Tokugawa Neo-Confucians was to define the Way in Japanese terms and to evoke the model of the sage for their own period. The task was both personal and educational, secular and spiritual.

For individual scholars and teachers, then, Neo-Confucian thought provided the foundations for a personally meaningful philosophy as well as the texts and method for establishing a broader educational program and spiritual discipline. Thus, Neo-Confucianism was embraced by Ekken and others both for its path of self-cultivation and for its educational methods, which were identified as indispensable for the particular needs of seventeenth-century Tokugawa society.

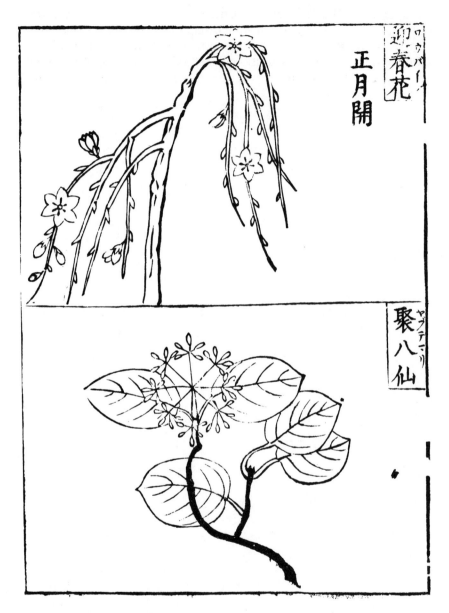

正月開　迎春花　ロフバー

聚八仙　ヤブテマリ

ABOVE: *Obai* (Chinese name), *Geishunka* (Japanese name). A yellow plum; opens in the first month of the year. BELOW: *Yabutemari*. "The gathering of eight hermits." A kind of Japanese snowball.

# 3

# Biography of Ekken

## EKKEN'S FAMILY

Kaibara Ekken's ancestors were said to have descended from the Fujiwara family.[1] They were hereditary Shinto priests at the Kibitsu shrine in Bitchū near the present-day city of Okayama. At the end of Muromachi period (1338–1573) one member of the family, Tahei, moved to Okayama. It was his son, Ichibei, who was Ekken's grandfather. He was also called Kyūbei, and after he took the Buddhist tonsure in his later years he received the name Sōgi. Kyūbei distinguished himself as a samurai and as a *han* (domain) official. Indeed, it was through his efforts that the position of the Kaibara family became firmly established in the Kuroda *han* in Kyushu. (In his later life Ekken, out of respect for his grandfather, took the name Kyūbei.)

In his youth Kyūbei served the renowned samurai warrior and ally of Oda Nobunaga, Takeda Shingen (1521–1573), in Kai, present day Yamanashi prefecture. Takeda later broke with Nobunaga, and after Takeda's death, Kyūbei wandered through several provinces seeking employment. He was eventually employed by the Mori family, who were stationed in Chōshū in southern Japan for defense of the nation's borders. It was here that Kyūbei married a daughter of the Yagi family, and they had two sons and two daughters. The eldest, Toshisada or Kansai, was Ekken's father.

Kyūbei did not remain in Chōshū but moved to Hyōgo in Kyushu after he was summoned there to serve Kuroda Josui (1546–

1604), a Christian *daimyo* (domain lord). His career as a samurai was quite active at this time, as Toyotomi Hideyoshi had selected Josui to be part of the vanguard in his campaign to subjugate Kyushu. Kyūbei gained great merit in this campaign, and after the Kuroda were appointed the ruling family of Buzen province, he was employed as a magistrate until his death in 1616. As a samurai of the Warring States period and as a talented domain official, he had a distinguished career.

Ekken's father, Kansai, was born in Chōshū in 1597. Moving with Kyūbei to Kyushu, he was also eventually employed by the Kuroda domain and served Kuroda Tadayuki for many years. At the age of eighteen, he married a daughter of the Mikado family, one of the ruling clans of Buzen province. With her he had five sons, although the eldest, Tarosuke, died at an early age. The next son was Kyūbei, named after his grandfather. The third was Mototada, also known as Sonzai, and the fourth son was Yoshitada, also known as Rakken. The youngest son was Atsunobu, also known as Sonken and later as Ekken. While several of the sons served the Kuroda domain, it was Ekken in particular who distinguished himself by following in the footsteps of his father and grandfather in their service to the Kuroda domain.

Ekken's father, Kansai, was said to be a milder and calmer man than Ekken's grandfather had been.[2] He was considered to be a model of behavior toward servants and guests. Most significantly, he was interested in education, was himself trained as a doctor, and encouraged learning among his sons. Although his wife was Buddhist, he rejected Buddhism and revered Confucianism. He served the Kuroda family for many years, and yet he was subject to the fluctuations of political favor. Thus, for reasons which are not completely clear, he was forced to move fairly frequently during Ekken's youth. At one point he lost his stipend and spent several years as a masterless samurai (*rōnin*).[3]

In 1630, when Ekken was born, his father had been living for some time within the Fukuoka castle and was employed as an attendant doctor. The following year, however, he was forced to move into a dilapidated house in Hakata, Katabarachō. It was here that Ekken's mother died when he was five. Although his father remarried, his stepmother also died during Ekken's childhood, when he was twelve. Thus he and his brothers were raised by a faithful servant woman to whom Ekken became deeply attached.[4]

Okada Takehiko has pointed out that although Ekken was from a samurai family, he grew up surrounded largely by townspeople (*chōnin*).[5] Samurai children traditionally grew up within the castle, but Ekken and his brothers lived principally in Hakata, outside the castle walls, and were cared for by a *chōnin* servant woman. These early contacts with townspeople may well have influenced his later decision to write for a wide audience and not simply for the educated samurai.[6]

## HIS EARLY EDUCATION

Ekken was said to have been a precocious child, teaching himself the native Japanese syllabary system (*kana*) and demonstrating an ability to read at an early age.[7] In 1638, his father and older brother participated in military operations to suppress the Shimabara rebellion. During this time Ekken was living with his father and brothers in the countryside of Yagiyama. It was here that he began to learn Chinese characters from his brother Sonzai.[8] Books were difficult to buy due to his family's financial condition, and so he borrowed such classics as *Heike monogatari*, *Heiji monogatari*, and *Hogen monogatari* from a neighboring samurai family.[9] He was also familiar with recently published Japanese dictionaries such as *Setsuyōshū*, which contributed to his lifelong interest in finding a language that would be comprehensible for many people. It has been said that he read avidly during this period.[10]

Because of his family's limited financial resources he was not given the kind of education usually provided for the children of the samurai of his day. Instead, he was taught largely by his father and brothers, Sonzai in particular. When Ekken was nine, Sonzai was commissioned by the *han* to study medicine in Kyoto. He remained there for almost five years, during which time he came in contact, as would Ekken later, with the great Confucian scholars of his day. Ekken, meanwhile, continued to live with his father, who encouraged his studies and introduced him to books on medicine and nutrition. It was from his father's medical interests that he acquired his lifelong concern for health care, from which his famous book on the subject, *Yōjōkun* (Precepts on Health Care), later was written.

In his youth Ekken had accepted Pure Land Buddhism under the influence of his mother and stepmother. When Sonzai returned home from Kyoto in 1643, he began to teach Ekken the importance of the Confucian classics. It was Sonzai who urged Ekken to reject Buddhism and to immerse himself in Confucianism.[11] In the following year, when Ekken was fourteen, his father was sent by the *han* to Edo and Ekken went to live with Sonzai in Fukuoka. His father remained in Edo for many years, returning intermittently to Fukuoka. Under Sonzai's guidance, Ekken thus continued his studies of the Confucian classics and Chu Hsi learning.

By all accounts Sonzai was an outstanding scholar with remarkable moral characteristics. His personal influence on Ekken was enormous. After Sonzai's return from Kyoto at the age of twenty-six, he became the physician for Kuroda Mitsuyuki, Tadayuki's heir as *han* lord. He remained in this post for seven years, until he resigned and retired to the countryside. Here he opened a private school and people came from great distances to study with him. According to Inoue Tadashi, public instruction in the Kuroda domain began under the direction of Sonzai.[12] In the seventh volume of Ekken's complete works there are lengthy passages extolling the virtues of Sonzai as a Confucian scholar.[13] The fact that Sonzai was a model of learning for Ekken can be seen in the similarity of these passages to many lines in the chapters on "The Pursuit of Learning" in *Yamato zokkun* (Precepts for Daily Life in Japan).

## EMPLOYMENT BY THE HAN AND VISITS TO NAGASAKI

When he was eighteen Ekken was employed as an attendant by the domain lord, Tadayuki. He was placed in charge of accounts for clothes and supplies, and he received a four-person stipend for his work.[14] This was the beginning of service to the Kuroda family which lasted for well over four decades and spanned the rules of Tadayuki, Mitsuyuki, and Tsunamasa, respectively.

In 1648, the same year that he received employment, he went with his father to Edo as an attendant for the domain lord's alternate year of residence (*sankin kōtai*). This was the first of twelve trips to Edo during his life. In the spring of the following year he returned to Fukuoka and that summer his coming of age ceremony (*genpuku*) was held. Shortly afterward he accompanied the domain lord by sea to Nagasaki for defense inspection.

Since the closing of the country by the series of seclusion edicts in the 1630s, the Fukuoka and Saga domains were responsible for the defense of Nagasaki. For this purpose, a thousand soldiers were stationed there to control trade and prevent any foreign ships from entering. There had been a secret entry by some Italian missionaries who drifted ashore shortly after the beginning of the seclusion period. There was also an incident of Portuguese ships entering

Nagasaki as late as 1639. This caused alarm to Bakufu officials who urged tighter controls by the Kyushu lords.

Ekken made numerous trips to Nagasaki, both with domain commissions carrying out these defense plans and also as a *rōnin*. It was here he came in contact with certain aspects of Western learning through books and through various Dutch interpreters. In addition, he had access to Chinese learning through books which were secretly imported despite the ban on foreign materials under the seclusion edicts. On his first visit to Nagasaki in 1649 he obtained a translation of a book on astronomy that recorded the astronomy of the European Middle Ages. Inoue Tadashi has suggested that it was also during this visit that he encountered, through books and interpreters, the idea of universal brotherhood among peoples (*shikaidōhō*).[15] Two years afterward when he was in Nagasaki as a *rōnin* intending to study medicine, he obtained a copy of Chu Hsi's work *Chin-ssu lu* (Reflections on Things at Hand), which had a profound influence on his thinking. It was seventeen years later that he wrote a commentary on this work entitled *Kinshiroku bikō*.

## RŌNIN PERIOD

Ekken's employment by Tadayuki was short-lived, for in 1650 he was dismissed and spent the next seven years as a *rōnin*. Tadayuki was considered to be a tempermental person and, enmeshed in domain factionalism, he was apparently unable to recognize Ekken's talents. Nonetheless, Ekken's scholarly interests progressed, and he spent some time in Nagasaki pursuing his study of medicine.

Meanwhile, his father, who was still in Edo, bequeathed all his property to his third son, Rakken. Yet he was eager to encourage Ekken's studies and summoned him to Edo for this purpose.[16] In 1655, Ekken made the journey by boat to Osaka, then overland to Kyoto and up to Edo by way of the Tokaidō road. He stayed in a lodging in Kawasaki before entering Edo. There, as was the custom, he cut his hair in preparation for becoming a doctor. He took the name Jūsai, meaning gentleness, to indicate his desire to conquer force with gentleness. He remained in Edo about a year and a half. Through his father he was introduced to the senior minister of the Kuroda clan and his chief retainers. He also met frequently with Hayashi Gahō (1618–1680), the leading Bakufu Confucian scholar. This marked the beginning of his contacts with numerous scholars in both Edo and Kyoto, which lasted throughout his life.

## REEMPLOYMENT AND STUDY IN KYOTO

Upon his return to Fukuoka with his father in 1656, Ekken was employed by Mitsuyuki, the new lord of the Kuroda domain. Mitsuyuki was involved in the conversion of the domain bureaucracy to a civil administration system, and he employed Ekken for a six-person stipend. Ekken was assigned to serve a senior *han* samurai, Tachibana Kanzaemon, who took a special interest in him and eventually became one of his strongest supporters.

In 1657, through Tachibana's influence, Ekken was sent by the *han* to Kyoto to continue his studies. He stayed there for the next seven years, meeting the great scholars of the day, hearing their lectures, and embarking on various series of lectures himself. His access to these scholars and to Kyoto's cultural life and numerous bookstores continued to be a source of stimulus throughout his life. Indeed, the rich cultural life of Kyoto, in addition to fostering his varied intellectual pursuits, sparked his avid interest in dance, poetry, and music. It was in Kyoto that he began to attend dance performances, hold poetry gatherings and perform on various musical instruments.

When Ekken first arrived in Kyoto he met the eminent Confucian scholar, Matsunaga Sekigo (1592–1657), who was a pupil of Fujiwara Seika (1561–1619) and the teacher of Kinoshita Jun'an (1621–1698).[17] Unfortunately Matsunaga died shortly after their meeting, but Ekken's friendship with Jun'an continued for many years. Like Ekken, Jun'an was interested in both education and practical learning, and Ekken admired his open spirit and comprehensive breadth as a scholar.[18] In addition to hearing Jun'an's lectures, Ekken attended those of Yamazaki Ansai (1618–1682). In contrast to Jun'an, Ansai appeared severe, dogmatic, and more interested in strict moral discipline than in the investigation of principles for practical learning. For these reasons Ekken was critical of his thought. The noted Confucians, Kumazawa Banzan (1619–1691)[19] and Ishikawa Jōzan (1583–1672), were also in Kyoto at this time, but apparently Ekken did not meet them. Some years later he did meet with Itō Jinsai (1627–1705) of the *Kogaku* (Ancient Learning) school. They did not become intimate, however, because Ekken disapproved of Jinsai's rejection of Chu Hsi learning in favor of a return to the early Confucian classics.[20]

Because of Ekken's wide interests, his acquaintances in Kyoto were not limited to the Confucians with whom he discussed Confucian texts. He had animated exchanges with Nakamura Tekisai (1629–1702) on subjects concerned with practical learning varying from astronomy to botany. Indeed, Nakamura's publication in 1666 of a classification of natural objects no doubt influenced Ekken's work in this field. Ekken also knew the historian, Matsushita Kenrin (1637–1704), the physician, Kurokawa Dōyū (d. 1691), and the herbalist, Inao Jakusui (1655–1715).

Inao, a leading naturalist of this period, was a great stimulus to Ekken in his own study of plants.[21] In 1692, Inao published a catalogue of the natural products of Japan, and four years later published one on edible plants. In 1697 he began to compile a massive encyclopedia of natural products, intending to fill a thousand volumes. This project was patronized by the Kaga lord, Maeda, on the recommendation of Kinoshita Jun'an. It was, however, left incomplete at the time of Inao's death. The encyclopedia, known as *Shobutsu ruisan*, was eventually finished in 1735 under Yoshimune's order. Ekken, who died a year before Inao, was no doubt inspired by his dedicated scholarship in the natural sciences. It was in 1709 that Ekken published his own contribution to this field *Yamato honzō* (Plants of Japan). Both Ekken and Inao published editions of the famous Ming compilation of Li Shih-chen, *Pen-ts'ao kang mu*. (Ekken's appeared in 1672 and Inao's appeared posthumously in 1717.)

In 1659 Ekken became acquainted with Mukai Genshō (1609–1677), a doctor and botanist who eventually became a lifelong friend. Mukai founded the Confucian academy, Tateyama, in Nagasaki and he and his descendants at the academy were appointed book examiners as part of the Bakufu's censorship efforts against books on Christianity.[22] In addition to being an herbalist, Mukai was a scholar of medicine and astronomy, and thus had intellectual concerns similar to Ekken's. Mukai, Inao, and Nakamura were a great stimulus for Ekken's interest in plants and their classification.

Ekken also developed a friendship with Miyazaki Yasusada (1623–1697), who became well known for his book on agriculture (*Nōgyō zensho*),[23] published in 1696. To compile this book Miyazaki had traveled to various provinces investigating farming methods and talking to local farmers. He eventually settled in a village near Fukuoka, where he became an authority on farm production. His correspondence and visits with Ekken in Fukuoka continued throughout his life. It was through Ekken that Miyazaki came in contact with Chinese books on agriculture, which were a great stimulus to his research. Moreover, it was Ekken's personal interest in Miyazaki's work which resulted in its publication.[24]

Ekken's conscientious study in Kyoto did not go unnoticed by the domain lord, Mitsuyuki. In 1659, on a visit to Kyoto, he presented Ekken with kimonos and books as a reward for his diligence.

In the following year Ekken was sent to Edo for four months to continue his studies. There he heard Hayashi Gahō lecture on divination. After returning to Kyoto he himself began to lecture more frequently, choosing as his topics the classics of *Elementary Learning*, *Filial Piety*, the *Great Learning*, and the *Analects*. In 1662 he began lecturing on the *Doctrine of the Mean* and *Mencius*. In the spring of the following year he lectured for the first time on Chu Hsi's *Reflections on Things at Hand*. These remained some of the principal topics of his lectures throughout his life.

In 1664 he was ordered to return to Fukuoka, and this marked the end of his seven years of study in Kyoto. In the three years after his return to the *han*, two major events occurred in his personal life. In 1665 his father died in Fukuoka. This was a great personal loss to Ekken, who was still single. Three years later, at the age of thirty eight, he was married to Tōken (1652–1713), the daughter of the Esaki family, who were local administrators of Akizuki, a village in Chikuzen province. Tōken has frequently been praised as a highly educated and talented woman who was skilled in calligraphy and in playing the *koto*.[25] She often kept diaries and wrote notes for Ekken when he traveled.[26] It was apparently a happy marriage of rare intellectual compatibility. While there were no children, Ekken later adopted his brother Sonzai's son, Shigeharu, to continue his family line. Ekken's marriage to Tōken lasted for some forty-five years, and his death occurred within a year of hers.

At the time of his marriage he took the name Kyūbei, after his grandfather. The *han* honored him by raising his stipend to two hundred *koku*. This was one of the largest amounts given to a Confucian scholar at that time, and it remained at this amount for the next twenty-eight years. Then, when he was sixty-six, his stipend was raised to three hundred *koku*, again a singular distinction for a scholar of this period. It remained at that level until his death seventeen years later.

## SERVICE AS HAN SCHOLAR

From the time of his return from Kyoto, Ekken's years of study were utilized in service to the domain. Despite his delicate health, he embarked on a rigorous program of lecturing, tutoring, research, and writing that was to continue for the next fifty years. The modern scholar Inoue Tetsujirō noted the intensity of Ekken's scholarly efforts citing his tendency to forego sleep in his eagerness to study and to write.[27] In addition, he traveled frequently, accompanying the daimyo to Edo, visiting Kyoto to attend or give lectures, and investigating the history and topography of Chikuzen province. During the twelve years after his study in Kyoto he spent several months each year in Edo or Kyoto or both. He maintained or broadened his contacts with leading Confucian scholars, thereby having numerous opportunities for intellectual exchange. In addition, he had access to books imported via Nagasaki, and on occasion acted as a liaison for the domain when delegates from Korea arrived in Nagasaki to begin their journey to Edo.[28]

As a *han* scholar, his tasks came under three major headings: lecturing and tutoring, study and research, editing and writing. Ekken's career as a lecturer began a year after he went to Kyoto. Following the tradition of various other scholars in Kyoto, Ekken would give a lecture or a series of talks on one of the Confucian classics or on Chu Hsi's writings. His audience was comprised of other leading scholars or members of the nobility (*kuge*) interested in such topics. The lectures were apparently well attended and his reputation began to spread.

After returning to Kyushu he was frequently called upon to lecture within the castle in Fukuoka. In addition, he occasionally lectured the domain lord, Mitsuyuki, while accompanying him to Edo. He was often requested to speak on the classics or on Chu Hsi's thought at the *han* residence in Edo. His teaching skills were not confined to his peers, for he also taught young students in the domain. Inoue Tetsujirō observed that while Ekken never established a private school in his *han*, as did other contemporary Confucians, nonetheless, his influence on education in this period was substantial.[29] In 1672 he was appointed the official tutor for the daimyo heir, Tsunamasa, and on certain occasions when he was in Edo he was requested to tutor the shogun's heir as well. His constant concern in these lectures was to promote moral education, encourage spiritual cultivation, and develop political leadership. This was a natural outgrowth of his commitments and duties as a Confucian scholar in the service of the domain.

Although as a lecturer Ekken was close to the sources of authority in the domain, he generally remained removed from the direct conduct of political affairs. Instead, he apparently hoped to influence policy by the traditional Neo-Confucian practice of lecturing on the classics to illustrate the desirable moral path for both ruler and ruled. In 1674, however, a succession dispute arose in the domain, spurred on by a faction which opposed the powerful

Tachibana family. There was also unrest and distress in the *han* because of the severity of taxes. At this time Ekken intervened directly, writing letters to the Tachibana and Kuroda lords urging them not to neglect their responsibilities as political leaders.[30]

In the third volume of Ekken's collected works there are two letters which are addressed to domain leaders and contain advice on economic and political matters.[31] One of the letters concerns a problem of severe taxes and the other admonishes the lax behavior of the Kuroda lord. The first, dated 1679, is addressed to Tachibana Kanzaemon. In it Ekken notes that the domain's resources are insufficient to meet expenses because of the high cost of living needed in Edo for alternate attendance (*sankin kōtai*). He says, however, that people should not be impoverished by severe taxes, nor should the domain cut back samurai stipends. Rather, the domain should make an effort to reduce its expenses in Edo. He observes also that financial difficulties have arisen from the issuing of paper money. Economic reforms by the government are necessary.

The second letter, dated 1680, is addressed to Kuroda Shigetane and notes that the *han* government has declined considerably. This, he maintains, is because of the inappropriate behavior of the domain lord, about which public opinion is becoming outspoken. Ekken admonishes the lord to reform his selfish ways and to be more concerned for the public good.

In addition to these letters, in 1703 Ekken published a theoretical treatise on the *Precepts for the Noble Person (Kunshikun)*. Here he stressed the significance of humane government in maintaining order in the state and he suggested ways to implement this in administration as well as in the person of the ruler. He outlined various steps for the ruler, namely:

1. Keeping in mind that the essential aspect of learning is self-cultivation for the governance of people.
2. Realizing that the most effective method of study is uniting knowledge and action.
3. Being able to listen to criticism and correct one's faults.
4. Knowing the good and bad points of people, especially ministers.
5. Being just in rewards and punishments.
6. Clarifying human relations.
7. Practicing frugality in managing economic affairs.[32]

However, Okada Takehiko has noted that perhaps most essential to Ekken's political thought was his stress on filiality.[33] Ekken emphasized the need to practice a spirit of filiality and gratitude in relations between ruler and ruled. Thus, humane government involved extending the traditional Confucian principles governing family relations to the larger sphere of the country.

## RESEARCH AND PRACTICAL LEARNING

To fulfill this task of lecturing on both personal and political rectification, Ekken was constantly engaged in scholarly research on a wide range of topics. These revolved around a fundamental interest in practical learning (*jitsugaku*).[34] As Okada has indicated, "The scope of Ekken's *jitsugaku* was truly amazing, covering everything from the experience and practice of ethics to manners, institutions, linguistics, medicine, botany, zoology, agriculture, production, taxonomy, food sanitation, law, mathematics (computation), music, and military tactics."[35] One might also add to the list astronomy, geography, history, archeology, and genealogy. The German physician and naturalist Philip Franz von Siebold (1796–1866), who visited Japan in the nineteenth century, similarly recognized the remarkable scope of Ekken's studies, calling him "the Aristotle of Japan."[36]

Ekken's practical learning was evident in his support for a group of researchers in astronomy within the Kuroda domain. The head of this group, Yasui Shunkai (1639–1715), used Chinese astronomical instruments to develop his own original theories and to promote calendar reforms. When Ekken visited Kyoto he frequently observed the stars with the amateur astronomer, Nakamura Tekisai (1629–1702). He was also a close friend of the noted astronomer Hoshino Sanenobu.

In promoting mathematics, Ekken's practical concerns were again manifest. The attitude of the traditional samurai of the period was to disdain learning computations, for the samurai considered economic affairs as something relegated to the merchant class. Ekken rejected this view and in his ethical and educational treatises (*kunmono*) repeatedly stressed the need to know mathematics. He emphasized its importance for good domestic management in the family, for careful agricultural planning by the farmers, and for sound economic policies by the government.[37]

Ekken's motivation in undertaking practical learning was to carry out Chu Hsi's injunction to investigate things and examine their principles. To facilitate this process he advocated a method of investigation which was adapted from Chu Hsi's directives to his

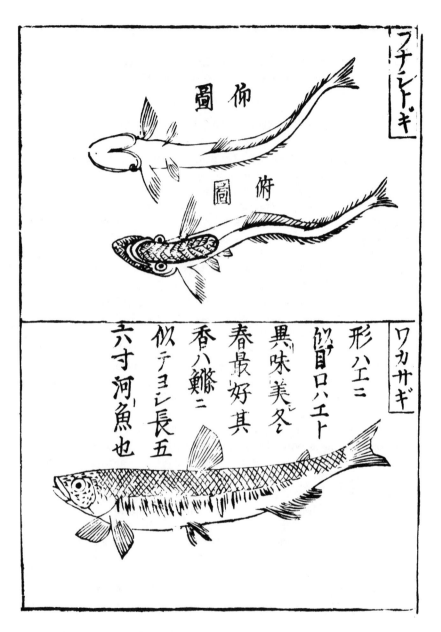

ABOVE: *Funashitogi*. A kind of shark sucker. Viewed from top and bottom. BELOW: *Wakasagi*. A fresh-water smelt. The shape is like *hae* (dace) although the eyes and mouth are different. The taste is quite good; in winter or spring it is best. It has a good smell, like a dace. It is about 7 inches long and is a river fish.

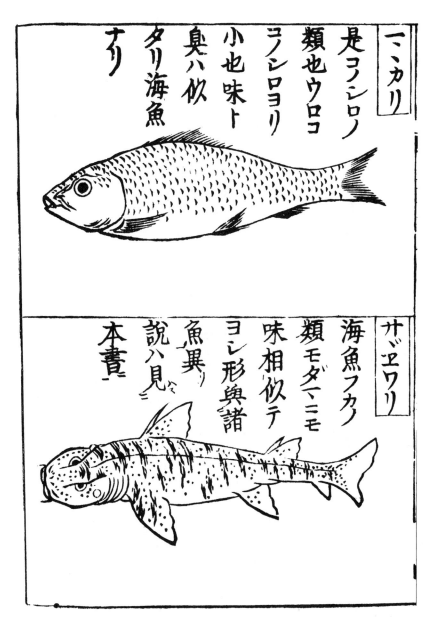

ABOVE: *Mamakari*. This is a kind of *konoshiro* (gizzard shad). The scales are smaller than a *konoshiro*, but the taste and smell are similar. It is a sea fish.
BELOW: *Sazaewari*. This is a kind of shark. The taste is good, like a *modama*. The shape is different from other kinds of fish.

students at the White Deer Grotto. In the introduction to *Yamato honzō* (Plants of Japan), Ekken described the unacceptable ways of scholarly study as follows:

> One should not blindly regard all one has heard as true and reject what others say merely because they disagree, nor be stubborn and refuse to admit mistakes. To have inadequate information, to be overly credulous about what one has seen and heard, to adhere rigidly to one's own interpretation, or to make a determination in a precipitate manner—all these four modes of thinking are erroneous.[38]

In contrast he suggested that a correct methodology should be marked by the following characteristics, which may be seen as elaborations of Chu Hsi's instructions:

1. Valuing broad learning and wide experience.
2. Not being overly credulous but remaining skeptical in regard to doubtful cases.
3. Being fair and objective in one's judgments.
4. Investigating thoroughly and reflecting carefully before making a judgment.[39]

With regard to the first principle of the need for broad knowledge, Ekken wrote, "The ancients said that all things under the sun are their province, and I too must become a man to whom the principles governing all things in the wide world are known."[40] His scholarly studies were by no means limited to textual exegesis or empirical analysis. It embraced popular culture as well. Indeed, he felt it was his mission both to study popular customs and to transmit Confucian values to the ordinary person. He asserted, "All that I have undertaken in my own humble writings has been the task of helping the young and the ordinary person to whatever extent I can."[41] He wrote of his studies of all classes of people:

> I followed up on what the townspeople spoke of, salvaged what I could prove out of even the most insane utterances, and made inquiries of people of the most lowly station. I was always willing to inquire into the most mundane and everyday matters and give consideration to all opinions. Forgetting about myself, I listened to others.[42]

Yet Ekken was aware of the need to maintain objectivity and rationality in the analysis of principles. He was not interested in simply collecting data or in becoming a specialist or technician of knowledge. He wanted to be able to bring together scholarly research and popular education, and to see empirical investigation and ethicoreligious practice as part of a single continuum.

Like many Confucians before him Ekken warned against the limitations of methods used by both the "humanist" scholar and the "scientific" researcher. For him the Neo-Confucian School of the Way (Ch.*Tao-hsüeh*, Jp. *dōgaku*), as an essentially ethicoreligious path, had to be distinguished from textual studies or technical skills, which might become ends in themselves. He urged scholars to maintain a reflective and contemplative posture when reading the classics, so as not to fall into the trap of empty exegesis or linguistic analysis for its own sake. Similarly, he rebuked both the scholarly specialists who were interested only in personal recognition and the technicians who were obsessed with manipulative processes. As Okada Takehiko has pointed out, Ekken felt that if one ignored moral principles, one was likely to become a narrow-minded specialist, and if one simply sought technical expertise, one was apt to become a manipulative technician.[43]

Thus, in terms of the content of education he sought to bring together "humanistic" and "scientific" studies. He advocated a practical learning which would foster self-cultivation while also assisting others. He urged that learning should be "preserved in the heart and carried out in action" (*juyō no gaku*).[44] Both traditional humanistic values and specific technical skills should be used for the benefit of self and society. In this way the scholar would be assisting in the Confucian aspiration to participate in the transformation of heaven and earth.

In order to bring together "humanistic" and "scientific" concerns, Ekken felt that a physician, for example, should practice humaneness while helping to "nourish life" (*yōjō no jutsu*).[45] His skills could not be dispensed without an understanding of his larger ethical responsibility. Similarly, to study horticultural techniques or to cultivate plants only because of their beauty was to trivialize their larger role in the natural order. By being concerned with manipulative processes of cultivation a person could fall into the danger of "trifling with things and losing one's sense of purpose."[46] Rather, horticulture and agriculture ought to be undertaken with an understanding of "the proclivity of nature to give birth to living things."[47] An appreciation of nature's mysterious fecundity as the source of life was essential to Ekken's form of practical learning. From this religious sense of reverence for the sacredness of all forms of life flowed a remarkably diverse range of research projects.

Ekken's encounters with leading scholars, his extensive travels, his wide reading, and his access to imported books via Nagasaki all contributed to his notable breadth of scholarly interests and research in practical learning. This was not simply surface knowledge, as can be seen in his development of an empirical method; his documentation of plant, fish, and animal species; his detailed investigation of agricultural techniques; and his experiments in astronomy and mathematics.

## EKKEN'S WRITINGS

The fruits of Ekken's lectures and research can be seen in his writings. He was prolific, producing more than one hundred and ten works. His collected works cover eight volumes which include:

Vol. 1  Essays on etiquette and philology.
Vol. 2  Essays written in classical Chinese (*kanbun*) concerning Confucian and Neo-Confucian texts.
Vol. 3  Collected essays on educational and moral precepts.
Vol. 4  Topography and history of Chikuzen.
Vol. 5  Records of the Kuroda family and histories of the local shrines.
Vol. 6  Botanical essays.
Vol. 7  Travelogues, Sonzai's writings, and essays on Chinese poetry.
Vol. 8  Essays on farming and on filial piety.[48]

Essentially these writings can be divided into those concerned with 1) Confucian thought and ethicoreligious practice, 2) *han* commissions of the Kuroda geneology and local topography, 3) studies in botany, and 4) agricultural and travelogue observations.

In order to promote Confucian learning, Ekken punctuated the Chinese classics and Neo-Confucian texts for easy reading by the Japanese. He also compiled his lectures on individual classics and wrote commentaries on the major works of Chu Hsi. His *Kinshiroku bikō*, one of the first Tokugawa commentaries on Chu's *Reflections on Things at Hand*, was published in 1668 and was admired by both Japanese and Chinese Confucian scholars. In his efforts to popularize Confucian ethicoreligious practices, he wrote essays of vernacular instruction (*kunmono*) designed for a wide audience. The majority of these were written after he retired from active domain service at the age of seventy. They included essays addressed to the samurai, the lord, the family, women, and children. He also wrote on health care, on learning, on calligraphy, and on literature. His treatises on *Precepts on Health Care* (*Yōjōkun*) and the *Learning for*

*Women* (*Onna daigaku*)[49] have remained to this day some of his best-known works. His essay on *Precepts for Daily Life in Japan* (*Yamato zokkun*) was included among these ethicoreligious treatises designed for a wide audience. In it he discussed the method of moral and spiritual discipline necessary for the practice of the learning of the mind-and-heart (*shingaku*). It was this *shingaku* cultivation which had been so significant in the development of Neo-Confucianism in both China and Korea and which, through Ekken and others, became an important force in Japanese Neo-Confucianism as well.

In addition to his Confucian writings, Ekken became involved in several projects for the Kuroda domain. In 1671 Ekken was commissioned by Mitsuyuki to compile the Kuroda family genealogy.[50] This was an enormous task which continued for seventeen years due to revisions and amendments made by both Ekken and Mitsuyuki. The first edition of the genealogy took seven years to compile, while the revised version took another ten years. Designed to demonstrate the loyalty of the Kuroda family to the Tokugawa rulers and to celebrate the meritorious battle deeds of their ancestors, it required the postponement of some of Ekken's major Confucian writings, including his ethicoreligious treatises and the *Record of Grave Doubts* (*Taigiroku*), until the end of his life.[51]

In 1688, the same year he completed the revised Kuroda genealogy, Ekken became absorbed in another major domain project, which was to last for fifteen years. He requested and received permission to compile a study of the topography of Chikuzen province. He became absorbed in gathering materials for this project and traveled extensively throughout the domain for his research. He was assisted in this work by his nephew, Yoshihisa (1664–1700) and his disciple, Takeda Shun'an. The extent of his success can be noted by the fact that his book on Chikuzen's topography is still consulted by experts in the field.

Ekken's writings on botany were first published in 1709 (in sixteen chapters) and included discussions of medicinal herbs, illustrations of various Japanese plants, and a taxonomy of names and types of plants. Inoue Tadashi has cited this work, known as *Yamato honzō* (Plants of Japan), as the first systematic botany text in Japan, and Shirai Mitsutarō has described it as a work "full of originality."[52] Indeed, Ekken's studies in this field captured the attention and admiration of Westerners who came to Japan after the Meiji restoration.[53] In the preface to *Yamato honzō*, Ekken spoke of the constant fecundity of heaven and earth in bringing forth the myriad things. He noted that scholars have responsibility to study the princi-

ple of things and to understand their usefulness; and he mentioned
that his own sickness when he was young gave him a lifelong interest in studying herbs and ways of nourishing life.[54]

Ekken acknowledged his familiarity with the famous Ming compilation of plant taxonomy by Li Shih-chen (1518–1593) known as
*Pen-ts'ao kang mu*.[55] This was published in China in 1596, and eleven
years later Hayashi Razan obtained a copy via Nagasaki and presented it to Tokugawa Ieyasu. Hayashi wrote a commentary on the
preface and translated the Chinese plant names into Japanese. Ekken published a revised edition of Li's work in 1672; Inao Jakusui
also prepared an edition, which was published posthumously in
1717. Ekken's edition of the *Pen-ts'ao kang mu* supplied Japanese
translations of Chinese names as well as a supplement of more than
two hundred species of natural objects.

Ekken's own *Yamato honzō* (Plants of Japan) appeared in 1709.
His basic categories of classification were comparable to Li Shih-
chen's but went beyond trees, plants, and flowers to include birds,
fish, and shells. (In addition to these basic categories, Li's compilation included metals and stones, insects, reptiles, and animals.) In
his *Yamato honzō*, Ekken classified natural objects in thirty-seven categories and described over 1,550 objects in detail. The careful descriptions and the detailed quality of the illustrations in both
Ekken's and Li's works demonstrates the highly developed observa-
tional skills in the field of natural science achieved in both Ming
China and Tokugawa Japan.

Okada has noted the importance of Ekken's contribution in this
area as follows: "He absorbed, modified, and surpassed the traditional Chinese herbological studies, applying the principle with creative insight to the Japanese context in his *Yamato honzō* which had
an enormous influence on the development of later pharmacological, botanical, and zoological research in Japan."[56]

In addition to his botanical and topographical concerns, Ekken
wrote various accounts of his travels in Kyushu, Kansai and Kantō.
Until the last years of his life, Ekken was an avid traveler either at
the request of the *han* or in pursuit of his own research. Indeed,
during his life he made some twelve trips to Edo and twice that
many to Kyoto. Inoue Tadashi has pointed out that his travelogues
contained much more than geographical observations or descriptions of the scenery.[57] They reflected a keen observation of local agricultural methods and production comparable to that of Miyazaki
Yasusada in his records of farming practices contained in *Nōgyō
zensho* (Compendium on Agriculture). Similarly, they provided an

important record of temple and shrine pilgrimages common in the seventeenth century. Ekken, for example, frequently visited the Ise shrine on his way to or from Kyoto or Edo. He likewise took a great interest in the shrines in Fukuoka province, traveling extensively to research and record their history.

Ekken's travelogues recorded or verified local legends which supplemented historical data. Furthermore, they documented archeological sites and demonstrated their historical significance. One particular incident is frequently noted in accounts of Ekken's early travels. In 1664 he was returning to Fukuoka at the end of his seven years of study in Kyoto. En route he stopped in Hyōgo (Minato-gawa) at the grave site of Kusunoki Masashige (1294–1336), the renowned hero of the *Taiheiki*. He was saddened to discover there was no tombstone to mark the grave of this famous imperial loyalist, and he made arrangements for one to be erected. After returning to Fukuoka he cancelled his original plan to have a wealthy merchant from Hyōgo construct the tombstone. It was later carried out by Tokugawa Mitsukuni the sponsor of the *Dainihonshi* (Great History of Japan). Inoue and Okada have used this incident to illustrate Ekken's love of travel to historical sites and his particular admiration for the loyalty and nobility of purpose which Kusunoki displayed in championing the imperial cause against great odds.[58]

Ekken's writings, then, are the fruits of his wide-ranging research interests, in addition to the commissions of the domain rulers. Through the variety of his works one can see the many roles Ekken was asked to play as a *han* scholar and the roles he felt compelled to fill as a Confucian teacher. Ekken, it is clear, wrote out of concerns that were both ethicoreligious and empirical and tried to embrace an audience from the domain bureaucrats down through the townspeople, artisans, and farmers.

## CONCLUSION

Ekken's life, spanning the greater part of the seventeenth-century, represents the possibilities and achievements of a Neo-Confucian thinker in early Tokugawa Japan. As a student and scholar, he was supported and educated by the domain leadership. He had the opportunity for extended study in Kyoto and for numerous return trips there as well as to Edo and Nagasaki. He was thus able to be in contact with the leading scholars of his time and, with apparently few restrictions, to purchase books and exchange ideas. As an adviser, lecturer, and tutor within the *han*, he had direct contact with its politically influential leadership for more than three generations of Kuroda lords. This included three years of service to Tadayuki, thirty-three years to Mitsuyuki, and eight years to Tsunamasa. It was thus possible for him to meet what he felt was his Confucian responsibility to bring ethicoreligious values into the sphere of political and social decision making. Furthermore, as a teacher and educator he was able to extend these same ethicoreligious values into the education of the common people. His own early contact with the townspeople in Fukuoka and the farmers in Yagiyama had left its imprint on Ekken, and he never abandoned his desire to make Confucianism available to the widest number of people. His egalitarian educational concerns remained at the heart of his scholarly studies and research. It was his desire to transmit a learning that was both rational and affective, moral and practical, that inspired his remarkably active life. According to Olaf Graf, Ekken's originality lay not simply in elaborating Chu Hsi's thought, but in applying this philosophy to education.[59]

As George Sansom has observed, it was Ekken's particular combination of rational and practical breadth which made him such a notable figure in this period:

> Ekken himself ranked high, perhaps the highest, among the Confucianists of his day, since he combined great analytical power with practical wisdom. In other words he was able to apply the rationalizing principle of Chu Hsi to the formulation of a simple code of everyday morals. Probably no Japanese thinker had so great an effect upon standards of behavior in Tokugawa society, especially in its middle classes.[60]

More than fifty years earlier W. G. Aston had similarly praised Ekken:

> His sole object of writing was to benefit his countrymen; and his style, though manly and vigorous, is wholly devoid of rhetorical ornament, and of those frivolities of language which were so freely indulged in by contemporary novelists and dramatists. . . . [T]hough perhaps the most eminent scholar of his day, there is not an atom of pedantry about him. . . . Yekken's writings are full of excellent morality of a plain, common sense description. It is hardly possible to over-estimate their influence or the service which he rendered to his country by his teachings.[61]

While a thorough verification of Sansom's or Aston's claims cannot be undertaken here, it is of utmost interest to examine in greater detail the content of Ekken's thought as a means of understanding its wide appeal. In so doing, we might expand upon Sansom's characterization of Ekken's thought as "rational" and "practical" to note its rich emotional and religious undercurrents. A deep reverence for heaven and earth as great parents and an obligation to repay one's debt to them permeates Ekken's thought. It is this essentially religious motivation which informs Ekken's teachings on self-cultivation. For him, it is this comprehensive religious context which serves to dynamize human actions and validate human goals.

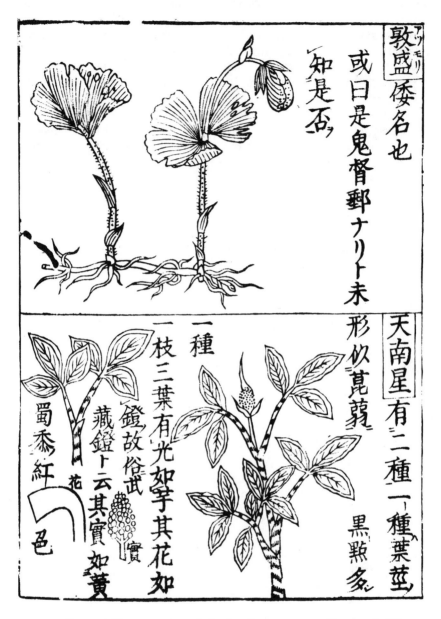

ABOVE: *Atsumori* (Japanese name). Lady slipper. BELOW: *Tennansei.* "Heavenly southern star plant." There are two kinds: (1) The leaf and stem are shaped like a *konyaku* (fragrant herb water plant). It has many black marks. (2) One stem has three leaves. Like a potato, the flower is shaped like a stirrup. Therefore, customarily it was called a *Musashi abumi* (Musashi stirrup). The berries are red like millet.

# 4

# Introduction to Ekken's Thought

Rooted in a sense of reverence and gratitude toward heaven and earth (*tenchi*), Ekken's religious concerns are both cosmic in scope and personal in focus. Heaven and earth are continually celebrated as the source and sustainer of life, and to him a primary goal of human existence is to realize one's sympathetic identity with these wellsprings of life.[1] Moral and spiritual cultivation for Ekken, then, becomes a means of recognizing the gift of the life principle (*seiri*) from heaven and earth and activating in human beings this natural connectedness to the universe through the extension of humaneness (Ch. *jen*, Jp. *jin*)[2] to all living things. A person's involvement in the social and political order is a further extension of this cultivation and the practical application of efforts at interior development. To experience a deep inner harmony with the myriad forms of life ("the ten thousand things") is the ultimate goal of this process which is most fully realized by the sage.

In these concerns Ekken is following some of the central ideas of the leading Sung Neo-Confucian, Chu Hsi. For Chu and for Ekken, humaneness is the source of human creativity and growth, just as the principle of origination is the root of productivity in nature. Thus for both these thinkers *jen* can be seen as "a cosmic love identified with the creativity of nature."[3]

Similarly, the other primary Confucian virtues have their cosmological and seasonal counterparts. While humaneness corresponds to "origination" and to spring, righteousness corresponds to "flourishing" and to summer, propriety to "advantage" and to

53

autumn, and wisdom to "correctness" and to winter.[4] Chu Hsi describes this correspondence of virtues and the seasons as follows:

> Humaneness, righteousness, propriety, and wisdom are origination, flourishing, advantage, and correctness. If in spring there were not the potential to bring forth, then when it came to summer there would be no cause for growth, in autumn and winter there would be no capacity to gather in and to store. The life force [ch'i] of the growth of spring permeates the whole and in humaneness is contained the impulse to movement and goodness.[5]

In other words, ethics and metaphysics are profoundly interrelated.[6] For Chu and for Ekken, moral transformation in human life is connected to and affirmed by larger generative processes in nature itself. This is a key element in Ekken's affirmation of Chu's basic philosophy, but it also becomes an important factor in his verbal disagreements with Chu. Above all, Ekken wished to emphasize the vitality implied in the life force, ch'i, as equated ethically with the generative principle of humaneness, jen.

## HEAVEN AND EARTH AS PARENTS: FILIALITY AND CO-CREATIVITY

Ekken continually spoke of the special relationship of human beings toward heaven and earth as similar to that of children toward their parents. In this respect he evokes the Western Inscription of Chang Tsai, the Sung Neo-Confucian, a work in which heaven is described as father and earth as mother. Since human beings are born from heaven and earth and receive the mind-and-heart of heaven and earth, they are endowed with intelligence and with moral virtues that distinguish them from other living things. This capacity for both rational and spiritual activity marks human beings as uniquely conscious of their connection to the cosmos and thus obligated to repay the great debt of having received the gift of life. It is for this reason that Ekken called upon people to serve heaven and earth with a heart of filiality and humaneness. He opened his treatise on Precepts for Daily Life in Japan with a summary of this position, which has strong antecedents in other Confucian writers in both China and Japan:

> The sages taught in the Book of History that heaven and earth are the parents of all things and that human beings are the spirit of the universe. This means that heaven and earth, being the source which gives

birth to all things, are the great parents. Since humans receive the purest material force of heaven and earth from birth, they surpass all other things and their mind shines forth clearly. Receiving a nature consisting of the five virtues [i.e. humaneness, righteousness, propriety, wisdom, faithfulness] their mind-and-heart is that of heaven and earth. Because among all things the position of humans is highest, they can be called the spirit of all things. That spirit is the bright shining essence in the mind-and-heart.

Heaven and earth give birth to and nourish all things but the deep compassion with which they treat humans is different from birds and beasts, trees and plants. Therefore, among all things only humans are the children of the universe. Thus humans have heaven as their father and earth as their mother and receive their great kindness. Because of this, always to serve heaven and earth is the Human Way.[7]

Ekken maintained that as a result of this unique connection to the natural order, human beings ought to extend the doctrine of filial piety to embrace the whole natural world.[8] Since nature is the source and sustainer of life, one should respond to it as to one's parents, with care, reverence, and consideration. He urged people to cherish living things and avoid wantonly killing plant or animal life.[9] In the introduction to Miyazaki Yasusada's *Collected Treatises on Agriculture* (*Nogyo zensho*) Ekken emphasized the importance of that book in explaining how human beings can assist heaven and earth by cultivating nature.[10]

This theme of co-creativity with the transformative processes of heaven and earth is an essential part of the Confucian tradition, and was especially developed by the Neo-Confucians. An early basis for the idea of co-creativity is found in the *Doctrine of the Mean*, where humans are urged to assist in the transforming and nourishing processes of heaven and earth and thus form one body with all things.[11] This is further elaborated by Chang Tsai in the *Western Inscription* and is central to the thinking of Neo-Confucians throughout East Asia.

As Donald Munro observes, in the Confucian context, "Personal development for the individual requires his deferring to and enabling the natural patterns of change to be fulfilled. The Confucian served as co-creator by such acts as not cutting grass, sparing tree saplings, saving the lives of pregnant animals, protecting pregnant women, comforting the aged, and nurturing the young."[12] Tu Wei-ming also emphasizes this idea of co-creativity as an essential role of the human in Confucian thought. He alludes to the conformity of humans with the rhythms of nature described in the *Doc-*

*trine of the Mean.* He writes, "Human beings, as the most sentient beings in the universe, are 'decreed' by heaven to embody the 'centrality' of the cosmic transformation as their nature. They are 'created' not as creatures, but as co-creators for the task of providing necessary assistance in the cosmic transformation of heaven and earth."[13] Tu notes, "The human transformation of nature, therefore, means as much an integrative effort to learn to live harmoniously in one's natural environment as a modest attempt to use the environment to sustain basic livelihood. The idea of exploiting nature is rejected because it is incompatible with the Confucian concern for moral self-development."[14] For Ekken, then, the understanding of filiality and co-creativity was central to his thought and provided an important basis for his educational treatises.

## Humaneness as Generative Principle

The key element in Ekken's doctrine of a cosmic filial relationship was an all-embracing humaneness or *jin* (Ch. *jen*). He spoke of humaneness as imparted by heaven and as a principle which generates and nurtures life. He wrote: "Humans have a heart of heaven and earth, namely the heart of compassion which gives birth to and nurtures all things. This heart is called humaneness. Humaneness is the original nature implanted by heaven into the human heart."[15]

Ekken followed Chu Hsi in seeing a direct correspondence between humaneness in persons and the origination principle in nature.[16] In this understanding, the creative dynamics of productivity in the universe find their richest expression in the capacity for reciprocity and transformation of human beings. The fecundity of nature and the wellsprings of the human heart were seen as two aspects of the all-embracing process of change and transformation in the universe. As Ekken wrote: "Grass and trees are produced ceaselessly and, similarly, within our hearts the originative process of nature flourishes and is an endless source of joyful energy—this is happiness."[17] When extended to others, it is humaneness.

For Ekken the human is the "spirit [or soul] of the universe" (*banbutsu no rei*)[18] and thus has both great privileges and awesome responsibilities in the hierarchy of the natural world. He repeatedly stated, "We are very fortunate to be born as human beings; we should not waste away our lives meaninglessly."[19] He felt people could give shape and meaning to their lives through studying the wisdom of the sages and through the activation of humaneness. He also cited the significant directive to follow the example of nature in achieving inner wisdom and contentment. With great detail Ekken described the seasonal changes with which one should harmonize one's own moods and activities.[20] He saw this as participating in the process of transformation which for the human is a key to both knowledge and moral practice:

> Every year without fail, from ancient times to the present, the sun and moon have circulated, the four seasons have changed, and numerous things have been born. This is the sincerity of the Heavenly Way, and should be revered. Those who are peaceful and experience this will have a deep joy; those who fully understand this truth will know the Way.[21]

Thus, for Ekken the process of self-cultivation and the investigation of things was directly connected to the natural cycles of change and transformation in the universe. How to harmonize with this change and investigate its dynamic patterned quality was a major concern in his thought. As Tetsuo Najita has observed, "While all phenomena in nature are in a state of dynamic movement, Kaibara . . . emphasized, this movement could be calculated in relatively accurate ways and ought not to be seen as merely 'flux' and 'ephemera' from which the human mind should seek spiritual distance."[22] Rather, humans are endowed with the "active potential to observe and order external things, to grasp patterns within a constantly moving natural field."[23] This applies to both ethics and practical learning. Thus as Najita writes: "The human mind could observe patterned regularity and formulate stable ethical concepts and rules of governance. It could also observe the stars and the movements of the heavens. It could make judgments as to when and what to plant in various geographical areas."[24] It was precisely this understanding of the interaction of humans and the natural world that lay behind Ekken's thought.[25]

## COSMOLOGY AND CHANGE FOR THE SUNG NEO-CONFUCIANS

This same theme of the interaction of humans with nature can be seen in all of the Sung Neo-Confucian thinkers. What is particularly striking about these early Neo-Confucians is their fascination with change and its dynamics. No doubt this was at least partially a reaction to the Buddhist view of sorrow as being caused by an attachment to the impermanent and transient nature of reality. The Neo-

Confucians, refuting this position and turning back to their own classical tradition, saw the possibility for developing a different cosmological view of reality and of understanding the interaction of flux and pattern. They were inspired in this effort primarily by the *I ching* (Book of Changes), where they found a rich storehouse of images of change.[26]

A corollary of their interest in change was a concern for creating a cosmological view that was functional in the human order. To situate human deeds within a cosmological framework that affirmed change was seen as increasingly imperative in the face of not only Buddhist but also Taoist tendencies toward withdrawal from social and political affairs. Consequently, the development of a functional cosmology that interpreted change and validated human actions became an underlying thread of early Neo-Confucian thought.

Of primary significance in the development of this cosmological framework was the elaboration of the idea of principle (Ch. *li*, Jp. *ri*) and its relation to material force (Ch. *ch'i*, Jp. *ki*). The Sung Neo-Confucians wished to stress the fact that just as there is constancy and inner direction in the midst of changes in the natural world, so are there moral constants to be followed amidst the fluctuations of human life. The means of harmonizing with change was through an understanding of the function of principle as both a metaphysical and a moral concept.

These ideas on the relation of principle (*li*) and material force (*ch'i*) were woven into the rich tapestry of correspondences of microcosm and macrocosm that is so characteristic of Neo-Confucian thought. Certain aspects of cosmology from the *Book of Changes* and from Han period doctrines of correspondences were important to the Sung Neo-Confucians, who developed a system which was simultaneously rational and moral, a vision of reality and a program for self-cultivation. Many of the Sung Neo-Confucians cited the Appended Remarks in the *Book of Changes*, which says: "Change is gushing life," namely, "Life giving life; procreation of procreation; the begetting of birth." In this process, then, "the greatest virtue between heaven and earth is to live"[27] and thus to participate in change in contrast to withdrawing from it.[28]

The manner, then, of active participation is elaborated by subsequent Neo-Confucian thinkers in their discussions of the relation between heaven, earth, and humans. In tracing these ideas of the human participation in change within a larger cosmological framework, the virtue of *jen* became essential to the process. It is the comprehensive activation of humaneness which joins the micro-cosm and macrocosm in a unique way. This is because *jen* energizes the capacity of the mind to extend to all things and thus overcome any sense of separation.[29] Thus, the underlying unity of all living things can be realized through the creative capacity of the human mind. This for the Confucians becomes the basis for participation in human social and political affairs.

In recent years various scholars have helped to define and re-fine our understanding of Confucian cosmology and self-cultivation. Tu Wei-ming, for example, has elucidated the Chinese understanding of the universe as an "organismic process" which is "spontaneously self-generating" and characterized by "continuity, wholeness, and dynamism."[30] The process of growth and transfor-mation essential to the natural order provides a unique context for self-cultivation of the human. Indeed, it is against this background that people are instructed to "model themselves on the ceaseless vitality of the cosmic process"[31] and to recognize their profound re-latedness with all things. Tu describes this relatedness of heaven, earth, and human as anthropocosmic, not anthropocentric.[32]

It is precisely in this anthropocosmic tradition that Ekken's thought lies. While deeply indebted to earlier Confucian thinkers in this vein, he nonetheless feels free to adapt this vitalistic form of Confucianism to his own time, place, and circumstances. This is one possible reason for his insistence on a monism of *ch'i* as a means of assuring a metaphysical basis for participating in the nat-ural order. In addition, this is, no doubt, part of his concern to show the parallels of Confucianism with Shinto, which had a simi-lar interest in affirming the natural world. In other words, Ekken's articulation of the role of the human as an integral part of the nat-ural world, responsive to nature's vital forces, was a means of pre-senting a dynamic form of self-cultivation in a society already appreciative of the cycles of nature.[33]

Indeed, Ekken's attempt to equate the Way of the sages with the Way of the gods (Shinto) is evident in his essay *Jingikun* (Precepts on the Gods).[34] He speaks of the principles of change and con-stancy in nature as essential to both Shinto and Confucianism, and he identifies the Shinto virtues of purity and sincerity with similar Confucian virtues. In both Shinto and Confucianism the unifying element of cosmology and ethics is the life principle (*seiri*). Specifi-cally for Ekken, the manifestation of this is the vital force of the universe, namely, *ch'i*. To be in harmony with *ch'i*, then, is to participate in the creative dynamics of nature. This is a process which is cosmological and metaphysical at the same time that it is ethical and spiritual.[35]

## CHU HSI'S SYNTHESIS OF NEO-CONFUCIANISM

In historical perspective, it was Chu Hsi (1130–1200) who completed the work of the early Sung philosophers and brought Confucianism to new depths of insight with a greatly enlarged sense of cosmology. While Chu was interested in the same problems of metaphysics and ethics as were the earlier Sung thinkers, his main emphasis lay in the direction of the way to attain sagehood.[36] Chu's primary concern was to develop a program for a spiritual discipline which could be the means of personal integration and social participation.

Chu's synthesis of Neo-Confucianism was recorded in the classic anthology *Chin-ssu lu* (Reflections on Things at Hand). In this work he provided for the first time a comprehensive metaphysical basis for Confucian thought and practice. In response to a Buddhist metaphysics of Emptiness, with its apparent tendency to withdraw from an active life in favor of one valuing meditative practices, Chu formulated a this-worldly spirituality based on a balance of religious reverence and ethical practice. The ultimate goal of this practice was the attainment of sagehood.

Unlike the Buddhists, who saw attachment to the world of change as a source of suffering, Chu affirmed change as the source of transformation in both the cosmos and the person. Thus, spiritual discipline involved cultivating one's moral nature so as to bring it into harmony with the larger pattern of change in the cosmos. Each moral virtue, then, had its cosmological correlate: humaneness corresponded to origination, righteousness to flourishing, propriety to advantage, and wisdom to correctness. The central virtue of humaneness was seen as that which was the source of fecundity and growth in both the individual and the cosmos. Thus, by practicing humaneness and cultivating virtue one could affect the transformation of things in oneself, in society, and in the cosmos. In so doing, one's deeper identity with reality was recognized as "forming one body with all things" (Ch. *wan wu i-t'i*, Jp. *banbutsu ittai*).

The identity of the human and the cosmos through humaneness had been acknowledged by all of the Sung thinkers. Yet Chu wanted to clarify this relationship so that it would not simply be prey to a vague mystical sense without discipline or direction. He wrote, "to talk about *jen* in general terms of the unity of things and the self will lead people to be vague, confused, neglectful, and make no effort to be alert."[37] He felt there might be many bad effects of this general sense of considering other things as oneself. It could lead people to forget their real objectives or to try artificial methods to help the mind develop. Thus, there arose for Chu the need to clarify the relation of the human to the cosmos through the discipline of the mind and investigation of principle. To achieve humaneness that forms one body with all things, it was necessary to "preserve the mind" and "nourish the nature." This involved a reverent self-watchfulness when desires were aroused, until one eventually came to experience a deep personal integration and to realize one's essential identity with heaven and earth.

In Chu Hsi's thought this path of moral and spiritual discipline required an ability to distinguish between substance (*t'i*) and function (*yung*), between the underlying unifying principle of things and its active manifestation. This distinction of substance and function was central for Chu and was the pivotal point of his system of relating the microcosm to the macrocosm. In essence, this clarification involved the problem of relating the metaphysical to the phenomenal order in the broadest yet most dynamic manner possible.

Ekken seems to have been drawn to Chu Hsi's thought precisely for its breadth and comprehensiveness. He was especially attracted to Chu's ideas on self-cultivation and the investigation of things. Ekken developed these two poles of Chu's thought, one in the direction of making moral cultivation more accessible to the common people, and the other toward exploring principles in the natural world through practical or empirical research. In doing this, Ekken was directly indebted to Chu's idea of complete substance and great function. To trace the significance of substance and function in Chu's thought and its influence on Ekken let us now examine its role in Chu's cosmology, psychology, and ethics.

## Cosmology

Chu began his *Reflections on Things at Hand* with a chapter called "On the Substance of the Way." This set forth his basic metaphysical suppositions underlying the moral and spiritual path. It is significant that he opened this chapter with Chou Tun-i's *T'ai-chi-t'u shuo* (Diagram of the Great Ultimate), thereby reaffirming the cosmological framework which was to become the basis for all subsequent Neo-Confucian thought. Despite the controversial associations with

Taoism,[38] the Diagram embodied both a picture of the universe and a means for achieving sagehood. Understanding it revealed one's intrinsic relation to the universe and one's innate capacity for moral and spiritual practice.

Chu Hsi expanded on Chou Tun-i's Diagram by identifying the Great Ultimate (t'ai-chi) with principle (li).[39] In doing this, however, he had to face the problem of relating principle as one unchanging substance running through all things yet beyond all things. In other words, the question of transcendence and immanence became an important issue. T'ang Chün-i describes Chu Hsi's efforts to answer this question by explaining the Great Ultimate in terms of substance and function.[40] Substance becomes identifiable with the Great Ultimate while its function is seen in terms of activity and quiescence. Yet how to account for production is still not completely answered by this t'i-yung formula.

Chu Hsi asserted that the principle of production lies within the Great Ultimate itself, for it triggers both activity and quiescence.[41] The Great Ultimate, then, is the principle of creativity which operates in the phenomenal world yet remains distinct from it. Chu Hsi wrote: "As regards the production of the myriad things, from beginning to end the flux of the heavenly decree never lacks this principle."[42]

This is because although li (principle) is logically prior to ch'i (material force), it is nonetheless always connected to ch'i. "The Great Ultimate is principle, and activity and quiescence are matter; when matter moves, principle does the same. The two always comply and are never separated."[43] Thus, the relation of the Great Ultimate to the material world is explained as a dialectical connection between li and ch'i as substance and function.

The dialectical articulation of the delicate mutual dependency of subject and object, of inner-ordering principle and of dynamic matter-energy, was crucial to both Chu and Ekken because it is precisely this interpenetrating relation of substance and function that accounts for the fecundity of the universe. For Chu, the t'ai-chi as principle is in fact "the principle of unending production (sheng-sheng pu-hsi-chih-li); the cessation of its function makes it naturally tend once again toward the manifestation of it."[44] Ekken, however, chose to identify the t'ai-chi with the primal material force of ch'i rather than with principle. Following the late Ming thinker, Lo Chin-shun, Ekken reformulated Chu's dualistic articulation of the relation of li and ch'i in favor of a monistic doctrine of ch'i. In particular, he took issue with Chu's explanation of principle as permanent and as logically prior to material force.[45] His *Taigiroku* (Record of Grave Doubts) is largely concerned with the diplomatic task of remaining true to the spirit of Chu's thought while altering the letter.

## Psychology

Chu Hsi's central concept of substance and function was essential to his theory of nature and of the mind. Chu Hsi saw the quiescent state of the mind before the feelings are aroused as its substance. The active state of response to external objects is its function. Yet he understood this as a concurrent process in which "substance and function are never separated from one another whether the mind is absolutely quiet . . . or in circulation and ingression."[46]

Chu Hsi extended his *t'i-yung* concept to explain the operation of the mind in relation to the changing quality of reality. He elaborated on this by saying: "Its substance is called change, its principle *tao* and its function spirit (expansion)."[47] The mind then, by its function, is able to respond to change in the universe because the same dynamic principle of change is within the mind itself. Thus, the mind dialectically expands to meet the external world rather than simply withdrawing from it or being a passive recipient of change.

Again, Chu Hsi saw the changing, generative powers of the cosmos as achieving their highest expression in the creative power of the human mind. He wrote:

> The mind is that which is said to produce unceasingly. Its substance is said to be the *tao* of origination, flourishing, advantage, and correctness. . . . Its function is said to be the *ch'i* of the four seasons . . . Hence, although substance is concretized within the mind by virtue of its being substance it is truly as great as heaven and earth.
>       . . . Although function is manifested within the mind, by virtue of its being function it truly flows through and penetrates heaven and earth. . . . The reason why the mind is mysterious is because it connects activity and quiescence, unifies the manifest and the hidden, and penetrates the without and within so that there is no gap between ending and beginning.[48]

Here we have an understanding of the mind as the source of the generative principles of change and as the unifier of both the hidden and the manifest. Chu Hsi's theory of the substance and function of the mind is both a synthesis of early Confucian thought and a unique contribution to the tradition itself.

To Ekken this idea of the mind as containing the principle of change (substance) and therefore able to respond to change (function) was central to his whole effort to articulate a moral and spiritual discipline. For Ekken, as for Chu, the mind contains the connatural principles of creative production, namely, beginning, growing, storing, and harvesting. Through cultivation the mind actively nourishes these principles as moral virtues, thus connecting the inner transformation of the human to the dynamic process of transformation in the cosmos.

## Ethics

The basis of Chu Hsi's ethics is the pivotal role of the mind in connecting, synthesizing, and empathizing. He realized in particular that, as Chang Tsai stated, it is "the mind which connects [or commands] the nature and feelings."[49] Thus for Chu and for Ekken the way one regulates the mind becomes key to moral and spiritual discipline and to a larger identification with all things.

To this end, Chu Hsi's ethical synthesis was most clearly centered in his concept of humaneness. In terms of substance he saw humaneness as the principle of the mind; as function it is the virtue of love. He felt this distinction to be particularly important because "there must be substance and afterwards function so that the significance of the 'mind governing the nature and the feelings' will become apparent."[50] For Chu Hsi, the nature was substance and the feelings were function, while humaneness was the principle of the mind which coordinates the two.

Humaneness was seen by Chu as similar to the spirit of life and growth: "*Jen* as the principle of love is comparable to the root of a tree and the spring of water."[51] Elsewhere he wrote, "It is like the will to grow, like the seeds of peaches and apricots."[52] Following the Ch'eng brothers, he saw humaneness in the human order as the generative source of all other virtues, just as origination in the cosmic order is the source of plentitude and change. Thus, humaneness is like the "vital force of spring"[53] which blossoms in humans, linking them to heaven and earth and all things. "For *jen* as constituting the Way (*Tao*) consists of the fact that the mind of Heaven and Earth to produce things is present in everything."[54]

For Chu humaneness is both the principle of origination and its dynamic activation in human love. Accordingly, the mind embraces the whole cosmic-human order. Such extensive penetration lends special meaning and direction to human activities. Furthermore, it allows human beings to nurture and sustain the cosmic order by their own capacity for generative sympathy with all reality.

Ekken was in essential agreement with Chu's articulation of humaneness and continually stressed its connection to production and reproduction in the natural world. In emphasizing the primary quality of *jen* as creative fecundity he sought an ethical position which also affirmed the emotions and senses as part of this natural process. Indeed, the appropriate expression of the emotions was central to Ekken's ethical teachings. In terms of self-cultivation this meant that he particularly advocated the importance of both sincerity and spontaneity in moral practice. He claimed to diverge here from Chu's stress on seriousness, which, he felt, often led to rigidity or artificiality,[55] but this becomes a matter of further discussion at this point.

## THE NATURE OF EKKEN'S DISAGREEMENTS WITH CHU HSI

Ekken followed Chu Hsi's basic interests in a world-affirming spirituality that combined a profound inner authenticity with a participation in practical affairs. Yet he also developed doubts about some of Chu's formulations. While Ekken affirmed Chu's dialectic of the interaction of substance and function, he came to disagree with Chu's articulation of the dialectic as a dualism of *li* and *ch'i*. Ekken's interest in articulating the dynamic relationship between the cosmological and human orders led him towards a naturalism expressed as a monism of *ch'i*. Central to this reformulation was his concern for fecundity and generation in the natural order as having their counterpart in the principle of humaneness in the human order. All his ethicoreligious treatises reflect this naturalistic emphasis.

Thus, Ekken identified the basic inspiration for moral behavior as lying in an active response to the natural order's great generative processes, which provide benefits and blessings in the human order. To understand these generative processes in relation to the human became a central motivation of his empirical studies as well. Ekken commented in his *Precepts for Daily Life in Japan* that simply living the moral Way is not sufficient. He felt people must also know the Way of heaven and earth as the source of the human Way.[56] He stressed the need to understand the intimate connection of the human with the cosmos as a grounding for assisting heaven through human action and investigation.

Ekken's desire to penetrate intellectually the principle within material force subtended his emphasis on empirical research. In this way he gave a special direction to the Neo-Confucian mandate of investigating principle that had heretofore privileged the study of the ancient classics and of history. Ekken opened up this investigation in two directions: one toward examining and extending ethical principles in the current lives of the common people, and the other toward observing the operation of principle in the natural world through empirical studies that would be useful to a broad spectrum of people. For both of these tasks, namely his ethical and his empirical concerns, Ekken's monism of *ch'i* was a significant basis of his thought. An understanding of the natural, creative process of *ch'i* at the source of the universe was both a motive for responsive moral action and a stimulus to scientific research. While this monism was not fully articulated until the composition of *Taigiroku* at the end of his life, it was nonetheless implicit in many of his earlier works such as *Rakkun* (The Way of Contentment), *Gojōkun* (Precepts on the Five Cardinal Confucian Virtues), *Shogakkun* (Precepts for Beginning Study) and *Shinshiroku* (Record of Careful Thoughts).

## INTERPRETATIONS OF EKKEN'S MONISM

While Ekken's monism of *ch'i* was the common grounding for both his ethical teachings and his empirical research, many contemporary scholars have tended to bifurcate these aspects of his thought. They have thus been unable to reconcile his religious orientation with his so-called rational or proto-scientific interests. In their search for "modern" thought, free from the constraints of "medieval" Neo-Confucianism, certain contemporary scholars have lost sight of the fact that the rise of science or "secularism" was often accompanied by religious motives.[57] Moreover, as David Dilworth has observed, it is precisely the "stadial character" of Japanese culture and thought which accounts for its adaptability and continuity, namely the "coexistence of various sediments of Japanese value traditions in a variety of integrative contexts."[58] This coexistence of ethical and empirical concerns permeates Ekken's writings.

In his introduction to *Principle and Practicality*, Wm. Theodore de Bary has emphasized the complexity involved in any discussion of a movement from medieval to modern thought and warned that such a shift "cannot be taken simply as one from the sacred to the secular or from the metaphysical to the material, but rather must be seen as a complex ramification and interaction of individual and social needs; moral, intellectual, and religious concerns; rational and intuitive methods."[59] Thus, spiritual and secular issues are not mutually exclusive, nor is the triumph of the latter over the former to be seen as the key signal of the emergence of modernity. Rather, as de Bary notes, "Where the spiritual is seen as the most distinctively 'human' aspect of man, and the secular is viewed as sacred, there can be a deepening and broadening of spirituality in the midst of secular change."[60]

It is precisely this merging of spiritual and secular concerns which typifies Ekken's thought and marks him as part of what de Bary has called a humanistic revival resulting in a transformation of spirituality rather than in a decline of it.[61] Indeed, de Bary has observed that within Neo-Confucian thought itself there is a dynamic polarity of "exploring principle" (Ch. *ch'iung li*, Jp. *kyūri*) and "abiding in reverence" (Ch. *chü ching*, Jp. *kyo kei*).[62] Exploring principle in turn may be interpreted subjectively or objectively: investigating principle internally within oneself or externally in things. Such polarities are a catalyst in the creative unfolding of the Neo-Confucian tradition. Therefore, they ought not to be seen as mutually exclusive entities or modes of transmission which separate "secular" and "sacred" concerns. In a figure such as Ekken they coalesce, resulting in a new kind of religious humanism. Ekken represents the ongoing effort of Neo-Confucianism to achieve a synthesis of "man's rational powers with his capacity for both moral commitment and spiritual self-transcendence."[63] In this sense, Ekken saw the empirical study of natural science as part of the investigation of principle in things.[64] Similarly, his investigation extended to moral principles in human society, as is evident in his numerous ethical treatises.

## Maruyama Masao and Modern Thought

It was Maruyama Masao's influential work *Studies in the Intellectual History of Tokugawa Japan* (first published in Japan in the early 1940s) that established the tone for many subsequent analyses that set modern rational thought against medieval or Confucian thought.[65] Maruyama saw Yamaga Sokō (1622–1685), Itō Jinsai (1627–1705), and Kaibara Ekken as part of a trend in the early Tokugawa period toward breaking up the unity of morality and metaphysics so characteristic of Chu Hsi's thought. Maruyama described this dissolution as a separation of "norm" and "nature" which had several distinct expressions. One tended to separate human nature from the natural world, another to break the link between individual moral cultivation and government, and still another inclined toward a relativism that no longer depended on absolute principle.

Maruyama claimed that these trends culminated in the thought of Ogyū Sorai, who completed the separation of norm and nature and thus prepared the way for a modern, rationalistic thought. Maruyama cited the *Taigiroku* as evidence for Ekken's defection from Chu Hsi and as support for his own argument of the collapse of Chu Hsi's unified system in Tokugawa Japan. It can also be demonstrated, however, that Ekken was not intent on disavowing Chu Hsi, but rather was eager to reclaim and develop anew some of Chu's essentially vitalistic concerns as a framework for his own ethical and empirical thought. Thus, far from breaking up the continuity of Chu's thought, Ekken further developed it for his own time, place, and circumstances.[66] Furthermore, it is somewhat misleading to characterize Ekken's monism of *ch'i*, which he outlined in *Taigiroku*, as a form of materialism. Clearly this cannot account for the religious quality in Ekken's writings, which constantly advocates serving heaven and earth.[67]

## Abe Yoshio's School of Principle and School of Material Force

Abe Yoshio, writing some twenty years after Maruyama and with a rather different focus, nonetheless seemed unable to avoid completely the legacy of Maruyama's bifurcating analysis. While Abe's masterful treatment of the influence of Korean Neo-Confucianism on Japan is a seminal work,[68] he based his discussion on a distinction of schools which could not always adequately encompass the broad concerns of particular thinkers. He identified the two major trends of Japanese Neo-Confucianism as the *rigaku* (school of principle) and the *kigaku* (school of material force). Abe claimed that the former emerged from the ideas of Fujiwara Seika (1561–1619), who was influenced by Yi T'oegye (1501–1570), among others, and that the latter emerged from the thought of Hayashi Razan (1583–1657), who carried on the tradition of Yi Yulgok (1536–1584), Lo Ch'in-shun (1465–1547), and Wang T'ing-hsiang (1474–1544). Abe indicated that Yamazaki Ansai (1618–1682) and the Kimon school were a further development of the school of principle, while such thinkers as Ekken, Andō Seian (1622–1701), Itō Jinsai (1627–1705), and Yamaga Sokō (1622–1685) became part of the school of material force.

He cited the significant impact among the *ki* school of Lo Ch'in-shun's *K'un-chih chi*, which was published in Japan in 1658.[69]

Abe identified the *ki* school as essentially "materialistic," seeing it as preoccupied with broad learning. The *ri* school, on the other hand, he claimed was more concerned with spirituality, for its proponents considered *ri* to be a transcendent principle. Thus, the *kigaku* became absorbed in book learning and the *rigaku* became primarily interested in moral cultivation. While Abe's distinctions have a definite usefulness, their application to individual thinkers may not always allow for the varied concerns found in one thinker. Ekken, for example, cannot be seen as a "materialist" interested only in book learning, for his religious and ethical concerns were essential to his thought as a whole.

## Minamoto Ryōen and Jitsugaku

The same inclination to separate "spirituality" from "rationalism" appeared in Minamoto Ryōen's work, which has also been seminal in the field of Tokugawa intellectual history. In his discussion of "*Jitsugaku* and Empirical Rationalism," Minamoto distinguished two types of practical learning, namely, the moral-idealistic and the empirical-realistic.[70] As examples of the former he cited Nakae Tōju and Yamazaki Ansai, while as examples of the latter he discussed Ekken and Sorai. Once again, these general categories may reflect certain trends in the Tokugawa period, yet they often tend to obfuscate rather than clarify the all-embracing thought of a figure like Ekken. Minamoto himself recognized this and yet, following Maruyama, claimed that the problem lay in an inherent contradiction in Ekken's thought, rather than in the limits of his own categories. He acknowledged that Ekken "mapped out new ground by developing the concept of *li* (principle) in Chu Hsi's philosophy in the direction of empirical rationalism." Yet he criticized Ekken, saying that he "uncritically maintained the continuous way of Chu Hsi's thinking that the *li* (principle) of things is also the *li* of morality."[71] He asserted that because Ekken described *jitsugaku* in moral terms, he was thus not able to "free" Chu Hsi's thought from its inclination to identify physical and moral principles.[72] Minamoto acknowledged that, in his empirical and ethical endeavors, Ekken held a position which saw the principles of things and principles of the mind as a unity. Thus, "Ekken advocated neither a pure idealism which would abandon the principles of things nor a thorough going empiricism which would abandon the principles of the mind."[73] Indeed, that is because he refused to adopt a dualistic approach; instead, he embraced a position that was both ethical and empirical, spiritual and rational.

## Tetsuo Najita's Views of Ekken

Tetsuo Najita's earlier insightful treatment of Ekken[74] is formulated with some of the same suppositions discussed above, namely, Maruyama's account of the separation of norm and nature, Abe's equation of kigaku as materialistic, and Minamoto's division of thinkers that were either moral and idealistic or empirical and realistic. In discussing the significance of Ekken's difficulties with Neo-Confucian dualism, Najita cited the Taigiroku as a key document in the history of Tokugawa Confucianism. He did not fully acknowledge Lo Ch'in-shun's important influence on Ekken's formulation of a monism of ch'i. Rather, he saw the Taigiroku as "a pioneering statement of a trend within Tokugawa Neo-Confucianism that seeks a more empirical approach to the study of nature unfettered by the constrictions of metaphysical ethics."[75] Najita thus felt that Ekken played a part in the separation of ethics and nature described by Maruyama.

Ekken's monism, according to Najita, led him to see a single life-principle (seiri) as running through all life, but for Ekken this was a natural, not an ethical, principle. Because Ekken "stripped nature of explicit ethical content,"[76] Najita claimed that Ekken came to an "essentially materialistic conclusion about the nature of the universe."[77] This entails the same difficulties as Abe's tendency to equate kigaku with materialism. Furthermore, it does not account for Ekken's identification of humaneness in humans with the creative principle of origination in nature, i.e. with an empathetic creativity as the most fundamental force in humans and in nature.

The logical outcome of Ekken's thought, in Najita's analysis, is that the physical world and the study of it gained in importance; in other words, empirical research superseded ethics. He thus followed the same separation as Minamoto of Confucian thinkers into categories of moral-idealistic and empirical-realistic. But Najita was unable adequately to reconcile the fact that ethics and empiricism coexist in Ekken's thought. He conceded that "a commitment to Confucian ethics and to an empirical approach to nature concurred, each valid and each as important as the other."[78] He also recognized Ekken's deep-seated spiritual orientation, acknowledging that "religious humility and reverence remained central to Kaibara's personality, especially when articulated with the concept of nature's 'blessing.' "[79] Ultimately, Najita relied on the idea of substance and function (*ti-yung*) to explain the coexistence of these factors. He wrote, "Ethics as essence and science as function could be seen as instrumentally distinct, mutually separate, and not competitive."[80]

It could be argued more convincingly, however, that ethics and empiricism do not simply coexist as separate entities, but that they are mutually reinforcing and supportive. They are both integral parts of Ekken's all-embracing system of a unified life-principle based on a monism of *ch'i*. In other words, precisely from out of his religious reverence for nature and his appreciation for the dynamic material force in all reality arises his urgency to investigate things in an empirical manner and to harmonize with change in an ethical manner.

In his more recent work, Najita seems to have moved toward such a reconciliation when he writes, "Deeply concerned about the relationship between firm knowledge and the alleviation of the sufferings of the peasantry, Kaibara rested his philosophy on the ground that all knowledge, practical and moral, must ultimately derive from universal nature."[81] He develops this point, arguing that the recognition of the shared life-principle gives humans the impetus for reverent treatment of all things. He observes, "Moral society, therefore, cannot be distinguished from nature as a mere fabrication as Ogyū Sorai had contended but must remain epistemologically related in a close and reverential manner to it."[82] Indeed, Najita says Ekken does not fall into the same category as Ogyū Sorai allegedly did in separating norm and nature. Rather, Ekken "argued that reverence for nature was a universal human capacity and constituted the ultimate basis for self-reflection regarding the moral character of human beings."[83] Najita notes the importance of this position as a basis for practical learning that would help both the peasants and the merchants. Indeed, as Najita demonstrates, Ekken's thought in this regard became one of the major influences on the scholars, teachers, and students involved in the Osaka Merchant Academy, the *Kaitokudō*.

## Ishida Ichirō's "Secularized Religion"

Ishida Ichirō has also attempted to resolve some of these seeming dichotomies between the moral and the empirical modes of thought. Specifically, he has tried to show that Neo-Confucianism was more than a secular or ethical system; rather, it was a "secularized religion."[84] Furthermore, he has demonstrated that the Neo-Confucian imperative to investigate things was not limited to the moral sphere but included natural science as well. Thus, the religious and the empirical elements are part of a single, integrating continuum.[85]

With regard to the religious dimension of Neo-Confucianism in the Tokugawa period, he outlined the central role of heaven as both a creative and a regulating force. It was the task of the human to assist the operations of heaven both internally through moral action and externally through productive work. Ishida noted that it was similarly from a motivation to understand heavenly laws and assist heaven's work that the mandate to investigate things was directed toward the natural world. There is, therefore, a confluence of religious motivation and empirical investigation which distinguishes many of the Tokugawa Neo-Confucians, including Ekken. It is necessary, then, to examine how Ekken's monism of *ch'i* became a basis for unifying his ethical and his empirical concerns as he struggled with his loyalty to Chu Hsi while acknowledging the force of Lo Ch'in-shun's critique.

## EKKEN'S LOYALTY TO CHU HSI

It was in 1665, when Ekken was thirty-five, that his first works were published, establishing his position as an advocate of Chu Hsi learning. These were *Ekigaku teiyō* (Manual of Divination) and *Dokusho junjo* (The Order of Reading). Prior to that he had read and enjoyed the writings of Lu Hsiang-shan and Wang Yang-ming.[86] He thought he could combine their ideas with those of Chu Hsi, but in 1665, after reading Ch'en Chien's book, *Hsüeh-p'u t'ung-pien* (General Critique of Obscurations of Learning), he realized this was impossible. Through Ch'en's book he became aware of the excesses of the followers of Wang, their tendency toward anti-intellectualism, and their emphasis on sudden enlightenment over long-term effort.[87] He thus became an avowed adherent of Chu's thought while retaining certain reservations which are evident in his subsequent writings.

In 1668 he completed a volume of commentary on Chu's *Reflections on Things at Hand* (*Kinshiroku bikō*), in which he assembled comments of great Confucian scholars. Inoue suggested that even at this time Ekken indicated certain disagreements with Chu Hsi's thought.[88] In particular, he emphasized the mutuality of *li* and *ch'i* in contrast to Chu's explanation of *li* as logically prior to *ch'i*. Nonetheless, his respect for Chu was evident in the publication the same year of *Shushi bunpan* (Model Compositions of Chu Hsi). This consisted of punctuated selections of significant passages in Chu's writings so as to make them more readily available for Japanese readers.

Lest he be misunderstood as a rebel outside the Chu Hsi school, Ekken declined to publish his *Record of Grave Doubts* (*Taigiroku*) during his lifetime. It was not until some fifty years after his death that it was published by Ōno Hokkai, one of Ogyū Sorai's followers. When Sorai himself first saw the manuscript three years after Ekken's death, he remarked, "It gives me great pleasure to find that there is a scholar in a faraway place who has anticipated my own thoughts."[89]

Yet Ekken never wished to be identified with the *Kogaku* (Ancient Learning) school or with those who he felt were somehow abandoning Chu Hsi's legacy. Indeed, he wrote at length of his disagreements with Itō Jinsai in his *Dōjimon higo* (A Critique of 'Boy's Questions').[90] Ekken thus wrestled with the tension created by both his loyalties and his disagreements with Chu. Like Lo Ch'in-shun, the Ming Confucian whom he strongly admired, Ekken sought to avoid tendencies in some Neo-Confucians, allegedly due to Buddhist or Taoist influences, toward quietistic practices. The crux of this argument, for both Lo and Ekken, lay in Chu's discussion of the relationship of *li* and *ch'i*.[91]

## THE INFLUENCE OF LO CH'IN-SHUN

While Chu Hsi no doubt intended a mutual interaction of *li* and *ch'i* to be the pivot of his cosmological and ethical system, he nonetheless attributed a certain priority, permanence, and superiority to *li*. He maintained that *li* is above form and therefore perfect, while *ch'i* is within form and therefore coarse. Lo Ch'in-shun disagreed with this dualistic characterization of *li* and *ch'i*, arguing against the notion of *li* as an autonomous, regulating power which becomes somehow linked to material force. As Irene Bloom has indicated, for Lo principle was neither causative nor determinative but "the pattern itself, the actual reality, rather than the origin or cause of what is true of the natural process."[92] Lo elaborated on the concept of principle in a manner which, no doubt, struck a responsive chord in Ekken more than a century later:

That which penetrates heaven and earth and connects past and present is nothing other than material force (*ch'i*), which is unitary. This material force, while originally one, revolves through endless cycles of movement and tranquillity, going and coming, opening and closing, rising and falling. Having become increasingly obscure, it then becomes manifest; having become manifest, it once again reverts to obscurity. It produces the warmth and coolness and the cold and heat of the four seasons, the birth, growth, gathering in, and storing of all living things, and constant moral relations of people's daily life, the victory and defeat, gain and loss in human affairs. And amid all of this prolific variety and phenomenal diversity there is a detailed order and an elaborate coherence which cannot ultimately be disturbed, and which is so even without our knowing why it is so. This is what is called principle. Principle is not a separate entity which depends on material force in order to exist or which 'attaches to material force in order to operate.'[93]

For Lo and for Ekken a monism of *ch'i* was an articulation of a naturalism which expressed the dynamics of change and thus became a basis for a unified doctrine of human nature and an affirmation of human emotions. In contrast to Chu Hsi's dualism, they both attempted to penetrate the patterns in the midst of process and to articulate the quality of renewal and regeneration in nature and in human life. It was this dynamic vitalism that Ekken found so appealing. He often quoted Lo, who wrote:

Li is only the *li* of *ch'i*. It must be observed in the phenomenon of revolving and turning of *ch'i* . . . If one gains a clear understanding of this phenomenon of revolving and turning, one will find that everything conforms to it.[94]

Both Lo and Ekken wished to avoid the subjective position of Wang Yang-ming who gave priority to principles in the mind. They both affirmed that principle within material force ought to be investigated.[95] Precisely because principle was the principle of material force, Ekken believed it contained within it both constancy and transformation (*ri no jōhen*) and was thus neither prior nor absolute. His desire to articulate a clear understanding of the constancy and transformation of principle is the subject of sections of *Shinshiroku* (Record of Careful Thoughts) and *Yamato honzō* (Plants of Japan) and is an underlying theme of the *Taigiroku* (Record of Grave Doubts). Ekken felt the need to articulate a cosmology that was dynamic and naturalistic, thus reflecting the actual state of fecundity and generation in the universe. When the great source and operation of this productivity was effectively understood, humans could be in harmony with the ongoing processes of life. They would be able to realize their fundamental continuity with the cosmos and, consequently, the dynamic potential of human nature for moral action. Just as heaven and earth generate the myriad things, so human beings, through their efforts at moral and spiritual cultivation, might come to realize their essentially life-inducing capacity.

## RECORD OF GRAVE DOUBTS

In *Taigiroku* we find a central statement of Ekken's thought which may be discussed under three major themes.[96] The first is doubt as a method of scholarly inquiry; the second is Ekken's metaphysical position, namely his naturalism expressed as a monism of *ch'i*; and the third is Ekken's doctrine of human nature and ethical practice.

### Doubt as a Method of Inquiry

Ekken's doubts about Chu Hsi's teachings were clearly a source of much anxiety for him. It is the authenticity of his doubts along with his sincere attempts to resolve them that are so immediately striking in *Taigiroku*. What emerges in this treatise is a portrait of a deeply reflective scholar with many concerns similar to Chu's, and yet with the overriding mandate to state respectfully and forcefully the nature of his particular disagreements. Doubt for Ekken was a means of genuine scholarly inquiry, not a sign of a break with the Confucian tradition.

Precisely for this reason, *Taigiroku* is a significant work, for it reflects the dynamics of both dissent and continuity within a tradition. At the same time that Ekken criticized Chu Hsi, he was concerned with issues similar to those discussed by Chu and the Sung Confucians, especially the nature and implications of change. These poles of dissent and continuity are pivotal in articulating Ekken's thought as well as situating him within the larger framework of Chinese and Japanese Neo-Confucianism. Indeed, Ekken's strong assertions of respect for Chu Hsi, his humble efforts to articulate his doctrine of a monism of *ch'i*, and his rigorous attempt to distinguish his position from *Kogaku* scholars such as Itō Jinsai, while closely aligning himself with Lo Ch'in-shun, would lead one to conclude, as has Okada Takehiko, that Ekken is not a renegade Confucian but a "reformed" Chu Hsi scholar.[97]

Irene Bloom makes a similar point with regard to Lo Ch'in-shun, Ekken's principal source of inspiration concerning the monism of *ch'i*. She notes Lo's work is not "imitative or mimetic," but rather it is "informed by a lively skepticism and a resolute insistence on cogency and consistency as against established authority as the basis for accepting any philosophical position."[98] She notes that Lo saw himself as "heir to a tradition that was constantly evolving" rather than simply a closed system.[99] For Lo "the principal criterion of orthodoxy was not the acceptance of received doctrines, but an essential fidelity to the tradition and to the richness of human experience that it embodied."[100] This is as apt for Ekken's position in the *Taigiroku* as it was for Lo's in *K'un-chih chi*.

Ekken opened the Preface to the *Taigiroku* by first citing Lu Hsiang-shan and then Chu Hsi on the importance of doubt for making progress in one's intellectual and spiritual endeavors. As Chu said, "If we have great doubts we will make great progress, if we have small doubts we will make little progress, and if we have no doubts we will make no progress."[101] Ekken himself stated that the process of scholarly and moral attainment necessarily implies doubts and reexamination of accepted positions. He wrote, "After one studies one has doubts, after one doubts one has questions, after one questions one can think, after one thinks one can understand."[102]

He acknowledged that he had been studying the writings of the Sung Neo-Confucians from an early age but had been unable to resolve certain doubts which had persisted. Lacking the assistance of an enlightened teacher in this process, he felt the need to state the reason for his doubts. He traced the path of Confucian thought from the times of the sage-kings to Confucius and Mencius and finally to Chu Hsi and the Sung Neo-Confucians. He asserted there was room for development within the tradition over such vast periods of time. Moreover, while the Ch'eng brothers and Chu Hsi were unquestionably worthy of respect, he felt that there were points in their discussion which differed from the views of Confucius and Mencius due to certain Buddhist and Taoist influences in the Sung. He suggested that one must examine the similarities and differences in their thought with an open mind, treading a narrow path between belief and scepticism. He noted that one should avoid the extremes of following blindly or of doubting indiscriminately. Thus, he called for a process of careful selectivity in differentiating between the original teachings of the sages and those of the Sung Neo-Confucians. When doubt emerges in the form of scholarly debate, positions should be argued, he felt, calmly and deliberately rather than belligerently or carelessly. The form of a critical scholarly debate should be similar to the proper method of admonishing people with regard to moral behavior. According to Ekken, a Noble Person (Ch. *chün tzu*, Jp. *kunshi*) does not berate others carelessly or try to make them yield by force. Even if there is some truth in what that person is saying, the listener will not follow or act upon it if the speaker is angry or irrational. Rather, one needs to have a sincere attitude and a calm tone, employing an indirect persuasiveness rather than a confrontational or deliberately provocative style.

He felt, for example, that the Ming Neo-Confucians frequently attacked the Sung Neo-Confucians in a manner that was abusive and offensive. Such an attitude, he maintained, would only breed resentment and factionalism, not rectification or reform. In scholarly debates one should be conscious of speaking for a larger truth, not simply arguing in favor of one's personal opinions. Ekken pointed out that one must therefore learn how to "wash away old opinions" so as not to lapse into habitual or confused ways of thinking.[103] One must try to be impartial, open-minded, and humble, and above all one must avoid succumbing to scholastic factionalism.

He suggested that the Way of the Noble Person is not difficult to know or to practice for it is in fact close at hand. By continual effort one will make gradual progress toward sagehood. He regarded the essence of early Confucianism as practicing filiality, obedience, loyalty, trust, and love. The later Sung Neo-Confucians, he asserted, emphasized the importance of seeing the truth of the *t'ai chi* (Great Ultimate) and the *wu chi* (Non-finite) and of encouraging the practice of quiet sitting, purifying the heart, and abiding in reverence. In so doing, he maintained, they became overly scrupulous in contrast to the early Confucians who stressed simplicity and the practice of basic virtues.

The Sung Neo-Confucians, he suggested, were not infallible, and by their strict adherence to trivial things they often lost sight of the dynamic process of learning and the holistic goal of sagehood. He continually stressed the fact that the Sung Neo-Confucians were not all sages, and while worthy of respect, they were subject to various biases and mistakes in their thinking. Just as a pearl is rarely perfect, he wrote, they too were not without flaws or failings.[104] For Ekken there was an urgency to return to fundamentals so that Confucianism would be adaptable to the contemporary age and not become fossilized into abstract academic debates or overly rigid ethical practices. He called for a shift from an interest in minute details back to essentials and from an obsession with trivia back to a concern for whole integration.

Ekken discussed the reasons for his doubts at considerable length. He especially wanted to stress the way doubt may be used as a scholarly method of inquiry within the Confucian tradition as

well as a means of reasserting the essential Confucian vision. While
he did not go to the extremes of the philological studies that so engaged the Ancient Learning scholars in their search for an authentic, classical Confucianism, nonetheless, his questions with regard
to Chu Hsi's thought were sometimes comparable. These can be
said to fall into two major categories, namely, his metaphysical doctrine and his ethical thought.

## Naturalism: The Metaphysics of Ch'i

Ekken's doubts were focused on the issue of cosmology, for his pivotal disagreement was with Chu Hsi's formulation of the nature of
the universe. While this concern with metaphysical issues may appear somewhat rarefied, its implications for his ethical and empirical thought are far from abstract.[105] From his naturalism outlined as
a monism of ch'i, there emerges both an affirmation of human nature and human action which affects his ethical ideas and an affirmation of nature and its transformations which informs his
empirical thought.

Ekken quoted the *Book of Changes* to explicate his naturalist cosmological view: "In the Changes there is the Great Ultimate and it
creates two forms."[106] He maintained that the Great Ultimate is the
name of the primal material force before it is divided into yin and
yang, whereas yin and yang are the names of the Great Ultimate
after division and change takes place. This flow of yin and yang is,
in fact, principle and is called the Way. Thus, the Great Ultimate as
the primal ch'i, and yin and yang as the Way are two aspects of the
same dynamic material force. It is this material force which constitutes the origination, growth, and transformation of all life. The
Way, then, is one of constant productivity and does not arise from
emptiness. He quoted the *Doctrine of the Mean* (Chapter 27) to illustrate his point: "The great Way of the Sages being vast, it causes the
development of all things." He continued, "It flows through the
seasons and it never stops. It is the root of all transformations and it
is the place from which all things emerge; it is the origin of all that
is received from heaven."[107] He indicated that this was different
from the emptiness or nothingness which is spoken of in Buddhism
and Taoism.

Ekken elaborated on this point when he claimed that "the *wu
chi* and the *t'ai chi*" was a phrase which appeared in the text *Hua-
yen fa-chieh kuan* (The Hua-yen View of the Realm of the Dharmas),
by Tu Shun (557–640).[108] It is clear that Ekken wished to establish a

linkage between this phrase and Buddhist or Taoist beliefs, for he maintained that the idea of the Great Ultimate originating from the Non-finite leads to the practice of "making quietude central."[109] Thus, although this phrase concerning the *t'ai-chi* had been incorporated into Chou Tun-i's *Diagram of the Great Ultimate* and consequently was used in the opening passage of Chu Hsi's *Reflections on Things at Hand*, Ekken claimed that its seemingly Buddhist and Taoist flavor was not suitable for Confucian cosmological understanding or ethical practices.

In identifying the *t'ai chi* with the primal material force, Ekken's position differed from that of Chu Hsi, who had identified *t'ai chi* with principle, which was prior to material force. Chu had claimed that there is a need to speak of both the *wu chi* and *t'ai chi*, for if one doesn't have the *wu chi* then "the *t'ai-chi* becomes the same rank as things and we can't regard it as the basis of transformation in all things."[110] Ekken vehemently disagreed, saying that to do this would be to deny the dynamic, life-affirming quality of a unified material force. Existence, not emptiness, he maintained, is the origin and essence of all things. It is only the Buddhists and Taoists who say that existence arises from nothingness.

Ekken returned to the basic source of Confucian cosmological speculation, namely, the *Book of Changes* in his attempt to reformulate Confucian cosmology. Indeed, his efforts may be seen, as were those of Lo Ch'in-shun, as a conscious attempt to return to classical sources as a means of reasserting a unified view of reality.[111] He cited, as had Ch'eng Hao before him, three of the key lines of the *Book of Changes*. He then commented on them in relation to Sung cosmological formulations:

> In heaven configurations are created;
> On earth physical forms are created.

> What is manifest we call configurations;
> What has physical form we call concrete objects.

> What is above physical form we call the Way;
> What is below physical form we call concrete objects.[112]

With regard to the first statement, he maintained that the "configurations" which arise in heaven were the material forces of yin and yang which have no particularized substance. Yet they are manifest through their operation of ceaseless alteration. He observed that this operation of yin and yang above form is called the Way of heaven, and it is this flow which causes growth in all things. It constitutes, then, a primordial flow of energy which lies at the heart of the universe and out of this continual process, production and re-production arise.

From these great creative configurations of energy, he noted, forms emerge and take shape. Physical forms, namely, humans and all the myriad things, are the actual substance of the configurations of energy. They are thus called concrete things. Being within the realm of form, they constitute the Way of earth and have various characteristics such as hardness or softness.

Ekken wished to maintain the unity and dynamic creativity of this vast process. He did not wish to see it divided as he claimed the Ch'eng brothers and Chu Hsi had done. Opposing *li* and *ch'i* as distinct entities, they identified *li* with the Way and *ch'i* with yin and yang. Thus, they maintained that the material force of *yin* and *yang*, being within the realm of forms, was therefore a concrete thing. This metaphysical position could lead toward an abstraction of the Way as separate from concrete reality and to a bifurcation of principle or reason from energy and matter.

Ekken hoped to avoid such a dualism because he felt it resulted in an idealism that both undervalued objects of this world and tended toward life-denying rather than life-affirming ethical practices. Such a dualistic idealism forced the Sung Neo-Confucians to posit an origin for the absolute principle which was prior to and above material force. This led to the use of the *wu chi* in the *Diagram of the Great Ultimate*. But to interpret emptiness as the source of existence was for Ekken precisely what he felt Confucianism should avoid.

Ekken claimed, as did Lo Ch'in-shun, that although Chou Tun-i used the term *wu chi* in his *Diagram* he never mentioned it in his *T'ung-shu* (Penetrating the Book of Changes).[113] While the *Diagram* was the product of his younger years, the *T'ung-shu* was written much later, so Ekken felt that Chou realized his mistake by not mentioning *wu chi*. He also claimed that the Ch'eng brothers never used *wu chi* in their writings and this indicated their lack of interest in it. Similarly, it was not a concept used in classical Confucianism, and Ekken indicated there was no mention of *wu chi* in the *Book of Changes*.

The central phrases that Ekken used to support his arguments against dualism were derived from Lo Ch'in-shun's *K'un-chih chi*. These were Ch'eng I's formulation: "Principle is one, its particularizations are diverse" (Ch. *li-i fen-shu*, Jp. *riichi bunshu*) and Lo's phrase: "Principle is the principle of material force."[114] Ekken used these to assert the essentially unified, dynamic, and creative nature of reality. Principle is not something separate from, or prior to, material force, nor is it eternal and unchanging. He thus disagreed with Chu Hsi, who maintained that while *ch'i* was subject to the transformations of life and death, *li* was not. He argued that because *li* is the principle of material force, when something is living it has principle, and when it dies principle is destroyed. He used the analogy of water and fire having the nature of being cold and hot, damp and dry, respectively. When water and fire are extinguished these attributes also disappear. Thus, the principle within material force is constantly undergoing change and transformation.

Ekken, then, argued for a naturalism that saw the universe as emerging and continuing solely due to the operations of primal energy. This primal energy above forms is the configuration of yin and yang while within the realm of forms it becomes concrete objects. This ceaseless process of generation and transformation is a unified organic whole. Bifurcation or dualism does not adequately describe the process or provide a satisfactory basis for an understanding of human nature and action in the midst of change.

Drawing on the *Book of Changes*, Ekken summarized his argument for the Way as being the dynamic operation of the yin and yang, which is the root of the generation and transformation of life:

> Ancient sages regarded yin and yang as the Way, and they did not speak of the Way outside of yin and yang. Sung Confucians regarded the Way as separate from yin and yang and as something empty and void of oneness and without vitality and power. They regarded the root of all things to be the marvel of the Great Ultimate, but it was not the 'Way of the sages.' The 'Way of the sages' is the principle of life and growth of heaven and earth; the original *ch'i* harmonizing the yin and yang is ceaseless fecundity.[115]

Ekken felt he was returning to the basic inspiration of classical Confucian thought in its concern to express the intimate relation of the human to the cosmos.[116] The primacy of the life process was emphasized by Ekken, for it is understanding and harmonizing with this vital operation which becomes the basis of moral and spiritual cultivation. His attention to primary processes may also be indicative of the indigenization of Confucian thought which was undertaken, both consciously and unconsciously, by many of the Tokugawa Confucians. Ekken was clearly interested in adapting Confucian teachings to time, place, and circumstances and thus making them appropriate to the Japanese context. His doctrine of a monism of *ch'i* may also be interpreted in this light as an effort to return to immediate, intuitive processes often associated with the native Japanese tradition of Shinto. Ekken, like many of the Tokugawa Confucians, was as eager to demonstrate Confucianism's compatibility with Shinto as he was to illustrate Buddhism's inherent incompatibility with it.[117] For Ekken, both Confucianism and Shinto affirmed the life-giving processes of the natural world and advocated the development of a purity and sincerity which mirrored these processes. From a sensitivity to this native resonance with the natural world arose Ekken's detailed articulation of the primary vitalistic operation of *ch'i* in the universe. His effort to return to a simple and naturalistic metaphysical formulation is paralleled by his concern with spontaneity and sincerity in ethical practices.

## Human Nature and Ethics

The consequences of Ekken's monistic and naturalistic position can be seen in his doctrine of human nature. Following Lo Ch'in-shun, he claimed that because *li* and *ch'i* are one, there is no distinction between an ideal nature and a physical nature.[118] He particularly disagreed with the position adopted by Chang Tsai, Ch'eng I, and Chu Hsi that there was a distinction between the original or heavenly nature as perfect and the physical nature as imperfect.[119]

Ekken denied such a dichotomy, relying on arguments from both Lo Ch'in-shun[120] and Mencius. Maintaining, as had Lo, that nature is principle, he felt one could not argue that a heavenly conferred nature was separate from physical nature. If they were separate, he asked, how could one then account for the origin of the physical nature? It, too, he maintained is received from heaven and earth. All people receive a heavenly bestowed nature, and this is principle. Following Mencius he argued that this human nature is essentially good because all people receive the four seeds of commiseration, shame, modesty, and conscience. While there are differences in what is conferred due to the varied nature of *ch'i*, the essence of what the human receives is the same. Just as the universe is irregular and many divergences exist, so also there are naturally differences in human beings due to the purity or impurity of one's *ch'i*. Thus, variations arise between wise and foolish people and good and evil people, respectively.

Ekken cited Lo Ch'in-shun's use of the phrase "Principle is one; its particularizations are diverse" (*li-i fen-shu*)[121] to illustrate this distinction of principle being present in all things but in a varied and distinctive manner in each particular thing. This phrase was as indispensable to Ekken as it had been to Lo both for articulating the relationship of the one and the many on a metaphysical level and for describing human nature and its concrete manifestations on an ethical level. Thus, Ekken collapsed the distinction of heavenly nature and physical nature using this formula. He asserted that while things have their original form and their distinctive characteristics, these are not two separate things. He used the analogy of water to illustrate this point, saying that the original form of water is its purity while its characteristics are its tendencies to have currents, to overflow, and to moisten.[122] The implication of Ekken's doctrine of human nature is most clearly seen in his efforts to affirm rather than deny or suppress the emotions.[123] He urged a careful balance between their control and, when appropriate, their expression. His discussions of spiritual discipline frequently focused on the way to achieve this balance.[124]

With regard to ethics, Ekken called for a return to the primary virtues of the sages, namely, honesty and faithfulness.[125] This basic sincerity of attitude he considered far more important than what the Sung Confucians had emphasized in their call for constant "seriousness" or "reverence" (Ch. *ching*, Jp. *kei*). While he did not deny the importance of *ching*, he felt the emphasis on seriousness had often led to overly austere and artificial practices which missed the creativity of an ethical path connected to a dynamic metaphysical basis of *ch'i*. As in the *Doctrine of the Mean* he saw the practice of sincerity in human life as reflecting the authenticity and spontaneity of the universe, revealed in its seasonal cycles and natural biological rhythms.

Ekken thus believed that sincerity was fundamental while seriousness was a "secondary method of practice."[126] One should not misplace priorities or confuse the order implied here. Without sincerity, seriousness would lose its life-connected function, for it then tends toward restrictive and overly intense attitudes, with a loss of naturalness and spontaneity. Ekken maintained that such a severe attitude was part of the Sung Neo-Confucian's obsession with lofty, abstract ideas at the expense of what was essential, dynamic, and close at hand, and often led to a misplaced sense of superiority and a distance from other people. He spoke of those concentrating only on seriousness as being too rigid and narrow-minded.[127] Such people tended to become withered, dried up, and without harmony or compassion in human relations.

Ultimately for Ekken the purpose of cultivating one's authenticity and fostering virtue was not to set oneself above or apart from others in a rigid, moralistic fashion. Rather it was to eliminate the separation between oneself and others so that one's heart would extend to everything.[128] He likened this, as had Mencius, to the process of the circulation of blood in the human body. If one is healthy the circulation is good; if not, one's hands and feet may become paralyzed. This latter state reflects a lack of humaneness. The former state of healthy circulation, however, is like the extension of humaneness to all things. He thus defined humaneness, as had Chang Tsai in the *Western Inscription*, as experiencing heaven and earth and all things as one body.

This ultimate identification of the human with all life forms reflects the dynamic process of the flow of *ch'i*. Just as *ch'i* is the life-inducing material force in the natural order, so is humaneness the creative principle of the moral order. To see these as two aspects of an unfolding continuum was for Ekken essential to the whole enterprise of becoming authentically and fully human. He wrote that the principle of life and the principle of humaneness are intimately connected:

> What is the heart of heaven and earth? It is nothing but birth (*sei*). The great virtue of heaven and earth is [nourishing] life (*sei*). What is birth and life? Chu Hsi said, 'Heaven and earth become the heart of living things.' He also said, 'Heaven and earth does nothing else but give birth to all things.' This is birth. The Way to obey and not hinder this [process] is only through humaneness. In other words, heaven and earth are the heart of living things. Humans receive this heart and it becomes their own. This is humaneness. Nourishing life and [practicing] humaneness are not two different things. Nourishing life belongs to heaven and humaneness belongs to humans.[129]

It is this understanding of the generative power of *ch'i* and of *jen* which informs all of his ethical treatises and is the underlying theme of his method of moral and spiritual cultivation. This cultivation is essentially a dynamic process of self-transformation which participates in the nourishing and life-giving processes of heaven and earth. While for Ekken the framework of such cultivation is a naturalism expressed as a dynamic monism of *ch'i*, and while a primary goal of that cultivation is to activate a humaneness and sincerity which is spontaneous and natural, nonetheless the actual method and program of moral and spiritual discipline which he advocated is carefully defined so as to be rigorously followed. In other words, to achieve an authentic spontaneity, he realized, required continual moral effort and intense spiritual discernment. True effortlessness demanded effort. It is this process of Neo-Confucian self-cultivation that was developed in Ekken's treatise on the *Precepts for Daily Life in Japan*.

# 5

# Analysis of *Yamato Zokkun*

## INTRODUCTION TO THE TEXT

### *The Learning of the Mind-and-Heart*

Ekken's teachings on spiritual cultivation lie within the tradition of the learning of the mind-and-heart (Ch. *hsin hsüeh*, Jp. *shingaku*), which has been discussed at length by Wm. Theodore de Bary in his books, *Neo-Confucian Orthodoxy and the Learning of the Mind-and-Heart* (1981) and *The Message of the Mind* (1988). According to de Bary, *hsin hsüeh* developed amidst the teachings of the Sung Neo-Confucians in their efforts to articulate an alternative to Buddhist doctrines of the mind and to develop an appropriate method for the cultivation of the mind-and-heart.[1] This arose as a Neo-Confucian response to the intensive methods of disciplining the mind advocated by the Buddhists, particularly within the Ch'an sect. While initially related to the "Learning of the Emperors and Kings" as a means of governance, it was also understood as a mode of self-governance. It thus came to have a universal application for both educated leaders and commoners. Its appeal as a teaching also transcended national and cultural boundaries, extending to the Mongols and other non-Han Chinese as well as to the Koreans and Japanese. Being both traditionalist and reformist, its rich humanistic character and religious tone distinguishes it as an important mode of East Asian moral and spiritual cultivation.

The learning of the mind-and-heart, while originating amidst earlier Neo-Confucian teaching, was formulated by Chen Te-hsiu (1178–1235) in his *Hsin ching* (Heart Classic). Although based on various passages from the Confucian classics and later Neo-Confucian writings, Chen gives this teaching a distinctive and enduring synthesis by his arrangement of passages and selection of commentaries. Since de Bary has outlined the contents of the *Heart Classic* in some detail, it is sufficient here to underscore the significance of this work as a guide to a this-worldly method of moral and spiritual discipline which later attracted many adherents in Korea and Japan, as well as China.

In Korea the learning of the mind-and-heart was especially favored by Yi T'oegye, and through him it had a strong impact on Japan as well. Yamazaki Ansai and others of the *Kimon* school were among those influenced by Yi T'oegye.[2] Ansai formed his own syncretic system of Confucianism and Shinto called Suika Shinto which relied on methods of reverent self-cultivation based in part on the learning of the mind-and-heart. While Ekken and others criticized Ansai as being overly rigid and intensely moralistic, his teachings nonetheless claimed ardent followers down into the present century.

Ishida Baigan (1688–1744) was born several years after Ansai's death, and his form of self-cultivation (*shingaku*) spread rapidly among the common people, especially the merchants. Bellah has called Baigan's teachings a "this-worldly mysticism" intended to rid the human heart of selfish desires.[3] The means for doing this were the practice of meditation and asceticism, devotion to one's obligations and occupations, being filial to one's parents, respectful to superiors, and honest in all one's dealings. While Baigan's form of *shingaku* was clearly adapted to the needs of the Tokugawa merchant class, he relied on the earlier Neo-Confucian teachings of the Ch'eng-Chu school for methods of cultivating the mind-and-heart.[4]

Ekken developed his own form of *shingaku* intended for all classes and occupations of people. As the foundation of his system of education, the learning of the mind-and-heart figures prominently in the *Precepts for Daily Life in Japan* and in his other ethico-religious treatises (*kunmono*). This became the core of his moral and spiritual teachings, for he saw self-cultivation as the primary task of human beings in repayment for their heavenly appointed nature. In developing his particular form of *shingaku*, Ekken relied on the *Elementary Learning*, the *Great Learning*, the *Doctrine of the Mean*, and Chu Hsi's commentaries on these texts. Furthermore, he was clearly familiar with Chen Te-hsiu's *Heart Classic*, which was the basis for his two chapters in *Yamato zokkun* on the "Discipline of the Mind-and-Heart."[5] Okada Takehiko noted that he was also influenced by his reading and annotation of the *Ta-hsüeh yen-i* (The Extended Meaning of the Great Learning) by Chen Te-hsiu, the *Hsin ching fu-chu* (Commentary on the Heart Classic) by the Ming scholar Ch'eng Min-cheng, and the *Ta-hsüeh yen-i pu* (Supplement to the Extended Meaning of the Great Learning) by Ch'iu Chün.[6] An analysis of the text of *Precepts for Daily Life in Japan* will help to reveal the particular form of Ekken's learning of the mind-and-heart. In addition, such a discussion can provide the basis for understanding the considerable body of ethicoreligious treatises produced by Ekken and other Neo-Confucian scholars in the Tokugawa period.

## The Text as a Discussion of Neo-Confucian Spiritual Discipline

*Precepts for Daily Life in Japan* begins by establishing the context for Neo-Confucian spiritual discipline in an overarching religious conception combined with specific moral practices. Ekken thus outlines the general cosmological framework for his *shingaku* teachings and suggests the appropriate method of self-cultivation for humans in this framework. These two themes are interwoven throughout the text and provide its fundamental unity. The eight chapters of the text are not tightly organized, however, and there is frequent reiteration of points. This rambling and repetitious style seems well suited to the inculcation of Ekken's teachings among a wide audience. Similarly, the use of a polite conversational Japanese in contrast to the stylized conventions of Chinese-style prose (*kanbun*) distinguishes his writing from other Confucians of the same period. By their very repetition, certain key ideas can be identified as constituting the principle components of Ekken's form of *shingaku*: namely, the religious impetus, the learning imperative,[7] personal integration, and modes of practice.

## The Religious Impetus: Gratitude to Heaven and Earth

In the preface and throughout the *Precepts for Daily Life in Japan* the religious motivation for self-cultivation is clearly expressed. Ekken believes that the special quality of human life is due to the fact that human beings receive the mind-and-heart of heaven and earth. Given a capacity for reflective moral behavior, humans have a heavenly bestowed nature which sets them apart from the plant and animal world and marks them in a special way as children of heaven and earth.[8]

This unique status of humans brings with it both privileges and responsibilities. The human being is seen as extremely fortunate to be born a human and must develop his or her heavenly bestowed nature by serving heaven and earth. To this end an individual practices filiality and reverence toward heaven and earth as the great parents and as the source of all life and blessings.

This religious sense of profound indebtedness to the cosmos for the gift of life, sustenance, and support is at the root of Neo-Confucian spiritual practice or *shingaku* as seen in the *Precepts for Daily Life In Japan*.[9] Moreover, it is also part of the larger process of Neo-Confucian cultivation, namely, the attainment of sagehood through the realization of one's moral nature as linked to heaven and earth and all things.[10] The recognition of this potential for a profound experience of identity with the ultimate reality becomes both the impetus and the goal of cultivation.

By receiving the mind-and-heart of heaven and earth the human becomes a natural vessel for containing and nurturing virtue. As such he is the "spirit of the universe," or the "soul of creation" (*banbutsu no rei*). Through human beings the great consciousness and compassion of the heavenly mind-and-heart may be expressed in moral practice.

The essential characteristic of this great mind-and-heart is its creative and nurturing capacity. Humans receive with their heavenly bestowed nature a rational, moral sense which gives them a capacity for nourishing life in the same way as does the heavenly mind-and-heart. They can therefore express its nurturing qualities in the primary virtue of humaneness. For humans this implies an extension outward in concentric circles of a profound love for other people, as well as a compassion for birds and beasts, trees and plants.

This primary virtue of humaneness encompasses the other principal virtues or constants, namely, righteousness, decorum, wisdom, and faithfulness. In order to avoid too general and diffuse a sense of morality, the practice of virtue is particularly emphasized in the context of the five relationships, namely, between lord and retainer, parent and child, husband and wife, older and younger siblings, and friends. These establish a model for interpersonal relations which implies a mutual bonding of human emotions to a sense of reciprocal obligation as a guide to human behavior.[11]

Accordingly, the preface of *Precepts for Daily Life in Japan* sets forth a cosmological framework in which to situate human beings and to discuss the privileges and responsibilities that human life entails. A religious reverence toward heaven and earth as the source of one's heavenly bestowed nature is at the heart of the moral practice of the human. Implicit in this is the larger Neo-Confucian goal of sagehood, or the profound realization of the essential identity of one's nature with all things. Ekken is deeply concerned that human beings might not recognize the unique religious and ethical obligations that the gift of life entails or that the goal of sagehood demands. He warns repeatedly against wasting time or living without a sense of purpose. He considers this to be a source of great regret and sorrow, for by so doing one fails to reciprocate the beneficence of heaven and earth.

In order to realize their responsibilities as human beings, he believes people must know the "Way of the human" and adopt it. Guidelines exist for following this path, and they should be sought out. There arises, then, an overriding need to know the Way so as to discover and discern the most authentic mode of human behavior. This can be called the learning imperative of Neo-Confucian spirituality. It is the source of the constant emphasis on learning and on education in the Confucian tradition. In *Precepts for Daily Life in Japan* it is the subject of the first two chapters on the "Pursuit of Learning".

The learning imperative is never an end in itself but rather an ongoing process of learning which Tu Wei-ming notes "requires an ultimate and a continuous commitment."[12] This process finds its natural outlet in personal integration. Here the pursuit of learning becomes the transformation of the self through moral and spiritual cultivation. This transformation is the core of Ekken's *shingaku* teachings and is the subject of chapters three and four on the "The Discipline of the Mind-and-Heart" (*shinjutsu*).[13] The last four chapters of the text are principally concerned with modes of practice based on the steps of internal cultivation outlined in the first four chapters. They serve to recapitulate and further develop specific points stated in the earlier sections.

## A DISCUSSION OF THE PRINCIPAL CHAPTERS

*Learning Imperative: The Basis, Method, and Extension of Knowledge*

As their titles indicate, Ekken's first two chapters are primarily concerned with the "Pursuit of Learning," namely, its basis, method, and extension. While these are not systematically developed, there is, nonetheless, a progression in the text which can be noted by the use of terms such as root or basis ( 本 ), method or technique ( 法 ), and extension of knowledge ( 致 知 ). These set forth the method of education and self-cultivation based on the essential teachings of the *Great Learning* and other later Neo-Confucian texts and commentaries on the same subject. This substructure of Ekken's work emphasizes the importance placed in Neo-Confucian education on the need for sequence and method in learning. A gradual progression is deemed necessary to attain inner authenticity and personal integration.

THE BASIS: BALANCING THE SUBJECTIVE AND THE OBJECTIVE

For Ekken the basis of learning is establishing a dynamic balance between subjective and objective knowledge. Over-emphasis on one or the other poles of knowledge could lead to a distortion of learning as a moral process. For this reason, Ekken is critical of the subjective tendencies of Buddhism, Taoism, and of the Lu-Wang teaching of the mind. At the same time he does not believe that a purely rational or empirical approach is satisfactory. He notes that those who are overly subjective tend to sink into quietistic or solipsistic practices, and those who try to be rational and objective are inclined to become simply technically adept at external investigation while ignoring the process of inner cultivation. Thus, Ekken emphasizes a learning that is based on a balancing of subjective and objective knowledge, leading to an expression of that knowledge in action.

With regard to subjectivity in knowing, Ekken, following Chu Hsi before him, states that learning begins with things close at hand. There is no need to search for an abstract wisdom in distant places. He stresses the need to rely on one's own innate knowledge of the good in trying to understand the teachings of the sages. The reason that people can recognize truth is because of their subjective capacity for "good knowing" (Ch. *liang-chih*, Jp. *ryōchi*). This affirmation of the potential of all humans for discernment and the confirmation of the goodness of that innate nature are at the heart of Neo-Confucian learning and self-cultivation.

Along with this dynamic reliance on subjectivity, there is a recognition of the need for objectivity so as to avoid the danger of depending exclusively on one's own opinions. Ekken stresses the importance of relying on teachers, on friends, and on the sages of the past. He believes that it is difficult to master even small arts without a teacher, and he notes that the sages also learned by studying with a teacher. It is essential to select good teachers and to respect them fully. In addition to teachers, people should learn and consult with trusted friends who will objectively point out their shortcomings and correct their mistakes. The biases of one's disposition can thus be rectified. Finally, the sages themselves are important models to be followed, both through the example of their lives and through their writings. Ekken is, however, aware of the need for a constant reevaluation of Confucian scholars, for he wishes to avoid an uncritical acceptance of their ideas.

In order to bring together the objective and subjective standards of knowledge, two factors are indispensable for Ekken. The first is establishing a resolute goal or aim for one's learning and the second is adopting humility as the foundation. These are key elements of the learning imperative which are reiterated throughout the text.

For Ekken establishing a goal is essential for all later progress. Within the context of Neo-Confucian self-cultivation, the ultimate goal for Ekken was understood to be the attainment of sagehood, namely the full realization of one's own nature and the experience of a oneness with heaven, earth, and all things. Perhaps in an effort to maintain a sense of the accessibility of such a goal and to stress the availability of Neo-Confucian practice for all classes of people, he speaks less about this ultimate goal than simply the goal of transformation of one's nature through moral cultivation. The process, he realizes, is demanding, human nature is weak, and thus a consciousness of a larger goal is essential. Without such a goal one may waver, become lazy, or be distracted by ephemeral things. For Ekken, establishing a goal means having a resolute aim and being constantly diligent toward this end. Thus he calls for a firm will which is single-minded and not divided or faltering. This dedicated effort of the will is the basis of study and the dynamic motive behind the learning imperative.

Lest a person become self-absorbed in this resolute drive toward a goal, Ekken advocates humility as a correlative principle for the learning process. Arrogance and pride are seen as destructive of genuine learning. Rather, a person should take pleasure in questioning others, listening carefully to instructions, and welcoming admonishments. People should be modest about their knowledge or accomplishments and be quick to correct their errors when necessary. Ultimately, Ekken follows the important directive of Confucius to learn for oneself, not to impress others. This was a cornerstone of Chu Hsi's teachings and was continually cited by Neo-Confucians in China, Korea, and Japan.[14]

Ekken urges those involved in learning not to come in conflict with illiterate people who dislike all forms of scholarly endeavor and thus err in their subjective prejudices. He says scholars should not argue angrily as such biased people do, or they will only justify such antagonism toward all scholarly endeavor. He feels the reason some uneducated people dislike learning is because frequently scholars do not practice the Way and are arrogant and disdainful of others. He makes a special plea for sincerity and humility in learning so that Japan may become "an enlightened nation of Noble Persons."[15]

Ekken continually returns to these two principles of resoluteness and constant humility as the basis of all learning. He urges people to make their goal great and lofty at the same time that they make their heart small and lowly. Thus, objectivity and subjectivity balance and refine each other, providing counterpoints for a steady progression on the Way.

THE METHOD: INTEGRATING KNOWLEDGE AND ACTION

The essential method of the learning imperative involves steps for integrating knowledge and action. These are the fundamental principles originally stated in the *Doctrine of the Mean* and emphasized by Chu Hsi, namely, study widely, question thoroughly, think carefully, judge clearly, and act seriously.[16] The method of studying widely is an elaboration of the subjective and objective elements previously discussed as the basis for learning. "By first delving into the Way and its principles in our own hearts, and then widely searching out the principles in all things, we will apprehend a truth in the center of our own being."[17] This requires an investigation of both the past and the present by a reliance on the books of the sages and on the teachings of other people. Similarly, questioning thoroughly builds on the basis of humility and becomes a method for resolving doubts and clarifying principles. Thinking carefully means reflecting with discretion so that one will acquire knowledge for oneself. Judging clearly means investigating right and wrong and distinguishing between good and evil. These four steps, namely, studying, questioning, thinking, and judging, Ekken describes as "techniques of knowing in order to discern the Way clearly."[18] The first two involve the specific "external" activities of studying and questioning while the latter two revolve around the more reflective "internal" activities of assimilating what one is learning through dispassionate reflection. This involves the important idea of "getting it for oneself" (Ch. *tzu-te*, Jp. *jitoku*) so essential to Neo-Confucian self-cultivation.[19] These steps have their natural culmination in the fifth directive, to act seriously. Ekken advises that one would be cultivating oneself in this direction if one were sincere in words and careful in actions.

More specifically, Ekken outlines the proper method of daily study as: learning with a teacher in the morning, reviewing in the afternoon, studying again in the evening, and reflecting on mistakes at night. Referring back to a passage from the *Book of Rites* which was often stressed by Chu Hsi, he encourages the student to be conscientious through "daily renewal."[20] This means trying to eliminate the mistakes of the previous day through examination, thereby facilitating a return to goodness.

He continually urges students to make an effort in their youth to use time wisely. He emphasizes careful attention when one is young to learning characters and understanding the meaning of words, so that one's education will progress steadily. At the same time, one should have a calm, natural approach in order to know how to wait and be open to wisdom. If students are conscientious in their youth and yet are patient with gradual progress, they will succeed in achieving their goals of intellectual and moral development. Ekken believes that these general directives on the method of learning apply to all classes of people and all walks of life.

Similarly, people can be educated by the methods established in the *Hsiao-hsüeh* (Elementary Learning) and the *Ta-hsüeh* (Great Learning). Ekken describes in some detail the program of Neo-Confucian learning based on these two texts. According to Chu Hsi, the *Elementary Learning* begins when a child reaches the age of eight, while the *Great Learning* begins at the age of fifteen. Ekken summarizes the teachings as follows: "What they were taught was to have filial piety toward their parents, respect their seniors, and serve their lord; the way to receive guests, sweep the rooms, prepare food and drink, advance and withdraw in the presence of notable people, and respond to questions and requests; and they were also taught the skills of the six arts for daily use, namely, ritual, music, archery, driving [a horse or chariot], reading, and arithmetic."[21] This was the traditional beginning of a Neo-Confucian education and the basis of the next stage, namely, the *Great Learning*. While the *Elementary Learning* is concerned with two essential virtues (filiality and respect), with external decorum (serving, sweeping, preparing, etc.), and with basic skills (six arts), the *Great Learning* concentrates on the truths of governing the people through self-discipline.[22] Clearly, however, one can not enter into the *Great Learning* without the prior preparation of the *Elementary Learning*.

Ekken is especially concerned to explicate the method of the *Great Learning*, namely, the three guiding principles and eight steps, so that their essentials would be understood and practiced by a large number of the Japanese people. He follows Chu Hsi's preface and commentary in explicating the doctrines of the *Great Learning*. The three guiding principles of the text are the goals of "manifesting illustrious virtue, renewing the people, and resting in the highest good."[23] The eight steps embrace a comprehensive program of social-political involvement (bringing peace to all under heaven, effecting order in the state, and regulating the family); moral and spiritual discipline (cultivating oneself, rectifying the mind, and making the will sincere); and intellectual realization (extending knowledge and investigating things). These are the essence of the method of Neo-Confucian education and are discussed throughout the text as the core elements underlying both the pursuit of learning and the "Discipline of the Mind-and-Heart" (*shinjutsu*).

THE EXTENSION OF KNOWLEDGE: THE INVESTIGATION OF THINGS

After outlining the basis and method or program of learning, Ekken discusses the importance of the extension of knowledge through the investigation of things. Here he elaborates on both his general directives and his more specific instructions for a curriculum of study. He summarizes his general directives in the following passage, which is based on the steps of the *Great Learning*:

> The way to extend knowledge is by first knowing the Way of the five constant virtues and the five moral relations. We should extend this to the principle of regulating the family and governing the people. Next we should seek to know the principles of all things and affairs. Since all things in heaven and earth lie within the ken of our own mind-and-heart, we should learn their principles. The way of investigating principles first gives priority to what is primary (the root) and what is close at hand and then follows up with what is secondary (the branches) and things farther away. We should not forget the order of sequence and priority.[24]

Ekken states that the beginning of all efforts at self-discipline and governing the people is clarifying truth through investigating things and extending knowledge. Investigating things means examining the truth of objects and events, beginning with moral virtues and relations close at hand and moving outward. Extending knowledge implies a careful examination of the mind-and-heart so that one will arrive at an authentic self-knowledge. These two poles, then, of internal reflection and external investigation are the pivotal points of the process of the *Great Learning* and are essential to all Neo-Confucian spiritual practice. While Ekken is primarily concerned in this text with moral and spiritual cultivation, he observes that merely investigating human relations or moral virtue as a separate entity is not sufficient. He feels this must be seen in relation to the dynamic life process of nature itself. Thus he believes people must also study the Way of heaven and earth as the basis of the human Way. The cosmological context and the role of principle within material force is, for Ekken, essential to an understanding of the "root from which truth emerges" so one may be able to "recognize the natural principles inherent in human beings."[25] This becomes the metaphysical basis for Ekken's efforts to investigate objects in the natural world. He thus extends the idea of investigating principles from a primarily ethical concern to an empirical and naturalist enterprise as well.

Ekken further notes that one should take an approach to investigation which is open-minded. To be open-minded one should realize that there is not only one way to investigate principles (ethically or empirically). Rather, there are a variety of approaches and numerous layers to be examined in one's studies. Taking up Confucius' directive to study for oneself rather than for others, Ekken urges the reader not to be concerned with impressing people or with seeking honor or fame through learning but to investigate principle with vigor, perseverance, and sincerity.

Following these general directives Ekken gives more specific instructions on investigating things and extending knowledge through a curriculum of study. He suggests which books should be read by beginning students and which ones should be used for more advanced studies. The *Four Books* and the *Five Classics* naturally form the heart of a Neo-Confucian program for learning. He emphasizes, as had Chu Hsi, the importance of the *Four Books*, saying, "Reading them is like listening to the teachings of the sages directly."[26] To fully understand their meaning he urges the student to consult the commentaries on the *Four Books*, as well as those on the *Five Classics*. Next he suggests reading the books of the Sung Neo-Confucians, namely, Chou Tun-i, the Ch'eng brothers, and Chu Hsi. He singles out the Ch'eng brothers and Chu Hsi as meriting special attention. He also cites the *Elementary Learning* as an important guide to self-discipline.

After these have been read thoroughly, Ekken urges the student to look at the histories, especially the *Tso chuan* (Tso's Commentary on the Spring and Autumn Annals), *Shih chi* (Records of the Historian), and Chu Hsi's *T'ung-chien kang-mu* (Outline and Digest of the Great Mirror). These could serve as guides to government by helping one understand the past so as to lead intelligently in the present. The historical records of Japan could similarly be of assistance in this respect. Ekken also includes collected works and literature in his list of books to be consulted.

He warns against dilettantism, however, saying that merely trying to read widely is not enough. One should not lose sight of one's true aim by becoming absorbed in superficial, broad learning. Rather, people should keep in mind the overarching concern to understand moral principles in order to extend knowledge and practice it in daily life. Thus, as in all Neo-Confucian programs of education, breadth should be balanced by selectivity and restraint.

## Personal Integration: The Discipline of the Mind-and-Heart

Chapters three and four describe the purpose and the method of moral and spiritual cultivation involved in the learning of the mind-and-heart. They expand upon the essential point of the *Great Learning* that, through disciplining oneself, one's family can be regulated and other people can be governed. If this self-discipline is not thorough, one's social or political participation will be ineffective. To rectify the mind-and-heart one must first make one's will sincere in loving good and disliking evil. Then a person will be able to maintain and express the seven emotions (happiness, anger, sadness, enjoyment, love, hate, desire) in correct proportion. With a balancing of emotions, an effective social-political activity can be undertaken and a deep spiritual harmony can be maintained.

In substance these two chapters are based on the rectification of the mind-and-heart as advocated in the *Great Learning* and by Chu Hsi and Chen Te-hsiu. Relying on these prior teachings, Ekken articulates the learning of the mind-and-heart, which is essentially a means of moral and spiritual cultivation. As discussed by Ekken, this discipline is undertaken primarily for religious motivations, for like the pursuit of learning, the impetus for undertaking such a discipline is the repayment of one's debt to heaven and earth as the source and sustainer of life. This method of cultivation culminates

in an experience of harmony among heaven, earth, and human beings. To achieve this final union, Ekken outlines a rigorous program
of moral and spiritual practice. This includes initial discernment
and resolution, moral purification and emotional control, the practice of virtue, and achieving spiritual harmony.

### THE RELIGIOUS IMPETUS OF SELF-CULTIVATION

Ekken indicates the importance of cultivating the mind-and-heart as
a means of following the Way of heaven and earth, thereby repaying our debt to nature for the gift of life. The compassion, kindness,
and nourishment which humans receive from heaven and earth
should be acknowledged by their own care for all living things. People should not allow themselves to be unrestrained, or "to be unfilial and harm people and things which nature has created and
nourished, disturbing the life principle, wasting the things of nature, and violating the heart of heaven and earth."[27] For Ekken the
primary motive of this ethicoreligious discipline is to acknowledge
one's filial obligation to nature, to respect the basic processes of life,
and to revere and assist the heavenly Way that is manifest in these
natural processes. A profound religious reverence underlies the
practice of *shingaku*. Moreover, behind this moral and spiritual discipline lies the larger goal of Neo-Confucian practice, namely the
attainment of sagehood by full realization of one's heavenly bestowed nature.

### DISCERNMENT, RESOLUTION, BALANCE: HUMAN MIND AND WAY MIND

At the core of Neo-Confucian moral and spiritual cultivation is the
learning of the mind-and-heart which arose among the Sung masters and was formulated in the *Heart Classic* of Chen Te-hsiu. Ekken
relies on the first quotation in the *Heart Classic* originally taken from
the *Book of History* and attributed to the sage king, Yü: "The human
mind is precarious, the Way mind is barely perceptible. Having utmost refinement and singleness of mind we should hold fast to the
Mean."[28] Like Chen, Ekken follows Chu Hsi's interpretation of
these lines to expound his teachings on self-cultivation. He begins
his discussion, as does Chu Hsi, by advocating a method which
combines intellectual discernment, volitional effort, and emotional
and aesthetic balance.[29]

Ekken first notes the importance of distinguishing between the
human mind and the Way mind. The human mind is seen as the

seat of emotions and desires while the mind of the Way is the root of moral principles and virtues. Recognizing the difference between the two is the beginning of moral and spiritual cultivation. This process of discernment is difficult because of the unstable nature of the human mind, which is connected to physical forms and precariously balanced between selfish and unselfish desires, and the subtle nature of the mind of the Way, which is "hidden in the depths of the heart."[30]

In discerning between the two, one can begin to learn how to control the human mind and preserve the Way mind. This is the fundamental basis of moral and spiritual discipline. This process of distinguishing between the human mind and the moral mind is what is referred to by the phrase "having utmost refinement." The next phrase, "singleness of mind," indicates the resolution to unify the will so that the Way mind is dominant and the human mind does not run rampant (i.e. selfish desires do not dominate the human mind). Finally, "holding fast to the Mean" implies achieving a balance of the emotions and the senses so that they are "neither excessive nor deficient."[31]

Having set forth the general motivations and methods of the learning of mind-and-heart, Ekken then outlines some of the specific problems that arise in the attempt at self-discipline. This involves a lengthy discussion of obstructions to achieving an inner harmony and ways to overcome these obstacles. Specifically, he advocates a program of moral purification along with suggestions of how to express one's emotions and yet control them effectively.

MORAL PURIFICATION AND EMOTIONAL CONTROL

Ekken cites three major obstacles to the practice of the learning of mind-and-heart: selfish desires and evil thoughts; a biased disposition; and faults. All of these obstacles must be carefully eliminated in order to progress in virtue. "Selfish desires" he describes as pleasures of the senses, namely, greed for fame, profit, sex, or possessions. "Evil thoughts" he sees as oppressing people, arguing angrily with others, boasting about ourselves, criticizing or slandering others, and flattering or deceiving people. "A biased disposition" means the partiality with which one is born, namely, having a rough and boisterous nature, a soft or weak nature, a dull or greedy nature. "Faults" refers to unwitting mistakes or habits which one should reform quickly. He emphasizes that it is extremely important

to purify oneself of these deficiencies or attempts at spiritual cultivation will be useless.

In connection with moral purification Ekken also engages in
specific discussions of the problem of the emotions. He is concerned
with the question of how and when to control the emotions or to
express them so as to live morally but also humanely. He is aiming
at an authentic integration of the person so that the emotions are
not suppressed or eliminated but are restrained when appropriate
and expressed when appropriate. He wishes to avoid the extremes
of puritanism or libertarianism. He specifically cites the directive in
the *Book of Changes* to "restrain anger and contain the desires,"[32]
considering these two to be the deadliest of the emotions. He warns
against the irrational, harmful aspect of anger and its inability to
move people. He gives other examples of appropriate emotional expression with regard to the circumstances. It is the mind that must
act as the master of the emotions so it will be able to control and
not be controlled by them. When such control is achieved then a
person will be better able to practice virtue with a sense of ease and
with assurance that his emotions will be expressed naturally and
spontaneously in response to specific circumstances.

## MODES OF PRACTICE

After purification and emotional balancing one can then effectively
practice virtue, beginning with love and respect toward others. This
implies having humaneness and decorum so as to show compassion
and sympathy rather than disdain toward people and things. Ekken
identifies the virtue of humaneness with the life-principle in the
universe. He writes that compassion "is the great virtue of heaven
and earth and it is the principle of life."[33] He also says, "humaneness is a heart which loves and sympathizes with others; in other
words, it is a heart which gives life to the things of heaven and
earth."[34] He speaks of an order and sequence in extending humaneness, namely, from family and lord outward to relatives, retainers,
and friends. Ekken also includes in this sphere animals, fish, birds,
insects, trees, and vegetation. From the lower forms to the higher
forms of life all are worthy of love, respect, care, and nourishment.
He elaborates at length on this all-encompassing virtue of humaneness which allows for no separation between ourselves and others.
He also discusses the importance of reciprocity, which is the ability
to imagine others as ourselves and to treat them accordingly.

Ekken describes the culmination of this path of virtue as the practice of hidden virtue, which does not seek recognition or repayment from others. Such hidden virtue is concerned with the public good rather than any private gain. He portrays this virtue in the following passage:

> In order to have compassion and kindness toward others, grieving with their sorrows and rejoicing in their happiness, we should give priority to the widowed, orphaned, and childless, bring relief to the hungry, give clothes to those who are cold, help the tired and sick, repair roads and bridges, eliminate things which harm people, and do things which benefit them—making peace among people; praising their goodness, concealing their faults, overlooking their small mistakes; developing and utilizing their talents; not being angry at people indiscriminately; not having resentments against them; stopping the angry disputes of others; not slandering people even slightly; not despising, depriving, or hindering others; fostering their virtue; reproving their errors; not injuring birds, animals, insects, or fish; not killing recklessly; not cutting plants and trees wantonly. All this is hidden virtue.[35]

If people choose such a generous and public-spirited path they will be "in accord with reason, with the will of heaven, and with the human heart."[36] In so doing they will have a broad tolerance toward others, will not harbor resentments, or agonize over mistakes. Instead, they will move with an inner calm in the rigorous practice of hidden virtue and humaneness.

Consequently, Ekken emphasizes the virtue of reverent mindfulness as something which should be constantly cultivated. He notes how this virtue, which implies both moral seriousness and religious reverence, had consistently been the touchstone of the learning of the mind-and-heart of the sages. Referring back to his discussion of moral purification, he warns people to be especially careful about things they are attracted to in order to avoid becoming immersed in sensual pleasures.

Similarly, rulers should have hearts which are morally serious and sympathetic toward others. If they do, they will give the people what they need and not selfishly indulge their own pleasures. Ekken points out that this method for ruling with moral seriousness will be effective because it will not create resentment among the people. Rather, "if the rulers love the people with sincerity, the people will definitely sense that and be happy."[37]

Ekken also discusses the importance of reverence as a religious virtue in conjunction with the state of inner harmony. He speaks of this kind of reverence as a constant state of mindful respect, while he sees harmony as a calm enjoyment. These two go together like the wheels of a cart or the wings of a bird. By reverence he means people are mindful of themselves and others in relation to heaven and earth. By harmony he suggests that people be content with their position in life, make an effort at their vocation, and avoid striving after external goals or seeking trivial satisfaction. Ekken speaks of this state of reverent, joyful contentment as a natural quality which is enriched by "harmony with external things."[38]

Thus, he says that by contact with "the wind and the flowers, the snow and the moon, the original contentment of the heart is deepened."[39] That is because the reverent contentment of the heart reflects the natural harmony of the universe. He writes, "birds fly, fish leap, birds chirp, animals cry out, vegetation flourishes, flowers bloom, fruit is produced—these are expressions of the will of heaven and the natural delight of all things."[40] Appreciating this, the Noble Person is not led astray by desires but reverently nurtures the natural contentment of the heart, which is part of the ceaseless fecundity of the universe. Such an inner harmony in the human Way reflects the sincerity of the Way of heaven and earth.

SPIRITUAL HARMONY AND INTELLECTUAL ILLUMINATION

For Ekken, when a person comes to this stage of integration, the mind-and-heart will be illuminated, clear, and not vacillating in discerning right from wrong. Through the acquisition of true knowledge the mind will indeed be the master of the body and the controller of the emotions and senses. Heavenly principles will progress within, as human desires decrease and thus the person's nature will be fully realized. The result will be an inner calm which reflects the peaceful harmony of the workings of heaven. The microcosm and the macrocosm will thus mirror each other through the inner harmony of the individual. In Neo-Confucianism this can be expressed as attaining sagehood. It is this type of spiritual integration that is the ultimate aim of Ekken's learning of the mind-and-heart. It is an integration which is in harmony with change and constantly reverent before the myriad life processes. Through an arduous effort at discernment, purification, and practice the individual can experience himself as a vital part of larger, cosmic processes. It was toward this end that Ekken advocates his "Discipline of the Mind-and-Heart," based on a dynamic naturalism articulated as a monism of *ch'i*.

## SUMMARY OF ADDITIONAL CHAPTERS

While the first half of *Precepts for Daily Life in Japan* outlines the necessary components of the Confucian learning imperative and the steps towards inner personal integration, the second half of the text concentrates on modes of practice based on these earlier efforts at intellectual and spiritual cultivation. The final four chapters are divided into one on "clothes and speech," two on "practice," and one on "responding to others." The main thrust of these four chapters is to recapitulate the major points of the earlier sections and to reemphasize certain forms of moral practice through examples. Ekken's conscious use of repetition as a teaching device underscores his intention to reach a variety of less-educated people who found such repetition familiar and helpful. Moreover, his colloquial style and use of examples from daily life are intended to free his writing from the artificiality inherent in Chinese-style prose (*kanbun*) conventions often used by Japanese Confucians.

In the two chapters on "Practice" Ekken develops points made earlier. He discusses the goals of moral practice, obstacles to their realization, the means of overcoming these obstacles, and the underlying motivations of such efforts. Ekken sees the goals of moral practice as self-cultivation and the practice of the five relations. He summarizes self-cultivation as: having sincerity in speech and discretion in action, suppressing anger and controlling desires, turning toward the good and vigorously practicing it, and knowing one's faults and reforming quickly. The principal obstacles to cultivating oneself are the psycho-physical disposition, selfish desires, and habits. These he describes as the root, trunk, and branches, respectively, of evil practices. The means to overcome these are through graciously accepting admonitions of others and vigorously making an effort to change one's disposition. Ekken notes that just as heaven moves ceaselessly, so should one's efforts be unflagging, and just as earth is still and quiet, so should one not arouse the heart but keep it calm and restrained. Above all, Ekken urges people not to despair or give up on themselves, but to have a constantly open and honest heart.

In his chapter on clothes and speech, Ekken advocates simplicity and understatedness in both. He warns against inappropriateness in dress or in conversation and calls for efforts at modesty and restraint.[41] His general instructions for speech involve first being calm internally and then speaking with discretion and brevity. He underscores the need for simplicity in speech, namely, keeping one's promises and fulfilling one's obligations. One should avoid speaking of people behind their backs or slandering them; instead one should aim at being tolerant and not holding grudges. Ekken particularly asks that superiors listen to inferiors with regard to their own failings. The lord, for example, should be open to criticism from his retainers. If the lord suppresses speech then evil rumors will only be propagated. Ekken also notes that the correct way to admonish people is either by personal admonition (directly) or by suggestive exhortation (indirectly). Excess in praise or criticism is to be avoided.

As a means toward self-cultivation he urges fidelity to principle, noting that one cannot serve two masters. Therefore, people should concentrate on three essential tasks, namely, being diligent in their work, caring for their health, and practicing righteousness. The overarching motivation for all of these efforts at moral practice is to repay one's great obligations to heaven and earth, to one's parents, to one's lord, and to the sages. In moral practice Ekken notes that people must ultimately trust the will of heaven and have respect for the gods. Once again Ekken's religious concerns are evident in his teachings.

In the final chapter of the text Ekken discusses the appropriate manner of responding to others as a culmination of earlier efforts at cultivating one's self. This involves having a correct propriety and a dignified manner which expresses itself as love and respect in mingling with others. He urges people to control their material force (*ch'i*) so that it is peaceful and then extend reciprocity to others. This implies a sympathetic understanding of others by inferring their feelings from one's own experiences.

## CONCLUDING COMMENTS

Ekken's *Precepts for Daily Life in Japan*, then, is an important text for its detailed discussion of the method of spiritual discipline based on the learning of the mind-and-heart. As the last and most developed of his ethicoreligious treatises, it serves as an appropriate summary of Ekken's teachings. When considered in conjunction with the *Taigiroku*, one can see how his naturalist metaphysics provide a dynamic basis for his ideas on cultivating the self in relation to change in the natural order. Finally, one can appreciate, as an example of Tokugawa Neo-Confucianism, Ekken's considerable efforts to make this a teaching text so as to spread moral education and the method of *shingaku* to a wide audience.

ABOVE: *Aosagi*. A blue heron. BELOW: *Toki*. A crested ibis.

# 6

# A Comparative Treatment of Ekken's Ethical Treatises

Ronald Dore has said that Ekken was "responsible for one of the most systematic accounts" of the rationale for moral education in the Tokugawa period, and he cited *Yamato zokkun* as the principle example of this effort.[1] As part of Ekken's attempt to codify Neo-Confucian ethics, he also wrote more than a dozen other treatises. One of his primary concerns was to make Neo-Confucian teachings understood and practiced by a broad spectrum of people. To this end he spent a great deal of effort in writing these moral essays (*kunmono*), which were instructions directed at specific groups in the society, namely, the lord, the samurai, the family, and women and children.[2] Other treatises concerned the beginning of study, composition, the five constant virtues, health care, and achieving contentment. Together these essays comprise over seven hundred pages in the third volume of his collected works. While the *Precepts for Daily Life in Japan* and *Precepts on the Five Cardinal Confucian Virtues* (*Gojōkun*) are the most extensive discussions of his moral teachings, the more widely known texts are *Precepts on Health Care* (*Yōjōkun*) and *Learning for Women* (*Onna daigaku*).[3]

The significance of these writings lies in their role of fostering popular education and adapting Neo-Confucianism to the Japanese context.[4] Their pedagogical style, a simplified Japanese, and the use of detailed instructions make them a valuable source for understanding this attempt to indigenize and codify Neo-Confucian val-

105

ues in seventeenth-century Tokugawa society. They also give a picture of some of the issues which Ekken identified as most significant for education in this period, namely, encouraging broad public education, making use of the Chinese classics for understanding one's moral duty in the contemporary society, and connecting one's vocation or family business to the performance of this duty.

Furthermore, Ekken was eager to explain the need for specific steps so individuals could progress in learning and gradually internalize it with a sense of proper sequence. Underlying these teachings was a recognition of the importance of a practical and functional spirituality based on the learning of the mind-and-heart. To illustrate some of these particular concerns, three of his essays will be discussed in comparison with other treatises of the period addressed to the samurai, to the family, and to children, respectively.

In lieu of an exhaustive survey of his ethical treatises, a comparative discussion of these three essays may serve to highlight the particular characteristics and objectives of Ekken's ideas on education. It may suggest, too, possibilities for further research in the areas of Tokugawa education, modes of ethical instruction, and the indigenization of Neo-Confucian values among various groups in the society.

## PRECEPTS FOR THE SAMURAI

Ekken's discussion of *Precepts for the Samurai* (*Bukun*)[5] represents a conscious concern to combine military (*bu*) and cultural (*bun*) pursuits, which he feels balance each other like the wheels of a cart or the wings of a bird. Ekken uses the metaphor of roots and branches throughout his essay to make distinctions which he believes are crucial to joining the two.[6]

First he identifies the roots of the military profession as the virtues of loyalty, filiality, righteousness, and bravery, while as branches of the martial arts he cites the use of the bow and arrow or sword and halberd. He says that a true samurai ought to be primarily concerned with the practice of virtue, and only secondarily with the mastery of the martial arts. He further subdivides these two areas of virtues and skills into internal and external components or roots and branches.

He notes, for example, that humaneness and righteousness are the roots of all military virtues, while bravery and courage are the branches.[7] Without these two primary Confucian virtues at the core of all military efforts, any external attempts at bravery or military prowess are meaningless.

With regard to skills, Ekken stresses the need for both physical and mental discipline as the root and branches of samurai training. Thus, in addition to recommending the practice of archery and horsemanship, he speaks in some detail of keeping one's mind-and-heart steady, calm, and single-minded.[8] This discussion represents a further elaboration of the learning of the mind-and-heart as outlined in chapter four. In essence, then, Ekken advocates an education that embraces both effective military preparedness, planning, and strategy along with mental control, endurance, and restraint.

He is particularly critical of the kind of Japanese *bushidō* (way of the samurai) that stresses bravado over virtue and, consequently, loses a proper sense of human relations.[9] He also disparages those who try to acquire the name of a warrior by claiming other people's deeds as their own. He feels many samurai are deceitful and are only motivated by personal profit and subjective desires. By acting in this way, they disregard their duty and ignore both military and cultural values.

Ekken's ultimate interest in combining cultural and military arts is to join together the virtues of humaneness and righteousness. He feels that through the pursuit of moral cultivation and learning one acquires an expansive sympathy with people which is expressed through humaneness. At the same time, knowing how to overcome an enemy and control disorder is practicing righteousness. These are the essential virtues to be cultivated in balancing the civilizing influence of culture with the discipline required by military training.

## Comparison and Contrast

The ideas which Ekken set forth in his *Bukun* can be compared to other contemporary treatises addressed to the samurai. Ekken was, for example, elaborating the general directive in the *Buke shohatto* and other unofficial treatises to join military and cultural interests. His particular emphasis on the need for broad education and self-cultivation of a Neo-Confucian type was also similar to that advocated by his contemporary, Mitsukuni (1628–1700), a lord of the Mito han.

In his "Instructions of a Mito Prince to his Retainers" (*Gikō meirei*), Mitsukuni was eager to combine Confucian moral teachings with the *bushidō* code.[10] Indeed, Mitsukuni was involved in a lifelong commitment to Confucian learning and employed the Ming refugee, Chu Shun-sui (1600–1682), to assist his efforts.[11] He was also particularly open to listening to advice from his retainers as is evident in the preface. Like Ekken, he urged his retainers to be attentive to both learning and virtue. He advocated reading of the classics as well as the diligent practice of filial piety and loyalty.[12]

He warned, as did Ekken, against imitating hypocritical people who might seem clever or wise on the exterior but were, in fact, degenerate or worthless men. In this spirit, he called for the samurai to remember politeness and humility and to avoid arrogance or rudeness. Like Ekken, he recognized the importance of military preparations and therefore asked that his retainers be observant and conscientious without being obsessive or impetuous.[13]

He also commented on the need for simplicity and frugality in entertainment, in military equipment, in one's house, and in one's possessions. He closed his treatise with the question: If each of the four classes had its particular function, what is the role of the samurai? His answer was reminiscent of Yamaga Sokō:

> Its only business is to preserve, or maintain, *giri* [duty]. The people of other classes deal with visible things, while the samurai deals with invisible, colorless, and unsubstantial things . . . But if there were no samurai, right [*giri*] would disappear from human society, the sense of shame would be lost, and wrong and injustice would prevail.[14]

Mitsukuni, then, is a Confucian lord who, like Ekken, took his role as an ethical teacher quite seriously, seeing moral cultivation and learning for the samurai as more important than military prowess.

This was in marked contrast to the ideas in the text entitled *Hagakure* (Hidden Among Leaves), which was also concerned with the role of the samurai in peacetime.[15] This treatise was the teaching of Yamamoto Tsunetomo (1659–1719), a Kyushu samurai who retired to the Buddhist priesthood. It was recorded by his student, Tashiro Tsuramoto, two years after Ekken wrote his *Yamato zokkun* (1708). Essentially, *Hagakure* reflected Yamamoto's attempt to transmit the core of the samurai spirit to a new generation which appeared to be soft and self-indulgent. His teachings were apparently passed down to subsequent generations of samurai in Saga, and even in twentieth-century Japan it has had considerable appeal.[16]

The virtue of loyalty to the lord above all things was Yamamoto's primary teaching. It was from this essential loyalty, even to the point of death, that the samurai's life derived its meaning and purpose. This devotion of the retainer took precedence over any other secondary claims on the samurai; indeed, its absolute quality makes it difficult for an outsider to fully understand the logic of *bushidō*.[17]

The urgency of Yamamoto's concerns is evident from his remarks about the laxity of the contemporary samurai. Yet, unlike the Neo-Confucian thinkers of the period, such as the Mito lord, and very much in contrast to Ekken, he enjoined the samurai to avoid scholarly learning or frivolous academic pursuits. Rather, he said, "Look at unschooled and unlettered men who fervently serve their masters straightforwardly or who strive to rear their families. They can lead [an] admirable life all through their days."[18] For Yamamoto learning might interfere with loyalty rather than promote it.

The mode of *bushidō* presented in *Hagakure* emphasized loyalty over learning, and fighting prowess was valued above any commercial endeavor. *Hagakure* might thus be seen as representing a fundamentalist (indeed, extremist) revival of Yamaga Sokō's earlier attempts to articulate the Way of the Warrior and the importance of the martial arts.[19] Yet Yamaga himself never denied the need to join military and cultural pursuits. In disputing this, Yamamoto's position was unique and clearly at odds with Ekken's ideas.

## PRECEPTS FOR THE FAMILY

Ekken's instructions for the samurai have characteristics in common with another genre of moral treatise called *kakun* ("house codes" or "family precepts"). These treatises consisted of exhortations of a clan head written for the moral edification of his family and descendants. Those described as house codes were usually addressed to the lord's retainer-descendants, while those known as family precepts were directed to the family as a whole. In this section the former type is represented by the codes of the Kuroda lords, while the latter is represented by Ise Teijō's instructions.

Carl Steenstrup has described family codes as "freely revocable expressions of patriarchal will" while noting their importance in revealing the value system of a particular period.[20] According to Steenstrup, most *kakun* were in a free-flowing personal style.[21] In discussing one by Hōjō Shigetoki, he observed that the ideas were linked by "analogy and association, not by chains of inference or subordination."[22] This is an apt description of Ekken's instructions for the family, as well as of his other ethical treatises.

The custom of writing family codes came to Japan from China in the seventh-century. A major influence on early Japanese *kakun* was the scholar Yen Chih-tu'i (531–591) who wrote *Family Instructions for the Yen Clan*.[23] Family precepts continued to be written by court nobility throughout the Heian period. One of these, dating from the ninth-century, was cited as important reading for Emperors as late as 1615 in the *Kuge shohatto*. There also exist major examples of Kamakura *kakun*, written by Hōjō Shigetoki and other samurai leaders.[24] In the Tokugawa era, the *Buke shohatto* and regulations for the *hatamoto* (banner men) have been seen by Steenstrup as essentially forms of house codes.[25] During this period there also began to appear similar family codes among the merchant class.[26]

Ekken, then, could not have been unaware that he was speaking within a tradition of family precepts that long preceded the Tokugawa era. He was, however, also intent on enlarging that tradition and adapting it to the needs of the contemporary family. This will become clearer in comparing his instructions with those of the Kuroda lords and with those of Ise Teijō. The choice of these *kakun* helps to illustrate the various types of precepts that were written and to identify what might be considered distinctive about Ekken's. For example, the Kuroda lord's treatises are forms of house codes that a clan leader passed on to his retainer-descendants. Because they are addressed to those who would inherit positions of leadership in the clan, they deal mainly with questions of benevolent government. As such they have certain similarities with the more general instructions for the samurai. Ise Teijō's instructions represent a broader category of family precepts that were intended as a spiritual legacy for the entire family. Thus, while the focus of the house codes was on governing, the concern of the family precepts was on regulating the family. Both might be seen as elaborations of basic Confucian teachings on the importance of moral rule and harmonious family relations for the establishment of a peaceful society.

Ekken's *Precepts on the Way of the Family* (*Kadōkun*)[27] have more in common with Teijō's instructions, while his precepts for the samurai have similar elements to the Kuroda lords' *Kakun*. His instructions for the family were characterized by greater detail and length of discussion than was found in most *kakun*. This is no doubt due to his aim as a Neo-Confucian moral educator, to reach a wide audience with a universally applicable code of ethics, rather than simply to address his own family. As in the *Precepts for the Samurai*, where he brought together cultural and military values, in the *Kadōkun* he joined moral and economic concerns in a pragmatic manner. Thus, Ekken synthesized Neo-Confucian teachings on human relationships, learning, and self-cultivation with practical suggestions for one's family business or professional occupation. In doing this he significantly expanded and developed some of the themes of traditional *kakun*.[28] He also suggested new grounds for joining morality and economics, the latter being a subject not often addressed directly by Neo-Confucians, their primary concern being self-cultivation of the scholar-official.

As in all of his moral treatises, Ekken's *Precepts on the Way of the Family* elaborates on the general directives in the *Great Learning* for regulating the family and the society through self-discipline. In his instructions for the family he develops this fundamental teaching by emphasizing the importance of preserving both a disciplined propriety and a humane reciprocity in relationships. He feels that the rise or fall of the household rests on valuing human relations and thus respecting the individual as part of a defined group. Distinctions of role and function are necessary to allow for both individual integration and social harmony. He repeatedly cites the need to moderate one's desires and to be frugal with material goods. This is intended not only for personal self-discipline but also to foster the success of the family business or professional occupation. These instructions illustrate the joining together of morality and economics which was a distinctive aspect of Ekken's family precepts.

To promote an effective morality and to encourage smooth personal relations within the family, Ekken stresses the importance of educating one's children and managing one's servants.[29] Many of his instructions with regard to children and servants are similar to those in his *Precepts on Japanese Customs for Children*, namely, how to avoid making children and servants angry and resentful, and how to counsel them in times of need. He enjoins against looking down on servants even if they make mistakes. He encourages teaching children to have respect for all living things and not to harm plant or animal life.

For sound economic planning within the family, Ekken advocates continual effort in the family business or professional occupation, thrift in every aspect of family affairs, controlling greed for profit, and avoiding borrowing or loaning money or goods.[30] Recognizing the need for long-range planning for the individual family and for the government, he urges the adoption of the ancient Chinese well-field system for farmers.[31]

Although stressing thrift, Ekken does not favor parsimony; rather, he urges the practice of "hidden virtue" towards the poor and destitute.[32] Here his moral and economic teachings coalesce in an impassioned call for humane treatment of others such as has

been noted in *Precepts for Daily Life in Japan*. In the tradition of acknowledging a familial relationship with all of humanity such as is
represented in Chang Tsai's *Western Inscription*, he continually ex-
horts people to give to the hungry, the sick, and the needy. He
urges families who are blessed with material comfort to be mindful
of those who are not by recalling people of the past who lived in
more primitive conditions and endured great physical hardships.

Ekken realizes that natural biological bonds of the family are the
model for all forms of reciprocal morality in the larger society. From
the most essential unit of the family, the pattern of mutual affection
and obligation is extended outward. Ekken notes that if the individual is responsible to the society as a whole, mutual benefits are
more likely to ensue and social harmony can be maintained. Consequently, he emphasizes the need for people to fulfill their role in
the society while being sensitive to the needs of others. In this respect, he stresses the communal nature of reciprocal obligations and
responsibilities of each of the four social groups, namely, samurai,
farmer, artisan, and merchant.

Ekken also discusses the specific measures necessary to a
householder both in his daily affairs and in the five stages of his
life. The latter consist of: attention to parental education of the
young until age twenty, application to education in the classics and
the arts between twenty and thirty, supporting the family and managing its business affairs between thirty and forty, planning for descendants until age fifty, and, in the remaining years, preparing for
things after death.[33] As a head of a family one should be mindful to
perform daily tasks so that external order is maintained in the
household.

This ordering of external things reflects the inner ordering of
the heart. Ekken says that keeping the house clean and bright is like
keeping one's heart clear. Similarly, he feels that by planting and
tending a garden one cultivates the heart. He describes in great detail the best method of planting fruit trees and flowering trees,
herbs and vegetables.[34] This theme of cultivating oneself through
caring for nature recurs throughout his ethical treatises and reflects
the dynamic naturalism underlying his thought.

In the *Kadōkun*, for example, moral discipline combined with
practical effort is interpreted by Ekken as reflecting the natural operations of heaven and earth. Heaven he describes as ceaselessly
active, while earth is reflective and mindful. This is what humans
should try and imitate so their lives might acquire a natural harmony and contentment. He writes:

An old maxim says, "If we make an effort we will overcome poverty, if we are mindful we will overcome misfortune." These words are very beneficial. People who diligently make an effort in the family business inevitably become rich. If we are mindful of ourselves there will be no misfortune. These two words [effort and mindfulness] we should always protect and practice. By actualizing these ourselves, our family members will do likewise. Making an effort is the Way of heaven; heaven revolves without ceasing. Being mindful is the Way of earth; earth is quiet and does not move. Making an effort and being mindful is basing our model on the Way of heaven and earth. This is the Way which humans ought to practice, for these are profound principles.[35]

Ekken thus encourages the householder to use his property and resources wisely so as to be able to pass them on to his descendants. However, most importantly, he should pass on to them not simply goods, but an understanding of the Way which is in harmony with the operations of nature. His legacy, then, was one that combined economic efforts with moral and spiritual discipline.

## Comparison and Contrast

Two of the most noted *kakun* that have been preserved from the early Tokugawa period are those of the Christian daimyo, Kuroda Josui (1546–1604), written seventeen years before he died, and of his successor, Kuroda Nagamasa (1568–1623), written a year before his death.[36] These are of particular interest to our discussion because they represent the legacy of the predecessors to the three Kuroda lords under whom Ekken served throughout his life.

The principal themes of the Kuroda's house codes were the placing of public duty over private gain and, as in the samurai precepts, the uniting of the military and cultural arts. Both treatises stressed the need to transcend personal interest for the sake of the public good. The ruler should serve as a model for his retainers and for each of the four groups in the society.[37] Humane government was the ideal toward which the lord and his retainers should aim. To accomplish this the military and cultural arts had to be employed. The Kurodas observed, as did Ekken, that these two go together like the wheels of a cart. As in the precepts for the samurai, culture was understood as learning based on moral insight and restraint, while military knowledge meant having both appropriate courage and skills.

The Kuroda house codes reflected significant themes of the early Tokugawa period, when peace had very recently been established. In urging the union of the military and cultural arts these house codes represented an attempt of the Kuroda lords to establish the roots of a sound provincial bureaucratic government that their heirs would later develop further.[38]

In contrast to the Kuroda lords, and like Ekken, Ise Teijō's *Kakun* was directed to his entire family and not only to his retainer-descendants.[39] The contents of Teijō's instructions were primarily Neo-Confucian inspired. His principal emphasis was on the five constant virtues and the five relations needed for regulating the family. These he discussed in some detail so as to allow for no mistakes in the appropriate manner of practicing them.

For example, when he discussed the five relations he stated emphatically that the term father also included mother. He described the intimacy of parents and children as "a deep mutual affection."[40] The same mutuality applied in the relations between the lord and retainer. He particularly stressed the need for liberality and tolerance on the part of the master toward his retainer.

Thus Ise's instructions for his family, being of a distinctively Neo-Confucian nature, demonstrated numerous similarities with Ekken's treatise written half a century earlier. It is, perhaps, not incorrect to suggest that many of the *kakun* in this period, reflecting the growing influence of Neo-Confucianism, followed a basic line of argument which included special emphasis on Neo-Confucian cultivation through the practice of the five virtues and five relations. In this respect Ekken's treatise on the family had more in common with Ise Teijō's treatise, while his essay on the samurai had definite similarities with the Kuroda house codes. The major difference between both the Kuroda and the Ise treatises and Ekken's was his particular attention to economic affairs.

## PRECEPTS FOR CHILDREN

At the heart of Ekken's family precepts was his evident interest in the education of children, for whom his writings stand in contrast to the popular collection, *Teachings for Children* (*Dōji-kyō*), and to Ogyū Sorai's more scholarly *Instructions for Students* (*Gakusoku*).

Ekken's *Precepts on Japanese Customs for Children* is divided into five chapters which follow a brief preface.[41] The first two chapters are general introductory remarks on the importance of learning. The third chapter consists of detailed instructions on what to teach a child between the ages of six and twenty. This chapter also includes specific guidelines on reading books, such as appear in

*Precepts for Daily Life in Japan.* Chapter four contains a detailed discussion of the method of writing based on the principle that handwriting reflected the condition of the mind-and-heart. Chapter five is concerned with the manner of teaching women, in which he outlines the steps necessary for their moral and intellectual formation.

In the preface, Ekken quotes the passage from the *Book of Changes* on the need for the Noble Person to be cautious at the beginning.[42] He emphasizes that, at birth, everyone's human nature is the same, but individuals can easily learn bad habits. Thus, the sages realized the need to instruct children from an early age. He goes on to explain his use of a simplified Japanese as a means of teaching people who are in country villages and do not have the benefit of teachers or scholars in their midst. Yet he also stresses that for those who have access to teachers it is important to select responsible tutors for their children.

In training a child, he feels people should always be honest and sincere and not deceive the child or permit lying. Parents should encourage the child to be humane and sympathetic, not despising others or causing them to suffer. If parents act in this way, children will follow their example.

With regard to discipline, Ekken repeatedly warns against being overly indulgent.[43] He feels that if parents are too affectionate they will harm the child. In both their physical and mental training, children should not be pampered. It is better that they know hunger and cold than that they become overfed or overly protected from the elements. Similarly, in moral and intellectual training, when the parents are strict, the child will be respectful and mindful. Yet, he notes, parents should reprimand gently and not angrily.

This moral discipline, combined with humble self-examination and earnest study, is designed to encourage the natural development of children toward appropriate and responsible behavior. It is not intended to be artificially or rigidly imposed. The larger goal is to foster maturity in children so they will be better prepared to meet unexpected changes or difficulties in later life. They will then be able to endure hardships and challenges with an inner resilience.[44] Ekken says that when adults raise children in this way they are truly loving them.

While Ekken states that the root of learning is moral training that develops the sense of humaneness and duty, he also emphasizes the importance of the six arts mentioned in the *Elementary Learning* as a practical application of learning.[45] He especially encourages learning how to write and count. In the past, he notes, some people looked down on mathematical skills, but Ekken believes these are necessary for managing daily affairs, supervising a family business, counting crops, and organizing political and military programs. Furthermore, he emphasizes the importance of both moral and political education for the nobility, so that they may know the principles for governing others. He points out the danger of extravagant ways among the upper classes and calls for the rulers to retain a deep sensitivity to human feelings (*mono no aware*) when in positions of power.[46]

Ekken then discusses the steps to be taught to children between the ages of six and twenty.[47] By careful consideration of his points, Ekken underlines the need for gradual but steady progression in learning until one has internalized what one has studied. This follows the traditional pattern of Neo-Confucian education, namely, teaching the *Elementary Learning* until age fifteen when the study of the *Great Learning* is begun.

After these early years of training, a young person is ready for a more serious and systematic reading program which Ekken outlines. This program includes a broadly based education centered on the *Four Books* and *Five Classics*, along with specific instructions on how to absorb the larger meaning of these texts for contemporary life.[48]

In trying to understand the past, Ekken stresses the importance of reading history.[49] In addition to the authorized official histories, Ekken observes that unofficial histories are also worth reading. He sees older relatives or family friends as an important source of oral history and urges young people to listen to their stories and pass them down to posterity.[50]

When an young man turns twenty, his coming of age ceremony is held. Because it marks his rite of passage to adulthood, Ekken emphasizes that the ceremony ought not to be for external show, but should represent the attainment of a certain dignified inner maturity. He notes that in Japan at that time the *kuge* (nobility) families still held a capping ceremony, while the samurai families cut the young man's hair to mark his coming of age.[51]

Ekken concludes his treatise with a discussion on the way to teach women.[52] Parents, he observes, are the most important teachers of women. While at first raising a girl is not radically different from raising a boy, the parents have to make sure they give their daughter a sense of womanly virtue at an early age. Because she will eventually marry and leave home, and because a woman's role in the family is so central, it is important that she be taught this well.

By means of her virtue she maintains harmony between family members and has a deep sense of sympathy for others. Ekken summarizes the four important tasks of a woman as being careful with regard to her virtue, speech, manners, and honor.[53] The six things to be avoided are obstinacy, resentment, anger, slander, jealousy, and foolishness. Her education should consist of learning *kana* (Japanese syllabary) at the age of seven and reading the *Classic of Filial Piety* and the sections on learning in the *Analects*. At age ten she is instructed within the house on the arts of weaving, sewing, and arithmetic.

Ekken notes thirteen modes of conduct which should be taught a young woman before her marriage:

1. remaining in the house and practicing filiality towards parents-in-law;
2. having no other master than her husband and serving him with respect;
3. having deep feelings for her sister and brother-in-law as members of her husband's family;
4. not allowing jealousy to arise;
5. admonishing her husband gently if he does not fulfill his duties;
6. being restrained in speech and not being involved in slandering others;
7. being careful in all her actions, i.e. rising early and going to bed late, not indulging in tea or sake, not watching theatrical performances;
8. not being led astray by *miko* (shamanesses); rather, by carrying out her household duties she is assured of divine protection;
9. preserving her family by avoiding extravagance;
10. not mingling with young men, male servants, or male relatives, but maintaining a proper separation between the sexes;
11. being unobtrusive and subdued in dress;
12. not returning frequently to her original family, but making her in-laws and their relatives her primary family;
13. not acting like an uneducated woman or maid servant or believing their gossip.[54]

Finally, Ekken gives the following traditional reasons for divorcing a woman: if she is disobedient to her parents-in-law, if she is barren, if she is immoral, if she is jealous, if she has a serious illness, if she frequently engages in gossip or slander, or if she steals.[55]

Some of these injunctions no doubt appear unduly severe to modern sensibilities. However, before interpretive evaluations can be made, the role of women in Confucian societies in East Asia needs further study as does the role of women in pre-modern societies in general. Ekken was simply codifying and developing the contemporary ethical practices of the period. In so doing, he provided a larger rationale for such practices by citing Neo-Confucian teachings on the need for harmony among family members. In his interest in education for women he was ahead of many of his contemporaries. Although this is within a traditional context and values, by stressing the importance of basic education of both a moral and practical nature for women and children, he contributed to the growing concern for cultural advancement of both sexes which began to emerge in seventeenth-century Tokugawa society.

## Comparison and Contrast

In contrast to Ekken's detailed precepts for children, Dōji-kyō (Teachings for Children) was short and relatively simple.[56] It was widely used in the temple schools (terakoya) for the commoners and was intended to be a general explanation of moral principles for the young. It was a text with a long history originally attributed to the ninth-century Tendai monk, Annen. He was believed to have composed it to teach children who came to his temple seeking instructions. Written in simple Chinese, it combined a Buddhist religiosity with Confucian ethics. Its influence as an educational text in Japan cannot be underestimated, and many of its moral precepts have become common proverbs. Indeed, Ronald Dore observed that, together with a similar treatise called Jitsugo-kyō, the Dōji-kyō "ranked among the most important influences on the ethical ideas, or at least the ethical vocabulary, of generations of Tokugawa commoners."[57] The contents of these texts "became folk knowledge and many of their phrases passed into the language."[58]

Although attributed to a Buddhist monk, Dōji-kyō consisted largely of Confucian moral teachings derived from classical Chinese sources such as the Analects, Confucius' Family Sayings, the Book of Poetry, the Book of History, and the Classic of Filial Piety. Stressing the importance of learning and filiality, it reflected direct Confucian influences, especially in the citation of exemplary Chinese figures who excelled in these areas.[59]

While *Dōji-kyō* was clearly effective as a basic learning text, Ekken's *Precepts on Japanese Customs for Children* (*Wazokudōjikun*) significantly expanded the content, method, and purposes of teaching children. Although trying to reach a broad audience, Ekken wished to avoid simply stringing together moral proverbs for repetition and memorization by children. Instead, he gave the rationale and outline for a comprehensive program of educating children from childhood to adulthood. He stressed a curriculum and a method of study which was concerned with the overall growth of the individual child. Memorization was deemphasized; internalization was stressed. By attention to detail and gradual progression, Ekken provided a ready handbook for teachers and parents in their educational concerns for their children.

Furthermore, Ekken was persistent in his life-long interest in education for women. While many of his teachings for women may appear antiquated today, his concern for women's education, nonetheless, was an important contribution in his own time and distinguishes him from other of his contemporaries who did not regard this as a necessary undertaking. Indeed, well into the twentieth century, Ekken's *Onna daigaku* (Learning for Women) was considered an essential part of a Japanese bride's trousseau.

A further illustration of the particular features of Ekken's precepts for children may be seen in contrast to Ogyū Sorai's *Instructions for Students*.[60] Although clearly intended for a more sophisticated audience than *Dōji-kyō*, this text may serve to illustrate how Ekken's ideas differed from those of other Confucian scholars of his time.

In writing about Sorai's *Instructions for Students*, Richard Minear has described it as "the finest introduction into the content of his thinking as a whole."[61] Written between 1711 and 1717, it was published at the same time as his well-known philosophical works, *Benmei* (Distinguishing Names) and *Bendō* (Distinguishing the Way). As a text written in Chinese, it clearly contrasts with Ekken's efforts to popularize Confucian teachings through the use of a simplified Japanese. Moreover, Sorai did not believe, as did Ekken and other Neo-Confucians, that all people could potentially become sages. He felt that there were definite distinctions between people due to different abilities.

Sorai opened his instructions with a lengthy explanation of why students should abandon contorted and artificial Japanese readings of Chinese texts and return to the original Chinese word order and pronunciation. He urged students to try and understand the meaning of an original text by relying not on commentaries but on an intuitive and meditative effort.[62]

This direct intuition of the truth of the classics did not proceed, according to Sorai, by a process of naming and theorizing. Rather, in trying to grasp the truth of something in itself, he felt one should not intellectualize but "wait for understanding to grow."[63] This naturalness in discovering and practicing the Way was an important theme of Sorai's work, and in this his concerns were similar to Ekken's. He wrote, "The Way of the sages is like soft wind and sweet rain. Things receive its sustenance and are born. Born, they mature."[64] This natural growth of the Way was something to be cherished, and he lamented its disintegration in his own time. Moreover, Sorai placed a particular value on diversity and breadth in scholarship and disliked what he perceived to be the narrow-mindedness of some of the Neo-Confucians.

Sorai's educational concerns were similar to Ekken's in certain respects, namely, his interest in preserving naturalness over artificiality and his emphasis on the importance of history. Major differences between Sorai and Ekken arose, however, from the fact that Sorai rejected Sung commentaries and Sung scholarship in his effort to return to the classics, whereas Ekken saw these commentaries as an invaluable part of the learning process. Ultimately Sorai's belief that all people could not become sages limited his readership considerably and determined the scholarly Chinese style in which he wrote. These beliefs were in marked contrast to Ekken's efforts, in his instructions for children, to make Neo-Confucian teachings accessible to a wider audience.


## CONCLUDING COMMENTS

What emerges, then, in this brief comparative study is a broader framework in which to situate Ekken's ideas on education so as to evaluate his objectives and summarize his particular style. Ekken expressed himself in the traditional genre of ethical precepts for the samurai class when he wrote his *Bukun* and *Kadōkun*. Yet he was also conscious of enlarging the scope of this genre in terms of the expanded content, the detailed instructions, and the wider audience he hoped to address. Similarly, in his teachings for children and for women, he aimed to broaden the scope and method of learning for these two groups.

In each of these treatises he joined the theoretical aspects of Neo-Confucianism to the practical exigencies of daily life. He was attempting to bring the "learning of the sages" close at hand, and to make that which was regarded as abstract and lofty more comprehensible for ordinary people. In so doing, he was particularly concerned to make Chinese Neo-Confucianism adaptable to the Japanese context. This can be seen in his effort in *Bukun* to join cultural and military pursuits, in *Kadōkun* to combine moral and economic efforts, and in *Wazokudōjikun* to relate education to its practical application.

Thus, the cultural, moral, and educational themes of Neo-Confucianism were consciously articulated in relation to the military, economic, and practical considerations of the contemporary society. While these objectives were not those of Ekken alone, the breadth and intensity of his efforts mark him as a foremost educator of his time and one still consulted in our own.[65]

ABOVE: *Anaguratsubame*. A type of swallow. BELOW: *Mimizuku*. A horned owl.

# 7

# Conclusion

## THE SIGNIFICANCE OF EKKEN'S THOUGHT

Both as a scholar grappling with key philosophical issues of the Chinese Neo-Confucian tradition and as a popular educator transmitting Confucian values to the Japanese context, Kaibara Ekken's contributions were wide-ranging. By embracing the subtle aspects of Neo-Confucian metaphysics and the broad concerns of the society of his time, Ekken was a fitting heir to a tradition which advocated careful attention to scholarship along with an interest in its practical application.

In Ekken's life and thought there emerged a unified effort toward research and self-cultivation that combined scholarship and spirituality in a distinctive manner. Ekken's thought may be summarized as a religious humanism based on a vitalistic naturalism that found expression in a practical empiricism. From this one can distinguish three abiding areas of his concerns: spirituality and ethics, cosmology and metaphysics, and practical learning. In each of these areas, his thought is distinguished by a particular confluence of Chinese and Japanese influences derived from both Confucian and Shinto sources.

### Spirituality and Ethics

One of Ekken's primary concerns was to describe the nature and function of human beings, and thus a central theme of his essays was the role of humans in the larger order of reality. In articulating this theme, Ekken used a style which was both poetic and metaphorical in an effort to express symbolically the profound connection that existed between humans and heaven and earth.[1] Based on the classical Confucian idea of the interpenetrating triad of heaven, earth, and human, Ekken developed the Neo-Confucian position of the unique role of the human in forming one body with all things.

Ekken, for example, frequently quoted the line from the *Book of History* indicating that heaven and earth are the great parents of all things. This metaphor of great parents was a means of articulating symbolically the primary sources of life. While in Confucianism there was no single creator God as in the Judeo-Christian tradition, there was an acknowledged self-generating and self-sustaining principle of life. Using the passage from the *Book of History*, Ekken spoke of this principle in anthropomorphic terms, namely as the great parents. In Confucian societies which placed primary emphasis on family relations, this metaphor clearly had a direct and lasting appeal. The process of begetting and nourishing life was thus seen as a function not only of humans but of the entire cosmos.

For Ekken, as a Confucian thinker, it is from heaven and earth as great parents that human beings received their heavenly bestowed nature. This nature distinguished humans from plants and animals and established the basis for a special link to the mind-and-heart of heaven and earth. It was, in fact, human nature which gave a person the capacity for consciousness and emotion that marked the human species as unique. Human nature, then, was seen by Ekken as a sacred gift to be cherished, reverenced, and cultivated. Above all, from an awareness of the sacrality of our nature there arose an instinctive gratitude for life and the sources that brought one into being and sustained one.

It is in this feeling of gratitude that elements of Ekken's Neo-Confucian spirituality merged with a native Shinto religiosity. Ekken joined a Confucian understanding of the human as the spirit of all creation with a Shinto sensibility of gratitude, humility, and pleasure for blessings received from nature. Thus, for example, the realization of a human being's unique role as the soul of creation (*banbutsu no rei*) along with a recognition of one's debt and obligation (*on*) to the cosmos became an underlying motivation of Ekken's spirituality and ethics. Ekken continually noted that humans have both great privileges and awesome responsibilities in the larger order of reality. Yet underlying this was his sense of contentment, harmony, and vitalism which savored the spontaneities of natural rhythms while avoiding an undue seriousness or artificiality. This

instinctive gratitude was expressed by Ekken as the spirit of pleasure and harmony in his essay on the *Way of Contentment*. Here the
affirmation of nature combined Confucian elements of an awareness of the operations of heaven and earth with Shinto elements
celebrating seasonal change and purification. This is evident in the
following passage:

> This spirit of harmony exists not only in human beings but also in
> birds and animals and in plants and trees. Animals play, birds sing,
> fish leap, and plants and trees flourish, bloom, and ripen. All have this
> spirit of harmony . . .
>
> The expansiveness of heaven and earth which is always replete be-
> fore us is a source of great joy—the light of the sun and moon; the
> continual return of the four seasons; the beauty of various landscapes;
> the changes from dawn to dusk in clouds and mists; the appearance of
> the mountains; the flow of the streams; the rustling of the wind;
> the moisture of the rain and dew; the purity of the snow; the array of
> flowers; the growth of fresh grass; the flourishing of trees; the diverse
> life of birds, animals, fish, and insects. If we constantly appreciate this
> varied beauty of creation, our spirit of harmony will be ceaseless
> by expanding our mind-and-heart, purifying our emotions, cultivating
> a moral sense, enkindling joy, and washing away all regrets from
> our heart. This is called being in touch with the mysteries of heaven.
> This means by contact with external things our inner goodness is
> aroused.[2]

From this feeling of reverence for the sources of life and of gratitude for the beauties of nature, there naturally arose a cosmic filiality towards heaven and earth as great parents. Ekken continually
stressed this primal filiality as essential for the process of self-
cultivation and indeed as the root of humaneness (*jen*). In the spirit
of Chang Tsai and the other Sung Neo-Confucians, Ekken celebrated the active identity of humans with all things through the
concept of humaneness. While this identity was implicit in the doctrine of human nature discussed above, its full realization emerged
with the activation of the deepest sources of one's nature in the
practice of humaneness. This virtue, then, had both cosmic and personal dimensions. Through its practice one realized one's connection to the vast and mysterious processes of natural life; at the same
time, one recognized that one was inextricably linked with the web
of human life. Through humaneness, then, care, reverence, and
consideration was extended to humans, animals, plants, and trees,
as is evident in the following passage.

> The principle of humaneness makes it a virtue to show kindness to-
> ward human beings and compassion for all things. The way to serve

heaven and earth is by preserving this virtue of humaneness without losing it, and deeply loving humanity, which heaven and earth have produced. Then, by having compassion for birds and beasts, trees and plants, and adhering to the heart of nature through which heaven and earth love humans and all things, we assist the efforts of the great compassion of heaven and earth and make the serving of heaven and earth the Way. This, the Human Way, is humaneness.[3]

Ekken's particular form of spirituality and of ethics was not simply anthropocentric but embraced the whole order of reality. In this sense it was a religious humanism in which a cosmic spirituality was balanced with personal and practical ethics. His religious awareness did not consist merely of a vague intuition into the oneness of creation, nor did his humanism become devoid of a larger cosmic significance. Rather, his ethics were expressed in particular practices such as the five relations in the human sphere and ecological stewardship in the natural sphere. Each dimension reinforced the other. Without the natural world humans would not be able to sustain life and culture, and without humans the universe would lack a self-conscious channel of reflection and transformation.

## Cosmology and Metaphysics

As indicated above, Ekken's form of naturalism combined Chinese and Japanese influences, especially mingling Confucian and Shinto cosmological elements. Inspired by classical sources such as the *Book of Changes* and aware of the affirmation of change among Sung and Ming Neo-Confucians, Ekken articulated his own vision of change in the cosmos and its implication for human actions. In particular, he evoked the essential wellsprings of Chinese Neo-Confucianism in its desire to harmonize with change rather than withdraw from it. At the same time he reflected the Japanese affinity for the power of the material force (*ch'i*) in all things. In native Shinto terms, the generative power of life was expressed as *musubi*. This has been translated as "the spirit of birth and becoming; also, birth, accomplishment, combination; the creating and harmonizing powers."[4] It was just such a vital, creative force that Ekken sought to illuminate in his discussions of cosmology and metaphysics. He relied on a basic Chinese Neo-Confucian concept of naturalism, joining this with a native Shinto sensibility which similarly celebrated the fecundity of nature.

Through his cosmology, then, Ekken was eager to affirm the dynamic quality of nature in its continual process of transformation.

He relied on the passage in the *Book of Changes* celebrating the source of life as the "begetter of all begetting," that constantly generated and renewed life. This dynamic pattern of production and reproduction was at the root of Ekken's organic thought, for fecundity was the source of the interweaving web of life forms. This is why in his *Record of Grave Doubts* (*Taigiroku*), Ekken was so careful to emphasize that existence, not emptiness, was the basis of Confucian cosmology. The principle of being rather than non-being most adequately expressed the pulsating principle of all life forms.

Moreover, Ekken did not want to articulate his cosmology from a dualistic metaphysical basis. He wished to avoid a bifurcation in which a transcendent principle (*li*) was regarded as prior and superior to an immanent force which was both matter and energy (*ch'i*). In so doing, Ekken affirmed the absolute, or the origin of life, as existing within the phenomenal order rather than separate from it. For Ekken, the source of being or fecundity was not something apart from reality but lay within its very dynamic processes.

Perceiving the creative force of existence in the natural world, Ekken felt that people would more readily understand its counterpart in the human sphere. In particular, he saw the natural operations of heaven and earth (*tenki*) as reflecting the sincerity (*makoto*) of the cosmos. The workings of nature thus became the inspiration for the practice of virtue. With a special sensitivity to the interaction of the human as microcosm and nature as macrocosm, Ekken recognized that the virtue of origination and regeneration lay in both spheres. The vitalistic force of *ch'i* was dynamized by the originative process in nature and similarly by the activation of humaneness in humans. Thus Ekken's vitalistic naturalism was the basis of his religious humanism. In this sense, he constantly demonstrated that human moral sensibility was grounded in the cosmic process and that, therefore, human beings had a vital role to play in relation to the cosmos and its creative process. The art of self-cultivation, especially as expressed in the learning of the mind-and-heart, thus implied harmonizing with change in the universe, purifying desires, bringing emotions into proper balance, and experiencing a fundamental unity with all things.

## Practical Learning

In the same way that Ekken's cosmology underlay his ethics, so his cosmology was an important framework for understanding his empirical interests. Ekken believed that until one understood something of the processes of nature, one could not really comprehend the human Way. Observing and recording various aspects of nature can be a foundation or support for a more fully human life. His empiricism was thus linked to his ethics.

Furthermore, although Ekken himself did not clearly explicate the relationship of his empirical studies to his cosmology, it seems apparent that his affirmation of the absolute within the phenomenal world (the *li* within *ch'i*) provided a theoretical basis for investigating principle within material force. In this sense, his desire to catalogue and describe various species of plants, fish, and shells can be seen as a drive to understand the unifying forms and underlying principles within reality itself. To investigate things came to mean seeking the patterns within change, uncovering the principles behind flux. While this understanding can be interpreted as being within the Chu Hsi tradition, investigation was more often directed by Neo-Confucian scholars toward illuminating the moral significance of texts, especially the classics. In Ekken, this impetus for investigation shifted toward the natural world. All things were seen as within its province—botany, topography, agriculture, medicine, arithmetic, and astronomy. The physical sciences and the pure sciences, theoretical speculation, and pragmatic observation came under this broadened concept of investigating things in order to determine their principle.

These diverse activities of Ekken were part of his over arching concern for practical learning. Rather than a dry or abstract approach to scholarship, he advocated a learning that would have practical implications for people. To be a technician of knowledge or of skills was not Ekken's aim; instead he called for a blending of humanistic and scientific studies that would combine theoretical and practical issues relevant to the people of his day. The scope and methodology of his own studies is an apt tribute to his ongoing efforts in this direction.

In content and in method Ekken's interest in practical learning had significant implications. Indeed, he saw this investigation as another aspect of self-cultivation and as a means of relating one to the vital force in the cosmos. To examine plants or agricultural methods, for example, was a way of understanding nature's life-giving capacity. Similarly, studying or practicing medicine was meaningless without the recognition that a person was nourishing life and practicing humaneness.

Ekken's empiricism, then, was rooted in his cosmology and was a further expression of his spirituality and ethics. To see the inter-relationship of these various components was to recognize the connecting thread underlying his holistic thought and practice. It is this interrelationship which distinguishes Ekken's life and thought. Moreover, it is his concern for illuminating the link between cosmology and spirituality, between metaphysics and ethics, and between each of these and a practical learning that made Ekken a noted figure in his own time and significant for our own.

## THE SIGNIFICANCE OF HIS TREATISES

The attempt by Ekken in his treatises to simplify, codify, and indigenize Neo-Confucian thought and practice was a major contribution to the spread of Neo-Confucianism in Japan. In particular, his advocacy of the learning of the mind-and-heart as expressed in moral discipline and spiritual practice make these texts significant in his own times, in the development of East Asian thought, and in comparative studies in the history of religions.

The learning of the mind-and-heart provided for Ekken's own era both a philosophical context and a practical method of self-cultivation that was a distinct alternative to the forms of Buddhism which had dominated medieval Japan. In these texts, Ekken developed a Neo-Confucian this-worldly spirituality emphasizing both the importance of human relations and of inner cultivation. His detailed articulation of the learning of the mind-and-heart was an important contribution to the spread of this teaching, which clearly had an appeal across class distinctions in Japan and which transcended cultural boundaries in East Asia.

The Neo-Confucian content of his treatises also distinguished them as important texts in the development of East Asian thought as a whole. While their general moral and spiritual teachings reflected the dominant influence of the Chinese Neo-Confucian tradition, their accommodation to Shinto elements makes them an important example of the indigenization process of Neo-Confucian thought. Furthermore, their simplified Japanese style and the examples cited to illustrate the teachings indicate an accommodation to the particular needs of the Japanese Tokugawa context. One can see the distinct impact of Chu Hsi and Chen Te-hsiu on Ekken in formulating a mode of moral and spiritual praxis. By adapting this praxis to each level of the society, he hoped to demonstrate its relevance for the Japanese of his day.

Finally, Ekken's treatises can be compared with texts in other religious traditions. Specifically, his teachings on the learning of the mind-and-heart can serve as an important basis of comparison with similar works on moral and spiritual discipline in other traditions.[5] In the current dialogue among the world's great religions, Confucianism has been regarded primarily as an ethical or a political system. With more detailed investigation of texts such as Ekken's, which discuss the learning of the mind-and-heart, the spiritual and religious components of Confucianism may be more fully appreciated, and a broad basis for comparative studies more firmly established. Such studies would help to illustrate the ways in which the human community has developed techniques of spiritual practice in very different cultural contexts. The variety as well as the universality of such texts would demonstrate the importance placed on such discipline and personal cultivation throughout history.

In the case of Ekken, we begin to see the vitalist basis of his thought and the thorough way in which he tried to find a balance between the needs for integration of the individual and the demands for participation in the society as a whole. From this perspective it is not adequate to interpret his treatises as simply reflective of a static feudal order. Rather, they can be seen as part of an ongoing and emerging process of humanistic education and moral and spiritual practice that was essential to Neo-Confucian thought in each of the countries it reached.

As the sense of context and perspective is widened, the texts themselves take shape and meaning beyond such categories as feudal or modern. What emerges is the dynamic personality and educational objectives of a teacher speaking to his own times in a voice that is conversational and tolerant, but with a breadth of concern admired by his contemporaries. Both the broad educational goals and the driving urgency of Ekken are discernible across the intervening centuries, lifting his particular concerns into the larger sphere of humanistic education shared by each age, and expanded by the next.

# Part II

## *Yamato Zokkun*

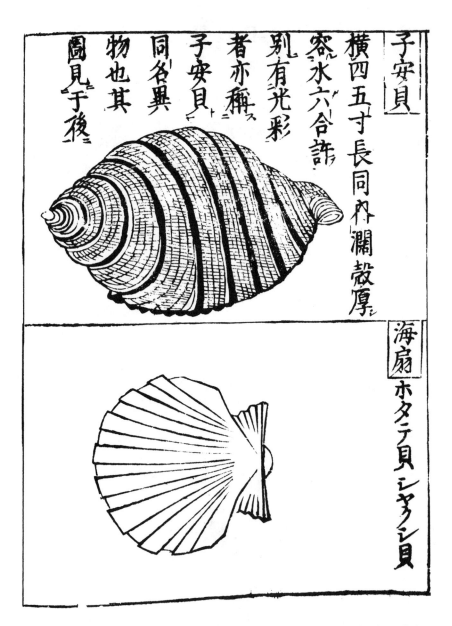

子安貝

横四五寸長同内濶殻厚
容水六合許
別有光彩
者亦稱
子安貝
同名異
物也其
圖見于後

海扇 ホタテ貝 シヤクシ貝

ABOVE: *Koyasugai*. A cowrie shell. The width is about 5 inches; the length is the same. The inside is wide; the shell is thick. It can hold about two pints of water. There are other bright shells that are called *koyasugai*, but this one is different from those. BELOW: *Kaisen*. A scallop. It is known as *hotategai* or *shakushigai*.

# 8

✤

# Translation of *Yamato Zokkun*

*The Japanese text of* Yamato zokkun *is provided in Appendix A following the translation. It appears in* Ekken zenshū, *volume 3 (Tokyo: Ekken zenshū kankōbu, 1910–1911), pp. 45–110. The full text comprises eight chapters. The first four chapters are translated here, as they are considered most central to the discussion of the learning of the mind-and-heart* (shingaku). *The following four chapters serve to recapitulate the major points of the earlier ones, and provide practical examples. They are concerned with "clothes and speech" (ch. 5), "practice" (chs. 6, 7), and "responding to others" (ch. 8).*

*All dates and ages are given according to the modern solar calendar except at the end of the preface. Here Ekken speaks of himself as being seventy-nine years of age when he wrote the text. By the Japanese system of calculating age, he was seventy-nine; by the Western system he was seventy-eight.*

*Because of Ekken's lifetime interest in the education of women, and because the Chinese character for human being includes both sexes, an effort has been made in the translation to use the word "human" instead of "man" in all cases where appropriate. The character* kokoro *has most frequently been translated as mind-and-heart, but occasionally for reasons of style or emphasis it has been rendered as either mind or heart.*

*Because of the quasi-scholarly, quasi-popular character of Ekken's work, he frequently uses both classical maxims and popular sayings without attribution. Moreover, because he was widely read in the Chinese classics and in Neo-Confucian texts he also tends to quote or paraphrase Chinese sources freely in Japanese without identification. In some cases the precise source of the quote remains unidentified; however, the general meaning is not in doubt.*

*The following standard abbreviations have been used in the notes:*

> SPPY  *Ssu-pu pei-yao*
> SPTK  *Ssu-pu ts'ung-k'an*
> TSCC  *Ts'ung-shu chi-ch'eng*

*The numbers in brackets refer to the pages of the Japanese text in* Ekken zenshū, *volume 3, which follows the translation.*

## PREFACE

[45a]  The principles of heaven and earth and the Way of the human were taught in the classics of the ancient sages, and
their teachings are as clear as the sun and moon shining in
the heavens. There is no one with eyes to see who does not
recognize this. It is reasonable to say that for the people of
old, had not heaven brought Confucius into this world, all
ages would have been like a long dark night. Subsequent
sages carefully followed his intentions and discussed and
transmitted the meanings of the classics so that they were understood by their descendants. That heaven brought forth
Confucius and that the sages transmitted his message has indeed been a great good fortune for those who have come
later. For those well able to read, understanding principle is
like distinguishing black from white during the daytime.
How is it that all people in the world do not venerate principle and study it to the end of their lives? It is greatly to be
regretted that in today's Japan there is a prejudice against
Chinese characters, and even among fairly intelligent people
there are many who do not know the teachings of the sages.
Younger generations in the poorer villages have few friends
or teachers who know how to punctuate texts. The children
of high-ranking families enjoy playing and idling away their
time, and they avoid any studies that will cause difficulties to
themselves. Consequently, not only do they know nothing of
the hardships of planting and harvesting rice, but without a
doubt, they do not even know who the ancient Chinese emperors and kings were.[1]

[45b]       That is why Confucians in our country have from long
ago been so few in number. This is truly regrettable. However, in the present enlightened period, culture is gradually
opening up and we can look forward to a time when Confucianism becomes clearly known throughout the land. Writing
books in Chinese to explain the Way of the sages, in order to
instruct ordinary people, is beyond my power. Moreover, we
already clearly have the explanations of the sages of previous
generations in China. If people who know Chinese characters
read these works and understood them, there would be no
need to dwell on the subject now.

[45b]       The Way of the sages is lofty and deep; to try to explain
even one part of it by writing in women's script is certainly

presumptuous.[2] We cannot observe the heavens through a
tube nor measure the sea on the basis of one clam.[3] Un-
skilled as I am [in such things], I was worried lest the deep
pools of the Asuka River[4] change and become shallow currents; but in order to climb to a high place one must start at
the bottom, and to go to a distant land one must surely begin
from somewhere close at hand. Thus for the sake of people
who are so unfortunate as not to know Chinese characters, I
have written in contemporary language about the principles
that have been received from ages past. I have gathered them
into eight chapters and named the work *Yamato zokkun* (Precepts for Daily Life in Japan).[5] I would only ask that this
book be made available for the instruction of husbands and
wives who know nothing of worldly matters, and even that it
be taught to small children who cannot distinguish beans
from barley.[6] By nature I am a person of meager talents and
have no ambition to be known as [a member of] the School of
the Way (*Dōgaku*), for which I would have no qualifications.
Therefore, not only because of this book, I suppose that by
trying to teach trivial things and making much use of the abbreviated script[7] of the rustic Japanese of old I will become
the laughingstock of scholars who have established a reputation in Confucian studies. But since I have committed myself
to this task, I am not fearful of the criticism of others.

[46a]          As I reflect upon it, I consider that we are fortunate to be
born as humans and to receive the limitless blessings of
heaven and earth. In several lifetimes it would be difficult to
repay even a fraction of that great blessing with my meager
talents. Even though I have written an insignificant work, I
want it to serve a purpose in the daily lives of the people and
to serve to teach ignorant people and children as well as men
and women who are not of high rank. In this way I who have
been born in the world, eaten to my own content, worn
warm clothes, and lived peacefully may manage to escape
blame for the sin of holding a sinecure which simply wastes
the treasure of heaven and earth. That being the case, I
would not worry about people's criticism. Now I am approaching eighty and I think it is regrettable to pass through
life like a calendar scroll, simply unrolling without having
done much of anything. Thus, being anxious lest I wither
away like grass and trees, I have boldly taken up my pen,
despite my lack of talent. Both mind and eyes are faltering in

this feeble old body of mine, and so I feel self-conscious about the number of mistakes I have made. If people who share my aims would correct the errors of this book and tell others about them, this would truly accord with my intentions.

> The beginning of winter in
> Hōei 5 (1708)
> Kaibara Atsunobu
> Age 79

## CHAPTER I

## THE PURSUIT OF LEARNING, PART 1

[47b]   The sages taught in the *Book of History* that heaven and earth are the parents of all things and that human beings are the spirit of the universe.[8] This means that heaven and earth, being the source which gives birth to all things, are the great parents. Since humans receive the purest material force of heaven and earth from birth, they surpass all other things and their mind-and-heart shines forth clearly. Receiving a nature consisting of the five virtues [i.e. humaneness, righteousness, decorum, wisdom, faithfulness][9] their mind-and-heart is that of heaven and earth. Because among all things the position of humans is highest, they can be called the spirit of all things. That spirit is the bright shining essence in the mind-and-heart.

[47b]        Heaven and earth give birth to and nourish all things, but the deep compassion with which they treat humans is different from [the way they nourish] birds and beasts, trees and plants. Therefore, among all things only humans are the children of the universe. Thus humans have heaven as their father and earth as their mother and receive their great kindness. Because of this, always to serve heaven and earth is the Human Way. What is the Way by which we should serve heaven and earth? Humans have a heart of heaven and earth, namely, the heart of compassion which gives birth to and nurtures all things. This heart is called humaneness. Humaneness is the original nature implanted by heaven in the human heart.

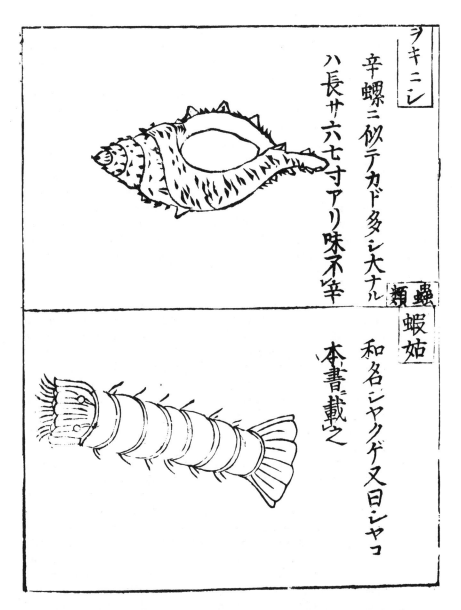

辛螺ニ似テカド多シ大ナル
ハ長サ六七寸アリ味不辛

ヲキニシレ

本書載之

和名ニシャクゲヌ又曰シャコ

蝦蛄
蟲類

ABOVE: *Okinishi*. A conch. This is like a whelk and has many rough edges on the surface of the shell. It is approximately 8 inches in length. The taste of the meat is not bitter. BELOW: *Shako*. A mantis crab (shrimp). The Japanese name is *shakuge* or *shako*.

[48a]        The principle of humaneness makes it a virtue to show
kindness toward human beings and compassion for all
things. The way to serve heaven and earth is by preserving
this virtue of humaneness without losing it, and deeply loving humanity, which heaven and earth have produced. Then,
by having compassion for birds and beasts, trees and plants,
and adhering to the heart of nature through which heaven
and earth love humans and all things, we assist the efforts of
the great compassion of heaven and earth and make the serving of heaven and earth the Way. This, the Human Way, is
humaneness. If we analyze the principle of humaneness, it is
composed of both humaneness and righteousness; if we analyze humaneness and righteousness they encompass decorum, wisdom, and faithfulness. These five innate qualities
together are called the five virtues (or constants). For example, if we divide one year we get yin and yang, and if we
divide it further it becomes the four seasons of spring, summer, autumn, and winter.

[48a]        Humaneness is the general name for the five constants
taken as a group. They are also called the five innate qualities, since they are Principles inborn in human beings. These
five innate qualities are called the five constants because everyone from ancient times to the present, high and low, wise
and foolish, has received these at birth from heaven and
earth, and this will remain unchanged for endless generations to come. "Constant" means unchanging. Among these
constants, humaneness is the mind of compassion and combines the other four virtues with it.

[48a]        "Righteousness" is appropriateness; it is behavior that is
appropriate to its object. "Decorum" is having a respectful
heart; it is being discrete and not despising others. "Wisdom" is penetrating to the principles of the Way with a mind
that perceives clearly. Though we have humaneness, righteousness, and decorum, should we lack wisdom, we would
not know how to act. Righteousness, decorum, and wisdom
all emerge from humaneness and are the principles which assist it. "Faithfulness" is sincerity (*makoto*). A mind of humaneness, righteousness, decorum, and wisdom is faithful
and without deceit. Humaneness, righteousness, decorum,
and wisdom do not exist without sincerity.

[48b]        The Human Way is to follow the nature of these five constants, and to act warmly and sympathetically in human re-

lations. There are five human relations, namely, those between ruler (lord) and minister (retainer), parent and child, husband and wife, older and younger, and between friends. These are the five relations and they are also known as the five categories.[10] Although there are many people in this world, none fall outside of these classifications. These five relations require that the lord should have compassion for his retainer and the retainer should serve his lord with utmost loyalty. Parents should love their children and children should serve their parents with utmost filial devotion. Husbands should behave with decorum and justice toward their wives and wives should be respectful and deferential toward their husbands. Those who are older should be kind to those who are younger and those who are younger should respect their elders. Older and younger brothers are included in the terms "older" and "younger." Friends should be mutually sincere and trust each other and there should be no duplicity. The five moral relations are put into practice when we follow the nature of the five constants as they emerge in conduct. It is not a Way that can be sought outside of our own basic nature.

[49a]     Since humans have heaven and earth as their great parents, just as they receive the kindness of their own parents, so they receive the limitless kindness of heaven and earth. Humans are not only brought into being through the beneficence of heaven and earth, but they receive nourishment throughout their lives, just the same as after a person is born he is raised through the parents' care. Consequently, since we are born in this world, we must always serve heaven and earth and feel [the need] to somehow repay the kindness. This is filial devotion which serves heaven and earth. Humans should always bear this in mind and not forget it. There is no other way to serve heaven and earth than to obey the mind-and-heart of the universe.

[49a]     Obeying this heart means not losing the virtues of humaneness and love which are received at birth from heaven and earth, and it implies extending warmth, compassion, and respect toward other human beings who are also born of heaven and earth. This is the proper and only Way for human beings.

[49a]     Humans are born through the beneficence of nature; they receive its heart and make it their own. They live amidst na-

ture and partake of its nourishment. Thus they receive an infinitely great favor, but most people do not realize it. This is what is meant by "Peasants use it every day and are unaware of it."[11] Disobeying the principle of heaven by not serving nature and following human desires is to receive the great favor of heaven and earth and at the same time to act contrary to nature. As a child of the universe this is extremely unfilial. It is as though a child were to love other people without loving his own parents; thus he betrays his parents and commits a great act of unfiliality. An unfilial child cannot establish himself within heaven and earth. As a child of the universe, by acting contrary to heaven and earth he is all the more unable to establish himself. Even though one has good fortune and no misfortune occurs, it is dreadful to disobey heaven and earth. I have already said that we must revere and serve heaven and earth, but [it is necessary] to repeat it again and again because people cannot be told too often. No doubt I will repeat it again in the future.

[49b]     Heaven is the source of human life and parents are the root. Humans take heaven and earth as their great parents and look upon their own father and mother as a microcosm of heaven and earth. The blessings of heaven and earth and of father and mother are equal. Therefore, practicing humaneness by serving heaven and earth is like practicing filiality by serving one's parents.

[49b]     Thus in the *Book of Ritual* it says, "A humane person serves heaven as he serves his parents. We must never be negligent. We must serve our parents as we serve heaven and treat them with awe and reverence."[12] To be negligent is to lack love, to lack respect is to lack reverence. In serving both heaven and earth and our parents we must, to the same degree, love and respect them and not be negligent and never show contempt. Those who serve heaven and earth well are humane people and they preserve a heart of humaneness. Children who serve parents well are filial and they earnestly endeavor to practice filiality and righteousness. The Way which serves heaven and earth and the Way which serves parents is the same. Therefore, serving heaven and earth is of great importance for human beings, and we must not forget that for an instant. Most people do not even know the Way that serves parents close at hand and they are not conscientious. How much more ignorant are they of bear-

ing a great and limitless debt toward heaven and earth; they think that serving heaven and earth has nothing to do with them. The blessings of heaven and earth are equal to those of one's parents. Therefore, it is an extremely important duty of human beings to always serve [them] diligently and make a great effort throughout their whole lives. People must understand this principle.

[50a] There are a myriad of things between heaven and earth, and among these nothing is as exalted as human beings.[13] Therefore, humans are called the "spirit of the universe." Because humans are the spirit, they have the five innate qualities in the heart and the five moral relations in their person. They distinguish the five colors with the eyes, recognize the five tastes with the mouth, discern the five sounds with their ears, and know the five smells with their nose.[14] There are no birds or beasts who can do these varied things. As a human, to receive such an exalted body is truly to have acquired a great blessing between heaven and earth. Is it not lamentable to be born as a human and not know the way to be human, being little removed from the birds and beasts and passing one's time in vain?

[50b] Yen Chih-t'ui said, "It is difficult to be born with a human body. Do not pass your time in vain."[15] The reason he says this is because being born as a human and being superior to other things is truly fortunate. If people could be reborn in this world, even if they were negligent this time and did not know the Human Way, they could rely on being born again next time as a human. However, since we cannot be reborn, we ought to live as a human being by learning the Way and by cultivating ourselves morally. We should not waste time carelessly. If we do not know the Human Way and if we live aimlessly, it is of no avail to have been born as a human. This is lamentable.

[50b] Among all living things, being born a human is extremely difficult. Birds, beasts, insects, and fish are born every year and are limitless in number, but the number of humans is small—not even a small fraction of the birds, beasts, insects, and fish. Moreover, humans are superior to all things and receive the deep blessings of heaven and earth. Since human beings are thus ennobled, it is very difficult to be born as a human. Although people are fortunate to live as human beings, by not studying they disobey the Way

of heaven and earth, and by not knowing the Way they cannot practice it. They forget the joy of being a human. By
spending their lives vainly and living the same as birds and
beasts, they will not have a good reputation after death. Is it
not indeed regrettable that they will simply decay like grass
or trees?

[51a]    Since being born a human is extremely difficult, we
ought not to forget to relish the fact that we received our precious body miraculously. Also, we should feel anxious about
living aimlessly in this world and not knowing the Way of
humans. Throughout our life we should remember two
things, happiness and sorrow.

[51a]    Humans should know the Way of being human. If we
seek to know the Way of being human we ought to respect
the teachings of the sages and study their Way, because the
sages are the highest of the humans. By following the Way of
heaven and earth they are the teachers of countless ages who
taught the Way of the human. The teachings of the Four
Books and the Five Classics, which were left for posterity, are
a mirror throughout history.[16] The clarity of their moral principles is like that of the sun and the moon in the heavens;
although the world is large, there is no place where these do
not shine. People who read carefully will know the moral
principles of the world clearly, just as they can distinguish
between black and white in bright daylight. How can we not
study this? For humans the Way of morality is innate, but
without a will [to learn] this Way, we will be satisfied only to
eat until satiated, to wear warm clothing, and to live
comfortably.[17] If we do not study the teachings of the sages
we will lack the Human Way and will be not far removed
from the birds and beasts. If this happens, having been born
a human being would be meaningless. We could not be considered the spirit of the universe. Therefore, the sages, being
deeply concerned about this, caused the Way of morality to
be known by making wise retainers the teachers of the people.

[51b]    This is why people must definitely learn the Way of the
sages. I believe that being born as a human and not studying
is the same as not having been born. If we study and do not
know the Way it is the same as not having studied it. If we
know the Way and do not practice it this is the same as not
knowing it. The reason is that if we are born a human and do

not study we will not know the Human Way and then it is meaningless to have been born a human. This means that, although we are a human being, if we do not study, it is the same as not being born a human. Study is for the sake of knowing the Way. If we study poorly and do not learn the Way it is the same as not having studied. Moreover, knowing the Way is for the sake of practicing it. Although we study and know the Way, if we do not practice it, it is the same as not having learned it. Therefore, being born a human, we must definitely study. Those who study definitely must learn the Way. If we know the way we will inevitably practice it well. Not to practice it is still not to know the Way. If we want to know the Way we ought to follow the method of respecting the teachings of the sages and taking the instructions of wise men as a guide. This is the correct way of learning by which we should know the Way. If we do not have a will to know the Way, if we have bad teachers, and if the path of scholarship is wrong, even though we make an effort throughout our life and study diligently, there will be no results. Therefore, if we think that we will study the Way, we must set our minds upon learning the Way at the beginning, follow illuminating teachers, associate with friends of good quality, and choose the art of learning. The art of learning is the method of study. If it is a bad method, although we make a lifetime effort, we will not understand the Way. Once we lose the Way, it is difficult to return to the correct Way. Therefore, we ought to first choose the [proper] art of learning.

[52a]     The path of knowledge is extremely broad and lofty with abstruse doctrines. However, that which is close at hand is the daily practice of filial piety and faithfulness. Therefore, even foolish people can easily study, know, and practice this Way. It is not a Way which is lofty or strangely different [from daily life].

[52b]     Even the ancient sages were instructed by their teachers. How much more so ordinary people of the present! Unless we study we are unable to know the Way. It is difficult to learn even small arts without a teacher. How much more difficult is the Human Way, in other words, the Way of heaven and earth, which is vast. Although we study, if we study poorly we will not understand the Way. Without studying, obtaining the Way is absolutely impossible.

[52b]          Learning takes as its basis first establishing one's resolve. This resolve is the direction of the mind-and-heart. Establishing a resolve is knowing and practicing the Way by thinking incessantly and fervently with a mind-and-heart which aims to become a Noble Person (*kunshi*). If we study without a goal we will not be successful. Therefore, the ancients said, "Persons who have a fixed resolve will in the end accomplish their task,"[18] and, "Establishing one's resolve is half of learning."[19] For example, establishing one's resolve is like shooting an arrow aiming at the target, or setting out on a road aiming at a destination. For all tasks we must first make an effort at the beginning. Establishing a goal is the root of learning. In establishing a goal we must have courage and not be lazy or timid. If we are lazy and ineffectual we will not progress. An earnest resoluteness in seeking the Way is the same as being hungry and seeking food or being thirsty and seeking water. When we are even slightly lazy and careless, we will lose our resoluteness. Therefore, it is good to keep single-mindedly on the Way and not become enamored of extraneous things.

[53a]          In the *Book of History* it is written, "If we trifle with things we will lose our aim."[20] Trifling with things means that we distort the mind-and-heart by pampering the senses, indulging the desires, being fond of extraneous things, or becoming overly fond of various useless skills. If we become enamored of extraneous things we will lose the goal of becoming a Noble Person by studying the Way. By trifling and enjoying extraneous things we will lose our resolve. Master Ch'eng said, "Unless we are single-minded, we will not accomplish our task immediately."[21] This means that it is difficult to achieve something without single-mindedness. Single-mindedness is like a cat watching for a mouse or a hen warming her eggs; they cannot have other aims. When the mind is divided, moving here and there, the aim of learning and of morality declines and falls into disuse.

[53a]          Since the samurai naturally practice civil and military arts, they should study them diligently. However, the arts are the branches while the study of morality is the root. If they love the arts exclusively, inevitably they will be carried away and lose their resolution to learn. Moreover, they must not indulge selfish desires or give in to personal preferences. They should be careful. Establishing a goal, for example, is

like a person of a western country thinking, "I will go east." Each day while he walks he constantly thinks, "Day and night I will proceed east." This is establishing one's resolve to go east. If he does this he will surely arrive at his destination in the end. We must be similarly resolute in the Way.

[53b]     In general, in studying we ought to establish a basis on which to receive the teachings and preserve prohibitions. The "basis" is the foundation on which one builds a house. A person who studies takes humility as the basis. Humility is modesty, which means not being proud or haughty toward others. It is having a clear mind and enjoying questioning people but not displaying one's own talents. It is respecting teachers and friends and, although we have talents or strengths, hiding them. It is listening carefully to instructions and being glad for the admonishments of others. Even though we know something already, acting as though we do not know it and not putting our knowledge ahead of others; even though we have already done something well, regarding it as though we had not yet done it; not admonishing others but correcting ourselves—all of this is modesty.

[53b]     This is the basis on which to apply oneself to learning and to receive instructions. It is the same as first setting a firm foundation when building a house. When we have this foundation, by listening each day to good speech and realizing our own mistakes, our knowledge will become clear and the good will grow daily. Our progress in learning will be without bounds. Furthermore, we must observe prohibitions. Prohibitions refer to what one is warned against and does not practice. People who study first prohibit pride. (The character for pride is read *hokoru*).

[54a]     Pride is being boastful with regard to oneself and being arrogant toward others. Boastful people claim to know what they really do not know, and they take their own bad points as being good. By only using their own knowledge and not consulting with or utilizing the admonishments of others, they do not criticize themselves but they criticize others. When people act this way evil will grow daily. Persons who are beginning to study should first observe these prohibitions and establish a foundation. Without this, even though they study, there will be no benefit; instead there will be harm. People ought to be aware of this as the first principle for those who are studying and reading books.

[54a]       Human nature is originally good, but in ordinary people
            this goodness is lost by the obscuration of the physical dis-
            position and by human desires. Disposition is what we are
            born with. Human desires means indulging the sense desires
            beyond the proper limit. If one's disposition is bad, human
            desires arise easily. Therefore, all humans should return to
            their original good nature by studying the teachings of the
            ancient sages, learning the Way to be human, reforming the
            bad habits of their physical nature, and avoiding the obscura-
            tions of the senses. This is the Way of learning, and it was for
            this reason that the ancient sages established their teachings.
            The reason that they taught it to all people was that, since
            human nature is good, it was a way of returning to goodness
            through study.

[54b]       All people have an innate knowledge of the good. Even
            though they are not taught, from their youth they love their
            parents, and as they grow up, they respect their brothers. All
            people have a heart of humaneness; they feel compassion
            when they see a child about to fall into a well.[22] All people
            have a sense of what is their duty. [When it is a matter of
            honor] even foolish servants are not afraid of dying. Even
            beggars will not eat food if it is trampled upon.[23] This is
            proof that human nature is good. The teaching of the sages is
            not something that could be taught or practiced if people did
            not have an inborn nature. Although the way might be
            taught, it would be difficult to practice, but taking as one's
            basis the moral sense with which people are originally born,
            one can lead and enlighten them and broaden their minds.

[54b]       The nature of all people is good and, based on this fact,
            they can be induced to activate their innate goodness. There-
            fore, the teachings of the sages are easy to practice. For ex-
            ample, in order for a woodsman to make a new axe handle,
            he takes the handle of the axe which he is holding in his
            hand and compares it by lining it up with the branch of a tree
            which will become the handle of the new axe that he is try-
            ing to make. There is no difference in size or shape. As a
            close model there is nothing better than this.[24] However, if
            there is a disparity between the axe handle that he has in his
            hand and the branch of the tree that he is trying to make into
            the handle of a new axe, it will not serve the purpose. The
            teachings of the sages are not like this. Taking innate moral
            sense as the root, they have a Way which nourishes it and

does not invent teachings or go on deviant paths in teaching people. In general, if people are induced and led by the Way, whether they are Chinese or Japanese, western warriors or southern barbarians, they will certainly revere and believe in this Way and will not fail to follow it.

[55a]     There are many paths of learning. There is the study of interpreting old texts, namely, philology and exegesis; there is memorization; there is the study of poetry and prose; and there is the learning of the Confucians.[25] Exegesis means trying to learn in detail the meaning of the sentences in the books of the sages. Memorization is reading widely the books of past and present and remembering the historical facts and evidence. The study of poetry and prose is learning to compose poems and essays. The learning of the Confucians is understanding the Way of heaven, earth, and human, and learning the way of self-discipline for the governance of people. If that involves the "pursuit of learning" it must be the study of the Confucians. Although exegesis is a mode of comprehending the meaning of sentences in the Four Books and the Five Classics, if we do not understand moral principles it is of little use. Memorization and the study of poetry and prose are still farther from the Way and are not the learning of the Confucians. If one is single-minded in the pursuit of Confucian learning it is all right for one to combine with it the practice of exegesis and memorization.

[55b]     Besides this there is also the study of stories. This is a study which does not favor the reading of classical or historical texts; it is merely a study which tries to remember and enjoy many things by appreciating books which describe various miscellaneous, detailed, and unusual events. Furthermore, the study of stories, like exegesis, the study of poetry and prose, and memorization, fails to provide a basic logic and order for scholarly work. Nevertheless, in a degenerate age this kind of learning exists. It is the lowest of the scholarly arts.

[55b]     With regard to Confucian learning, someone might ask: is it not all right just to learn the Human Way? Why is there a need to learn the Way of heaven and earth? In reply I would say: the Way of heaven and earth is the root and source of the Human Way, and unless we know the Way of heaven and earth we will not understand the root from which truth emerges. If we do not know the root, the Human

Way will not be clear because we will not recognize the natural principles inherent in human beings, and we will not
understand the unity between heaven and humans which we
receive from nature. Therefore, after first learning the Way of
daily human relations (i.e. morality), we should learn the
Way of heaven and earth. Is not this why the Sage studied
the *Book of Changes?*[26] However, the Way of heaven and earth
can not be known easily.

[55b]      In establishing our aim in life we should make it comprehensive and lofty. If it is small and narrow we will be satisfied with minor achievements, and true accomplishment will
be difficult to attain. We should have a constant resolve to
become a superior person. We should not aim at what is unworthy and low as do common people. If, by setting our goal
in this way, we work diligently over a long period of time,
our success will accumulate and we shall be sure to surpass
others. If we aim for the highest we may achieve middling
success, and if we aim at middling success we may end up at
the bottom; but if we aim at the bottom we shall have no
success at all.

[56a]      Yet we should also make our heart small and lowly. We
should be humble toward others and modest in our everyday
conduct of matters close at hand. If we are proud of heart
and lacking in respect for others we cannot be punctilious in
small matters. If we are aloof and arrogant toward others we
will lose humility.

[56a]      In the pursuit of learning, knowledge and action are both
essential. We call being diligent in these two essentials "extending knowledge" and "being vigorous in practice."[27] Extending knowledge is penetrating to the limits of knowledge.
Vigorous practice is making an effort in action. When knowledge of the Way is not clear, we cannot act. For example, it is
like those who are blind; even though their legs are strong,
they do not know the way they ought to go and it is difficult
to progress. If we are not conscientious in our practice, even
though we know something, it is useless. For example, although one can see clearly, if one cannot stand one cannot
proceed. Knowledge and conduct are like seeing with the eye
and progressing with the legs. When we cannot see we are
unable to discern the way in which we ought to proceed. If
we cannot stand we cannot proceed. When we are not
equipped with both sight and movement it is difficult to
progress along the path.

[56b]     First we have knowledge, then we have action. When we do not know which is first, it is difficult to act. In order of precedence, knowledge is first. Knowledge is for the sake of action. Although we know something, if we do not practice it, it is useless. In order of relative importance, action is most significant. If either action or knowledge is missing, it is like a bird with one wing or a cart with one wheel. The pursuit of learning is a parallel progress of knowledge and action. Parallel progress means practicing what we know. There is a slight priority in knowing over acting, but they must progress side by side without one getting ahead of the other. By simply knowing and not acting one will not be able to proceed in a parallel manner.

[56b]     If we divide the two methods of knowledge and action into greater detail there are five steps. They are stated in the *Doctrine of the Mean* as: study widely, question thoroughly, think carefully, discern clearly, and practice earnestly.[28] This is the method for the pursuit of learning by knowing the Way and practicing it.

[56b]     The method of "studying widely" implies diligence with respect to seeing and hearing. It is seeking truth by reading the books of the sages, hearing the Way from others, and reflecting on past and present. The Way of human moral relations is recorded in the writings of the sages and worthies. For people who read well it should be like distinguishing black and white in broad daylight. There is no limit to the Way and its principles in this world. If we do not learn the Way and its principles, and do not know the method by which we should act, our mistakes will be numerous. The Way and its principles are established in our hearts and it functions in all things and affairs. Thus, by first delving into the Way and its principles in our own hearts, and then widely searching out the principles in all things, we will apprehend a truth at the center of our own being [lit. "get it for ourselves"]. This is learning widely. The ways to learn widely are numerous; however, there is nothing so beneficial as reading books. The ancients also said, "To increase wisdom there is nothing equal to books."[29] However, simply the love of words without the seeking of moral principles is not wide learning.

[57a]     In "questioning thoroughly," we should resolve our doubts by clarifying these principles through association with enlightened teachers and good friends. We may ques-

tion them in greater detail concerning things which we have already learned but may still have doubts about.

[57a]　　　As for "thinking carefully," with regard to doubtful things in what we have already investigated, we should try to understand them by calming our mind-and-heart and reflecting seriously upon them until we understand. Even if we investigate something, if we do not completely understand it, it will not become our own. Therefore, we should grasp that principle by seeking the Way and principle in our hearts. This means that by thorough reflection we will discern truth, but without careful thought it will be difficult to do so. The pursuit of learning values "getting it oneself." Getting it oneself means acquiring knowledge by careful and thorough consideration and, by realizing the Way and principles within our hearts, making them our own.

[57b]　　　When we "discern clearly," if there is still a confusion of good and evil after we have already considered something carefully, then by clearly investigating the rightness or wrongness of the situation we can distinguish good and evil. The four [steps] mentioned above are all techniques of knowing in order to discern the Way clearly.

[57b]　　　As for "practicing earnestly," if we learn a truth through studying, questioning, and discerning, we must deliberately practice the truth that we know. When we do not, the Way will not be established. The way of practicing earnestly is being true to our words, being without deception, being prudent in action, and having few faults. Self-conduct takes many forms, but the forms are nothing more than words and actions. Therefore, if we are sincere in words and careful in actions,[30] our self-conduct will be controlled.

[57b]　　　There are seven functions which arise in the heart which are called the seven emotions.[31] They are happiness, anger, sadness, joy, love, hate, and desire. The actions of people arise through these seven things. Being careful of the emotions and keeping them in proper proportion we can accord with the Way and principle. Among the seven emotions, anger and desire are especially harmful to our heart, injurious to our body, and damaging to others. Thus by repressing anger and obstructing desires we control these emotions when they first arise. Moreover, in returning to the good, if we find there is a good that is better than our own, we should abandon our own and follow that superior one. If we have faults

we should correct them immediately. We must not hesitate to reform our self-attachment. Furthermore, in dealings with others, if they do not follow us we should not blame them but should reflect on and reproach ourselves.

[58a]     All of this is the way to practice earnestly. If we do not study and question, the Way will not be clear. If we do not think and discern, it will be difficult to obtain the Way in our heart. If we do not practice earnestly, although we may understand, it will have no substance. These five steps are the methods of learning indicated in the *Doctrine of the Mean*. Master Ch'eng said if you lose even one of these five you will not learn.[32]

[58a]     Always reflecting on ourself and also listening to the criticisms of others, knowing our own faults and mistakes, we should correct our mistakes and return to the good.[33] It is important to seek instruction and listen to admonishment by seeking out and associating with good companions who are wise and honest and will correct our faults. As for learning, since it is a way of changing the evil within ourselves and returning to the good, if we think that we have wisdom and are a good person, even though we study there will be no benefit; on the contrary, we may increase wickedness. People are not sages.[34] How can they exhaust the good in everything? We should not think that it is sufficient to make ourselves good. Even the sages could not make themselves good by [simply] loving learning. How can ordinary people of today be without faults?

[58b]     In general, the way to extend knowledge is by first knowing the Way of the five constant virtues and the five moral relations. We should extend this to the principle of regulating the family and governing the people.[35] Next we should seek to know the principles of all things and affairs. Since all things in heaven and earth lie within the ken of our own mind-and-heart, we should learn their principles. The way of investigating principles first gives priority to what is primary (the root) and what is close at hand, and then follows up with what is secondary (the branches) and things farther away. We should not forget the order of sequence and priority.

[58b]     Those who pursue learning should not be satisfied merely with the state of their own knowledge and conduct. Even if we possess much learning, intelligence, and skill, we

should not think that we have much knowledge or take pride in our own talents. All people have knowledge; and furthermore, they have their strong points. We should not look down on others as foolish. We should not take ourselves as correct and resist admonitions from others. To give up our own mistaken ways and to follow and adopt the good points of others is proper self-conduct. To think of ourselves as knowing everything is a vice. Do not succumb to it. Those who know their ignorance are not great fools; those who know their own errors do not have major faults. However, those who make excuses for themselves out of pride are definitely foolish, because if they lack self-understanding and are not basically open-minded, willing to learn and advance toward the good, they will end up being fools. Those who look down on others will inevitably have the reproach of heaven and be criticized by others. Those who slander people will certainly be spoken ill of by others. Even the Noble Person of the past who was wise and perceptive guarded himself against foolishness.[36] How much more foolish is it for people of a degenerate age to boast of their knowledge and talents!

[59a]      In the *Book of History* it says, "If we boast about a certain good, we lose the good; if we boast about a talent, we lose the talent."[37] If we praise ourselves and think we are good, since we do not know our faults we cannot correct them and we won't be able to return to the good. Evil will increase daily while good will decrease. Such being the case, even if we were to receive instructions from the sages from morning until night it would be useless. Although we read and studied books diligently, it would be of no benefit to us at all. On the contrary, guile would increase and harm would come from boasting of one's talents. The reason that pride is a vice is clear from the admonitions of the ancients. Those who pursue learning must first forswear pride. Illiterate people say that if one pursues learning, one's character worsens and there is no benefit from it, but only harm. Illiterate people say such things indiscriminately because they see that there are such people in the world who really want to stay as they are and, indeed, dislike learning from the beginning. If we really study with a view to disciplining ourselves, how could it not be beneficial, much less be harmful?

[59b]     In searching out principles or learning facts we should not think of things as on one level. Just as a crinum plant on the shore has many layers [on the stem], we should search out principle in its several layers.[38] Shallow-minded people know only one layer and they extend it to other things. It is superficial to think that there is nothing other than this one level. Every day we ought to act by peeling off one layer today and peeling off another layer tomorrow. Peeling off the skin, we should look at the meat, taking off the meat we should look at the bone, breaking up the bone we should look at the marrow. Learning which penetrates all principles cannot be pursued by coarse, careless people. We must have a calm, precise mind.

[59b]     Confucius said, "In ancient times one studied for one's own sake; nowadays one studies for the sake of others' [approbation]."[39] "For one's own sake" means real [practical] learning to cultivate oneself. "For others" means learning for fame and profit, which is learning to be known by others. The original meaning of learning is cultivating ourselves without concern for whether or not we are known by others. For example, it is the same as eating to satisfy our hunger and to nourish our body. Realizing that our stomach is full, we have no desire that others should know we have already eaten. Learning ought to be only for the sake of cultivating ourselves. It should not be in any way for the sake of making ourselves known to others. Moreover, Confucius said to Tzu-hsia, "Be a scholar in the manner of a Noble Person, not in the manner of a petty person."[40] This means that the true Confucian learns for his own sake. This is real [or practical] learning. However, the Confucianism of the petty person is learning in order to be known by others. This is simply having in mind to seek fame and profit without having the aim of disciplining oneself. It is false learning.

[60a]     Therefore, the mind-and-heart of the Noble Person advances towards the good each day, while the mind-and-heart of the petty person falls back toward evil each day. With the same expenditure of effort we ought to become a Noble Confucian and not a small-minded one. It is regrettable if one studies hard only to become a small-minded Confucian. From the beginning scholars must first establish it as their aim to learn for their own sake. For those who pursue learn-

ing this should be their first priority. If we don't do this, even though we study and read widely, there will be no benefit. On the contrary, there will be harm.

[60a]     If we read books, it should be our single-minded aim to assimilate them for ourselves. Assimilating means receiving, using, observing, and practicing the teachings of the sages which are written in books. Although we read books and hear about moral principles, if we do not internalize and practice those principles, they are useless and without benefit to us. In reading the *Great Learning* we see: "It is similar to disliking bad smells and enjoying pleasant colors."[41] Assimilating means that truly despising evil is the same as disliking bad smells, and loving the good is the same as enjoying pleasant colors.

[60b]     When we read the *Analects,* we find the passage: "Serving one's parents well by using great effort; serving one's lord by devoting one's life."[42] Serving one's parents in this way means that without sparing our energies or resources we ought to practice filial piety. As a retainer we should not regard our life as our own but should forget ourselves and be completely loyal to our master. In other cases we should do the same. This is reading books and assimilating them. Although we read many books, if we do not assimilate them it is only what is called "learning of the mouth and ear,"[43] for it is only what comes in the ear and immediately goes out of the mouth, without being kept in the heart or personally practiced. This is useless learning.

[60b]     When people begin their studies they should first earnestly read the Four Books and then carefully read the Five Classics. The Five Classics are the teachings of the sages of high antiquity; they represent the fountainhead of letters and the ancestral source of moral principles. The Four Books are the teachings of the Confucian school. Reading them is like listening to the teachings of the sages directly. We ought to respect them. If we wish to understand the meaning of these writings we should first look at the commentaries on the Four Books, then at the *Questions Concerning the Great Learning* and the *Questions Concerning the Doctrine of the Mean,*[44] and then at the commentaries on the Five Classics. Next one should look at the books of [the Sung Masters]: Chou Tun-i, the Ch'eng brothers, Chang Tsai, and Chu Hsi. Among these we ought to read thoroughly the books of the Ch'eng broth-

ers and Chu Hsi. The *Elementary Learning*[45] is concerned with an especially important method for self-discipline. The Way of human moral relations is almost completely supplied there. By reading this at an early age we should learn its meaning. Furthermore, it is good to look at the histories of past ages, namely, *The Commentary on the Spring and Autumn Annals, Records of the Historian,* and Chu Hsi's *Outline and Digest of the General Mirror.*[46] This is the method of learning by which we understand the Way and penetrate past and present. If we understand the classics, the commentaries, and the histories, we will not fail to grasp the principles of events, past and present.

[61a]     The books of the sages are called classics. Classics are constants. The words of the sages reveal the constant Way throughout the centuries. The writings of the worthies are called commentaries. These commentaries recount the Way of the sages and transmit them to later generations. The Four Books and the Five Classics are constants. The annotations [on the classics] and the writings of the Sung Confucians are commentaries on these. The books which record past ages are called histories. These are records of past events. The philosophical texts include those by Hsün Tzu,[47] Yang Tzu,[48] Huai-nan Tzu,[49] Wen-chung Tzu,[50] and the *Shuo Yüan.*[51] These books are not as clear or detailed as the books of the Ch'eng brothers or Chu Hsi in clarifying the Way and its principles, but they are useful as an aid to [understanding] the moral principles expressed in the classics and we should read them.

[61a]     The "collected works" (*shu*) are books with essays and so forth by various authors. These also reveal moral principles. These four types of books, namely, classics, histories, philosophical treatises, and collected works, are of varying importance, but they are all useful in the pursuit of learning. If one wishes to learn the Way one should mainly devote oneself to diligent study of the classics for one's whole lifetime. Next are the histories, which are also of great benefit. Then we should look at the philosophers and collected works. *The Outline and Digest of the General Mirror* by Chu Hsi is an especially good book. It is not simply for learning about the remaining records of past ages, their periods of order and disorder, rise and decline, but it is also a great help for the study of moral principles. It is especially a clear mirror for

those who rule the country. Also, since it shows the way to victory or defeat in war, it is definitely helpful for people studying military arts. In this book there are numerous important events of the past and present; there are many things of great benefit, and we should apply ourselves to reading them over and over. Truly it is one of the great classics for the governance of the world.

[61b]    In addition, we ought to look as much as possible at the records of China and Japan. If one still has free time, it is good to look at the writings of the hundred philosophers in order to clarify the meaning of the classics and broaden one's grasp of moral principles.

[61b]    Nevertheless, one should be careful lest reading widely and unselectively should cause us to lose our sense of direction and commitment. In learning there should be both breadth and restraint (selectivity). If there is breadth there will be a wealth of detail to prepare one [for any eventuality]. If there is restraint the moral implications will all be precise and clear. Those who do not have time to study broadly or who begin their study after middle age should be restrained (selective).[52] Of old it was said, "Being broad and diffuse is not as good as being selective and precise."[53] Studying and reading books is for the sake of learning the Way. If we do not learn the Way, although we read widely among books of past and present, and learn to write poetry and prose, it will be to no avail. It is not the true meaning of learning. Although people may penetrate the meaning of the Four Books and the Five Classics and read widely among the books of ancient and modern times, there are many who still do not understand moral principles throughout their whole life. It is because they have not committed themselves to seek the Way. Even if they have such a commitment, if their method of learning is not good, they will not learn the Way their whole life long. It may be because they lack wisdom. We must continually strive to broaden our knowledge.

[62a]    People who are committed to the learning of the mind-and-heart should use the method of daily renewal. Daily renewal means starting each day anew by changing the old vices of yesterday, returning to the new goodness of today, and renewing oneself by surpassing yesterday.[54] If we do this we will understand that today we are right while yesterday we were wrong. If we are constantly diligent our practice will

progress each day and change each month so we will not be the same each year. In one day we will accumulate the merits of the day, in one month the merits of thirty days, in one year the merits of 360 days, and in three years the merits of 1,000 days. If we continue to progress toward virtue and return to the good, our joy will be boundless and unconsciously we will be leaping with our feet and dancing with our hands [for joy].[55] Thus when we progress we can certainly expect that we will become a Noble Person. If today we do not change from yesterday, if this month we don't change from last month, if we are the same this year as last year, without the strength to begin anew each day, we will end up our lives as fools—to our own regret.

[62a]    The same is true if we exert ourselves in learning. If we make an effort each day without stopping, our study will progress daily. At the end of a number of years, we will come to understand and enjoy the meaning of moral principles in the classics and the commentaries. Our meritorious deeds of ten years will be exceedingly great and our learning will be half accomplished.

[62b]    In all things if we are lazy and do not struggle from the beginning, afterward there will be no meritorious achievement or enjoyment. In other words, it is the same as if we apply hot moxa or drink unpleasant medicine so as to become free of illness later. In the pursuit of learning it is the same. A person who struggles in youth will have many joys when he becomes older.

[62b]    In reading, first we should earnestly study the Four Books and the Five Classics, remember many characters, and become familiar with the readings. "Readings" refers to the meaning of words. When we do not know words or their meaning, it is difficult to understand books, we have no zest for it, and we lag behind in reading. Lack of progress in reading is due to not knowing words.[56] However, to get stuck over the recognition and reading of characters so that one does not have the satisfaction of "getting" moral principles for oneself means one cannot learn to become a Noble Person.

[62b]    The pursuit of learning is the way which enlarges our wisdom, and so by listening widely, seeing much, and coming to understand moral principles, patiently we await the natural enlargement of wisdom in our hearts. Seeking en-

lightenment we must not press for it by drawing upon our own wit and knowledge. We should draw on the good words of others without deprecating the wit and intelligence of others. Even people of high rank or seniority, or those with talent and education, should not boast of their rank or age or talent. Simply questioning others humbly is the way to increase wisdom gradually.

[63a]          To be diligent in study from one's youth, we must use time wisely. Emperor Yü [founder of the Hsia dynasty] was a sage [i.e. naturally gifted] and, yet, he used every second carefully. How much more should we ordinary people of today do so![57] We should not waste time by being indolent and careless. The seasons flow like the arrow of time; consequently we should not let time be lost thinking that we can rely on our being youthful [forever]. During our time in this world it is difficult to study when we are too young, old, or sick. Moreover, there are numerous household duties and tasks to be performed by the four classes of people [samurai, farmer, artisan, and merchant],[58] so there is little time left for study. Those who spend their life squandering precious free time, being excessively lazy and carefree, or wasting time doing useless things are definitely foolish. Realizing that this day, this year, will never come again, we should not waste even a moment. We ought to keep this in mind throughout our whole lives. Of old it was said, "It is difficult to outdo a person who keeps at it, trying hard all the time."[59] Likewise, "A careless person who does not do anything and always has a lot of free time cannot surpass others."[60]

[63ab]          For example, farmers and merchants work without wasting time. Farmers work in the fields from dawn until dusk and merchants definitely surpass other people in diligence. Their houses are full of wealth and there is no lack of clothing and food. Of old it was also said, "If human beings toil and are diligent they will not be poor."[61] If one exerts one's self with great care for the administration of the state, the country will definitely be well ordered. When we apply ourselves fully to scholarship, we will inevitably surpass others and our talents will progress. Many things are like that. When we make an effort for a long time, without wasting time, we will surely succeed. There is nothing so valuable for people as time. The gentleman makes an effort to study, conducts the administration of the country, serves his parents

and lord, and studies various arts. The farmer cultivates his fields, the merchant buys and sells, the artisan makes things, women weave and sew. All of them do things by using time prudently; therefore, using time well is more precious than a golden treasure. There is an old saying: "The sages did not value great treasures; they valued time."[62] People who do not value time and do not study or make an effort definitely will not have wisdom, virtue or skill. If the gentleman does not use time prudently, he will not be able to discipline himself or regulate his family. The farmer, artisan, and merchant will lose the work of their family and cannot escape poverty, starvation, and cold. Scholars will assuredly lack refinement in learning and have no capabilities. Doctors will inevitably become like lowly craftsmen. Various skills will be lost if we do not use time wisely. Therefore, time is a treasure for people and we should use it well.

[64a]      Especially in youth we have little work and a lot of time and our energy and memory are strong. What we remember by observing once we will never forget our whole life. If we study diligently during this time there will be many results. If we make an effort when we are strong and have time in our youth, our reading will make great progress and be very rewarding. After thirty one's tasks are numerous, one's free time decreases, one's energy gradually declines, and one's memory fades; even though we may use great effort, we forget easily, and although we work hard our success will be small. Young people, recognizing this well, should be prudent about their time when young and study hard. Truly this should be a treasure throughout their life.

[64a]      In a poem of T'ao Ch'ien it says: "Youthful years never come again; today only comes once. Thus we should exert ourselves at each moment, for time waits for no one."[63] Again in an old poem it says: "If we do not make an effort in youth, we will regret it in old age."[64] Considering this well in youth, we should make an effort to use each day wisely and not have regrets later. Even though we make an effort, when our method of study is poor, there will be no benefit, we will be confused and anxious, and we will not know the correct Way. We should deem this foolish.

[64b]      The learning of the Noble Person considers the Way to consist in earnestly practicing the five moral relations by having the three virtues of wisdom, humaneness, and courage as

the basis. Wisdom, humaneness, and courage are the virtues of the heart which put into practice the Way of the five moral relations. Wisdom is understanding the Way of the five relations, humaneness is preserving and exercising them, and courage is practicing them diligently. Knowing and practicing is having courage and making an effort. These three virtues are the method of the mind-and-heart, which is the learning of the Noble Person. The Way which we ought to practice is that of the five moral relations. These three virtues and the five moral constants have the same principle. The five constants are the nature with which one is born and the three virtues are the discipline of the mind-and-heart cultivated by learning. These are summarized in the five virtues.

[64b]      Confucius said, "Study unceasingly. Cease only at death."[65] Being born as a human, knowing the Human Way, and cultivating one's person well, we ought to strive to become a Noble Person. In so doing, one makes it worthwhile to be born a human. Therefore, we should not be negligent in studying the Way to become [truly] human. Our study should be unceasing even until our last remaining breath. Only with death should it cease.

## CHAPTER II

## *THE PURSUIT OF LEARNING*, PART 2

[65a]   The teachings of the *Elementary Learning*, as something studied by children, are a form of learning for the young.[66] In the past all children at the age of eight, regardless of rank, became students and learned by receiving the instruction of a teacher. This was elementary learning. What they were taught was to have filial piety toward their parents, respect their seniors, and serve their lord; the way to receive guests, sweep the rooms, prepare food and drink, advance and withdraw in the presence of notable people, and respond to questions and requests;[67] and they were also taught the skills of the six arts for daily use, namely, ritual, music, archery, driving [a horse or chariot], reading, and arithmetic. From their youth they nurtured their mind-and-heart by these means, and as they became older they made them the basis for study of the great [higher] learning. In general, the *Elementary Learning* teaches such matters.

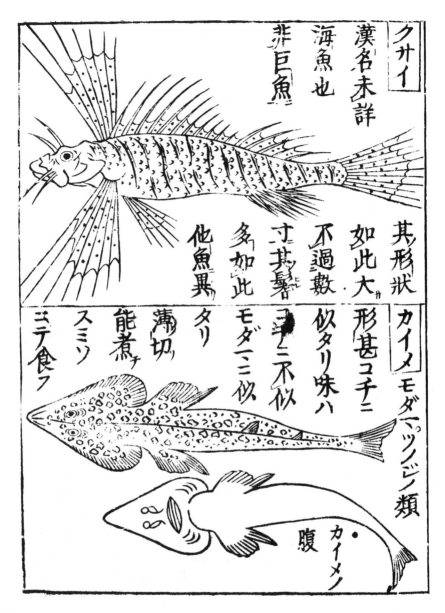

ABOVE: *Kusai*. The Chinese name is unknown. It is a sea fish. It is not large, approximately 5 inches. It has many fins and is different from other fish. BELOW: *Kaime*. A kind of shark. This is a kind of *modama* (shark). Its shape is very similar to a *kochi* (flathead). The taste is not like a flathead, it is like a shark. Cut it thin, boil it well and eat it with vinegared bean paste. The diagram shows the stomach of the *kaime*.

[65ab]    The *Great Learning* is the learning for adults from the age of fifteen, and it is concerned with the important principle of governing the people through self-discipline. The earth is extensive but it consists [essentially] of nothing but the self and others. The study of the Way of governing the people through self-discipline is the greatest and most important of studies. Therefore, it is called the *Great Learning*. "Making clear one's luminous virtue" [i.e. manifesting the moral nature] is to discipline oneself. "To renew the people" is [the means of] governing the people.[68] "Resting in the highest good" means that by manifesting illustrious virtue and by renewing the people we attain the highest goodness and should rest there. Therefore, there is no way to rest in the highest good other than by manifesting illustrious virtue and renewing the people. These three structural principles are the great essence of the *Great Learning*. There are eight specific items in the method that leads to the three guiding principles. The eight items are the detailed methods included within the three structural principles. The investigation of things and extension of knowledge is a way which opens up knowledge by exploring and understanding the principle of things and affairs. [The items that come] after "making one's intention sincere" constitute the way of vigorous practice. Above all, sincerity, honesty, and self-discipline are the Way to cultivate oneself. Ordering the family, governing the state, and bringing peace to all under heaven is a Way of ruling the people. In general, the *Great Learning* teaches these principles.

[65b]    In the *Great Learning* the clarifying of principles by investigating things and extending knowledge is the beginning of "governing people through self-discipline." "Investigating things" is thoroughly exploring and attaining the principles of all things and affairs; "extending knowledge" is fathoming what is known in our own mind-and-heart and clarifying it. The order of investigation of things begins with the Way of the five constant virtues and five moral relations and proceeds from things close at hand such as disciplining the self and regulating the family and, following this sequence, gradually reaches up to fathoming the principles for governing the country. This is the investigation of things. When we exhaustively fathom the principles concerning the myriad things and events, our self-understanding will naturally be

clarified. This is the extension of knowledge. There is no method of extending knowledge other than investigating things. This is the beginning of the endeavor [to internalize] the *Great Learning*.

[66a]     Next is making our intentions sincere. Intentions are like seedlings; they indicate when the mind-and-heart is first aroused. The substance of the mind-and-heart is quiescent before good and evil appear. When it is first moved, both good and evil arise and so do likes and dislikes. To dislike means to hate. At this point, making ones intentions sincere means loving the good, disliking evil, being honest and not deceitful. For example, loving the good is like loving beautiful colors, disliking evil is like shunning bad smells. We should be honest in such things, for it is the beginning of effort and practice.

[66a]     When we are not honest in loving the good and disliking evil, the foundation will not be firmly established and we cannot practice the Way in all things. This method [described in the *Great Learning*] of "Rectifying the heart, disciplining oneself, regulating the family, ruling the country, and making peace under heaven," begins with making our intentions sincere. Thus the eight articles of the *Great Learning* have as their essence the investigation of things and making the intentions sincere. The investigation of things is the beginning of knowledge. Making our intentions sincere is the beginning of action. If we do not investigate things we cannot thoroughly explore all principles and so our knowledge will not be clear, it will be difficult to distinguish good and evil, and we will be confused and unenlightened. This is like still being in a dream and not waking up. If we do not make our intentions sincere in loving the good and disliking evil, we will be without a basis on which to practice the Way, and we still cannot be called a good person. Therefore, is it not natural that one takes these two [loving good and disliking evil] as the beginning of the extension of knowledge and vigorous practice?

[66b]     All people definitely have the innate capacity to know, and even foolish people can distinguish somewhat between good and evil. In addition, when knowledge gradually opens up, by thoroughly exploring principles through study, the mind-and-heart which sees good as good and evil as evil becomes increasingly clear. However, if we are not genuine in

loving good and disliking evil, the good will not be practiced. Should we not shun evil, both the power of innate
knowledge and what we know through study are rendered
useless. Therefore, if scholars wish to practice the Way they
must first be genuine in loving good and disliking evil. Consequently, the method of making the intentions sincere is indeed important.

[66b]      There are two essentials for learning. When we still do
not know, we should seek to know, and if we already know
we should practice it. If we do not know it is difficult to act.
If we know but do not practice, it is the same as not understanding, which makes it useless. Thus the Way of learning
is just these two: knowing and acting. Furthermore, although
we may read numerous volumes, if we do not know the Way
and don't practice it, it is the same as not reading. This is
because we lack resoluteness in pursuing the Way. Thus the
Way of the *Great Learning* is expanding our knowledge by
fathoming the principle of everything through the investigation of things and the extension of knowledge. Then, making
our heart sincere by loving the good and shunning evil, we
practice what we know. This is making the intentions sincere.
If our knowledge is insufficient we cannot distinguish between good and evil in everything. If we do not make our
intentions sincere by loving good and shunning evil, we will
lack genuineness and cannot carry out the Way. These two
are the essence of the Way of the *Great Learning*, and they
represent the method [both] of knowing and acting.

[67a]      Even people who teach moral principles by emphasizing
broad learning and the understanding of the classics are inferior to common people if their spiritual discipline and conduct are not good. This is because without resoluteness in
pursuing the Way they do not find the Way in their own
hearts. Even though we observe with our eyes and recite
with our mouth, if we do not take principle into our hearts it
is useless. To give an analogy, even if much lavish food and
fragrant wine are put before one, if we do not eat and drink
them it is the same as not having enough to eat or drink.
Some people doubt that there could be people who read
books and yet act wickedly, but we should dispel their
doubts on this score. Although we may read books, if we are
not committed to the Way, it amounts to no more than learning the words without benefiting the mind-and-heart. This is

useless learning. The pursuit of learning must be based on a
prior commitment [to the Way].

[67a]        In the morning we learn from a teacher, in the afternoon
we review what we learned in the morning, and in the
evening we study it again. At night we reflect on our mistakes during the day, and if there are no failings we can sleep
peacefully. If there are failings we should be repentant and
ashamed and take this as the lesson for the following day. We
should consider this the method of learning which is spoken
of in the *Kuo-yü*.[69]

[67b]        If we speak of this for the benefit of people who have not
yet learned to read, making a commitment to practice the
Way should truly be given the first priority. However, if a
person beginning with the classics does not read the books of
the sages widely, he will not understand their teachings. He
will be ignorant of the Way and may well make mistakes in
both speech and action. Furthermore, when a person does
not know the ancient chronicles he cannot take them as a
mirror for the present. Therefore, reading diligently day and
night, we should reflect on the past. No matter how much
talent people may have innately, unless they study the past
they will not be able to learn the Way by themselves or understand all the changes from past to present. If we speak of
this for the benefit of people who can already read books,
learning should concentrate on the practice of correcting mistakes, returning to the good, and disciplining oneself.
Though we may read widely and come to understand past
and present, if we do not correct our mistakes and actualize
the good, it will be pointless. Thus, learning should put
commitment to the Way and personal practice [of it] as its
first priority. Reading books comes second.

[68a]        The Way to pursue learning is to respect the teacher. In
respecting the teacher we naturally honor the Way; in honoring the Way, we revere the Way of the people. Therefore,
even though a person may have a high rank as a lord, he
should not look down on the teacher as a retainer. In ancient
times, in the Royal College, the teacher did not face north
when teaching the Emperor. This was because the teacher
was venerated.[70]

[68a]        In this world the Way and principle are to be found first
of all in one's own heart. If we are mingling with people
there is a Way of appropriate conduct between lord and mas-

ter, father and son, older brother and younger, husband and wife, and friends. There is a definite principle appropriate to each and all of our personal involvements, and one may not depart from this Way even for a moment. Even an ordinary person is furnished with the principles which he ought to practice; in this he is no different from a sage or a worthy. Furthermore, no matter how foolish a person is, he has a heart which loves the good and dislikes evil, and by this innate knowledge of the good he knows the Way to some degree and uses it daily. Otherwise, it would be difficult to live even one day in the world. A person will not last very long if he disobeys his lord or father, creates disturbances, fights with people, violates or robs others, or commits crimes.

[68a]     Nevertheless, it is difficult for ordinary people to know and practice the Way well. Therefore, the ancient sages made their appearance in the world, established their teachings, made clear the Way and principles, and expressed these in books. There is nothing which is not clearly presented in the writings of the sages concerning the principles of all things under heaven, whether great or small, fine or coarse. Just as the sun and moon in the midst of the heavens illuminate the shape of everything, so all people who have eyes can see this. Those who read the classics are bound to clarify the Way, preserve principles in their heart, discipline themselves, engage in moral relations, make an effort in all things, and endeavor to govern the people. In this way we should seek to fulfill our duty as human beings and thereby take our place between heaven and earth. If we do not do this we will lose the Way to be fully human, we will obfuscate our duty, and we will betray the principles of heaven and earth.

[68b]     Everything has its role. Heaven and earth have a mind-and-heart which create and nourish things; heaven covers them and earth bears them up. This is the role of heaven and earth. Even the least of the myriad things has its particular function. The cock greets the dawn, the dog acts as guardian of the evening; by being diligent in the performance of their innate functions they carry out their respective roles.

[68b]     Human beings are the soul of all things. The human heart is originally clear and it contains all principles. If the principles which we possess cannot be practiced, we should say that our human role is unfilled. Would not this make us as human beings inferior to the birds and the animals?

[68b]     People who read books should first correct the line of their scholarship and then rectify their practice of the mind-and-heart. Following the Way of heaven and earth and the sages without deviating toward evil even a little, both scholarship and the discipline of the mind-and-heart should be pure. Even though someone may be attracted to the Way of the sages, if there is the slightest deviation from this Way, we cannot say it is pure. When one's pursuit of learning is pure, one's discipline of the mind-and-heart is without evil and is correct. When the discipline of the mind-and-heart is correct, what emerges in action will all be proper. This is the same as someone who, in following a path, first of all inquires and learns the direction of the path. If we only make an effort to proceed without knowing the direction of the path, it is like a person from the capital [Kyoto] who thinks he will go to Ōshū [the northern provinces] and first proceeds toward Yodo and Yamazaki [toward Osaka]. The more he makes an effort to proceed, the further he will get from Ōshū. This is simply to know that one may hasten on the path without knowing that one has missed the way.

[69a]     Confucius said, "Children are endowed with heavenly nature; their habits are spontaneous."[71] This means that habits formed in youth become like dispositions one is born with. What becomes ours after a long-time practice, be it good or evil, is arrived at naturally with no effort on our part. Our good and evil actions more often arise from habit than from inborn nature. Thus in our habits we ought to be cautious in choosing good or evil. What becomes habit is like what is natural from birth. To pursue learning is to adhere to the practice of the good. People who do evil are not only those who are born that way; there are many who become evil by falling into bad habits. Therefore Confucius said, "By nature human beings are nearly alike; by practice they become far apart."[72]

[69b]     What is the reason that some people are unfilial and disloyal, do various evil things, have selfish desires, and destroy themselves and their families? It is because they do not know better. Furthermore, what is the reason that people do good, raise a family, preserve their body, and earn praise? It is because they know. If they know, they clearly recognize good and evil. Realizing that they should do good, they practice it, and recognizing what they should not do, they do not

practice it. Knowledge is thus a great treasure. If scholars aim at the Way, they must first seek to know. Expanding one's knowledge will be difficult if one makes no effort at learning.

[69b]    Master Ch'eng said, "The fact that people do evil is due to a lack of knowledge."[73] This means that the reason people do evil is because they do not know the reason for not doing evil. If we knew something well, why would we make bad mistakes for ourselves or for others? That is to say, the fact that a child crawls and may fall into a well is not the child's fault. It is because children do not know yet that if they fall into the well they will die. That people do evil is like this and is much to be pitied. Therefore, endeavoring to learn the Way by studying and expanding our knowledge is of utmost importance for human beings.

[70a]    In learning we ought to be careful at the beginning about the technique we adopt. If the technique of learning is not correct in the beginning, once we make a mistake and fall into the wrong way, that mistake becomes a habit and it becomes difficult to change and return to the correct Way. We don't realize that we are led astray by our mistakes until the end of our life. On the contrary, we begin to dislike the correct Way and speak ill of it. Disobeying the Way of heaven and earth, and losing the Way of humans, for the rest of one's life one becomes, regrettably enough, confused and unenlightened. If we intend to study we should definitely adopt a method of learning by following enlightened teachers and good friends. This is being careful at the beginning. In the *I-wei* it says, "The gentleman exercises great care at the beginning. If there is the slightest deviation [at the outset] it becomes an error of a thousand miles in the end."[74] The first error may be small, but eventually it becomes an error of greater proportions. Should we not be careful, from the start, of what technique of learning we adopt?

[70a]    Even a lengthy journey begins with one step.[75] For example, in going to a distant place, if from the first step we are careful and continue without letting up, we will eventually arrive [at our destination]. Attaining the Way through study is the same. By fixing our aim, studying the Way, practicing earnestly and ceaselessly, year after year, will we not attain success and arrive at great heights? For example, it is like

shopowners who are careful with every cent and accumulate money; over the years they become very wealthy.

[70b]    There is the knowledge of seeing and hearing [observation] and there is true wisdom.[76] Knowledge of seeing and hearing is learned from reading books and from listening to people. This knowledge is shallow. True wisdom proceeds from the knowledge of seeing and hearing to a genuine understanding of the principle of the Way in our hearts. This knowledge is deep. The pursuit of learning proceeds first from the knowledge of seeing and hearing. If we do not read books or hear the Way, we have no way to attain true knowledge. But we will not know the Way if we stop at the learning of seeing and hearing and do not truly learn. If we really know [something], we will practice it well; if we know and do not practice, we still do not really understand it. Thus scholars should begin with the knowledge of seeing and hearing, and then they should seek true wisdom. They should not stop at learning by seeing and hearing.

[70b]    If we pursue learning by reading books, knowledge of seeing and hearing will increase daily. However, if we do not practice what we know, virtuous deeds will daily decline and will not increase. If we do not act, what we know is not true knowledge. Today's scholars greatly distort what is learning and what is practice because they do not "learn for their own sake."[77] Scholars should make sincere resolution their first priority and proceed through the knowledge of seeing and hearing to the practice of what they have learned, until they arrive at true knowledge.

[71a]    The Way to pursue learning is to empty the heart, be humble, pretending that we do not know what we actually know quite well, pretending that we do not do what we actually do very well, not boasting of our talents or actions, nor displaying our knowledge, questioning others, listening and using the criticisms of others, rectifying our faults, and returning to the good. If we act in this way, our pursuit of learning will bring results and our progress toward the good will know no bounds. If we are proud and consider ourselves right and others wrong, if we ignore the criticisms of others and dislike hearing about our faults, then as we advance in talent and in study our heart will become evil. Not only will our pursuit of learning yield no benefit, but on the contrary,

it will bring harm. If we do not learn for our own sake but only to impress others, we will become not a Noble Confucian but a petty one.[78] If this is the result, it is worse than not learning.

[71a]  In scholarship there is both useful and useless learning. Our Confucian studies are useful, which means that they are beneficial to ourselves and to others. For this reason, the Way of scholarship should be useful and not useless. Practical learning is cultivating oneself and sincerely practicing the Way of morality, and it especially lies in earnest loyalty and filiality and in helping people by doing good.

[71b]  Even poor people, if they only have the resolve to do good, encounter many instances where they can help people. How much more, then, do the rich and noble have the power to do good on a wide scale? Thus the learning of people of wealth and rank should not be simply concerned with their self-cultivation, but should, by taking a heart of humaneness and love as the basis, concentrate exclusively on helping others. All of this is useful learning. Even though we may speak of lofty things, favor correctness in our hearts, and do very difficult things, if we do not seek a heart of humaneness and righteousness, or if we fail to practice the Way of morality or do good things that are of benefit to others, then it is useless learning. Furthermore, composing prose or poetry, fretting needlessly, wasting a lot of time, cleverly showing off one's talents, seeking the praise of others, not being resolute in the way of daily morality—all of this is without benefit and in vain. It is useless learning.

[71b]  Yang Tzu said, "Learning is for the sake of becoming a Noble Person."[79] The meaning of this is that if one asks the purpose of learning, it is to become a Noble Person. A Noble Person is one who has virtue. The meaning of a Noble Person is described in *The Correct Meaning of the Book of Changes*[80] as "a person who possesses virtue [sufficient] to become the ruler of others and to treat all the people as though they were one's own children." Even though one be poor or of low rank, if one has that virtue one may be called a Noble Person. To become a Noble Person means to become fully human. A person who does not study is not worthy of being called a Noble Person. Even if a person studies, if he does not become a Noble Person, it is the same as if he did not study, and it is in vain that he was born a human. Becoming

a Noble Person is not easy. However, if we are resolute and not negligent we will inevitably have success. An old saying has it, "One who is resolute will finally succeed."[81] Learning goes on until death; as long as one breath still remains we must not neglect this goal. This is one's lifelong duty.

[72a]    Since, for the most part, people are not sages, they are bound to have a natural tendency to do evil. This is the bias of their psycho-physical disposition. Therefore there is nothing for it but to follow the Way of self-discipline, examining the bad points of our own dispositions, listening to the criticisms of others, and overcoming and reforming the bad habits toward which we are inclined. If we fail to do this and if we leave things to our natural dispositions, our heart will not be correct and we will not discipline ourselves. Although we may think that we love the Way and practice it by reading and studying, we may simply be activating the biases of our disposition. Thus it becomes a vain pursuit.

[72a]    The fact that the biases of our disposition may become a detriment is like having harmful weeds amidst a planted field. Even though we plant seedlings and give them water and fertilizer, if we do not pull up the weeds the seedlings will not grow. Cultivating with fertilizer and water benefits only the weeds and becomes fruitless. Therefore, recognizing and reforming the bad habits of our disposition ought to be the principal effort of people who pursue learning. Those who pursue learning must be constantly concerned about this.

[72b]    The evil deeds and mistakes of most people all arise from inclinations which they have from birth. Therefore, scholars must by all means reform their faults by transforming their physical dispositions. This is the essence of learning. People who are aware of the biased aspects of their temperament and know their own weak points are rare. We ought to detect and realize our mistakes through reflection. We should seek beneficial friends who will honestly tell us our faults, and we should draw to ourselves loyal retainers, and listen to and utilize their criticisms. It is like people who are playing *go* and cannot see the required move, while people who are observing from the side can clearly see it.

[72b]    A Noble Person has no predisposition to evil or bias and has no weaknesses. Because many people have weaknesses arising from a biased temperament, their faults are numerous

and they become sick. By getting rid of this sickness one becomes a Noble Person. We should not foster evil by leaving
the illness as it is. If we want to eliminate the sickness, we
should try to meet good friends and enlightened teachers
and receive their instructions in order to reform the bad aspects of our disposition. It is the same as when sick people
have a good doctor and have their ailments cured. If they do
not summon a doctor and do not drink medicine, it is difficult for them to become healthy. So it is with people having
weaknesses in their physical dispositions. If we do not seek
to remedy and get rid of the weaknesses in our physical dispositions by meeting with teachers and friends and admonishing ourselves, it will naturally be difficult to become a
Noble Person. To dislike friends who correct our faults and to
fend off the criticisms of retainers is the same as a patient
disliking doctors and refusing medicine, and not realizing
that he may even be so sick as to die. What a pity!

[73a]          An old maxim says: "There is no greater pleasure than
the reading of books. There is nothing more important then
the instructing of children."[82] Furthermore, an old Chinese
poem says, "The greatest pleasure in the world is to be at
one's desk throughout the day."[83] Even if one has neither
wealth nor rank, the pleasure of reading books is great. Even
without wine or sex, the pleasure [of reading] is deep. Even
though one is not in a mountain forest, reading gives a sense
of tranquility. Another old saying has it: "Even if we can read
only one volume, there is the benefit in that one volume; if
we can read books for even one day, there is that day's benefit to be gained."[84] And also, "There is nothing like reading
books for increasing the wisdom and knowledge of
peopie."[85] Those of wealth and high rank who are fond of
books derive extensive pleasure from them; similarly those
who are poor and of low rank who are fond of books derive
deep enjoyment from them. Further, in teaching children it is
good to establish one's aim. This is essential. Not to teach
children and not to inform them of the Way is to fail as a
father. We should say this is to be inhumane.

[73a]          Inquiring of people about one's doubts is the way to seek
wisdom. Reflecting on truth in our own hearts is a basis for
opening up wisdom. Questioning is seeking wisdom in others while reflecting is seeking wisdom in ourselves. If we do
not question people, what we know will be narrow, con-

fused, and unclear in our mind. If we do not think for ourselves, even though we observe widely, we cannot attain truth deeply in our heart. Therefore, the two acts of questioning and thinking are necessary for study as ways to thoroughly investigate principles and to clarify knowledge.

[73b]     People who are not resolved to pursue the Way are not worth mentioning, but even if they are resolved to pursue the Way and engage in broad study, if they do not study in the right way they will remain ignorant of the Way all their life. And even though they may like the Learning of the Way, they may be preoccupied with philology and fail to comprehend moral principles. We call this "exegetical study." These people think of themselves as studying the Learning of the Way and may even boast of this to others, but do not realize that it is [simply] "exegetical study." Furthermore, there are those who are enamored of the name of "Learning of the Way," yet lack its real substance. What we should love is the substance of the Learning of the Way. Simply to be enamored of the name "Learning of the Way" is dishonest and of no benefit. Moreover, there is a "learning" that dispenses with exegetical studies and neglects to follow the methods of the sages, but seeks only to learn from one's own mind-and-heart. This may be better than no learning at all, but it is not sagely learning. Even though it is transmitted from great teachers, it is our own exclusive learning. If we think to pursue true learning we should resolve to pursue the Way, revere virtue, take the teachings of Confucius and Mencius as our basis, and make the teachings of the Ch'eng brothers and Chu Hsi our guide. This is the lineage of true learning. In this degenerate age there are numerous bad methods of learning. We must make a choice and not let ourselves become confused.

[74a]     Scholars are often zealous in literary and philological pursuits, but rarely do they make an effort in the daily practice of virtue. This is to lose the true purpose of learning. Not to be diligent in the practice of virtue but to be enamored of literature is like throwing away the *sake* to get to the dregs. Not to take and use the good points is to prefer the bad points.

[74a]     Knowing the Way is very difficult. If we pursue the conventional learning of the world, even though we study diligently until the end of our life, the Way will be difficult to

learn. If we first love learning and have a sincere resolve, by following enlightened teachers and good friends, seeking out the path of ancient learning, and exerting our minds-and-hearts for a long time, we should succeed. People who speak cleverly, are proud of their own talents, and rely on their own knowledge are people who have a disposition that is far from the Way. To the end of their lives they will find it hard to learn the Way. However, a person with a disposition close to the Way is one who is simple by nature and without affectation, who, in the stillness of his mind-and-heart, recognizes moral principles, is humble and does not try to flatter himself. If he is single-minded in his resolve and studies hard, by the end of his life he will learn the Way.

[74b]     People often like the arts and do not like scholarship. The arts are, so to speak, the leaves and branches, while scholarship is the root and trunk of the tree. To fail to attend to the roots and instead to attend to the leaves and branches, to abandon what is essential while concentrating on the trivial, is folly. Since it is not the Learning of the Way, even though one takes up many arts, the foundation will not be there and it will not enable one to become a Noble Person. Yet, if one lacks the arts one will be unfamiliar with many things and will not derive benefit [from the arts] in the pursuit of virtue. Such a person is a country bumpkin.

[74b]     In youth we ought to take Confucianism as the base, be familiar with many books, and learn various useful arts. From the middle years one ought to give up encyclopedic reading and concentrate on the essence of the classics, become well-versed in the principles of the Way, and find the Way for oneself in one's own heart.

[74b]     Not yet knowing the Way is like having a dream without waking up. This is why the extension of knowledge in the *Great Learning* is called the gateway to awakening from dreams. It is the boundary between dreaming and awakening. When we are not sincere in liking the good, we cannot avoid being drawn into the world of evil people. Therefore, in the *Great Learning* "making the intentions sincere" is called the border [pass] between good and evil. It is the boundary between good and evil people. The border means the boundary between inner and outer.

[74b]     The sages represent the ultimate in human morality. For someone like myself to speak of this is presumptuous. However, from the outset, those who shoot arrows have a target,

and likewise people who take a trip have a specific aim. Taking the sages as our guide we must make the idea of establishing our goal a high priority. Even for a long journey there is the initial step of departure, and thus by first beginning with daily, familiar, humble places, gradually we reach a point where we climb to higher places. From the beginning, if we try to bypass the stages and go higher it is the same as trying to climb to heaven without wings. We certainly know that is impossible. For example, in climbing a high mountain our first step begins from the foot of the mountain; we cannot reach the mountaintop in a single bound. If all things did not follow an order, it would be difficult to achieve one's aim. A shortcut is pleasant to talk about, but without the principle of the Way we will not succeed, and so inane speech and useless explanations are pointless.

[75a]     Since we will not be reborn in this world, learning and enjoying the highest path of heaven, earth, and human is truly worthwhile, and even at the end of life we will have no regrets. I think it is extremely unfortunate to end our life without knowing the Way to be human, to suffer on account of our own desires, and to be confused by the base ways of the world. We must be careful.

[75b]     People who pass their days by reading the books of the sages and loving the Way will indeed be superior to most people and will have enjoyment throughout their life. They will, no doubt, live a memorable life. If this is the case, it will be worth having been born, for if one has heard of the Way in the morning, even if he dies in the evening, he will have no regrets.[86] To be poor and not blessed by good fortune is not a cause for gloom. If we do not study and do not know the Way of the sages our time in this world will be similar to that of birds or beasts and our life will be useless. After death we will decay just as grass and trees, we will not leave an honorable reputation, and there will be no one who will know us in the next generation. Is it not unfortunate that people are prone to make their lives similar to those of birds and beasts, grass and trees? If we think it is regretful, should we not avoid such mistakes? It is difficult to obtain a human body a second time, so we should not waste time in this world uselessly.

[75b]     Since there are people who try to pursue learning by reading books, those who dislike them say harmful things

and slander learning. There are many people who, thinking that what they say is true, give up the pursuit of learning. Furthermore, although we try to make our children read, people who dislike study try to intimidate them, saying, if you read you will become sick, your vital spirit will decrease, and your life will be shortened. Thus parents, out of a deep love for their children, thinking this is true, stop them from reading; these children will be illiterate their whole life and will end their lives being ignorant.

[76a]     People who do not read books dislike and detest people who do and speak ill of them, saying, "If people read their vital spirit will decrease, they will become sick, their mind will become stupid, and even those engaged in the Way of the samurai will become weak, like priests and courtiers." People who read, when they hear this, frequently argue angrily, and dispute these ideas, and their fighting becomes an example of this type of criticism. Common people are attracted to what is similar to themselves and they dislike what is different from themselves. Through their own ignorance they disparage what others know. This is the normal mentality of common people. Those who hear such mistaken views and dispute them angrily become just like ignorant people, and it is regrettable. Reading and studying is to avoid becoming like such uneducated people. Realizing that foolish people disparage learning and even attack us on account of their ignorance, we should pity and forgive them, but not make it a cause for anger. We should not make an issue of this, giving as our reason the fact that ignorant people say foolish things. The sages pitied such stubborn people and they did not get angry. It is good to have them as our model.

[76b]     The reason common people speak ill of learning is that even though scholars read books, they often fail to practice the Way. On the contrary, they praise themselves arrogantly and their hearts become evil by despising others, and there is no benefit to their learning. People who study the Way should be restrained and examine themselves. It is regrettable that, on the contrary, some people become petty individuals through reading.

[76b]     Boasting of their own talents, making themselves seem good and despising others, they do not utilize the talents of others but only make use of their own talents. There is an old saying: "If we rely on our own talents alone we will become

petty."[87] Those who utilize the wisdom of others are broad-minded, those who rely on their own wisdom alone are small-minded. Those who boast of their own scholarly ability and despise others only harm their own virtue for the sake of clever scholarship. Even greater than the sin of an ignorant person who violates the Way is the failing in virtue of one who, though he reads many books of the sages, has no resolve to pursue the Way. When scholars are like this, common people who dislike scholarship say that there is no benefit in learning and, on the contrary, it does much harm. This then becomes evidence that the pursuit of learning is harmful. We ought to be careful out of concern lest we too become evidence bearing out what common people say when they criticize learning.

[77a]     Scholars should practice the good with daily effort by making filiality and loyalty their highest priority and aiming at always liking the good and loving people. They should make reading books secondary. When they do not love the good first of all, even though they read books, they have no basis on which they can practice the Way, and although they may read thousands of volumes it is useless. By thoroughly experiencing the chapter in the *Great Learning* on making the intentions sincere, they should be genuine in disliking evil and loving the good.

[77a]     In fixing their resolve, scholars should take honesty as primary. They should strive to put into practice the Learning of the Way, and not simply love the name of Confucianism. Being worried about our own reputation is petty. Between heaven and earth there is no one with whom we are so familiar as ourself. If we pursue learning it should be for our self, not for the sake of our reputation. However, in both China and Japan, both in the past and in the present, there have been many people who coveted the name of the Learning of the Way. People who pursue the Way in order to enjoy its reputation have an appearance which resembles a good person, but there is little sincerity in their love of the good. Lacking rank or virtue, they make pretensions to high position and imitate the appearance of sages and wise men. They make a show by saying things which are inappropriate to their status. They do not know their own rank, they blame the past and present, they criticize the small mistakes of others and reproach the inabilities of people. They are even

more excessive in their cruelty than uneducated people, and their compassion toward others is almost nonexistent. They deserve to be called "inhumane."

[77b]     Without realizing that people and eras change, we try to apply the ancient rituals directly in the modern world. This is a lack of knowledge. If we do this, although we may startle the world and obtain a reputation for pursuing the Learning of the Way, it probably will be fruitless. If ignorant people look at such scholars, they think that Confucians are prejudiced in one direction, that they flout human feelings and the ordinary customs of the country, and that they are useless persons who do not understand the times. This is why the Learning of the Way is more and more abandoned. Ch'en Chi-ju of the Ming said, "Priests need to be truthful, they do not need to have a high position."[88] Confucian scholars are the same. Confucians should value honesty and be faithful to the Way. Those who lack sincerity, even though they are highly placed, should be scorned.

[77b]     The Confucian school of Japan has already passed through two millenia. Even though scholars have been few, since the days of the great peace continue, human culture is gradually developing. Because this is so, within one hundred years from now the study of letters will become skillful and the understanding of moral principles will be clear. We will become an enlightened nation and will truly attain the reputation of a country of Noble Persons. From here on we can only pray that the art of scholarship will be correct and not base, and that scholars with sincere resolve will revere and strongly believe in the Way of the sages.


CHAPTER III

## *THE ART OF THE MIND-AND-HEART,* PART 1

[78a]  The mind-and-heart is the master of the body and the root of all things. Thus, when it is not correct we cannot discipline ourself and it is difficult to regulate the family and govern the people. It is analogous to the roots of trees and plants not being firm, in which case the branches and leaves will not flourish; or to the master of a household not being virtuous, in which case the family can not be governed. The Way to rectify the mind-and-heart involves first loving the good and

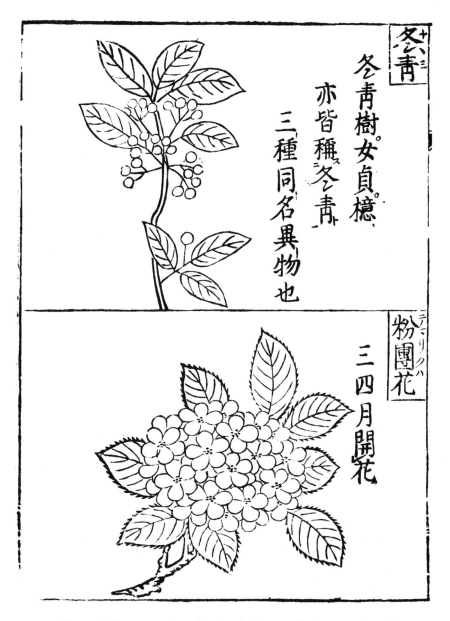

冬青

冬青樹女貞檜亦皆稱冬青三種同名異物也

粉團花

三四月開花

ABOVE: *Nanami*. There are three kinds of plants called *nanami* but they are each different. BELOW: *Temarika*. A Japanese snowball. A flower which opens in the third or fourth month.

disliking evil—this is the root of honesty. Without sincerely loving the good and disliking evil, we can not avoid the world of evil people, and thus we will not have a method to rectify the mind-and-heart.

[78a]     In the Way of the *Great Learning*, if we want to rectify the mind-and-heart, we must first make our will sincere. If we are already sincere in loving good and disliking evil, rectifying the mind-and-heart should be easy. Rectification means that the seven emotions of happiness, anger, sadness, enjoyment, love, hate, and desire which arise in the mind-and-heart are in correct measure with neither excess nor deficiency. This means being happy when we should be happy, but not being excessive in that happiness; being angry when we should be angry, but not being excessive in anger. Other emotions should also be expressed in a similar manner. If the seven emotions are balanced with neither excess nor deficiency, we will not be swayed within the heart and there will always be harmony. This is rectifying the mind-and-heart.

[78b]     In the *Book of History* it is written: "The human mind is precarious, the Way mind is barely perceptible. Having utmost refinement and singleness of mind we should hold fast to the Mean."[89] When the illustrious ancient sage Emperor Shun passed on the reign to the sage King Yü, he transmitted this method of the mind-and-heart for ruling the kingdom. The human mind refers to [that which is aroused by virtue of] the physical form of the senses responding to what they desire. The preferences of physical forms means liking things by their physical appearance; for example, enjoying color with the eyes, sound with the ears, taste with the mouth, and comfort with the body. Moreover, the seven emotions of happiness, anger, sadness, enjoyment, love, hatred, and desire arise in the human mind-and-heart heart due to physical forms. Liking to eat when we are hungry, seeking clothes when we are cold, or resting the body when we are tired—in this way the seven emotions must all be called human emotions, and even the sage has a human mind.

[78b]     However, if humans allow the preferences of the senses to have their way and, if they let the seven emotions run rampant, they will forget what is appropriate, and soon they will follow their own desires and fall into wicked ways. This is the reason the human mind was said to be "precarious."

"Precarious" is like a child being near fire or like a drunken person about to fall into a moat. Moral sense is the mind of the Way which arises from one's innate nature of humaneness, righteousness, decorum, and wisdom. "The Way mind is barely perceptible" means that it is diminished and neglected. Since the human mind originates from physical form, it moves and is expressed externally, and that energy flourishes easily. The Way mind is hidden in the depths of the heart, and being faint, it has difficulty manifesting itself. Therefore, it is called "barely perceptible." The human mind prospers easily; the Way mind is easily hidden. Since the two of them coexist in one's breast, if we do not know how to control them, the human mind becomes even more precarious and is carried away by human desires; the Way mind becomes increasingly imperceptible and finally is overwhelmed by the human mind and dies. We must have a way to control the human mind and preserve the Way mind. "Utmost refinement" means that by distinguishing between the human mind and the Way mind, we will know [the difference] clearly and in detail. "Singleness of mind" means if we have already distinguished the Way mind and the human mind by making the Way mind primary, we should not let the unreliable side of the human mind have its way. When one does this, the actions of a unified mind will emerge from the mind of the Way and the human mind will follow the commands of the Way mind. "Hold fast to the Mean" implies that the actions of the human mind and the workings of the senses and the seven emotions are neither excessive nor deficient. This is indeed the principle of the Way and should be our objective. "Utmost refinement" and "singleness of mind" means in everything we do having neither excess nor deficiency, but conforming exactly to the Mean. If we take eating and drinking as an example, it is the human mind which likes food and drink. The mind of the Way realizes that we should not be excessive in food and drink. When we allow our preference for food and drink to have its way, we immediately lose a dignified manner and harm our digestive organs. This is the unreliability of the human mind.

[79b]     Even though we have a Way mind which is concerned that such excess may harm the body, when the human mind flourishes the cautious mind naturally becomes weak and barely perceptible. This is the Way mind becoming faint. If

we rely in this manner on a mind that loves food and drink, and if our cautious mind becomes faint, immediately our self-ish desires for food and drink become excessive, our cautious mind disappears, and finally we cannot control our desires. However, refinement is not vacillating but knowing clearly the selfishness of the human mind and the reverent control of the Way mind. If we realize that there is harm in excessive eating and drinking and that there is benefit in moderation, by principally having reverent control and making the Way mind the master, by restraining the desires and greed of the human mind, we will then naturally be without excess or de-ficiency. In conclusion, "The human mind is precarious and the Way mind is barely perceptible" refers to two aspects of the human mind and Way mind, respectively. "Utmost re-finement" and "singleness of mind" are methods of making the Way mind the master through clarification. "Hold fast to the Mean" implies that centrality, with neither excess nor de-ficiency, is the highest principle of the Way. Having the method of "utmost refinement" and "singleness of mind" is not losing the principle of the Way, which implies not being excessive or deficient. This is the important method of the mind-and-heart which the great sage-kings transmitted when they transferred the reign, and thus it is the highest truth. These sixteen characters are the origin of the learning of the mind-and-heart for all generations. From the king and nobles down to the common people, all should revere it, understand it well, and take it to heart.

[80a]     There is no limit to heaven's compassion and kindness toward humans. Heaven and earth produce and give to hu-man beings various things to cultivate life such as food, clothing, shelter, and utensils. All human beings take and use these and nourish themselves. Among all people, both high and low, there is no one who cannot receive these bless-ings. There is nothing to which we can compare the extent of our debt, even to the [expanse of] the seas or mountains, and so we can not express it in words. Furthermore, we can save life by creating medicine. Materials in this world which help and nourish humans are plentiful and without limit. All of this is the rich blessing of heaven and earth for humans. Na-ture's nourishment for birds and beasts does not amount to even a fraction of its nourishment for human beings. In addi-tion, animals and birds are killed and used for food by hu-

mans, and bushes and trees are cut and used by them. Thus, humans are more valued than all other things, and from this we should realize how richly blessed by nature we are. Foolish people do not recognize this and do not practice ordinary goodness even though they receive the kindness of nature. They do not carry out the Way which would repay their debt and serve heaven and earth. How much more negligent is it to be unfilial and harm people and things which nature has created and nourished, disturbing the life principle, wasting the things of nature, and violating the heart of heaven and earth. This can be called being unfilial and not recognizing our obligation to nature and losing the human Way. We must be in awe of the heavenly Way.

[80b]       Human beings at the very least should not disobey the Way of heaven and earth or harm things which nature created, even if they are foolish like myself and do not have the ability to repay a fraction of the great obligation to nature. The sages knew the heavenly Way was before them and they respected the Way from morning until night and did not violate it. People today should also do this. In the *Book of Poetry* it says, "Revere the majesty of heaven and preserve its favor."[90] Scholars should always honor the heavenly Way in their hearts. The human Way should definitely be like this.

[81a]       If we have even one selfish desire or evil thought we should quickly banish it by continual self-reflection. Selfish desires means greed for fame, profit, lust, or possessions; these are the pleasures of the senses which are the selfish desires of the body. Evil thoughts means oppressing people, arguing angrily with them, boasting about ourselves, criticizing or slandering others, and flattering or deceiving others. All of these involve an evil heart. If we have these tendencies even in the slightest, it is good to remove them quickly, because the harm to our heart will be great. If we have a biased disposition we must overcome it. A biased disposition is the partiality with which we are born. This means a rough and boisterous nature, or an excessively soft and weak nature, or an extremely dull nature, or a greedy and angry nature. These are all the biases of the physical disposition, and they are harmful to one's mind-and-heart. It is very difficult to change the evil parts of a disposition. We must subdue them by always being careful, and moreover, if we have faults we must change them quickly. Having faults does not mean do-

ing evil on purpose; it means that without knowing good and evil we violate the principle of the Way. Our faults are numerous due to our biased dispositions and the obstructions of selfish desires. Since we are not sages, everyone has numerous faults. If we know our faults, we should be willing immediately to reform and return to the good. Being unwilling means that we are reluctant to give up our faults and we cannot change.

[81b]     There are three obstructions to the art of the mind-and-heart: 1) selfish desires and evil thoughts; 2) a biased disposition; and 3) faults. Even if we rectify the heart and practice the Way, when we have these failings and cannot banish them, we will not progress in virtue. For example, when in cultivating a field we cannot get rid of the weeds, even though we add water and fertilizer, the weeds will flourish and the seedlings will not benefit. We should pull up the weeds first and then use water and fertilizer in the same way that, after sickness in the body is cured, we supplement our diet.

[81b]     In mingling with people, we take love and respect as the method of the mind-and-heart. This is extremely important and everyone should know it. Love is having compassion for people and not despising them. Respect is honoring people and not looking down on them. Compassion for people is humaneness; respect for people is decorum. In preserving humaneness and decorum within the heart we must respect and sympathize with people. This is goodness, which we ought to practice toward others. We need not speak of love toward parents and respect toward one's lord [which is a natural thing]; we should also have a similar love and respect toward people whom we do not know, and toward lowly people we should show proper respect according to distinctions. We should not look down on people. This is the way to associate with people.

[82a]     In the human heart at times one's conscience becomes aroused due to one's having a nature of humaneness, righteousness, decorum, and wisdom. We should extend the exercise of conscience and not let it become frustrated. Extending it means not allowing what arises from one's moral sense to be deflected in the slightest but fostering and nourishing it, making it flourish, fulfilling it according to one's capacity, and extending it wherever one goes. "It is like

the flow of water that comes if one does not let it become stopped up at the beginning, or like a fire that warms up if one does not let the initial flame become extinguished. If conscience is extended it is more than enough to rule the wide world; if we do not extend it, we cannot serve even our parents close at hand."[91] This is the teaching of Mencius, and it is an especially important teaching. Scholars definitely must take this to heart and practice it earnestly.

[82a]      Humaneness is the moral sense which is compassionate toward people and nurtures things. This is the human heart that receives the blessings of heaven and earth. Therefore, Mencius said, "Humaneness is the heart of humans."[92] It is the original heart which is born to each person. The Noble Person does not lose his original heart but has a heart which loves others as much as himself and does not separate himself from others. The petty person loves only himself and does not love others; the separation between himself and others is deep. This is because he has selfish desires. This is called being inhumane. Human beings should have a heart of humaneness. A person who lacks this loses his original heart, destroys the human Way, and violates the Way of heaven. For this reason we should reprove a lack of humaneness more than anything else. Because it is something abhorrent to heaven, earth, and human beings, it is an evil which eventually results in heaven's punishment. Moreover, even our descendants will have this retribution. We must stand in awe of the heavenly Way. There are many instances of this truth in the past and present, in China and Japan; and, there being no instances to the contrary, we should have no doubts about it.

[82b]      In the *Book of Changes* it says, "To be life-giving is the great virtue of heaven and earth."[93] We should learn and experience this principle thoroughly. "Life-giving" means living and not dying, not killing but being ceaselessly fecund. Therefore, heaven and earth are the parents who give birth and growth to all things. In having compassion we love letting things live and we dislike killing things. This is the great virtue of heaven and earth and it is the principle of life. Because the human is the child of the universe, the great virtue of heaven and earth and the principle of life is replete in our hearts, and we are born with a heart filled with the blessings of nature. This is humaneness. Humaneness is a heart which

loves and sympathizes with others; in other words, it is a
heart which gives life to the things of heaven and earth. All
things are created by heaven and earth and among these humanity is especially blessed by heaven and earth; among all
things it is particularly valued and thus regarded as a child of
heaven and earth. Because of this we must be especially
warm in human relations, obeying the heart of nature and
loving things with a humane heart. Having warm relations is
following the heart of nature. Even for loving humanity there
is an order. The root of the practice of humaneness is, first,
loving parents and brothers and sisters. The lord is equal to
parents. Next, we should love relatives, retainers, and
friends, and all other people. Then we should love and not
wantonly kill birds, beasts, insects, and fish. Finally, we
should love and not recklessly cut down grass and trees. This
is the order of showing compassion toward people and living
things. However, killing wicked people is righteous and may
be sanctioned by humaneness. Moreover, cutting trees in an
appropriate time, or killing animals for a reason, is righteous. Whether it is birds, beasts, vegetation, or trees, killing
or cutting them carelessly is a lack of humaneness.

[83a]      "The humane person forms one body with all things."[94]
Thus we must, of course, love humanity but we should also
love all things. Even Confucius said, "Cutting one tree, killing one animal, if it is not at an appropriate time, is a lack of
filiality."[95] Thus even birds and animals, grasses and trees,
are all made by nature—if we damage them recklessly, we
should realize that it is a lack of filiality toward nature. In
order for people to love things they ought to extend [this fil-
iality] from intimate things to distant things, from things that
weigh heavily on one to things with less claim on us. To
make no distinction between light and heavy claims, intimate
obligations and more remote ones—in short, to love indiscriminately —is not righteousness. Mo Tzu called it universal
love.[96] Loving all people equally is the same as going off and
leaving one's parents. This is not knowing the Way of humaneness, and it is not being in accord with righteousness.

[83b]      As children of heaven and earth, human beings must
take heaven and earth as the model for their conduct; heaven
and earth have nothing else at heart than to be sympathetic
to all things. They have no other purpose or function than to
bring forth and nourish all things. Humans also receive this

heart and should always aspire to have a heart which is sympathetic and kind to others. They have no other function than to help others. Thus there are good deeds which should be performed daily by all people from the king and nobility down to the common people, each being in a position to do what is proper to his station in life. One should never be idle, but always be engaged in timely action. This is to serve heaven by endeavoring to do heaven's work.

[83b]     A humane person loves others; there is no separation between himself and others. Not loving others and simply loving ourselves is separating ourselves from others; this is selfish. A person of humaneness is not selfish; he loves others as he loves himself; "what he does not wish done to himself he does not do to others"[97]; "seeking to establish himself he also seeks to establish others."[98] To forget the distinction between self and others is to be impartial. To be impartial is to be unselfish.

[84a]     The heart of a humane person does this effortlessly and naturally, but scholars who have still not attained humaneness need to make an effort in the practice of humaneness. If we infer from our own hearts what the hearts of others feel, their hearts are seen to be no different from our own. What we ourselves like other people will like, and what we dislike others will also dislike. If we practice humaneness toward others, first by imagining the heart of others through our own heart, then what we wish for ourselves, we will do to others and what we do not wish for ourselves we will not do to others. When we do this it will not be displeasing to others and people will be put at ease in their respective circumstances. This is the practice of humaneness. This is called "Inferring from ourselves and extending it to others."[99] This is reciprocity. Reciprocity is a method of extending humaneness toward others. Humaneness is loving people naturally without effort; reciprocity is making an effort to practice humaneness. This is the difference between humaneness and reciprocity. The sages spoke of reciprocity as being a Way which one should strive to practice until the end of one's life.

[84a]     Human beings ought to obey the heart of heaven and earth, and act by making their heart one of humaneness and love. Loving others as one loves oneself is humaneness, and this is the heart of humans. Animals know only that they love themselves, and they cannot love things. If people lack

humaneness, and only love themselves but do not love others, in what respect would they be different from birds and beasts? When we lack humaneness we lose the human heart, and when that happens, even if we have other talents they will not be worth noticing.

[84b]     Humility is being modest and not arrogant toward others. When we have humility we do not boast about ourselves, we are modest, we like to inquire of others, we listen to the admonishments of others and reform our own faults. Consequently, there is no limit to our opening up of knowledge and moving toward the good. It was for this reason that the ancients regarded humility as the most beautiful virtue under heaven. The opposite of humility is pride, which is boasting about ourselves. This is being vain. If we boast, we will be self-righteous and we will not inquire of others. If we are like this there will be no limit to our moving toward evil. Therefore, the ancients think pride is an evil thing. I have spoken before of the good of humility and the evil of pride; however, I am repeating it for the sake of people who are just beginning to study.

[84b]     The character for reverence (*kei*) has a Japanese reading, *tsutsushimu*. This means taking admonitions to heart. *Tsutsushimu* is from the Japanese word *tsutsumu* [meaning "enwrap"] and the syllable *shi* does not change the meaning. Having reverent mindfulness within is not allowing anything to emerge carelessly. If we have reverent mindfulness we will preserve our original heart and not lose it. Practice is conforming to principles and not making mistakes. Thus reverence preserves a unified heart and is the root of all good. Therefore, if we have reverent mindfulness we will discipline ourselves, but if this is lacking there will be confusion. We must have reverent mindfulness in all things. All good is actualized by mindfulness and all evil arises from its absence. Therefore, the five virtues are established with this and the Way of the five relations are practiced with this. For this reason, the learning of the sages makes reverence essential, and from beginning to end it makes this its touchstone. The learning of the mind-and-heart of the sages and worthies in past and present takes the one character of reverence as its essence. People who study the Way ought to make the greatest effort. If they are completely mindful, they will have good fortune; if they are not, they will have misfortune. Po Chü-i

said, "Good fortune or misfortune depends on whether or not one is mindful."[100] Our misfortunes are due to not having mindfulness. Therefore, he said that mindfulness overcomes misfortune.

[85a]     An old maxim observes that people are not sages, "Everyone has faults. We should rectify our faults well. There is no greater good than this."[101] Master Ch'eng also said, "The Way of learning has no other path; if we know that something is evil we should quickly reform and follow the good."[102] "Evil" means our faults. Knowing one's faults and changing them is the essence of study. However, there are few people who know their own faults. Ordinary people do not know their own faults and mistakes. If we do not know many other things it is not such a great concern, but not knowing our faults or mistakes is definitely foolish. Is there anything more regrettable than this? It is good to learn our faults by examining ourselves and listening to other's criticisms.

[85b]     We should be mindful about things which we like. When one does not restrain one's preferences, it undermines one's resolve to pursue the Way, squanders resources and wastes time. Therefore, an excessive fondness for something may become the cause of misfortune. To cite the most serious cases, if we do not restrain our liking for food and drink, sexual desires, and wealth and profit, we will suffer a loss of virtue and eventually even our lives. In other things of which we are [excessively] fond, it will be the same. So generally it is good to restrict the number of things that we like. Even though our desires may be small, if they deepen and become extreme they become evil. The ancients said, "By looking at what people are fond of, we can tell what is good and bad about those people."[103] We should be restrained in what we indulge in.

[85b]     Fang Hsiao-ju said, "Pleasures not yet enjoyed but anxiously longed for become selfish human desires."[104] Is this not true? When we are greedy and wish to enjoy food, drink, and sensual pleasures, even before the enjoyment has been satisfied, these faults and anxieties may emerge and we may harm ourselves with food and drink and sensual desires. This all arises from human desires. The method of reducing desires is controlling them and not thoroughly indulging ourselves. We should not satiate ourselves with what we like.

If we are more than half satisfied we should stop. When the desires are completely satisfied, misfortune will definitely arise, and although we have regrets afterward, it is of no use. It is like an old expression, "*Sake* should be drunk until one is half intoxicated and flowers should be seen half opened."[105] In *Shan-yu wen* it says, "If we are excessive in temporal pleasures even once, we will inevitably have misfortune."[106]

[86a]    Those who rule the people, since they are the parents of the people, ought to take as their basis a heart which is sympathetic toward the people. Taking the people's heart as their own, they enjoy providing what the people like, and dislike imposing what the people dislike. They are the parents of the people since they regard the people as their children. Those who stand over the populace know that they have received a mission from heaven to nourish the people; they obey the heavenly Way and do not allow the people to suffer. Indulging in one's own pleasures and allowing many people to suffer goes against the heart of the heavenly Way.

[86a]    We ought to revere the Way of heaven. All people both high and low are the same and so the enjoyment and the suffering of people is the same as our own. We should be compassionate by correctly inferring the heart of others through our own heart and by thinking of the suffering and anxieties of others. A person who lacks humaneness does not have compassion for the people. He says, "I do not have sympathy for the people because, if I love the people, they will be arrogant and will not respect their superiors." These are the words of a person who is inhumane. All people have an obedient heavenly nature. If the rulers love the people with sincerity, the people will definitely sense that and be happy. They will not have resentment and will serve the rulers with sincerity. When there is deceit and lack of humaneness from the rulers, the people will also certainly be deceitful. The principle of this mutual response has not changed in Japan or China in past or present. We cannot doubt it. If the rulers love the people and in addition make the laws strict and forbid the mistaken practices of the people, there will not be contempt or arrogance toward the rulers.

[86b]    The rulers should not indulge in their own pleasures, but ought to share their enjoyment with the people.[107] This is

true enjoyment. There is a principle which says that all people, both high and low born, are brothers and sisters.[108] Knowing that we have one origin and imagining the heart of others through our own heart, we must not cause anxiety and suffering to others. With our own energies, we ought to help the poor and the hungry, the sick and the disabled, the widowed and orphaned and childless who are suffering and anxious, being unable to earn a living. Widowed, orphaned, and childless refer to the following: those who are old and without wives are widowers; those who are old and without husbands are widows; those who are young and without parents are orphans; those who are old and without children are childless. These four are the distressed people of the world. They are people who are hungry and cold, and cannot depend on receiving the kindness of others. We must be very compassionate. The government of the sages of old first quickly gave assistance to these distressed people. Indeed, we should not cause suffering for many people by loving ourselves and not loving others. We must be aware not to harm or obstruct others even in small ways. We must think of others, stand by them, and relieve their sufferings and anxieties. We must not be negligent.

[87a]     Even low-ranking people, if they have the financial resources and are able to give, should help relieve poverty according to their means and compassionately assist suffering people who have no one to rely on, such as the widowed, orphaned, and childless. We must not be stingy with financial resources. Next we must extend this compassion to animals, insects, fish, plants, and trees. This is not because of their being our brothers amidst heaven and earth, but since they are born within heaven and earth as we are, and share the same material force, we should remember this and thus not harm them carelessly. However, this should not include animals which are harmful to humans.

[87a]     All of this is the method of practicing humaneness. If a person is a lowly rustic peasant, it is difficult to help others. However, even poor, lowly people should give to others as much assistance as possible each day by simply having a humane loving heart, and using effort and care. Thus even lowly people should earnestly try to practice humaneness. This is the way to serve heaven and earth by receiving and following the heart of the universe.

[87b]        Hidden virtue is doing good and not seeking to be
known by people. It is secretly preserving humaneness and
love in one's heart and acting it out. The ancients said, "Hidden virtue is just like the echo in one's ear; it is known to
oneself but not known to others."[109] In order to have compassion and kindness toward others, grieving with their sorrows
and rejoicing in their happiness, we should give priority to
the widowed, orphaned, and childless, bring relief to the
hungry, give clothes to those who are cold, help the tired
and sick, repair roads and bridges, eliminate things which
harm people, and do things which benefit them—making
peace among people; praising their goodness; concealing
their faults; overlooking their small mistakes; developing and
utilizing their talents; not being angry at people indiscriminately; not having resentment against them; stopping the angry disputes of others; not slandering people even slightly;
not despising, depriving, or hindering others; fostering their
virtue; reproving their errors; not injuring birds, animals, insects, or fish; not killing recklessly; not cutting plants and
trees wantonly. All this is hidden virtue.

[88a]        Hidden virtue is not known by others; yet it accords with
the heavenly Way. Consequently, we will surely be happy afterward and will be able to bring prosperity to our descendants. Therefore, if we seek happiness there is no prayer
which can do better than this. The principle by which the
heavenly Way bestows happiness in return for goodness, and
evil for evil, is self-evident in past and present, in China
and Japan. However, generally people do not know this, and
without loving the good, they do evil; they seek happiness
through mistaken things and they pray obsequiously at the
shrine of a deity whom they should not worship. If we do
not have the ability to reflect on the past, we should at least
try to reflect broadly on the present time and recent past,
learning from this that there is benefit in doing good and no
benefit in reckless flattery toward other people and toward
the gods. However, the heart of a Noble Person does not
practice hidden virtue in order to seek rewards. If we practice
hidden virtue without seeking rewards, blessings will be
there within.

[88a]        Clarity of foresight is knowing clearly beforehand things
that are in the future. This is what intelligent people can do
and we should respect it. A foolish person like myself, with-

out clarity of foresight, is apt to make many mistakes and have many regrets. Although I am foolish, if I reflect well with a quiet heart, these worries will diminish. If we want to have fewer regrets, we should reflect constantly and not abandon ourselves to the enjoyment of things. [Otherwise,] wants will increase and our mistakes and regrets will multiply.

[88b]     Once it was said, "There is no greater misfortune than acting on our desires selfishly. There is no greater evil than finding fault with others."[110] These are both ways which not only do harm to moral principles but also lead to self-destruction. We must constantly bear this in mind.

[88b]     The everyday method of the mind-and-heart is to be honest and not deceitful. In the *Doctrine of the Mean* it says, "Sincerity is the Way of heaven. The attainment of sincerity is the Way of humans."[111] "Sincerity is the Way of heaven" refers to the action of the yin and yang, the circulation of sun and moon, the orderly procession of the seasons; and this has not changed in past or present. Grass and trees are planted in the spring, grow large in the summer, bear fruit in the fall, and lie dormant in the winter. Without change each year, all of this is the sincerity of the heavenly Way. "The attainment of sincerity" means that by our own effort we endeavor to become sincere. Since humans are children of heaven and earth, we must act by taking and following the sincerity of the heavenly Way as a model. Thus it is said [in the *Doctrine of the Mean*], "The attainment of sincerity is the Way of humans." Confucius also said, "Make loyalty and faithfulness the master."[112] This means that we ought to make sincerity the lord of the human heart. Being true, in other words, is having sincerity. While Confucius did not say "sincerity" in this case, he used the term "being true." Not having deceit in the heart is being true and not being false in word or deed is faithfulness. Sincerity refers to the naturalness of the heavenly Way. Being true refers to the sincerity which is to be diligently practiced by humans.

[89a]     Principle is one, but there is a distinction between acting naturally and making an effort. Master Ch'eng said, "The human Way is simply loyalty and faithfulness[113]; if we do not have sincerity we do not have anything."[114] If in serving one's lord or parent there is no sincerity, there is no loyalty or filiality. If in all our actions there is no sincerity, no matter

how many good deeds we do, because we are not sincere, they are not true deeds. Even if we act diligently there will be harm every time and our actions will be meaningless. If we earnestly do good deeds, we should act with authenticity and not for the sake of fame or profit. This is true goodness.

[89a]     Our words and actions must not be two-faced. Even if we do many good deeds, if we lack sincerity it is like trying to contain treasures in a bottomless vessel. Yoshida Kenkō said, "Even though it not be genuine, if one studies to be a worthy he should be called a worthy."[115] These words are very harmful to learning. The human Way is simply loyalty and trustworthiness. Once there is any deception, it is not worth looking at the rest. If one is deceitful in studying wisdom we call him a petty person. How can we call him a worthy? Wang Mang of the Han and Wang Ching-kung [Wang Anshih] of the Sung[116] were deceitful and yet studied to be worthies. Thus, initially they obtained the distinction of [being called] a "Noble Person" but eventually they usurped the kingdom and caused havoc. Can we call this being a worthy? The Way of the Noble Person is pure and not sullied. We must not harbor false thoughts within. Even if we practice good outwardly, if we don't have inner authenticity, it is not the Way of the Noble Person. For this reason, in cultivating oneself we ought to practice only the Way of sincerity. If we are speaking for ordinary people, whether their practice is sincere or insincere, it will require the same effort, so we might as well be sincere in all things. Although practicing the good disingenuously is better than clearly doing evil, nonetheless, it is not sincerity. Consequently, disobeying the Way of heaven and the Way of humanity is a grave sin. When we are sincere we can move heaven and earth, we can reach the gods and spirits, and we can know the human heart.

[89b]     That even one evil thought about others inevitably reaches heaven is a general principle. There is a saying, "Heaven is in a high place but hears the lowly."[117] We should not deceive heaven; we should revere it. If we mislead people, in the end this duplicity will be apparent. "If we are inwardly sincere it will surely be outwardly apparent."[118] We should not cheat others; we ought to feel shame. Deceiving heaven and other people is because we deceive ourselves. If we know the evil in our own heart and act on it, it is self-deception. We should not mislead our own heart. We should

not deceive heaven, others, or ourselves; we
sincere. In this way, the heart of the Noble J
like a clear sky on a bright day. The heart of a ɾ
always cloudy and difficult to understand clearly.

[90a]     In the *Book of Changes* it says, "Restrain anger and contain
the desires."[119] Restraining anger is controlling it. Anger is
affiliated with yang; it is like a fire burning things. Being easily angered is harmful to others and injures the virtue in our
own heart. When one is angry we should first try to forget
the anger, calm our mind-and-heart, and then consider what
is right and wrong. Moreover, we should not discuss something when we are angry. When we are upset and try to
speak, we will certainly make mistakes, and afterward we
will have many regrets. We should be silent and have reverent self-control. If someone does something wrong in word
or deed we should not be angry but we should gradually balance our spirit, make our mind-and-heart gentle, and discuss
the issue of right and wrong in detail. Even if people do not
obey us we must not be swayed by anger or make our spirit
violent. When the heart is not calm or gentle, even if it seems
reasonable, it is incorrect. Thus if we are swayed by anger, it
goes without saying that our behavior will be irrational.

[90a]     Desire is not only coveting material goods. It is also doing as we please by liking and being absorbed in fame and
profit, food and drink, sexual indulgence, lewd music, material things, drinking bouts, or selfish pleasures. Stopping
these obsessions means that when an avaricious thought
arises we can quickly control our desires. If our desires are
already flourishing, the heart will be confused and it will be
difficult to restrain. When desires first occur, if we stop them
quickly by using a little effort, the end result will be significant. Desires are affiliated with yin, and it is easy to drown
in them just as water drowns a person. Many evils are frequently generated from anger and desire. Among the seven
emotions these two are the most harmful. We may harm ourselves and others and should thus be careful. Furthermore,
anger and desire do great harm to our practice of caring for
our health.

[90b]     The seven emotions are all human feelings, and so to be
without them is not appropriate. Moderation without going
too far or falling short is the Mean. To go to excess is the
most harmful, but to fall short is also contrary to reason.

Having compassion toward people is truly good. However, being excessive in our love for our wife, child, or concubine, saying it is because they please us and giving them favors to the utmost, is not a love which emerges from the Way. This is the extreme tendency of a selfish heart. When we drown a person in love, we will not know the dark side of that person; when we love someone too much, that person will surely be arrogant and will violate the Way. Thus, it will become the downfall of that person and our own downfall as well.

[90b]     Being angry when we should be angry is a way to admonish people's vices. But if we are angry when we should not be angry, or if we are excessively angry when we are justified in being angry, we will injure ourselves and others.[120] When we are excessive against things we dislike we cannot know or use the good in others; when we admonish the small faults of others to an extreme degree they will be hurt and resentful. All our emotions have excesses. Yet if we are not compassionate when we should be compassionate, it is a lack of humaneness. This is the greatest evil.

[91a]     Not being sad when we should be sad, and not enjoying when we should enjoy, can be said to be unfeeling. This is being deficient in emotion. Even when the seven emotions arise we should have neither excess nor deficiency but should stop at what is right and proper. The ancients said, "When we are aroused by emotions we should stop at what is right and proper."[121] Truth is a path which attains the Mean without excess or deficiency, and it is the highest good. Even if we have only one thing to eat, when we are moderate without excess or deficiency, it will nourish the body. This is the Mean; it is the Way. When we eat too much we damage our stomach, and when it is not enough our nourishment is insufficient. This is not the Mean.

[91a]     There is an old expression: "When a person's blood does not circulate he will be sick; if a person's mind does not function he will be ignorant."[122] Saying "the mind functions" means reflecting carefully according to circumstances. It is exercising the mind. It is like the saying in *Mencius*, "The work of the mind is thinking."[123] Without reflection the mind does not function; we will not know right from wrong and will be ignorant. If we think carefully and activate the mind according to circumstances, we will distinguish right from

wrong and will not become foolish. A foolish person does not clearly distinguish good and evil because he does not reflect.

[91b]    We must make a great effort to control our desires. Control is restraint. If scholars try to control their desires without making a real effort, their learning will be worthless. This can be called a lack of effort. They should especially use their lifelong learning capacities.

[91b]    We must take these teachings as basic when we try to correct the mistakes of children and servants. We should not correct them in a spirit of anger. When we act calmly we gain the trust of the children or servants and they become obedient without resentment. It is a useful method for admonishing children and servants.

[91b]    The Chinese character for wisdom is read *satoru* in Japanese. It means the illumination of the heart. If the heart is bright and not cloudy we will clearly penetrate all truths, we will not vacillate in distinguishing right and wrong and good and evil. For example, it is like a bright light which fully illumines things. If we do not have wisdom, even though we love the good, we will vacillate and will not know the way we ought to follow, and our mistakes will be numerous. Moreover, without knowledge we will not know others. If we take to being a petty person and give up being a Noble Person, our misfortunes will be numerous. If we have wisdom, by carefully distinguishing the rightness and wrongness of truth, we will preserve ourself without acting unjustly. By clearly discerning the good and bad points of people, we will get close to the Noble Person and avoid the petty person. In disciplining oneself so as to govern others, one brings benefit and not harm. Hence, wisdom is a great treasure for oneself and for others. To be wise is to be clear in mind-and-heart. When these are clear we can fully perceive the good and evil of others. In the *Analects* it says, "Fan Ch'ih asked about knowledge and Confucius said, 'Know people'."[124] This means that knowing people is having clarity of perception.

[92a]    An ordinary disposition should be quietly and calmly peaceful. It should not be rash or restless. A peaceful harmony reflects the workings of heaven which is innate in the human heart. We must be always mindful of the workings of heaven. Moreover, we should not worry or lose contentment by thinking of unprofitable things. This is foolish. Easily con-

trolling what is premature within the heart and also admonishing laziness, always pacifying the heart, not being quick or
slow but just right—this is the method for governing the
mind-and-heart.

[92a]          The mind-and-heart is the master of the body. Since it is
the basis of everything, we must always be quiet and peaceful and not move carelessly. If the mind moves carelessly it
will be confused and unclear; responding to the myriad affairs of life, it will make many mistakes. When we are busy
our limbs move; when we speak, if we are not quick we will
be too late. Thus our mind should not be too busy. Our
senses and our limbs should be like servants. The mind is the
master of the body, and it has the role of correcting the good
and evil of the senses and limbs. Therefore, if the mind is not
calm we cannot reflect. In order to do something without being remiss, being relaxed, and not hurrying recklessly, we
should act by distinguishing in detail the good or evil of a
situation through careful reflection. The sages called this "attending." This means one acts by attending upon the appropriate time and not hurrying something, but seeking the
truth by thorough reflection. It is not being negligent. If we
decide quickly and carelessly we will surely make a mistake
and have regrets afterward.

[92b]          Becoming bored with our efforts and not working hard
over a long period is not usually because one's energy is
weak. By being self-indulgent and disliking to make an effort
we become impatient, find things difficult, and become
bored. If we calm our mind and are not prejudiced against
things, and if we follow a sequence and make a gradual effort, we will not be exhausted even when something requires
a long time. If we are not lazy and do not slacken our efforts
we will quietly make good progress.

[92b]          Thoughts of desire, fame, and profit are all human emotions, and so they sometimes arise easily. It harms virtue to
indulge them. In order to restrain these thoughts when they
arise, it is good to use the method of "subduing the self."[125]
Subduing oneself is most difficult. We must use sufficient
willpower and not be negligent. However, it is very easy to
have control by [being aware of] the signs when the desires
first arise. This is the essential method of "subduing the
self." If one resolves to pursue learning and love what is

right, naturally thought of fame, profit, lust, and material goods will weaken. If heavenly principles advance; human desires retreat; if human desires advance, heavenly principles retreat. In general, you cannot have these two things at the same time.

[93a] Within the mind-and-heart we should be open and clear, like a blue sky on a bright day. We should not harbor or cover up things in the heart. Our thoughts must be deep and well-informed; we should not be shallow. In doing things we should enjoy thinking deeply and should not decide things quickly or imprudently. It is good to reflect quietly and not quickly. If we decide quickly, inevitable there will be mistakes.

[93a] We must not bear a grudge or be angry at people who lack a sense of righteousness or decorum. This is because people's mistakes need not be connected to us. The ordinary practices of petty people are not worth criticizing. Why dispute right and wrong with them by being angry and bearing a grudge? We should simply try to reflect and blame ourselves for our lack of righteousness or decorum. We should not accuse others. If we examine and discipline ourselves there is no time to criticize others.

[93b] In the *Book of History* it says, "If one endures something, he will accomplish his purpose. If one is tolerant, his virtue will be great."[126] Enduring is bearing things patiently. If we endure patiently, we will control our anger, we will not damage things, and there will be no misfortune. Between ourselves and others there will be peace; and because everything is in order, we use the expression, "accomplish one's purpose."[127] An old saying has it: "Things will go well after one has endured."[128] If we have patient endurance, there is sure to be rejoicing. When we do not bear the evil of people, anger arises, we fight with people, and the relationship between ourselves and others worsens and it is difficult to live in this world. If we endure patiently, disputes cannot occur; if there are no arguments there will be no cause for shame. Having a peaceful heart, our joys will be numerous.

[93b] When we are tolerant our mind-and-heart expands, we utilize the goodness of people and forgive their faults. If we are tolerant, the vessel of virtue will be large. For example, if the volume of a vessel is large, we can put many things in it.

It is like a saying in an ancient poem: "The sea's expanse allows for the jumping of fish; the sky being spacious allows for the flying of birds."[129]

[93b]      Endurance is using effort and bearing patiently. Tolerance expands that virtue, and so we need not call it endurance. First, we exert ourselves and are patient, and after this practice matures, we speak of having tolerance. Endurance is still immature, but having tolerance is maturity. However, from the beginning it is good to practice tolerance. We should accept the goodness of people and overlook their faults from the beginning.

[94a]      A long time ago two people boarded the same boat and one of them had an impatient nature. The weather was bad, and he was worried about the boat being late. From morning until night he was distressed, and he became numb with cold. Now, the other person had a calm nature and was not worried that the boat was late. He ate well, slept easily, and his color was good. Since they were going to the same destination, they disembarked at the same time. Thus, what did it profit the man who was so worried, complaining all along that the boat was late? He only made himself anxious. Impatient people should learn a lesson from this. It is difficult to rely on our own power but it is good to rely on heaven. It is foolish to be anxious.

[94a]      In mingling with the world we should have few words, act diligently, be humble, and not boast of our talents. We should respect and not look down on people or speak ill of them. Knowing human nature we should not bear grudges against people; knowing the movement and changes of the world we should respond to the times. Finally, preserving trust we should not break our promises; being pure we should not be corrupted by wealth or profit. When we act in such a way, our faults will decrease; nowhere will we be disliked or slandered by others. In a poem it says: "There, not being hated; here, not being disliked."[130] To dislike means to become tired of something.

[94b]      Those who resent being neglected do not know human nature, and should be regarded as people who are not familiar with the ways of the world. Even though we are the master of our own body, there are many things which do not go as we would like; it is difficult to fulfill expectations. How can others fulfill expectations for us in the way that we

would like? Furthermore, there is no telling how many obstacles there will be which will prevent us from carrying out our intentions. Realizing that there is a reason for everything, we must not reproach people or bear grudges easily. Criticizing and resenting people who have no faults simply because something is distasteful to us is a very serious failing. Those who realize this and do not slander or resent others know human nature well and they understand the mutability of the world.

[94b]     In the *Book of Poetry* it says, "There is certainly a reason if someone does not come for a long time."[131] This means that there is some reason if a person does not come to our place for a while; either they do not have time, or they are sick, or they have an excuse not to come. We should not resent it if a person does not come for a long time, but we should imagine that they have something hindering them. In Chu Hsi's *Commentary on the Book of Odes (Shih chuan)* this poem is praised as reflecting a knowledge of human nature. A person who has a narrow mind and shallow knowledge does not know human nature or the changeability of events. Since he only feels that something is disagreeable to him, he has resentments and is troubled. This is a person who has a narrow mind and is unaccustomed to the ways of the world.

[95a]     If people speak ill of us we should reflect on our own faults and not bear a grudge. If we have no faults, even if they speak falsely, it will not harm our virtue. If we have faults and someone speaks ill of us, if there is truth to it from the beginning, we should not resent it. Moreover, if we hear this and rectify our faults, our happiness will be exceedingly great. We should not get angry. Confucius said, "I am fortunate! If I have faults, people will definitely know them."[132] If we are reproached and made aware of our faults, we are fortunate. We should respect the words of the sage.

[95a]     Recently there has been a saying in colloquial speech, "Being cautious is being discreet,"[133] which is very true. In small matters when we think, "What is there to worry about?" and we act boldly as if we had nothing to fear, this becomes the beginning of mistakes and the root of evil. A very big mistake or misfortune will inevitably occur due to lack of reverence or mindfulness even for a short time or in a small deed. Therefore, being reverent and mindful in small matters and not being overconfident is the way to prevent

misfortune. This is the meaning of the inscription of King Wu which says, "Don't speak of what evil may befall or it will surely come."[134]

## CHAPTER IV

## *THE ART OF THE MIND-AND-HEART,* PART 2

[96a]  It is said that the mind-and-heart is the heavenly lord and the master of the body.[135] Therefore, it is by thinking that we fulfill our function [as human beings]. The five senses are called the five organs of control. An organ directs or performs a role. The ears are in charge of hearing, the eyes are in charge of seeing, the mouth is in charge of eating and talking, the nose is in charge of smelling, the hands and feet are in charge of moving. These five controlling organs have their respective roles; they have nothing to do with anything else but that. Since the mind is the heavenly lord, it is the master that governs and controls the five senses. There will be no regrets and no mistakes in the operations of the five senses if we act by carefully considering whether or not a thing is correct or if we reflect thoroughly about the actions of the five senses. If the mind fails in its function, if without forethought we yield to the desires of the five senses, and if we do not consider the moral propriety of what we do, then human desires will do as they please and heavenly principles will be destroyed. This is because the mind loses control and cannot think clearly.

[96a]       Human desire is simply selfishness which allows the five senses to have their way. Seeing impropriety and being tainted by it, listening to impropriety and being tempted by confused voices, saying inappropriate things, being greedy for food and drink, loving fragrant smells, being lazy or doing things that we should not do, are all human desires. The principle of heaven is nothing other than conforming to the principle of the Way by controlling the five senses. Since the mind is the heavenly lord, employing the five senses is as natural as the master employing a retainer. If the mind fails to serve us and we indulge the senses without reflection, the body, conversely, will put the mind to its own uses. That is to say, it is like a master being used by a retainer. This is backwards.

ABOVE: *Sankōdori*. A type of crested fly catcher. Picture shows male (with long tail feather) and female. BELOW: *Tadehiwa*. A type of finch.

[96b]       We should act solely with a humane mind-and-heart by
exerting ourselves in planning for the people, or recommending their talents to the lord or to councillors, sparing people
harm, being compassionate and helpful toward those who
are poor and distressed, and treating people with kindness.
We must not expect that other people will gladly repay us,
nor should we act with a view to gaining a [good] reputation.
This is hidden virtue. If we do good for our own sake or if
we give to people and then expect repayment, our heart's humaneness will be empty. If we act like this, even if we exert
ourselves to do good, our actions may be right but all in
vain, because our heart is wrong. This is because it is not the
Way of sincerity.

[97a]       Ignorant people not only cannot discern moral principles,
they also do not distinguish between benefit and harm, gain
and loss. Without reflecting on the consequences of their
deeds, they make mistakes. Thinking that they will establish
themselves, on the contrary, they destroy themselves and
their families. It is sad. By not curtailing our wickedness we
invite heaven's censure. We do bad things, thinking it will be
to our own benefit, and we enjoy ourselves while hurting
others—not realizing that all of this is harmful to ourselves.

[97a]       When we do not put the Way ahead of all else, our mind
gives free rein to anger and happiness, likes and dislikes; it
follows our selfish desires and becomes caught up with profit
and desires, fear of loss and hope of gain. Confused by foolish things that others say, it takes evil for good and good for
evil. Acting selfishly on behalf of relatives and friends, or
thinking only of how one can profit from dealing with people's petitions, one does not adhere to the Way or serve the
public good. Not studying the Way, we fail to understand it;
consequently, we have no way to distinguish right from
wrong. We act selfishly and put our own preferences ahead
of all else. Even though they read books, many selfish people
do not put the Way first but just follow their own desires;
consequently, no matter how much they study, it is of no
benefit to them.

[97b]       Within the home we should not be critical and angry,
saying that the efforts of our wife, children, or family members in serving us are not satisfactory. In mingling with others, we should be tolerant and make allowances for their
mistakes. Moreover, we should not demand that the basic ne-
cessities of life be completely supplied. It is good to always be

in some need. When one is fully satisfied, there will be misfortune. It was said of old, "The roof of a house should lack three tiles,"[136] and a kimono should lack a collar.

[97b]    The world is a sea, the body is a ship and one's purpose is the rudder. If we hold the rudder incorrectly, we will not go where we ought to; [we will be like] a ship overturning when it encounters wind and waves. What goal we hold to is important. If we hold to the wrong goal, we will be overturned. It is like grasping the rudder incorrectly and letting the boat be overturned.

[97b]    If we know what is sufficient for ourselves, even if we are poor, we will still be content. When we do not know what is sufficient, even if we are wealthy, we will not be content.

[97b]    We should not rejoice or be fearful in noticing the praise or blame of others concerning the goodness or evil of our actions. We ought to have our own method [of judgment] through reason. If our actions conform to reason, we have nothing to fear even if everyone criticizes us. If our actions are contrary to reason, even though the whole world praises us, we should not rejoice. The Noble Person is one who is praised by good people and criticized by wicked people. We are, on the contrary, suspicious of people who are praised by everyone, for there are many who can skillfully put on airs.

[98a]    It is not proper to seek to be praised in our efforts at self-discipline. We should only think about not having faults. If we conform to the principle of the Way, it will not matter whether people praise or criticize us; [what people think] is not sufficient [cause] for happiness or anxiety. We should endeavor to follow the path of constancy and courage of a true warrior, and not be tainted by selfish desires, but be honest and without greed. By these two means we may act in such a way as generally to be spared the criticism of others. If we are in the right, no harm is done us even if our reputation suffers. So long as these two things hold, nothing else need concern us.

[98a]    If we abandon doing good for fear of what people may say, our love of the good is not sincere. A petty person, in his love of material goods and passions, is not concerned about the criticisms of others. This is because he is absorbed in his pleasures. The good deeds of a scholar should be like this.

[98a]    Generally if we rely on ourselves alone[137] it will inevitably become our downfall. When we rely on our own talents and neglect other people we will be overcome by them.

When we depend on our courage and despise other people, we will be destroyed by them. When we have [too much] confidence in our strength and do as we like, sickness will occur and we will lose our life. When we rely on our own strength we will become arrogant and be destroyed. If we depend on our own wisdom and are proud we will make mistakes.

[98b]     In both mind and deed we should concentrate on [the unity and purity of] heavenly principle and not taint it with even a little [selfish] desire. This is reaching the highest good. The mind and the deeds of a Noble Person should definitely be this way. If one part of human desire mixes with ten parts of heavenly principle, it is like mixing black and white, or having the fragrant and the putrid together in one vessel. When ten parts of white are mixed with one part of black, we cannot call it white. If a fragrant thing is added to something even a little putrid, it is the same as if the fragrant thing smelled bad.

[98b]     Since ancient times, sincerity has been declining daily while ostentation has been flourishing. Extravagance is gradually becoming widespread while frugality is slowly being abandoned. Simplicity is despised and gaudiness is praised. If we practice the Way in today's world we should cease from deceit and ostentation, return to old customs, be gentle, and strive to value honesty. If we are honest, it will be easy for people to acknowledge it and follow it. We should not be tainted by vulgar customs of the times.

[99a]     Even if we are unlucky and suffer misfortunes and false charges, or if there is a lack of humaneness and decorum between lord and retainer, or between one's parents, brothers, or friends, still we should compare [our situation] to that of others, in both Japan and China, who have met even greater misfortunes in the past and present, and we can console ourselves and be relieved; we should not be distressed. This is the teaching of the sages. There is also another method by which the Noble Person accepts [hardship and disappointment] as heaven's decree. The former method, however, is an easier one, and we should all learn it.

[99a]     Although there are unexpected misfortunes in the world, realizing that this is the fate of human beings in the past and in the present, we should not suffer or be distressed. A poem by Yoshida Kenkō says, "We can console ourselves by recog-

nizing that something is unavoidable and that it is not simply one's own fault but it is the nature of the changing world."[138]

[99a]        If people are disrespectful and unreasonable toward us, or if they are improper in their behavior, or if things do not turn out as we would like, we should rededicate ourselves to the pursuit of learning which arouses our moral sense and restrains personal desire, seeing these as occasions for advancement in virtue; enduring the improprieties of others, we should examine ourselves, control our mind, repress our anger, restrain our desires, and turn toward the good and correct our mistakes. We should not think of these occasions, when we make an effort to cultivate the "art of the mind-and-heart," as of no significance nor should we let them pass in a purposeless manner. By coping with those situations which are not to our own liking, both our virtue and our learning will advance. If we do not do this, we shall make no progress in our effort to control the mind and suppress desires.

[99b]        The heavenly Way implies that in spring there is birth, in summer there is growth, in autumn there is harvest. The three seasons all have their activities. In winter, however, the life-force is simply hidden and quiet and there is no activity. Just as during the night when people are sleeping they rest without doing anything, so during the winter the life-force is closed up and stored, yet it is the root of the coming spring and the genesis of life. During the winter when the cold is severe, the vital spirit is controlled and thus it will flourish in the following season. Therefore, in a mild winter when there is lightning and the vital force moves and dissipates, the growth of the following spring is weak and in autumn the five kinds of grain do not ripen well. When people do not sleep through the night, their blood is not quiet and the next day their energy is weak. By nourishing the human mind in times of quiet, we should make it the basis of movement. When the mind is not quiet but is restless, there will be no energy to be diligent in our work and we will vacillate and make many mistakes.

[99b]        Liu Hsing-chien [a Sung scholar] said, "The affairs of this world should accord with the hearts of human beings below, with the intentions of heaven above, and with the great Way in between. This, in a word, is impartiality [public-mindedness]."[139] Impartiality is not being selfish [pursuing

private interests]. To be selfish means trying solely to benefit ourselves and not considering the benefit of others. This is separating ourselves from others. Impartiality means not separating ourselves from others; it is benefiting ourselves and others equally.

[100a]    If one is impartial and not selfish one is in accord with reason, with the will of heaven, and with the human heart. Therefore, the sincerity of the heart is expressed naturally, the praise and happiness of people is warm, there is no hatred or doubt on the part of others. Without grasping for it, this is [receiving] the blessings of the heavenly Way and the love and respect of others. Furthermore, in a word, it is selfishness which violates the heavenly Way above, is contrary to the human heart below, and does not conform to the great Way in between. That is to say, although we practice good deeds to such an extent that they are heard of throughout the realm, if it is done selfishly, it is not the Way of sincerity.

[100a]    If we act selfishly, and profit from it on occasion, even though no misfortune strikes us down, the anger of heaven and the resentment of others will eventually be visited on us. Misfortune will surely befall us, we will be shamed and our name dishonored. The Way of heaven is truly to be feared! It is not only a matter of not knowing the truth of the Way, it is foolishly not knowing what is beneficial or harmful to oneself. Although we think we are establishing ourselves and obtaining wealth through selfish acts, on the contrary we will meet disaster and cause our own downfall, so that we do not even understand what is truly in our own interest. This is indeed extremely foolish.

[100a]    In people's mind-and-heart lies the principle that virtue is to be most highly valued and enjoyed. The Noble Person knows this, values and delights in it, and seeks nothing else. The petty person does not know this, damages virtue, loses the Way, and does not value and delight in this truth. Simply liking despicable things of vulgar pleasure, he is concerned solely with greed and loses contentment in long periods of anxiety and worry. To be fully human means to value the knowledge of this true delight. If we do not know this, there is no benefit in being human. If we wish to know this contentment, by making an effort at authentic learning we should come to understand this principle.

[100b]  Remorse is truly a good thing, for it has the benefit of anticipating and warning against later mistakes. Thus, Chia I said, "Not forgetting our past deeds is the [best] teacher of later deeds."[140] However, if we agonize over and harbor something within for a long time, our mind will inevitably become stagnant and sick, and will destroy our sense of peace and well-being. After admonishing ourselves once, we should abandon that fault and not cause mental suffering from continual remorse. We should take precautions for the future and try not to make such a mistake again.

[100b]  Within a person's mind-and-heart there should always be reverence and harmony. Reverence is mindful respect. When we do not have reverence, the mind becomes self-indulgent and flows in a bad direction, and the basis of ritual decorum is not established. Harmony is calm enjoyment. When we do not have harmony we are anxious and distressed, we cannot follow the principle of the Way, and we cannot establish the basis of enjoyment. Reverence and harmony are like the two wheels of a cart and the two wings of a bird. Lining them up together, we must not damage either of them. No matter how vulgar the people we meet may be, we should not follow the common stream and lose our sense of reverence and respect. No matter how many kinds of misfortune we may encounter, we must not lose harmony by worrying. In the *Book of Ritual* it says, "Rites and music should not be separated from ourselves even for a short time."[141]

[101a]  Although we attain wealth and honor, if we indulge human [selfish] desires we never satisfy our wants, and we will probably be inferior to those who are poor with few desires. Delighting in moral principles, we shall be ennobled even without rank and wealthy even without a stipend. This kind of delight knows no bounds. It comes from having contentment within and no desires without.

[101a]  Not knowing our own foolishness or mistakes, thinking much of ourselves and seeking to make ourselves known, being unaware of our own lack of ability—all are because we have not clarified our own mind. Knowing people is truly difficult because within people's breast good and evil hides and cannot be seen. We think we can easily know the good and evil within our own heart since it is our own, but on the contrary, it is more difficult than knowing others. This is be-

cause we are selfish and do not know our own faults. Therefore, of old it was said, "To know others is simply knowledge. To know oneself is enlightenment."[142] Knowing other people is very difficult; however, since knowing ourselves is more difficult, we term this "clarifying" which is even superior to knowing. When we clarify our mind we know our own faults. Therefore, people who are self-satisfied and boast to others do not know their own evil because their mind is obscured.

[101b] In the *Book of Changes* it says, "If we listen to good advice and do not believe it, it is because we are not hearing clearly."[143] If we listen to the admonishments and good advice of others, yet do not believe these words, but regard them simply as mistaken and useless, it is because our mind is obscured and we cannot hear their essence. If the mind is clear we will listen, understand, and believe what is true in these words. If a person has worldly talents and is skillful with words, people will listen and believe even things which lack principle. If, however, someone is not skillful with words, even if there is truth in what he says, people will not believe it. This is because the people who listen are not clear [in their thinking].

[101b] To control our desires for food and drink, passion and wealth, is like using all of our strength; we must fight and defend ourselves as if against a strong enemy. If we do not act like this we cannot control our desires. This is a good method of conquering desires. If we are even slightly weak we cannot conquer our desires, and eventually the desires take over and it is hard to forestall them. Human desires are the great enemy of people. We must not be careless; by whatever means we must conquer them.

[102a] Human failings occur because of the proclivities of our psycho-physical disposition. The way to change the bad parts of our disposition is by controlling our faults and making an effort to overcome our deficiencies. People who are too forceful should try to become gentle and gentle people should endeavor to be more forceful. Quick people should slow down and slow people should become quicker. It is good for people with other proclivities to do likewise. An ancient sage called Hsi-men Pao [a wise retainer of the Warring States period][144] was impetuous and always admonished himself by tying a leather string. The string was [a symbol of] softness and flex-

ibility. Tung An-yü [a loyal retainer of the Spring and Autumn period] was slow by nature and always admonished himself by tying a bowstring to himself. The bowstring was [a symbol of] quickness. If we have resolve to correct our faults in this way, no matter what kind of disposition we are born with, how could we fail to change our disposition? Study requires knowing our faults and conquering them. This is a path whereby our mistakes become few. When we do not do this, learning will be profitless.

[102a]     Although we are busy and have many things to do, the mind should not be agitated and hurried. When the mind is irritated and hasty, not only does it suffer by losing contentment, but our thinking is not clear and our mistakes are numerous.

[102b]     The Noble Person rarely blames others and frequently criticizes himself. For such a person to be hateful toward or bear a grudge against others is rare, while to be tolerant of and patient with others is common. The petty person is the opposite. Therefore, the mind of a Noble Person is always balanced and his joys are numerous. A petty person's mind is always angry and his sorrows are many.

[102b]     By reflecting carefully about everything, we should plan so as to have no mistakes afterwards and no regrets. There will be misfortune when we fail to reflect and do not avoid anger and desires. These are not the activities of a wise person. There will surely be mistakes and regrets if we act foolishly and with a lack of thought. If we must act quickly, we should act with even more careful reflection. If we do this, there will be no mistakes later. When we are quick, agitated, and not calm, without reflecting there will certainly be mistakes and regrets.

[102b]     Due to our anger and desires when we do not bear with petty irritations for a short time, we will make big mistakes, and these will plague us for the rest of our life. In the end we will lose ourselves.[145] We must be careful, for to encounter disaster by being careless even for a moment is extremely foolish.

[103a]     The misfortunes of ourselves and others frequently occur because of selfish desires. There would be no misfortune if we did not yield to these desires. It is rare that disaster falls unexpectedly from heaven. Even if this happens, according to the situation we may escape it. The misfortune which we in-

vite on ourselves by carrying out our selfish desires and committing offenses will be greater than the misfortunes which we receive from heaven, and it will be difficult to avoid. If we try to gain something for ourselves, we will certainly hinder others. The consequences of obstructing others is inevitably harmful to ourselves. Even if we hinder others, for example by obtaining profit unexpectedly, and we are not blamed by others, we will eventually receive the reproach of heaven and misfortune will occur. Those who commit crimes and are punished publicly are visible to all. The reproach of heaven, however, cannot be seen, and since it can fall at any moment, people do not know it. It is a mistake to think that when these disasters come they come unintentionally.

[103a]     When we seek profit there will inevitably be harm. If we seek good fortune there will certainly be misfortune. Because of this, in *Han-shih wai chuan* it says, "Profit is the root of harm; good fortune is the forerunner of misfortune."[146] It is fine when good fortune comes naturally without seeking it. Good fortune which we seek for ourselves, however, will surely turn to disaster. One should serve the will of heaven by simply being careful of one's person, being content with one's lot, and endeavoring to fulfill one's function. Profit is not to be found in wealth alone. Whatever is of benefit solely to ourselves is all profit. What a person calculates as advantageous to oneself is harmful to others. Therefore, our profit becomes another's loss and harm to others becomes harm to ourselves. It is like an endless circle, turning and returning. We should understand this principle well and not covet profit.

[103b]     Confucius said, "We should not grieve about not being known by others but we should grieve over not knowing others."[147] People who do not know us are foolish people. We should not be sad because it is not our fault [that we are not known]. Not knowing the good and evil of others is our own foolishness and we should be ashamed. Seeking to have one's own good known by others is having the heart of a petty person. This is unworthy of us.

[103b]     We must not shame others by complaining about their mistakes and making a fuss about their wrongdoings. There will definitely be resentment from these people. We may momentarily feel good by attacking those who are at fault, but if those people seek retribution and are not patient, it will be

inviting disaster. Controlling our anger and thinking carefully about our mistakes to come, we must not seek to be entirely satisfied. We should deal with low-ranking people, too, in the same spirit.

[104a]    People who have few desires and know what is sufficient for themselves are at ease about their status in life, and even if they are poor they still are able to be content. People who have contentment are always satisfied. People who have many desires and do not know what is satisfying, even though they have wealth and honor, do not know their own limits and are not satisfied. People who are not satisfied and contented are always seeking something else. This often leads to many misfortunes.

[104a]    In *Pao-p'u Tzu* it says, "The cicadas who eat clear dew do not envy the dung beetles who consume excrement."[148] This means that cicadas drink the clear dew and they are hungry with an empty stomach, but they do not envy the dung beetles who eat excrement and are satisfied. In other words, it is better to be poor and lowly yet honest, than to have wealth and honor but to lack righteousness. We should not be envious of those who have wealth and honor but lack righteousness. Obtaining riches by flattery and greed provides no grounds for satisfaction; rather there is reason to believe that being poor and lowly surpasses being rich and honored. We should think about this often and understand it well.

[104a]    In all things there is correctness and a mean. Correctness means not being wrong. This is good. A mean implies being just right, without excess or deficiency. This is attaining the highest good. It is correct to drink water when we are thirsty and to eat when we are hungry. It is not wrong. To drink too much, saying it is because we are thirsty, or to eat too much, saying it is because we are hungry, is not the mean. Eating and drinking just enough is the mean. From this we may know how it can be applied to all other matters. Even if we are correct, if we do not strike the mean we do not attain the highest good. The mean means being just right, being without excess or deficiency in all things. This is, in other words, where the Way lies. When there is excess or deficiency, and we are not just right, then even if we do a good deed we are not in accord with the Way.

[104b]    Even if we have talents we should not boast about them. If we boast of our talents we will inevitably go wrong. More-

over, people will not believe in us. Even if we have some
small talent, if we do not read widely in the writings of the
sages and gain a broad understanding of history, it will be
difficult for us to judge right and wrong in the world
whether in the past or the present. Failing to know the Way
through our ignorance of the classics, and failing to reflect on
the past and the future because we have not become well acquainted with ancient and contemporary matters, but just relying on our own small talents, we will often err when we
try to understand the principles of the world. It is like trying
to measure the weight of things on a scale without a mark, or
like trying to distinguish the beauty of something in a mirror
which is cloudy. We should be humble, ask questions of people, think of ancient times, and try to clarify moral principles. We should not be foolish, praising or blaming others,
relying on our meager talents, or deciding good and evil by
ourselves.

[105a]      People who work hard and play hard are not sad but enjoy life, and are not lazy but diligent in their work. They realize that in human life this day is not repeatable; thus they
make one day like a month, one year like ten years, and ten
years like one hundred years. Working hard and enjoying
things, we go through life; that's how it is with intelligent
people. People who do not know how to be diligent or enjoy
things may live as long as one hundred years, but if they are
constantly lazy, they will not do any good during their lifetime. This is because they are not diligent. Their sufferings
and sorrows will always be numerous because they cannot be
content. When this happens there is no value in being human. To have only an awareness of being alive cannot be
called living. Although one may enjoy various pleasures,
when one's desires are numerous and unrestrained one will
harm oneself, and when one's pleasures are still not satiated,
anxieties will soon come. This is how it is with foolish people. In the *Book of Ritual* it says, "The Noble Person is content
to obtain the Way; the petty person is content to obtain the
things he desires."[149] If we control desires by means of the
Way, we will have contentment and will not be led astray; if
we lose the Way on account of desires, we will not have contentment and will be confused. The true person passes his
days in contentment; the petty person passes his days in anx-

iety. I am a foolish old man, and since my remaining days are few, I should have a method of making a day into a month, and making a month into a year. It is foolish to waste time carelessly and not enjoy even one day or one hour.

[105b]      The capacity for joyful contentment is implanted by the workings of heaven in the human heart and thus we possess it originally. However, when we have selfish desires we are harmed by the cravings of the senses, we are overtaken by feelings of joy and anger, pity and fear, and we lose contentment. The Noble Person is not destroyed by emotions and desires and never loses contentment. No matter what calamities he may encounter, they do not alter the natural happiness which is his. Moreover, when we are in contact with the wind and the flowers, the snow and the moon, the original contentment of the heart is deepened through harmony with these external things. This does not mean that enjoyment comes for the first time through contact with external things. Rather, external things only augment our original joyful contentment. The Way of heaven and earth, the transformations of yin and yang, the cycle of the four seasons are always harmonious. This is the joyful contentment of heaven and earth. This joy, however, is not only for humans; birds fly, fish leap, birds chirp, animals cry out, vegetation flourishes, flowers bloom, fruit is produced—these are expressions of the will of heaven and the natural delight of all things. Through these expressions, we should realize that there is joyful contentment from the beginning in the human heart. To be led astray by desires and lose this contentment is contrary to the Way of heaven and earth.

[106a]      No matter what hardships or misfortunes we may encounter we must never lose this [innate] happiness. So it was with the sages, who taught people to be contented. We should realize that contentment is something which is essential for people. The contentment of a Confucius or a Yen Hui[150] is something beyond the comprehension of foolish people like us, but even we should know that enjoyment is innate in all of us and we should learn how to keep from losing it. Everyone knows that if desires multiply, people will no longer recognize this joyful contentment. Contentment and desires are opposed to one another. If we are content, we do not have desires; if we have desires, we are not content.

We should think carefully about this principle and be discriminating. It should not be said that contentment is never to be found in human life.

[106a]     The mind-and-heart is the heavenly lord and the master of the body. We ought always to be peaceful and not be troubled. Even if we are poor and lowly and have unexpected troubles, since this is the will of heaven, we must not be sad or lose contentment. Moreover, if people wrong us we should have forbearance and forgiveness and should not be anxious. If we act like this, we will not suffer and our happiness will be great. We should not cause pain and harm our mind-and-heart by being distressed about our poverty or being unnecessarily angry or hateful toward people. Even if people lack decorum and have contempt for us, we must not look down on them, but think that they do this because they are ignorant. Even if our children are negligent toward us, we must not be angry with them, but think that it is because they do not understand the Way. There is no use in worrying. As for servants, since their habits are especially poor, they are foolish and difficult to enlighten. Teaching and reprimanding their bad habits is good but we should not attack them in anger or be violent in speech or in demeanor. By destroying our inner harmony we invite the resentment of others. Even without being stern in speech or fearsome in demeanor, just by being correct in our conduct and refraining from ridiculing others, we can make others naturally respect us and not despise us.

[106b]     When there is no control of the heart and we try to do something, we will be too quick and noisy, or too slow and lazy, or we will be ahead of things and in error, or behind in things and not on time. If we have a master, the heart will always be settled, neither too fast nor too slow but always just right, and so our mistakes will be few.

[106b]     It is said that Hsü Hsiao-chieh[151] from his youth warned people against killing things and, fearful of treading even on an ant hill, tried to avoid them. Such a heart can be called good. Expanding this compassionate heart, first by loving our parents and siblings, then by extending this love to humanity, and finally by extending it to the myriad creatures, the Way of humaneness can and should be practiced widely. The method of expanding virtue should always be practiced in this way. Being fond of living things and not liking to kill

them is having the mind-and-heart of heaven. In receiving the compassionate heart of heaven, the human heart is made humane. People who lack this humaneness do not have a heart which is compassionate toward things and merciful toward people, and they are fond of killing. When people lack humaneness in this way, even though they may have many other talents, their disobedience to the heavenly Way and lack of the human Way makes them unworthy of consideration.

[107a]    Since all gain is derived from heaven and earth and is a principle of nourishment open to all, it is a public thing. It is not something which ought to be for oneself alone. If we gain some benefit together with others, there is no harm in each one obtaining it individually. If we are selfish and try to obtain the profit for ourselves alone, conflict will arise and, on the contrary, we will be harmed. Gain which comes naturally and fairly is genuine and is beneficial to us. Gain which we seek greedily is not genuine, and inevitably it will bring misfortune. This is not to pursue gain but to pursue one's own harm.

[107a]    There is an ancient saying: "We cannot see even a large mountain if we cover our eye with a finger."[152] Although our mind is originally clear, if we have many selfish desires and the mind and body become obstructed, we will be ignorant and will not understand the principle of the Way. Therefore, if we make our mind clear and resolve not to vacillate between good and evil, we should dispel selfish desires. When we drive away desires the mind becomes clear. It is written in the poem of Shan-ku, "The original mind is like the sun and the moon; selfish desires resemble their eclipse."[153]

[107b]    From of old the misdeeds of people who do not follow the Way have not been limited to one thing but have been of all kinds. However, men of old said, "There is no evil as great as the anger which resists the admonitions of others."[154] From ancient times in both China and Japan, the fact that people do evil, destroy themselves, and ruin their families, is all because they ignore the admonitions of others. We must take this deeply to heart.

[107b]    Living in the world we should express our criticisms and disapproval of others lightly and not sternly. This is because, even though many read books and study the past, there are not many who keep to the Way. If they do not study, they

become all the more ignorant of good and evil in the world, and since in their ignorance they do foolish things unwittingly, we should not hate them but have compassion. It is written in the *Book of History,* "We must not get angry and dislike obstinate people."[155]

[107b]     Even we ourselves cannot [always] be in accord with our own mind and heart. There are many times when we mistakenly do things which we had intended not to do. How much less, then, can we expect that what others do will conform to our own thinking. Moreover, the fact that people's mind-and-hearts are different is the same as with faces, and we should not bear a grudge when people's minds-and-hearts are different from ours.[156]

[108a]     People's minds change easily according to the times. We should not rely completely on either another person's mind or on our own mind. This is the Way to have no regrets.

[108a]     People who know contentment do not resent heaven and do not reproach people; they do not seek something else in the world and they are at ease in their own position. Those who do not know contentment are the opposite of this.

[108a]     In dealing with others, all business should be conducted with a heart that is calm, gentle, and quiet. When the heart is not quiet and when the vital spirit is disturbed and wild, what is right and reasonable will not be clear and it will be difficult to follow the Way. Therefore, we should first control the mind-and-heart and make it calm and harmonious. When the blood is aroused the vital spirit will be stirred up and the heart will likewise be unsettled. For example, when we are sick with a rising temperature we cannot control the mind-and-heart. When we are drunk with *sake* the vital spirit rises and the heart is confused. In building a new house, if the pillars, beams, and rafters are not firmly secured, it will be easily blown down in a typhoon. When we have assembled the timbers securely, even if a typhoon comes, the house will not be easily blown down.

[108a]     With people too, when they are not calm, their heart will not be steady towards others and since they are not calm but fickle, neither their words nor their actions will be in accord with principle. In fighting with an enemy on the battlefield, if the vital spirit becomes heated up and the mind-and-heart is not calm, one's movement will be agitated so that it will become difficult to prevail and easy to concede defeat. In

writing too, skillful calligraphy involves achieving a rich appearance through calmness in forming each character. A lack of steadiness in one's characters means poor brushwork. In all things and affairs, when the spirit is unrestrained and lacking in composure, it is difficult to be in accord with principle.

[108b]     When the mind-and-heart is peaceful and does not find fault with others, but instead examines and finds fault with oneself, one will conduct oneself well and derive much satisfaction. This method is extremely beneficial and we should discipline our mind-and-heart with it. When we neglect this method we are sure to lose the Way and fail to find contentment. An ancient expression says, "The Noble Person looks within oneself; the petty person looks at others."[157]

[108b]     Narrow-mnded people use their own knowledge and think that they understand everything without utilizing the knowledge of others. There is an ancient saying: "If we rely on ourselves, we become small-minded."[158] Relying on our own knowledge and not making use of the knowledge of others, we have difficulty understanding the multifarious affairs of the world. Because the things we do not know are numerous, one should term this "a little knowledge." People with an expansive mind-and-heart do not simply use their own knowledge but question and listen to other people. Because they take and use what is good by combining together the knowledge of others, they make it their own wisdom. This can be called "much knowledge." All people have something they individually have gotten and things they have learned for themselves. Among ten people they have the knowledge of ten. Among one hundred people they have the knowledge of a hundred. It is good to take and use the strengths of others. No matter how talented the person, in the past or the present, it is difficult for him to know everything himself. There is a saying, "The knowledge of one person is limited, the knowledge of many unlimited."[159]

[109a]     Heaven's mandate flows from itself and we receive it. A mandate is like a command; it means an order. It is called heaven's mandate because it is bestowed from heaven. There is constancy and variability in heaven's mandate. That doing good brings good fortune and doing evil brings misfortune represents constancy. That the good person may suffer misfortune and the evil person good fortune represents variabil-

ity. All of our good luck or bad luck, misfortune or fortune, long life or short life, wealth or success, poverty or lowliness, happiness or unhappiness, are due to the mandate of heaven. There is nothing that happens to people which is not derived from the mandate of heaven. For some, destiny is determined at birth, for others, it is received unexpectedly; we meet prosperity or misfortune by chance. If we seek something, but it is not mandated, it will be difficult to obtain. Even if we do not seek something, if it is mandated it will be easy to obtain. All we need to do is observe human laws and await heaven's mandate. The usual rule is that good deeds are rewarded by good fortune; however, even if we meet adversity, since this is due to the variability of heaven's mandate, we should not be unhappy. Generally people should follow the method of discerning heaven's mandate, resign themselves to fate, and be happy. If we do not discern heaven's will, we do not realize that it is established by fate and that fortune is difficult to seek and misfortune difficult to escape. It is unseemly to try to exploit gain and escape loss by currying favor with people and with the gods. We should deem this foolish. Therefore, in the *Analects* it says, "One cannot become a Noble Person unless he learns the mandate [of heaven]."[160]

[109b]　　　When a person's heart is always content in ordinary peaceful times, no matter what misfortune occurs, he will not suffer. For example, even if a rich person has an unlucky year, he will not starve; and a strong, vigorous person will not feel discomfort even if there is a severe cold spell.

[109b]　　　When a person does not have contentment in peaceful times, if suddenly things happen and misfortunes arise, there will be sorrow and suffering, disorder and agitation in his heart. We should deepen contentment by using this method carefully in ordinary times and by cultivating the mind-and-heart. With the mind-and-heart as the lord of heaven, we should always be content and not be troubled or worried by external things.

[109b]　　　If we have unexpected misfortunes, even if we do not understand why, we should not be anxious and lose contentment. If we reflect quietly, there will emerge a method whereby we can escape misfortune. We must not be brought to an impasse but must think deeply and adequately by broadening the mind-and-heart.

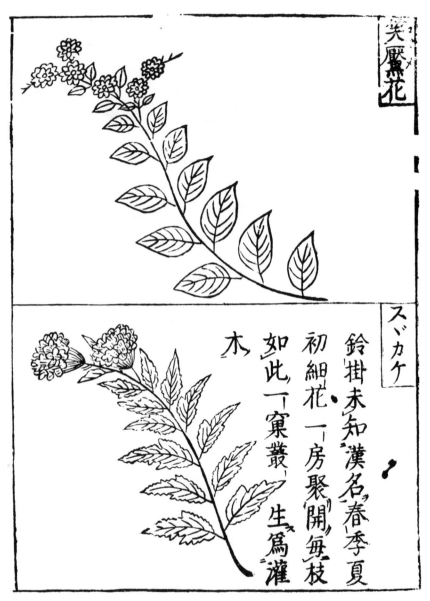

ABOVE *Kogomebana* Literally means "laughing dimple flower". BELOW *Suzukake* "Bell hanging flower". The Chinese name is unknown. In the spring season and the beginning of summer the flower is thin. One cluster gathers and opens at each branch as depicted. Each bunch has very dense growth. It is a shrub.

# 9

## Japanese Text of *Yamato Zokkun*

# 大和俗訓 自序

あめつちのことはり、人の道は、古の聖人これを
經典にしるし給ひ、其の明らかなること、日月の
天にかゝれるが如くなれば、天下の目ある者は見
ざることなし。いにしへの人、天もし仲尼を生せ
すんば、萬世長夜の如くならんといへりしも、む
べなり。後世の諸賢又よく其の志をつぎ、其の事
を述べ、經義を傳へて、來裔をさとし給ふ。かれ
これまことに天下後世の大なる幸なるべし。よく
よまん人は、其の理をしられんこと、たとへば日
中に黑白をわかつが如くならん。あに世こぞりて、
これをたふとび、身をおはるまで誦せざるべけん
や。うらむらくは、わが日の本の俗のならひ、文
字にかたくなにて、さばかり聰明の人も、おほく
は聖學にうとし。又窮鄉の晩進は、句讀をならひ
うべき師友にともしく、高貴の家の子弟は、たは
ふれあそびをたのしみ、安逸にならひて、學問な
どに身をくるしめんこと、いと遠ければ、稼穡の
艱難をすべてしらざるのみならず、五帝三王をも、

是何物ぞと思へる疑をまぬかれがたし。こゝを以
て、わが國聖學の寥々たること、古よりすでに久
し、うらみても猶うらめしきかな。しかれども、
今まさに聖明の御世にあたりぬれば、人文やうや
く開けて、聖學の世に明らかになりなんことたの
もし。今の世の俗をさとさんため、からの文字を
作りて、聖の道をとかんことは、わが輩のちから
になしうべからず。況もろこしのもろ〳〵の先正
の説、すでに明らかに備はれるをや。漢字をしれ
る人は、よんでしるべければ、今更贅言を用ゆべ
からず。夫聖人の道の、至りて高大にして、ふか
くおくまりたるは、此國のをんなもじを以て、其か
たはしをもまなびて、説かんことゝおほけなくて、管
にて天をうかがひ、蠡にて海をはかるが如くなれ
ば、つたなき筆にてしるさんこと、飛鳥川のふか
き淵の變じてあさき瀬となり行きなんうれひに、
猶まされりといへども、高きにのぼるには、必ま
づ下よりし、遠きにゆくには、必近きよりはじ
むる理あれば、世の不幸にして漢字をしらざる人
の爲に、いさゝかむかしきける所のことはりを、

今の俗語を以てかき、あつめて八卷とし、名づけ
て大和俗訓といふ。世の中の夫婦の愚なるも、あ
づかりしらしめ、兒女のいときけなくて、菽麥をわ
さまへざるをも、さとさむとをこひねがふのみ。
わが材器もとより拙なければ、身にも應ぜぬ道學
を以て、名を立てんことを好まず。この故にこの
書にかぎらず、いにし年より、かゝる鄙俚なるか
らやまとの、小文字を多くつくり、瑣細なる事を
も何くれとしるせしこと、世の道學の名を立つる
君子の、わらひ草とならんことも思ひかけぬれど、
わが志たるすぢもあれば、世のそしりをも、あな
がちにおそるべきにあらず。つらく思ふに、わ
が輩天地のきはまりなき御めぐみをかうぶりて、
人と生れたる幸は、おろかなる身にては、その大な
る德の萬一を、幾世をふとも、むくひ奉らんこと
かたかるべし。せめてかゝるあさはかなることを
つくりて、もしくは世の中の無學なる人、小兒の
輩、しづのをの、しづのめをさとして、民用の小補
にもなりなば、わがこの世に生れ、食にあき、衣
をあたゝかにき、居り所をやすくして、天地のた

からを多くついやせる素餐の罪を、すこしまぬか
るゝよすがともなりぬべし。こゝを以て、人の誹を
うれひざるなるべし。今われ犬馬のとしすでにや
そぢにせまり・なす事なくて、この世くれ行くな
べに、こよみのぢくわらはれたるごとくなれば、
やがて草木と同じくはかなくくちはてなんと、う
らめしくて、わが身のざえのつたなきをわすれ、み
だりにつとめて筆をおこし侍べる。老らくの身は、
心も目もたどくしければ、いかなるひが事を書
きけんもうしろめたし。世の中にわれと志を同じ
くする人もありて、この書のあやまりおほくして、
ひがくしきことをよく改めつくりて、世をさと
し給はゞ、まことにわがねがはしきほいにかなへ
るなるべし。

寶永五年立冬日

益軒　貝原篤信　書

時年七十有九

# 大和俗訓目次

# 大和俗訓　卷之一

## 爲學上・

貝原篤信著

天地は萬物の父母、人は萬物の靈なりと、尙書に聖人とさ給へり。言ふこゝろは、天地は萬物をうみ給ふ根本にして、大父母なり。人は天地の正氣をうけて生るゝ故に、萬物すぐれて其の心明らかにして、五常の性をうけ、天地の心を以て心として、萬物の內にて其の品いとたうとければ、萬物の靈とはのたまへるなるべし。靈とは、心に明らかなるたましゐあるを云。天地は萬物をうみ養ひ給ふ中にも、人をあつくあはれみ給ふと、鳥獸草木にことなり、こゝを以て萬物のうちにて、もはら人を以て天地の子とせり。されば人は天を父とし、地を母として、かぎりなき天地の大恩を受けたり。故に常に天地につかへ奉る道はいかんぞや、およそ人は、天地につかへ奉る道を以て人の道とす。天地の萬物をうみそだて給ふ御めぐみの心を以て心

とす。此心を名づけて仁と云。仁は人の心に天よ
り生れつきたる本性なり。仁の理は人をめぐみ物
をあはれむを徳とす。此仁の徳をたもち失はずし
て、天地のうみ給へる人倫をあつく愛し、次に鳥
獸卓木をあはれみて、天地の人と萬物を愛し給ふ
御心にしたがひ、天地の御めぐみのちからを助く
るを以て、天地につかへ奉る道とす。これすなは
ち人の道とする所にして、仁なり。仁の理をわか
てば仁義となり、仁義をわかてば禮智信となる。
五の性をすべて五常といふ。たとへば一年をわか
てば陰陽となり、又わかてば春夏秋冬の四時とな
るが如し。仁は五常をすべて其の總名なり。五常
は人に生れつきたる理なれば五性といふ。性とは
人の心に生れつきたる理をいふ。此五性は、いに
しへ今天下の人高きいやしきも、さかしおろかな
るも、おしなべて天地より生れつきて、萬世迄も
相かはることなき故に五常といふ。常とはかはら
ざるなり。中につきて、仁はあはれみの心なり、
是を以て四德をかねたり。義は宜しきなり、行ふ
所各其の物に相應ずるを云。禮はうやまふ心、つ

つしみてあなどらざるを云。智はあきらかにさと
る心、道理に通ずるなり。仁義禮も智なければ行
ふすべをしらず。義禮智は、みな仁より出で、仁
をたすくる理なり。信はまことなり、仁義禮智の
心、信にしていつはりなきを云ふ。まことなけれ
ば、仁義禮智にあらず。凡この五常の性にしたが
ひて、人倫に對してなさけふかく、あつく行ふを
人の道とす。人倫とは、君臣父子夫婦長幼朋友の
五なり。是を五倫といふ。又五品ともいふ。天下
に人多しといへど、その品をわかてば、この五
品の外にはいでず。五倫にまじはる道は、君は臣
をあはれみ、臣は君に忠をつくすべし。父は子を
いつくしみ、子は親に孝をつくすべし。夫は婦に
禮義あり、婦は夫をうやまひて和順なるべし。長
者は幼をめぐみ、幼きは長者をうやまふべし。兄
弟も長幼の内にあり。朋友はたがひにまことあり
て、たのもしく表裏なかるべし。此五倫の道は仁
義禮智信の五常の性にしたがひて、人倫にまじは
る時に行ひ出せる**なり**。わが本性の外に**求むる**道
にあらず。

人となるものは天地を以て大父母とする故、父母の
恩をうくるがごとく、きはまりなき天地の恩を受
けたり。天地のめぐみにて生れたる恩のみならず、
身を終るまで天地のやしなひをうくること、たと
へば人の身の父母より生れて後も、父母のやしな
ひによりてひとゝなるがごとし。こゝを以て、こ
の世に生れては、つねに天地につかへ奉り、いか
にもして天地の恩をむくひんことを思ふべし。是
天地につかふる孝なり。人たる者は、つねに是を
心にかけてわするべからず。天地につかへ奉る道
は別にあらず、天地の御心にしたがふを以て道と
す。天地の御心にしたがふとは、我に天地より生
れつきたる仁愛の徳をあつくあはれみうやまふして、天地の生
める所の人倫をあつくあはれみうやまふをいふ。
是則人の行ふべき所にして、人の道なり、人の
道とする所、さらにこの外にある可らず。夫人は
天地のめぐみによりて生れ、天地の心をうけて心
とし、天地の内にすみ、天地のやしなひをうけた
り。かくのごとく、極りなき大恩をうけたれども、
凡人はしらず。所謂百姓は日々に用ひてしらざ

るなり。然るに天地につかへ奉らずして、人欲に
したがひ、天理にしたがはざるは、天地の大恩を
かうふりて、天地にそむく故、天地の子として大
不孝なり。人の子としてそむきてその親を愛せずして、他
人を愛し、父母にそむきて不孝を行ふがごとし。
不孝の子はその身を天地の内に立てがたし。いは
んや天地の子として、天地にそむき不孝なるをや。
幸にしてわざはひなしといへども、天地にそむけ
るがおそるべし。天地をたふとびつかへ奉るべ
きこと、前にもすでにいへれど、返すぐよく人
につげんために、同じことをいくたびもくりかへ
していふなり。猶此後にもいふべし。

およそ天は人の始なり。父母は人の本なり。人は天
地を以て大父母とし、父母を以て小天地とす。天
地父母その恩ひとし。故に天地につかへて仁を行
ふこと、父母につかへて孝を行ふが如くすべし。
こゝを以て、禮經にも仁人の天につかふるは、親
につかふるが如くし、疎なるべからず、親につか
ふること、天につかふるが如くすべし、畏愼しむ
べしといへり。おろそかなるは愛なきなり。おそ

四九

れざるは敬なきなり。天地につかへ奉るも、父母につかうまつるも、同じく愛敬をいたして、おろそかならず、あなどるべからず。天地によくつかふるは仁人なり、仁心をたもつ人なり、父母によくつかふるは孝子なり、孝養をよくつとむる子なり。天地につかへ父母につかふるの道同じ。しかれば、天地につかへ奉るは、人間の大事にて、しばしもわするべからず。常人はちかき父母につかふる道をだにしらずして、心を用ひず。況や天地は、きはまりなき大恩あることをわきまへずして、天地につかへ奉るは、身にあづからざることをおもへり。夫天地の恩は父母の恩にひとし、こゝを以て身をはるまで、常につゝしんでつかへ奉り、力をつくすべきこと、是人の職分にて、至りておもき大事なり。人たる者この理をしらずんばあるべからず。

天地の中に萬物あり。萬物の内、人ばかりたうとき物なし。かるがゆへに萬物の靈といふ。その靈たるゆへに、心に五性あり、身に五倫あり、目に五色をわかち、口に五味をおぼえ、耳に五音をわきまへ、鼻に五臭をしる。鳥けだものには、このあまたのこと一もなし。人となりて、かゝるたふとき身を得たること、まことに天地の間の大なる幸を得たるなり。しかるに人となれる道をしらず、禽獣にちかくして、空しく此の世を過し、人と生れたる身をいたづらになすこと、くやしからずや。

顔子推は、人身得がたし、空しく過ることなかれといへり。萬物にすぐれて人とかく生れたるは、誠に幸の至りなれば、人身得がたしといへり。人たる者もしふたゝびこの世に生れば、たとひこのたび怠りて、人の道をしらずとも、かさねて又人とむまれん時をたのむべきこともありなん。この身再び人となることを得ざれば、道を學びこの身をよくをさめ、人となりてをはるべし。むなしくこの世を過すべからず。もし人の道をしらで、空しくこの世を過しなば、人と生れたるかひなかるべし。をしむべきかな。

萬物の内、人と生るゝこと甚かたし。いかんとなれば、鳥獣虫魚は年々に多く生ることその数かぎり

なし。人の数は鳥獣蟲魚の萬が一もなくして、き
はめてすくなし。その上人は萬物にすぐれて、天
地のめぐみをうくることあつし。かく貴き人身な
れば、萬物の内人と生るゝこと、きはめてかたき
ことなるを、幸に人と生れたるわが身を持ながら、
學ばずして天地の道にそむき、人の道をしらずし
て行はず、人とかく生れぬるたのしみをわすれ、
いたづらに一生をむなしく過して、鳥獣と同じく
いき、身死して後は、よき名をのこすことなく、
草木と同じくくちなんこと、あにうらみ多きこと
ならずや。

人と生るゝは、きはめてかたきことなれば、わくら
はに得がたき人の身を得たることをたのしみて、
わするべからず。又人と生れて、人の道をしらで、
むなしくこの世を過ぎなんことうれふべし。この
樂と憂との二を、身を終るまでわするべからず。
およそ、人となる者は、人の道をしらずばあるべ
からず。人の道をしらんとならば、聖人の教をた
ふとびてその道を學ぶべし。いかんとなれば、聖
人は人の至極なり、天地の道にしたがひて、人の

道をおしへ給へる萬世の師なり。後代にのこしお
き給ふ四書五經の教は萬世の鑑なり。その道理明
らかなること、日月の天にかゝれるが如く、天下
ひろしといへども、てらざる所なし。よくよきん
人は、天下の道理をしらんこと、白日に黒白をわ
かつが如くなるべし。あに是を學ばざるべけんや。
しかるに人となる者、人倫の道は天性に生れつき
たれども、その道に志なくして、食にあき、衣をあ
たゝかにき、居所をやすくしたるまでにて、聖人の
教を學ばざれば、人の道なくして鳥けだものにち
かし。かくの如くなれば、人と生れたるかひなし。
萬物の靈とすべからず。このゆへに聖人是をうれ
ひ、賢臣を以て萬民の師として、人倫の道を教へ
させ給ふ。是人となるものは、必道を學ばずんば
有べからざればなり。愚おもへらく、人と生れて
學びざれば生れざると同じ。道をしらず
ざれば學びざると同じ。道をしりても行はざれば
しらざるに同じ。その故いかんとなれば、人の道を
しらざれば、まなばざると同じ、道をしりても行は
れてまなばざれば、人の道をしらずして、人と生
れて學ばざれば、人と生
たるかひなし。是人とむまれて學びざれば、生れ

ざると同じきなり。學ぶは道をしらんがためなり。もし學びやうあしくて道をしらずんば、學びざると同じきなり。又道をしるは行はんがためなり。まなんで道をしりても、行はざればしらざるに同じ。故に人とむまれては、必學びずんばあるべからず。學ぶ者は必道をしらずんばあるべからず。道をしれらば必行はずんばあるべからず。道をしれば必よく行ふ。行はざるはいまだ道をしらざるなり。道をしらんと思はゞ、聖人の教をあふぎ、賢人の説を階梯として、その法に隨ふべし。是道をしるべき學問のすぢなり。道に志なく、師傳あしく、學術のすぢちがへば、一生精力を用ひ、つとめ學んでもしるしなし。故に道を學ばんと思はゞ、初學より道にふかく志をたてゝ、明師にしたがひ、良友にまじはり、學術をえらぶをむねとすべし。學術とはまなびやうのすぢを云ふ。學のすぢあしければ、一生つとめても道をしらず。一たび迷ひぬれば、よき道に立ちかへりがたし。故にまづ學術をえらぶべし。

學問の道は、極めて廣大高妙にして深奧なり。しかれども其近き所は、孝弟忠信の日用常行にあり。故にいかなる愚なる者も、この道をまなびやすく、しりやすく、行ひやすし。高遠にしてあやしく異なる道にはあらず。

古の聖人すら、猶師にしたがひて學び給ふ。況や今時の凡人學ばずしては道をしりがたし。小藝だにも師なく習ひなくしてはなしがたし。況や人の道は即天地の道にて、極めて大なるをや。學んでもまなびやうあしければ道をしらず、學ばずして道を得んことは萬々此の理なし。

學問はまづ志を立つるを以て本とす。志とは心のゆく所なり。道を知り行ひて、君子に至らんと思ふ心つねにをこたりなく、念々やまざるを、志を立つると云ふ。志たゝざれば學ぶこと成就せず。故に古人も志ある者はその事つひに成るといひ、又志たつは學の半なりといへり。たとへば弓いる者の的に志し、道ゆく者の宿りに志すがごとし。よろづの事まづ本をつとむべし。志を立つるは學問の本なり。志を立つるには勇猛なるべし。柔弱にしてをこたるべからず。をこたれば、しるしな

くしてはかゆかず。道を求るにせちなる志は、たとへば飢ゑて食を求め、渇きて湯水を求るが如くなるべし。わづかに悠々としてをこたれば、志すたる。只此道に心を一すぢにすべし、外物に心をうばゝるべからず。物を翫べば志をうしなふと尚書にもいへり。言ふ意は、耳目口體にこのむ所の外、欲に耽り外物をこのむ、或は無益の雜藝を一向にすきこのみて、心をかたぶくるの類は、皆是物をもてあそぶなり。かくのごとく外物に心をうつせば、道を學び君子となる志をうしなふ。萬の外物の翫び、このみ、皆志をそこなふものなり。程子曰、專一ならざれば直に遂ぐることあたはず。言ふこゝろは、一すぢになさゞれば行ひとぐること成りがたし。專一とは、たとへば猫の鼠をねらふがごとく、鷄の卵をあたゝむるがごとく、他念なかるべし。心あなたにわかるれば、學問道義の志はおとろへすたる。文藝武藝は誠に士たる者の習ふべきことなれば、つとめ學ぶべし。されども藝は末なり、道義の學は本なり。藝をひたすらこのめば必學の志をうばゝれて失ふものなり。

いはんや私欲のなぐさみこのみにまかするをや。志を立つれば、たとへば西國の人のあづまへゆかんとおもひ立ちて、日々にゆくに、その間晝夜あづまへゆかんと思ふ心は、念々つねにやます。是あづまへゆく志たつなり。かくのごとくなれば、つひにこゝろざす所に行きとゞかずといふことなし。道に志すも亦かくの如くなるべし。

凡學をするには、敎をうくる基を立て、又禁戒を守るべし。基とは家をつくる土臺なり。學問する人は謙を以て基とす。謙とはへりくだるなり。我が身にはこらず、人に高ぶらずして、心をむなしくし、人に問ふことをこのみ、わが才をたのまず、師友をうやまひ、我が身に才力有ても、なきが如くし、をしへをよくきゝ、人のいさめを悅び、すでにしれることもしらざるが如くにして、わが知を先だてず、すでによく行ふことも、いまだ行はざるが如く思ひ、人をせめずしてわが身をせむを、へりくだると云ふ。是學問をつとめ、敎をうくる基なり。たとへば家を作るに、先基を立つる

が如し。この基あれば、日々に善言をきゝ、わが

過をしりて、知明らかになり、善日々に長ず、學

の進むことはまりなし。又禁戒を守るべし。禁

戒とは、いましめて行はざるを云ふ。學問する人

は、まづ粉の字を禁戒とす。粉はほこるとよむ。ほ

こるとはわが身に自滿して、人にへりくだらざる

を云ふ。いまだしらざるをすでにしれりとし、よ

からざるをよしとす。もはら我が知を用ひて、人

にとはず、人のいさめを用ひず、身をせめずして

人をせむ。かくのごとくなれば惡日々に長ず。初

學の人は先この禁戒を守り、又此基を立つべし。

然らざれば學んでも益なきのみにあらず、かへつ

て害あり。是書をよみ學問する人の第一心得べき

事なり。

人の性は本善なれども、凡人は氣質と人欲に妨げら

れて善を失ふ。氣質とは生れつきを云ふ。人欲と

は、人の身の耳目口體に好むことのよき程に過ぐ

るを云ふ。生れつきあしければ人欲行はれやすし。

されば、すべて人たる者は、古のひじりのをしへを

學んで、人となれる道をしり、氣質のあしきくせを

改め、人欲の妨を去りて、本性の善にかへるべし。

是學問の道なり。故にいにしへの聖人、をしへを

立て、天下の人に學ばしめ給ふは、人の性皆善な

る故、學んで善にかへる道あればなり。

人皆良知あり。をしへざれども、幼よりおやを愛し、

少し長じては兄をうやまふ。人皆仁心あり、孺子

の井におち入るを見てはあはれむ。人皆義理あ

り。節にあたつては、おろかなる下部も命ををし

まず、なき食をも食をけちらしてあたへられはくはず。

是人の性の善なる證なり。聖人の敎は天下の人の

生れつかざることをしらしめ行はしめんとにはあ

らず。心生れつかざることは、をしへてなしがた

し、その人にもと より生れつきたる善心あるを

本として、みちびきびらきて是をおしひろめさせ

んとなり。天下の人その性皆善なり、その善なる

に本づきて、その生れつきたる善を行なへとみち

びき給へるなり。故にその敎行はれやすし。たと

へば山人が斧の柄をきるに、我が手に持ちたる斧

の柄を以て、新しく作らんとする斧の柄になるべ

き木の枝に、おしならべくらぶれば、大小長短少

しもたがはず、まづかき手本になること、是に過
ぎたる事なし。しかれども我が手にもてる斧と、
新しく斧に作らんとする木の枝とは、別の物なれ
ば猶以て遠しとす。聖人のをしへはしからず、即
その人に生れつきたる善心を本として、是をそだ
て養ふ道なれば、敎をつくりいだし、別の道をもち
來りて、その人にをしふるにはあらず。然れば天
下の人、おしなべて、この道を以ていざなひみちび
かば、およそ血氣ある人類は、唐もやまとも西戎南
蠻も、この道を尊信して、したがはずといふこと
なかるべし。

學問にすぢ多し。訓詁の學あり、記誦の學あり、詞
章の學あり、儒者の學あり。訓詁の學とは、聖人
の書の文義を、くはしくしることをつとむるを云
ふ。記誦の學とは、廣く古今の書をよみ、故事事
迹を覺ゆるを云ふ。詞章の學とは、詩文を作るこ
とを學ぶを云ふ。儒者の學は、天地人の道に通じ
て、身ををさめ人ををさむる道を知るを云。學問
をせば儒者の學をすべし。訓詁の學は四書六經等
の文義に通じても、義理をしらざれば用ひがた

し。いはんや記誦詞章の學は、いよ〳〵道に遠し、
儒者の學とすべからず。儒者の學に專一ならば、訓
詁記誦詞章の習を略其内にかねてよし。此外に又
小說の學あり。是は經史文章の學をこのまず、た
だもろ〳〵の雜細の事、又あやしき事などをしる
せる書をめでゝ、多く兒おぼえ、樂しみとする學な
り。又小說の學は訓詁詞章記誦などにならべて、
學術の條理を立つるにはたらず。しかれども末世
には又この學あり。學術の最下品なり。

或人の曰、儒者の學は只人道をしらば可ならん、天
地の道をしるに及ぶべからずと。予答へて曰く、
天地の道は人道の本なり、天地の道をしらざれば
道理のよつて出づる所の根本をしらず、根本をし
らざれば、天理の人にそなはり、人の天地にうけ
たる天人合一のすぢめをしらずして、人道明らか
ならず、故にまづ日用人倫の道を學んで後、天地
の道を學ぶべし。聖人の易を學び給ふも此の故な
らずや。されども天地の道は猶容易知がたし。

志を立つることは大にして高くすべし。小にしてひ
きければ、小成に安んじて成就しがたし。天下第一

等の人とならんと平生志ざすべし。世俗と同じく、いやしくひきくすべからず。かく志をたてゝ、日日々につとめ行はゞ、久しくしてその功つもりて、必人にまさるべし。上をまなべば中にいたり、中を學べば下にいたる、下を學べば功をなさず。又心は小にしてひきくすべし。人にへりくだり、日用常行のひきゝあしもとより行ふべし。心大なれば、をごりてつゝしみなく、細行をつとめず。高ければ人にたかぶりて謙徳を失ふ。

學問の法は知行の二を要とす。この二をつとむるを致知力行とす。　致知とは、しることをきはむるなり。　力行とは、行ふことをつとむるなり。道をしること明らかならざれば行はれず。たとへば目なきもの、足すくやかなれど、ゆくべき道をしらで、ゆきがたきがごとし。行ふことゝするどならざれば、知りても用なし。たとへば目明らかなりといへども、足たゝざれば、ゆくことかなはざるが如し。知と行とは目に見て足にてゆくがごとし。目くらければ行くべき道見えず。足立たざれば行くことかなはず。　目足ともにそなはらざれば道をゆきがたきがごとし。知を先とし、行ひを後とす、萬のこと先しらざれば行ひがたし。故に前後をいへば知るを先とす。しるは行はんためなり、知ても行なはざれば用なし。故に輕重をいへば行ふをもおもしとす。知ると行ふとの二は、一をかぐべからざること、鳥の両翼のごとく、車の両輪のごとし。學問は知と行と並進むをよしとす。並進むとは、知れることは即必ず行ふを云ふ。知と行と少しの前後はあれど、さきだちおくれず、一度につれだちてゆくをならび進むといふ。しれるばかりにて行はざるは、ならびすゝむにあらず。

知行の二の工夫を、こまかにわかてば五あり。中庸に曰、博く學び、審に問ひ、愼んで思ひ、明かに辨へ、篤く行ふ。　是道をしりて行ふの工夫にして、學問の法なり。

博く學ぶの道は、見ると聞くとの二をつとむ。聖賢の書をよみ、人に道をきゝて、古今を考へて道理を求むなり。人倫の道はのせて聖賢の書に有り、よくよきん人は、白日に黒白をわかつがごとくなるべし。天下の道理はきはまりなし、その道理を

しらざれば、行ふべきすべをしらでであやまり多し。道理はわが一心にそなはり、その用は萬物の上にあるなれば、まづわが一心の道理をきはめ、次には萬事につきてひろき道理をもとめて、わが心中に自得すべし。是ひろく學ぶなり。博く學ぶの道多けれど、書をよむほど益あるはなし。古人も、人の知惠をますは、書にしくはなしといへり。されど文字をのみ好みて、義理を求めざるは、博く學ぶにはあらず。

審に問とは、すでに學べる事のわが心にうたがはしき事を、明師良友にちかづきて、つまびらかに問ふて其理を明らかにし、うたがひをとくべし。愼んで思ふとは、すでに學び問ひたることのうたがはしきことは、心をしづかにし、つくしんで思ひて、よくがてんすべし。まなび問ひても、よくがてんせざれば、わが物にならず。故にわが心に道理をもとめて、その理を會得すべし。是よく思案して道理に通ずるなり。愼しんで思ふにあらざれば、道理に通じがたし。學問は自得をたふとし。自得とは愼んでよく思ひて、心中に道理をがてんして、わが物にし得たるなり。

明に辨ふとは、すでに愼んで思案して、猶善惡のまぎらはしきこととあらば、あきらかにその是非をきはめて、善惡をわかつを云ふ。以上の四は皆知の工夫にして、道をあきらかにするなり。

篤く行ふとは、すでにまなびとひ、思ひわきまへて、その道理をしらば、即吾身に其しれる道理をあつく行ふべし。行ふことあつからざれば道たがたがし。篤く行ふの道は、ことばを忠信にしていつはりなく、行をつしみてあやまちをすくなくす。人の身のわざ多けれど、言と行との二にはいです。故に言をまことにし、行をつししめば、身をさまる。又心のおこる處の用七あり、七情と云ふ。喜怒哀樂愛惡慾なり。人の身の用はこの七よりおこる。是をつしみて、過不及なくして道理にかなふべし。中につきて、七情の内いかりと慾との二、尤わが心を害し、身をそこなび人をそこなふものなる故に、いかりをこらしやめ、慾をふさぎ去りて、其はじめておこる處のきざしにかつべし。又善にうつりて、我善より猶よき事あらば、おのれ

が善をすてゝ、まされる方にしたがふべし。身に
過あらばはやく改むべし。わが身に執着して、改
むるにはゝかるべからず。又人に對して行ふに、
人われにしたがはざる事あらば、人をせめずして
わが身をかへりみとがむべし。是皆あつく行ふ道
なり。學び問ふにあらざれば道明らかならず。思
ひ辨ふるにあらざれば道をわが心に得がたし。篤
く行ふにあらざれば知りても實なし。右五のもの
は中庸にしるせる所、學の工夫なり。程子もこの
五のもの、一をかげば學にあらずといへり。

常に我が身をかへりみ、又人のいさめをきゝて、わが
不善なると、我あやまちとをしりて、善にうつり
あやまちをあらたむべし。知ありて忠直にして、我
が過を正す良友を求めて、交りしたしみて、いさめ
をきゝ、をしへをもとむべし。學問は我が身のあし
きをあらためて、よきにうつる道なれば、我を知あ
りとし、我をよしと思はゞ、學ぶとも益なくして、
かへりて邪氣を長すべし。人聖人にあらず、なんぞ
事ごとに善をつくさんや。聖人すら學問をこのみて、
べからず。自是とし自足れりとす

ず。今の凡夫いかでかあやまちなかるべき。
凡致知の法は、五常五倫の道をしるを以て先とし、
家をとゝのへて民ををさむる理にいたるべし。次
に萬事萬物の道理をもしりきはむべし。天地の内
にあらゆる萬事萬物は、皆我が心の分内のことな
れば、その理をしらずんばあるべからず。天下の
理をきはめしるの道は、本とちかきとを先とし、
末と遠きとを後にして、前後緩急の次第を失ふべ
からず。

學ぶ人は只我が知のくらく、わが德のすゝまざるこ
とをうれふべし。われに學問才智技藝ありとも、
我を知ありとし、我が才にほこる心あるべからず。
人各知あり、又長ずる所あり、人をおろかにしあ
などるべからず。いさめをふせぎ我を是とすべか
らず。おのれが不善をすてゝ人の善にしたがひ、
人の善を用ひて我身に行ふべし。我を知ありとす
るものは大愚にあらず。いましむべし。その愚をしる
のは大愚なり。其過をしるものは大なる過な
し。故に高滿にしておのれをゆるすものは必愚人
なり。いかんとなれば、自知の明なく、知をひらき

善にす〻むの基なくして、終に愚にてをはる。人をあなどる者は必天のとがめあり。人のせめあり。人をそしる者は必人にそしらる。古の君子は聡明審知なれども守之以愚。いはんや末世の凡夫、わづかなる智恵才能にほこるは甚おろかなりといふべし。尚書にも、その善にほこれば其の善をうしなひ、その能にほこればその能を失ふといへり。わが身にほこれば、みづから是として吾に過惡あることをしらざる故に、過を改め善にうつることあたはず。惡日々に長じ、善日々に消えぬ。しかれば、たとひ聖人と同じく居て、朝夕をしへをうくとも益なかるべし。つとめて書をよみ學問すとも、其の身に益なきのみにあらず、却て邪智をまし、才能にはこりて害あり。こゝを以て矜は天下の惡徳の由〻古人のいましめ明らかなり。學問する者まづ第一これをいましむべし。文盲なる人のことばに、學問すれば人品あしくなる、益なくして害ありといふは、世上にかやうの人あるを見て、そのくひせを守り、その上その人もとより學問をきらふ故に、妄にかくいふなるべし。もし己が身をを

さめんために實にまなばゞ、なんぞ益なからんや。害をはなるゝも事をしるも、一重に物を思ふべからず。うらのはまゆふの百重なることを思ひて、幾重にも理をきはむべし。心あさき人は一重をしりて、はやことはり至極して、この上なしと思ふははかなきことなり。今日一重をさりて、明日又一重をさり、日々かくのごとくすべし。皮をつくして肉を見、肉をつくして骨を見、骨をつくして髓を見るべし。凡理をきはむる學問は、心くはしかるき人は、なしうべからず。心くはしく静にすべし。

孔子曰「古之學者爲己。今之學者爲人。爲己とは我が身を修めん爲にする實學なり。爲人とは、人にしられんがためにする名利の學なり。學問の本意は己が身ををさめんためなれば、人の知と不知とにかゝはらず。たとへば食する者のわが飢をやめ、身を養はんためにするがごとし。只わが腹にみちなんことをのみ思ひて、さらに我が食したるを人にしらせんと願ふ心なし。學問はたゞ我が身を人にしられんことをのみ思ひて、さらに我が身をををさめんためにすべし。聊人にしられん爲にす

べからず。又聖人の子夏に、女爲ニ君子儒ニ無レ爲ニ
小人儒ニとの給へり。此意は、君子儒は只己が身を
をさめんために學べり。實學なり。小人儒は只人の
みにて、我が身をさむるに志なし。是名利をねがふ心の
みにて、我が身をさむるに志なし。僞學なり。
こゝを以て君子の心は、日々に善にすゝみて上達
し、小人の心は日々に惡におちいりて下達す。同
じく力を用ひて學問せば、君子儒となるべし。小人
儒となるべからず。つとめまなんで小人儒となる
はロをし。學者まづ初より己が爲にせんとする志を立つ
べし。是學問する人の第一に心得べきことなり。
しからざれば博く書をよみ學問しても、益なくし
てかへつて害あり。

書をよまばわが身に受用することを專一に志すべ
し。受用とは、書にしるせる聖人の敎をわが身に
うけ用ひて、まもり行ひ用ひるを云ふ。もし
書をよみ義理をきゝても、身にうけ用ひずして行
はざれば、何の益もなきいたづらごとゝなり。大學
をよんで、如レ惡ニ惡臭ニ如レ好ニ好色ニとあるを見て
は、我が心にこれをうけ用ひて、實に惡をきらふ

こと惡臭の如く、善を好むこと好色のごとくすべ
し。論語をよんで、父母につかへてよく其力をつ
くし、君につかへて能くその身をゆだぬとあるを
見ては、そのごとくおやにつかへて、わが身の力も
財の力も、をしまずして孝をつくすべし。臣とし
ては我が身をわがものにせずして、わたくしをわ
すれ、專ら君に忠をつくすべし。自餘も皆かくの
ごとくすべし。是を書をよんで受用すると云ふ。
もし書を多くよんでも受用せざるは、口耳の學と
いひて、耳にきゝて頓て口に言ひたるまでにて、
心にまもり身に行はざるは無用の學なり。

初學の人、書をよむにはまづ四書を熟讀し、又五經を
よくよむべし。五經は上代の聖人の敎なり、又五經
の祖義理の宗と云ひて、文字のはじめ義理のをし
への本なり。四書は孔門のをしへなり。是をよむ
はまのあたり聖賢の敎をきくが如し。愼ふべし。
文義やうやく通ぜば、四書の註、大學中庸の或問
を見て、後五經の註を見るべし。次に周程張朱四
家の書を見るべし。中につきて程朱の書尤よくよ
むべし。殊に小學の書は身をさむる大法をしる

せり。人倫の道はゝ備れり。はやくよんで其の義を習ひしるべし。又歴代の史、左傳史記朱子通鑑綱目を見るべし。是道をしり古今に通ずる學問の法なり。經傳及歴代の史に通ぜば、天下古今の事理明らかならずといふことなかるべし。聖人の書を經と云ふ、經とは常なり、聖人の言は萬世の常道なり。賢人の書を傳といふ、傳とは經なり。其註並周程張朱の書は傳ふるなり。四書五經は經なり。逃べ、後代に傳ふるなり。歴代の事をしるせる書を史と云ふ、記録のことなり。子は荀子楊子淮南子説苑文中子等の諸子の書を云。是は程朱の書のごとく、道理精明なるにはあらざれども、經書の義理を助くる益あり。見るべし。集は諸家の文章等の書なり、是文義理を發明せり。この經史子集の四の書は本末輕重あれども、皆學問のため用ある書なり。道をしらんとならば、經學を專として一生つとむべし。次に史學是もその益大なり。次に諸子諸集を見るべし。朱子綱目尤好書なり。古代の治亂盛衰の事迹をしるのみにあらず、義理の學にも亦大に助あり。殊に國土ををさむる人の明らかなる鏡なり。又軍の勝敗の道を記して、兵術を學ぶ人にも甚益あり。古來要用の故事も亦この内に多し、彼是尤益多し、つとめて數遍見るべし。誠に經世の大典とすべし。その外和漢の記録ちからにまかせて見るべし。又いとまあらば諸子百家の書を見て經説を發明し、義理の趣をひろむべし。しかれども、もはら博覧をつとめて雜學にうつり、志をうしなふべからず。學問は博くして又約にすべし。博ければ義理詳にして、備らずといふことなし。約なれば義理精しくして、明かならずといふことなし。博く學ぶにいとまなく、又中年以後はじめて學ぶ人は約にすべし。古人も博くして雜なるは、約やかにしてくらきにしかずといへり。およそ書をよみ學問するは、道をしらんがためなり。道を知らざれば、廣く古今の書をよみ、詩文章をよく作りても要用なし。學問の本意にあらず。又四書五經等の文義に通じて、古今の書をひろく見ても、一生義理をしらざる人多し。道に志なければなり。又志ありてもまなびやうあしければ、一生道をしらず。或は聰明の足らざる故にもよれり。

知をひらくことを勤むべし。

心學に志す人は日新の工夫を用ゆべし。日に新にす
とは、昨日のふるき惡をあらためて、今日あたら
しく善にうつり、けふはきのふにまさりて新しく
なるを日に新にすといふ。如ㇾ此くなれば、今日は
是にして、きのふは非なることを覺ふべし。かや
うにつとめてやまざれば、日々に工夫進み、月々
に異にして、年々に同じからず。一日は一日の功あ
り、一月には三十日の功あり、一年には三百六十
日の功あり、三年には千日の功ありて、德にすゝ
み善にうつりゆかば、其樂極りなくして、手の舞
ひ足の踏むことをしらざるべし。かくのごとくす
みゆかば、君子となること必期すべし。若けふ
はきのふにかはらず、今月は前川にことならず、
ことしはこぞに同じくば、日に新にするちからな
くして、いつまでも愚者にて世を終らんこと口を
し。

文學をつとむるも亦同じ、日々につとめてやまざれ
ば文學日々にすゝむ。數年の後は經傳の義理に通
じて樂となる。十年の功は甚だ大なり。文學半は
成就す。

萬の事はじめに苦勞せずしてをたれば、後に功な
らずして樂なし。たとへばあつき灸をこらへ苦き
藥をのめば、後に無病の人となるが如し。學問に
おいて尤このしるしあり。わかき時辛勞する人は
老て後樂多し。

書をよむには、まづ四書五經などを熟讀し、文字を
多くおぼえて訓詁に通ずべし。訓詁とは字義をい
ふ。文字訓詁をしらざれば、書を見わけがたく、
ちからなくして、書をよむにはかゆかず。文學の
すゝまざるは、字をしらざればなり。されども文
字訓詁にかゝはり止まりて、義理を自得せざるは
君子の學にあらず。

學問は智惠をひらく道なれば、廣く聞き多く見て義
理に通じ、我が心に智惠のおのづからひらくるを
待つべし。聰明をたのみ、我が才智を先だて用ゆ
べからず。人の才智をおさへずして、人の善言を
取りもちゆべし。位たかく年たけたる人、或は才
學の名ある人も、其の位と年と才とにほこるべか
らず。只人にへりくだりて尋ねとふは、知者のま

すく智をます道なり。

凡幼よりつとめまなぶに、ひまををしむべし。いに
しへの禹王は、聖人なりしだに、猶寸陰ををしみ
給ふ。いはんや今の凡人をや。いたづらに悠々と
して、むなしく時日をつひやすべからず。光陰箭
のごとく、時節は流るゝがごとくなれば、年わか
きをたのんで時をうしなふべからず。人の世にあ
るは、老幼の時とやまひする時は學びがたし。又
四民ともにその家のことわざしげくして、もの學
ぶひまはすくなし。そのすくなき隙ををしまず、
怠りてむなしく過ぎ、或は無益の事をなして時を
費し、一生をはかなくをはらんこと、いとおろか
なりといふべし。今年の今日ふたゝび得がたきこ
とを思ひて、かりにもいたづらに時をわたるべか
らず。是一生の間心を用ゆべきことなり。古人も
常にしておかず、つねに行ひてやまざる者には及
びがたしといへり。又いたづらになすことなく、
常に隙多き人は、人にすぐるゝことはなきものな
りといへり。たとへば農人商人のつとめていとま
ををしみ、朝夕田を作り、あきなふ者は必人にす

ぐれて、その家とみて衣食ともにしからず。古人も
人生はつとめにあり、つとむれば則まどしからず
といへり。國家の政をくはしくつとむれば、其國
家必をさまる。學問をくはしくつとむれば、必諸
人にすぐれてその才すゝむ。萬の事皆しかり。隙
をゝしみて久しくつとむれば、成就せざることな
し。それ人の寶はいとまに過ぎたるはなし。いか
んとなれば、君子の學問をつとめ、國家の政を行
ひ、父母主君に仕へ、諸藝をまなび、農の田を作
り、商人のひさぎ、百工の器物を作り、婦女の布
帛をおりぬるも、皆いとまを用ひてなし出すわざ
なれば、人の尤おもんじをしむべきこと、いとま
に過ぎたるはなし。故にそのをしむべきこと、
金玉にも過ぎたり。古語にも、聖人は尺璧を貴ば
ずして、寸陰を貴ぶといへり。隙をゝしまざる人
はまなぶことも、つとむることもなければ、必才
智も徳行も藝能もなきものなり。いとまををしま
されば、君子は身ををさめ、家をとゝのふる事あ
たはず。農工商はその家事を失ひて、貧窮飢寒を
まぬかれず。學者は必粗學にして不才なり。くす

しは必賤工なり。よろづの道々のたくみも、いとまををしまざれば、必つたなし。是いとまは人生の寶にしてをしむべき故なり。就中年少の咋は事すくなく、いとま多し、精力つよく記憶つよく、一たび見きヽて覺えしこと、身を終るまでわすれず。この時つとめまなべばその功多し。故に書をよむとは、少年の氣力つよくいとまある時、よくつとむれば大にすヽみて益あり。三十歳以後は、よろづつとめ多くなりて、いとまなく、精力やうやうよわくなるにしたがひて、その覺えおとろへぬれば、力を多く用ひてもわすれやすく、勞すれども功すくなし。年少なる人はこれをよく心得て、わかき時隙ををしみ、學問をつとむべし。誠に一生の寶となるべし。淵明が詩に曰。盛年不▷重來○一日難▷再晨○及▷時當▷勉勵○歳月不▷待▷人○又古詩に。少壯不▷努力○老大徒傷悲○といへり。わかき時是をよく考へ、後悔なからんことを思ひて、時日ををしみてつとむべし。又よくつとむれども、學問の術をえらばざれば一生益なきことにまよひ、心を用ひくるしみて、よき道をしらず。是又おろかなりといふべし。

凡君子の學問は知仁勇の三徳を本とし、五倫をあつくするを道とす。知仁勇は五倫の道を行ふ心の徳なり。知は五倫の道をしり、仁は五倫の道を身にたもちおこなひ、勇はつとめてしり、つとめて行ふ。しるも行ふも勇を以てつとむ。君子の學問をするに、その心法とする事三徳なり。行ふべき道とするは五倫なり。三徳と五常とは理同じ。五常はむまれつきたる性なり。三徳は學問をする心法なり。五常をつヽめていへり。

孔子曰。學而不▷止。闘▷棺而止。人と生れては人の道をしり、この身をよくをさめて、君子となることをつとめとすべし。是は人と生れたるかひあらんとなり。しかれば、人となるべき道を學ぶことをこたるべからず。一息も猶のこれる内は學ぶことやむべからず。死して後やむべし。

大和俗訓卷一卷終

# 大和俗訓 卷之二

## 爲學 下

貝原篤信 著

小學の敎は小子のまなぶ所少なる學問なり。いにし
へ八歳になれば、たかきいやしき、凡天下の人の
子となり弟となれる者、師のをしへをうけてまな
べり。これ小學なり。そのをしへは、父母に孝し、
兄長をうやまひ、君上につかへ、賓客に對する道、
或は座敷をはき、飮食をそなへ、賓者の前にす
みしりどき、いらへこたへをする禮ををしへ、又
日用の禮樂射御書數の六藝のわざをもをしへ、是
を以ていとけなき時より、その心をやしなひ、年
長じて、大學の道をまなぶもとゐとせり。凡小學
はわざををしふるなり。

大學とは、十五歳以上成人のまなぶ所、身を治め人
ををさむる大なる道理の學問なり。天下ひろしと
いへども、己と人より外なる物なし。己をををさめ人
ををさむる道をまなぶは大なる學問なれば大學と

いふ。明德を明らかにするはおのれを治むるなり。
民をあらたにするは人をををさむるなり。至善にと
ゞまるは、明德をあきらかにし、民をあらたにする
に、皆至極の善にいたりてとゞまるべしとなり。
故に明德新民の外に、至善にとゞまる道あるには
あらず。右の三綱領は大學の大要なり。此三にいた
る工夫の條目八あり、八條目は三綱領の内のこま
かなる工夫なり。格物致知は事物の理をきはめし
りて、知を開く道なり。誠意より以下は、皆力行
の道なり。就中誠意正心修身は、ともに身をををさ
むる道なり。齊家治國平天下は、人をををさむるの
道なり。凡大學は理を敎ゆるなり。

大學に、格物致知を以て、道理を明らかにするを、
身をををさめ人をををさむるつとめのはじめとす。格
物とは、萬事萬物の道理にきはめいたるを云ひ、
致知とは、わが心の知をきはめて、明らかにする
なり。格物の次第は、まづ五常五倫の道、身を治め
家をとゝのふるちかきとよりして、次第を以てや
うやく國天下をををさむる理にきはめ至る。是格物
なり。かくのごとく萬事萬物につきて理をきはむ

れば、わが心の知おのづから明らかになる。是致知なり。故に格物の外に致知の工夫なし。是大學のつとめのはじめなり。その次は誠意にあり、意とは心のはじめておこる所の苗なり。心の體はしづかにして、善惡いまだあらはれず、その初めてうごく時、善も惡もあらはる。意のおこる時にこのむと惡むとの二あり。惡むとはきらふなり。この時善をこのみ惡をきらふこと、眞實にしていつはりなきを誠意といふ。惡をにくむことは、好色を好むが如くにして、惡臭をきらふがごとくに眞實なるべし。善をこのみ惡をきらふこと眞實ならざれば、本たゞずして萬の道行はれず。故にこの後正レ心修レ身齊レ家治レ國平二天下一の工夫も皆是を以て初とす。されば大學の八條目は格物と誠意を以て要とす。格物は知のはじめなり。誠意は行のはじめなり。格物なくして萬の理をきはめざれば智明らかならずして、善惡をわかちがたければ、まよひてさとらず、夢のいまださめざるがごとし。誠意なくして、善をこのみ惡をきらふ、意誠ならざれば道を行ふべき基なくして、いまだ善人とはいひがたし。故にこの二を以て、致知力行のはじめとするこ とむべならずや。

凡人には必生れつきたる良智ありて、いかなる愚者も善惡をすこしはわきまへしれり。その上學問して理をきはめ、其智やうやくひらけぬれば、善を善とし、惡を惡とする心、いよいよ明らかになりぬ。されども善をこのみ惡をきらふに、誠なければ善行はれず。惡去らずして、生れつきたる良智のちからも、學問してしれる所も皆無用となりぬ。この故に學者道を行はんと思はゞ、まづ善を好み惡をきらふに誠わるべし。故に誠意の工夫尤大切なり。

學問の要二あり。いまだしらざる時は知らんことを求め、既にしれらば行ふべし、知らざれば行ひがたし。行はざればしらざるに同じく、無用の事となりぬ。こゝを以て學問の道は、只知と行との二にあり。又萬卷の書をよんでも、道をしらず行はざればよまざるに同じ。是道に志なければなり。こゝを以て大學の道まづ格物致知して、事物の理

をきはめ、わが知をひらき、さて知れる所の善を
このみ惡をきらふ心實にして、知れる所を行ふ、
是誠意なり。知ることいたらざれば、萬事の善惡
わきまへがたし。意誠ならざれば、善をなし惡を
さること、實ならずして道行はれず。この二は大
學の道の要にして、知行の工夫なり。

博學にして經書に通じ、義理をとく人も、その心術
行迹あしくして俗人におとれるもあり。是道に志
なくして、道を我が心に得ざればなり。口によみ
ならひて、目に見おぼえても、その理を心に得ざれ
ば益なし。たとへば美食芳樽前に多くつらなれど
も、これをのみくらはざれば、食にあくこともな
く、酒にゑふこともなきが如し。書をよんで、行
がひをはらすべし。書をみても道に志なくは、
文字をしれるのみにて、心において益なし。是無
用の學なり。こゝを以て學をするにはまづ志を本
とすべし。

朝は師にまなび、晝は朝まなびたることをつとめな
らひ、夕はこれをいよ／＼かさぬ。夜は一日の間

のあやまりをかんがへて、あやまちなければ、夜
をやすくいぬべし。もし過あらば、悔ひはぢて來
日のいましめとすべし。是國語にいへる所學問の
法とすべし。

いまだ書をよまざる人のためにいはゞ、この道を行
はんと志を立つることは、まことに第一なるべし。
されど經書をはじめとして、ひろく古の書をよま
ざれば、聖人の敎をしらで道にくらく、言ふこと
行ふことひが事のみぞあるべき。又古來歷代の事
をしらでは、今日のかゞみとすべきやうなし。こ
こを以て、つとめて朝夕書をよみ、いにしへをか
んがふべし。いかに生れつきたる才ありとも、稽
古なくては、おのれと道をしり、古今天下の變を
しるべからず。もし又すでに書をよめる人のため
にいはゞ、學問はたゞわが身のあやまりをあらた
め、善にうつりて、身ををさむる工夫を專一にす
べし。書をひろくよみ、古今天下のことに通ずと
も、もし我が身のあやまちをあらためず、善を行
はずばいたづらごとなり。しかれば、學問はまづ
志を立て、身に行ふを第一とすべし。書をよむは こ

れ第二義なり。

學問の道は師をたつとぶにあり。師尊くして道尊ぶ
べし、道尊くして民道をうやまふ。故に君として
位高しといへども、師をば臣としていやしめず。
いにしへ大學にしては、天子にをしふるにも北面
せず。師をたつとぶばなり。

此道理の天下にある處は、まづ吾が心を本とす。人
にまじはれば、君臣父子兄弟夫婦朋友の間行ふべ
き道あり。又我が身の萬のわざに皆十定の道理あ
りて、暫時もこの道をはなれがたし。凡夫といへど
此行ふべき道理のそなはること聖賢とかはらず。
又いかなる愚人も、善をこのみ惡をにくむ心あり、
生れつきたる良智ありて、この道のかたはしを少
しはしりて、日々用ひ行ふ。しからざれば一日も
世にたつことかたし。君父にそむき、亂逆をなし、
人とあらそひ、人ををかしかすめ、非法をおこな
ひては、しばらくも世に立つべからず。されども、
凡夫はこの道を能くしり、能く行ふことかたし。
故にいにしへの聖人世に出で給ひて、教をたてゝ
道理を明にして、これを書にあらはし給ふ。天下

の事大小精粗萬事の道理、一として聖賢の書に明
らかに備はらざる事なし。たとへば日月の天に中
して、萬物のかたち分明なるは、凡目あるもの是
を見ざることなきが如し。其書をよむものは必そ
の道をあきらめ、その理を我が心にたもち、身に
行ひて、人倫にまじはり・萬事をつとめ、人民を
をさむ。かくのごとくにして、人の職分をつくし
て、天地の間にたつべし。若如く此ならざれば、人
たるの道をうしなひ、人の職分かけ、天地の理に
そむけり。凡物皆職分あり、天地は物を生じやし
なふを心とし給ひ、天はおほひ地はのする、これ
天地の職分なり。萬物の微細なるも皆各職分あり、
雞の晨をつくり、犬の夜を守るの類、みなその物
に生れ得たるわざをつとむるを以て、其物の職分
を行ふとす。人は萬物の靈なり、其心本明らかに、
萬理備はれり。若人として身に備りたる理を行は
ず、人の職分をむなしうすといふべし。人を以
て鳥獸にだもしかざるべけんや。

書をよむ人は、まづ其學問のすぢを正しくし、又心
術を正しくすべし。學問も心法も、一すぢに天地

聖人の道にしたがひて、一點も邪をまじへずして純一なるべし。聖人の道をこのむとも、その間に又少しにても聖人の道に似ざる所あらば、純一なりといひがたし。學純一なれば、その心法も邪なくして正し。心法正しければ、行事にあらはし發するも皆正し。たとへば道をゆく人の、まづ道のすぢを尋ねしるが如し。道のすぢをしらずして、ただに行くことをのみつとめば、たとへば都にある人奥州にゆかんとて、まづ淀山崎へむかひ行くが如し。いよ〳〵つとめ行くほど、いよ〳〵奥州には遠ざかることをしらざるなり。是只道をいそぐことをしりて、道をあやまることをしらざるなり。

孔子曰。幼成如二天性一習慣如二自然一とは、幼少より習ひて成就したることは、天性にうまれつきたるが如くなり。又ひさしくならひなれてそみぬることは、よきもあしきもつとめずして、自然によくするが如しとなり。善惡ともに性に出でたるよりも、習より出づること多し。然れば習ひなること、善惡をえらびつゝしむべし。ならひてなれぬることは、生れつきたる自然の如し。學問をするも善にならびなるゝわざなり。人の惡をするも必生れつきてするのみにはあらず、惡人にならひてすること多し。故に孔子も、性は相近し習へば相遠しとのたまへり。

およそ人の不孝不忠、もろ〳〵の惡を行ひ、慾をほしきまにゝし、身をほろぼし、家をほろぼすにいたるは、何にかよれるや。知なければなり。又善を行ひて家をおこし、身をたもち、ほまれを得るは、何の故ぞや。知あればなり。知あればよく善惡をしる。善のなすべきことをしりて行ひ、惡のなすまじきことをしりて行はず。この故に知は身の内の大なる寶なり。學者道に志さば知を求むるを第一とすべし。知をひらくことは、學問の功にあらずんば成りがたし。

程子の曰、人の不善をするは只知らずとす。言ふころは、世人の惡をするは惡のすまじき理をしらざればなり。よくしれらばなどか人のためわがため、あしきがことをば行ふべき。たとへば赤子のはらばひて井に入らんとするは、赤子のとがにあらず、いまだ知あらずして、井に入れば死ぬる

學問はそのはじめをつゝしんで、その術をえらぶべし。もしそのはじめ、學術正しからず、一たびわやまりてあしき方にふみまよへば、其あやまりにならびて、改めてよき道に立ちかへりがたく、身を終るまで、ひがことにまよへることをしらず、かへりて正しき道をきらひそしる、天地の道にそむき人の道を失ひ、一生の間まよひてさとらず、かなしむべし。學問せんと思はゞ、必まづ明師良友にしたがひて學術をえらぶべし。是はじめをつゝしむなり。易緯に、君子愼レ始、もしたがふことはじめのたがひは少なれど、後のあやまりは千里の遠きにいたる。そのはじめ學術をえらぶこと、毫釐なれば、あやまるに千里を以てすといへり。

千里の道も一歩よりはじまる。たとへば遠き所に行くに、出でたつ足もとよりはじまりて、つとめゆ

ことをしらざればなり。世の人の惡をするも亦かくのごとし。あはれむべし。故に學問して知をひらき、道をしることをつとむるは、人間の一大事なり。

きてやまざればとゞかざることなし。學んで道にいたるも亦かくのごとくなるべし。志を立てゝ道をまなび、つとめ行ひてやまず、久しく年をつまば、などかその功を成して遠大にいたらざらん。たとへば商人の一錢をつみ、つみかさねて、久しく年ふれば大なる富人となるがごとし。

聞見の智あり、眞智あり。聞見の智は、書をよみ人に聞きてしるを云ふ。是しることゝあさし。眞智とは聞見の智によりて、わが心に道理を眞にしるをいふ。是しることゝふかし。學問はまづ聞見の智より入るべし。書をよみ道をきかざれば、眞にしるきやうなし。聞見たるまでにとゞまりて、眞にしらざるは道をしるにあらず。眞にしれどもとゞまりて、眞にしりても行はざるはいまだ眞にしらざるなり。故に學者は聞見の知を初として、後には眞智を求むべし。聞見の學にとゞまるべからず。

書をよみ學問すれば、聞見の智は日々にすゝむ。されども知れることをおこなはざれば、德行は日々におくれてすゝまず、行はざれば其しれる所眞智にあらず。故に今の學者は其まなぶ所とおこなふ

所と、大にそむけり。是己がためにまなばざれば
なり。學者まづ誠の志を本とし、聞見の智より入
りて、知れることをも行ひ、眞智にいたるべし。
學問の道は心をむなしくし、へりくだり、よくしれ
ることをもしらざるが如くにし、我が才と行とにほこらず、
わが智を先だてずして、人に問ひ、人のいさめを
聞き用ひ、我が過を改めて善にうつるべし。かく
のごとくすれば、學問の益あり、善にすゝむこと
はまりなし。もし自ほこり、我を是とし、人を非と
し、人の諫をふせぎ、我が過をきく事をきらはゝ、
才學に長ずるにしたがひて、その心あしくなりて、
學問の益なきのみにあらず、かへりて害となるべ
し。是己が爲にせずして人のためにする故、君子
儒とならずして、小人儒となるなり。かくのごと
くならんは學ばざるにおとれり。

學問に有用の學あり、無用の學あり。わが儒の學は、
有用の學なり。有用の學とは、學問をすれば、わ
がため人のため益となるを云ふ。この故に學問の
道は有用の學をすべし、無用の學をすべからず。

有用の學は身ををさめて、人倫の道をあつく行ひ、
ことに忠孝をつとめ、善をなして人を助けすくふ
にあり。貧賤なる者も善を行ふ志だにあれば、人
を救ふこと多し。いはんや富貴の人は、そのちか
らによりて其のほどこしひろし。故に富貴の人の
學は我が身を修むるのみならず、仁愛の心を本と
し、人を助けすくふことを、專つとめ行ふべし。
是皆有用の學なり。もし口に高きことをのみ、心に
いさぎよきことをこのみ、身に艱苦なることを行
ふとも、仁義の心を求めず、人倫の道を行はず、善
をなして人に益あることをなくば、無用の學なるべ
し。又詩文を作り、心をくるしめ、多く隙をつひ
やし、たくみにかざりて、人にほめられんことを
求めて、日用人倫の道に志なきは、益もなきいた
づらごとなり。皆是無用の學なり。

楊子曰。學者所=以求=爲=君子=也。言ふこゝろは、
學問をするは何の爲ぞや、君子とならんが爲なり。
君子とは有徳人を云ふ。君子の字義は、易の正
義に、人の君となりて萬民を子のごとくする德あ
る人といへり。いやしくして下にありても、その

德あれば君子と稱す。君子となるとは人となるなり。學ばざる人は云ふにたらず、學んでも君子とならずんば、學ばざるに同じくして人と生れたるかひなし。君子となること容易からず。しかれども、志を立ておこたらずんば、必その功あるべし。古語にも、志あるものはその事つひに成るといへり。學は終〻身のことなり、一息もいまだのこれる内は、この志おこたるべからず。是れ人の一生の間のつとめなり。

およそ、人聖人にあらざれば、必あしき生れつきのくせあり。是氣質の偏なり。故に身ををさむる道は他なし、たゞ我が氣質のあしき所をみづから察し、人にいはせてきゝ、其の偏なるあしき所にかちて改め去るべし。かくのごとくせずして、生れつきて偏なる所にまかせぬれば、心正しからずして身をさまらず。書をよみ學問し、道を好み行ふと思ふも、皆我が氣質の偏なることを行ふ。故にいたづらごとくなる。氣質の偏の害となること、たとへば田を作るに莠あるがごとし。苗を植ゑて水をそゝぎ肥しても、莠を去らざれば苗長せず。

水と肥しの養ひも、皆莠のためになりて、いたづらごとなり。故にわが氣質のあしき所を知りて改むること、これ學問する人の專つとむべきことなり。學者必ここに心を用ふべし。およそ、人のあやまりあしきことは、皆その生れつきの偏なるくせよりおこる。こゝを以て、學者は必氣質を變化じて過を改むべし。こゝを以て、學者は必氣質を變化じて過を改むべし。我が氣質の偏惡と、我が過をみづからしる人まれなり。かへりみて察し知るべし。是學問の要なり。我が氣質の偏惡と、我が過をみづからしる人まれなり。正直にして過をつぐる益友を求め、忠臣を近づけて諫を聞き用ふべし。碁をうつ人は手見えず、傍より見る人は、眼よく見ゆるがごとし。

君子は氣質の偏惡なし、無病の人なり。衆人は皆氣質の偏なる病ある故、過のみ多し、皆病人なり。その病を去りて君子にいたるべし。病を其まゝおきて、其惡を長ずべからず。病を去らんと思はゞ、明師良友にあひて、その敎をうけ、其氣質の惡しきを改むべし。たとへば病人の良醫にあひて、其の病をいやすが如し。病人は醫を招きて藥を服せざれば、無病の人となりがたし。衆人に氣質の病あ

るも亦しかり。師友にあひ、又みづからせめて、其
氣質の病を改め去らずんば、君子とはなりがたか
るべし。朋友の我が過を正すをきらひ、臣下のいさ
めをふせぐは、病人の醫をきらひて藥を用ひず、病
死すれどもさとらざるがごとし。かなしむべし。

古語曰。人生至樂。無レ如レ讀レ書。至要無レ如レ敎レ子。
又古人の詩曰。至哉天下樂○終日在二几案○書をよむ
の樂、いたれるかな。富貴ならずしてその樂大な
り。酒色ならずしてその樂ふかし。山林ならずし
てその樂しづかなり。古語に、書をよむこと一卷
なれば、一日の益あり。又人の神智をますこ
と・書をよむにしくはなしといへり。富貴にして
書を好む人はその樂ひろし。貧賤にして書をこの
む人はその樂ふかし。次に子ををしへて、我が志
をつがしむべし。是肝要のことなり。子を敎へず
して、道をしらしめざるは父のあやまりなり。不仁
と云ふべし。

うたがひを人に問ふは、智を求むる道なり。みづ
から心に道理を思ふは、智をひらく本なり。問ふ

は智を人に求るなり。思ふは智をわれに求るなり。
人に問はざれば、知ることせばくして心に迷ひと
けず。みづから思はざれば、見きくことひろしと
いへども、道理をわが心にふかく自得せず。この故
に、問ふと思ふとの二は、理をきはめ智を明らか
にする道にして、學の要なり。

道に志なき人は、いふにたらず。たとひ道に志あり
て、ひろく學ぶとも、學びやうあしければ一生道
をしらず。或は道學をこのめども、文句にかゝは
りて義理に通ぜず。是を訓詁の學と云ふ。その人
はみづから道學をすと思ひ、自是とし人にほこれ
ども、訓詁の學なることをしらず。又道學の名を
むさぼりこのみて、その實なき人あり。只道學の
實をこのむべし。道學の名を好むは、不實にして
益なし。又古訓を學ばず、聖人の法にしたがはず
して、ひとへに我が心に求る學あり。是無學にま
されりといへども聖學にあらず。師傅ありといふ
とも私の學なり。眞の學問をせんと思はゞ、道に
志し德をたつとびて、孔孟の敎を本とし、程朱の
說を階梯とすべし。是すぢみよき眞の學なり。末

世にいたりてあしき學術多し。えらぶべし、迷ふべからず。

學者、文學言句に求るつとめは常に多く、日用徳行に心を用ふるつとめは常にすくなし。是學問の本意を失へり。もし徳行をつとめずして文學を好むは、たとへば酒をすてゝ糟をくらふが如し。よき所をば取りて用ひずして、よからざる所をこのむなり。

道をしること至りてかたし。よのつねの俗學の習にては、身を終るまでつとめ學びても道を知りがたし。まづ學を好むに誠の志ありて、明師良友にしたがひ、いにしへの學のすぢをたづねもとめ、心を用ふること久しくば、その功あるべし。利口にして我が才にほこり、このんで我が智をたのみ用ふる人は、道に遠き生れつきなり。身をはるまで、此道をしることかたかるべし。只生れつき質實にしてかざりなく、その心しづかに、義理にさとく、へりくだりて自是とせざる人あらば、これ道にちかき生質なり。かゝる人、志專一にしてよく學ばゞ、この道をやうやく晩年にしてしるべし。

世の人、多くは藝をこのみて學問をこのまず。藝は、たとへば木の枝葉なり。學問は、たとへば木の根本なり。根本をつとめずして枝葉をつとめ、本をすてゝ末に專なるはひがごとなり。道學なければ、藝多くしても根本たゝず。君子とすべからず。又技藝なければ、事に通ぜずして其德の助なし。野人といふべし。

わかき時は、經學を本として、ひろく群書に通じ、且又有用の諸藝を習ふべし。中年以後は、博覽をやめて經傳の要文をつゝまやかにあぢはひ、道理をくはしくし、心に自得せんことを求むべし。いまだ道をしらざれば、ゆめ見てさめざるが如し。故に大學の致知を夢覺の關と云ふ。ゆめみると、さむるとのさかひなり。善をこのむと誠ならざれば、惡人の境界をまぬがれず。故に大學の誠意を善惡の關と云ふ。善人と惡人とのさかひなり。關とは内外のさかひなり。

聖人は人倫の至りなり。吾がともがらの口にかけまくは、いともかしこし。されど弓ゐる者は、はじ

めより的に志し、道ゆく者は初より家に志すがごとし。聖人をめあてとして、その志を立つることは高くすべし。然るに千里の道も、出でたつ足もとの一歩よりはじむる理なれば、道を行ふことは、まづ日用のちかくひきゝ所より行ひて、やうやくへのぼりて高きにいたるべし。はじめよりしなをこえて、高くいたらんとするは、つばさなくして、天に上らんとするに同じ。必この理なきことをして天に上らんとするに同じ。萬事は次第にしたがはざれば成就しがたし。ちか道なることは、口にいふところは快したし。たとへば高山にのぼるにも、先ふもとの一足よりはじむるがごとし、一とびに山上には上りがたし。萬事は次第にしたがはざれば成就しがたし。ちか道なることは、口にいふところは快したし。たとへば高山にのぼるにも、先ふもとの一足よりはじむるがごとし、一とびに山上には上りがたし。ちか道なることは、口にいふところは快したしといへども、道理のなきことは、ならざるものなれば、虚妄の説、無用の辯はいたづらごとなり。ふたゝび生れ來るべきたのみなき此世の間なるに、天地人のいたれる道をまなんで樂しまんこそ、いけるかひありて、身終る時もうらみなかるべけれ。我が身の私慾にくるしめられ、世俗のいやしきならはしにまよひて、人の道をしらずして一世を終らんこと、かへすぐゝ口をしと思ひ、かねて心を

用ゆべし。

聖人の書をよみ、道をこのみて日を送る人は、誠に諸人にすぐれ、一生の間常に樂しみて、思いで多き世なるべし。かくのごとくならば、人とむまれたるかひありて、朝にすでに道をきゝなば、夕に死ぬともさらにうらみあるべからず。貧賤にして時にあはざるは憂ふるにたらざるべし。もし聖人の道をまなばずして、道をしらずば、此世にいける時は禽獸と同じくして、人とむまれたるかひなく、死して後は草木とおなじくくちはてゝ、人のほむべき佳名を殘すことなく、後世にいたりてしる人なかるべし。われも人も、皆かくのごとくなれど、人とかく生れし身を、とりわけだもの草木に同じくせんこと、はいなきこととならずや。これを口をしと思はゞ、あにこのうれひをまぬかるべき道なかるべきや。人の身はふたゝび得がたし、むなしく此世を過すべからず。

書をよみ學問せんとする人あれば、彼のきらふ人、色々いひさまたげて、學問することをそしる。まことゞと心得て學問をやむる人多し。又我が子に

七五

254

書をよませんとするに、かのきらふもの書をよめ
ば、病者になり、氣へり、いのちみじかくなるな
どといひておどせば、おやは子をいつくしむ心ふ
かくして、もし左もあるべきかと思ひて、書をよ
ませざるゆへ、其子は一生文盲に、おろかにて身
ををはる。あはれむべし。

書をよまざる人は、書をよむ人をきらひにくみて、
書をよめば氣へり病者になり、心うつけてぬるく
なり、出家長そでのごとく、武道もよはくなると
いひてそしる。書をよむ人、これをきゝて、いか
りあらそひ、口論となり、たゝかひに及ぶことそ
のためしあり。凡人は、ひとの我に同じきをよろ
こび、我にことなるをにくみ、わがしらざるを以
て人のしるをそしる。是凡人のつねの心なり。か
るひがことをきゝて、いかりあらそふは、われも
亦彼のおろかなる人と同じくなるは口をし。書を
よみ學問するは、かゝるおろかなる人になるまじ
きがためなり。愚人の學問をそしり、我ををかす
ば、不智なる故なりと思ひて、あはれみゆるすべ
し、いかるべき理にはあらず。又愚人のあだごとを

云ふとて、我が心にかけてあづかるべからず。聖人
は、かゝる頑なる人をあはれみて、いかりにくみ
給はず。是を以て則とすべし。

俗人の學問をそしるは、學者書をよんでも、道を行
はずして、かへりて高滿にしてみづからほこり、
人をあなどりて、心ざまあしくなりゆき、學びた
る益なきが故なり。學者つゝしみて身をかへりみ
るべし。書をよむによつて、かへつてかくのごと
くなる小人となるはくちをし。

我が才にほこり、自是として人をあなどり、人の才
智あるを取用ひず、只我が才智のみを用ゆ。古語
にも自用ふれば即小なりといへり。諸人の智を用
ゆるは大なり、われ一人の智を用ふるは小なり。
我が學才にほこり、人をあなどるは是才學のため
にわが德をそこなはるゝなり。かゝる惡德あらん
よりは、才學なきがはるかにまされり。聖賢の書
を多くよんでも、道に志なくして不德なるは、無學
なる者の心あしく道にそむくよりも、其つみ猶ふ
かし。學者如此なれば、學をきらふ俗人の言に、
學問は益なし、かへりて害ありと云。その證據に

なりて、學問の道の害となる。つゝしみて學をそ
しる俗人の證據にならんことをうれふべし。
學者はまづ孝弟忠信を先として、常に善を好み人を
愛するを以て志として、日々につとめて善を行ふ
べし。書をよむをば第二義とすべし。第一善を好
まざれば、書をよんでも道を行ふべき基なし、萬卷
の書をよむとも無用の事なるべし。大學誠意の章
をよく味はひて、善を好み惡を嫌ふに誠あるべし。
學者志を立つること、真實なるを以て本とす。只道學
の實をつとめて、道學の名を好むべからず。名聞
のため、わづらはさるゝはいやし。　天地の間に、
我が身はどうしたしき物なし、學問せば只身の為
にすべし、名の為にすべからず。しかれども、から
やまと、いにしへ今道學の名をむさばる人多し。名
を好む學者は、形は善人に似たれども、善を好むの
誠すくなし、位も德もなくして、我が身を自置くこ
と其高く、賢人君子の模樣をなし、其身に應せぬ
言を出しふるまひをなせり。みづから其外量を知
らずして、古今をそしり、人の小過をとがめ、不能
をせめ、刻薄なること無學の人より甚しく、人をあ

はれむ心うすし。不仁と云ふべし。人情時變をし
らずして、古禮を當世に直に行はんとす、不智と
いふべし。もしかくのごとくならば、時俗の耳目
をおどろかして、道學の名を得ても益なかるべし。
無學なる人、かゝる學者を見ては、儒者は一向に
偏にして、國俗と人情にそむき、時宜をしらざる
無用の者と思へり。是道學のますゝゝすたれる所
なり。明の陳繼儒が、僧は真ならんことを要む、
儒者は只道を信じて、真實なるを貴しとす。人に
高ぶりて、誠すくなきはいやしむべし。
儒者は只道ならんことを要めずといへり。儒者も亦しかり。

○本朝の儒術、古來二千歲・寥々たりといへども、
太平日久しければ、世の人文もいよゝゝやうやく
開けぬべし。しからば、今より百年の後は・文字
の習も拙からず、義理の學も大に明らかになるべ
し。文明の國となりて、誠に君子國の名にかなふ
べし。只今より後、學術の正しくしていやしから
ず、學者の志真實にして、聖人の道をあつくたふ
とび信ぜむことをこひねがふのみ。

# 大和俗訓 卷之三

## 心術 上

貝原篤信 著

心は身の主にて萬事の本根なり。この故に心正しからざれば、身をさまらずして、家をとゝのへ人をさめがたし。たとへば、草木の根堅からざれば枝葉さかえず、家の主不德なれば家をさまらざるが如し。心を正しくする道は、まづ善をこのみ、惡を嫌ふこと、眞實なるを本とすべし。心の内に、善をこのむ誠なく、惡をさらふことまめやかならずんば、猶惡人の境界をまぬかれがたきゆへ、心を正しくすべきやうなかるべし。是大學の道、心を正しくせんとはつしては、先其の意を誠にするにあり。既に善をこのみ惡をさらふこと誠わらば、心を正しくすることやすかるべし。心を正しくすとは、心よりおこる所の喜怒哀樂愛惡慾の七情、よきほどに過不及なくして、かたおちざるを云ふ。喜ぶべくしてよろこび、その喜すぐすべからず。

いかるべくしていかり、その怒過すべからず。自餘も亦かくのごとくなるべし。七情過不及なくして、かたおちざれば、心の内とゝこほりなくして、常に和平なり、是心正しきなり。

尙書曰。人心惟危。道心惟微。惟精惟一。允執二厥中一。

是いにしへの大聖虞舜の帝の、天下を治し聖人にゆづらせ給ふ時、天下を治め給ふ心法を傳へ給ふ御敎なり。人心とは、人の身の耳目口體の形氣の好む所によつておこるを云ふ。形氣の好む所とは、目に色をこのみ、耳に聲を好み、口に味を好み、形には安らかなることを好むを云ふ。又よろこび、いかり、かなしみ、たのしみ、この み、にくみ、ねがふの七情も、是形氣よりおこる人心なり。うゑて食をこのみ、寒くして衣をもとめ、つかれて形をやすむるの類、又七情も。皆是人情のなくて叶はざることとなれば、聖人といへども、人心なきことあたはず。然れども、衆人は耳目口體の好むにまかせ、七情のおこるにまかせぬれば、ほどよきことをわすれ、たちまちに、私欲にながれ惡におちいる。故に人心はこれ危しとの

たまふ。あやうしとは、たとへば、小児を火のは
たに置きたるが如く、酔へる人のがけほりにおち
入らんとするが如し。道心とは、仁義禮智の本性
よりおこる善心なり。道心惟微とは、微はすこし
きにしてかくるゝなり。人心は形氣よりおこる
故、外にあらはれうごきて、その勢さかんになり
やすし。道心は心底にかくれ、かすかにしてあら
はれがたし。故に道心は惟微とのたまふ。人心は
さかんになりやすく、道心はかくれやすし。二の
者、胸中に相まじりて、そのをさめやうをしらざ
れば、人心はいよいよあやうくして、人欲になが
れ、道心は彌かすかにして、つひに人心におほは
れてほろぶ。こゝにおゐて、人心をおさへ、道心
をたもつ道なくんばあるべからず。惟精とは、人
心道心二の間をわかちて、明らかにくはしくしる
なり。惟一とは、すでに、人心道心をわかちしれ
ば、專一に道心を主として、人心のあやふき方にま
かせざるを云ふ。かくの如くなれば、一心のしわ
ざ皆道心より出で、人心は道心の下知にしたがふ。
允執二厥中一。中とは、人心のなす所、耳目口體七情

のわざ、皆過不及のあやまりなきを云ふ。是道理の
至極にて、目あてにする所なり。惟精惟一なれば、
萬の身のわざ、皆過不及のあやまりなくして、よき
ほどの中にかなふなり。飲食ふわざを以ていはゞ、
酒食をこのむは人心なり。酒食を過すべからずと
思ふは道心なり。酒食をこのむ心にまかせぬれば、た
ちまち威儀を失ひ、脾胃をそこなふにいたらんと
す。是人心は危きなり。酒食を過せば、身の害に
ならんことをおそるゝ道心はありといへども、人
心さかんなれば、おそるゝ心はおのづからかすか
にしてあらはれがたし。是道心惟微なるなり。か
くの如くに、酒食を好む心にまかせ、おそるゝ心
かすかなれば、たちまち、酒食をほしいまゝにす
ごし、おそるゝ心はなくなりて、つひに人欲にか
たず。然るに人心のわがまゝなると、道心のつゝ
しみあるとの二を、明らかにしりてまよはざるは
惟精なり。すでに酒食の過ぎて損あり、節にして益
あることをくはしくしれらば、專一につゝしみて
道心を主とし、人心のむさぼりこのむ欲をいまし
めをさへて、おのづから過不及のあやまりなかから

しむべし。すべて論ずるに、人心惟危。道心惟微。惟精惟一は、心を

むさらめ、道心を主とする工夫なり。允執二厥中一は、中は過不及なき至極の道理なり。必惟精惟一は、人心道心二の有さまなり。道心を主とする至極の道理なり。

の工夫ありて、過不及の過なき道理を失はざるべしとの意なり。是大聖人の天下をゆづり給ふ時、傳へ給へる大事の心法なれば、眞理至極なるべし。この十六字は、萬世心學の敎の根源なり、王公より以下庶人にいたるまで、皆たつとんでよく心得、受用あるべきことなるべし。

天地の人をあはれみめぐみ給ふことかぎりなし。食物衣服居所器物、もろ〳〵の人の、身を養ふ物を生じてあたへ給ふ。もろ〳〵の人、是をとりて用ひ、我が身をやしなふ。天下の人、たかきもひきゝも、一人もそのめぐみをうけざる人なし。その恩のふかく高きこと、海山にもくらべがたく、言語にも逃べがたし。又藥物を生じて生を救ふ。凡世にあらゆるよろづの物、人の身を養ひ助くる品々、多きことゝあげてかぞふべからず。是皆天地の人をあつくめぐみ給ふ所なり。天地の禽獸を養ふこと

は、人を養ひたまふ百分が一にもあらず。其上、禽獸は人にころされて食と成り、草木はきられて用となる。然れば人の萬物より貴くして、天地のあつきめぐみをうくること思ひしるべし。かくのごとく、天地の恩をあつくかうぶりても愚なる人はしらず、平生一の善事をもなさずして、天地につかへ奉り、恩を報ずる道を行はず。いはんや不仁にして、天地のうみやしなひ給ふ人物をそこなひなやまして、天地の生理を妨げ、天地の物をつひやし、天地の御心にそむくをや。是れ天地の恩をしらず、天地に不孝にして、人道を失へりと云ふべし。天道おそるべし。我輩愚にして、天地の大恩の萬一を報ずるほどのちからこそなくとも、せめて天地の道にそむかず、天地の生じ給ふ物をそこなはゞざるべし。古人は、天道の眼前にあることをしりて、朝夕おそれをなしてそむかず。今の世の人も、亦かくのごとくなるべし。詩曰、天の威をおぢて、こゝにこれをたもつといへり。學者は、つねに天道をおそるゝを以て心とすべし。人道はかならずかくの如くなるべし。

つねに心の内をかへりみて、一點の私欲邪念あらば
はやく去るべし。私欲とは、名利色貨（シキクワ）の欲とて、
名聞を好み、色を好み、貨（タカラ）を好むの類、並に耳目
口體の好む所の身に私する慾をいふ。邪念とは、
人をしへたげ、人といかりあらそひ、我が身には
こり、人をあなどり、人をそねみそしり、人にへ
つらひ、人をあざむきいつはるのたぐひなり。
皆是れ、邪惡の心なり。もし是等のことつゆばかり
もあらば、すみやかに去るべし。心を害すること
甚しければなり。又氣質の偏あらば勝つべし。氣質
の偏とは、生れつきにかたおちたる所あるをいふ。
氣のあらきとさわがしきと、又やはらかすぎてよ
わきと、或ははやすぎると、にぶくゆるすぎたる
のたぐひ、或は生れつきて、いかりおほく、慾お
ほきのたぐひをいふ。是皆氣質の偏なり。心を害
す。凡氣質のあしき所を變化することを、きはめて
かたし。平生心を用ひて恥に勝たずんばあるべか
らず。又あやまちあらばすみやかに改むべし。過
とは、たくみて惡をするにはあらず、是非をしらず
して、不意に道理にそむくをいふ。氣質の偏によ

り私慾の妨によりて過をなすこと多し。人聖人に
あらず、誰も過多し。過としらば速に改めて善にう
つるべし。やぶさかなるべからず。客なりとは、過
ををしみて改めかぬるをいふ。凡私慾邪念と氣質
の偏と過と、此三の者ありては心術を害す。心を
正しくし、道を行はんとすれども、是等の過惡あ
りて去らざれば、慾にすゝむべきやうなし。たと
ば田を作るに莠（アザ）を去らざれば、水をそゝぎこやし
しても、莠のみしげりて苗に益なし、まづ莠をさり
て水と肥（コヤシ）しを用ゆるがごとし。又身の病を去りて
後、補養するが如し。
人にまじはるに、愛敬の二を心法とす。是簡要のこ
となり、誰もしらずんばあるべからず。愛とは、人
をあはれむをいふ、にくまざるなり。敬とは、人を
うやまふをいふ、あなどらざるなり。人をあはれ
むは仁なり。人を敬ふは禮なり。仁禮を心の内に
たもちて人をあはれみ、人をうやまふことわする
べからず。是人に對して行ふべき善なり。父母を
あはれみ主君をうやまふはいふに及ばず、うとき
人いやしき人に對すとも、其位にしたがひて、よ

きはどに愛敬すべし、あなどりおろそかにすべからず。是人にまじはる道なり。

およそ人の心、必仁義禮智の性あるゆへに良心時におこる。其良心をむなしくせずして擴め充つべし。おしひろめみつとは、善心のわづかにおこるをそこなはずして、そだてやしなひさかんならしめ、其分量を十分にみてゝ、いづくにも行きわたらしむるをいふ。たとへば水のはじめて流れ出づるをせきとめずしてながし、さかんにおこらしむるが如くすべし。この良心をおしひろめば、遠き四海ををさめて餘あり。おしひろめざればちかき父母につかふるにだにたらず。是孟子の説、殊に親切なる教なり。學者必服膺してつとめ行ふべし。

仁は人をあはれみ物をそだつる善心なり。是天地のめぐみの心をうけて人の心とする所なり。故に孟子に、仁は人の心なりといへり。人ごとに生れつきたる本心なり。君子はこの本心を失はず、おのれを愛する心を以て人を愛し、人我のへだてなし。小人はひとへに我が身を愛して人を愛せず、人我

のへだてふかし、是私欲あればなり。是を不仁といふ。人たるものは仁を以て心とすべし。不仁の人は本心を失ひ、人道をほろぼし天道にそむく。この故に人の尤いましむべきと不仁より先なるはなし。不仁は天地人のにくむ所なり。故につひに天罰をかうふりてわざはひあり。その上子孫までもむくふものなり、天道おそるべし。この道理古今、からやまと、ためし多し。たがふことなし。

易に、天地の大德を生ずといふ。この理よくあぢはひてしるべし。生とはいきて死なず、いかしてころさず、生々してやまず、この故に、天地は萬物をうみてそだて給ふ萬物の父母なり。物をあはれみていかすことをこのみ、ころすことをきらひ給ふ。是天地の大德なり、生の理なり。人は天地の子なれば、其心に天地の大德、生の理そなはりて、天地のめぐみの心を生れつきたり、是を仁と云。仁は人物をあはれみ愛するの心にして、是即天地の生物の心なり。萬物は皆天地のうめる所なり。その中に取分人倫は最天地のめぐみあつし、萬物

の内にていと貴くして、天地の子とする所なり。
この故に天地の御心にしたがひ、仁心を以て物を
愛するには、人倫におゐてことさらにあつくすべし。
人倫をあつくするは、是天地の御心に順ふなり。
人倫を愛するにも次第あり。まづ父母兄弟を愛す
るは、仁を行ふ本なり。次に親類臣下朋友、次に萬民を愛すべし。次
に鳥けだもの蟲魚を愛してみだりに殺さず。次
に草木を愛してみだりにきらず。是人をあはれみ物
を愛する次第なり。されど又惡人をころすとも、是
義にして仁にかなへり。又樹木も時を以てきり、
鳥獸も道理を以てころすは義なり。みだりにころしきるは不仁なり。
とて、みだりにころしきるは不仁なり。
物を一體とす。故に人倫はいふに及ばず、物とし
て愛せざることなし。孔子も、一樹をきり、一獸
をころすに、其時を以てせざるは、孝にあらずと
のたまへり。されば禽獸も草木も、皆天地の生ず
るものなれば、みだりに是をそこなふは、天地に對
して不孝なりとしるべし。人物を愛するに、した
しきよりうときに及び、重きよりかろきにいたる

べし。輕重親疎の差別なく、平等に愛するは義に
あらず。墨子が兼愛とて、天下の人を一様に愛する
は、父母をも路人と同じくするなり。是仁の道を
しらずして、義にかなはざるなり。

人は天地の子なり、天地を法として行ふべし。天地
は別に心なし、萬物をあはれむを以て心とせり。
別にしわざなし、萬物をうみ出しやしなふを以て
わざとせり。人も亦この心をうけて、常に人にめ
ぐみあはれむを以て心とすべし、別の念あるべか
らず。人をたすけすくふを以てわざとすべし、別
のわざあるべからず。故に天下の人、王公より以下
庶人にいたる迄、日々行ふべき善事あり、善を行
ふべき位にあり。時にあたらば、むなしくすぐべ
からず。是天につかへ奉りて、天職をつとむるな
り。

仁者は人を愛す、人我のへだてなし。人を愛せずし
て、ひとへに我を愛するは、人我のへだてなり。
是私なり。仁者は私なし、我を愛する心を以て人
を愛し、わがきらふ事は人にほどこさず、我が身
を立てんとして、又人を立つ。かくの如く人我

をわすれてわかたざるを、公と云ふ。公とは、私
なきなり。仁者の心つとめずして、おのづからか
くの如し。學者はいまだ仁にいたらず、つとめて
仁を行ふべし。我が心を以て、人の心をおしはか
るに、人の心も亦わが心にかはらず、わがこのむ
ことは人も好み、わが嫌ふことは人もきらふ。こ
ゝを以て仁を人にほどこし行はんとせば、まづ我
が心を以て人の心をおしはかり、我が好むことは
人にほどこしあたへ、わがきらふことは人にほど
こさず。かくの如くすれば、人の心にかなはざる
ことなくして、人々各その所を得てやすんず。是
仁の行はるゝなり。是を推し己及し人と云ふ、恕な
り。恕は仁にいたらんとする人の行ふべき工夫な
り。仁者はつとめずして、おのづから人を愛す。
恕はつとめて仁を行ふ。是仁恕のわかちなり。恕
の一字は人の身終る迄つとめ行ふべき道なりと、
聖人のたまへり。

人となる者は天地の心に隨ひ、仁愛を以て、心とし
行ふべし。己を愛する心を以て人を愛す、是仁な
り、人の心なり。禽獸は、おのが身を愛すること

のみしりて物を愛せず。人もし不仁にして、只わ
が身を愛して人を愛せずんば、人の心にあらず、
禽獸と何ぞことならんや。不仁なれば人心を失ふ
故、その餘の才能のよきことは見るにたらず。
我が身をへりくだり、人にたかぶらざるを謙と云ふ。
謙なれば、我が身にほこらず、人にくだり、問ふ
ことをこのみ、人のいさめを聞きて、我があやま
ちを改むる故、智をひらき善にうつるときはまり
なし。この故に古人謙を以て天下の美徳とす。謙
のうらは矜なり、矜は、ほこるとよむ。ほこると
は、我が身を自滿するを云ふ。かくのごとくと
して人に求めず。かくのごとくなれば、惡にうつ
る事きはまりなし。この故に古人矜を以て天下の
惡事とす。謙と矜との善惡のこと、前に既にとけ
りといへども、繰返して初學の人に知らしめんが
爲なり。

敬はつゝしむと訓ず。つゝしむとは、心にいましめ
おそるゝを云ふ。和語の意はつゝむなり、しはや
すめ字なり、内につゝんで、みだりに外に出さざ
るなり。敬めば本心をたもちて失はず、行ひな

すこと、理にかなひてあやまりなし。これを以て、
敬は一心のまもり、萬善の根本なり。故に敬めば
身修り、敬まざれば亂る、萬のこと敬まざること
なかれ。萬善皆つゝしみによつて行はれ、萬惡皆
不レ敬よりおこる。故に五常の德是によつて立ち、
五倫の道是によつて行はる。これを以て、聖學は
敬を以て要とす。故に聖學の始終、皆敬を以て宗
とす。古來聖賢の心法、皆敬の一字を要とす。學
者の尤つとむべき所なり。又よくつゝしめば福あ
り、つゝしまざれば禍あり。身のわざはひは、皆つ
つしまざるによれり。故につゝしみは、禍にかつ
といへり。

古語に、人聖人にあらず、誰か過なからん、過まつ
てよく改む、善これより大なるはなしといへり。
程子も學問の道他なし、その不善をしれば、速に
改めて善にしたがふのみといへり。不善とは即過
なり。過をしりて改むるは學問の要なり。されど
も我が過をしる人すくなし。すべて凡人は我が身
に私して、その身の過と惡とをしらず。よろづ外

のことは、事ごとにしらずとも、さほどのうれひ
にあらず。我が身の惡と過を知ざるは、はなはだ
愚なるかな。是何よりもおそれらるべきことならずや。
身をかへりみ人の諫をきゝて、我が過を知るべし。

何事も、すきこのむことをつゝしむべし。このみて
やまざれば道の志をうばゝれ、財をつひやし、ひ
まをつひやす。この故に、すぐれてすきこのむと
は禍の基なり。その大なるをあげていへば、酒食
と色慾と財利とをこのみてやまざれば、德を損ひ
て、後は身をうしなふ。その餘の事をこのむも亦
しかり。凡このむことは、多きをいむ。すくなけ
れども、すぎてふかく好めば、又わざはひとなる。
古人の言にこのむことを見て、その人の善惡を知
るといへり。好むことをつゝしむべし。

方孝孺が、樂未レ既而憂繼レ之者。人之欲也。といへ
る事、あにしからずや。酒食好色などをむさぼりた
のしみて、その樂いまだつきざるに、はやそのわ
ざはひ忽出來て、酒食にやぶられ、色欲に
そこなはる、皆是人欲よりおこる。欲をすくなく
するの工夫は、欲をこらへて、好む所十分にいたる

べからず。只六七分或は七八分に至らば、はやく
やむべし。十分にいたれば、必ずわざはひ出來て、
後悔すれども益なし。古語に、酒は微醉に飲み、
花は半開に見るといへるがごとくなるべし。善誘
文にも、一時我が心に快きこと、過れば必ず身のわ
ざはひとなるといへり。

民を司どる人は民の父母なれば、民をあはれむ心を
本とすべし。民の心を以て心として、民の好むこ
とをこのみてほどこし、民のきらふことをきらひ
てほどこさず、父母の子を思ふが如くする故、是
を民の父母といふ。民の上に立つ人は、民をやし
なふ職分を、天よりさづけ給ふことをしりて、天
道にしたがひ、民をくるしましむべからず。我一
人の樂をきはめんとて、おほくの人をくるしむる
は、天道の御心にそむけり。天道おそるべし。す
べて人は高きもひくきも、同じ人なれば民の樂し
み苦しみも我と同じ。我が心を以て、民の心をお
しはかるにちがはず、民のうれひ苦しみを思ひは
かりて憐むべし。不仁なる人は民をあはれまずし
て、民を愛すれば、おごりて上をあなどるとて、

民をあはれまず。是不仁の人のいふ詞なり。すべ
て民はすなほなる天性あり、上なる人誠を以て民
を愛すれば、民も亦必感悦して、わだかまらず、
誠を以て上につかふ。上より不仁にして、いつは
りを行へば、民も亦必いつはる。この感應の理、
からもやまとも古も今もかはらず、うたがふべか
らず。民をいつくしみ、その上に法を嚴にして、
民のひがことを禁ずれば、上を侮らずおどるべき
やうなし。

民の司となる人、我一人のたのしみを好むべからず、
民と共に樂しむべし。是まことの樂なり。天下の
人は、たかきもひくきも皆我が兄弟の理ありて、
本は一體なることを知り、我が心を以て人の心を
おしはかり、聊人のうれひくるしむることをなすべ
からず。貧窮にして、うゑこゞゆるもの、病者か
たわなる者、世をわたりかねて、うれひくるしめ
る鰥寡孤獨の類をば、我がちからを以てすくふ
べし。鰥寡孤獨とは、老いて妻なきを鰥といひ、
老いて夫なきを寡といひ、いとけなうして父なき
を孤といひ、老いて子なきを獨といふ。この四の

者は世の中の困窮せる民にて、人のめぐみをうくべきたよりなく、うゑこゞえする人なり、いとあはれむべし。いにしへの聖人の政は、まづかやうのふびんなる民を、はやくめぐみ給ふ。かへすぐ我が身ひとつを愛して人を愛せず、おほくの人をくるしむべからず。かりにも、人に妨なく害なからんことを思ふべし。人のうれひくるしみを救ひ、人のためにはかりて忠あるべし、疎略にすべからず。位ひきゝ人も我に財ありて、ほどこす力あらば貧窮をすくひ、鰥寡孤獨のたよりなく苦しめる人を、分限にしたがひてあはれみたすくべし。財ををしむべからず。次には禽獸蟲魚草木に至るまで。ひろくあはれむべし。是等は天地の内にて、我が兄弟の列にはあらざれども、同じく天地の内に生ずる物にして、もとは一氣なれば、同類の思ひをなして、みだりにそこなふべからず。但人に妨わる禽獸をば除くべし。是皆仁を行ふ工夫なり。下にあるいやしき匹夫のともがら、諸人の補ひにならんことは、もとより力に及ばざる所なり。されどもいやしくして下にある者も、仁愛の心だにわらば、その分に應じ、その力にしたがひて、天用ひて人を救ふこと、日々に多かるべし。然れば仁愛は、いやしき人も、心にかけてつとめ行ふべきことなり。是即天地の御心うけしたがひて、天地につかへ奉る道なり。

陰德とは、善を行ひて人にしられんことを求めず、只心の内にひそかに仁愛をたもち行ふをいふ。古人の日、陰德は耳の鳴るが如し。我ひとりしりて人しらず。およそ人の患ひをうれひ、人のよろこびをよろこび、人をあはれみめぐむに、鰥寡孤獨のたよりなき人を先にし、人の飢ゑたるをすくひ、こゞえたる人に衣をあたへ、つかれたるをたすけ、病者をすくひ、道橋を修理し、人に害あるをのぞき、人に利益あることをなし、人の中を和らげ、人の善あるを譽め、人の過を隱し、人の小過をゆるし、人の才藝を用ひすゝめ、みだりに人にいからず、人をうらみず、人のいかり爭ひをやめ、かりにも人をそしらず、人をあなどらず、人をいはず、人を妨げず、人の善をすゝめ、人の惡をいさめ、禽獸蟲魚をくるしめず、妄にころさず、草

木をみだりに切らざる、皆是陰徳なり。凡陰徳は
人しらざれども、天道にかなふ。故に後は必わが
身のさいはひとなり、子孫の繁榮を得る道理あり。
かるがゆへに、さいはひを求るに、是にまされ
る祈禱なし。天道の善にさいはひし、惡にわざは
ひし給ふ理は、古今和漢明白なりといへども、凡
その人は是をしらずして、善をこのまず、惡を行ひ、
ひがことをなして、さいはひを求め、我が身の祭
るまじき淫祠にへつらひいのる。いにしへを考ふ
にちからなくば、せめて近き古と今の世の中を廣
く考へ見て、善を行ひて益あると、みだりに神と
人とにへつらひて、益なきをしるべし。されども
君子の心は、福をもとめんために、陰徳を行ふに
はあらず。陰德をおこなへば、求めずして福は其
中にあり。

よく後來のことをかねてしるを、先見の明といふ。
是知者のしる所、たつとぶべし。我輩の愚者は、
先見の明なくして、やゝもすればあやまち多く、
後悔多し。愚なりとも心しづかに、よく思案せば
このうれひすくなかるべし。後悔すくなからんこ

とを思はゞ、常に思案をこのみて、みだりに事を
好まざるべし。事を好めば事多くなり、あやまち
多く悔多し。

我が身の慾をほしいまゝにするより大なる禍なし、
人の非をそしるより大なる惡なしと、古人いへり。
この二は義理に乖くのみならず、身を亡す道なり。
常に心にかけていましむべし。

凡平生の心法は眞實にして僞りなかるべし。中庸に、
誠天之道也。誠之者。人之道也。といへり。誠天之
道也とは、陰陽のしわざ、日月のめぐり、春夏秋冬
の次第、いにしへ今かはらず、草木の、春生じ、
夏長じ、秋みのり、冬をさまりて、年々にかはりな
きも、皆是天道の誠なり。誠之とは人のちからに
て、つとめて誠にするをいふ。人は天地の子なれ
ば、天道の誠を法とし、したがひて行ふべし。是誠
之とは人之道なり。孔子も主忠信とのたまへり。
この意は、誠を以て人の心の主とすべしとなり。
忠信は即ち人の誠なり。誠といはずして、忠信と
のたまへるは、心にいつはりなくするは忠なり、
言と事とにいつはりなくするは信なり。誠は天

理の自然をいふ。忠信は人のつとめ行へる誠を
いふ。理は一にしておのづからなると、つとむる
とのわかちあり。程子も、人道は只忠信にあり。
誠ならざれば物なしといへり。君父につかふるに
も、誠なければ忠孝にあらずといへど、萬の事誠な
ければ、さばかりの善事をなすといへど、偽りとなれば實
事にあらず。つとめ行ふも、あだごとなり。是無レ
物なり。善事をつとめ行はゞ、名利のためにせず
して、誠を以て行ふべし。是誠の善なり。
言と行ふと、心の言と、表裏なかるべし。よろづのこ
といみじくとも、誠なくんば玉の盃のそこなきが
如くなるべし。吉田の兼好が、偽りても賢をまな
ばんを賢といふべしと云ふ。このことは甚敷に害
あり。およそ人道は只忠信にあり。すでにいつは
りあらば、その餘は見るにたらず。偽りて賢を
なぶ、是を小人と云ふ、なんぞ賢といはんや。漢
の王莽宋の王荊公など、いつはりて賢を學びし故、
はじめは君子の名を得るといへども、つねに天下
をうばひ天下を亂れり。是を賢といはんや。君子
の道は純一にして偽りなかるべし、かりそめにも、

いつはれる念を心にさしはさむべからず。たとひ
外に善を行ふとも、内に誠なくば君子の道にあら
ず。故に身ををさむるは只一すぢに誠の道ゞ行ふ
べし。もし凡夫のためにいはゞ偽りてするもまこ
とにするも、力を用ふるその勞は同じければ、と
てものことに只まことを行ふべし。偽りて善を行
ふは、あらはれて惡をするにまされども、誠あら
ざれば、天道人道にそむきて、其つみふかし。誠
いたれば天地をうごかし、鬼神を感ぜしめ、、、
を和らぐ。
およそ、人の一念の不善も、かならず天に通ずる理
あり。天は高きに居て、ひきゝにきくといへり。
上天をあざむくべからず。おそるべし。人をあざ
むけば、つひに其偽りあらはる、内に誠あれば、必
外にあらはるといへり。下人をあざむくべからず。
恥づべし。天を欺き人をあざむくは、共にわが心を
あざむくによれり。我が心に不善としりながらこ
れを行ふ、是自欺なり。我が心と、我が心あざむくべからず。
およそ天と人と、我が心と、皆あざむくべからず。
只一すぢに誠あるべし。こゝを以て君子の心は、

つねに青天白日の如くなり。小人の心は、常に陰暗してはかりがたし。

易に、懲￯忿窒￯慾。といへり。忿をおさふるなり。怒は陽に屬して、火の物をやくが如し、おこりやすくして人を害し、我が心の德をそこなふこと甚し。いかる時、先いかりをわすれ、心を和平にして、後理の是非を見るべし。又いかる時、言をいだすべからず。いかる時云出す詞は、必ひがごとありて後悔多し、つゝしみこらへて、いふべからず。人のいふこと、行ふこと、あしきことあらば、いからずして彌氣を平らかにし、心を和らかにして、その是非を詳にのぶべし。人隨はずとも、いかりて心を動かし、氣をあらくすべからず。心氣和平ならざれば、たとひそのいふこと理に當るとも、その心はまづ非なり。いはんやいかりて心をうごかせば、そのいふこと理にあたらざるをや。慾とは、只財寳をむさぼるのみにあらず、名利、酒食、好色、或は淫樂、器物、酒宴、佚遊を好みおぼれて、我が私をなすは皆慾なり。慾をふさぐとは、慾心おこらば、はやく其慾をお

さゆるをいふ。すでに慾さかんになりぬれば、心まよひて慾にかちがたし。慾のはじめておこる時、はやくふさげば、ちからを用ふることやすしにて、そのしるし多し。慾は陰に屬す。たとへば水の人をおぼらすが如く、おぼれやすし。およそ萬の惡は、多くはいかりと慾よりおこる。七情の内の二の者尤害多し。我が身をそこなひ、人をそこなふ。おそるべし。又怒と慾との二は、養生の道に甚害あり。

七情は、皆是人情なれば、なくてかなはず、過不及なく、よき程なるは中なり。過ぎたるは尤害多し。不及も亦理に合はず。人をあはれむは誠に善なり。されど我が心にあへりとて、妻子從妾などを、ひたすらに愛し過し、あくまで恩をほどこすは、道より出でたる愛にあらず。是私の心の甚しきなり。愛におぼれては、その人の惡しきをしらず、愛すればその人必おごりて道にそむく故、かへつてその人のわざはひとなり、又わが禍となる。いかるべきを怒るは人の不善をいましむるの道なり。怒るまじきに怒り、或はいかるべきことにも、い

かり過ては人をそこなひ、我が心をそこなふ。に
くむこと過ぬれば、その人の善あるを知らずして
用ひず、小のあやまりを大にいひなして、せめた
れば、その人うらみそむく。又あはれむべきをあはれまざるは不仁なり。
是尤不善なり。哀しむべきをかなしまず、樂しむ
り。又あはれむべきをあはれまざるは不仁なり。
べきをたのしまざるは、ひたすら情なしといふべ
し。是等は皆情の不及なり。七情おこれども、過
不及なくして、禮義にとゞまるべし。是古人の發二
平情一止二于禮義一と云へるなり。およそ天下の道
理は、過不及なき中にいたるが至善にして、是れ
道のある所なり。食する一事を以ていはゞ、過不
及なくよき程くらへば、身をやしふ。是中なり、
過れば脾胃をやぶり、不及な
れば、身の養たらず、是皆中にあらず。
人の血氣めぐらざれば病とす。人の心めぐらざれば
愚なり。是古語なり。心めぐるとは、事に當りて心
を用ひ思案するを云。運動するなり。孟子に、心
の官は則思ふといへるが如し。思案せざれば心
ぐらずして、是非をわかつことなく愚なり。事に

當りて心をめぐらし、よく思案すれば是非をわか
つ故愚ならず。人善惡をあきまへずして、愚なる
は思案せざればなり。

欲を忍ぶことつとむべし。忍ぶとはこらゆるなり。
學者もし欲をこらふるに、力を用ひずんば、學べ
る甲斐なし、力なしといふべし。平生の學力、こ
こにおゐて用べし。

子弟及奴僕に對して、その過をたゞさば、教を本と
すべし。いかりを先だつべからず。如レ斯なれば、
子弟奴僕の心を得て、恨なくしたがひやすし。是
子弟奴僕をいましむるの要法なり。

智はさとるとよむ。心の明らかなるなり。心あきら
かにしてくもりなければ、萬の道理によく通じ、
是非善惡をわきまへてまよはず。たとへば燈明ら
かにして、よく物を照すが如し。智なければ善を
このめどもくらく、まよひて、行ふべき道をしら
ず、あやまりてひがこと多し。又智なければ人を
知らず。君子をすてゝ、小人を用ふれば禍多し。
智あればよく道理の是非をわきまへ、非義を行は
ずして身をたもつ。よく人の善惡をしりて、君子

をちかづけ小人をしりぞく。是は身ををさめ、人を
をさむるに、益ありて害なし。この故に智は人身
の大寶なり。心明らかなるは智なり。心明らかなれ
ば、よく人の善惡を知る。これ人を知るは、知の明らかなる所なり。樊遲問▷知。子曰知▷人。

平生の氣象は、從容としづかに和樂なるべし。輕卒
急迫すべからず。和樂は人心の生れつきたる天
機なり。つねに和樂を失ふべからず。又益なきこ
とを思ひて、心をくるしめ、樂しみを失ふべから
ず。是不智といふべし。心のかろき速さをおさえ、
又おこたりをいましめ、つねに心を定め、早から
ず遲からず、よきほどとなるが心ををさむる法なり。
心は身の主にて、萬事の本なれば、つねにしづか
にやすらかにして、妄に動くべからず。心みだりに
動けば、亂れて明らかならず、萬事に應じてあや
まち多し。事いそがしき時は、手足のうごき、口
の物いふことは、はやからざれば事に及ばず、心
はいそがしかるべからず。手足と、目口耳鼻は、
たとへば下人のごとし。心は身の主にて、目口耳
鼻手足の事のよしあしをたゞすやすくなり。故に心

はしづかならでは、思案はなしがたし。およそ事
をなすに、しづかならざれば、思案はなしがたし。緩の字を用
ひて、みだりにいそがず、よく思案して、詳に
事の是非をわかちて行ふべし。古人これを待とい
ふ。待とは事をいそがずして時をまち、詳に思案
して道理を求め行ふことゝなり。ゆだんするにはあ
らず。みだりにはやく決定すれば、必その事をし
そんじ、後悔あるものなり。

凡つとめにたいくつし、久しくつとめがたきは、おは
かたは精力のよはきにはあらず。氣ずいにして、事
をつとむるをきらひ、心いそがはしくてみじかき
故、むつかしく思ひて、はやく退屈するものなり。
心しづかにして事をきらはず、次第に隨ひて一ツ
づゝ漸につとむれば、久しく勤めてもつかれず。
をこたりなくたゆみなければ、しづかにしてもは
かゆくものなり。

色慾名利の念、皆是人情なれば、時としておこりや
すし。其まゝおきては德を害ふ。其おこる時に、
いましむるには克己の工夫を用ゆべし。己に克つ
こと尤かたし、十分のちからを用ゆべし。おろそ

かにすべからず。但はじめて慾のおこるきざしに
かつこと、甚だやすし。是克己の要法なり。平生
學問し道義を好む志ふかくば、おのづから名利色
貨の念はうすくなるべし。天理すゝめば、人欲し
りぞく。人欲すゝめば、天理しりぞく。凡物は二
ながら一時に立たざる理なり。

心の中は灑落にして、青天白日のごとく明白なるべ
し。心の中に物をたくはへ、おほひくらますべか
らず。思慮はふかくはしくすべし。あさくあら
くすべからず。事をなすには、ふかく思案をこの
みて、かるゝしくはやく決定すべからず。思案
はしづかにして、いそがざるをよしとす。はやく
決定すれば、必あやまりあり。

人の我に不義無禮なるをば、いかり恨むべからず。
それは人のあやまりなれば、我が心にあづからず、
是小人の常情なれば、せむるにたらず。なんぞい
かりうらみて、かれとその是非をあらそふべけん
や。只我が身をかへりみて、我が不義不禮なるを、
みづからせむべし。人をとがむ可らず。我が身を
かへりみをさむれば、人のうへをとがむるにいと
まなし。

尚書曰。必有(レ)忍。其乃有(レ)濟。有(レ)容德乃大。忍ぶとは
堪忍するなり。堪忍すれば、怒をおさへ事をやぶ
らずして禍なし、人我の間和平にして、萬事とゝ
のふ故に有(レ)濟と云ふ。古語に、忍過ぎて事堪(レ)喜と
いへり。堪忍しすませば、必よろこびありとなり。
人のあしきを堪忍せざれば、怒起り人にあらそひ
て、人の間和順ならず、世に立がたし。堪忍すれ
ばあらそひ出來ず、口論にも及ばずして恥辱なし、
心中平らかにして樂み多し。有(レ)容とは、心廣くし
て人の善を取て用ひ、人の過あるをばゆるすを
いふ。容るゝことゝわれば、その德の器大なり。たと
へば大なる器の、その量ひろければ、物を入るこ
と多きが如し。古人の詩に、海濶從(二)魚躍(一)天空任(二)
鳥飛(一)といへるがごとし。忍は力を用ひて堪ふる
なり。容はその德ひろくして大なれば、忍ぶはい
ふに及ばず、まづ務めて忍びて、其工夫熟して後、
有(レ)容にいたるべし。忍は生しきなり。有(レ)容は、
熟するなり。されどはじめより、容の工夫もある
べし。人の善を取り、人の過をゆるすこと、はじ

めよりなくんばあるべからず。

むかし二人同じ船にのりてゆくに、一人は性急なり、日和あしく、舟のおそきをくるしみて、晝夜心をなやまし、形かじけたり。一人は性おだやかなり、舟のおそきをくるしまず、よく食し、やすくいねて顔色うるはし。其所につきしかば、二人一時に陸にあがる。此間船おそきとて、心をくるしめし者、何の益あるや。只みづからくるしましめるのみ。

是心みじかき人のいましめとすべし。天下の事我が力になしがたきことは、只天に任せ置くべし。心をくるしむるは愚なり。

世に交るに言すくなく、わざをよくつとめ、へりくだりて、我が才にほこらず、人をうやまひてあなどらず、人をそしらず、人情をしりて人をうらみとがめず、世變をしりて時宜に應じ、信義をかたく守りて約を變ぜず、身をいさぎよくして財利のけがれなし。かくのごとくなれば、過すくなくして、いづくにても人のにくみそしるべきやうなし。詩曰、かしこにあつても、にくまるゝことなく、こゝにあつても、いとはるゝことなし、

是を云ムなり。いとふはあくなり。

人のわれにうときときをうらむるは人情をしらず、又は世になれぬ人といふべし。それだに心にまかせざること多くして、わが道をつくしがたし。いかんぞ人の方より、我が心にかなふやうに、わがために道をつくさんや。又世にはいかなるさはりもありて、心にまかせざることも有りぬべし。何事もさだめて故あらんとおもひやりて、人をたやすくうらみとがむべからず。我が心にかなはざるとて、あやまりなき人をうらみそしるはいとつみ深し。かくのごとくおもひはかりて、人をうらみそしらざる人は、世變と人情をよくしれる人なるべし。詩經に曰。何其久也。

必有以也。いふこゝろは、人のわがもとに、何しに久しく來らざるや、必ひまなきか、病あるか、ゆへありて、來らざるべしとなり。是人の久しくおとづれざるをうらみずして、いかさまにもさはりありて、來らざるなるべしと、思ひなだめしなり。朱子の詩傳にも、此詩は、人情をよくしれりとて、ほめ給ふ。心せばく智あさき人は、人

情事變をしらで、少しわが心にかなはざることあれば、はやく人をうらみいかりて、心をくるしむるは、心せばく世なれぬ人といふべし。

人われをそしらば、わが身のあしきをかへりみとがめて人をうらむべからず。もしわが身にあやまりなければ、誇あゝても、我が徳に害なし。もしわが身に過あらば、そしらるゝは、もとより其のことわりなればうらむべからず。いはんやそしりを聞きて、身のあやまちをあらたむれば、わが幸甚し。いかるべからず。孔子曰、丘幸あり、もし過あれば、人必知レ之。わが過を人にしられて、とがめらるゝは、わが幸なりとのたまへり。聖人の言、たふとぶべし。

ちかき頃の俗語に、用心は臆病にせよといふこと、まことに道理によくかなへり。是ほどの小事は、何のうれひかあらんと思ひて、けなげにしておそれざるは、あやまちのはじめ、わざはひの本なり。莫大のあやまちわざはひは、必しばしの間、少なることをおそれずして、つゝしまざるよりおこるゆへ、小事をおそれつゝしみて、けなげならざる

が、わざはひなき道なり。武士の銘に、勿レ言何害。其禍將レ至。とのたまひしもこの意なり。

大和俗訓卷之三終

# 大和俗訓卷之四

## 心術 下

貝原篤信 著

心は天君と云ふ。身の主なり。思ふを以て職分とす。耳目口鼻形は五官といふ。官はつかさどるなり。役をつとむるをいふ。耳はきくことをつかさどり、目は見ることをつかさどり、口は物くひものいひ、鼻は香をかぎ、手足の形はうごくことをつかさどる。この五官は、各一づ～のやくありて、他事に通せず。心は天君なれば、五官をさしつかふ主なり。五官のしわざ、見ること、聴くこと、言ふこと、嗅ぐこと、動くことに付きて、心によく思案して、義理に當るか、あたらざるかをかんがへ行へば、五官のしわざあやまりなく、後悔なし。もし心その職分をうしなひて、思案もなく耳目鼻口形の欲にまかせて、義理の當否を察せざれば、人欲ほしいまゝにして天理ほろぶ。是心の官をうしなひて、よく思はざるによれり。人欲とは他にあ

らず、五官のしわざにまかせて、わがまゝなるをいふ。目に非禮をみていろにそみ、耳に非禮をきゝて聲淫にまよひ、口に非禮をいひ、飲食をほしいまゝにむさぼり、鼻は香をめで、かたちはをこたり、或はなすまじきしわざをなすは、皆是人欲なり。又天理といふも、他にあらず、五官のなすこと、よきほどの道理にあたるをいふ。心は天君なれば、耳目口鼻形の五官をつかふは、君として臣をつかふがごとく順なり。もし心のやくを失ひ、思案なくして五官にまかせしたがへば、かへりてかたちより心をつかふ。たとへば君として臣につかはるゝがごとし。是逆なり。

人のためにはかりて心をつくし、或はその才能を君相にすゝめ、人のため害をのぞき、貧困をめぐみ救ひ、人に恩をほどこすこと、只ひとすぢに、仁心より行ふべし。人の悦びてその返報せんことをのぞむべからず。我が名聞のためにすべからず。是隱德なり。若名聞のために善を行ひ、又人にはどくして、其報をのぞめば、仁心むなしくなる。如此すれば、ちからを用ひて善を行へども、其

事は是にして其心は非なること、をしむべし。誠
の道にあらざればなり。

不知の人は義理をわきまへざるのみにあらず、又利
害損得をもしらずして、わが身のわざはひとなる
ことをかへりみず、ひがことをなして、身を立て
んと思ひ、かへりて身をほろぼし、家をやぶるに
いたる。かなしむべし。これわが身の惡をやめず
して、天のせめをまつものなり。わが身を利せん
とて惡しきことを行ひ、人をくるしめて身をたの
しむ。是みなわが身の害となることをしらず。
道を主とせざれば、わが心のいかり、よろこび、こ
のみ、にくむにまかせ、わが私欲にしたがひ、利欲
損得にかゝはり、或は人のひがことにまよひ
て、惡を善とし善を惡とす。親類朋友に私し、或
は人の請託をうけて私する故に、道にかなひ公に
したがふことなし。是無學にして、道をしらざる
故、何をより所として、理非をわきまふべきやう
なし。たゞわが身の私意を主として、わがまゝに
行ふ。或は書をよめども、私多き人は道を主とせ
ずして、欲にしたがふ故、まなべども益なし。

家の内、妻子家人の、われにつかふるつとめ、十分
にわが心にあはざるとて、せめいかるべからず。

人にまじはるには、恕を以て人の非をゆるすべし。
又わが衣食家居器物財用など、事ごとにわが心に
十分にたりなんことを求むべからず、常に不足の
事あるがよし。十分心にかなへばわざはひあり。
家のいらかをふきて、三瓦をおははず、衣のゑり
をかくも、この意なりと、古人いへり。

世は海なり、身は舟なり。志はかぢなり。かぢをあ
しくとれば、行くべきかたにゆかず、風波にあへ
ば舟くつがへるが如し。あしく志をもてば、身をくつがへ
り。あしく志をもてば、身をくつがへす。かぢの
とりやうあしくして、舟をくつがへすがごとし。
わが身に事たらぬことをしをれば、貧賤にしても亦たの
しむ。たることをしらざれば、富貴なりといへど
もたのしまず。

我が身の行の善惡は、世人のほめそしりを、あなが
ちに氣にして、よろこび、おそるべからず。たゞ
道理を以て法とすべし。わが行ひ道理にかなはゞ、
世こぞりてそしるとも、おそるべからず。わが行

ひ道理にそむかば、世こぞりてほむるとも、よろこぶべからず。よき人にほめられ、あしき人にそしらるゝこそ、君子とはいふべけれ。人ごとにはむる者は、かへりてうたがはし。おほくはたくみにして、かざれる人なるべし。

わが身ををさむるには、ほめられんとすべからず。我が身だにあやまちなからんことを思ふべし。我が身だに道理にかなはゞ、人のそしりはまるれは、さもあらばあれ、よろこびうれひとするにたらず。但士の節義武勇の道と、又利欲のけがれなく、廉潔にしてむさぼらざる、この二はなべて人のそしらざるやうに、心がけつとむべし。名ををしむも義におほて害なし。この二のことかけなば、その餘は見るにたらず。

善をなすに、人の誹をおそれてやむるは、善をこのむこと誠あらざるなり。小人財と色とをこのむには、人のそしりをかへりみず。是好むこと誠あればなり。學者の善をなすことも、亦かくのごとくなるべし。

凡わが身にあることをたのめば、必身の禍となる。

才をたのめば、人をないがしろにして、人にやぶらる。勇をたのめば、人をわなどりて、人にほろぼさる。氣力をたのめば、慾をほしいまゝにして、勢をたのめば、おごりてほろぶ。智をたのめば・身にほこりてあやまる。

心も事も、天理に專一にして、人欲をすこしもまじゆべからず。是を至善といふ。君子の心事、必かくのごとくなるべし。もし十分の天理に一分の人欲あひまじはらば、たとへば黒白のあひまじはり、香臭の一器にあるが如し。十分の白き物に、一分の黒き物まじはれば白きとはいひがたし。香ばしき物も、少し惡しき臭をくはふれば、にほひよからざるがごとし。

上代よりこのかた、誠は日々におとろへ、かざりは日々にさかんなり。おごりは彌まさり、儉約は彌すたる。質朴をばいやしみ、華美をばはむ。今の世に道を行はゞ、いつはりかざりをやめて、古風に立ちかへり、すなほにして、眞實なるをたつとびつとむべし。眞實なれば、人も感じてしたがひやすし。時俗にうつり行くべからず。

我が身不幸にて、災にあひ、讒言にあひ、或は主君父母兄弟朋友の不仁無禮にあふとも、古來和漢の内、なほそれよりも、甚しきわざはひにあへる人を思ひくらべて、みづから心をなぐさめやすんじて、うれふべからず。是古人の說なり。君子の天命をやすんずる工夫は、別に有るべし。されど是は一のやすき手だてなり。しるべし。

およそ世間のはからざる、不意のわざはひいできたるとも、是古今の人間にあるならひぞと思ひて、心をくるしめうれふべからず。兼好が歌に「ならひぞと思ひなしてやなぐさむ、わが身ひとつのうきよならねば。」

人の我に對して無禮横逆あり、又事不順ありて、わが心にかなはざることあらば、是すなはち、善心をおこし私欲をこらゆる學問のつとめ、德のすむ所なりと思ひ、人の不順なるを堪忍し、わが身をかへりみ、心をせめおさへて、いかりをこらし、欲をふさぎ、善にうつり、過を改むべし。かやうのわが心術をつとむべき折節を、あだに思ひて、いたづらにすごすべからず。かく心にかなはざる

所を、よくこらへつとめてこそ、わが心の德も增もすゝむべき理なり。かゝること凶あはされば、心ををさめ、欲をしのぶ工夫すゝます。

天道は、春は生じ、夏は長じ、秋はをさむ。三時は皆事あり。冬はたゞ生氣のかくれしづまるまでにて、しわざなし。冬ふけて人のねいりたる時、無事にしてやすむが如し。冬の氣閉藏するは、即是來春發生の本なり。冬寒氣はげしくして、陽氣をさまりかくるれば、來春の陽氣さかんなり。故に冬あたゝかに、雷なりて陽氣うごきもるれば、來春の發生の氣よわく、秋穀のみのりもうすし。人夜半ののちいねざれば、血氣しづまらずして、明日氣力よわし。人心も靜なる時に養ひて、動く時の本とすべし。心しづかならず、うごきさわげば、わざをつとむるにちからなく、まよひてあやまり多し。

劉行簡曰、天下の事下人心に合ひ、上天意に合ひ、中大道に合ふ、惟一言あり。曰、公のみ。公とは私なきを云ふ。私とはひたすらわが身を利せんことをこのみて、人のためをかへりみざるをいふ。是人我をへだつるなり。公とは人我のへだてなく、

我と人とともに同じく利するをいふなり。公にし
て私なければ道理にかなひ、天意にかなひ人心に
かなふ。故にその心の誠おのづからあらはれて、
人のほまれもよろこびもあつく、人のうたがひに
くむことなく、もとめずして天道のめぐみも人の
愛敬もこれあり。又一言にして、上天道にそむき、
下人心にちがひ、中大道にかなはざることとあり。
私の一字なり。たとひ天下に聞ゆるほどの善事を
行ふとも、心に私あらばまことの道にあらず。凡
私を行ひて、たとひ一旦利を得て、わざはひなくと
も、天のいかり、人のうらみにくみ、身にむくひて、
かならずわざはひにあひ、身はづかしめられ、名を
けがす。天道はまことにおそるべきかな。是たゞ
道理をしらざるのみならず、私を行ひて身
の損得をしらず、私を行ひて福祿を得、おろかにしてわが身
んと思へど、かへりてわざはひにあひ、身をほろぼ
すは、わが身の損得をもしらざるなり。いたりて
おろかなりといふべし。

人の心の内、道徳の至りてたふとく、至りてたのし
むべき理あり。君子はこれをしりて、たふとびた

のしみて外に求めず。小人はこれをしらず、徳を
そこなひ道を失ひて、これをたふとびたのしまず、
たゞ俗樂のいやしきわざをのみたのしみとし、利
欲をもつぱらとし、長くうれひくるしみてたのし
みを失ふ。是をしらずんば、人となれるかひなかるべし。
この樂をしらんとならば、まことの學問をよくつ
とめて、其理をしるべし。

後悔は前にたちて、後のあやまりをいましむる益あ
れば、誠にこれ善事なり。されば、賈誼も前事を
わすれざるは、後事の師なりといへり。然れども
ながく心の内にとゞめてくるしめば、滯りて必
心の病となり、和樂をやぶる。一旦いましめて後、
その事をすて、かさねて、しばゝ後悔して、心
を苦しむべからず。たゞ後日をいましめて、か
かるあやまりなからんことを思ふべし。

人の心の内は、常に恭敬和樂なるべし。恭敬はつゝ
しみうやまふなり。恭敬ならざれば、心はしいま
まにして、おしかたにながれて、禮の本たゝず。
和樂はやはらぎたのしむなり。和樂ならざれば、

心うれひくるしみ、道理にしたがはずして、樂の
もとたゝず。此二は車の兩輪鳥の兩翼のごとし。
ならび行はれて、そむかざるべし。いかなるあし
き俗人に交るとも、ながれて恭敬をうしなふべか
らず。いかなる不幸なることにあふとも、心をく
るしめて、和樂を失ふべからず。禮經に、禮樂は
しばらくも身をはなるべからずといへり。
富貴をきはむといふとも、人欲だにあらば、そのね
がひつくることなくて、貧賤にして慾すくなきに
おとるべし。道義の樂は、位なくして貴く、祿なく
して富めり。其樂みきはまりなし。いかんとなれ
ば、內に樂ありて外にねがひなければなり。
我が愚をしらず、我があやまりをしらずして、自是と
し自知とすると、吾が藝能のつたなきをしらずし
て、みづからほこるは、皆心明らかならざる故な
り。人をしるはまことにかたし、人の胸中に、善
惡かくれて見えざればなり。わが心中にある善惡
は、わが身のことなれば、しりやすかるべくして、
かへつて人をしるよりもかたし。いかんとなれ
ば、わが身に私して、そのあしきをしらざればな

り。故に古語に曰、知人之謂知。自知之謂明。人
をしるは誠にかたしといへど、わが身をしるは、
人をしるよりもかたければ、是を明といふ。明は
知より猶まされり。わが心明なれば、わが身のあ
しきをしるものなり。故にわが身に自滿して、人
にほこるものは、その心くらきゆへ、わがあしき
をしらざるなり。
言を聞きて信せざるは、聞くことあきらかならざる
なりと、易にいへり。人の善言といさめをきゝな
がら、その言を信せず、只益もなきあだごとのや
うに思ふは、その心くらくして、善言を聞きわけ
ざればなり。心明らかなれば、よくその言の道理
あることをきゝわけて信ず。又世俗の才辯ありて
言たくみなるものゝいふことは、理もなきことを
も聞きて信す。その言貌ふつゝかなれば、その言
に道理あれども信せず。是きく人のくらき故なり。
わが身の飲食色欲財利などの慾にかつには、たと
ば強敵に對して、我が十分のちからをつくして、
ふせぎ戰ふが如くすべし。かくのごとくせざれ
ば、私慾にかちがたし。是欲にかつ良法なり。もしす

こしもよわげなれば、欲にかちがたく、つねに欲かちてふせぎがたし。人欲は人のため大敵なり。ゆだんすべからず、いかにもしてかつべし。人のあやまちは、氣質の偏なる所よりおこる。我が氣質のあしきを變ずるみちは、己が過ぎたるをおさへて、たらざる所をつとむべし。つよすぎたる人はやはらかなるべし。よわき人はつとめてはげむべし。はや過ぎたる人はゆるやかなるべし。にぶき人はつとめてするどに行ふべし。その餘もみなかくのごとくすべし。むかし西門豹といひし人は性急なり、つねに韋をおびていましめとす。韋はやはらかなるものなり。董安于といひし人は性緩し、常に弓の弦をおびていましめとす。弦は急なるものなり。かやうにわがあしきを改むるに志あらば、いかに偏性なりとも、などか氣質を變せざるべき、學問は氣質のあしき所をしりてかつを要とす。是あやまりをすくなくする道なり。かくの如くならざれば學問の益なし。

事急にして多しといへども、心はせはらしくいそがはしかるべからず。心せまりいそがはしければ、和樂を失ひて心をくるしむるのみならず、思案もつまびらかならずして、あやまりおほし。

君子は人をせむる心つねに少し。人をせむる心つねにすくなく、おのれをせむる心常に多し。人をうらみにくむ心つねにすくなく、人をゆるし堪忍する心つねに多し。小人はこのうらなり。この故に君子の心は、常にたひらかにして樂多し。小人の心は常にけはしくして憂おほし。

萬の事つらつら思案して、後のあやまりなく、悔なからんことをはかるべし。思案なくして、いかりと慾をさらざれば、後のわざはひとなる。是智者のしわざにあらず。事を思案せずして、かるぐしく行へば、必あやまりあり、後悔あり。もし急なることあらば、ことさらよく思案して詳に行ふべし。如此せば、後のあやまりなかるべし。いそぎて心さわがしく、しづかならざれば、思案なくして、必あやまりあり、悔あり。莫大のあやまりとなり、少の間少の事を堪忍せずして、一生のわざはひとなる。怒と慾とによりて、はては身をうしなふにいたることあり。つつし

むべし。すこしの間つゝしますして、わざはひに
いたるは、いたりて愚なり。

人の身のわざはひあること、多くは私欲よりおこる。
私欲をほしいまゝにせざれば、わざはひなし。凡
人のわざはひは、思はざるに不幸にして、天よりた
まゝくゝだるはまれなり。もしあれども事によつ
てのがれやすし。私欲を行ひ、つみをおかして、み
づからなせるわざはひは、天よりくだる禍より多
くしてのがれがたし。それわが身を利せんとすれ
ば、必人に妨あり。人を妨げたるむくひは、必わ
が身の害となる。人を妨げて、たとひ一旦幸にして
利を得、人のせめをまぬかるゝといへども、必天
のせめ身にむくひて、わざはひ來る。凡とがをお
かして、公につみせらるゝは、目に見えて明らか
なり。天のせめは目に見えずして、いつとなく
だれるゆへ、人しらず。其わざはひ來れば、只不
意にふり來るやうに思ふは、ひがことなり。故
利を求むれば必害あり。福を求むれば必禍あり。
めざるに自然に福來るはよし、われより求むべか

らず。我より求めたる禍は、必禍となる。只わが
身をつゝしみ、分をやすんじ、わが職分をつとめ
て、天命にまかすべし。利とは財利のみにあらず、
一切わが身のために便よきことをはからば、皆人に害あり。我が
爲に便よきことをはからば、皆人に害あり。故に
わが利は人の害なり、人の害は又わが害となる。
たとへばたきのはしなくして、めぐりて又かへ
るが如し。よくこの理をしりて、利をひさぼるべ
からず。

子曰。不患人之不己知。患不知人也。人のわれ
をしらざるは、人のおろかなるなり。わがとがに
はあらず、うれひとすべからず。人の善惡をしら
ざるは、わがおろかなるなり。みづからはづべし。
又我がよきことを、人にしられんと求むるは小人
の心なり。いやしむべし。

人のあやまちをそしり、不善あるをはなはだしくせ
めはづかしむべからず。必人のうらみとなる。或
はとがある人をうちたゝきて、一旦心に快くすと
いへども、その人もし堪忍せずしてむくへば、大
なるわざはひとなる。いかりをおさへて、後のわ

萬の事正あり中あり。正とはよこしまならざるをい

く思ひてしるべし。

賤なるは、かへつて富貴にまさる道理もあり。よ

さぼりて、富を得るは樂しむべき理にあらず。貧

義の富貴うらやむべからず。世にへつらひ、人をむ

賤ならんは、不義にして富貴なるにまされり。不

腹空しけれど、蜣蜋の糞土をくらひて、常に飽け

るをうらやますとなり。しかれば、廉潔にして貧

いへり。言ふ心はせみはきよき露を飲み、うゑて

抱朴子といへる書に、玄蟬潔饑。不‐羨二蜣蜋穢飽一と

ひとなること又多し。

をしらずして、外に求めてやまず。つねにわざは

なるは中なり。あきたらざる者は、たのしむこと

てあきたらず。あきたらざる者は、富貴にしても

しらざるものは、富貴にしても、分限をしらずし

しむ者は、常にあきたる。慾多くして足ることを

分限をやすんじて、貧賤にしても亦樂しむ。たの

慾すくなくして、わが身の足ることをしるものは、

ひ有べし。

べからず。いやしき下部に對しても、この心づか

ざはひをよくかんがへ、わが心に十分快きを求む

---

なはず。

て、よきほどならざれば、善事なりとても道にか

なるは中なり。是即道のある所なり。過不及あり

れば至善ならず。凡萬のわざ過不及なく、よき程

中にあらず。よきほどにのみくふは、よき程よ過ぐ

以て萬事をおしてしるべし。正なれども中ならざ

かはくとてのみ過し、うゑたるとてくひ過すは、

らゑて食するは是正なり、よこしまにはあらず。

ふ。是善なり。中とは過不及なくしてよきほどな

るをいふ。是至善なり。のどかはく時湯水をのみ、

我が身に才ありてもほこるべからず。才にほこれ

ば必あやまる。其の上人信服せず。小才ありとて

も、聖賢の書をあまねくよまず、歴代の史にひろ

く通ぜずんば、古今天下の是非をわきまへがたし。

經書にくらくして道をしらず、古今に通ぜずして

ふるきあとを考へず、小才をたのみ、あながちに

世のことはりをわかたんとすればあやまり多し。

たとへば星なき量を以て、物の輕重をはかり、く

もれる鏡を以て、物の妍媸をわかたんとするが如

し。只へりくだりて人にとひ、古を考へて義理を

明らむべし。愚なるわが心を以て、人をほめそし
り、わづかなる才をたのみて、みづから是非を決
すべからず。

人生この日の再び得がたきことをしりて、時々その事
をつとめてをこたらず、日々この生を樂しみてう
れへず、よくつとめ、よくたのしむ人は、一日を
以て一月とし、一年を以て十年とし、十年を以て
百年とす。つとめとたのしみを以て身を終る。智
者のしわざ、かくのごとし。勤とたのしみをしら
ざる人は、たとひ百歳の長壽をたもつとも、常に
怠りて、一生の間何のなし出せる善事なし。是つ
とめざればなり。常にうれひくるしみ多し。是樂
しまざればなり。かくのごとくなれば、人となれる
かひなし。いけるばかりにて、生を得た
りといひがたし。飲食聲色を樂しむといへども、
欲多く節なくしてかへりて身をそこなひ、たのし
みいまだつきざる内に、憂はやく來る。愚者のしわ
ざかくのごとし。禮記に、君子は道を得ることを
たのしみ、小人は欲を得ることを樂しむ。道を以
て欲を制すれば、たのしみて迷はず。欲を以て道

を失へば、迷ひて樂しまずといへり。君子は常に
たのしみて日をおくり、小人は常にうれひて日を
おくる。衰老の身は殊に餘日すくなければ、一日を
以て一月とし、一月を以て一年とする工夫をなす
べし。一日一時も樂しまずして、あだに時日をお
くるは愚なりといふべし。

樂みは人の心に生れつきたる天機にして、本自これ
あり。されども私欲あれば、耳目口體の欲にそ
なはれ、喜怒哀懼の情におほはれて、この樂を失
ふ。君子は情慾にやぶられずして、常にこの樂を
失はず。いかなる患難の事にあひても、この天然
自有の樂を改めず。又風花雪月の外境にふるれば、
心の内にある本然の樂、外物と相和して彌樂しむ。
是外物を以て、はじめて樂とするにはあらず。外
物來りて本然の樂をたすくるなり。天地の道陰陽
の化、四時のめぐりはつねに和氣あり。是天地の
樂なり。この樂たゞ人にあるのみにあらず、鳶の
とび、魚のをどるも、凡禽獸のさへづりなくも、草
木のさかえ、花さき、實のるも、みな是天機の發生
する所、萬物自然の樂なり。これを以て人の心に、

もとより樂あることをしるべし。もし欲にひかれて、この樂をうしなふは、天地の道にそむけり。いかなる横逆にあひ、不幸にあふとも、常に此の樂を失ふべからず。聖人やゝもすれば、此樂をとき給ふ。この樂の人に切なることにあらず。仲尼顔子の樂は、我輩愚者のしるべきことにあらず。たゞ愚人にも、各生れつきたる樂あることをしりて、樂を失はざる工夫あるべし。われも人も人欲さかんなれば、この樂をしらず。樂と欲と両立せず、樂しめば欲なし、欲あれば樂なし。この理をよく思ひて、わきまへしるべし。樂は常人の事にあらずといふべからず。

心は天君にて身の主なり。つねに樂しましむべし、くるしむべからず。わが身貧賤にして、或は不意の禍ありとも、これ天命なれば、うれふべからず、樂を失ふべからず。又人のわれにあしきをば、忍びてゆるすべし、うれふべからず。かくの如くすれば、心のくるしみなく樂多し。身のまどしきをうれひ、又みだりに人をいかりにくみて、わが心をくるしめそこなふべからず。人の無禮にして、我

をおかしあなどるとも、おろかなる故と思ひ、いかりにくむべからず。子弟のともがら、われにおろそかなりとも、道をしらざる故と思ひ、いかるべからず。心をくるしめて益なし。下部などはことにならはしあしければ、おろかにしてさとしがたし。そのあしきをいましめをしふるはよし。いかり怒めて、ことばと色とをはげしくすべからず。我が心の和樂をやぶり、人のうらみをとる。言と顔色とはげしからざれども、わが行正しく言にたはふれなければ、人おのづからおそれてあなどらず。

心にあるじなければ、事をつとむる時、はや過ぎてさわがしく、又おそ過ぎて怠りとなり、或は事に先だてあやまち、或は事におくれてまにあはず。主あれば心つねに定りて、遲速なくよきほどなるゆへ、あやまちすくなし。

徐孝節といふ人、幼少より物をころすことをいましめ、蟻のむつまり居る處をも、ふみころさん事をおそれ、よきて道をゆけり。其心善なりといふべし。此の心をおしひろめて、まづ父母兄弟を愛し、人

倫に及ぼし、次に萬物に及ぼさば、仁愛の道ひろ
く行はるべし。善心をおしひろむる工夫、常にか
くの如くすべし。夫いかすことをこのみ、ころす
ことをにくむは天の御心なり。天の物をあはれみ
給へる御心をうけて、人の心とする所、即仁なり。
不仁の人は人をめぐみ、物をあはれむに心なくし
て、ころすことをこのむ。かくのごとく不仁なら
ば、他の才多しといへども、天道にそむき人道か
けて、見るにたらず。

利は天地より生じて、天下の公物なり。われ一人の私ものにす
なれば、天下の人にあたへ養ひ給ふ理
べからず。人とゝもに、同じく利を得れば、人々
各その所を得て害なし。身に私して我一人利を得
んとすれば、爭出來て、かへつて我が身の害とな
る。義を行ひて自來る利は眞の利なり、わが益と
なる。むさぼり求むる利は、眞の利にあらず、必
身の禍となる。是利を求むるには非ず、害を求む
るなり。

一指目をおほへば、太山も不見と古語にいへり。人
の心はもと明らかなる物なりといへども、私欲の

おほひありて心體をふさげば、くらくして道理に
通ぜず。故に心を明らかにして、是非にまよはざ
らんことを思はゞ、私欲を去るべし。欲されば心
明らかなり。本心如三日月。嗜欲食之既。と山谷が
詩にも見えたり。

ひにしへより、無道の人、その惡行、まことに一事
にとゞまらず、その品多し。されども其内人のい
さめをふせぎ、いかるより大なる惡なしと古人い へ
り。からや、まと、むかしより人の行あしくて、身を
うしなひ、家をほろぼすも、皆いさめをふせぐよ
りおこれり。ふかくいましむべし。

世にをるには、人をにくみせむる心かろかるべし、
重くすべからず。いかんとなれば、およその人書
をよみ古をまなんでも、道にそむく人おほし。況
や學ばざれば世のことはりの、よきもあしきもしら
ず、しらずしてなせるひがことなれば、にくむべ
からず、あはれむべし。頑なるをいかりにくむて
となかれと、尚書に見えたり。

我が身すらわが心にかなはず、みづからせじと思ひ
しことをもあやまりてすること多し。いはんや人

のわざ、わが思ふごとくなるべきやうなし。其上

人心の同じからざることその面のごとく、人のわ

が心にかなはざるをうらむべからず。

人の心は時によりかはりやすし。人の心も、わが心

も、皆たのむべからず。是後悔なき道なり。

樂をしる人は天をうらみず、人をとがめず、世に求

めなくして、その分をやすんず。樂をしらざるも

のは是に反す。

人倫にまじはり、萬事を行ふに心平かに、氣和して

しづかなるべし。しづかならざれば、氣さわがし

くわらくして、道理明らかならず、道を行ふこと

かたし。故にまづ心氣ををさめ、和平にして靜な

・るべし。血氣さかんなる時は、氣さかのぼりて、

心もともに定まらず。たとへば氣の上る病あれば、

心氣をさまらず。酒にえひたる時は、氣のぼりて心

みだる。家を新に作りて、棟、杈首、梁、柱などいま

だおちつかざる時、大風にあへばたふれやすし。材

木をりあひて後は、大風ふきてもたふれがたし。

人も血氣をさまらざれば、人に對するにも、心さ

だかならず、浮氣にておちつかざれば、言も行も

理にあたらず。戰場にて敵と戰ふにも、氣上りて

心しづかならざれば、うごきさわぎて敵にかちが

たく退きやすし。文字をかくにも、字ごとにその

所におちつきて、ゆたかにみゆるは能書なり。文

字おちつかずして、せはしきは惡筆なり。萬の事皆氣の下にを

りあひて、しづかなる時ならでは、道理にかなひ

がたし。

心氣和平にして人をとがめず、わが身にかへり求め、

己をせむれば、身をさまりて樂多し。この工夫甚

益あり。常にこれを以てわが心ををさむべし。も

しこの工夫をわすれば、必道をうしなひ樂をうし

なふ。古語に曰、君子は己にもとむ、小人は人に

求むといへり。

心のうつはものせばき人は、わが智ひとつを用ひて、

萬の事に通ずとおもひ、人の智を用ひず。古語に、

自用ゆれば小なりといへり。わが智ひとつをた

のみて、人の智を用ひざれば、世間の萬事わが一人

にてしりがたし。しらざること多ければ、小智と

いふべし。心のうつはものひろき人は、わが一人

の智を用ひず、ひろく人にとひてきゝ、そのよさ

をとり用ゆる故、もろ人の知を合せてわが智とす。是大知とすべし。凡人は各得たる所あり、なれたることあり。十人には十人の知あり。百人には百人の知あり。各その人の長ぜる所を取用ゆべし。さばかり才ある人も、天下古今もろくのこと、われ一人の知にてはしりがたし。一人の智は限あり、衆人の智はきはまりなしといへり。

天命は天のくだす所、人のうくる所なり。命は猶令のごとくして、下知の意なり。天よりくだる故に天命といふ。天命に常あり變あり。善を行へば福あり、惡をすれば禍あるは常なり。善人に禍あり惡人に福あるは變なり。人の吉凶禍福壽夭富貴貧賤、萬の幸不幸、皆天の命ずる所なり。人間の萬事天命にあらざるとなし。或は生れつきて定まり、或は時により、不慮に命くだりて、偶然として福にあひ、わざはひにあふ。求めても命なければ得がたく、求めざれども命あれば得やすし。只人の法を行びて、天命をまつべし。善を行びて福來るは、常の理なれども、もし福あるは是亦天命の變なれば、うれふべからず。およそ人天命をしりて

命にまかせ、うれひなき工夫をなすべし。天命をしらざれば、命のさだまりありて福の求めがたく、禍の去りがたきことをしらず。利につき害をさけんとし、人にへつらひ神にへつらふは見ぐるし。愚なりといふべし。故に論語に、不レ知レ命無三以為二君子一也といへり。

人の心平生無事なる時、つねに樂みおほければ、いかなるわざはひ出來てもくるしまず。たとへば富める人は、凶年にあひてもうゑず、血氣つよき人ははげしき寒暑にあたりても感ぜざるが如し。もし無事なるとき樂なければ、にはかに事いできて、わざはひ來るとき、うれひくるしみ、心をうごかし慌してとりうしなふ。つねの時よく工夫して、心を養ひて樂をふかくすべし。心は天君なり。つねにたのしましむべし、外事にわづらはされて、くるしむべからず。

不意なるわざはひにあひて、すべきやうなくとも、心をくるしめて、樂を失ふべからず。心しづかに思慮すれば、そのわざはひをのがるゝおもんばかりもいでくることあり。行つまり、心せはしかる

べからず。心ひろくしてよく思ひをのぶべし。

大和俗訓巻之四 終

# 大和俗訓巻之五

貝原篤信著

## 衣服

衣服は身のおもてなり、人に對すればまづみゆ。この故に古人身をつゝしむの名目をつらぬるに、まづ衣服、次に言語、次に行と、つゐでをなせり。言行と同じく相ならべるほどのことなれば、衣服をもつゝしみて、身に相應せる正しきをえらび用ふべし。相應せざるは、正しからざるなり。相應とは年と位と時と處とに似合たるを云ふ。染色繪様、わかき人も、其年のほどよりは、すこしくすみて老いらかなるは、人の目にたゝずして宜し。かくのごとくなるは、わかきも老いたるも、たかきもいやしきも、むかしも今も似合はざることなし。年と位よりわかやかに、ざればみたるはいやし。大なるかた、大もん、大すぢ、すべて人の目にたちてけざやかに、又あやしくことやうなる染色の服きたるは、たれもその身に似げなくして、むげに

人に見おとさるゝものなり。かやうのきぬきたる
入は、位高き人も、いやしく見ぐるしくして下部
の如し。是を好むは何のためぞや。大かたは衣服に
ても、人の心はおしはからるゝものなり。位なく
ても、みづからおもんずる人は、下着にもすべか
らず。凡人の目たつべからざるを用ゆべし。
目にたつは相應せざる故なり。おびもいにしへは、
男女共にちいさかりしが、今やうはひろくして見
ぐるし。何の益ありやしらず。

衣服は儉素に、かざりすくなく、よのつねにしてい
やしからざるがよし。又まどしき人も、つとめて
潔くあかづきけがれざるを用ゆべし。富める人も
美麗をこのみ、無用の服多くすべからず。又甚質
朴に過ぎて、けがらはしく鄙野なるもあしゝ。染
色は正色を用ゆべし。紫もえぎなどの間色、すべ
て女子の服にちかきを用ゆべからず。　紅紫をば、
褻の服・衾、褥にもすべからず。

身のかざりに心を用ひ過すべからず。ひまついえて
益なし。俗人奴婢のともがらにほめられんとて、
衣服をかざれば、識者にいやしめらる。何の益も
なくはかなきことむなり。

左傳に、服の不衷身の災なりといへり。きる物のた
だしからずして、その身に似合はざるは、身のわ
ざはひとなる。このためし世に多きことなり。い
ましむべし。國語曰、服心之文也。心のこのむこ
とを身にも必服する故に、衣服は心の外にあらは
るゝ文なり。正しからざる服きたるは、心の内見
えてはづかし。つゝしんでえらび用ゆべし。

衣服は常に用ひて、いつもよき製法染色あり。時の
好みにしたがひ、世のあしき俗にうつるべから
ず。

### 言　語

言は心の聲なりと古人いへり。人の心の內にあるこ
と、ことばによりて外にいづ。一言みだりに發す
れば、駟馬も追ひがたし。よきこともあしきこと
も、皆口よりいづ。口をつゝしめば、あやまちす
くなく、耻辱なくわざはひなし。故に人の身のつ
つしみは、口をつゝしむを第一のつとめとす。言
おほければ、口のあやまち多く、人ににくまれ、

二一一

わざはひおこる。つゝしみて多くいふべからず。
殊に人をそしるは莫大の惡事なり、いましめて、
人の非をいふべからず。

易に、心をやすんじて、後かたるといへり。人に物
いはんと思はゞ、先わが心をやすくしづかにし、
思案していひ出すべし。かくのごとくせば、言の
あやまちとがめすくなかるべし。

人に對して、ことばを出すに、事によりて道理をい
ひつくさず、意を内にふくみ、ことばをのこせば、
言に餘味ありて、人感服してしたがひやすし。人
をいさむるにも、辭はげしからず、氣象和順にし
て、かすめなしていひて、その人の過惡をさしあ
らはさず。是かへつて人の心を感せしむ。

言をつゝしみて、一言を出すにも、よく思案して
をいへば、言語はおのづからすくなし。むりに口
をとぢて、いはざるにはあらず。

ことばをば、必信にすべし。かりそめのすこしなる
ことにも、いつはるべからず。その事は少なりと
も、心を害する咎は大なり。まことの道を失へば
なり。故に萬のことうるはしくとも、いつはりを

<hr/>

いふは人にあらず。我が心の神は則ち天地の神な
り。おそるべし。心にいつはりとしらば、いふべ
からず。偽としりて、わが心をあざむくは罪ふか
し。

人と約をなさば、必其信をかたく守るべし。一度
約したる事をたがへば人にあらずと思ふべし。若
その契約義にかなはざることか、又ちからの及び
がたきことにて、後に約を守りがたからんと思は
ば、かねて約をなすべからず。かるゝしくうけ
あへば、その約たがふ。つゝしむべし。論語に、
信近二於義一則言可レ復也。といへり。人と約束した
ること、首尾ちがはざるやうにせんと思はゞ、約す
ること義理にかなへば、うけ合ひたる言のごとく
行ひとげられて、いつはりなくして、首尾相違せ
ずとなり。

あやまちをはぢて、いつはりかざるべからず。是心
をあざむき、人をあざむくなり。既にわが過あ
らんは、すべきやうなし。あやまらば直にいひあ
らはすべし。かくしていつはりかざるべからず。
あやまりて又人をあざむくは、あやまりをかさぬ

るなり。いよ〳〵つみふかくなる。

言を出すに、その言さわがしからず、おだやかなる
は、その心のやしなひあるなり。もし言を出すに、
さわがしくけはしきは、心のやしなひなしとしる
べし。

人あやまちありて、もしいさむべき人ならば、目前
にてそのあやまちをいさめ、かげにてはその過を
いふべからず。目前にて諫めず、かげにてそしる
は、うしろめたし。もれきこえては、その人のう
らみもふかし。面前にてしたがひ、退きて後言す
るは、聖人の誡なり。晋の世の崔洪と云ひし人は、
目前に人の過をいさめ、かげにてその人をそしら
ず。故に人これを重んじけるとかや。宋の劉貢父
といひし人も、亦かくのごとくなりしなり。

一言のあやまちにて、莫大の禍となり、一事のあやま
ちにて、一生の憂となる。愼むべし。平生つゝし
みある人も、事により時によりて、をこたりたゆ
みぬれば、一言一事のあやまちによりて、思ひの
外に大なるわざはひとなることあり。一言一事も
つゝしまずんばあるべからず。

古語に、病は口より入り、禍は口より出づといへり。
ことばをつゝしみて、みだりに口より出されば
わざはひなし。飲食をつゝしみて、みだりに口に
入れざれば病なし。病と災との出くることは、天
より降るにあらず、皆口よりおこると古人いへり。
口の出し入れ、つゝしむべし。

人のあしきことは、わが心の中にしりわきまへて、
口には出すべからず。

人をそしり、人を言ひおとすこと不仁の甚しきなり。
その上わが身におゐて、つゆばかりも益なし。そ
の人もしきけば甚害あり。そのそしる所その實に
たがはずとも、人をそしるは、厚くおとなしき道
にあらず。況凡夫の人をそしるは、多くは理にあ
たらず。つゝしむべし。

人をそしれば、人また我をそしる。人をそしるは即
我をそしるなり。たとへば天にむかひてつばき吐
くが如し。そのむくひ甚はやし。言さかりて出づ
れば、又さかりて入る。我に出づるつみは、やが
てわれにかへること、車の輪の如し。おそるべき
かな。人を一分そしれば、人より三分そしりかへ

二三

さる。その上人に見おとされ、いやしめらるゝ。
益なくして損あり。愚なりといふべし。

人をそしるは是不仁なるのみならず、必身のわざは
ひとゝなることをしらず。是不智なり。人をそしる
一事にして、仁智の大德を失ふ。殊に我が同官同
藝の人をそしるは、人をおさへて、わが身をたて
んとするなり。又不義不禮といふべし。卑狹の甚
しきなり。是小人のわざなり。みづからはぢて戒
むべし。

人をそしるは、その人に對せず、かげにてひそかに
いふことなれば、その人しるべからず、何の害か
あらんと思ふは愚なり。そしりは必もれやすし。
俗語に、惡事千里を行くといひ、又壁に耳ありとい
ふが如し。人のしらんことをおそれればいふべから
ず。孟子に、人の不善をいふは、後の患をいかん
かすべきといへり。

言を出すにも、わが身をかへりみて、分に過ぎたる
ことをばいふべからず。分に過ぎたることをいへ
ば、人にそしりわらはる。恥づべし。また人きゝ
て信ずべからざることは、事實なりともいふべか

らず。この心づかひあるべきことゝなり。
わが善をばかくして、みづからほむべからず。人の
善をばあらはして、はむべし。わがあやまりをばか
ざるべからず、あらはして改むべし。人のあやま
ちをばあらはすべからず、おほひかくすべし。
わが身にいかなる才能善行ありとも、口に出しては
ほこるべからず。その才能をうしなひ、その善行を
うしなひ、その善行にほこれば、その善行を失ふ。

我が身をはめざれども、わがよきもあしきも、人の心
にしるものなり。たとひわが才行あらはれずして、
人しらずとも、わが身の德に害なし。わが身の才
能いみじくとも、みづからあらはしほむるは自嫌
すと云。いやしむべし。其不德のほどあらはれて、
むげに人に見おとさるゝわざなり。

凡人のいみきらふこと、いふべからず。人の生れつ
き、不具かたわなる者あり。又その行ざきに大な
る過ありしものあり。或は親先祖いやしかりしも
のあり。此のたぐひ、いひいだせば、きく人きら
ひてうらみいかる。是世俗のいはゆるさしわひな

二一四

り。心を用ひていふべからず。

ことば多く無用の枝葉しげ〴〵れば、相對する人つかる。同じことをくりかへせば、きく人あく。如此なれば、さし立ちたる用ある道理はきこえず。ことばすくなく、用あることを言ひて、道理明らかに詳なるべし。辭は簡要をたつとぶと古人もいへり。無用の言を出さず、有用のことをいふべしとなり。

人のしわざ、わが心にかなはずとも、なだめゆるして、左こそありなんと思ひて、いかり恨むべからず。もし心の中にいかり甚しくとも、いかりやみて本心になるまでは、こらへて言を口に出すべからず。いかりのさかんなる時、はやく口にいだせば、必過言いで〻、後悔あり。心をやはらげ、氣を平らかにし、怒やみて後言ふべきことはいひ、なすべきことはなすべし。酒に醉ひたる時も、尤言をつ〻しみて、いふべからず。酒さめて後ことばを出すべし。人にふみを途るも同じ。いかりやみ酒さめて後、文をかくべし。是皆後悔なき道なり。言よりも、げに文はあとにのこるものなり。

ふみをかくに殊につ〻しみて、いかりの内にかくべからず。

世俗のかたり傳ふること、そらごと多し。こと〴〵く信ずべからず。ことにあやしきこと、多くはいつはりなり。神佛の奇特も、俗人のかたり傳ふることはそらごと多し。きくわいあるは正法にあらず。凡正法には奇恠なし。奇恠なりとて貴ぶべからず。神佛をはめむとて、なきことをつくり出し、或は似たることを、まことにいひなし、奇異なることを言ひつげて、かへつて神佛の德をけがすことを知らず。鬼魅狐狸のしわざには、奇恠なることもあり。それも多くはそらごとあり、ことごとく信ずべからず。おろかなる人は、そ〻うなるそらごとを信じてまよひやすし。そらごとをつくりて、かたりつたふること、世におほし、信ずべからず。妄に人のことばにまかせて、かたり傳ふべからず。人の胡亂なる言を信じて、又人にかたれは、我も亦虚言をいふの罪あり。つ〻しんで人にかたるべからず。

あやしきことを耳にきくとも、目に見ざることの、

一一五

たしかならざるをば、口にいふべからず。必虚說
多し。人のみだりにかたりつたふる神變奇怪なる
ことを、我も亦かたれば、世につたはりて、人を
まよはすこと多し。おろかなる人は、きくことに
いつはりを信じやすし。すべてあやし
きことは、かたるべからず。たしかに見たること
にも、心目の病によりて、あやしきことゝみゆ。又
あやしとみゆることも、ゆへありて、あやしから
ざることとおはし。

人のあやまちを正して、**いひきかせ、** 改めんこと
をしへすゝむるは善事なり。既に過去りたる過を
かへすぐ〜言出しとがむべからず。凡人のあやま
りてしつることゝか、又しらずしてしそんじたるこ
とは、ちから及ばず。そのあやまりをばつげきか
すべし。**しばぐ〜云出して、** せむべからず。その
人わが身をばせめずして、うらみいかりてそむく。その
**古語に、** その國に居ては、その大夫をそしらずとい
へり。いはんや君をそしるは、大なるとがなり。
**古語に、** 臣の不忠、君をそしるより大なるはなし
といへり。たとひ君にひがことありとも、臣たる

ものは、かくして語るべからず。又我が身その位
にをらずんば、國政の是非を評議すべからず。下
として上をそしるは不忠不敬なり。つゝしむべし。
上をそしる人ありとて、それに雷同すべからず。わが
口をとぢてかたることなかれ。上たる人は、
行のあやまりを、下なるものにいはせそしらせて、
ひろくきくべし。下のそしりをきくは、是上たる人
の幸なり。人の口をとづるはあしく、口をとづれ
ばかへつてそしり多し。そしらすれば、後はそし
りなし。このこと古人の教明白なり。川の水は、
下をはり流せば、水のうれひなし。下をせきとむ
れば、ふさがりて、横流のわざはひとなる。人の口
をとむるも、亦かくのごとし。故に明君は人の口
をとむるずして、人にいはせ、下のそしりをきくこ
とをこのめり。帝堯は、諫の鼓を置きて、いさめ
をきゝ給ひ、殷の湯王は、誹謗の木を立てゝ、政
のあやまりをそしらしめ給ひしとかや。
およそ、人を知ることは、いたりてかたきことなれ
ば、人の口とわが目きゝにまかせて、みだりに人
の善惡を決すべからず。然るゆへに、ほむるもそ

二一六

295

しるも、かる〳〵しく妄にすべからず、歳月を待
つべし。即時にはやく人を譽め毀れば、必あやま
りて後悔あり。われひとりあしきことゝおもへど、さ
もなくてかへつてよきことあり。人のほめそりも、
又あしき人あり。人の口と我が心二ながら證とし
がたし。人の口と我が心二ながら善惡を定むべか
らず。人をはむるは諂にちかし。
面前に人をはむるは諂にちかし。もしはむべきこと
あらば、その人に對せずして、他人に對してほむ
べし。その人の感も亦ふかし。面前に人の過を正
すはよし。退けてかげにてそしるべからず。

凡ほめそしること・あやまりて理にたがへば、わが
人をしらざる不智のほどあらはれて、はづかし。
人の小惡を大惡にいひなし、小過を大過にいひな
し、虚なることを實にいひなすは、讒言なり。又
左程なきことを、甚しく人をほめ過すも、正直の
道にあらず。へつらひてその人に私するなり。は
めそしること、かる〳〵しくすべからず。たとへ

ば權量を以て物の輕重をはかるが如くなるべし。
一毫もかろくし重くして、過不及あるべからず。
ほむべからざる人をほめ、そしるべからざる人を
そしり、或ほめ過し、そしり過すは、ともに不智
なり。論語に、子貢曰、君子は一言以て智とし、一
言以て不智とす、言つゝしまずんばあるべからず
といへり。よき人は、許川をつゝしむとて、人を
みだりにゆるしはめず。されども小善をもすてず、
一藝をも用ふるは、君子のする所なり。人の善を
ばもてはやして稱譽すべし。惡をかくして、善を
あぐるは、聖人の行なり。まなぶべし。

およそ人をいさむるには法あり。たとひわが子我が
弟をいさむるにも、聲をあらゝげ、言をあらくし
て惡口し、はづかしむるはあしゝ。如此すれば、
きく者はらだちうらみて、心に服せず、かへつて、
そのいさめにそむきてしたがはず。こゝを以て、
人をいさむるには、心を平和にし、ことばを順に
し、道理を正しくいさむべし。まづ人のよきこと
をほめて、人の心をよろこばしむべし。いかりて
よろこばざれば、いさめてもうけ用ひがたし。こ

れ人をいさむるてだてなり。およそ人をいさむる
には、人の氣質によりて、直諫諷諫の二の法あり、
しらずんばあるべからず。その心和順にて、義理
明なる人ならば、直諫すべし。直諫とは、過を言
ひあらはし、理をすぐにのべて、是非をまげず、
つよくいさむるなり。かくの如くなれば、聞く人
おそれてしたがふ。孔子の、法語の言とのたまふ、
是なり。又氣質和順ならず、義理くらき人ならば、
諷諫すべし。諷諫とは、すぐにその人の過惡をさし
あらはしていはず、まづその人のよき所をあげて
はめ、その人をよろこばしめ、その人の心にした
がひてさからはず、たゞその事の損あると、益わ
るとをときて、得心せしむべし。或は他事によそ
へて、善惡得失をのぶべし。かくのごとくすれば、
きく人はらたゝずして、よろこびていさめをき
したがふ。孔子の、巽與の言とのたまへる是なり。
人をいさむる法は、この二なり。その人の氣質に
よりて、いさめの法かはるべし。直諫するこそ本
意なれども、正直につよくいさめても、きく人の
耳にさからひて、うけ用ひざれば益なし。明君賢

者ならでは、直諫によろしき人は稀なり。よのつね
の人ならば諷諫すべし。諷諫をよくして、人のよ
くゝいれたるためし多し。是いさめのよき手立
なり。いさめの道をしらで、ことばをあらくして
人にさからひ、みだりにいへば、人いかりて必さ
きいれず。人に益なくして、我身のわざはひとな
る。ことに我が親に直諫してはらたゝしめ、親よ
ろこびざれば、親子の中らとくなる。大なる不幸
なり。おやをいさむるには法あり。
易曰、納約自牖 などは明らかなる所なり。たとへ
ば家の内にある人に、外より物をいひ入るゝに、
かべでしにいへばきこえず、まどよりいへばきこ
ゆ。いさめをいふも、またかくのごとし。いかな
るおろかなる人も、必いづくにぞ片はしに道理開
けて、明らかなる所あり。或は好む所の欲あり。
その所をよく見つけて、言ひ入るれば、きゝ入れ
やすし。この諫めやうのよきこと、古もさるため
し多し。ふさがりたる處をしらずして、いかに忠
をつくしていさむとも、きゝ用ひざれば益なし。
人の過をいさむるには、誠あまりありて、ことばた

らざるがよし。心を内にふくみて、言すくなく云ひつくさず、餘味ふかゝるべし。人のあしきことをいひ、そのあやまりをさとらしむるをよしとす。人のあしきことを、ことごとくいひ顯し、はげしくわらそしひぬれば、人いかりてうけ用ひず。是をいさむる道にあらず。温厚にして理明らかなるか、還てよく人を感せしむ。是はげしくせむるにまされり。

徐偉長曰。君子非二其人一則弗二與之言一。其人にあらずとは、道理ををしへつげても、よくその理をきゝわかつべき智なく、聞きて信じ用ふべき誠なき人を云。かやうの人に、善言をつげても益なし。凡善言を聞きても、さとらず信せざるは、其人愚なればなり。

人のあしきをいさむるに、はじめよりうちつけに、其事をすぐにさしていへば、おほやうは聞入れず、かへりていかりをもよほす。只その事となくかすめなして、人の心につくからずして、聞入るゝこそよろしかるべけれ。

よろこぶ時の言は誠すくなし。いかる時の言は敬すくなし。喜び怒るとき、殊に言語をつゝしみて、喜怒のために心をやぶらるゝことなかれ。

末の世には風俗うすくなりて、からやまとの文をつくるにもへつらひかざりて、いつはり多し。政のよきをほむるとて、舜の御世にもこえつべしといひ、人の善をほむるとて、聖賢のごとく云なし、或は知仁勇の三德そなはれりなどいひ、武略をほめては、孫呉にもおとらずといひ、手跡をほむるとては、王羲之にも及ぶべしといひ、詩文をほむるとて李杜蘇黄に同じかるべしといひ、和歌は貫之躬恒にもおとらず、和文は紫式部清少納言が如しといふの類多し。さほどになき事とは、心の内にしりながら、風俗のあしきにしたがひて、いつはりへつらひとなることをしらず。かゝるあしきならはしにしたがひて、正直の道理を失ふべからず。かゝる時の

君子は人の善をあげて、人の惡をかくし、人の長ずる所をとりて、短なる所をゆるす。厚しと云べし。

小人は人の善あるをばほめずして、その過をあげてそしり、人の才の長じたる所をばあげずしてか

くし、その才の不得手にして短なる所をあらはし
てそしる。薄きことの至なり。人の不得手なる所
を云あらはせば恨をとる。

主君はいふに及ばず、父母兄夫のわれに物いひかけ
たるに、そのこたへ明らかに聞えざるはうらめし。
甚無禮なり。父兄夫など我に問ふことあらば、こ
とわりの正しく聞ゆるやうに答ふべし。おや兄を
つとは、いづれもしたしければ、そのしたしきを
たのみて、答のなめげなるはあしゝ。よき人はわ
れより下ざまなる人に對してもあなどらず。故に
こたへ明らかなり。いはんやわれより上なる人を
や。

人のいふことをば、きゝいれずして、たゞわが道
理のみをいひたてんとするは甚無禮なり。人にも
道理をいはせて、きゝて後わが思ふ處をのぶべし。
古語に、流丸は甌臾（オウユ）にとゞまり、流言は知者にとゞま
るといへり。甌臾とはくぼき所なり。丸き玉をな
ぐれば轉じてやまず。されどもくぼき所にとゞま
る。流言は根なしごとなれば、質もなきあだなる
雑説なり。愚者は是を誠ぞと心得て、信じてかた

り傳ふれば、世にあまねく流布してやまず、知者
は不實なることを信ぜずして、耳に聞けども口に
いはず。その耳にとゞまりて言ひちらさず。是流
言は知者にとゞまるなり。

やむことを得ずんば、人をそしり、人をほむること
なくんばあるべからず。されどもみだりに、この
んで人をほめそしりて、口に是非おほき人は、古
人のいましむる所なり。やむことを得ば、みだり
に人をほめそしるべからず。あやまること多し。

大和俗訓卷之五 終

# 大和俗訓 卷之六

## 躬行上

貝原篤信 著

善をこのみ、惡をきらふことの誠なるは、大學の誠意のことにて、身を修め道を行ふ初なり。善を好み惡をきらはざれば、道い行はるやうなし。學者の最初よりつとむべきこと、是より急なるはなし。善をこのむことは、たとへばよき色をこのむがごとく、惡をきらふことは、あしき臭をきらふがごとくすべし。是誠にこのみきらふなり。人のきらふこと多けれど、惡臭ほどいむべき物なし。このむこと多けれど、好色に過ぎたるものなし。是皆諸人の、眞實にこのみきらふものなれば、善をこのみ惡をきらふことも、亦如此眞實なるべしとなり。是誠によく人をさとすべきたとへなり。もし心の内に、すでに善惡をしれども、このみきらふこと實ならずして、善を行はず、惡を去らざるは、これを自欺と云ふ。自欺とは、わが心の内實ならざるをいふ。善を好み、惡をきらふこと誠ならざれば、萬の行みないつはりとなりて、道行はるべからず。たとへば草木の根なきが如く、家をつくるに基なきがごとし、行の本たゝず。こゝを以て、道を行はんと思はゝ、先この志を立つるを初とすべし。

力行の道は、その大綱は身ををさめて、五倫をあつくするにあり。身ををさむるは道を行ふ本なり。身ををさまらざれば、五倫の道行はれず。身ををさむる條目は、言を忠信にし、行をあつくつゝしみ、いかりを懲しおさへ、慾をこらへ行ひ、見きゝする所の善に、はやくうつりてつとめ行ひ、わがあやまちをしりて、すみやかにあらたむるにあり。その上人に對して道を行へども、人したがはずして、行はれざることあらば、人をせめずして自からへりみ求めて、わが善のいたらざることをせむべし。

およそ人の身のわざ多けれど、つゝめていへば、言と行との二にすぎず。言をつゝしみて信にし、行をつとめて篤くつゝしめば身をさまる。故に言行を

つゝしみあつくするは、身ををさむるのみちなり。言行をわかてば、人の身のわざ四となる。視聽言動なり。この四のわざに、皆なすべき所の定れる法あり。是を禮といふ。禮にしたがひて、視聽言動をなすべし。四の事のなすまじきことをなすは、非禮なり。禮はたとへば工のすみかねの如し。すみかねを用ひざれば、材木工あれども用にたゝず。およそ人の人たる所は禮なり。禮なければ禽獣にちかし。故に禮は身ををさめ、道を行ふ則なり。君子は常に禮を守り行ふ。小人はつねに禮にそむく。君子の視聽言動は、人の身の四のわざなり。思は又心の動にしてその本なり。善を好み、惡をきらふことを誠にするは、思をつゝしむの道なり。善を行ふに、その心に義と利とのわかちあり。義とは我が行ふべき公の理なり。私なくして我が爲にせざるなり。わが身のためにするは義にあらず。利とはわが身のためにする私の心なり。公ならざるをいふ。萬の事を行ふに、まづ義か不義かをか

へりみて、義にしたがひ行ふべし。その行ふこと善なりとも、その心義にしたがはずして、わが身の利分のためにせば、是私なり。君に仕ふる一事を以ていはゞ、奉公をよくつとむるは善なり。眞實に忠をなして、わが身をわするゝは、義を正しくするなり。もし奉公をつとめて、つゆばかりも、君の恩寵を得んためにつとむる心あらば、是利をはかるなり、義にあらず。凡義とは、なすべきことをなして、わが身の利のためにする私なきをいふ。されども、義理にかなへば、人よろこびしたがひ、事とゝのひ行はるゝ故、利は求めずして自來る。自來る利は義に害なし。求めて得る利は義に害あり。たとへば、天下にきこゆるほどの善を行ひても、身のためにするに志あるは利なり、義にあらず。義と利とをわかつこと、第一つとむべき心術なり。善を行ふとは、天性に生れつきたる仁義禮智の本心にしたがひて、孝弟、忠信、慈愛、恭敬、温和、辭讓、剛勇、廉恥などを、時に隨ひ、事に隨つて行ふをいふ。さばかりの善を行ひても、名利をね

がふ心ありて行ふは誠の善にあらず。善を行ふに
は、たゞ一すぢに、義理に専にして名利の心なか
るべし。

衆人の行、萬事につきて過と惡とあり。過とは心に
惡なけれども、しらずして理にたがひ、或は心つ
かずして理にちがふをいふ。惡とは善惡は知りな
がら、慾にひかれて理にたがふをいふ。是自欺な
り。身ををさむるには、過惡をあらためて、善に
うつるをつとめとすべし。聖人は過なし。賢者以
下は、過なきことなし。殊に凡人は過多し。何ぞ
今の世に過なき人あらんや。人のいさめをきて
も用ひず、われに過あれどもしらずして、あやま
ちなきと思ふ人あり。是自修むるに志なきゆへな
り。もし自修むる人は、過多きことをしるべし。
自省みてわが過をしり、人の諌を聞きて、わが道
をあらため善にうつるべし。

常に我が身をかへりみて先我が過をしるべし。すで
に過をしりなば、速にあらたむべし。尚書に過を
改めて吝ならずといへり。吝とはをしむなり、あ
やまちををしまずして早く改むるを云ふ。孔子も、

過つては則改むるにはゞかることなかれとのたま
へり。わが身の過をしらざるは愚なり。過をしり
て改めざるは即惡なり。しらずして過つより猶そ
のつみおもし。

過は必氣質の偏よりおこる。剛なる人は、心つよき
所より過おこり、柔なる人は心よわき所より過お
こる。氣質の偏なる所にかちて、過なからんこと
を求むべし。學者つねに、わが氣質の偏を察し、
その過をかへりみて改むべし。かくのごとくせざ
れば、學問の益なし。是學者の專つとめ行ふべき
所なり。過を改むるは、氣質の偏にかつ道なり。
氣質の偏なる所にはかちがたし。つねにつとめて
十分の力を用ゆべし。

わが身、聖人にあらずして、過多きはうべなりとて、過
をしりながら、改めざる人は、無下に道に志なき
人なり。自暴自棄といふべからず。かゝの志なき人
にならひて、わが過をゆるすべからず。

人の目は、百里ゝ遠を見れどもその背を見ず。明
鋭といへどもそのうらをてらさず、離婁が明目な
るも、そのまつげをみることなし。こゝを以て人

知ありといへども、わが身のあやまりをしりがた
し。故に君子の學は、專わが身をかへりみ、人の
いさめをきゝ用ひ、あやまちをしりて改むるを
ねとす。子路は我過を人の告るをよろこべり。故
に百世の師なりと程子もいへり。人をしること、
まことにかたしといへど、わが身のあしきをしる
は、又人をしるよりも猶かたし。こゝを以て、わ
が過をつげしらする人あらば、まことによろこぶ
べし。人わづかなる財をおくり、或は酒肴をおく
るをも、うくる人これをよろこぶ。いはんや、い
ひがたき諫をいひ、みづからしりがたき過をきく
をや。わが身におゝてかゝる大なる益なし。いさ
めをきくこととあに幸ならずや。子路のよろこべる
ことむべなるかな。過をきくことをきらひ、諫を
ふせぐはあしきことの至りなり。諫をきゝて過を
改むるは、醫を招きて病をいやすが如し。もし過
あれども、諫をふせぎて人の正すことをきらふは、
病をそだてゝ醫をきらふが如し。その身をうしな
へどもかへりみず、かなしむべし。いふこゝろは、一度

顔子は、あやまちをまたせず。いふこゝろは、一度

あやまちとしれることは、ふたゝび行はず。又顔子
は、不善あれば未三嘗不ν知ν知ν之未三嘗復行一と易
に見えたり。いふ意は、わが身に過あれば必しる。
是知ることの明らかなるなり。過をしれば必行は
ず。是行ふことのつよきなり。

論語に、君子のあやまちは日月の食のごとし、あや
まてば人皆是をみる、更むれば人皆仰ぐといへ
り。君子の心は、青天白日のごとく、洒落にして
一點のおほひなし。故にあやまちをおほひかくさ
ずしてはやく改む。日食月食をば、天が下の人、
たれもあふぎ見てかくれなし。しばし光かくれど
も、やがてもとのごとく明になれば、日月の光明
に少もきずなし。君子の過かくの如し。又論語に、
小人過也必文といへり。小人は過をはぢてかざり、
その過をおほひかくせば、正直の道理をうしなひ、
是非をいひまげ、いつはりてつひに過を改めず。
甚見ぐるし。尚書に、あやまちをはぢて、非をなすこ
となかれといへり。賢人すら過あり、況凡人をや。
只過つてよく改むるを君子とすべし。

人の善を見ては、我も亦この善あらんことを思ひ、是をまなび行ふべし。人の不善を見ては、我も亦この不善ありやと、身をかへりみおそれて、もしあらば改むべし。如此すれば、見きゝする所の善惡、皆わが助となる。老子の善人は不善人の師、不善人は善人の資といへるもこの意なり。

いにしへの賢者は、わが過をきくことをのみ、人のいさめをよろこべり。いさめをきゝて、過を改め善にうつれば、道にすゝむことはまりなし。善なること、これより大なるはなし。又古の賢者は、人にほめらるゝをよろこばず、わが善をきくことをこのます。わが善をきゝては、益なきのみならず。もしすこしもわが身にほこる心いでゝ、善をなすにをこたらば大なる害なり。今の人はわが過をきくことをもこのます、人の我をほむるを悦び、わが善をきくことをこのむ。世にへつらへる小人多き故はむる者多し。それをまことゞと心得て身にほこり、善を行ふにをこたるはおろかなり。末の世の人は、からもやまとも、すべて人のいさめをこのます。故に人を諫むるを、ひとへに世な

れぬかたくなゝる人とおもへり。父として子をいさむれば、わが父は老耄せりといひ、また老人は今の風をしらずとてそしりうらむ。臣として君をいさむれば、おのれり無禮なりとていかり遠ざく。こゝを以て、人ごとに世の俗になれ、人の欲にしたがひ、へつらひていさめず。この風もし世に行はれ、風俗となりなば、善は日々にすたり、惡は日々にさかんになりて、道行はるべからず。かなしむべし。およそ諫をいふ人有りがたし。古來からもやまとも、諫をよろぶ人は尤有りがたし。故にいさむる人もまれなり。

人に對して道を行ふに、人われにしたがはずば、人をせむべからず。たゞわが身に立かへりて求むべし。是を自反と云ふ。この工夫かんようなり。人を愛して、人われをしたしまずば、わが愛のいまだいたらざる故とおもふべし。人を禮して人われに無禮ならば、わが禮いまだいたらざるゆへと思ふべし。人ををさめてをさまらずんば、わが智の至らざる故とおもふべし。是人をせめずして、わが身にかへり求むる工夫なり。かくのごとくすれ

ば、人したがひやすし。したがはざるは、猶われが
誠のいたらざるとおもひ、その質をつとむべし。
われに誠あれど、人そむくは道埋もなき妄人なり。
禽獸にちかき人なれば、其人と是非をあらそふべ
からず。

中庸曰、言顧行、行顧言。いふ意は、言と行とは相
違なかるべし。言を出すに、わが身の行をかへり
みていふべし。事を行ふには、己が言をかへりみ
て行ふべし。言ふことはやすく、行ふことはかた
し。故に言はひかへていひ、行は言より過すべし。
如此すれば、言と行と相違なし。口にいふことあ
まり有りて、身に行ふことたらざるは、是言行の
そむけるなり。はづべし。

善も惡も、かならず小をつみて大にいたる。故に善
は小なりとてすつべからず。惡は小なりとて行ふ
べからず。

古語に、忠臣は二君につかへず、烈女は兩夫にあら
ためずといへり。君子の道、節義を守るをおもし
とす。節義とは、臣の君につかへ、婦の夫につか
ふるに、一すぢに忠節義理ありて二心なく、二君

につかへず兩夫にあらためず。もし不幸にしてわ
が身艱難にくるしむとも、君をすて夫にそむきて
身命をおしむべからず。命を失ふとも、忠貞の志
を改めざるを節義と云ふ。よろづのこと、いみじ
く才能ありて、うるはしき人も、節義をうしなひ
て、君にそむきて難をのがれ、夫をすて二人にし
たがはゞ、その餘は見るにたらず。一たび節義を
うしなひて、利ある方につき、害ある方をのがれ、
或は死ぬべき時にしなざれば、一生の名をけがす
のみならず、後代までもながき惡名をながす。お
よそ人生前の血肉をのみ、わが身と思ふべからず。
死後の善惡の名も、亦わが身の内なることを思ふ
べし。生けるもの、必一たび死なずといふことな
し。節義をうしなひて、かひなき命をいき、たと
ひ百年のよはひをたもち、富貴をきはむとも、人
の道をうしなひて、世にいけるかひなくば、何の
たのしみがあらんや、是人のつとめ行ふべき大節
なり。

凡、人のつとめ行ふべきわざ三あり。願ふ所もまた
三有り。一には務業、二には養生、三には行義

なり。務業とは、四民ともにその家のわざをつとむるなり。士は君につかへ、農工商は、各その家業をつとめて、その衣食を求むるをいふ。家業をつとめざれば、飢寒貧窮をまぬかれず、是諸民の先つとむべきことにて、財禄あらんことをねがふ所なり。業を務むれば、衣食と居處を得て、身をやしなふ生計は其内にあり。二には、養生は飲食色慾七情の内、慾をうすくし、起居動静の形氣をつつしみ、風寒暑濕の外邪をふせぎ、生命を養ひて、病なく長壽を得んことをねがふをいふ。生を養はざれば、必病生じて、身をくるしめ、又むまれつきたる天年をたもちがたし。是また人のよくつとむべきことなり。三には、行義は身ををさめて人倫の道をあつく行ひ、道理にかなはんことを得て、義を行はざれば人道を失ふ。凡業を務めて富貴に居り、生を養ひて長生を得ても、人の道なくんば、禽獣にちかくしていけるかひなし。古の聖人、これをうれひて、師を立て學を立て人倫の道ををしへ、義理をしらしめ給ふ。この三の内、務業より養生はおもく、養生より行義はおも

もし。いかんとなれば、務業は富貴をさはびるを宗とす。國土を領し、高位にのぼるは、富貴のきはまりなり。されども、壽命なければ富貴も用なし。たゞ今人ありて、汝に國土をゆづり、高位をさづくべし。然らば汝が命をうばふべしとならば、至りて欲ふかき愚なる人も、命を失ひて國土を得んと思ふ者あるべからず。しかれば富貴より命をもきにあらずや。故曰、務業より養生はいのちおもきにあらずや。又君父のために命をすつるは云に及ばず、朋友とつれ立ちて道をゆくに、もしむかひより人來りて、朋友と口論し、たゝかはゞ、士ほどの者はその友を見すてゝ、にぐる人あるべからず、たゝかひて死すれどもかへりみず。又わづかなる禄を得て、君に仕ふる下部も、主人のため命をすつるはめづらしからず。是生命より義理はおもきにあはらずや。凡この三は、天下の人むまれつきて、各その心にねがふ所にして、又行ふべき常然の道なり、つとめてをこたるべからず。その内に、輕重あることかくの如し。義理の生命よりも富貴よりも重く貴ぶべきこと、是を以てしるべし。然れば

命ををしみて、義理を失ふは輕重をしらざるなり。いはんや利欲によりて、大なる義理を失ふはいふにおよばず。

凡の人、財祿を得ることをこのまざるはなし。これをこのまば、家業をよくつとむべし。これをこのまば、養生の道をよくつとむべし。又長生を好まざるはなし。これを好まば、養生の道をよくつとむべし。又義を好まざるはなし。これを好まば、學問をつとめて義理をしるべし。

恩を報ふこと、人道の大節なり。恩をしらざるは、禽獸にひとし。是人と禽獸とわかるゝ所なり。是を以て、恩を報ずるは、人道の大節なりといふことむべならずや。恩をしらば、必報ふべし。しりて報ぜざるは、しらざるに同じ。恩を報ずるには誠を以てすべし。

人に四恩あり。天地の恩、父母の恩、主君の恩、聖人の恩。この四恩、わするべからず。天地は人の大父母なり。父母の氣は、即天地の氣なり。人は天地の氣より生る。又むまれて後は、天地の養をうけて身をたつ。故に天地の恩は、廣大にしてき

はまりなし。何を以てか、その恩をむくひんや。天地の御心にしたがひてそむかざる、是天地につかへ奉りて、孝をつくし、その恩を報ずる道なり。天地の御心にしたがふとはなんぞや。人たるものは、天地の萬物をうみやしなひ給ふ、その御心をうけて心とす。是仁なり。仁とは、あはれみの心なり。仁を失ざるは、天地の心にしたがふなり。仁を行ふ道いかん。天地は、そのうめる所の人をあつく愛し、次には萬物を愛し給ふ。その心にしたがひて、人倫を厚く愛し、次に鳥獸以下の萬物を愛してそこなはざる、是天地の御心にしたがふなり。即是仁なり。仁を行ふは、天につかへ奉りて、その大恩の萬一をむくふ道なり。天地は人の大父母なり、人は天地の子なれば、是より大なるはなく、是より急なるはなし。天地につかへ奉る孝の道なり。人となる者の一生つとめ行ふべき道、是より大なるはなく、是より急なるはなし。人となる者、必しらずんばあるべからず。此こと前卷に既にいへり。初學の人にしらせんために、しばゝゝいふなり。父母われをうめりといへども、その生をうけし初は、

天地の氣をうけて生ず。是天地は生の本なり。そ
の上うまれて後、いとけなきより身をはるまで
天地の養をうけ、天地の生ずる物を食とし、衣と
し、家とし、器として、身をやしなふ。天地の性を
うけ、五常の徳を心にむまれつきて、萬物の靈と
なり、天地の内にすみて、天地のあつさめぐみを
うく。生をうけし初より身をはるまで、天地の
恩をうけしとてとかくのごとし。かゝる大恩ある
ことをさとりて、身ををはるより天地につかへ奉り
て、孝を行ひ、そのきはまりなき徳に報ひんこと
を思ふべし。是人間の一大事なり。故にたび〲
くりかへしていふなり。

父母の恩、きはまりなきこと、天地にひとし。父母
なくんば、何んぞ我あらん。その恩、海よりふか
く山より高し。海山は限りあり、父母のめぐみはか
ぎりなし。いかんしてか、その恩をむくひんや。
たゞ孝を行ひて、その恩い萬一ヲ報ずべし。父母
につかへて、その力をつくして、をしむべからず。父母
力とは身と財との力をいふ。身の力のかぎりをつ
くしてつかへ、財の力のかぎりをつくして發ひ、

そのちからをゝをしむべからず。わかき時はいわれ
も人も、父母の恩を思はず、力をつくさずして、
不孝を行ひ、父母をはりて、後悔すれど益なし。
是一生のかぎりなき、父母をはりて、人の子たる者、後悔
なからんことを思ひ、父母のいける時、ちからをつ
くして孝を行ふべし。父母につかふる年は久しからず。
一日も孝を行はずしてわだ
に過すべからず。孝する日をのをしむ。といへることに心にかくべし。

父母われを生むといへど、君の養ひにあらざれば、
我が身立たず。君の祿をうけて、わが身を養ふの
みならず、父母妻子をやしない、奴婢をつかひ、
衣服居宅器物、萬の用ともしからずして、安樂に
世をわたること、ひとへに君のたまものなり。是
又父母にならびて、その恩大なり。君につかふる
には、我が身をわすれて、身をわが物とすべから
ず、君に奉りおくべし。是身をゆだぬるなり。論
語に、子夏の曰、事二父母一能竭二其力一。事レ君能致二其
身一とは是なり。

父母に生れ、君にやしなはるゝといへども、聖人の敎
なければ人の道をしらず。道をしらざれば、食に

あき、衣をあたゝかに着、居り所をやすくしても、人の道なくして禽獸にちかければ、人にむまれたるかひなし。今をしへをうけたるいにしへの聖人の恩は、君父にひとし。聖人は萬世の師なり、萬世の後までいとたふとぶべし。聖人の恩をむくんとならば、聖人の敎にしたがひ、その道にそむかざるべし。是聖人の恩を報ずる道なり。

およそ、天地父母主君聖人の恩・相ならびて至りておもし。この四恩をわすれそむくは、人にあらずと思ふべし。むくいずんばあるべからず。これをむくいんと思はゞ、道をまなびて行ふにあり、他の道あるべからず。

今の世に、道を敎ふる師は有りがたし、もしあらば貴びつかふべし。道の敎をうけたる師は、その恩ふかきこと君父にひとし。又書をよみならひたる師を、句讀の師といふ、その勞はなはだし。藝術の師は又その次なり。是等は君父聖人の恩にはならべがたしといへども、その苦勞の恩わするべからず。この外、人の生涯には、恩をうくること多し。およそ、人の恩をうけば、心に銘してわする

べからず。一言の情をも感し、一事の志をも心にかけて思ふべし。人の情あれども感せず、人の志をもむなしくするは、無下に心なきなり。

司馬溫公の曰、人の恩をうけて、そむくに忍びざる者は、その人必忠孝ならんと。この言道理至極せり。然れば、恩をうけてわする〻ものは、忠孝ともになかるべし。忠孝も君父の恩を忘れざる道なり。俗語に、恩を知らざれば木石にひとし。といへるも、恩をしらざるは人の心なきなり。君子の道、天地につかへて仁を行ひ、父母に孝を行ひ、君に忠をつくし、故舊にあつくするは、皆恩をむくふる道なり。人の性によりて、無學なる俗人にも、恩をわすれずして、節義をつとめ、禮をかゝざるものあり。是その天性のすぐれたる所なり。その善行貴とぶべし。又よのつねのことは、才ありて惡人ならざれども、舊恩をわする〻者あり。義なしといふべし。

古語曰。施㆑恩勿㆑念。受㆑惠勿㆑忘。人に恩をほどこさば、是わがなすべき常然の道とおもひて、かさねてそのほどこしたることをわするべし。思ひ出す

べからず。恩をほどこしたるとて、恩だらしくす
るは見ぐるし。又人のめぐみをうけば、その恩を
わするべからず。必むくひんことを思ふべし。小
人は人の恩をうけては必むくひんことを思ふべし。
どことしては、必わすれして、そのむくひを求む。
その人むくひざれば、うらみいかる。凡天地の人
を生し育なひ給ふは、其めぐみ廣大なれど、君子
にあらざれば、其洪恩をしらず、天地につかへむ
と思ふ心なし。父母の恩をうけしことは、猶ちか
くして、誰もしれることとなれど、それだにわすれ
て不孝なるは、凡夫の生れつきならはしなり。い
はんや、その餘の人倫の交の内にて、たとひそく
ばくの恩をほどこしたりとも、父母のめぐみにく
らべば萬が一なるべし。人皆君子にあらざれば、
恩をふかくうけながら、十人に九人は必わすれて
むくはず。恩をうけてわするゝは、凡人のならひ
ぞと思ひて、われより恩をほどこせりとて、ほこる
べからず。ほどこしてむくひをのぞめば、人その
恩をわすれたる時、うらみいかりてわが德をそこ
なふ。是人情をしらずといふべし。恩をうけてわ

するゝは、小人のくせなり、めづらしからずと思
ひ、人をとがむべからず。是人情をしれるなり。
たゞわが身は恩をわするべからず。
およそ人のほどこしをうけ、恩をかうふり、或は我
を君にすゝめたる恩あらば、ながく忘るべからず。
折節の禮義をつとむべし、久しくして、をとたる
べからず。或は初めにつとむれども、誠すくなき
人は、久しきをふれば、必舊恩をわすれて訪ひく
ることだになし。始終一の如くなるべし。凡恩を
しらざるは世の凡人のならひなれば、せむるにた
らず。我が身、かゝるうすき人情にならひて、恩を
わするべからず。恩をわするゝは、人にあらずと
思ふべし。犬はいやしき獣なれど、養をうけし主
人をしたひてわすらず。他の富める家に引きよせつ
なぎ置きて、食にあかしむれども、まどしきもとの
主人の家ににげ歸る。或は數十里の道をもかへり、
はるかなる海をおよぎてもかへることとあり。され
ば恩をしらざるは、人を以て犬にもしかずといふ
べし。
人倫をあつく愛し、四恩を感じむくひて、又神を た

るとぶべし。古人の曰、民は神之主也。是を以て、

王は、先民を養ひて後神に力を用ひ給ふ。人事をつ

とめずして、神に助を求むべからず。神に三あり、

天神、地祇、人鬼なり。天神は天の神霊をいふ、日

月星も其の内にあり。地祇は地に在る神霊なり、

名山大川の神、社稷の神もその内にあり。地祇と

は國土と五穀とを守る神なり。人鬼とは人死して

神にいはへるをいふ。わが家の父母先祖の神あり、

是を祭るべし。王公の先祖宗廟の神あり、たとぶ

べし。これを祭るは恐多し、無禮なり。又先祖に

あらざれども、人民に功徳ありし人あり、これ皆

人鬼なり、是亦たつとぶべし。およそわが身に應

ず。天神地祇人鬼ともに、人の位によりて、わが

身にあづかりて祭るべき神あり。身にあづからず

して祭るまじき神あり。わが祭るべき神にあらざ

れば祭らず。是を祭るは諂なり。非禮なり。神は

非禮をうけ給はず、わが身にあづからずして、祭

るべき神にあらざれば、正しき神にても淫祀とい

ふ。淫祀は無し福とて、わが祭るまじき神を祭り

て、いのりへつらひつかへても、非禮なればうけ

給はず、利生なし。わが祭るべき神と、祭

るべき神と、祭るまじき神とをよくわきまふべし。

利生なくて、神罰はかりがたし。天子諸侯の

祭り給へる所の及びなき天地神明を、いやしき者

けがしくあなどりて祭るは、大なる非禮なり。天道神

明は公にして、人間のごとく、即時にその非禮を

とがめ、罰を行ひ給はざれども、久しきをつみて、

必わざはひをかうふるは必然の道理なり。いやし

き者の日月を祭り、又祭るまじき神を祭り、久し

くして大なる禍にあへる人多し。わがしばしば見

る所なり。おそるべし。鬼神を敬ひて遠ざくと、聖

人のたまへり。いふ心は、神はおそれうやまふべ

し。ちかづきあなどるべからず。たとへば、王公

大人などに、おそれてちかづかざるが如し。是遠

之なり。神のやしろに入るにも、此心得ありて、

みだりにちかづきあなどるべからず、おそれて遠

さかるべし。

よく人の言を用ひ、人の諫をさく人は、必過すくな

く、行正しく、よき譽あり。人の言を用ひざる者は、
ひがこと多くそしり多し。もろこしに、岳飛とい
へる忠臣あり、すぐれたる良將なりしが、この人、
大將として出陣する度ごとに、まづかねてその下
にしたがへる諸司をよび集め、饗應して、この度
の戰、敵にかちぬべき手立をたづね、人々にいは
せ、まけぬべきさわしきますぢをもいはせてきゝ、そ
の內にて、よさを撰び用ひて、かねてよくはかり
ごとを定めて、十分にかちぬべきと議定して後、
出陣せしかば、戰ふたびごとに、かち軍のみして敗
軍せず、向ふ所敵なかりしとなり。是軍のみにか
ぎらず、大事小事、皆此ごとく、衆と人とよくにか
かりて事を行はゞ、過なかるべし。孔子の、三軍
を行ふに、つねの時事にのぞんでおそれ、謀をこ
のんでなさん者にくみせんと、のたまひしも、此
意なり。

人の性、もと善なれば、惡をする心もとよりなし
いへども、利害喜怒愛憎の私欲にひかれて、惡心生
じ惡事を行ふ。故に善をする人常にすくなく、惡
をするものつねに多し。わが心の中をかへりみて、

その惡のおごる所をもとめ去りて、善心の生ずる
をそだて、おしひろめ行ふべし。

孟子の曰、志士は、溝壑にあるにわすれず。勇士はそ
の元をうしなふに忘れず。いふ心は義理に志ある
士は、たとひわが身不幸にして、いふ心は義理に志ある
しまろびて死ぬるとも、その時までは義理を忘れ
ず。又義理にいさむ士は、たとひ人と戰つて、我が
かうべをうしなふ時にいたるといへども、義理を
忘れずとなり。士たる者は、必この語を常に心に
たもちて失ふべからずと古人もいへり。人の命は
おもき物なれど・義理は又命より甚おもし。故に
生死の大事にのぞんでも、義理を忘るべからざる
ことかくのごとし。いはんや名利好色財寶は、皆外
物の輕き物なれば、なんぞ是をむさぼりて、おも
き道義を失はんや。およそ人の慾は富貴をきはむ
るにより。然れどもいたれる富貴にも換へがたき
は命なり。命なくては富貴も用なし。命はかほど
重きものなれども、義理にあたりては、命をもかろ
くすつること、君子はいふに及ばず、凡夫も能く
するは、是人の本心なり。然れば義理ほどおもき

312

ものはなしとしるべし。かほどに一命より甚重き義理をすてゝ、きはめて輕き私欲にしたがふは、本心を失へるなり。誠におろかなりといふべし。怒はつよく慾はふかき故、是にかちがたし。力をつくして堪忍すべし。ちからよわければ、怒と慾にかちがたし。忍の字は、心の上に刃を書く。怒と慾の心おこるをたちさること、刃を以て切りたつが如くなるべし。又敵にむかひて戰ふが如く、十分のちからを用ゆべし。如此せざれば、怒と慾とにまけやすし。堪忍の工夫なく、怒と慾とにかたざれば、平生の學文も用に立たず、いたづらごとなり。是吳臨川が、忍の卦をつくりし説なり。

人と生れては、道に志さして、つねに仁を心にたもちて、毎日人に利益ある善事を行ふべし。主君父母舅姑兄長などによくつかへ、家人を愛するは、皆善なり。又人をめぐみ救ふこと亦善なり。是皆心をつくして行ふべし。人をめぐみ救ふことは、必財を用ゆることの多少によらず、只人の難儀をすくへばその功大なり。富める者には、財を多くあたへても益なし。貧しき者にほどこせば、少しあたへてもその利益大なり。たとへば食にあきたる者に、又食をあたふるは、益なくして、かへつて病となる。うゑたる者には、少し食をあたへても利益とかきが如し。財を多くついやしても、無益のことに用ゆれば、人の助とならず。たとへば萬燈をともしても、あたら油をついやしたるのみにて利益なし。その費を以て、貧人をやしなはゞ、大なる利益なるべし。善を行ふとは、たゞ人の利益になることを行ふにあり。人を利益すれば、天地神明の御心にかなひて、つひにそのむくひありて、さいはひを得る理、古來そのためし多し。およそ善を行ひて人をすくふこと、上は王公より、下は乞丐にいたるまで行ふべき道あり。富貴貧賤によらず、たゞ善を行ふべき志だにあらば、善行はれずといふことなし。善を行ふべき時にあたりて心をつくすべし、をこたるべからず。まづしくいやしき人も、仁に志さして行へば、その身に應じ、日々に人に利益あること多し。いはんや富貴の人、その志あれば、人をすくふことひろく、その功大なり。たかきもいやしきも、をこたりなく、久しく行へ

313

ば、善をつひことかぎりなし。あにたのしまざるべきや。かく心の內に陰德をたもち、善を行ふこと久しければ、天道のむくひありて、あはれみをかふむり、そのさいはひ子孫にいたる。この理は古今からやまと、そのためし多し、うたがふべからず。されども、君子の善を行ふは、そのむくひをのぞむにはあらず、自然のしるしをいふのみ。

世俗は、耳目口腹の欲をほしまゝにするを樂とす。しからざれば、わが身人と生れ、富貴なるかひなしといふ。是まことに世俗のいやしき志なり。人の道をしり、善を行ひ、道にしたがひ、人をすくふほどの樂、この世の中に何かあるべきや。たかきいやしき、たゞ善を行ひ、みちにしたがふを以て樂とすべし。天理にしたがひ、人道を行ひて、人をあはれむを以て、樂とせずして、そゞろなる俗樂をねがふは、富貴の人といへども、誠に不幸なる人といふべし。ことさら、富貴の人は、貧困なるものをあはれみ、ほどこすことを樂むべし。然らざれば、富貴を得たるかひなし。是富貴を得たる福德なり。耳目口腹の欲も、よき程なるは、

道にそむかずして樂となる。よきほどに過ぎて、欲をほしまゝにするは、身のわざはひとなり、人に害ありて樂にあらず、かへりてうれひとなる。

後漢明帝の弟東平王、その國より都に參勤ありし時、明帝問うて曰、家に居て何か樂しきや。東平王答へて申さく、爲善最樂といへり。いふ心は、われ國にありて、臣を愛し、民の貧窮飢寒をすくひ、鰥寡孤獨を養ひて、善をするは尤たのしきことなり。およそ人間の樂は、善をするほどの面白きことはなし。いやしき匹夫も、善を行ふ志あれば、善をすること多く、其樂多し。日々善を行ひてやまず、その樂きはまりなかるべし。況富貴の人、善を行はゞ、その功大きに廣くして、その樂も亦甚しかるべし。凡善をすれば、我が心快く、人も亦よろこび隨ふ。またたのしからずや。

尚書○有レ備無レ患。といへり。いふ心は、萬のことかねて早く用意をすれば、にはかなることにあひても、うれひなしとなり。つねに善を心がくる人は、無事の時の用意ある故、俄に兵亂ありても行きあた

りてうれひなし。常に儉約して財のたくはへあれ
ば、にはかなる變にあひても困窮せず。その費の
諸事皆かくの如し。當時いつひえをはぶき、私欲
をこらへて後の用意をしおくべし。常の時に、變
にあへる時の覺悟なければ、不意に變にあひてつ
まづく。明日のことは、今日より心を用ゆ。來年
のことは、今年より心を用ゆ。一生の事は、只今
よりつとむべし。すべて萬の事、後悔なきやうに、
かねて思ひはかるべし。人遠き慮なければ、必近
きうれひありと、聖人のたまへり。

大
和
俗
訓
卷
之
六
終

---

# 大和俗訓卷之七

貝原篤信著

## 躬行下

人の身に氣質のあしき所と、あやまちとあるは、身に
病あるが如し。病ある人、醫をまねき藥を服し、
針灸をして、病をせめざればいえず。身にあやまち
ある人、その過をせめざれば、たとへば病ある人
の藥を用ひ、針灸をして、病をせめざれば病いえ
ざるが如し。氣質を變じ改むるはきはめて難し、
つねに心を用ふべし。故に前にもいへれども、又
くりかへして人につぐるのみ。

天は常にめぐりうごきてやまず、人これにのつとり
て、つねにつとめてやまざるべし。地は常にとゞ
まりしづかにしてうごかず。人是にのつとりて、
つねにつゝしみ、しづかにして、心をうごかさゞる
べし。つとむるにあらざれば人の道行はれず。つ
つしむにあらざれば人の道たゝず。つとむるとつ
つしむとは、即天地の道にして、人の法として行

ふべき道なり。

人の身になすわざ、何事にも道あらずといふことなし。坐するには坐するの道あり。臥すには臥すの道あり。行くには行くの道あり。飲食には飲食の道あり。言ふには言ふの道あり。動くには動くの道あり。視るには視るの道あり。聽くには聽くの道あり。道を行はんと思はゞ、事ごとに道あることを思ひて、謹ぜいたして、しばらくも道をはなるべからず。是身を修むる道なり。

不仁にして、客嗇なれば、財多くもちても、人をすくひめぐむことなし。客嗇ならざる人も、仁愛に心を用ひざれば、その施なくして、かへりて無益の事に財をついやす。一両事をあげていはゞ、門内に儀に及べる乞食貧人來りて食をこへども、心を用ひて是をめぐまざれば、家のやつこも食をあたへず。又寒夜に客來りて語るに、客にしたがひ來れる下部などを、屋の内寒からざる所に入れ置き、こゝえざるやうにするは、いとやすきことなるに、客に對するに專にして、まぎらはしく、從者の寒氣にくるしむべきを心にかけざれば、彼が

うゑこゝえをしらずして、いたはることなし、是心を用ひざればなり。善を行ふに志あらん人は、萬の事、折ふしにつけて、心を用ひて、人のくるしみなからんことを思ひはかりて、人をすくふべし。

• 程子曰、財ををしみては、よく善を行ふことなりがたし、誠なくしては、善をなすことはなりがたしと。この言むべなるかな。財を用ひずして、たゞ言を以て人をかたらふとも、人をすくひがたし。人も亦よろこばずして、その人のために、忠をつくさゝれば、功をなすこと成りがたし。項羽を婦人の仁といひしも是なり。又凡の事、いつはりを以て善を行へば、中心よりいでざる故、善を行ふに專一ならずして、その事成就せず。誠の善とすべからず。人も亦信とせず、感通の理なし。

禮義廉耻の正しくいさぎよき道を以て、わが身を正すべし。かくのごとくすれば、あやまちすくなし。これを以て、人をせむべからず。人のうへを、事ごとにせめたゞして、わが思ふごとくに、よくせんとすれば、人とあらそひ、人のうらみ多くして、世に交りがたし。人の善をばほめすゝむべし。人

の不能をばあはれみて、みだりにそしりとがむべ
からず。

聖人を以てわが身を正すべし。聖人を以て人を正す
べからず。凡人を以て人をゆるすべからず。凡人を以
て我が身をゆるすべからず。

人のあしきをばゆるすべし。わがあしきをば人にゆる
さるべからず。人のあしきをゆるさゞるは、心の量
せばし。わがあしきを、ひとにゆるされんことを
思ふ人は、鄙狭の至りなり。

わが身は、十分に善ならんことを求むべし。人の身
には十分に善ならんことをせむべからず。人に一
の善あらば、又一の善を求むべからず。是一を得
ば、二を求むべからざるなり。

君子は己をせむ。小人は人をせむ。己をせむれば身
をさまる。人をせむれば、人のうらみなし。小
人はこのうらなり。人をせむる心を以て、わが身
をせむれば過すくなし。己をゆるす心を以て、人
をゆるせば、人のうらみなくして交を全くす。

徳行はわれより上なる人を見てうらやみ、かれに及
ばんことをおもふべし。ひきゝにのぞみて、わが

身を高しとおもふべからず。財禄はわれにおとれ
る人を見て、みづからたのしむべし。世には身の
福禄・我ほどもなき人多し。人各その分をやすん
ずれば、世にうらみなく、もとめなくしてたのし
み多し。上を見てわが身をあきたらず思へば、大
富貴なる人も、願多く、その欲かぎりなくして樂
なし。下をみれば、分をやすんじて樂多し。或人
の歌に、上見ればはてしもあらぬ世の中にわれは
ども下なき人もこそあれ。とよめるが如し。

酒食をすごすは、病を生ずるの本なり。言をつくし
まざるは、わざはひの本なり。思案せざるは、あ
やまちの本なり。私欲ふかきは、身をころすの本
なり。怒をこらへざるは、爭の本なり。儉約なら
ざるは、困窮の本なり。この六本さらざれば、身
と家とをたもちがたし、つとめてこれを去るべ
し。

善をすることはやすく、善を行ひてその名聞をもと
・めざることはかたし。是まことの善なり。人を犯
さゞることはやすく、人の我を犯せども、その返
報をせざるはかたし。

心には、古の道を守り行ひ、身の作法は、今の世の
風俗にそむくべからず。今の世に生れ、古の法に
かゝはりて、必行はんとするはひがごとなり。道
に害あり。古法の内、常世にも行はるべきことは
行ふべし、常世の時宜にそむくべからず。又常世
の風俗にながれて、古の道にそむくは 甚わるし。
是は道に志なきなり。道は五常五倫といふ。法は禮
なり、作法をいふ。

世にまじはるには、和してながれざるをよしとす。
和すれば人にそむかず。ながれざれば道をうしな
はず。是世にまじはるよき程の中道なり。

五常五倫の道は、古今和漢同じ。誠の道にあらず。
法は時により所に
りてかはらば、よろしきと宜しからざることあるゆへ
によりて、よろしきと宜しからざることあるゆへ
に、古今和漢異なり。その國の禮法を行ふべか
らず。國法にそむきて、古の禮法にそむくべか
むけり。但古の禮法の中に、國法に背かずして、
今の世に行ひて宜しきことは行ふべし。もろこし
の古の禮法ありとて、今の世の時宜にかなはずば
行ふべからず。

忠信を主としていつはりなく、仁愛ふかくして人を
あはれみ、義理をかたく守りて行ふべき節を失は
ず、父母兄弟に孝友をあつくし、主君につかへて
身をわすれ、親戚をしたしみてうとからず、朋友
に信實にしてたのもしく、家にありては嚴にして
内行正しく、儉約にして奢なく、貧窮をめぐみ、
艱難をすくひ、利欲すくなく、權勢にへつらはず、
舊恩を忘れず、武をたしなみ、軍用をかゝず、一
度約諾したることを、後までそむかざるを、良士と
すべし。

古語曰、人のきかんことをおそるれば、いふべからず。
人のしらんことをおそれば、行ふべからず。是過
すくなく、悔すくなく、また禍なき道なり。
善は必日々行ひ、久しく積みかさねて後、その功な
りぬ。たとへば、補藥を用ひて元氣を補ふが如し。
そのしるしおそし、久しく服してその驗あり。惡は
少なりともおそるべし。たとへば、毒をくへばた
ちまち害あるが如し、其しるしはやし。惡を去る
ことは、つよき藥を用ひて、病を去るが如くすべ
し。たちまちにせめざれば身に害あり。

古語に、人生在レ勤。勤則不レ匱。といへり。つとめは
利の本なり。よくつとめておのづから得るは、眞の
利なり。利を專むさばれば必害あり。農の田をつ
くりて五穀を多く得るも、工のたくみをいとなみ、
商のあきなひて利を得るも、皆つとめよりなし出
す利なり。士は佞巧を以てへつらはざれども、た
だ忠勤をだに專一にすれば、求めざれども君の寵
ありて、祿を得さいはひを得る。農は歳の凶にあひ
ても、をこたらず耕作に專一なれば、自なりはひを
得る。工は器を精しく作りて粗糙ならざれば、必
其利を得る。商人は、いつはりなく正直にして、利
分をすくなくとれば、諸人の信愛あつく、たのもし
げありて、必あきもの多くうるゝ故利を得ること
多し。是皆本をつとめて、おのづから來る所のま
ことの利なり。もし工は器をそざうに作りていつ
はり、商はあきものをいつはりて、利を多くむさ
ぼれば、人信せずして、かれが器、うりものをか
ふ人すらなくなり。かへりて利を得ることすくな
し。漢書に、貪買三二之。廉買五レ之。といへるもこ
の意なり。いふ心は、欲ふかき商人は三分の利を

得、欲すくなき商人は五分の利を得る。欲ふかき
者は利を得ることすくなく、欲すくなき商人はか
へりて利を多く得るとなり。

終日つとひつゝして、ゆふべにいたりても、おそれつ
つしむは易の敎なり。天道は日俊めぐりてやます。
これを手本としてつとむべし。古人はつとに起き、
よはにいねて、日夜つとめししるしあり。

古語に一生のはかりごとは、つとめにありといへり。
つとめざれば、萬の事行はれず、身を立つること
かたし。又一生のつとめはわかき時にあり。人の
身をたつるはかりごとは、三十歳の内に覺悟すれ
ば、一生の家業成立つ。その内覺悟なく怠れば、
一生立ちがたし。一年のはかりごとは春にあり、
春の間怠たりぬれば、一年のこと成りがたし。一
月のはかりごとは上旬にあり、朔日より十日まで
の内につとむれば、一月の事成りやすし。十日の間
に、すゑ二旬の日數をたのみてをこたれば、其事
成就しがたし。一日のはかりごとは朝にあり、朝
に一日の間の事をよく考へ定め、早くつとむれば
はかゆく。若朝の間をこたれば、一日のつとめは

かゆかず。又明日のはかりごとは、今夕にあるべ
し。明日のことを、明日はからんとて、今日さだ
めざれば、つまづきてはかゆかず。

古人は人の朝早くおくると、おそくおくるとを以て、
家の興廃を知るといへり。朝早くおくるは、家の
さかふるしるしなり。おそくおくるは、家のおと
ろふるもとなり。朝つとにおきて、事をつとむ
るを以て、身のならはしとし、家のつとめの則と
し、見ならはしむべし。凡の人を見るに、朝おし
ては學ぶこととならず。家業をこたりて、富めるも
のまれなり。朝居するは、おこたりのはじめ、貧
窮のもとゐなり。よく事をつとむるものは、一日
を以て十日とす。つとめてをこたりなくするどな
れば、はかゆく故なり。をこたるものは、十日を
以て一日とす。日數多くふるといへどはかゆかず。
凡善をつとめて、をこたらざるを良士とす。必家
をおこす。家業をつとめて、をこたらざるを良民
とす。必とむ。

知れば行ひやすく、行へば知りやすし。二の者たが
ひに相助けて、道明らかにして行はる。たとへば

道路をゆくが如し。道をしらざれば行きがたく、
行かざれば行路をしりがたきが如し。

わが身の過すくなく、悔すくなからんことを思はゞ、
事にさき立ちてはやく思案し、その事の是非をか
んがへはかり、その事にのぞみて、又義か不義か
をかへりみて、その理にかなはんことを思ひはか
るべし。かねて思案なくして、その時にいたりて、
にはかにまどひつまづくべからず。たとひいそが
はしき事にのぞむとも、思ひめぐらして理の當否
をえらび行ふべし。わはたゞしく、思案なくして行
へば、必義理にちがひあやまること多し。すでに
一たびよく思ひさだめても、又一ぺんに心得そこ
なふこと多し。その事の外に、心をめぐらし、其
變をかんがへて、二たび思ふべし。孔子曰、人遠き
慮なければ、必ちかき悔あり。さしあたりたるこ
とを思ふは、いふに及ばず、後の事を思ひはかり、
あやまりなく、悔なからんことを思ふべし。たと
へば、古語に、旱に簑笠を備ふべしといへる如く、
たいまやどりを出でゝ、他所に行くに、天は
晴れ日和よくして、雨ふるまじき景色なりとも、遠

き所にゆかば、天變はかりがたければ、簑笠を持ち
ゆくべし。たとひ天氣よく雨ふらずとも、簑笠も
たるいたづがはしきのみにて、さほどの妨にあら
ず。若思はざるに雨ふりなば、ぬれそぼちて、衣
ぬらすのみかは、心をいたましめ、身をくるしま
しめ、折節人にも用あるべき簑かさを乞ひかりて、
又もたせかへすも、われ人のためいたづがはし。
よろづのこと、かねて心を用ひ、おそれつゝしみ、
ふかく思ひ遠く慮りて事を行へば、あやまちすく
なく悔すくなし。やつこ下部などの心ならひは、
さしあたりて、わが身のたよりよきことのみを思
ひて、後のわざはひをしらず。たとへばやがて雨
ふりなんと見ゆるそらにも、雨衣の用意もなく出
づる時、主人もてゆかんことを命ずれども、雨ふ
るまじきよしをあらがふ。やがて雨にぬれてくる
しめどもこりず、いくたびも亦かくの如し。かく用
意なくて、後のうれひをかへりみざるは、いやし
きものゝくせなれば、よからぬことをしるべし。
すべて人の惡を行ふも、あやまちをするも、皆事
にのぞみて、思慮せざるよりおこる。酒食をほし

ぬまゝに過して、病をおこすも、その時にのぞみ、
思案なくして、只欲にまかせてのみくらふゆへに、
病を生じ、はては身を失ふにいたる。よく思案し
てつゝしむは、欲にかち、禍をまぬかるゝみちな
り。

わが身のあやまちを改めんため、人の諫を好むこと
眞實ならば、いさむるもの多からん。酒食は人の好
む物なれば、人辭退してふせげとも、しゐて飮ま
せくらはしむるは、世のならひなり。是人の眞實
に酒食を好むことをしれればなり。酒食をこのむ
ごとく、諫をこのみ、わが過をあらためば、諫をい
ふ人多くして、我が身の過なかるべし。

子曰、躬自厚くして、人をせむるに薄ければ、うらみ
に遠かる。いふ心は、わが身の行をあつくし、十分
によくせんことを求めて、常に我が身の行ひのた
らざることを思ひて、つとめ行ふべし。人のたら
ざるをゆるくしてせむべからず、かくの如くすれば
人のうらみなし。

能く詩文を作る人は、妄に輕々しく文字を下さず。
久しく沈思して、一字一句に心を用ふること精し

くして後、好き詩文を作り出せり。和歌をよむも
同じ。如此ならざれば、詩聖歌仙といへども、好
き詩文和歌を作ることもかたかるべし。碁をよく
打人の、碁子を下すをみるに、久しく思ひて後
に下す、一子もみだりにはやく下さず。こゝを以て、
碁子をくだせば、その所にかなひてよく人にかつ。
是を以て思ふに、賢者の言行も亦如此。よく思案
して後、ことばを出し事を行ふべし。この故に、
賢者の言行は、あやまちすくなし。もしはやく決
定して、かるがくく行はゞ、賢者といへども過
多かるべし。孔子の、必也臨事而懼。好謀而成者
也。とのたまふを以てみつべし。常世の愚人より、
聖賢のなす所を見ば、はかゆかずにぶくしてもど
かしかるべし。常人も思案をこのめば、わが心を
つくすゆへ、事をはやく決定せず、にぶきやうにみ
ゆれど、あやまちすくなく道理に當ること多し。決
斷早き人は、はかゆけども、必過多く後悔多し。
順境とは、思のまゝなる境界をいふ。逆境とは思ふや
うにならざる境界をいふ。世間の事、順境に居る
はやすく、逆境に居るはかたし。故に逆境に居れ

ば敬畏出來て、身の過すくなくして、かへつて禍
となる。順境に居れば、驕怠の心出來て、身の過
多くして身の禍となる。たとへば高に登るものは
たふれがたし、勢逆にしてかたければなり。ひきき
に下るものはたふれやすし、勢順にしてやすけれ
ばなり。孟子の、愛患に生きて安樂に死ぬる。との
たまふもこの意なり。うれひおそれあれば生命を
たもつ。安樂にして放逸なれば、死をまぬかれがた
し。敵ある國は長久し、敵なき國は、かへつて亡び
やすきが如し。
周武王席銘曰。安樂必敬。無行可悔。この銘の意
は、艱難にうれひある時は、おそれつゝしみて、
あやまちすくなきゆへ禍なし。心やすくたのしむ
ときは、必おごたりゆだんして、あやまちおほく、
わざはひおこる。かゝる心やすき時殊につゝしむ
べし。つゝしめば、あやまちすくなく、行ふこと
ごとに後悔なし。のぼり坂は、なやみなくしてまろび
づかず、くだり坂は、なやみなくしてまろびやす
きが如し。
日々行ふことごとに、過なからんことを思ふべし。

過あれば必後悔あり。後悔はあやまりよりおとる。いかりと欲とをこらゆれば、過すくなく後悔すなくして後の禍なし。又事ごとに、早く行はずして、しづかによく思案して、是非のうたがはしきことは、みづから決定せず、人に問ひてわが善悪を考ふべし。いそぎて、にはかに事を決斷すべからず。早く決斷すれば過多し。諺に悔はさきだゝずとはいへれど、事に先立ちて、よく思ひつゝしみて、しづかに行はゞ、あやまちすくなくして後悔なかるべし。あくまで思案し、十分にはかりて後あやまちあらんは、わが心の分量をつくしたれば、ちからに及ばず。その上は天命に任せて、うれふべからず。

君子は、朝夕つとめて善を行ふ。小人は朝夕つとめて利を行ふ。君子小人、ともにつとめ行ふといへども、その志は利と善とかはれり。善に志すは、聖人の徒なり。利に志すは盜蹠が徒なりと、孟子のたまへり。利とは、財利をむさぼるのみにあらず、われひとり勝手よきやうに、便利をはかるも利心なり、是私なり。私を行へば必人に害あり。

人に害あれば、必わが身の禍となる。善を行はん人は、必づ利心を去るべし。利を心にさしはさんでする善は、誠の善にあらず。

君子の道は、すべきことを行ひ、すまじきことをせず。これ義なり。このむべきことをのみ、このむまじきことをこのまず。是善なり。君子の道は、かくの如きのみ、是孟子の語意なり。

人の知は目のごとし。人の目はよく百里の外を見れども、わが睫を見がたし。人の知よく、他人の惡をしれども、わが身の惡をしらず。人をみることは常に明なり、わが私なければなり。自見ることは常にくらし、私あればなり。こゝを以て、人の過をせむることはきびしく、わが惡をゆるすことはゆるやかなり。

富貴の人、善をこのめば、富貴の力によって人をすくひ、善を行ふこと廣し。是まことに樂多かるべし。富貴にして、善をこのまざれば、富貴のちからによって、おごりて人をくるしめ、惡を行ふこと廣し。かくの如くなれば、富貴なるも、かへつてわざはひとなり、貧賤におとる。何の樂かあら

ん。貧賤なる人、もし艱難によりて、よく身をつつしみて過をあらため、善をつとめ行はゞ、禍なくして樂多かるべし。かくのごとくして福となるも、かへつて福となり、富貴にまさる。

敏事とは、行ふべき事を、ゆだんなく、するにつとめて行ふをいふ。何事もつとめずして、をこたれば事行はれず。行へどもはかゆかずしてなすこと成就せず。よく事をつとむる者は、事をいそがざれどもをこたりなき故、一日に十日の事をなす。をこたる者は十日に、たゞ一日の事をなす。をこたるとつとむるとは、その功はるかにかはれり。

自信とは、わが行ふ所理に當れりと、あきらかに思へば、人のそしりをかへりみずして、心をうごかさゞるをいふ。古詩に、禮義不レ愆。何憂二人言一。といへるが如し。小人非義を行ひて人の誹をかへりみざるとは甚別なり。君子善を行ひて、人のそしりをおそれざるべし。小人不善を行ひて、人のそしりをおそれずんば、その惡きはまりなかるべし。

耐煩とは、むつかしきことをきらはずして、攝忍してつとめ行をいふ。もし孝弟忠信など、諸のつとめを、むつかしとをこたり、人の附託をうけて、いたつがはしとて、おろそかにするものは、善を行ひとげず。是善をこのまざればなり。わがこのむことは、日夜つとめても勞せず、何事もつとめをむつかしとて、苦しむ者は氣むすぼれて、必病おこる。

今日は明日の計をなし、今月は來月の計をなし、今年は明年の計をなし、平生は一生の計をなし、生前に早く死後の計をなすべし。をこたるべからず。

明日行ふべきことあらば、必今日よりその事を思ひはかりて定むべし。明朝便をつかはし、文をおくらんと思はゞ、今夕よりかきとゝのへて使を命ずべし。その日の事をその日はじめて思案し、いとなめばはかゆかず。事にのぞみて、或はさまたげ出來、まぎらはしくて過多し。

中庸に、凡事豫則立。不レ豫則廢。言前定則不レ跲。事前定則不レ困。といへり。豫とはかねてと云意、事を前に定むるなり。萬事かねて思案して定むれば、

事立ちて行はる。さなければ事すたりて行はれず。物いふにも、かねて先思案していへば、言つまづかず。事を行ふにも、かねて思案して定むれば、

事にのぞみて行さあたりくるしまず。

世に住むこと一日なれば、一日の善人となるべし。一日も善を行はずして、日を送ること一日ならば、公儀。

の官職にあづかりて、官に居ること一日ならば、一日の善事をなすべし。一日も善を行はずして、官をむなしくすべからず。世に久しく住みて善行

なきは、一生を空しくするなり。官職に居て善行なきは、官職を空しくするなり。この二は大なるはぢなり。

衆人の行ふわざは、かねて思案なく、又事にのぞみては、慮もなくはやく決定するゆへに、毎事あやまり多くして、後悔すれども、それにもこりず、つねに事ごとにかくの如し。一事あるごとに、必

後のあやまり悔あらんことをおそれ、しづかに思慮して行ふべし。何の害かあるべきと思ひ、思慮もなく其まく決定すべからず。もし即時にきはめがたくば、かさねてよく思案して行ふべし。事にあ

たりて、十分に道理にかなひ、此上は思案に及ばずと思ふとも、又いかなるあしきこともあらんかと猶豫して、俄に決断すべからず。是あやまちすくなく、悔すくなくする道なり。

思慮して、善悪をよく明らめたらば、必決断して猶豫なく行ふべし。思慮して理明らかになりても、決断つよからざれば行はれず、悠々としてむなしく時を過すはあし。所謂見而不レ爲無レ勇也。

思慮と決断との二こそはりてよし。思慮なくして、みだりに早く決断すればあやまる。是不智なり。思慮して、道理はわかれぬれど、悠々として時を失ふは、をこたりなり。是無レ勇也。二の者はいづれも悔あり。

凡あやまりは、おほくは初一時の快さを求むるよりいでゝ、後はながきくるしみとなる。はじめ少し心や用ひ、少し慾をこらゆれば、其ちからを用ゆることはすこしなれど、しるしを得てさいはひとなることは大なり。少しの間少しの事をこらへずして、大なるわざはひとなること多し。

夜にして後、けふのわが身のなせるわざを、よくか

へりみて、ひがことあらば、後日のかゞみとして、改めんことを思ふべし。毎夜かくのごとくすべし。人の身の上、さしあたりてなすべきこと多し。よく思ひてゆだんなく、はやくつとむべし。ゆだんあれば、急なること、さしおきていそがず、急ならざることを、いそぎてつとむ。前後の次第を失ふべからず。さして用なきことをつとめ、いたづら事をこのみて、日をおくりてはかなしといふべし。わかき時は、ことにすべきわざにも、心を用ひずしてむなしくすごすこと多し。よくよく心をつくべし。人のしらんことをゝれふることならば、悪事なるべし。心にきざすべからず。ことさら身に行ふべからず。

人のあしきをそしる人は多し。わが身のあしきをかへりみて、改むる人すくなし。わが身をわすれて、人の上をそしることおろかなり。わが身の上を、つねにかへりみをさむべし。人のほめそしりは、あながちにうれひよろこびとするにめ、なにことゞやゝ、思案するを云なり。そしる人必皆たらず。いかんとなれば、ほむる人そしる人必皆

賢者ならざればなり。人われをそしらば、たゞわが身のあやまちをかへりみるべし。もしわが身に過あらば、そしる人は即わが師なりと思ひ、うらむべからず。わが身に、少しもあやまりなきをそしらば、彼人は妄人なり。かれとあらそひにくむにたらず。

人の悪をすること三の故あり。氣質の偏より悪をなすあり、又あやまちとはしれども、人欲の私によりてなすあり、又ならはしの誘によりてなすことあり。この三の内、氣質の偏なるは悪の本なり、人欲の私は悪の幹なり、俗習の誘は悪の末なり。身の禍となることは共に同じ。氣質のあしきをば變化して改むべし。人欲をば忍びて、ほしゐまゝにすべからず。俗習をばその非をしりてうつるべからず。

よき人は、心を用ふこと多き故、事ごとによくをさまりて過すくなし。よからざる人は、心を用ひずして過多し。下部などの智慮なくして用にかなはざるは、皆心を用ひざればなり。心を用ゆるとは、

古語に、つとむれば貧にかち、愼めばわざはひにかつといへり。いふこゝろは、つとむる人は必富む、つゝしむ人は必わざはひなし。

過ぎにしことをおもへば、あやまり多くして、くやしきこと多けれど、一たびあやまりて、かへらざることは、悔のやちたびかなしめども益なし。今より後をつゝしみて、過なく悔なからんことを思ふべし。又あやまりて後、はやく改むれば過なくなること多し。易に所 v 罰、遠からずしてかへる、悔にいたることなかるべし。萬のことはじめによくつゝしみおもむばかりて、後悔なからんことを思ふべし。愼 v 終于 v 始と尙書にいへり。はじめに思慮なければ、あやまりて悔あり。

身の禍福は天命に任すべし、人に求むべからず。身の徳行はわが心に求むべし、人をせむべからず。君子は人道の行ふべき法を行ひて、身の上の吉凶は天命を待つ。是則とすべし。

人のために益ある善事を毎日多く行ふべし。その善事とは、富貴なる人は、ひとにほどこしすくふことを自由にしてひろく行ひやすし。心にかけて行はば、その功大にその樂も亦大なるべし。貧賤なる者も、志だにあれば、人の利益となること多し。

て、人の利益となれば、所にしたがひ時にしたがひわが家の内、または外なる道に、人の往來に足にさはりとなる物あれば、これをのけて他所へうつし、のんどかはく人には、一盃の水をあたへ、つかれたる者に、一椀の食をあたふる、かやうのたぐひ、少なることながら、人の益になることはまりなし。上は王公より、下は庶人乞丐にいたるまで皆行ふべし。年久しく積行はゞ、其善大にしてきはまりなかるべし。常に善を行ふを以て樂とすべし。

天地父母は、わが生れし本にして、わが身のよつて來れる初なり。わするべからず。天地の恩をしらずして、仁にそむき、父母の恩を思はずして、孝を行はざるは、わが身の生れ來れる本初を忘れたるなり。人と生れたるかひなしといふべし。われ人のはぢておそるべきこと、是より大なるはなし。

善をするは、のぼり坂をのぼるが如し、つとめざればなしがたし。惡をするは下り坂をくだるが如し、つとめざれどもなしやすし。しかれば、善はこの

みて力を用ひつとめ行ふべし、惡はにくみてつゝ
しみおそるべし。

大和俗訓卷之七
大和俗訓卷之七終

# 大和俗訓卷之八

貝原篤信著

## 應接　事に應じ人にまじはる道をしるす

人にまじはるには、つねに禮義を正しくすべし。禮
義のはじめは、先威儀をとゝのふべし。衣服を正しくし、顔色をとゝの
へ、形を厳にし、ことばを順にするを威儀といふ。威儀とは
身の形儀をいふ。言のなめげなるは下部の交なり。言語容
貌は、内心の外に見ゆる符なり。ことばとかたち
を見きゝて、その内心の善惡はしれやすし、つゝ
しむべし。又ことばのうやまひ過ぎたるも、禮に
あらず、へつらへるなり。過不及なかるべし。

人にまじはるには、貴賤と親疎によらず、愛敬をむ
ねとすべし。愛とは、人をいとをしみてにくまざる
なり。仁の用なり。敬とは、人をうやまひてあな
どらざるなり、禮の用なり。人に交はるに愛敬な
ければ、人我の間へだゝりて、人倫の道行はれず。

父母につかへ、兄弟夫婦に對し、賓客に交るも、皆愛敬を以て心法とす。おやには、愛を主として、敬はざれば、犬馬をやしなふに同じ。君には、敬を主として、愛を行ふべし。君をうやまひおそれたるのみにて、心まことに愛せざれば忠にあらず、臣たるの道たゝず。

したしき人を愛し、貴き人をうやまふはいふに及ばず、うとき路人に對し、いやしき乞丐に對するも、皆これ天地のうめる人なれば、その分にしたがひて愛敬すべし。にくみあなどるべからず。うときしたしきにより、貴さいやしさにしたがひて、愛敬する厚薄はあるべけれど、愛敬せざることなかるべし。

凡愛敬を行ふには、信を本とすべし。信とは、愛敬を行ふに、その心眞實にして偽なきなり。信なければ、眞の愛敬にあらず。信は人にまじはる道なり。信なくては人と我との心感通せず。いかに言と貌に愛敬をあらはすとも、信なければ、人まことゝせずして、愛敬の道行はれず。

人に對するに、温和にして謙り、おのれにほこらず、人をあなどらず、ことばすくなく、信實に愛敬ありて、むかひよからんこそ、善人とはいふべけれ。我身かろ〴〵しからずして正しければ、温和なれども人あなどらず。

朱子曰、平心和氣は、是學問の根本なり。この語よくおもふべし。人の萬事は心氣を本とす。心氣和平ならざれば、萬事の本たゝずして、道理行はれず。人に交るに尤和平なるべし。父母につかふるには、かならず氣を下し、色を怡ばしめ、聲をやはらぐるには、是心氣の和平なるなり。たゞ父母につかふるに、かくのごとくにすべきのみならず、すべて人に交はるに、皆かくのごとくにすべきなり。人一言わが心にそむけば、たちまち心にいかり、色にあらはれ、目をいからし、ことばをはげしくする。これ心氣の和平ならざるなり。心氣すでにうごきみだれては、本みだれて末をさまらず。なんぞその言行よろしかるべきや。

人にまじはるに、恕を以てすべし。恕とは己をおし

て人に及ぼすなり。いふ意は、わが心を以て、人の心にくらぶるに、たがふことなし。わが好むことは、必人もこのめり。故にわが心を以て、人の心をおしはかり、わがきらふことを、人にほどこすべからず。わが好むことは、人にほどこすべし。是仁を行ふ道なり。又人あやまちあらば、凡夫はかくこそあらめと思ひてゆるすべし、とがむべからず。人の得ざる所は、せむべからず。おろかなるをば、いかるべからず。人の我に無禮を行はゞ、理しらぬ故と思ひて、うらむべからず。聖人頑なるをいかりにくむことなかれとのたまふ。頑とは、心愚にして道理に通ぜざるなり。頑愚に生れつきたれば、すべきやうなし。赤子の井におち入るがごとし。おろかにして、道理をしらざる故に、ひがことを行ふはあはれむべし。是皆恕の道なり。わが身に善を行ひて、人に善をすゝむべし。我が身に惡をさりて、人の惡をいましむべし。かくのごとくなれば、人したがひやすし。是己をおして人に施すなり。是も亦恕の道なり。

人にまじはるには、自反をむねとすべし。自反とは、みづからにかへるなり。人をとがめずして、わが身に立ちかへりて、善をおのれに求むるをいふ。人われにしたがはず、我にそむかば、わが過をせめて、人をとがむべからず。わが身をかへりみて、わが行のいまだいたらざる故と思ひ、人をせむべからず、いかりそしるべからず。是自反なり。自反は身をさめ、人にまじはり、世にをる要道なり。自反のこと、前にもすでにいへり、又くりかへしていふなり。

凡人に交るには、言もかたちも禮をあつくすべし。人のことばをとがむべからず。もしやむ事を得して、人のあやまちをたゞさば、禮義を以てその道理を眞實にのぶべし。いかりて言を過し、無禮をなすべからず。

古人の言に、天下皆非なるの理なしといへり。この言よく慊認すべし。世の中の人のしわざ、わが心にかなはずとも、皆ひがことにてはあらじ。何事ぞ、故ありてかくあるべしと思ひ、みだりに人をと

がむべからず。わが心にあしきと思へど、又さな
きことあり。故ありてなせる事には、過ならざる
ことあり。又かへつて道理にかなへる事あり。わ
が心かならず、道理の寸尺のかねになるべからず。
わが心にあしきと思ふとも、みだりに人をせめそ
しるべからず。愚なる人は、人情事變をしらず、
人のなすわざ、心に叶はざれば、故ありと故なきと
をかへりみず、みだりに人をそしりうらむ故に、
うらむるもそしるも、義理にかなはざること多し。
人われをそしらば、そしるものをとがむべからず。
わが身にかへりみて求むべし。わが身に一分の過
あり、人われをそしることありとも、わが
やまりより、おこりしことなれば、恨むべからず。
わが過をせむべし。これそしりをやむる道なり。
左もなくて、たゞ人をとがめ、人をうらみて、我
に求めざれば、人のそしりはやむべからず。喧嘩口論
朋友の間、禮あつければ、あらそひなし。
は、必無禮よりおこる。人に交るに禮義正しく懇
懇なれば、人と我との間、滯なくして和らぎむつ
まじ。人に交るに無禮なるは、これいやしき俗人

下部の風俗なり、士の交にあらず。いましむべし。
晏子が人にまじはるに、久しくして敬ひしことを
聖人もほめ給へり。久しく交りて、たがひに心や
すくなりゆくまゝに、無禮をなすべからず。
人われに無禮なりとて、わが耻辱にならざることは、
とがむべからず。人の無禮をなだめゆるして堪忍
すれば、わが心和平にして樂をうしなはず、人にあ
らそはずして無事なり、われに耻辱なし。古語に、
忍過ぎて事よろこぶにたへたり。といへるがごと
く、堪忍して後よろこびとなる。もし人の無禮を
とがめて、われよりもまた惡言を出し、無禮を行
へば、人も亦いかりて堪忍せず。わがとがめしよ
り、猶すぎて甚しく無禮をわれにほどこせば、堪
忍なりがたくして、即時にたゝかひに及ぶ。この
ときにいたりて、はじめてそのわざはひをおそれ
て、堪忍するも見ぐるし。たゞはじめより、禮義
正しくして、人もし無禮を行ふとも、わが耻辱に
ならざる程は、堪忍して我より又人を惡口すべか
らず。かれが愚なるに對して、いかりをおこし、無
禮をほどこせば、われも亦愚なり。

古語に、和なればかたきなし、忍べば辱なしといへ
り。いふ意は、温和にして人とあらそはざれば、
かたき出來ず。人の無禮をゆるして、いかりを
らゆれば、人のいかりもおこらずして、我身に恥
辱なしとなり。しばしの間、いかりをこらへずし
て、人とあらそひたゝかひ、人をころし身を失ふ。
一朝の怒に、その身をわすれて、その親に及ぼし
て、父母をうれへしむ、不孝の至なり。君父の大
事に死ぬべきあたら命を、かゝるよしなきことに
すつるは、至りておろかなり。忠孝の道しらざる
みならず、武勇を心にかけざればなり。死ぬるこ
とはやすく、死して道理にかなふことはかたし。
臍下三寸を丹田といふ。人の一身の氣を、つねに丹
田にをさめて、胸にあつむべからず。是氣をさ
むる良法なり。人に交り、事に應じ、物をいふに、
まづ心をしづかにして、又氣を丹田にをさめて、物
をいひ、事をなすべし。是氣の本を立つるなり。
本たてばちからありて道生ず。しからずして、氣
のぼりて、むねにあつまれば、心うごきさわぎて
をさまらず。この時ものいひ、ことをなししいだせ

ば、ちからなくて、必あやまり多し。學者身をさ
めんと思はゞ、心を平にし、氣を和らかにすべし。
氣をむねにあつめずして吐出し、丹田にをさむる
こと、術者の言に似たりといへども、よく習ひな
せば、甚そのしるしを得ることあり。物をいひわ
ざをつとむるに、氣をさむる良法なり。

人われに無禮なりとて咎むべからず。おろかなる人
か、或は酒にゑひたる人は、狂人と同じければ、堪
忍したりとて、いさゝか恥辱にはあらず。かれに
對して、いかりあらそふは、我も亦おろかなりと
いふべし。敵對すべからず。

小人の我に對して、ひがことをいひ行ひて、さとし
がたきはすべきやうなし。もし小人にたてあひて、
我が顔色と言語をはげしくし、いかりあらそひて、
その是非をいひひかせても、かれもとよりかしこ
からざればきゝわけず、かへりていよいよいかり
をあらそふ。かくのごとく、かれといかりあらそへ
ば我も亦小人なり。いよいよわが身をつゝしみを
さめ、顔色を和らげ、ことばを順にして道理をい
ひきかせ爭はざれば、彼もしすこし人心地あらば、

みづからその非をさとるべし。かれさとらずと
も、わが心法に害なし。

人に交るに、小人としらば、其人をゆるくして、彼と
善惡を爭そふべからず。又小人としれども、はな
はだへだてなくとがめざれば、小人我を害せず。
およそ、人に善ををしへて行はしむるに、その人の
生れつきたる所につきて、すゝめ行はしむべし。
もし生れつかず、その人の不得手にて、心になき
ことを、しゐてせしめすゝめても、つゐに從がはざ
れば益なし。必我が心のごとくにせんとおもふべ
からず。

凡夫の心はたのもしげなし。親しみあつければども、
變じやすし。今親しむといへど、後を保ちがたし。
人の心を賴みて、あやまつことなかれ。

およそ、人の心の同じからざるは、その面のごとし。
世間の人ごとに、各心かはれるゆへに、人のなすわ
ざ、わが思ふごとくならざるは、人の心のありさ
まかくのごとしと思ひ、我が心にかなはざるとて、
人をとがむべからず。これが堪忍していからず、
ことばに出さゞれば、無事にしてわが心やすく、

人にさはりなし。是世にまじはる道なり。

君子はみづからせめて人をせめず、故に善を己に求
む。小人は人をせめて、みづからせめず、故に善
を人にもとむ。小人は人をせめて、我
が身をせむることかろし。人を愛することうすく、我
わが身を愛することあつし。君子はしからず。人
をせむる心を以て、わが身をせむれば過すくなし。
わが身を愛する心を以て、人を愛すれば仁をつく
す。

人に交る道は厚きをむねとす。厚しとは、人をせめ
ずして我をせむるをいふ。如此すれば、我が心和
樂にして人をうらみず。人もまた我をうらみずし
てしたがひやすし。うすければそのうらなり。人
のあやまりをきびしくせむれば、子弟の輩も、う
らみふかくそむきやすし。況他人をや。

世には愚なる人多し。世にまじはるに、わが道理を
專に立てんと思ふべからず。我に道理あり、人に
非ありとも、人とあらそふべからず。人に十分の
あやまりありとも、人にも少しは道理をつけ、少
しは人にまけて、人にかたんことをこのむべから

ず。かやうにすれば、人とあらそはず、われと人との間和して、人の心をうしなはず、無事にしてさはりなし。

明月の玉にも、きずなきことあたはず。過なき人、なんぞ今の世にあらんや。今の人、ひとの小過のるをみて、その人をいやしみ、すこし短なる所あれば、長ずる所あれど、言ひおとし、すてゝ取用ひず。おろかなるかな。聖人は過なし、聖人を以て人をのぞまば、世に人なかるべし。人のあやまちをせめて、わがあやまちをしらざるは、おろかなるかな。是わが身をかへり見ざればなり。もしわれをかへりみば、我が身にも過おほかるべし。わが身をかへりみて、我が過をせめば、人の過をとがむるには、いとまなかるべし。我が田の草のおほきをば、其まゝおきてとらず、人の田をくさぎるに、古人もたとへたり。

君子は、禮儀を専にして爭なし。爭は小人のことなり。小人は人に交れば、わが才智藝能など、凡我が身に能あるを以て、人にほこりあらそふ。是禮儀の道にあらず。獸の角と牙とを以て爭ふが如し。

爭はざるは人に交るの道なり。凡節義をまもり、武勇を行ふは、進んで人に先だつべし。その外のことは、人に先だゝず、少し人におくれ、少し人にまけたるが、爭なくして禮にかなひ、その上禍なき道なり。

善人に交れば、日々に善言をきゝ、善事を見ならひて益あり。惡人に交れば、日々惡言をきゝ、惡行を見ならひて損あり。交る人えらぶべし。ふるきことわざに、朱にまじはればあかし、墨にちかづけば黑し。といへるがごとし。正直なる人にまじはれば、わが心につゝしみ出來、我があやまりをきゝて益あり。われにへつらふ人に交れば、いさめをきかず、わが心にしたがひほむる故、わが心をこたりて損あり。たとへば、味よき酒食を、多くのみくらへば病おこり、苦きくすりをのみ、あつき灸をすれば、やまひいゆるがごとし。

おろかなる人は、情こはくしてさとしがたく、義に移りがたし。かゝる人に對して爭ふべからず。我が身のふるまひだに、わが心にかなはざること多し。なんぞ他人のしわざ、わが心にかなはんや。人

のしわざの、我が心にかなはぬは、ゆるすべし。と
がむべからず。たゝ我が身をかへりみ、わが過を
しりて改むべし。

人の生れつきは、各同じからず、得たる所あり、得
ざる所あり。これに得たりといへども、彼に得ざ
る所あり。何事も一人の身に、よきこととそなはれ
る人なし。その人の得たる所を用ひて、得ざる所
をせむべからず。一事よきことあらば、取用ひて
その餘のよからざるをとがむべからず。わが身を
かへりみば、得ざること亦多かるべし。もし人の
得ざる所をせめて、得たる所をすてば、天下に用
ゆべき人なく、変るべき人なかるべし。得たる所
を取用ひ、得ざる所をゆるして、せめざれば、天
下にすてらるゝ人なかるべし。人に交はるにもかく
のごとくすれば、人のうらみなし。

人の得たる所を以て、得ざる所を信ずべからず。一
事得たりといへども、他事には得ざることあり。
又得ざる所を以て、得たる所をうたがふべからず。
一事えずといへども、他事に得たることあり。我
が得たる所を以て、人の得ざる所をそしるべから
ず。是恨をとるみちなり。

不智不才の人といへども、必すぐれて得たる所あり。
智者はその得たる所をとりて、得ざる所をゆるす。
故に天下にすたる人なし。いかなるいやしき草にも、よき能
あればこり用ゆ。大匠の材を用ゆるがごとし。す
ぐなるを柱とし、それるをうつばりとして、材を
すてず。

古語に、善をよみして、不能をあはれむといへり。人
の善事は賞翫し、得ざることをばあはれみて、せ
むべからず。是君子の心なり。

高位の人に對すとも、その勢に屈しへつらふべから
ず。又品くだれる人に對すとも、あなどりかろし
むべからず。孔子の大人をおそれ給ふは、その位
をうやまひ給ふなり。孟子の大人をかろんじ給ふ
は、その勢に屈せざるなり。聖賢の道、ならび行
はれて相そむかず、共に萬世の師なり。

人にまじはるに、おくり物を以てするはなんぞや。
是心の愛敬を外にあらはし行ふ禮なり。途物をも
ちひざれば、心にある愛敬の誠を外にあらはすべ

きやうなし。おくり物を用ゆるはこの故なり、是
人に交はるの道なり。いにしへ、神につかふるに、
蘋藻のすゝめ物あり、是いさぎよき水草を以て神
にそなふるなり。はじめて師にまみゆるに、束脩
の禮あり、是贄を持參して、師をうやまふなり。
神に事へ、人に交るに、かくのごとくならざれば、
その誠あらはれず。されど貧しき者は、貨財を以
て禮とせず、ちからに及ばざる送物を、つとめて
行ふにはあらず。老いたるもの、筋力を以て禮と
せざるがごとし。又よからざる物を人に送るは、
おくらざるにおとる。おくり物によりて、その人
の志の實不實あらはる。送物にも心を用ひて、愛
敬の誠を行ふべし。濫惡なる物
を人におくるべからず。下人にまかせて、

人に對して物いふに、我が位と年との品をしりて、其宜
み、又對する人の位と年との品をかへり
かなふは又禮なり。若いまだ物なれざる人は、すこ
しは人をうやまひ過すは、筋にあたらざれども、
大なるあやまりにあらず、わが位よりおごれるは、
無禮にして大なる過なり、見にくし。座につくに

も、我が身に宜しきよきほどの所につくべきを。
ゐなか人か、又禮しらぬ人は、ひとの請せざるに、
高座に上りすぎて、見ぐるしくわらふべし。わが
位より下座につくは、禮にあたらざれども、大な
る誤にのらず。

我が身を卑下して、人にたかぶらざるは誠によし。
されど、あまり卑屈にして、へりくだり過し、つ
くべき座敷などにも、たやすくつかず。道ゆくに
も、我がさきへ行くべき位なれど、辭してゆかず。
我が前にめぐり來れる盃をも呑ずして、人のこと
ばを多くつひやさしむるも、かへりて無禮なり。
たゞわが當然なるべき程をば、あながちによく
辭退すべからず。位あるん人、老いたる人、下座に
ありては、いやしくわかき人の居るべき座なくし
て、各その處を得ざることあり。しかれば、卑下
するにも過不及なかるべし。

人のほめそしりを聞くことよく察すべし。譽むる人、
そしる人、智なくして、人の善惡と事の是非をし
らず。その上私ありて、わが氣にあへるをほめ、
氣にあはざるをそしれば、善惡亂れて人をまよは

す。かゝる人のほめそしりは、必信すべからず。これを信ずれば、あやまりて、是を非とし、非を善とし、咎なき人をうらみ、善人を遠ざけ、悪人をちかづくれば、そのわざはひ甚し。人のほめそしりにまよふべからず。

心あらへば、千里も相したしみ、心あはざれば隣家も往來せず。或は日々に對談してもその心をしらず。或は千里をへだてゝも、その人を相したふ。是心の合ふと合はざるとによれり。心の合へる人まれなり。思ふこといはでたゞにやゝやみぬべき我にひとしき人しなければ。とよみけんことむべなり。世に相しれる人多けれど、同心の人まれなり。その上人をしること世に至りてかたし。人の我をしらざること世に多し。人の我をしらざるをうらむべからず。兄弟にても相しらざること世に多し。

賓客を久しくまたしめざるは、主人の禮なれば、古人のよしとすることなり。客來らば、我が位よりいやしき人なりとも、はやく出て對すべし、久しく待たしむべからず。客を久しく待たしむるは、無禮の至りなり。富貴權勢の家に、必此あやまりあり。もしゆへありて、はやく出であふことならずば、人をしてその由をつげやるべし。周公は文王の子、武王の弟にて、その位貴かりしかど、客來れる折ふし、髪洗ひ給へば、かみをにぎりて客にあひ、飯をくひ給へば、口中なる食をはきて客にあひたまふ、人の心をうしなはんことをおそれ給ひてなり。又家に敎なければ、そのやつこ、必客に對して無禮なり。ことに權勢の家のやつこ、主人の戒なければ、必主人の權勢にほこり、賓客におごりて無禮を行ふ。是諸人のいかりにくむ所なり。そのやつこはせしむるにたらず、そのとがは皆主人に歸す。主人たる人、是をしらざるべけんや。

陸宣公曰。寧レ人負レ我。我勿レ負レ人。是忠厚の道なり。忠厚とは、人を愛すること、眞實にして厚きなり。人のよきにめで、、我をよくするは厚といふべからず。人の我にそむき、われをそしるをいかり恨みず、我より人にそむかずして、いからず、恨みそしらず、人の我にしたがふと、したがはざるを心にかけざる、是厚といふべし。もし如此ならば

彼亦人なれば感じてしたがふべし。したがはずと
も、わが心法に害なし。

瘖は口物いはず。聾は耳きこえず。口耳に聲音の通
せざるのみにあらず、心にも亦生れつきて、瘖の
いはざるが如く、聾のきかざるがごとくに理の通
ぜざる人あり。その人と是非をあらそふべからず。
是とあらそふは、我も亦人をしらざるなり。愚と
いふべし。

わがもとに來るべき人、ひさしく來らずとも、故わ
るらんとおもひうらむべからず。こなたよりは、
したしき人には、したしみを失ふべからず。これ
あつき道なり。

人われに對して過あらば、心を廣くしてゆるすべし。
我が身に過あらば、心を小にしてせむべし。
對しがたき人に對せば、彌厚かるべし。したがたき
ことをなさば、彌緩なるべし。急なることに對せ
ば、彌靜なるべし。是古人の言なり。或人、祐筆
にふみをかゝするに、急用のことなり、静に書く
べしといへり。又俗語に、急がばまはれといへる
も其意同じ。

人の善言を聞きて、うつりやすきは誠によし。人の
不善なることばを聞きて、うつりやすき人あり。
まよへりといふべし。是知なければなり。よく心
の内に思案し、その言の是非をわきまへて、あし
き言にまよふべからず。

古人のことばに、衆人を以て人を望めば、人したが
ひやすしといへり。衆人とは、凡夫のことなり。
人の我に對し不義なるをば、凡夫なれば、かくこ
そあらめと思ひ、なだめゆるしてとがめざれば、
人われにしたがひやすく、人をむかずとなり。君子
の道を以てかねにして、一々にせば一も
かねにあはず、一人も全き人なかるべし。かくの
ごとくすれば、人われにしたがはず、そむきやす
し。ひがごと多さは、うき世のならひぞとおもひ
さとりて、人をとがめ世をうらみざること、君子
の心なり。

喜によつて、人に物をあたへ賞を行ひ、いかりによ
つて、人をせめ罰を行へば、必理にあたらずして
あやまる。喜怒の時、こらへて事を行ふべからず。
よろこびもやみ、いかりもやみ、常の心になりて

後事を行ふべし。くじをきく人、訟ふる者のこと

ばによりて、いかりを起し、悦をなすべからず。

怒れば必非分のせめを行ひ、悦べば罪あるをゆる

す。慎しむべし。人ををさむるには、さづわが心

ををさむべし。我が心をさまらずしては、理非を

分ちがたかるべし。いかりによつて理をまげ、是

を非とし、罪を重くするは、賄賂にふけりて、理

をまげて罪をかろくするに同じ。

事に處るには、よく思案し、しづかに行ふべし。よ

く思案すれば理にそむかず。しづかに行へば、あ

やまちすくなし。

我が心に合ひたるものをば、ひとへに愛し、氣に

不ㇾ合者をば、偏に惡むは是愛憎の私なり。如ㇾ此

すれば、人に施すに過不及ありて公ならず。衆人

は愛すぐればおごる、愛せざればうらむ。是偏愛

偏憎の私よりおこる。人に對し下に施すに私なく

して、その人の貴賤親疎功罪賢愚にしたがひて、

與ふべきほどわたへ、與へまじきにはあたへず。

かくのごとくなれば、幸不幸なく、過不及なくして

諸人のいきどほりなし。人々その處を得て、不足

のうらみなし、是たひらかにするなり。

いとまある人、さびしさのあまりに、いとまなく時

ををしむ人のもとに來り、心のどけくよしなき長

ものがたりし、あるじにいとはるゝこそ、むげに

心なきわざなれ。されど、かゝる人に對せんとき、

わが心にかなはずとも、ひたすらに面のけしきさ

しく、詞づかひ不順なるべからず。

人われに對して、不慮に無道なることをしかけ、云

かけして、はなはだわが心にそむくことあり。是

かゝる逆境にあひたる時ごとに、必堪忍の工夫を

なして、いかりうらむべからず。色にあらはし

言にあらはすべからず。是勤ㇾ心忍ㇾ性て、氣質を

變化し、心をみがきて學に進む時なり。空しく過

ぐべからず。かやうの時、つねに心にかけて、忍

べる工夫をなすべし。

横逆の人なり。かやうの處を逆境と云ふ。世にま

じはるには、必かくのごとくなる横逆の人あり。

人のするわざ、その善惡十分にしれて、明白なるこ

と有り。又その事の有りさま、その人の心の中・

よきもあしきも、あきらかにしらざること多し。
わが心にあしゝと思ふとも、その實をよくたづ
ぬれば道理あることあり。よしとおもふことにも
よからざることあり。天下皆非なるの理なしと
へり。何事も人のしわざに故なからんと思ひ、みだ
りに人をにくみそしるべからず。又みだりにほむ
べからず。

友をとるには、人をえらび、人の心をしりて後交り
を定むべし。しらずして交れば、後悔することあ
り、人心はかくれてしりがたし。同じ官職をつと
め、事に出合ひ、旅宿をともにするやうのことに
て、其人に馴るれば人の心みゆ。

人と共に、同じ官職をつとめ、同じ技藝をとる者、
われのみひとり身を立て、名を得んとすべからず。
かくすれば、人もまたあらそひて我をたてじとす。
是かへつて、身のわざはひとなる。かくすれば、人も亦
とせば、まづ人をたつべし。おのれ才にほこり、同官
あらそはず。才あるもの、わが才にほこり、同官
をないがしろにすれば、必同官ににくまれて、わ

ざはひにあへる人古今多し。愼しむべし。我一人
にて事をとらんとするは甚あしく、よきことは同
官にゆづり、我一人の才名をあらはさんとすべか
らず。

世に居るには、人情をしり、時變を考へて、天命に
やすんずべし。或老人のいへるは、としのつもり
に、世の中のありさまを、とかく思ひしりゆくま
に、わがうゆる子、わが祿をあたふるやつこだ
まに、わが心のまゝになりがたし。いはんや世の人
の心、さまぐ＼にかはれば、わが思ふまゝにした
がひがたし。畢竟たゞわが身ををさめて、人をせ
めざるべし。是世にをるの道なり。

およそ、人にまじはるに、その人よく物いひ、才は
たらきて、我が心にかなへりとも、その眸子正し
からず、心術うたがはしくは、まじはりをふかく
すべからず。後に必我が身の害となることあり、
悔ゆれども益なし。是久しく世をへて、おほく人
に交りてしる人のいふ所なれば、たがふべからず。
若後年で害なきは是幸なり。家臣をつかふに、殊
更この目きゝ心得あるべし。唐の張九齡が、安

二六一

340

山に叛相あることを兼て知りたるは、先見の明と
いふべし。才にぶくとも、邪なく忠實なる人を用
ゆべし。眼前は快からざれども、後のうれひなく、
且わがしらざる所にも益多し。小人を用ひ、小人
に交はれば必後の害となる。

さばかりよき所ある人をば、一のくせ、一事のあや
まりにより、すこし心にあはずとも、なだめてこ
そは有べきに、一向にすつること、をしむべし。
人のあしきのみをとがめて、わが身にかへり求めず、
みづからをさめざれば、いかりうらみおほくして、
わが心和せず。人と争ふことしげ〱れば、世に立
ちがたし。わが心におゐても、くるしみ多く樂な
かるべし。身にかへり求むる工夫を専一になすべ
し。かくのごとくすれば、人我相和して、人と争
なく世に立ちやすくして、其樂を失はず。是ひと
に交るの道なり。

我よりは、善をほどこすべし。彼よりも、亦善を以
てむくふることを望むべからず。かれは彼、我は
われ、我はたゞわが道を行ふべし。かれが善不善
は、わが心にあづかるべからず。

朋友親戚の間は、たゞ誠を以てまじはるべし。若わ
れより久しく音問をおろそかにせば、只わが情の
うすくして、疎略なることを謝すべし。餘事にこ
とをよせて、いつはりてわが罪を謝すべからず
是小事といへど、誠の道にあらざれば、心術を害
することは大なり。

易に、君子以遠＝小人。不＝惡而嚴。いふ意は、君子の小
人に對して遠ざからんとするは、顔色とことばを
あしくせず、只わが身を嚴にすれば、かれおのづ
から遠ざかる。

およそ人に交はるに、其人をよくえらぶべし。その
人の善惡見しりがたくば、先このんで交るべから
ず。かれよりしたしむとも、只こたへの禮をばつ
とめて、われよりはうとかるべし。その人小人な
れば、したしみて後必悔あり。すでにしたしく成
るぬれば、小人としれども、にはかにうとんじが
たし。うとんずれば害あり。初その小人なること
をしらず、しるといへども、かれよりしたしむゆ
へに、ふせぎがたくて、ときぐ〲交ることとあり。
小人に交りては、必後に何事ぞにつきて、大事か

小事かわが身の害となる。古語曰、いふことなか
れ、何の害かあらんと。その禍まさに至らんとい
へるが如し。古人の言、たがふべからず。小人と
しらば、わが方よりうとんずべし。しかれば、か
れおのづからうとくなる。

一人をしること、きはめてかたし。古人といへども、
人を知ることいとかたきことなりといへり。況今
の人をや。もしいつはりて忠言をあらはし、謹厚
なるやうにして、われに和順に善柔なりとも、そ
の心信じがたし。剛直なる人は、和順ならずとも、
も、かへつて忠實なり。わが子をたのみ、わが家
をたのみ、わが身後のことをたのむ、その人に非
ざれば、かへつて害あり。臣下朋友、すべて人を
用ひ、人をたのまば、知ありて忠信ある人をえら
ぶべし。かやうの人、世に有りがたし。もしなく
んば、その次には才力にぶくとも、忠實なるを用
ゐべし。忠實ならずば、才ありとて用ふべからず。
才ありて忠信なき人は、かならず害となる。おそ
るべし。

凡人倫に交りて、そのまじはる所の人、われに對し、

ほどこし行へること、もし禮義にあたらずして、
わが心にかなはずとも、人聖質にあらざれば、事
ごとに禮義にあたるべからず。是即凡人の常にし
て、古今天下の世のならはしぞと思ひなだめて、
心にかくべからず。いはんや、うらみいかるべけ
んや。わが身さへ、我が思ふごとくに行ひがたし。
なんぞ人われにほどこす所、わが心のごとくなら
んや。わが身さへ、道にちがはずば、人のわれに
施すこと、道にかなはざるは、わが身にあづから
ざることとなれば、心にかくべからず。我がうれふ
べきことにあらず。人倫の内、われより位たかき
君父と兄夫のわれに無禮なるはいふに及ばず、わ
が子弟臣僕のともがら、われよりいやしき者、我
に禮義なくとも、禮ををさめ人に交るに、その罪をいましむ
べからず。是わが身ををさめ人に交るに、みづか
ら心をやすくし、樂を失はずして、よく世をを
るはしかるべし、心にかけてふかくいかりうらむ
べからず。
の道なり。

大禹謨に曰、滿招レ損。謙受レ益。わが才德を滿てりと
するは、禍ありてわが損となる。謙れば、かへつ

て身の益となる。易曰。天道虧レ盈。而益レ謙。といへるも同理なり。

天下皆非なるの理なし。人の行をあしゝとのみ思ふべからず。わが身をかへりみおさへて、おのれをせむべし。人の非をのみ見て、わが身をかへりみざるは、是滿は損をまねくなり。

人つねにわが身をかへりみて、わが身に道を求むべし。實をつとめて、外をねがふ心あるべからず。人をせめ外に求むるは、實をつとむるにあらず。論語の内、孔子の言に、人の己をしらざることをうれへざれ、人をしらざることをうれへよ。かやうの語、數章あり。その語意大抵相似たり。聖人しばしのたまふは、皆人に實をつとむることを敎へ給ふなるべし。學者のつねに心にかけて行ふべきことなり。

大和俗訓卷之八大尾

# Appendix A

## *Chronology of Kaibara Ekken's Life*

A statue of Kaibara Ekken on his tomb at Kinryūji, a temple in Fukuoka city, Kyushu.

This life chronology (*Nenpu*) is adapted from the diaries of Ekken and the *Collected Works of Ekken* (*Ekken zenshū* Vol. 1), Inoue Tadashi's biography, *Kaibara Ekken*, and Okada Takehiko's study of Ekken's life and thought in Komoguchi Isao and Okada Takehiko, *Andō Seian; Kaibara Ekken*.

1630    Born in Fukuoka castle.

1631    Moves outside the castle to the port city of Hakata.

1635    His mother dies.

1636    Begins to learn *kana* (Japanese syllabary).

1637    Moves with his father to Honamigori, Yakiyama fief.

1638    His father and oldest brother participate in the suppression of the Shimabara rebellion. He begins to learn *kanji* (Chinese characters) from another brother, Sonzai.

1639    Sonzai goes by *han* order to Kyoto to study medicine.

1640    He moves with his father back to Fukuoka where his father tutors him.

1641    He moves again with his father to the village of Ihara in the countryside of Itogori.

1642    His stepmother dies.

1643    He begins to learn about nutrition and medicine from his father. His brother, Sonzai, returns from Kyoto and Ekken begins to study the *Four Books* with him. Under his influence he rejects Buddhism.

1644    His father leaves for Edo where he stays for four years.

1646    He begins reading the *Elementary Learning*.

1647    In the beginning of the year his father returns from Edo. Sonzai moves to Bungo and opens a school. Ekken lives with his youngest brother, Rakken.

1648    He is summoned to serve the *han* lord, Kuroda Tadayuki, as an official in charge of accounts. In the winter he accompanies his father to Edo for the first time.

1649    After returning from Edo he has a coming of age ceremony. He goes to Nagasaki with Kuroda Tadayuki.

1650    In the summer he serves as a guard in the Fukuoka castle. Later this year he falls out of favor with Kuroda Tadayuki and is forced to become a *rōnin*. (This lasted for seven years.)

1651    He first reads Chu Hsi's *Kinshiroku* (Reflections on Things at Hand) which he obtained in Nagasaki.

1654    He moves to Fukuoka and twice that winter goes to Nagasaki to buy books imported from China.

1655    He travels to Edo in order to help his father in the *han* residence there. In Edo he frequently visits Hayashi Gahō.

1656    Toward the end of the year he leaves Edo with his father and visits Ise shrine. Back in Kyushu he begins to serve Kuroda Mitsuyuki and he receives a six-person stipend.

1657    He begins to serve the *han* samurai, Tachibana Kanzaemon, who later becomes his disciple. He lectures on Chu Hsi's *Preface to the Great Learning*. He is sent by the *han* to Kyoto for further study. (He remains there for seven years.) He meets Matsunaga Sekigo, Yamazaki Ansai, and Kinoshita Jun'an.

1658    In Kyoto he lectures on the *Great Learning* and the *Analects*. He frequently hears Kinoshita Jun'an's lectures and also meets Mukai Genshō.

1659    In recognition of his accomplishments he receives a kimono and books from Kuroda Mitsukuni. At the end of the year his stipend is increased by ten. (Total is now twenty *koku*.)

1660    He lectures on the *Elementary Learning*. He becomes acquainted with Matsushita Kenrin. He goes from Kyoto to Edo and stays there for four months.

1661    In Edo he hears a lecture by Hayashi Gahō on divination. He returns to Kyoto and Miyazaki Yasusada visits him there. He lectures on the *Elementary Learning*, the *Classic of Filial Piety*, and *Great Learning*, and the *Analects*.

1662    While in Kyoto he meets frequently with Kinoshita Jun'an. He lectures on the *Analects*. He returns to Kyushu for several months and his stipend is increased by ten (now at thirty). He accompanies Mitsuyuki to Edo and tutors him en route. He returns to Kyoto where he lectures for the first time, and to large audiences, on the *Doctrine of the Mean* and on *Mencius*.

1663 In Kyoto he lectures for the first time on Chu Hsi's *Reflections on Things at Hand*.

1664 He returns to Kyushu with his disciple, Tsuruhara Shōrin. (En route they stop in Hyōgo and visit the grave of Kusunoki Masashige in Minatogawa.) He is given a stipend of 150 *koku*. He accompanies Mitsuyuki to Edo and begins lecturing Mitsuyuki's son, Tsunamasa, on the *Elementary Learning*. He visits the Bakufu Confucian, Toki Shigemoto, and afterwards corresponds with him.

1665 He lectures on the *Diagram of the Supreme Ultimate* at the *han* villa in Edo. He is sent to Kyoto to lecture and there he meets Itō Jinsai for the first time. He begins to lecture on the *Heart Classic* and the *Book of Changes*. He reads *Hsüeh p'u t'ung-pien* of Ch'en Chien and this convinces him to reject Lu Hsiang-shan and Wang Yang-ming and to follow Chu Hsi. This year he publishes *Ekigakuteiyo* (Manual on Divination) and *Dokushojunjo* (Reading books in the proper order.) At the end of the year his father dies at the age of 69.

1666 He leaves Kyoto and returns home to mourn his father. He goes ahead of Mitsuyuki to Edo and arrives there after visiting Kyoto en route.

1667 He leaves Edo and goes to Kyoto. Toward the end of the year he travels in various parts of Yamato.

1668 In Kyoto he meets with Itō Jinsai. He returns to Kyushu to marry Tōken, the 17-year-old daughter of a *han* samurai. He takes the name Kyūbei (after his grandfather) and his stipend is increased to 200 koku. He goes to Edo and lectures the shogun's heir. This year he writes *Daigaku kōryō jōmoku zokkai* (Essential points of the Great Learning explained in common language), *Shushi bunpan*, (Model compositions of Chu Hsi) and *Kinshiroku bikō* (Notes on Reflections on Things at Hand), and *Jikeihan* (Self-cautionary compilations).

1669 Goes to Kyoto for four months and returns to Kyushu. Writes *Shōgaku kutō bikō* (Annotated version of the Elementary Learning).

1670 He lectures on the *Analects* in the Kuroda *han*.

1671 Goes to Kyoto and visits Nakamura Tekisai, with whom he studies the constellations. In the middle of the year he leaves

Kyoto and returns home, where he builds a library. He is commissioned to compile the Kuroda family geneology.

1672    He tutors Kuroda Mitsuyuki's son, Tsunamasa. At the end of the year he goes to Edo on the recommendation of Hoshina Masayuki and tutors the shogunal heir, Tsunayuki, on the *Analects*. This year he publishes two compilations on plants called *Honzō kōmoku hinmoku* (List of items in Li Shih-chen's *Pen-ts'ao kang mu*) and *Honzō meibutsu furoku* (Supplement to *Pen-ts'ao kang mu*).

1673    He leaves Edo, spends a month in Kyoto and returns home.

1674    He takes issue with a local *han* Confucian, Shibata Fuzan, regarding the succession of the Kuroda *han* leader. He leaves Kyushu for Edo with Mitsuyuki and his son, Tsunamasa.

1675    In Edo he lectures on Chu Hsi's *Precepts of the White Deer Grotto Academy* and on the *Great Learning*. He is ordered to remain in Edo and he becomes a tutor for the new *han* heir, Tsunamasa. He investigates the Bakufu's medicinal-herb garden in Meguro. He leaves Edo and returns to Kyushu via Kyoto. This year he compiles his lectures on the *Great Learning* and on the *Precepts of the White Deer Grotto Academy*.

1676    He goes to Nagasaki to purchase books. During this year he gathers the principal parts of the *Elementary Learning*, the *Four Books*, *Reflections on Things at Hand*, the *Five Classics*, the *Extended Meaning of the Great Learning* and puts them in two volumes with commentaries.

1677    He is ordered to converse in writing with the Koreans who had drifted into Munakatagori at Ōshima and he accompanies them to Nagasaki. This year he corrects *Tenshin gyōjō* (Deportment before the heavenly spirits); he compiles *Seizoku bunshō kihan yoroku* (Supplementary record of model sentences); and he revises the punctuation of *Kinshiroku* (Reflections on Things at Hand).

1678    He presents Mitsuyuki with the *Kuroda kafu* (Kuroda family geneology). For the first time he sees a water clock within the castle. He compiles *Wakan meisū* (A number of items from Japan and China) and *Kokon shisen* (Anthology of poems from past and present).

1679 He lectures on the *Book of Documents*. He celebrates his 50th birthday by having a banquet. This year he publishes *Jōshokukikō* (Travelogue), *Shogaku shihō* (Method of beginning to study poetry).

1680 He goes to Kyoto via Osaka. This year he writes various travelogues including *Kinai ginkō* (Traveling minstrels in the region around Kyoto), *Keikikikō* (Travels around Kyoto), *Yamato Kawauchi jiki* (Travels in Yamato and Kawauchi) and a botany book, *Honzō kōmoku mokuroku wamei* (Japanese names and an outline catalogue of plants).

1681 Because of a famine he gives silver to the local farmers. This year he corrects *Tōshōgūikun* (Last Testament of Ieyasu) and *Kuroda kafu* (Kuroda family geneology).

1682 He corresponds with Korean messengers at Aijima. He goes to Edo where he is invited to the home of Sakai Kawauchi and he meets Hitomi Yuzan. (They later became closely associated for a long period of time.) This year he writes *Kokumeishō* (Summary of loyal duty).

1683 He leaves Edo, and goes sightseeing at the Ise Shrine and in the Yoshino mountains. This year he compiles *Shushi gorui senyo* (Essential selections from the sayings of Chu Hsi), *Shushi shosetsuyō* (Essential letters of Chu Hsi), *Sōju bunsui* (Pithy sayings of the Sung Confucians), *Nitei ruigō shūi* (Sayings of the Ch'eng brothers).

1684 He receives an order from the Bakufu to do research on the military deeds of the Kuroda family and makes two trips to Edo for his research. This year he writes *Kuroda senkō kunkoki* (Record of the meritorious deeds of the former Kuroda lords), *Dazaifu Tenmangū kojitsu* (Ancient practices of the Tenman shrine in Dazaifu), and *Daigaku shinso* (New comments on the Great Learning).

1685 He visits with the Shinto scholar Yao Yaheiji and with the Confucian scholars Jun'an and Sukemoto. He also visits Yoshikawa Tadashi. He leaves Edo and returns to Kyushu. A Confucian retainer from Mito comes with a group to Kyushu to obtain materials for the *Dainihonshi* (Great History of Japan). He had already investigated the records of the temples and shrines within the *han* and had them displayed at the Daizaifu shrine for the benefit of the Mito group.

1687 He presents an account of those who died in the Shimabara rebellion. He revises the Kuroda family lineage and he writes *Gakusoku* (Rules for study), *Waji kakun* (Precepts for the family in Japanese), and *Gojuroki* (Record of travels with my wife).

1688 There is a border dispute with the Saga *han* and Ekken is involved in settling it. He presents to Mitsuyuki and to his heir, Tsunamasa, a revised edition of the *Kuroda kafu* (Kuroda family geneology). He is commissioned to compile an account of Chikuzen's topography and he is permitted to travel within the borders for his research. He goes to Kyoto where he meets the mathematician, Myōgonin Rishōbō.

1689 In Kyoto he visits Matsushita Kenrin and hears a lecture on *Shindaikan* (The age of the gods). He visits various medicinal gardens with Inao Jakusui. He leaves Kyoto and returns home via Osaka and Sakai. His oldest brother, Kyūbei, dies. This year he publishes *Kōfu* (Encyclopedia of incense).

1690 He visits various temples and shrines of Fukuoka and investigates their ancient customs. A *han* mathematician, Hoshino Minoru, comes and he listens to his lectures. He celebrates his 60th birthday. (By Japanese calculation he reached the age of 60 the year before but the celebration had been postponed because of a death in his family.) He is invited by the Akizuki *han* lord to lecture on *Mencius* and the *Great Learning*. This year he publishes *Kashigū kiji* (Account of Kashi shrine) and *Tohikōyūki* (Record of travels in town and country).

1691 He leaves Kyushu and goes to Kyoto with his wife and nephew. After returning home he begins lecturing on the *Book of Changes* and the *Doctrine of the Mean*. This year he writes *Chikuzen nayose* (Famous places of Chikuzen), *Kōtō kikō* (Travelogue of Kōtō), *Sefuri yamaki* (Account of Sefuri mountain), and *Shinju heikōji fusō hairon* (Discussion of the parallels between Confucianism and Shinto).

1692 He is ordered to go to Edo where he pays his respects for the first time at the Yushima Seidō and also meets with Hayashi Takaoka. This year he writes *Zoku wakan meisū* (Continuation of items on Japan and China), and *Yamato junranki* (Diary of travels in Yamato).

1694 He lectures to Tsunamasa on the *Book of History* and on *Mencius*. He presents Tsunamasa with the *Kuroda kiryaku* (Abbreviated account of the Kuroda family). He goes to Kyoto where he sees a performance of Kagura at the court. This year he writes *Toyokuni kikō* (Travelogue through fertile provinces), *Kumano jiki* (Record of travels in Kumano), and *Kafu* (Flower encyclopedia).

1695      He leaves Kyoto and returns home. He asks permission to resign but is refused. His brother, Sonzai, dies at age 73.

1696      His stipend is increased by 100 koku. (It is now 300.) He invites guests to celebrate and they have a party for several days. Miyazki Yasusada's *Nōgyō zensho* (Compendium on agriculture) is published.

1697      Miyazaki Yasusada dies.

1698      He tours the Kyoto area accompanied by his wife. At the end of the year he obtains permission to adopt his nephew, Shigeharu, as his heir.

1699      Shigeharu has his coming of age ceremony and Ekken celebrates his 70th birthday. This year he writes *Wajikai* (Explanation of Japanese characters), *Nihon shakumyō* (Japanese dictionary), *Sanrei kuketsu* (The oral transmission of three ritual practices).

1700      Yoshihisa, his nephew, dies at age 36. He receives permission to resign.

1701      This year he writes *Kinsei buke hennen ryaku* (Abridged chronicle of samurai in recent times), *Shiyōhen* (Essential compilations), *Munekatagori fudoki* (Topographical record of Munekata province).

1702      His brother, Rakken, dies at the age of 77. This year he writes *Ongaku kibun* (Dictated record of music) and revises *Fusō kishō* (Account of Japan's topography).

1703      His nephew, Shigeharu, marries his wife Tōken's niece. He presents *Chikuzen no kuni zokufudoki* (Topographical record of the Chikuzen province) to Tsunemasa. In this year he writes *Tenrei* (Philology examples), *Waka kibun* (Dictated record of waka), *Kuroda Tadayuki kafu* (Geneology of Kuroda Tadayuki), *Gorinkun* (Precepts for the five moral relations), *Kunshikun* (Precepts for the Noble Person).

1704 During the spring and autumn Tōken is gravely ill but gradually recovers. This year he writes *Saifu* (Vegetable encyclopedia).

1705 A girl is born to his nephew, Shigeharu, but his wife dies in childbirth. Ekken gives his rice stipend to the needy to assuage their hunger. This year he writes *Hijiki* (Country diary).

1706 His nephew, Shigeharu, is remarried to a daughter of the Ide family. At the end of the year he administers Shigeharu's household affairs. Ekken is ordered to come to the castle to revise *Chikuzen no kuni zokufudoki* (Continual of Topographical record of Chikuzen). This year he writes *Wakan kogen* (Old sayings of Japan and China).

1708 He writes *Yamato zokkun* (Precepts for daily life in Japan).

1709 He entrusts his household affairs to Shigeharu, his nephew. Shigeharu gives a party for Ekken's 80th birthday. This year he writes *Kiso jinoki* (Roads of Kiso), *Yamato honzō* (Plants of Japan).

1710 He writes *Rakkun* (Precepts on contentment), *Wazoku dōjikun* (Precepts on Japanese customs for children).

1711 His pupils gather and celebrate his birthday. He sees a world map which has been brought from Nagasaki. This year he writes *Arima meishoki* (Scenic spots of Arima), *Gōjōkun* (Precepts on the five cardinal Confucian virtues), *Kadōkun* (Precepts on the way of the family).

1712 This year he writes *Shinga kihan* (Models for calligraphy), *Jigoshū* (Essay written to amuse myself).

1713 Tōken becomes ill and at the end of the year she dies at age 62. This year he writes *Yōjōkun* (Precepts on health care), *Shoshū junranki* (Diary of travels in various provinces), and *Nikkō meishōki* (Scenic spots of Nikkō).

1714 At the beginning of the year his health is poor and he refuses visitors. In the spring he writes *Shinshiroku* (Record of careful thoughts). In the summer he finishes *Taigiroku* (Record of grave doubts). He dies and is buried in Kinryūji in Fukuoka.

1911 He is granted the fourth court rank posthumously.

# Appendix B

## *A List of Ekken's Collected Works*

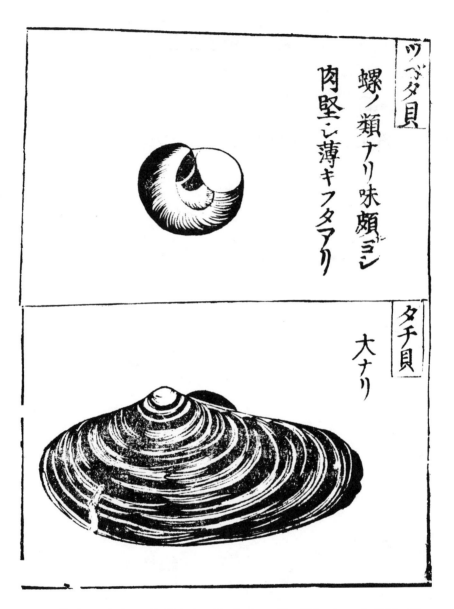

ツブタ貝

螺ノ類ナリ味頰ヨシ
肉堅シ薄キフタアリ

タチ貝

大ナリ

ABOVE: *Tsubetagai*. A snail. This is a kind of small edible river shellfish. The taste is exceedingly good. The meat is tough and has a thin covering. BELOW: *Tachigai*. A large razor clam.

# VOLUME I

1. Personal chronology of Ekken's life (Nenpu)
2. Chronology of his writings
3. Biography of Ekken

## Writings

4. Nihon shakumyō (Japanese dictionary)
5. Tenrei (Philology examples)
6. Wajikai (Explanation of Japanese characters)
7. Kafu (Flower encyclopedia)
8. Saifu (Vegetable encyclopedia)
9. Shorei kuketsu (Proper form of writing passed down orally)
10. Shokurei kuketsu (Proper form of eating passed down orally)
11. Charei kuketsu (Proper form of tea passed down orally)
12. Banpo hijikki (Record of household affairs)
13. Wakan kogen (Ancient proverbs of China and Japan)
14. Nihon saijikki (Record of yearly events in Japan)
15. Chūka kotohajime (Dictionary of Chinese events)
16. Yamato kotohajime (Dictionary of Japan)
17. Yamato kotohajime seigo (Revised dictionary of Japan)

# VOLUME II

1. Shinshiroku (Record of careful thoughts)
2. Taigiroku (Record of grave doubts)
3. Jigoshū (Essay written to amuse myself)
4. Kakubutsu yowa (Writings on the investigation of things)
5. Jikeihen (Self-cautionary compilations)
6. Shogaku chiyō (Necessary wisdom for beginning study)
7. Shōgaku kutō bikō (Notes on the punctuation of the *Elementary Learning*)
8. Kinshiroku bikō (Notes on *Reflections on Things at Hand*)
9. Wakan meisū (A number of items on Japan and China)
10. Zoku wakan meisū (Continuation of items on Japan and China

## VOLUME III

1. Shogakukun (Precepts for beginning study)
2. Yamato zokkun (Precepts for daily life in Japan)
3. Wazoku dōjikun (Precepts on Japanese customs for children)
4. Gojōkun (Precepts on the five cardinal Confucian virtues)
5. Bunkun (Precepts on literature)
6. Bukun (Precepts for the samurai)
7. Kunshikun (Precepts for the Noble Person)
8. Kadōkun (Precepts on the way of the family)
9. Yōjōkun (Precepts on health care)
10. Yōjōkun furoku (Precepts on health care continued)
11. Rakkun (Precepts on contentment)
12. Jingikun (Precepts concerning the gods)
13. Onna daigaku (Learning for women)
14. Ekken sensei saishin ni atōru sho (Ekken's letters to the chief minister)
15. Kokumeisho (Summary of loyal duty)
16. Shogaku tōsho (About calligraphy)
17. Shinga kihan (Models for calligraphy)
18. Gensō (On proverbs)
19. Kakun (Precepts for the family)

## VOLUME IV

1. Chikuzen no kuni zokufudoki (Topographical record of the Chikuzen province)
2. Chikuzen nayose (Famous collections of Chikuzen)
3. Chikuzen no kuni shosha engi (The history of various shrines in Chikuzen)
4. Chikuzen no kuni ni innen aru mono o osamu (Collecting things related to Chikuzen province)

## VOLUME V

1. Kuroda kafu (Kuroda family geneology)
2. Kuroda kiryaku (Abbreviated account of the Kuroda family)
3. Kuroda senkō chūgi den (Biographies containing the meritorious deeds of the former Kuroda lords)

4. Kuroda kashin den (Biographies of the Kuroda retainers)
5. Hachimangū hongi (Chronicle of the Hachiman shrine) [By Kaibara Yoshihisa, Ekken's nephew]
6. Daizaifu Tenmangū kojitsu (Ancient practices of the Tenman shrine in Daizaifu)
7. Chikuzen no kuni zoku shosha engi (History of the various shrines of Chikuzen province)

## VOLUME VI

1. Yamato honzō (Plants of Japan)
2. Yamato honzō furoku (Supplement to Plants of Japan)
3. Yamato honzō shohinzu (Illustrations of various items in Plants of Japan)
4. Yamato honzō hisei (Corrigenda for Plants of Japan) [Lectures of Ono Ranzan recorded by his disciples]
5. Yamato honzō furoku hisei (Corrigenda for the supplement to Plants of Japan) [Lectures of Ono Ranzan]
6. Honzō kōmoku hinmoku (List of items in Li Shih-chen's *Pen-ts'ao kang mu*)
7. Honzō meibutsu furoku (Supplement to *Pen-ts'ao kang mu*)
8. Honzō wamyōshō (A summary of Japanese names of plants) [that appear in Chapter 5 of *Pen-ts'ao kang mu*]

## VOLUME VII

1. Kyōjō shoran (Observations on the castles in Kyoto)
2. Kyōjō shoran dōshui (Similar gleanings on Kyoto's castles)
3. Washū junranki (Diary of travels around Japan)
4. Seihokukikō (Northwest travelogue)
5. Nanyukikō (Southern travelogue)
6. Zoku shoshū meguri (Touring the provinces, continued)
7. Azuma ji no ki (Record of travels in Azuma)
8. Nikkō meishō ki (Scenic spots of Nikko)
9. Kiso ji no ki (Record of travels in Kiso)
10. Arimayama onsen ki (Account of Mt. Arima hot springs)
11. Arimayama onsen ki tsuika (Supplement to account of Mt. Arima hot springs)
12. Fusō ki shō (Account of Japan's topography)
13. Wajiga (Dictionary of Japan) [compiled by Kaibara Yoshihisa, Ekken's nephew]

14. Isei shūyō (Compilation of sayings on health care)
    [edited by Takeda Shun'an]
15. Sonzai ishū (Posthumous collection of Sonzai)
    [Ekken's brother]
16. Waken ginsō (The writings of Kaibara Waken)
    [Ekken's nephew]
17. Waken zoku ginsō (Continuation of the writings of
    Kaibara Waken)

## VOLUME VIII

1. Chōya zassai (Miscellaneous historial records of Japan)
   [edited by Kaibara Waken]
2. Nōgyō zensho (Compendium on agriculture)
   [by Miyazaki Yasusada]
3. Dōfuroku (Supplement to compendium on agriculture)
   [by Kaibara Rakken, Ekken's brother]
4. Kōkyōshakugi benmō (Commentary on the *Book of Filial Piety*) [by Takeda Shun'an based on Ekken's lectures]
5. Dōfusan (Supplement to the commentary on the *Book of Filial Piety*) [by Takeda Shun'an based on Ekken's lectures]

# Notes

## CHAPTER 1
## INTRODUCTION

1. Tetsuo Najita, *Visions of Virtue in Tokugawa Japan: The Kaitokudō Merchant Academy of Osaka* (Chicago: University of Chicago Press, 1987), paperback, p. 54.

2. This term is used to indicate the dynamic quality of the universe as revealed in its processes of continual transformation. To express this idea the Neo-Confucians drew on the *Book of Changes*, on the vital concept of material force (*ch'i*), and on the role of human beings as participating in the transformation of heaven and earth.

Samuel Yamashita has used the term "naturalistic vitalism" in discussing the thought of Itō Jinsai. He points out that there are a variety of vitalistic cosmologies within the Confucian and Neo-Confucian tradition. See *Compasses and Carpenter's Squares: A Study of Itō Jinsai (1627–1705) and Ogyū Sorai (1666–1728)*, Ph.D. thesis, University of Michigan, 1981, pp. 78 and 120.

3. These themes have been discussed by Wm. Theodore de Bary in his Introduction to *Principle and Practicality* (New York: Columbia University Press, 1979), ed. by Wm. T. de Bary and Irene Bloom, paperback, pp. 22-23. See also Wm. T. de Bary, "Neo-Confucian Cultivation and the Seventeenth-Century 'Enlightenment' " in *The Unfolding of Neo-Confucianism* (New York: Columbia University Press, 1975), ed. by Wm. T. de Bary, paperback, pp. 141–216 and his Introduction to *Self and Society in Ming Thought* (New York: Columbia University Press, 1970), ed. by Wm. T. de Bary, paperback, pp. 1–28. On Korean Neo-Confucianism see Wm. T. de Bary and JaHyun Kim Haboush, eds., *The Rise of Neo-Confucianism in Korea* (New York: Columbia University Press, 1985); Michael C. Kalton, trans., *To Become A Sage: The Ten Diagrams on Sage Learning by Yi T'oegye* (New York: Columbia University Press, 1988); Young-chan Ro, *Korean Neo-Confucianism of Yi Yulgok* (Albany: State University of New York Press, 1988).

4. The term "monism of *ch'i*" has been used to describe what has also been called the philosophy of *ch'i*, namely, the collapse of a distinct dual-

NOTES TO CHAPTER 1

ism of *li* (principle) as prior and superior to *ch'i* (material force). Monism in this case indicates the position of Ekken and other earlier Neo-Confucians in both China and Korea, who maintained that reality was one organic whole composed of material force (*ch'i*). This will be discussed further in chapter three. To demonstrate the connection with Chinese Neo-Confucian thinkers that is evident in Ekken's writings, the term "monism of *ch'i*" (rather than *ki*) will be used throughout this work. On the philosophy of material force, see Onozawa Seiichi, Fukunaga Mitsuji, and Yamanoi Yū, eds., *Ki no shisō* (Tokyo: Tokyo Daigaku shuppankai, 1978).

5. This work has been translated with an introduction by Irene Bloom, *Knowledge Painfully Acquired: The K'un-chih chi by Lo Ch'in-shun* (New York: Columbia University Press, 1987). On Yi Yulgok see Young-chan Ro, *Korean Neo-Confucianism of Yi Yulgok* (Albany: State University of New York Press, 1988).

6. See Willard J. Peterson, "Fang I-chih: Western Learning and the 'Investigation of Things,' " in Wm. T. de Bary, ed., *The Unfolding of Neo-Confucianism*, pp. 369–411 and W. J. Peterson, *Bitter Gourd: Fang I-chih and the Impetus for Intellectual Change* (New Haven: Yale University Press, 1979). In *Bitter Gourd* Peterson stresses that while Fang I-chih was not a scientist in the modern sense of the term, the motivations for his research were similar to those of seventeenth-century European scientists. See p. 169.

7. Maruyama Masao, *Studies in the Intellectual History of Tokugawa Japan*, trans. by Mikiso Hane (Tokyo and Princeton: University of Toyko Press and Princeton University Press, 1974). See chapter 2.

8. See discussion in Wm. T. de Bary, "Human Rites—An Essay on Confucianism and Human Rites," in Irene Eber, ed., *Confucianism: The Dynamics of Tradition* (New York: Macmillan, 1986), p. 116.

9. Scholars who have helped to articulate the religious aspects of Neo-Confucianism include Mou Tsung-san, T'ang Chün-i, Chung-ying Cheng, Wing-tsit Chan, Tu Wei-ming, Ha Tai Kim, Wm. Theodore de Bary, and Rodney L. Taylor.

10. Frederick J. Streng, *Understanding Religious Life* (Belmont, Calif.: Dickenson Publishing Co., 1985), pp. 1–9. Also useful in this regard are Joachim Wach's criteria of authentic religious experience as 1) a response to what is experienced as Ultimate Reality; 2) a total response of the total being; 3) intensity; 4) the imperative to issue in action. See Joachim Wach, *The Comparative Study of Religion* (New York: Columbia University Press, 1958), chapter 2. I am grateful to Rodney Taylor for these references. See his discussion of defining religion in relation to Neo-Confucianism in "Neo-Confucianism, Sagehood and the Religious Dimension," *Journal of Chinese Philosophy* 2 (1975): 389–415.

11. See a discussion of this point in Winston King, "Religion," *The En-*

*cyclopedia of Religion* (New York: Macmillan, 1987), vol. 12, pp. 282–293. King argues that defining religion is largely a Western concern and that the categories many scholars use in relation to non-Western and tribal traditions are often inappropriate because they are largely determined by Western categories.

12. See Wilfred Cantwell Smith, *The Meaning and End of Religion* (New York: Macmillan, 1964), pp. 19–74.

13. Tu Wei-ming, "Neo-Confucian Religiosity and Human-Relatedness," *Confucian Thought: Selfhood as Creative Transformation* (Albany: SUNY Press, 1985), p. 132.

14. *Ibid.*, p. 132.

15. *Ibid.*, p. 133. Emphasis is Tu Wei-ming's.

16. An interesting comparative example of this can be seen in the thought of Tai Chen (1724–1777), who, like Ekken, based his ideas of investigating things and of cultivating the moral nature on a naturalistic monism of *ch'i*. See Cheng Chung-ying, trans. *Tai Chen's Inquiry Into Goodness* (Honolulu: East-West Center Press, 1971).

17. For an extensive discussion of Chu Hsi's proclamations as a means of public education, see Ron-Guey Chu, "Chu Hsi and Public Instruction." Wm. T. de Bary and John W. Chaffee, eds., *Neo-Confucian Education: The Formative Stage* (Berkeley: University of California Press, 1989). See also Wm. T. de Bary's article in the same volume, "Chu Hsi's Aims as an Educator."

## CHAPTER 2

1. João Rodrigues in Michael Cooper, ed., *They Came to Japan: An Anthology of European Reports on Japan, 1543–1640* (Berkeley: University of California Press, 1965), paperback, 1981, p. 32.

2. For an account of Ieyasu's life see Conrad D. Totman, *Tokugawa Ieyasu, Shogun: A Biography* (San Francisco: Heian, 1983). See also A. L. Sadler, *The Maker of Modern Japan: The Life of Shogun Tokugawa Ieyasu* (London: Allen & Unwin Ltd., 1937; Rutland, Vt.: Charles E. Tuttle Co., 1978). Of particular relevance for the discussion in this chapter regarding the transmission of ethics is the translation of the legacy of Ieyasu in the final chapter as well as a partial translation of Kuroda Josui's admonitions to his retainers. Kuroda Josui (1546–1604) was an important Christian daimyo in Kyushu, and it was his heirs that Ekken later served in the Chikuzen han.

3. The term *han* was first used by nineteenth-century historians but

has become the commonly used term for modern historians when referring to a Tokugawa-period domain. For a more detailed discussion of the politics and organization of the *Bakuhan* system, see Conrad D. Totman, *Politics in the Tokugawa Bakufu, 1600–1843* (Cambridge: Harvard University Press, 1967). Totman observes that "the stability of the Bakufu system is surprising in view of the high degree of daimyo autonomy." (p. 33) He maintains the Bakufu was able to wield authority through institutional controls, ideological claims, and nominal imperial approval. (p. 39)

4. See Herschel Webb, *The Japanese Imperial Institution in the Tokugawa Period* (New York: Columbia University Press, 1968); also Asao Naohiro and Marius B. Jansen, "Shogun and *Tennō*", in John W. Hall, et al., eds., *Japan Before Tokugawa* (Princeton: Princeton University Press, 1981), paperback, pp. 248–270. The authors maintain that in the early seventeenth-century "the emperor was fixed in a purely symbolic position of authority. At the same time, the shogun ceased to function as a court official. Instead, as Tokugawa Ieyasu had desired, the shogun emerged as the absolute head of his warrior aristocracy and the authority in actual control of affairs of government." (p. 264)

5. Theoretically, this bureaucracy consisted of a hereditary administrative system whose highest offices were restricted to vassal daimyo, bannerman, and housemen (*gokenin*). However, it had the feature of perpetuating factional rivalry among the bureaucrats which consequently minimized the importance of hereditary status and allowed for the emergence of informal governing techniques by cliques. This is the basic thesis of Conrad Totman's discussion of *Politics in the Tokugawa Bakufu, 1600–1843*.

6. Those who were his supporters before the battle of Sekigahara were the *fudai* or vassal daimyo, those who descended from Ieyasu's family were the *shimpan* or related daimyo, and those who swore loyalty after Sekigahara were the *tozama* or outside daimyo. For a discussion of the role of the *fudai* daimyo see Harold Bolitho, *Treasures Among Men, The Fudai Daimyo in Tokugawa Japan* (New Haven: Yale University Press, 1974). For an account of the development of the daimyo see John W. Hall, "Foundations of the Modern Japanese Daimyo," *Journal of Asian Studies* 20,3 (1961): 317–329.

7. See Toshio G. Tsukahira, *Feudal Control in Japan: The Sankin Kōtai System* (Cambridge: East Asian Research Center, Harvard, 1966). See also Constantine N. Vaporis, "Post Stations and Assisting Villages: Corvée Labor and Peasant Contention." *Monumenta Nipponica* 41,4 (1986): 377–414.

8. As Tashirō Kazui has observed, the term *sakoku* is relatively late and can be traced back to 1801 when part of Englebert Kaempfer's (1651–1716) *History of Japan* was translated into Japanese and titled *Sakoku ron* by a Nagasaki interpreter named Shizuki Tadao. Tashirō asserts that the term was invented by Shizuki by inverting the characters for *kuni o tozasu*. Tashirō's argument, relying on Itazawa Takeo's *Nichiran bunka koshōshi no kenkyū*, ap-

pears in "Foreign Relations During the Edo Period: *Sakoku* Reexamined." Trans. by Susan D. Videen, *Journal of Japanese Studies* 8,2 (1982): 283–306. See also Katō Eiichi, "Development of Japanese Studies on *Sakoku* (Closing the Country): A Survey." *Acta Asiatica* 22 (1972): 84–103 and Katō Hidetoshi, "The Significance of the Period of National Seclusion Reconsidered," in *Journal of Japanese Studies* 7,1 (1981): 85–109.

9. For accounts of the Christian missionaries and their converts see Charles R. Boxer, *The Christian Century in Japan 1549–1650* (Berkeley: University of California Press, 1951); Michael Cooper, ed., *They Came to Japan: An Anthology of European Reports on Japan, 1543–1640* (Berkeley: University of California Press, 1965, paperback, 1981); George Elison, *Deus Destroyed: The Image of Christianity in Early Modern Japan* (Cambridge: Harvard University Press, 1973). Also Ivan Morris, "The Japanese Messiah," in *The Nobility of Failure: Tragic Heroes in the History of Japan* (New York: Holt, Rinehart and Winston, 1975), pp. 143–179; Itō Tasaburō, "The Book Banning Policy of the Tokugawa Shogunate," *Acta Asiatica* 22 (1972): 36–61; Nagazumi Yoko, "Japan's Isolationist Policy as Seen Through Dutch Source Materials." *Acta Asiatica* 22 (1972): 18–35.

10. This point has been discussed by Tashirō Kazui in her article cited in note 8 above. Tashirō argues that trade and foreign relations were encouraged with China, Korea, and the Ryukyus and that *sakoku* was a positive effort of the Japanese to set them free of Chinese controls. Ronald P. Toby develops this argument still further in discussing the ongoing diplomatic relations with the continent that were important to the Bakufu legitimization processes. See Toby's article, "Reopening the Question of *Sakoku*: Diplomacy in the Legitimation of the Tokugawa Bakufu," *Journal of Japanese Studies* 3,2 (1977): 323–363, and his book, *State and Diplomacy in Early Modern Japan: Asia in the Development of the Tokugawa Bakufu* (Princeton: Princeton University Press, 1984). Toby demonstrates the impact of foreign delegations in Tokugawa Japan in his article, "Carnival of the Aliens: Korean Embassies in Edo-Period Art and Popular Culture." *Monumenta Nipponica* 41,4 (1986): 415–456.

11. The positive and negative effects of *sakoku* have been vigorously debated by Japanese scholars. While Tashirō Kazui and Minamoto Ryōen have cited its benefits in terms of internal stability, others such as Watsuji Tetsurō have claimed it had negative effects for Japan. See Watsuji's *Sakoku: Nihon no higeki* (Tokyo: Chikuma shobō, 1950). Iwao Seiichi gives a short survey of varying views of *sakoku* in his book of the same title (vol. 14 of Chūō Kōronsha series, Nihon no rekishi, Tokyo, 1966), pp. 456–464.

12. Ronald Toby, *State and Diplomacy in Early Modern Japan*, p. 234.

13. George Elison, *Deus Destroyed*, pp. 249–250.

14. Ronald Dore has pointed out that these four classes were by no means rigidly defined. "It was rather a world of infinite gradations in

which the dividing line between the samurai proper and the commoner was a blurred and shifting one." In *Education in Tokugawa Japan* (Berkeley: University of California Press, 1965), p. 226. Dore also observes that limited social mobility was possible through education. See his "Talent and the Social Order in Tokugawa Japan" in John W. Hall and Marius B. Jansen, eds., *Studies in the Institutional History of Early Modern Japan* (Princeton: Princeton University Press, 1968), pp. 349–361. The Japanese historian Kobayashi Tetsuya makes a similar point when he notes that Tokugawa society allowed mobility, although on a limited scale. See his *Society, Schools and Progress in Japan*, (Oxford: Pergamon Press, 1976), p. 20. While social roles within these classes were often prescribed by law or custom, this again should not lead us to conclude arbitrarily that this was a static society. Traditional societies have been subject to hierarchial order, as has been described by Louis Dumont in *Homo Hierarchicus* (Chicago: University of Chicago Press, 1980). On this subject Donald Munro observes, "The Western thinker may mistakenly infer from reference to fixed social roles that he is faced with a totally static holism. However, so strongly did Confucians believe that all things exist in a state of constant growth and change that their image of social roles is one of change as well." In Donald Munro, ed., *Individualism and Holism: Studies in Confucian and Taoist Values* (Ann Arbor: Center for Chinese Studies, University of Michigan, 1985), paperback, p. 18.

15. This was demonstrated by the case of Yui Shōsetsu, who was forced to commit suicide in 1651 after an apparent plot against the government was exposed. One of the most famous cases of a *rōnin* disturbance was the Akō affair of the revenge of the 47 *rōnin* in 1703.

16. See Thomas C. Smith, *The Agrarian Origins of Modern Japan* (Stanford: Stanford University Press, 1959) and his article on "The Japanese Village in the Seventeenth-Century," in *Journal of Economic History* 12,1 (1952): 1–20. For a discussion of the problems of rural life, especially in the eighteenth and nineteenth-centuries, see Hugh Borton, *Peasant Uprisings in Japan of the Tokugawa Period* (New York: Paragon, 1968) and Irwin Scheiner, "Benevolent Lords and Honorable Peasants: Rebellion and Peasant Consciousness in Tokugawa Japan," in T. Najita and I. Scheiner, eds., *Japanese Thought in the Tokugawa Period* (Chicago: University of Chicago Press, 1978), pp. 39–62. For a survey and commentary on the literature on Tokugawa peasants see Conrad Totman, "Tokugawa Peasants: Win, Lose, or Draw?" *Monumenta Nipponica* 41,4 (1986): 457–476. For an overview of Tokugawa peasant culture see Anne Walthall, "Peripheries: Rural Culture in Tokugawa Japan," *Monumenta Nipponica* 39,4 (1984): 371–392. Recent books on peasant protest include the following: Herbert P. Bix, *Peasant Protest in Japan 1590–1884* (New Haven: Yale University Press, 1986); William Kelly, *Deference and Defiance in Nineteenth-Century Japan* (Princeton: Princeton University Press, 1985); Stephen Vlastos, *Peasant Protests and Uprisings in Tokugawa Japan* (Berkeley: University of California Press, 1986); Anne Walth-

all, *Social Protest and Popular Culture in Eighteenth-Century Japan*, Association of Asian Studies Monograph 43 (Tucson: University of Arizona Press, 1986).

17. For a description of this agricultural revolution see Kozo Yamamura, "Returns on Unification: Economic Growth in Japan, 1550–1650," in John W. Hall et al., eds., *Japan Before Tokugawa*, pp. 327–372.

18. The economic history of the Tokugawa period has been analyzed by Honjō Eijirō in his *Economic Theory and History of Japan in the Tokugawa Period* (New York: Russell and Russell, 1965) and by Charles D. Sheldon, *The Rise of the Merchant Class in Tokugawa Japan* (Locust Valley, N.Y: J. J. Augustin, 1958). E. S. Crawcour has revised some of Sheldon's arguments concerning the merchant class to suggest that they did not continually struggle to free themselves of Bakufu controls. Rather he asserts, "Although official opinion was generally hostile to commercialization, some degree of commercial development was essential to the workings of the Tokugawa system. In their dealings with commerce the authorities sought to keep it within the bounds of what they considered necessary and to control it within established channels." In E. S. Crawcour, "Changes in Japanese Commerce in the Tokugawa Period," *Journal of Asian Studies* 22,4 (1963): 399. See also Sasaki Gin'ya with William Hauser, "*Sengoku* Daimyo Rule and Commerce" in John W. Hall et al., eds., *Japan Before Tokugawa*, pp. 125–148. More recently Tetsuo Najita has done an extensive study of the merchant academy in Osaka, the Kaitokudō. He provides a stimulating analysis of intellectual issues regarding virtue and education in relation to the role of the merchants in shaping the political economy of the Tokugawa period. See his *Visions of Virtue in Tokugawa Japan: The Kaitokudō Merchant Academy of Osaka.* With regard to urbanization, see the valuable study of John W. Hall, "The Castle Town and Japan's Modern Urbanization," in J. W. Hall et al., *Studies in the Institutional History of Early Modern Japan*, pp. 169–188.

19. For discussions of urbanization see Yazaki Takeo, *Social Change and the City in Japan* (Tokyo: Japan Publications Inc., 1968), esp. pp. 124–185. See also Gilbert Rozman, "Edo's Importance in the Changing Tokugawa Society," *Journal of Japanese Studies* 1,1 (1974): 91–112 and his *Urban Networks in Ch'ing China and Tokugawa Japan* (Princeton: Princeton University Press, 1973).

20. See Laurence Bresler, *Origins of Popular Travel and Travel Literature in Japan*, Ph.D. dissertation, Columbia University, 1975.

21. Kozo Yamamura, *A Study of Samurai Income and Entrepreneurship* (Cambridge: Harvard University Press, 1974). See especially pages 1–133. In discussing the *hatamoto* (bannermen), who formed a large section of the *Bakuhan* bureaucracy, Yamamura argues that their impoverishment was due to the fact that their income did not increase at a rate sufficient for them to be able to consume freely as did the daimyo in their visits to Edo.

22. See Kenneth P. Kirkwood, *Renaissance in Japan: A Cultural Survey of Seventeenth-Century Japan* (Rutland, Vt.: Charles E. Tuttle, 1970, reprint of 1938 edition) and Tsuda Sōkichi, *An Inquiry into the Japanese Mind as Mirrored in Literature: The Flowering Period of Common People Literature*, trans. by Fukumatsu Matsuda (Tokyo: Japan Society for the Promotion of Science, 1970).

23. See Abe Yoshio, "The Development of Neo-Confucianism in Japan, Korea and China: A Comparative Study," *Acta Asiatica* 19 (1970): 35.

24. Tetsuo Najita, *Visions of Virtue in Tokugawa Japan*, p. 61.

25. *Ibid.*, pp. 61–62.

26. In Peter Nosco, ed., *Confucianism and Tokugawa Culture* (Princeton: Princeton University Press, 1984), p. 26.

27. Tetsuo Najita, *Visions of Virtue in Tokugawa Japan*, pp. 60–61. In his article on "Intellectual Change in Early Eighteenth-Century Tokugawa Confucianism," Najita also notes ". . . there is little doubt as to the depth of the Tokugawa intellectual engagement with Confucion thought and of the profound legacy of that engagement for the modern history of Japan." *Journal of Asian Studies* 34,4 (1975), p. 931.

28. See Donald Keene, *World Within Walls* (New York: Holt, Rinehart and Winston, 1976), pp. 1–7; Richard Lane, "The Beginnings of the Modern Japanese Novel: *Kanazōshi*, 1600–1682," *Harvard Journal of Asian Studies* 20 (1957): 644–701; and Ronald Dore, *Education in Tokugawa Japan*.

29. Ekken himself was familiar with this dictionary in his youth. See *nenpu* in *Ekken zenshū*, 1:4. (Tokyo: Ekken zenshū kankōbu, 1910–1911).

30. On the Jesuit press see Charles R. Boxer, *The Christian Century in Japan, 1549–1650*, pp. 188–199. Boxer divides the types of works published into three main groups: 1) Those translated from European languages into Japanese. With the exception of Aesop's fables these consisted primarily of catechisms and religious calendars. 2) Works adapted from Japanese originals, e.g. *Heike monogatari*. 3) Linguistic works, grammars, dictionaries (p. 191). See also Ernest Satow, *The Jesuit Mission Press in Japan, 1591–1610* (London: Private printing, 1888).

31. Donald Keene states that this was due to aesthetic reasons, namely, the need to create the appearance of *hiragana* flowing together rather than as distinct entities, which was the case with moveable type. See his *World Within Walls*, p. 4.

32. See Donald Keene, "Characteristic Responses to Confucianism in Tokugawa Literature," in Peter Nosco, ed., *Confucianism and Tokugawa Culture*, pp. 120–137.

33. For an account of the reissuing of Ekken's works through the Tokugawa period see Yajima Genryō, ed., *Tokugawa jidai shuppansha shuppanbutsu shūran* (Sendai: Tōhoku Daigaku fuzoku toshokan, 1968).

34. João Rodrigues as quoted in Michael Cooper, ed., *They Came to Japan*, p. 243.

35. Ronald P. Dore, *Education in Tokugawa Japan*, p. 59. In this book and in his article on "The Legacy of Tokugawa Education," Dore argues persuasively for the emerging role of education in this period as an important factor in the rapid modernization process which occurred since the Meiji restoration. See his article in Marius B. Jansen, ed., *Changing Japanese Attitudes Toward Modernization* (Princeton: Princeton University Press, 1965), pp. 99–131.

36. On the *shijuku* see Richard Rubinger, *Private Academies of Tokugawa Japan* (Princeton: Princeton University Press, 1983).

37. Kobayashi Tetsuya outlines some of these points as the principal reasons for the growth of literacy in this period. See his *Society, Schools and Progress in Japan* (Oxford: Pergamon Press, 1976), pp. 19–20. Thomas Smith notes that upper-level peasants were literate beyond the fundamentals of reading and writing and lists examples to illustrate his point in his article on "The Japanese Village in the Seventeenth-Century," *Journal of Economic History* 12,1 (Winter 1952): 1–20.

38. Nakae Tōju (1608–1648) taught from a building erected near his home known as *Tōju Shoin*. Kumazawa Banzan (1619–1691) taught at the *Shizutani Gakkō* which was established in Okayama by the Ikeda lord.

39. Yamaga Sokō (1622–1685) served as advisor to the Akō lord from 1652–1660. In his autobiography, Arai Hakuseki (1656–1725) gives a detailed picture of his close association with the sixth shogun, Ienobu, both before and during his rule (1709–1712). See his account as translated by Joyce Ackroyd, *Told Round a Brushwood Fire: The Autobiography of Arai Hakuseki* (Princeton and Tokyo: Princeton University Press and University of Tokyo Press, 1979). See also Kate Wildman Nakai, *Shogunal Politics: Arai Hakuseki and the Premises of Tokugawa Rule* (Cambridge: Harvard University Press, 1988).

40. See *Fukuoka ken kyōiku hyakunen shi*, compiled and published by Fukuoka ken kyōiku iinkai, 1980, pp. 18–19. See also their high appraisal of Ekken's role in fostering education in the *han*, pp. 12–14. The descendant was Takeda Shun'an's grandson. Irizawa Sōju, *Kaibara Ekken: Nihon kyōiku sentetsu sōsho* (Tokyo: Bunkyō shoin, 1954), p. 101.

41. Englebert Kaempfer, *The History of Japan Together with a Description of the Kingdom of Siam 1690–1692*, vol. 2, bk. 3 (Glasgow: James MacLehose and Sons, 1906), p. 64.

42. Donald Shively, "Tokugawa Tsunayoshi, the Genroku Shogun," in Albert Craig and Donald Shively, eds., *Personality in Japanese History* (Berkeley: University of California Press, 1970), p. 125. Shively notes that Tsunayoshi "contributed to the century-long transformation by which the early Tokugawa state, dominated by a psychology of military strategic considerations, gradually turned into a more civil-minded warrior bureaucracy infused with ethical and humanitarian ideas. And because the state was the dominant force in the society, this contributed in turn to the diffusion of education and ethical concerns to all classes." (p. 86) Shively claims the most conspicuous changes in this area came around 1700 and were implemented by Tsunayoshi. See also the article on Tsunayoshi by Beatrice Bodart Bailey, "The Laws of Compassion," *Monumenta Nipponica* 40,2 (1985): 163–189.

43. Donald Shively, "Tokugawa Tsunayoshi, the Genroku Shogun," p. 125.

44. *Ibid.*, p. 125.

45. See for example Herbert Passin, *Society and Education in Japan* (New York: Teachers College and the East Asian Institute with Columbia University Press, 1965), paperback, pp. 60–61. Here he elaborates on the idea that Confucianism "may have served Tokugawa Japan better than most people are prepared to believe." Also John W. Hall observes, "On closer scrutiny, the ideas commonly associated with Confucianism are found to contain elements which proved congenial to the modern ethos—loyalty over self, national over personal goals, emphasis on self-improvement and achievement." In Introduction, Marius B. Jansen, ed., *Changing Japanese Attitudes Toward Modernization* (Princeton: Princeton University Press, 1965), p. 40.

46. Those who see the seeds of modernization in the Tokugawa period include Japanese scholars such as Minamoto Ryōen and American scholars such as Wm. Theodore de Bary, John W. Hall, Marius B. Jansen, and Edwin Reischauer. Some of those who cite the roots of authoritarian government are Tokutomi Sohō, Watsuji Tetsurō, John Dower, and E. H. Norman.

47. George Sansom, *A History of Japan, 1615–1867* (Stanford: Stanford University Press, 1963), vol. 3, paperback, p. 77. When discussing ideology in the pre-war period in her book, Carol Gluck cites Clifford Geertz's argument that all societies rely on some form of ideology to persuade their members that their life is meaningful. (p. 6) She further notes that the presumed existence of an ideology does not in itself demonstrate its efficacy. (p. 12) This is an important point with regard to discussions of so-called "Tokugawa orthodoxy" or "ideology." See Carol Gluck, *Japan's Modern Myths: Ideology in the Late Meiji Period* (Princeton: Princeton University Press, 1985).

48. See Herman Ooms, "Neo-Confucianism and the Formation of Early Tokugawa Ideology," p. 59, in Peter Nosco, ed; *Confucianism and Tokugawa Culture*. See also Oom's book, *Tokugawa Ideology: Early Constructs, 1570–1680* (Princeton: Princeton University Press, 1985).

49. Herman Ooms, *Tokugawa Ideology*, p. 80.

50. *Ibid.*, p. 76.

51. Herman Ooms, "Neo-Confucianism and the Formation of Early Tokugawa Ideology," p. 51, in Peter Nosco, ed., *Confucianism and Tokugawa Culture*.

52. *Ibid.*, p. 50.

53. Wm. T. de Bary, Introduction to *Principle and Practicality*, p. 19.

54. With regard to literary pieces, Richard Lane has cited didactic treatises and works aimed at popular education as special categories of *kanazōshi* which emerged in the seventeenth-century. See "The Beginnings of the Modern Japanese Novel: *Kanazōshi*, 1600–1682," *Harvard Journal of Asian Studies* 20 (1957): 668–675. The eighteenth-century *shingaku* movement of Ishida Baigan is an example of preaching and sermonizing. For a discussion of Baigan see Robert Bellah, *Tokugawa Religion: The Values of Pre-Industrial Japan* (Boston: Beacon Press, 1957). The nineteenth-century *hōtoku* movement of Ninomiya Sontoku is another instance of spreading morality through sermons. On Sontoku see Yoshimoto Tadasu, *A Peasant Sage of Japan: The Life and Work of Sontoku Ninomiya* (New York: Longmans Green, 1912). A sample of preaching from this period has been translated by M. Y. Aoki and M. B. Dardess in "The Popularization of Samurai Values: A Sermon by Hosoi Heishū." *Monumenta Nipponica* 31,4 (1976): 393–413.

55. On the *Buke Shohatto* see R. Tsunoda, Wm. T. de Bary and D. Keene, eds., *Sources of Japanese Tradition* (New York: Columbia University Press, 1964), vol. 1, paperback, pp. 326–329. Also George Sansom, *A History of Japan, 1615–1867*, vol. 3, pp. 7–8 and John Carey Hall, "Japanese Feudal Laws III: The Tokugawa Legislation." *Transactions of the Asiatic Society of Japan* 38,4 (1911): 269–331.

56. See Carl Steenstrup's discussion of earlier examples of moral codes in *Hōjō Shigetoki 1198–1261* (London: Curzon Press, 1979).

57. See R. Tsunoda, et al., eds., *Sources of Japanese Tradition*, vol. 1, paperback, pp. 325–326. ". . . in a feudal society, where the governmental structure was built upon personal relationships and so much depended upon the loyalty, fitness and discretion of the individual members of the ruling class, such a(n ethical) code served a vital need and its universal acceptance took the place to a large extent of centralized control backed by force. The Tokugawa appreciated that the voluntary, internalized restraints

of Confucian morality, reinforcing the rigid self-discipline of feudal tradition, could be a potent force in itself for the maintenance of order."

58. See Nakai's discussion of this topic in "The Naturalization of Confucianism in Tokugawa Japan: The Problem of Sinocentrism," *Harvard Journal of Asian Studies* 40 (1980): 157–199.

59. *Ibid.*, p. 157.

60. See his important discussion of this in relation to Ekken in "Intellectual Change in Early Eighteenth-Century Tokugawa Confucianism," *Journal of Asian Studies* 34,4 (1975): 931–944.

61. Richard Minear, "Ogyū Sorai's 'Instructions for Students': A Translation and Commentary," *Harvard Journal of Asian Studies* 36 (1976): 81. In recent times this tension is seen in the work of Tsuda Sōkichi, *An Inquiry into the Japanese Mind as Mirrored in Literature* (Tokyo: Japan Society for the Promotion of Science, 1970). Tsuda, like the early *Kokugakusha*, sought the essence of Japan in its literary tradition. Furthermore, his belief in the superiority of the Japanese language over the Chinese language for the expression of ideas is evident in his discussion of Ekken's use of Japanese in his ethical treatises. See Tsuda Sōkichi, *Jukyō no kenkyū* (Tokyo: Iwanami shoten, 1956), pp. 426–429.

# CHAPTER 3

1. Ekken's nenpu (life chronology) is based on several diaries written by Ekken and published by the Kyushu shiryō kankōkai in 1964. These were kindly made available to me by Professors Inoui Tadashi and Okada Takehiko of Kyushu University. The diaries include *Sonken nikkiryaku* (1656–1713), pp. 1–43, *Kanbun nikki* (1661–1672), pp. 45–141, *Enpō shichinen nikki* (1679), pp. 1–40, *Nikki 5* (1686–1688), pp. 1–140, *Nikki 6* (1688–1692), pp. 1–71, *Kyoka nikki* (1699–1713), pp. 1–140. Also included in these materials are various letters written by Ekken: *Shokanshū* Part 1, pp. 1–120; *Shokanshū*, Part 2, pp. 1–174.

Secondary sources on Ekken's life and thought include:

*Ekken zenshū*, vol. 1 (Tokyo: Ekken zenshū kankōbu, 1910–1911), "Kaibara Ekken sensei nenpu," pp. 1–42; and "Kaibara Ekken sensei den," pp. 1–72.
Olaf Graf, *Kaibara Ekiken* (Leiden: E. J. Brill, 1942).
Inoue Tadashi, *Kaibara Ekken* (Tokyo: Yoshikawa kōbunkan, 1963).
Inoue Tadashi and Araki Kengo, eds., *Kaibara Ekken, Muro Kyūsō. Nihon shisō taikei*, vol. 34 (Tokyo: Iwanami shoten, 1970), pp. 445–504.
Inoue Tetsujirō, *Nihon Shushigakuha no tetsugaku* (Tokyo: Fuzanbō, 1923), pp. 264–362.

Irizawa Sōju, *Kaibara Ekken. Nihon kyōiku sentetsu sōsho,* vol. 8 (Tokyo: Bunkyō shoin, 1954), pp. 1–121.

Ishikawa Matsutarō, ed., *Kaibara Ekken, Muro Kyūsō shū. Sekai kyōiku hōten* (Tokyo: Tamagawa Daigaku shuppanbu, 1968).

Iwabashi Junsei, *Dainihon rinri shisō hattatsushi,* vol. 1 (Tokyo: Meguro shoten, 1915), pp. 219–260.

Komoguchi Isao and Okada Takehiko, *Andō Seian; Kaibara Ekken* (Tokyo: Meitoku shuppansha, 1985).

Matsuda Michio, "Kaibara Ekken no Jugaku," in Matsuda Michio, ed., *Kaibara Ekken. Nihon no meicho,* vol. 14 (Tokyo: Chūō kōronsha, 1969), pp. 7–54.

Takigawa Masajirō, ed., *Kaibara Ekken shū. Kinsei shakai keizai gakusetsu taikei,* vol. 10 (Tokyo: Seibundō shinkōsha, 1939), pp. 3–93.

2. *Ekken zenshū,* vol. 1, "Kaibara Ekken sensei den," p. 5.

3. *Ibid.,* p. 10.

4. *Ibid.,* p. 10. The accounts of his life emphasize the difficulty of Ekken's childhood due to the loss of his mother and stepmother and because of his father's uncertain financial condition.

5. Komoguchi Isao and Okada Takehiko, *Andō Seian; Kaibara Ekken,* p. 86.

6. Similarly when he lived with his father and brothers in the country from 1637–1640 he was in contact with farmers. This no doubt contributed to his later interest in agriculture and in botany.

7. The *nenpu* says he learned this at the age of six (1636). *Ekken zenshū,* 1:3.

8. It is said that Sonzai also taught him *zekku,* a style of Chinese poetry. *Ekken zenshū,* vol. 1, "Kaibara Ekken sensei den," p. 13.

9. He is also said to have read the *Taiheiki* when he was eleven. *Ekken zenshū,* vol. 1, "Kaibara Ekken sensei den," pp. 13–14.

10. *Ekken zenshū,* vol. 1, *Nenpu,* p. 4. "Kaibara Ekken sensei den," pp. 13–14.

11. *Ekken zenshū,* vol. 1, *Nenpu,* p. 6. "Kaibara Ekken sensei den," p. 17.

12. Inoue Tadashi, *Kaibara Ekken,* p. 14. See also *Ekken zenshū,* vol. 1, "Kaibara Ekken sensei den," (p. 17) where it is stated that Sonzai promoted Confucianism in the *han.*

13. *Ekken zenshū,* 7: 186.

14. *Ekken zenshū,* vol. 1, *Nenpu,* p. 8.

15. See Inoue Tadashi, *Kaibara Ekken*, p. 20.

16. The *nenpu* indicates that Ekken was also anxious to care for his father in his old age. *Ekken zenshū*, 1:10.

17. For an account of Ekken's contacts in Kyoto see Inoue Tadashi, *Kaibara Ekken*, pp. 29–33; and Komoguchi Isao and Okada Takehiko, *Andō Seian; Kaibara Ekken*, ch. 6.

18. Kinoshita Jun'an encouraged his students to undertake various forms of practical learning, including agricultural studies, botany, and medicine. In addition to Muro Kyūsō and Arai Hakuseki, Jun'an also influenced Inao Jakusui, Sueyama Don'o, and Sakakibara Koshu. Inao produced an encyclopedia classifying natural objects entitled *Shobutsu ruisan*. Sueyama wrote voluminously on agricultural policies and techniques and Sakakibara made a study of Ming law. See Abe Yoshio, "The Influence of Lo Ch'in-shun's *K'un-chih chi* in the Early Edo Period and the State of Practical Learning Among the Students of the Schools of Kinoshita Jun'an and Yamazaki Ansai." Draft paper for the June 1974 ACLS conference on Neo-Confucianism and Practical Learning in the Ming and Early Tokugawa Periods held at the University of Hawaii.

19. For a detailed account of Banzan, see I. J. McMullen's Ph.D. dissertation from Cambridge University, 1968, titled *Kumazawa Banzan: The Life and Thought of a Seventeenth-Century Japanese Confucian*. See also his article, "Kumazawa Banzan and *Jitsugaku*: Toward Pragmatic Action," in Wm. T. de Bary and I. Bloom, eds., *Principle and Practicality*, paperback, pp. 337–371. For an interesting comparison of Banzan and Ekken, see Tsuda Sōkichi, *Jukyō no kenkyū* (Tokyo: Iwanami shoten, 1956), pp. 410–535.

20. Ekken wrote a critique of Jinsai called "Dōjimon higo"; See Inoue Tadashi's article on this titled " 'Dōjimon higo' ni tsuite," *Kyushu Daigaku kenkyū hōkoku* (1977): 121–177.

21. For a discussion of Inao's work see Shirai Mitsutarō, "A Brief History of Botany in Old Japan," in *Scientific Japan: Past and Present* (Tokyo: National Research Council of Japan, 1926), p. 26.

22. See Itō Tasaburō, "The Book Banning Policy of the Tokugawa Shogunate," *Acta Asiatica* 22 (1972): 38–40.

23. For discussion of Ekken's relationship with Miyazaki Yasusada, see Inoue Tadashi, *Kaibara Ekken*, pp. 32, 39–44; and Jeffery Marti, "Intellectual and Moral Foundations of Empirical Agronomy in Eighteenth-Century Japan," *Selected Papers from the Center for Far Eastern Studies*, No. 2 (Chicago: University of Chicago, 1977–78), pp. 41–80.

24. No doubt because Ekken helped to revise it, the *Nōgyō zensho* has been included in volume eight of Ekken's collected works along with a supplement written by Ekken's brother, Rakken. Abe Yoshio has pointed out

that the *Nōgyō zensho* was based in part on Hsu Kuang Chi's *Nung-cheng ch'uan shu* (Compendium on Agricultural Administration). This he describes as a "representative book on agriculture published in the Ming period which was based not only on previous Chinese studies of agriculture but also on the knowledge of hydrodynamics and geography of the West." See Abe Yoshio, "The Influence of Lo Ch'in-shun's *K'un-chih chi* in the Early Edo Period," p. 8.

25. Inoue Tadashi, *Kaibara Ekken*, pp. 56–59.

26. Matsuda Michio, *Kaibara Ekken*, p. 19.

27. Inoue Tetsujirō, *Nihon Shushigakuha no tetsugaku*, pp. 271–273.

28. On the significance of the Korean diplomatic missions to Tokugawa Japan, see Ronald Toby's article, "Carnival of the Aliens: Korean Embassies in Edo Period Art and Popular Culture," *Monumenta Nipponica* 41,1 (1986): 415–456.

29. *Ibid.*, pp. 269–270. R. P. Dore observes, however, that Ekken wrote a senior member of the Kuroda family, advocating the establishment of a school. He claimed that education would have the benefit of making the people "not only more conscious of their duties to their lord and more loyally cooperative in economy drives (thus helping to keep the fief solvent) but also more earnest in practicing their military skills." In *Education in Tokugawa Japan*, p. 69, Ekken's importance in promoting education in the *han* is noted in accounts of education in Fukuoka domain. See for example, *Fukuoka ken no kyōiku hyakunenshi* (Fukuoka: Fukuoka ken kyōiku iinkai, 1980), vol. 5, pp. 12–14; also in Ishikawa Matsutarō, ed., *Kaibara Ekken, Muro Kyūsō. Sekai kyōiku hōten*, pp. 3–62.

30. See discussion of this in Inoue Tadashi, *Kaibara Ekken*, pp. 82–86.

31. See discussion of these letters in Irizawa Sōju, *Kaibara Ekken. Nihon kyōiku sentetsu sōsho*, p. 19.

32. See discussion of these points in Komoguchi Isao and Okada Takehiko, *Andō Seian; Kaibara Ekken* p. 120–121.

33. *Ibid.*, p. 69.

34. For discussions of the place of *jitsugaku* in Japanese thought see Minamoto Ryōen, *Kinsei shoki jitsugaku shisō no kenkyū* (Tokyo: Sōbunsha, 1980) and Wm. T. de Bary and I. Bloom, eds., *Principle and Practicality*.

35. Okada Takehiko, "Practical Learning in the Chu Hsi School: Yamazaki Ansai and Kaibara Ekken," in Wm. T. de Bary and I. Bloom, eds., *Principle and Practicality*, p. 268. (Hereafter abbreviated to "Yamazaki Ansai and Kaibara Ekken.")

36. See the preface to *Yōjōkun, Japanese Secret of Good Health*, by Ayanori Onishi (Tokyo: Tokuma shoten, 1974), p. 7. For a discussion of von Siebold's work in Japan, see John Z. Bowers, *Western Medical Pioneers in Feudal Japan* (Baltimore: John Hopkins University Press, 1970), pp. 91–173.

37. This will be discussed further in chapter 5. See also Tada Akira, "Kaibara Ekken no keizai shisō ni tsuite," *Chiba Daigaku kyōeibu kenkyū hōkoku* A-3 (1970): 43–74.

38. *Ekken zenshū*, 6:2. Trans. by Robert Wargo in Okada Takehiko, "Yamazaki Ansai and Kaibara Ekken," in Wm. T. de Bary and I. Bloom, eds., *Principle and Practicality*, p. 270.

39. *Ibid.*, p. 270. It is important to note that while this method of observation was thorough and objective in its design, it does not contain the element of experimentation which was so essential to Francis Bacon's scientific method as developed in *Novum Organum*, published in 1620. It was the combination of theory and experimentation which gave birth to the scientific revolution in seventeenth-century Europe.

40. From the Introduction to *Chikuzen no kuni zokufudoki, Ekken zenshū*, 4:1. Trans. by Robert Wargo in Okada Takehiko, "Yamazaki Ansai and Kaibara Ekken," in Wm. T. de Bary and I. Bloom, eds., *Principle and Practicality*, p. 270.

41. *Ekken zenshū*, 3:320. Trans. by Robert Wargo in Okada Takehiko, "Yamazaki Ansai and Kaibara Ekken," in Wm. T. de Bary and I. Bloom, eds., *Principle and Practicality*, p. 283.

42. *Shinshiroku 6, Ekken zenshū*, 1:146. Trans. by Robert Wargo in Okada Takehiko, "Yamazaki Ansai and Kaibara Ekken," in Wm. T. de Bary and I. Bloom, eds., *Principle and Practicality*, p. 271. This passage reflects something of Ekken's humility, which is frequently noted by his biographers.

43. Okada Takehiko, "Yamazaki Ansai and Kaibara Ekken," in Wm. T. de Bary and I. Bloom, eds., *Principle and Practicality*, p. 276.

44. *Ibid.*, p. 279.

45. *Ibid.*, p. 277. See also Kumida Yoshio, "Kaibara Ekken no yōjōkan no tokushitsu," *Shisō*, no. 528 (June 1968): 82–94.

46. Introduction to *Kafu* in *Ekken zenshū*, 1:120. Trans. by Robert Wargo in Okada Takehiko, "Yamazaki Ansai and Kaibara Ekken," in Wm. T. de Bary and I. Bloom, eds., *Principle and Practicality*, p. 277.

47. *Ibid.* See a similar discussion of these ideas in Tsuji Tetsuo, "Kaibara Ekken no gakumon to hōhō," *Shisō*, vol. 11, no. 605 (Nov. 1974): 57–71.

48. See appendix listing Ekken's collected works.

49. While it is difficult to prove definitively, it has been suggested that Tōken, his wife, may have had a hand in the writing of *Onna daigaku*. See Sakai Atsuharu, "Kaibara Ekken and *Onna-Daigaku*," *Cultural Nippon* 7,4 (Dec. 1939): 43–51. See also the entry for Kaibara Tōken in *Nihon Rekishi Daijiten* (Tokyo: Kawada Shobō, 1956–60), p. 82.

50. *Kuroda kafu* appears in volume five of *Ekken zenshū*. The compilation was continued by Ekken's most noted pupil, Takeda Shun'an, and by later domain scholars over a period of some two hundred years. The work has been considered so valuable as a historical source that it was reissued in 1983. This newly revised edition was done by Fukuoka kobunsho yomukai and published by Bunken shuppansha.

51. Matsuda Michio laments that Ekken's talents were used for such a long period on this "burdensome task" and observes that his remarkable literary output in later years was compensatory for time lost on this project. "Kaibara Ekken no Jugaku" in Matsuda Michio, ed., *Kaibara Ekken, Nihon no meicho*, vol. 14, pp. 14–18. Inoue Tadashi notes that Ekken's prodigious writing after his retirement at the age of seventy occurred despite the losses he suffered in the deaths of his brothers Sonzai and Rakken as well as the wife of his adopted child, Shigeharu. See Inoue Tadashi, *Kaibara Ekken*, pp. 212–215.

52. Inoue Tadashi, *Kaibara Ekken*, p. 253. Mitsutaro Shirai, *Scientific Japan: Past and Present* (Tokyo: National Research Council of Japan, 1926), p. 218. Shirai observes that Ekken classified all natural objects in thirty-seven groups and described 1,362 types of objects in the work proper and 205 kinds in the supplement. See also the article on "Botany" by Yoshito Sinoto in *Science Education in Japan* (Tokyo: Kokusai shuppan insatsusha, 1937). Sinoto cites Ekken's *Yamato honzō* as the "first well-systematized book" relating to botany. (p. 32)

53. See R. Tsunoda, et al., eds., *Sources of Japanese Tradition*, vol. 1, paperback, p. 366. "Kaibara's contributions to the study of nature were nonetheless significant enough to attract the attention of Westerners, among them Dutch visitors, and also the American, Swingle, with the U.S. Agricultural Experimental Station after the Restoration, whose enthusiasm for Kaibara's works led him to collect a complete set of them in first editions."

54. Preface, *Yamato honzō, Ekken zenshū*, 6:7.

55. For a general discussion of Li Shih-chen see *Dictionary of Ming Biography*, pp. 859–864. Various reprints of the *Pen-ts'ao kang mu* were available during the Tokugawa period, and as late as 1931 another edition appeared. See *Dictionary of Ming Biography*, p. 863. For a discussion of its medical significance see William C. Cooper and Nathan Sivin, "Man as a Medicine: Pharmacological and Ritual Aspects of Traditional Therapy Using Drugs Derived From the Human Body." In Shigeru Nakayama and Nathan

Sivin, eds., *Chinese Science: Explorations of an Ancient Tradition* (Cambridge: Massachusetts Institute of Technology Press, 1973), pp. 203–272.

56. Okada Takehiko, "Yamazaki Ansai and Kaibara Ekken," in Wm. T. de Bary and I. Bloom, eds., *Principle and Practicality*, pp. 257–258.

57. Inoue Tadashi, *Kaibara Ekken*, pp. 124–127.

58. "Kaibara Ekken sensei den," *Ekken zenshū*, 1: 38–43. Inoue Tetsujirō, *Nihon Shushigaku no tetsugaku*, pp. 34, 274–278; and Komoguchi Isao and Okada Takehiko, *Andō Seian; Kaibara Ekken*, pp. 97–98.

59. Olaf Graf, *Kaibara Ekiken* (Leiden: E. J. Brill, 1942), p. 244. It should be noted that Graf's study of Ekken, published in German over forty years ago, is a generally sympathetic one. Graf, himself a Catholic priest, does express regret that Ekken did not make any references to Christianity, although Graf feels he must have been aware of its earlier presence in Kyushu. (pp. 275–282) Graf's study gives a detailed account of Ekken's life (pp. 16–157) and an overview of his writings (pp. 158–190). He then proceeds to discuss Ekken's thought, especially his monism of *ch'i* and his disagreements with Chu Hsi (pp. 193–262). Graf also summarizes Ekken's educational philosophy and treatises (*kunmono*) (pp. 283–339) and concludes with a German translation of the *Taigiroku* (*Record of Grave Doubts*). There are at least two major differences between Graf's work and the present study of Ekken. One is the effort here to situate Ekken against the background of Tokugawa society, and the other is the articulation in this work of the religious aspects of his thought. I am grateful to Greta Neelsen for her careful translation work in summarizing Graf's major points in each chapter.

60. George Sansom, *A History of Japan, 1615–1867*, vol. 3 (Stanford: Stanford University Press, 1963), paperback, p. 88.

61. W. G. Aston, *History of Japanese Literature* (London: Wm. Heineman, 1908), p. 237.

# CHAPTER 4

1. R. P. Dore discusses Ekken's religiosity as a reverence for *tenchi* in *Education in Tokugawa Japan*, pp. 34–35. Carmen Blacker has described Ekken's notion of *tenchi* in *Yamato zokkun* in the following manner: "Ekken's idea of *tenchi* was a good deal more personal and anthropopathic than was Chu Hsi's. He envisaged *tenchi* as 'loving' all creatures, but according man special favor in equipping him with a mind which was essentially the same as its own. Man thus owed a great obligation (*taion*) to *tenchi*, and it was his moral way to repay this obligation by according with the mind of *tenchi*," *The Japanese Enlightenment: A Study of the Writings of Fukuzawa Yukichi* (Cam-

bridge: Cambridge University Press, 1964), p. 147. See also a discussion of Ekken's theism in Morishita Sanao, "Kaibara Ekken no tendō shisō," *Rekishi to chiri* 17,5 (May 1925), pp. 412–420. Morishita contrasts the Taoist idea of heaven as "deistic" with the Confucian idea of heaven as "theistic." For a general treatment of the importance of heaven in the Tokugawa period see Matsumoto Sannosuke, "The Idea of Heaven: A Tokugawa Foundation for Natural Rights Theory," in Tetsuo Najita and Irwin Scheiner, eds., *Japanese Thought in the Tokugawa Period* (Chicago: University of Chicago Press, 1978), pp. 181–199.

2. For a discussion of the evolution of the virtue of *jen* in Chinese thought see Wing-tsit Chan, "The Evolution of the Confucian Concept *Jen*," *Philosophy East and West* 4,4 (1955): 295–319. See also Sato Hitoshi's article, "Chu Hsi's 'Treatise on *Jen*,' " in Wing tsit-Chan, ed., *Chu Hsi and Neo-Confucianism* (Honolulu: University of Hawaii Press, 1986), pp. 212–227.

3. In R. Tsunoda, Wm. T. de Bary and D. Keene, eds., *Sources of Japanese Tradition* (New York: Columbia University Press, 1958), paperback, p. 365.

4. These correspondences are referred to in the commentary on the first hexagram (*ch'ien*) in the *Book of Changes*. The terms appear in Chu Hsi's introduction to the *Hsiao hsüeh* (Elementary Learning) and in his "Treatise on *Jen*." See for example *Chu Tzu wen chi* in *Chu Tzu ta ch'üan* (SPPY ed.) 67: 20a–21b, as translated in Wing-tsit Chan's *Source Book*, pp. 593–596. In Ekken's works see *Gojōkun*, *Ekken zenshū* 3: 238, *Shogakkun*, *Ekken zenshū*, 3:7.

5. *Chu Tzu yü-lei* (reprint of 1473 edition, Taipei: Cheng-chung shu-chu, 1970), 20, 24b.

6. This interrelationship and the process of regeneration and growth in the natural and human orders has been discussed by Stanislaus Lokuang:

The principle of Heaven and Earth is perpetual renewal of life. The principle of man is humanity. From creation there is humanity. In the myriad things of the universe there is creation, and in man there is humanity. Perpetual renewal of life in Heaven and Earth passes through four processes, which are Origination, Flourish, Advantage, and Firmness. The spiritual life of man also passes through four processes which are humanity, righteousness, propriety, and wisdom. These belong to the substance of man and the characteristics of the substance. Thus ethical morality and the characteristics of the substance connect with each other.

Stanislaus Lokuang, "Chu Hsi's Theory of Metaphysical Structure." In Wing-tsit Chan, ed., *Chu Hsi and Neo-Confucianism*, pp. 75–76.

7. *Yamato zokkun*, *Ekken zenshū*, 3:47.

8. After Chang Tsai, other Neo-Confucians have similarly stressed this concept of a cosmic filiality. See for example the discussion of this in Monica Ubelhor, "On the Notion of Filial Piety in Wang Ken's Thought." (Paper presented at the Regional Seminar on Neo-Confucianism, Columbia University, March 1981) See also Nakae Tōju's understanding of filiality as translated in *Sources of Japanese Tradition*, pp. 374–375. The importance of filial piety in China has been discussed by Hsieh Yu-wei in his article, "Filial Piety and Chinese Society," in *The Chinese Mind*, ed. by Charles A. Moore, (Honolulu: The University Press of Hawaii, 1971), paperback, pp. 167–187.

9. This same theme of filiality appears in the classical Confucian text of the *Book of Rites* where it states: "Yang-tze said, 'Trees are felled and animals killed (only) at the proper seasons.' The Master said, 'To fell a single tree, or kill a single animal, not at the proper season, is contrary to filial piety'," *Li chi*, trans. by James Legge, vol. 2, chap. 18 (New Hyde Park: University Books, 1967), pp. 227–228. See also, Rodney L. Taylor, "Of Animals and Man: The Confucian Perspective," in Tom Regan, ed., *Animal Sacrifices: Religious Perspectives on the Use of Animals in Science* (Philadelphia: Temple University Press, 1986), pp. 237–263.

10. Kaibara Ekken, *Nōgyō zensho jo* (Tokyo: Iwanami bunko, 1948), p. 29. Jeffrey Marti stresses that Ekken's understanding of harmonizing with nature was particularly important for the peasants. He writes:

. . . ethical activity was not limited to those who could read and understand the classical texts. Indeed, since the text was nature itself, the peasants—who in their daily lives were in closest contact with the natural world—would benefit most by understanding the orderliness of nature and the necessity of acting in accord with that order. By following Nature in their daily activities, such as the planting and harvesting of crops, they would be performing duties as important in a moral sense as the task of ruling the country itself. According to Kaibara, the true purpose of the scholar was in providing the peasants and other classes with the knowledge to channel their activities in directions which would not only be beneficial to themselves but moral as well.

In "Intellectual and Moral Foundations of Empirical Agronomy in Eighteenth-Century Japan," *Select Papers from the Center for Far Eastern Studies, University of Chicago*, No. 2 (1977–78): 52–53.

11. *Chung yung* 22. See Wm. T. de Bary, W. T. Chan and B. Watson, eds., *Sources of Chinese Tradition* (New York, 1960), paperback, pp. 120–121. See also Tu Wei-ming, *Centrality and Commonality: An Essay on Chung yung*, Monograph no. 3 of the Society for Asian and Comparative Philosophy (Honolulu: The University Press of Hawaii, 1976), especially chapter 4.

12. Donald Munro, "Introduction," *Individualism and Holism: Studies in Confucian and Taoist Values* (Ann Arbor: Center for Chinese Studies, University of Michigan, 1985), paperback, p. 21.

13. Tu Wei-ming, "Subjectivity in Liu Tsung-chou," in Donald Munro, ed., *Individualism and Holism*, p. 231. Tu is referring to chapters 29–31 in the *Doctrine of the Mean*.

14. Tu Wei-ming, "The Value of the Human in Classical Confucian Thought," *Confucian Thought: Selfhood as Creative Transformation* (Albany: SUNY Press, 1985), p. 75. Tu also observes that because humans are potentially guardians and co-creators of the universe, "the idea of man as a manipulator and conqueror of nature would also seem to be ruled out." In "Neo-Confucian Ontology: A Preliminary Questioning," *Confucian Thought: Selfhood as Creative Transformation*, p. 158.

15. *Yamato zokkun, Ekken zenshū*, 3: 47–48.

16. As Irene Bloom has expressed it, "Following the lead of the Ch'eng brothers, who saw *jen* as a generative principle, resembling a seed and conveying the impulse to life and growth in the natural world, Chu identified the original substance of the human mind with the mind of heaven and earth and with the creative spirit or life force in the universe." Irene Bloom, "On the Matter of the Mind: The Metaphysical Basis of the Expanded Self," in Donald Munro, ed., *Individualism and Holism*, p. 314. This is more fully developed in the following section on Chu Hsi.

17. *Rakkun, Ekken zenshū*, 3: 605–606.

18. The term *banbutsu no rei* is originally found in *Shu ching, The Chinese Classics*, trans. by James Legge, vol. 3, bk. i, 3. Ekken uses the term repeatedly; see, for example, in *Ekken zenshū, Wazokudōjikun* 3:166; *Gojōkun* 3:236; *Kunshikun* 3:391; *Rakkun* 3:605; and *Yamato zokkun* 3: 47.

19. *Rakkun, Ekken zenshū*, 3: 605. See also *Yamato zokkun, Ekken zenshū* 3: 50–51.

20. *Rakkun, Ekken zenshū*, 3: 631. This is the principle theme of the *Way of Contentment* and is repeated in Ekken's other ethical treatises as well. See the discussion at the end of *Yamato zokkun* on having a natural contentment in harmony with external things in *Ekken zenshū*, 3:99, 105. As Jeffrey Marti has observed, Ekken stressed "the importance of understanding the dynamic relationships of natural activity and of uncovering the proper modes of human activity in response." Jeffrey Marti, "Intellectual and Moral Foundations of Empirical Agronomy in Eighteenth-Century Japan," p. 43.

21. *Rakkun, Ekken zenshū*, 3: 631.

22. Tetsuo Najita, *Visions of Virtue in Tokugawa Japan* (Chicago: University of Chicago Press, 1987), p. 59.

23. *Ibid.*, p. 54. Najita is speaking here of Nishikawa Joken, but his observations apply to Ekken, who also subscribed to the "natural ontology" which Najita describes.

24. *Ibid.*, p. 54. See also Najita's article, "Intellectual Change in Early Eighteenth-Century Tokugawa Confucianism," *Journal of Asian Studies* 34, 4 (1975): 935–936.

25. As Jeffrey Marti writes: "Because [Ekken] saw man and nature as interdependent, he felt that a detailed study of nature was essential to a proper understanding of man and his relationship to the universe." In Jeffrey Marti, "Intellectual and Moral Foundations of Empirical Agronomy in Eighteenth-Century Japan," p. 44.

26. As Mitukuni Yoshida demonstrates in discussing the Chinese concepts of nature, the Changes as described in the *I ching* are:

> . . . identical with heaven and earth, that is to say, with nature. Nature is transformation and this transformation arises out of the two *ch'i* of *yin* and *yang*. The activity of the spirit shows itself in the totality of phenomena; this is transformation. . . . The principles of transformation can be applied as they are directly to the human world, bringing it into correspondence with the Way of Heaven. . . .

Mitukuni Yoshida, "The Chinese Concept of Nature," in *Chinese Science*, ed. by Shigeru Nakayama and Nathan Sivin (Cambridge: MIT Press, 1973), pp. 73 and 74. It is precisely this classical Confucian understanding of change, transformation, and the role of the human that the later Neo-Confucians wished to revitalize and develop with a more comprehensive and metaphysical basis.

27. From the Appended Remarks in the *Book of Changes*. See Richard Wilhelm's discussion in *Heaven, Earth and Man in the Book of Changes* (Seattle: University of Washington Press, 1979), p. 189. Note Ekken's use of this idea in *Taigiroku* (NST, 34, p. 57): "The virtue of ceaseless production we call life." Also in *Gojōkun, Ekken zenshū*, 3: 230–231.

28. Okada Takehiko has cited study of the *Book of Changes* as providing a means for harmonizing with natural law by understanding both transformation and constancy:

> For this reason the *Book of Changes* regards the active mind of nature as the Way and establishes an active orientation toward the world. In fact, the title *Book of Changes* means precisely this. Change means constant transformation. It actually has been treated as having three separate meanings: continual transformation, constancy, simplicity.

Continual transformation means that things are not fixed or still. This is a far-reaching point of view; however, it is essential to know that this is also an unchanging law. Thus to be able to perceive an unchanging law in the midst of ceaseless transformations eases the difficulty of a human life constantly subject to change. Change, in addition to its meaning of continual transformation, also means what is simple and what is constant, though the root meaning retains the sense of continual change. Thus change is based upon a view of the world from the standpoint of activity.

In Rodney L. Taylor, *The Confucian Way of Contemplation* (Columbia: University of South Carolina Press, 1988), pp. 85–86.

29. As Irene Bloom writes: "It is precisely this capacity of the mind to unite with the mind of heaven—that is, to overcome any sense of opposition between self and other and to enter into a productive moral relation with all things—that Chu Hsi understood as the essential character of *jen*, the complete substance of the mind." In Irene Bloom, "On the Matter of the Mind," in Donald Munro, ed., *Individualism and Holism*, p. 314.

30. Tu Wei-ming, "The Continuity of Being: Chinese Visions of Nature," in *Confucian Thought: Selfhood as Creative Transformation*, p. 38.

31. *Ibid.*, p. 39.

32. Tu Wei-ming feels this vital cosmic-humanistic viewpoint is distinctively Confucian and he notes, "It contrasts sharply with the Taoist idea of non-interference on the one hand and the Buddhist concept of detachment on the other." *Ibid.*, p. 43.

Another approach to Confucian cosmology is given by Donald Munro in his essay, "The Family Network, the Stream of Water and the Plant: Picturing Persons in Sung Confucianism." Here he makes useful distinctions between three types of cosmological relationships in the Confucian framework. Using pictorial metaphors he describes these three cosmological theories as: 1) hierarchial (family network), 2) a single ordering unity (stream of water), and 3) organic (plant). In Donald Munro, ed., *Individualism and Holism*, pp. 259–291.

In outlining his cosmology Ekken uses all of these theories. For example, he draws on the hierarchical theme and family metaphor in describing the relation of humans to the universe as that of filial children to their parents. Secondly, he uses the theory of a single ordering unity in nature when he cites the important idea of interpenetration, namely, "Principle is one, its manifestations are diverse." Here *li* can be seen as similar to a stream of water, in other words, a unifying principle that flows through reality. Finally, Ekken relies on the organic metaphor of the human as microcosm and the universe as macrocosm. There is an organic relationship between all forms of reality because they are infused with a common source of life, "ceaseless production and reproduction" (Ch. *sheng, sheng;* Jp. *sei, sei*). For both Chu Hsi and Ekken this is present in the human as *jen,* the dynamic virtue of expansive growth or humaneness.

33. Thus many Japanese Neo-Confucians used Confucian concepts to express indigenous ideas frequently associated with Shinto. In the writings of Hayashi Razan, Yamazaki Ansai, Nakae Tōju, Kumazawa Banzan, and others, the effort to accomodate Confucianism to Shinto is evident. Najita alludes to this process in discussing Tokugawa Confucianism which he sees as "a thought system used initially by Japanese thinkers to order and explain an indigenous ethical and political reality which then triggered a metamorphosis of conceptual thinking that fundamentally altered the intellectual life of Japan." In "Intellectual Change in Early Eighteenth-Century Tokugawa Confucianism," *Journal of Asian Studies* 31, 4 (1975): 931.

34. Kaibara Ekken, *Jingikun,* in *Ekken zenshū* 3: 641–685.

35. As Tu Wei-ming has observed, the philosophers of *ch'i* can not be seen as only materialistic. Rather for them, *"ch'i* was not simply matter but vital force endowed with all-pervasive spirituality." In Tu Wei-ming, "The Continuity of Being: Chinese Visions of Nature," in *Confucian Thought: Selfhood as Creative Transformation,* p. 37.

36. See Wm. T. de Bary, "Neo-Confucian Cultivation and Enlightenment," in his *The Unfolding of Neo-Confucianism,* pp. 155–156 and "Neo-Confucian Individualism and Holism," in Donald Munro, ed., *Individualism and Holism,* p. 335. Also Rodney L. Taylor, "Neo-Confucianism, Sagehood and the Religious Dimension," *Journal of Chinese Philosophy* 2 (1975): 389–415.
Wing-tsit Chan has described Chu's synthesis as follows, "He synthesized Confucius' concept of *jen* (humanity), Mencius' doctrine of humanity and righteousness, the idea of the investigation of things in the *Great Learning,* the teaching of sincerity in the *Doctrine of the Mean,* the yin yang (passive and active cosmic forces) and the Five Agents (Water, Fire, Wood, Metal, Earth) doctrines of Han times (206 B.C.–A.D. 220), and practically all the important ideas of the Neo-Confucianists of early Sung (960–1279). . . ." (*Source Book,* p. 589.)

37. *Chu-Tzu wen chi* in *Chu Tzu ta-ch'üan* (SPPY ed.), 67:21b, trans. by Wing-tsit Chan in *Source Book,* p. 596.

38. See Fung Yu-lan, *A History of Chinese Philosophy* vol. 2, trans. by Derk Bodde (Princeton: Princeton University Press, 1983), paperback, pp. 434–442. See also Wing-tsit Chan, *Source Book,* pp. 460–465.

39. Yamanoi Yū argues that Chu Hsi never gave the *t'ai chi* a position superior to *li* and in fact rarely referred to it in his philosophical remarks. See his article, "The Great Ultimate and Heaven in Chu Hsi's Philosophy"

in Wing-tsit Chan, ed., *Chu Hsi and Neo-Confucianism*, pp. 79–92. In the same volume Teng Aimin summarizes Chu's understanding of the *t'ai chi* as follows: "Chu Hsi held that the Great Ultimate is supreme, infinite, and the highest good, and that it possesses activity and tranquility. All things in the universe are generated from it. It also stands as their archetype and purpose. He asserted that the Great Ultimate is prior to *yin* and *yang* and that principle is prior to material force." See Teng Aimin, "Chu Hsi's Theories of the Great Ultimate," p. 110.

40. T'ang Chün-i cited in David Gedalecia, "Excursion into Substance and Function: The Development of the *T'i-yung* Paradigm in Chu Hsi," *Philosophy East and West* (Oct. 1974), p. 445. This article has been the source of a number of ideas in this section. Also consulted were two papers: Julia Ching, "The Symbolism of the Great Ultimate (*T'ai-chi*): Myth, Religion and Philosophy" (unpublished) and Tomoeda Ryūtarō, "Yi T'oegye and Chu Hsi: Differences in their Theories of Principle and Material Force," in Wm. T. de Bary and J. K. Haboush, eds., *The Rise of Neo-Confucianism in Korea* (New York: Columbia University Press, 1985), pp. 243–260.

41. *Chu-Tzu yü-lei* (reprint of 1473 edition, Taipei: *Cheng-chung shu-chu*, 1970, hereinafter cited as CCSC) 94:10b, p. 3774. Quoted by D. Gedalecia, p. 446.

42. *Chu-Tzu yü-lei*, CCSC, 95:16b, p. 3864. Quoted by D. Gedalacia, p. 445.

43. *Chu-Tzu yü-lei*, CCSC, 94:10a, p. 3773. Quoted by D. Gedalecia, p. 446.

44. T'ang Chün-i, *Chung-kuo*, p. 456. Quoted by D. Gedalecia, p. 446.

45. Although Chu emphasized that principle and material force co-exist, when asked, "Does principle come first and material force follow it?" Chu replied, "Principle and material force as such are not sequential; but when we are reasoning, principle comes first and material force follows it." *Chu-Tzu yü-lei*, CCSC, 1:2b, p. 4.

46. *Hui-an hsien-sheng Chu wen-kung wen chi (Ssu pu ts'ung-k'an)*, 32:26b–27a. Quoted by D. Gedalacia, p. 447.

47. *Chu-Tzu yü-lei*, CCSC, 5:2b, p. 136. Quoted by D. Gedalecia, p. 447.

48. *Yu-tsuan Chu-Tzu ch'üan shu*, 1713 edition, 44:32a–33b. Quoted by D. Gedalecia, p. 448.

49. Quoted by Irene Bloom in "On the Matter of the Mind," in Donald Munro, ed., *Individualism and Holism*, p. 309.

50. *Chu-Tzu yü-lei*, CCSC, 98:6b–7a, pp. 3992–3993. Quoted by D. Gedalecia, p. 448.

51. *Chu-Tzu ch'üan shu* 47: 37a, trans. by Wing-tsit Chan in "The Concept of Man in Chinese Thought," in *Neo-Confucianism, Etc.*, p. 155.

52. *Chu-Tzu ch'üan shu* 47: 3a, trans. by Wing-tsit Chan in "The Concept of Man in Chinese Thought," in *Neo-Confucianism, Etc.*, p. 155.

53. *Chu-Tzu wen-chi*, CTTC, 67: 20a, trans. by Wing-tsit Chan in *Source Book*, p. 594.

54. *Ibid.*, p. 594.

55. *Taigiroku*, in *Kaibara Ekken, Muro Kyūsō. Nihon shisō taikei*, vol. 34 (Tokyo: Iwanami shoten, 1970), pp. 49–52).

56. *Yamato zokkun*, *Ekken zenshū*, 3: 55.

57. See *Creation: The Impact of an Idea*, ed. by D. O'Connor and F. Oakley (New York: Charles Scribner's & Son, 1969), pp. 1–104 for Western approaches to the idea of science. Also Hugh Kearney, *Science and Change 1500–1700* (New York: McGraw Hill, 1971); Mary Boas, *The Scientific Renaissance 1450–1630* (New York: Harper and Row, 1962). For a general discussion of "Science and Confucianism in Tokugawa Japan," see Albert Craig's article in Marius B. Jansen, ed., *Changing Attitudes Toward Moderniztion*, pp. 133–160. Craig acknowledges his debt to Maruyama's interpretive categories of a split between norm and nature leading to the disintegration of the Chu Hsi position in Japan.

58. See David A. Dilworth, "*Jitsugaku* as an Ontological Conception: Continuities and Discontinuities in Early and Mid-Tokugawa Thought," in Wm. T. de Bary and I. Bloom, eds., *Principle and Practicality, p. 472. "Stadial character" (jūsōsei) is a term used by Watsuji Tetsurō in his essay "Nihon bunka jūsōsei," in Watsuji Tetsurō zenshū* (Tokyo: Iwanami shoten, 1963), vol. 17, pp. 377–386.

59. Wm. T. de Bary, *Principle and Practicality*, p. 5.

60. *Ibid.*, p. 5.

61. *Ibid.*, p. 7.

62. *Ibid.*, pp. 19–20.

63. *Ibid.*, p. 171. Note also the comprehensive treatment of these ideas in Wm. T. de Bary, *The Unfolding of Neo-Confucianism*, pp. 141–216.

64. This point is also made by Masayoshi Sugimoto and David Swain, *Science and Culture in Traditional Japan* (Boston: MIT Press, 1978), p. 304.

65. Maruyama Masao, *Studies in the Intellectual History of Tokugawa Japan*. See his discussion of Ekken on pp. 61–68. Maruyama's thesis has come under closer scrutiny in recent years by both Japanese and Western schol-

ars. Jeffrey Marti points out, for example, that the difficulty with Maruyama's overarching schema is that the intentionality of individual thinkers is often subsumed into the larger schema. See his "Intellectual and Moral Foundations of Empirical Agronomy in Eighteenth-Century Japan," p. 41.

66. As de Bary has emphasized, Neo-Confucianism was not as rigid, unchanging, or authoritarian as Maruyama and others have described it. (See his discussion in Wm. T. de Bary and I. Bloom, eds., *Principle and Practicality*, pp. 15–20, 31) Rather, debate and dissent were very much a part of the tradition, so that "conflict and controversy cannot in themselves be taken as signs of disaffection or deviation from Neo-Confucianism as a whole." See Wm. T. de Bary, *Neo-Confucian Orthodoxy and the Learning of the Mind-and-Heart* (New York: Columbia University Press, 1981), p. 210. Ekken is an important example of this dissent within the traditiion. Note de Bary's discussion of the problems of orthodoxy and dissent in his introduction to *The Unfolding of Neo-Confucianism*. See also how his observations on the importance of doubt and independent thinking among Neo-Confucian thinkers in *The Liberal Tradition in China* (New York: Columbia University Press, 1983), pp. 62, 64, 68–69).

67. Irizawa Sōju makes this point quite clearly in his discussion of Ekken's monism of *ch'i*. Irizawa Sōju, *Kaibara Ekken* (Tokyo: Bunkyō shoin, 1954), pp. 31–32.

68. See Abe Yoshio, *Nihon Shushigaku to Chōsen* (Tokyo: Tokyo Daigaku shuppankai, 1965). See also his article on the "Development of Neo-Confucianism in Japan, Korea and China: A Comparative Study," *Acta Asiatica* 19 (1970): 16–39.

69. In addition to his *Nihon Shushigaku to Chōsen* (pp. 494–497 and 520–524) see Abe's discussion of this in "The Influence of Lo Ch'in-shun's *K'un-chih chi* in the Early Edo Period and the State of Practical Learning Among the Students of the Schools of Kinoshita Jun'an and Yamazaki Ansai." Paper presented for the June 1974 ACLS conference in Hawaii on Neo-Confucianism and Practical Learning in the Ming and Early Tokugawa Periods.

70. In Wm. T. de Bary and I. Bloom, eds., *Principle and Practicality*, pp. 375–469. See also Minamoto Ryōen, "The Development of the *Jitsugaku* Concept in the Tokugawa Period," *Philosopohical Studies of Japan* (1975): 61–93.

71. Minamoto Ryōen, "The Development of the *Jitsugaku* Concept in the Tokugawa Period," *Philosophical Studies of Japan* (1975): 67.

72. Minamoto Ryōen, "*Jitsugaku* and Empirical Rationalism in the First Half of the Tokugawa Period," in Wm. T. de Bary and I. Bloom, eds., *Principle and Practicality*, pp. 410–411.

73. *Ibid.*, p. 412.

74. Tetsuo Najita, "Intellectual Change in Early Eighteenth-Century Tokugawa Confucianism," *Journal of Asian Studies* 34,4 (1975): 931–944. See also his discussion of Ekken in his book, *Visions of Virtue in Tokugawa Japan*, pp. 45–48. In this recent work Najita seems to be emphasizing Ekken's practical learning (especially agricultural studies) not as an isolated movement toward empiricism per se, but rather as something directly linked to his ethical concerns, namely to alleviate the sufferings of society.

75. Tetsuo Najita, "Intellectual Change in Early Eighteenth-Century Tokugawa Confucianism," p. 933.

76. *Ibid.*, p. 935.

77. *Ibid.*, p. 936.

78. *Ibid.*, p. 940.

79. *Ibid.*, p. 943.

80. *Ibid.*, p. 943.

81. Tetsuo Najita, *Visions of Virtue in Tokugawa Japan*, pp. 45–46.

82. *Ibid.*, pp. 46–47.

83. *Ibid.*, p. 47. For another view of the connection between ethics and empiricism, see Samuel H. Yamashita, "The Early Life and Thought of Itō Jinsai (1627–1705)," *Harvard Journal of Asiatic Studies* 43 (1983): 453–480.

84. Ishida Ichirō, "Tokugawa Feudal Society and Neo-Confucian Thought," *Philosophical Studies of Japan* 5 (1964): 1–37. See p. 32 for discussion of "secularized religion" which he derives from Ozaki Hiromichi, a leading Christian in the Meiji period.

85. As Wm. T. de Bary, has noted, there are some fundamental problems with Ishida's argument that Neo-Confucianism provided a rationale for the Bakuhan system. (See Wm. T. de Bary and I. Bloom, eds., *Principle and Practicality*, pp. 135–137.) However, Ishida's discussion of Neo-Confucianism and science is quite useful, as is his understanding of the religious aspects of Neo-Confucianism.

86. Indeed, Ekken is said to have read Wang Yang-ming's *Instructions for Practical Learning* at least a dozen times. See Okada Takehiko, "Yamazaki Ansai and Kaibara Ekken," in Wm. T. de Bary and I. Bloom, eds., *Principle and Practicality*, p. 260.

87. See Okada Takehiko, "Yamazaki Ansai and Kaibara Ekken" in Wm. T. de Bary and I. Bloom, eds., *Principle and Practicality*, p. 260. Okada also points out that Ekken was similarly influenced by Feng K'o's attack on

the Lu-Wang school in *Ch'iu-shih pien*, p. 260. Irene Bloom notes that Jung Chao-tso and Yu Ying-shih have both suggested an affinity between Lo Ch'in-shun and Ch'en Chien in their criticisms of Lu Hsiang-shan and Wang Yang-ming. See Irene Bloom, trans., *Knowledge Painfully Acquired*, p. 26.

88. Inoue Tadashi, *Kaibara Ekken*, p. 62.

89. Letter of Ogyū Sorai to Takeda Shun'an, *Ekken shiryō*, 6:69. Quoted by Okada Takehiko, "Yamazaki Ansai and Kaibara Ekken," in Wm. T. de Bary and I. Bloom, eds., *Principle and Practicality*, p. 263. See also a discussion of Sorai and Ekken in Samuel Yamashita's article, "Nature and Artifice in the Writings of Ogyū Sorai (1666–1728)," in Peter Nosco, ed., *Confucianism and Tokugawa Culture*, p. 152.

90. For a discussion of Ekken's criticisms of Jinsai see Inoue Tadashi, "Kaibara Ekken no 'Dōjimon higo' ni tsuite," *Kyushu Daigaku kenkyū hōkoku* (1977), pp. 121–177.

According to Samuel H. Yamashita, Jinsai did acknowledge his affinities with Ekken although he did not see eye to eye with him. See Samuel H. Yamashita, *Compasses and Carpenter's Squares: A Study of Itō Jinsai (1627–1705) and Ogyū Sorai (1666–1728)*, Ph.D. thesis, University of Michigan, 1981, pp. 88–89. Yamashita describes Jinsai's "naturalistic vitalism" as embracing three aspects: 1) the cosmos is in constant flux; 2) the cosmos is composed of an original material force (*ichi genki*); and 3) the chief trait of the cosmos is life or liveliness (*sei*). (pp. 76–78) This vitalistic cosmology is similar to Ekken's. Yamashita argues, however, that Jinsai in fact rejected "the Ch'eng-Chu dualism of principle and material force" at the same time he created "a new dualism of material force and concrete things." (p. 83)

91. This is also true of Yi Yulgok's non-dualism, which is discussed by Young-chan Ro in his book, *Korean Neo-Confucianism of Yi Yulgok* (Albany: SUNY Press, 1988).

92. Irene Bloom, "Philosophy of Lo Ch'in-shun," in Wm. T. de Bary and I. Bloom, eds., *Principle and Practicality*, p. 84.

93. *K'un-chih chi*, 1623 ed. 1:11. Translated by Irene Bloom in *Knowledge Painfully Acquired*, p. 58. The first Japanese version of this text was based on a Korean edition copied by Hayashi Razan. See Abe Yoshio, "Development of Neo-Confucianism in China, Korea and Japan: A Comparative Study," *Acta Asiatica* 19 (1970): 22.

94. *K'un-chih chi*, 1623 ed. 3:3. Translated by Irene Bloom in *Knowledge Painfully Acquired*, p. 173.

95. As de Bary has observed, "Lo believed that he was only amending and not revoking the essential Ch'eng-Chu tradition, which he sought to

defend against an excess of moralistic idealism. A major point in the Neo-Confucian case against Buddhism had been its reaffirmation of the physical world." See Wm. T. de Bary and I. Bloom, eds., *Principle and Practicality*, p. 134. Ekken similarly felt he was emphasizing an important strain in Ch'eng-Chu thought, not departing from it.

96. Okada Takehiko indicates that both the handwritten and the original published version of *Taigiroku* have been preserved. See Wm. T. de Bary and I. Bloom, eds., *Principle and Practicality*, p. 263. He and Professor Inoue have kindly made available to me a photocopy of a hand-written copy of the original text. Along with this text I have relied on the version in *Kaibara Ekken, Muro Kyūsō. Nihon shisō taikei* 34:10–64 (hereafter referred to as *NST*) in consultation with the text in *Ekken zenshū* 2: 149–175.

For discussions of *Taigiroku* see Maki Katsumi, "Kaibara Ekken no ichigenki ni tsuite," *Shinagaku kenkyū* (Oct. 1960): 217–222; and "Kaibara Ekken no uchūkan ni tsuite," *Shinagaku kenkyū* (Nov. 1966): 42–49; and Tsuji Tetsuō, "Kaibara Ekken no gakumon to hōhō," *Shisō* 11, 605 (1974): 57–71. See also Kinugasa Yasuki, *Kinsei Jugaku shisōshi no kenkyū* (Tokyo: Hōsei Daigaku shuppankyoku, 1976), pp. 64–76.

97. Okada Takehiko, "Yamazaki Ansai and Kaibara Ekken," in Wm. T. de Bary and I. Bloom, eds., *Principle and Practicality*, p. 290.

98. Irene Bloom, "Introduction," *Knowledge Painfully Acquired*, p. 1.

99. *Ibid.*, p. 1.

100. *Ibid.*, p. 2.

101. *Taigiroku, NST*, p. 10.

102. *Taigiroku, NST*, p. 10.

103. *Taigiroku, NST*, p. 24.

104. *Taigiroku, NST*, pp. 14–15.

105. That his monism of *ch'i* was closely connected to his ethics is evident from the fact that within the first few pages of *Taigiroku* he argues that one's heavenly nature and one's physical nature are not two separate things. This was similarly argued by Lo Ch'in-shun in *K'un-chih chi*. (See Irene Bloom, "Introduction," *Knowledge Painfully Acquired*, pp. 17–21.) The monism of *ch'i* and the unity of the heavenly and the physical natures was also held by the seventeenth-century Chinese Neo-Confucian, Wang Fu-chih, and by Tai Chen in the following century. See Carson Chang's discussion of these two figures in *The Development of Neo-Confucian Thought*, vol. 2 (New York: Bookman Associates, 1962). Also note Ian McMorran, "Wang Fu-chih and the Neo-Confucian Tradition," in Wm. T. de Bary, ed., *The Unfolding of Neo-Confucianism*, pp. 413–467 and Chung-ying Cheng, "Reason,

Substance and Human Desires in Seventeenth-Century Neo-Confucianism," in Wm. T. de Bary, ed., *The Unfolding of Neo-Confucianism*, pp. 469–509, and Chung-ying Cheng, trans., *Tai Chen's Inquiry Into Goodness* (Honolulu: East-West Center Press, 1971).

106. *Taigiroku, NST*, p. 42. See Appended Remarks on the *Book of Changes*.

107. *Ibid.*, p. 54.

108. *Taigiroku, NST*, p. 43. Wing-tsit Chan, however, indicates that he has not been able to locate the words there. See his translation of *Reflections on Things at Hand*, note 2, p. 5. Okada notes that Ekken may have been arguing on the basis of similar criticisms found in *Shang chih pien* (1440) by K'ung ku Ching-lung, upon which Itō Jinsai also relied. See Okada Takehiko, "Yamazaki Ansai and Kaibara Ekken,"in Wm. T. de Bary and I. Bloom, eds., *Principle and Practicality*, p. 265.

It is important to note that in his discussion with Lu Hsiang-shan, Chu Hsi disclaims any association of the *wu-chi* with a Taosit first principle of nothingness. (*Chu Tzu wen-chi*, SPPY ed. 36: 10a–b and 11b–12a) He also asserts the inseparable qualities of *wu-chi* and *t'ai chi*. De Bary describes Chu's philosophy of these two principles in the following manner: "They were simultaneous aspects of a Way that was in one sense indeterminate and yet in another sense the supreme value and ultimate end of all things." In "Neo-Confucian Individualism and Holism," in Donald Munro, ed., *Individualism and Holism*, p. 337.

While this was no doubt true for Chu, the ongoing debates about the relationship of *wu chi* and *t'ai chi* (and *li* and *ch'i*) throughout the tradition indicate that the matter was by no means definitively settled by Chu's synthesis. That this was such an important issue to Ekken only reflects the vitality of the Neo-Confucian tradition some 500 years later.

109. *Taigiroku, NST*, p. 44.

110. *Ibid.*, p. 39, and discussion following pp. 40–46.

111. See Irene Bloom, "Introduction", *Knowledge Painfully Acquired*, p. 18 and the text, p. 59.

112. *Taigiroku, NST*, p. 39. See the *Book of Changes*, Appended Remarks, 7:18b.

113. *Ibid.*, p. 44.

114. *Ibid.*, pp. 17, 18, and 54. The phrase, "Principle is one, its particularizations are diverse," is thought to have originated with Ch'eng I, *I-ch'uan wen-chi* (Collection of Literary Works by Ch'eng I), 5:126. See Irene Bloom, trans., *Knowledge Painfully Acquired*, p. 65. For the phrase, "Principle is the principle of material force," see *Knowledge Painfully Acquired*, p. 173.

115. *Taigiroku, NST,* p. 54. Ekken is drawing especially on the phrase, "The succession of *yin* and *yang* is called the Way," from the *Book of Changes,* Appended Remarks, 7:7A. Lo Ch'in-shun similarly refers to this frequently. See I. Bloom, trans., *Knowledge Painfully Acquired,* pp. 59, 60, 76, 155, 156.

116. This is also the contention of Maki Katsumi in "Kaibara Ekken no ichigenki ni tsuite," *Shinagaku kenkyū* (Oct. 1960): 217–222, especially p. 220.

117. His opinions on the unity of Confucianism and Shinto are expressed in "Shinju heikō shite ai motorazaru no ron," in *Andō Seian; Kaibara Ekken,* by Komoguchi Isao and Okada Takehiko (Toyko: Meitoku shuppan-sha, 1985), p. 220–221. See also *Jingikun (Precepts concerning the gods), Ekken zenshū* vol. 2. A discussion of these views is in Aoki Yoshinori, "Kaibara Ekken no *Shinju heikō fusō hairon,*" *Shigaku zasshi* 50, 1 (Jan. 1939): 223–239.

118. *Taigiroku, NST,* pp. 17–18.

119. See discussion of this in Ira E. Kasoff, *The Thought of Chang Tsai (1020-1077)* (Cambridge: Cambridge University Press, 1984), pp. 72–76. Irene Bloom summarizes the Sung Neo-Confucian position as follows:

> Chang [Tsai] contraposed the original nature and the discrete physical endowment, identifying the physical endowment as the source of one-sidedness and partiality. Ch'eng I extended this idea by proposing a dichotomy between a common human nature, which is uniformly good by virtue of its association with *li,* and capacity (*ts'ai*), which is variable in its quality owing to its association with clear or turbid *ch'i.* Chu Hsi endors[ed] this idea and recogniz[ed] that it was without classical precedent. . . .

Irene Bloom, "On the Matter of the Mind," in Donald Munro, ed., *Individualism and Holism,* p. 307.

120. See Irene Bloom's analysis of Lo's position in "Introduction," *Knowledge Painfully Acquired,* pp. 17–20. Bloom discusses the arguments for and against the consistency of Lo's view that "the nature is principle."

121. *Taigiroku, NST,* p. 18.

122. *Taigiroku, NST,* p. 19.

123. In this Ekken also followed Lo Ch'in-shun, who saw the emotions as "natural and in conformity with principle." It was only selfishness which must be curbed. See Irene Bloom, "Introduction," *Knowledge Painfully Acquired,* p. 20 and text, p. 121. It is interesting to note the parallel movements in seenteenth-century China, namely, in a similar direction of a monism of *ch'i,* an anti-dualism of heavenly nature and human nature, and a concomitant affirmation of the emotions and feelings. This is developed by Chung-

ying Cheng in his article, "Reason, Substance, and Human Desires in Seventeenth-Century Neo-Confucianism" in Wm. T. de Bary, ed., *The Unfolding of Neo-Confucianism*, pp. 469–509. Cheng cites especially Wang Fu-chih, Yen Yuan, Li Kung, Huang Tsung-hsi, Ch'en Ch'ueh, Li Erh-ch'u, and Fang I-chih as part of this movement against the dualism of the Sung Neo-Confucians.

124. See *Yamato zokkun, Ekken zenshū*, 3: 78, 90–91.

125. *Taigiroku, NST*, p. 49.

126. *Ibid.*, p. 48.

127. *Ibid.*, pp. 49–52.

128. *Ibid.*, pp. 45–46.

129. *Jigoshū, Ekken zenshū*, 3:182–183.

## CHAPTER 5

1. Wm. T. de Bary, *Neo-Confucian Orthodoxy and the Learning of the Mind-and-Heart*, p. 69. The discussion that follows draws upon and develops de Bary's analysis of the significance of the learning of the mind-and-heart. De Bary stresses the importance of seeing this kind of Neo-Confucianism not as a philosophical system but as a "type and method of spirituality." Thus there is a need to study it in greater detail so as "to bring out the more religious aspect of orthodox Neo-Confucianism and suggest the need for a reinterpretation of the main line of development in Neo-Confucian thought." In *Neo-Confucian Orthodoxy and the Learning of the Mind-and-Heart*, p. 210. See also his discussion in *The Liberal Tradition in China* and in *The Message of the Mind*.

2. For a discussion of *shingaku* and its influence on Ansai via T'oegye, see Abe Yoshio, *Nihon Shushigaku to Chōsen* (Tokyo: Tokyo Daigaku shuppan-sha, 1971), pp. 244–246. For an insightful treatment of Ansai's philosophical and spiritual ideas, see Herman Oom's discussion in "Yamazaki Ansai: Repossessing the Way," in *Tokugawa Ideology*, pp. 194–232.

3. Robert Bellah, *Tokugawa Religion* (Boston: Beacon Press, 1957), p. 152. For a discussion of Baigan and *shingaku* see *Tokugawa Religion*, pp. 133–177. Bellah claims that Baigan did not actually use the term *shingaku* but rather *seigaku* to describe his teachings. It was his follower, Teshima Toan, who first used it in 1778, calling it *sekimon shingaku* (see p. 177). De Bary observes that Baigan's teachings, however, corresponded to the Chinese *hsin-hsüeh* and were an outgrowth of the Ch'eng-Chu school. See Wm. T. de Bary, *Neo-Confucian Orthodoxy and the Learning of the Mind-and-Heart*, p. 206.

For a discussion of the spread of *shingaku* in eighteenth-century Japan see Jennifer Robertson, "Rooting the Pine: *Shingaku* Methods of Organization," *Monumenta Nipponica* 34 (1979): 311–332.

4. See Wm. T. de Bary, *Neo-Confucian Orthodoxy and the Learning of the Mind-and-Heart*, pp. 206–208.

5. Ekken's *nenpu* indicates that he was lecturing on Chen's *Heart Classic* in 1665 when he was 35. *Ekken zenshū*, 1:14.

6. Okada Takehiko, "Yamazaki Ansai and Kaibara Ekken," in Wm. T. de Bary and I. Bloom, eds., *Principle and Practicality*, p. 282. Professors Okada and Inoue have made available to me a copy of the *Ganko mokuroku* (from *Kyushu shiryō sōsho*), which lists all the books Ekken read each year. From this and the discussion in Inoue's biography of Ekken one can get a detailed picture of the books with which Ekken was familiar. (See Inoue Tadashi, *Kaibara Ekken*, chapter 7, and the chart on pp. 186–187 where Inoue diagrams the types of books Ekken read.) Inoue indicates that in the first half of his life Ekken read principally Chinese books, whereas in the latter half he read primarily Japanese books.

7. This term has been chosen to emphasize the importance of the process of Confucian education. While learning was seen as a lifetime process for the Confucians, the necessary goal of Confucian education was a deepening of moral knowledge which led to action. Not everyone could expect to become a sage, but all had the obligation or imperative to learn. For a detailed discussion of Ekken's ideas on education, see Olaf Graf, *Kaibara Ekiken*, pp. 284–330.

8. On the human response to this heavenly bestowed nature see Thomas Berry, "Authenticity in Confucian Spirituality," *Riverdale Papers* III.

9. This same idea of repayment for blessings received is at the heart of Ninomiya Sontoku's teachings on *hōtoku* and his formation of societies by that name. See R. C. Armstrong, *Just Before Dawn, the Life and Work of Ninomiya Sontoku* (New York: Macmillan, 1912), pp. 175–195.

10. For a discussion of sagehood as a religious goal, see Rodney L. Taylor, "Neo-Confucianism, Sagehood and the Religious Dimension," *Journal of Chinese Philosophy* 2 (1975): 389–415.

11. In *Gojōkun* Ekken notes that not only humans have the five virtues, but that animals also have their own kind of virtue expressed in relationships and distinctions. See *Gojōkun* in Inoue Tadashi and Araki Kengo, eds., *Kaibara Ekken, Muro Kyūsō, NST* 34, pp. 79–80.

12. Tu Wei-ming, "On Neo-Confucianism and Human Relatedness." In George DeVos and Takao Sufue, eds., *Religion and the Family in East Asia* (Berkeley: University of California Press, 1986), p. 115.

13. In Chinese and Japanese one character is used to designate what we call mind and heart. Consequently there is a need for hyphens to indicate the rational and affective components of *hsin* (Ch.) or *kokoro* (Jp.). The term *shinjutsu* literally means the art or the exercise of the mind-and-heart. In this context, however, it clearly refers to the art of disciplining or cultivating of one's inner self. It is not unlike the idea of spiritual discipline in Western religious traditions. It was the title of one of the chapters of the *Elementary Learning* and in this text appears as a generic term to include the method of rectifying the mind-and-heart recommended in the *Great Learning* and in Chen Te-hsiu's *Heart Classic*.

14. See discussion of these ideas on the importance of the individual learning for himself in chapter 2 of de Bary's book, *The Liberal Tradition in China* (New York: Columbia University Press, 1983).

15. *Yamato zokkun, Ekken zenshū*, 3:77.

16. *Chung yung*: 20. See Wing-tsit Chan, *Source Book in Chinese Philosophy*, p. 107. Chu Hsi used these directives in his Instructions at the White Deer Grotto Academy.

17. *Yamato zokkun, Ekken zenshū*, 3:56.

18. *Yamato zokkun, Ekken zenshū*, 3:57.

19. Wm. T. de Bary, *The Liberal Tradition in China*, pp. 45–48 and 73–74.

20. *Yamato zokkun, Ekken zenshū*, 3:62.

21. *Yamato zokkun, Ekken zenshū*, 3:65.

22. *Yamato zokkun, Ekken zenshū*, 3:65.

23. *Yamato zokkun, Ekken zenshū*, 3:65.

24. *Yamato zokkun, Ekken zenshū*, 3:58.

25. *Yamato zokkun, Ekken zenshū*, 3:55.

26. *Yamato zokkun, Ekken zenshū*, 3:60.

27. *Yamato zokkun, Ekken zenshū*, 3:80.

28. *Yamato zokkun, Ekken zenshū*, 3:78.

29. See de Bary's discussion in *The Liberal Tradition in China*, pp. 17–18 and chapter 2.

30. *Yamato zokkun, Ekken zenshū*, 3:78.

31. *Yamato zokkun, Ekken zenshū*, 3:78.

32. *Yamato zokkun, Ekken zenshū*, 3:90.

33. *Yamato zokkun, Ekken zenshū*, 3:82.

34. *Yamato zokkun, Ekken zenshū*, 3:82.

35. *Yamato zokkun, Ekken zenshū*, 3:87.

36. *Yamato zokkun, Ekken zenshū*, 3:100.

37. *Yamato zokkun, Ekken zenshū*, 3:86.

38. *Yamato zokkun, Ekken zenshū*, 3:105.

39. *Yamato zokkun, Ekken zenshū*, 3:105.

40. *Yamato zokkun, Ekken zenshū*, 3:105.

41. No doubt Ekken's comments on clothing and his earlier discussion of food and drink were inspired by the chapter on "Reverencing the Self," in Chu Hsi's *Elementary Learning*.

## CHAPTER 6

1. Ronald Dore, *Education in Tokugawa Japan*, p. 35.

2. The so-called *Jikkun* (ten ethical treatises) of Ekken include: *Kunshikun* (1703), *Yamato zokkun* (1708), *Wazokudōjikun* (1710), *Rakkun* (1710), *Gojōkun* (1711), *Kadōkun* (1711), *Yōjōkun* (1713), *Shogakkun, Bunkun,* and *Bukun* (dates uncertain). Originally three others were included among his *kunmono*: *Wajikakun* (1687), *Gorinkun* (1703), and *Jingikun*. The *Jikkun* have been collected in two volumes by Tsukamoto Tetsuzō, ed., *Kaibara Ekken* (Tokyo: Yūhōdō shoten, 1927).

3. It has been argued whether Ekken or his wife actually composed *Onna daigaku*. Sakai Atsuharu doubts that Ekken wrote it, but he notes that the work surpassed others of its kind for women. See "Kaibara Ekiken and *Onna-Daigaku*," by Sakai Atsuharu, in *Cultural Nippon* 7, 4 (Dec. 1939): 43–51.
*Yōjōkun*, on the other hand, reflected Ekken's abiding interest in the physical (as well as psychic-spiritual) well-being of the individual. Here Ekken drew on his earlier training as a doctor. For an English translation of *Yōjōkun* see Masao Kunihiro, *Yōjōkun: Japanese Secret of Good Health* (Tokyo: Tokuma shoten, 1974).

4. Ekken's efforts to join Neo-Confucian educational and moral theories with Japanese customs and context can be seen as part of a larger attempt by Japanese *Jugakusha* to adapt Confucian and Neo-Confucian

thought to time, place, and rank. See for example the writings of Nakae Tōju and Kumazawa Banzan.

5. I have followed the edition of *Bukun* in *Ekken zenshū*, 3: 366–389.

6. *Ekken zenshū*, 3: 366, 371–373, 379, 389.

7. *Ekken zenshū*, 3: 366, 373.

8. *Ekken zenshū*, 3: 382–384.

9. *Ekken zenshū*, 3: 372.

10. See Ernest W. Clement, "Instructions of a Mito Prince to His Retainers," *TASJ* 26 (Dec. 1898): 115–153. Similar ideas with regard to the importance of learning are expressed in Mito Mitsukuni's address to the samurai in *Mitogaku zenshū* (Tokyo: Nittō shoin, 1934), vol. 4, pp. 12–20. Also important in regard to urging samurai to join the literary and military arts was the well-known Imagawa letter originally written in 1412. During the Tokugawa period it was used as a school primer and reproduced over 200 times. See a translation of this by Carl Steenstrup, "The Imagawa Letter," *Monumenta Nipponica* 28, 3 (1973): 295–316. An earlier example of a letter addressed to samurai in the Kamakura period is also translated by Steenstrup, "The Gokurakuji Letter," *Monumenta Nipponica* 32, 1 (1977): 1–34. See also William Wilson, *Ideals of the Samurai* (Burbank: Ohara, 1982).

11. On Mito Mitsukuni and Chu Shun-shui see Julia Ching, "The Practical Learning of Chu Shun-shui, 1660–1682," in Wm. T. de Bary and I. Bloom, eds., *Principle and Practicality*, pp. 189–229.

12. Yet he realized occasionally one might have to make a difficult choice between loyalty to one's lord or to one's parents, and he left such decisions up to the individual. "Instructions of a Mito Prince to His Retainers," *TASJ* 26 (1898), p. 130.

13. "Instructions of a Mito Prince to His Retainers," p. 126.

14. *Ibid.*, p. 135.

15. For Japanese versions of *Hagakure* see: *Hagakure* (Tokyo: Tokuma shoten, 1967), also in *Nihon shisō taikei*, vol. 26, and in *Nihon no meicho*, no. 17. For a selected English translation see *Hagakure: The Book of the Samurai*, trans. by W. S. Wilson (Tokyo: Kodansha, 1979) or *Hagakure: A Code to the Way of the Samurai*, trans. by Takao Mukoh (Tokyo: Hokuseido, 1980).

16. Yukio Mishima, for example, was strongly influenced by this text. See Kathryn Sparling, *The Way of the Samurai. Yukio Mishima on 'Hagakure' in Modern Life* (New York: Basic Books, 1977).

17. To bear this sense of loyalty and duty constantly in mind was the ultimate challenge of the samurai. Therefore, the constant readiness to sac-

rifice one's life was the means of single-minded self-discipline. Yamamoto said calmly:

> Bushidō, I have found out, lies in dying. When confronted with two alternatives, life and death, one is to choose death without hesitation. There is nothing particularly difficult; one has only to be resolved and push forward. (Yamamoto Tsunetomo, *Hagakure: A Code to the Way of the Samurai*, trans. by Takako Mukoh, p. 35.) [Elsewhere he urges:] Think anew of yourself as already dead every morning. Every day, in the morning, in a tranquil frame of mind, think of yourself as already dead without fail, cogitating upon a variety of forms of death, picturing your last moments. . . . (Yamamoto Tsunetomo, *Hagakure*, p. 150.)

The starkness of these directives are mitigated by such statements as "the lord-retainer relationship, I believe, is similar to love. That is the fundamental spirit of retainer service, far beyond logical reasoning." (Yamamoto Tsunetomo, *Hagakure*, pp. 92–93.)

18. Yamamoto Tsunetomo, *Hagakure*, p. 91.

19. The numerous treatises of Yamaga Sokō (1622–1685) on the Way of the Warrior are a prime example of an individual's efforts to provide a rationale for the role of the samurai in peacetime. Yamaga, however, rejected the Ch'eng-Chu approach to ethics as too theoretical and impractical and he sought a model in Confucius himself. Yamaga's principal treatises include: *Shidō* (The Way of the Warrior), *Bukyō yoroku* (Fundamentals of the Samurai Creed), *Bukyō honron* (Principal Discourses on the Samurai) and *Haisho zampitsu* (Autobiography in Exile). For a translation of his autobiography see Shizo Uenaka, " 'Last Testament in Exile': Yamaga Sokō's *Haisho zampitsu*," *Monumenta Nipponica* 32,2 (1977): 125–152.

20. Carl Steenstrup, *Hōjō Shigetoki 1198–1261* (London: Curzon Press, 1979), p. 56.

21. Carl Steenstrup, *Hōjō Shigetoki*, p. 82.

22. Carl Steenstrup, *Hōjō Shigetoki*, p. 211.

23. Carl Steenstrup, *Hōjō Shigetoki*, pp. 49–50. This text was called *Yen-shih chia hsün*. It is interesting to note that Ekken frequently quotes Yen, indicating that a familarity with his ethical teachings extended to the Tokugawa period. See for example *Yamato zokkun, Ekken zenshū*, 3: 50.

24. Two of these have been translated by Carl Steenstrup in *Hōjō Shigetoki*. See pp. 139–199.

25. Carl Steenstrup, *Hōjō Shigetoki*, p. 53.

26. See the examples in G. W. Sargent, trans., *The Japanese Family Storehouse* (Cambridge: Cambridge University Press, 1959).

27. *Kadōkun* appears in *Ekken zenshū*, 3: 421–475. Ekken also write a *kakun* which is considerably shorter. It is essentially a condensed version of some of his basic ethical and educational teachings and is not as concerned with economic matters as is his *Kadōkun*. It appears in *Ekken zenshū*, 3: 935–949, and is dated 1687.

28. The role of the merchant, however, was becoming increasingly important in Tokugawa society and a variety of efforts were made to rationalize their role in the political economy. For the most sophisticated treatment of this subject see Tetsuo Najita, *Visions of Virtue in Tokugawa Japan: The Kaitokudō Merchant Acadamy of Osaka*. See also G. W. Sargent, trans., *The Japanese Family Storehouse* (Cambridge: Cambridge University Press, 1950), and Mark Ramseyer, "Thrift and Diligence: House Codes of Tokugawa Merchant Families," *Monumenta Nipponica* 34,2 (Summer 1979): 209–230.

29. *Kadōkun* in *Ekken zenshū*, vol. 3. This is the basic concern of the second chapter, pp. 429–438.

30. *Ibid.* This is the principal theme of chapters four, five, and six.

31. This system, which was reputedly practiced during the Chou dynasty in China, was advocated by many later Confucian reformers. Theoretically, a large square of land was divided into nine equal plots. A plot was given to eight individual families for their own use and the central square was cultivated jointly for the government by all the families.

32. *Ekken zenshū*, 3: 424–425.

33. *Ekken zenshū*, 3: 438.

34. *Ekken zenshū*, 3: 445–447.

35. *Ekken zenshū*, 3: 430.

36. These appear in various *buke* (samurai) anthologies. I have followed the texts in Kondō Hitoshi, ed., *Sengoku jidai: Buke kakun no kenkyū* (Tokyo: Kazama shobō, 1978), "Kuroda shi no kakun," pp. 269–283. Kuroda Nagamasa's *kakun* also appears in Ishii Shirō, ed., *Kinsei buke shisō. NST*, vol. 27 (Tokyo: Iwanami shoten, 1974), pp. 10–32, and in *Nihon kyōiku bunkō* (Tokyo: Dōbunkan, 1910–1911), vol. 1, Kakuhen, pp. 361–387. In the history of education in Fukuoka prefecture the Kuroda lords are cited as beginning a tradition of education in the han which lasted over two hundred years. See *Fukuoka ken kyōiku hyakunen shi*, p. 10. Because Nagamasa incorporated parts of Josui's instructions directly into his text, the contents of the two treatises will be discussed as a unit.

37. "Kuroda shi no kakun," *Sengoku jidai: Buke kakun no kenkyū*. See Josui's treatise, p. 269; Nagamasa's treatise, p. 272.

38. Ekken himself was employed in 1656 by Mitsuyuki to assist in the conversion of the han bureaucracy to a civil administrative system. See Inoue Tadashi, *Kaibara Ekken*, pp. 23–24.

39. "Ise Teijō kakun" in *Nihon kyōiku bunkō*, vol. 1, Kakunhen, pp. 506–523. J. Carey Hall has translated this in "Teijō's Family Instruction: A Samurai's Ethical Bequest to his Posterity (1763)," *Transactions and Proceedings of the Japan Society, London*, 14 (1915–1916): 128–157.

40. "Ise Teijō kakun," in *Nihon kyōiku bunkō*, p. 508.

41. See *Wazokudōjikun* in *Ekken zenshū*, 3: 165–228.

42. *Ekken zenshū*, 3: 165.

43. *Ekken zenshū*, 3: 169–170.

44. *Ekken zenshū*, 3: 171, 184.

45. *Ekken zenshū*, 3: 177. The six arts were ritual, music, archery, charioteering, reading, writing, and arithmetic.

46. *Ekken zenshū*, 3: 180.

47. *Ekken zenshū*, 3: 194–197. At age six, while the reading and writing of *kana* and *kanji* was begun, the formation of sentences was also taught. At age seven, following ancient Confucian tradition, boys and girls were no longer allowed to sit or eat together. The teaching of reading and writing continued and instruction in etiquette was begin. When a child was eight, he was introduced to the *Elementary Learning*. This included the correct manner of standing and sitting, entering and withdrawing, and questioning and replying. Of special importance were the instructions on filiality toward parents and respect for superiors. From the spring of the eighth year, a child practiced both square characters and grass writing. He was also given short sentences to memorize to prepare him for studying the classics. At age ten, the child was taught the five virtues and the five relations and was gradually introduced to the *Four Books* and *Five Classics*. He was also instructed in the cultural and the military arts. At fifteen the child began studying the *Great Learning*, namely, the way of disciplining oneself for ruling the people. Ekken stressed this as especially important for children of high-ranking families so that they would be well prepared when they moved into leadership positions.

48. While he suggested studying the *Classic of Filial Piety* followed by the *Analects*, he placed special emphasis on *Mencius*. He valued this work not only as a means of learning duty, but as a way of studying the proper formation of sentences. He also devised a program of reading the *Four Books* aloud which he calculated, by the number of Chinese characters, would require a year and a half to complete.

In order to understand fully the significance of a particular text, Ekken described the necessary preparation for reading as constituting a kind of ritual of internal and external purification. Likewise, he emphasized the importance of using time wisely for studies yet not hurrying one's goal. This ordered, meditative, and reflective pose in studying was essential to develop a learning that was focused and purposeful rather than diffused or fragmented.

49. *Ekken zenshū*, 3: 203–204. He suggests Japanese histories such as the *Nihonshoki* as well as popular histories. In addition, he mentions the Chinese histories such as *Tso chuan*, the *Han Shu*, *Shih chi*, and Chu Hsi's *T'ung-chien kang mu*.

50. *Ekken zenshū*, 3: 190.

51. *Ekken zenshū*, 3: 197.

52. *Ekken zenshū*, 3: 213–228. Many of the ideas in this section are also contained in *Onna daigaku*. See *Ekken zenshū*, 3: 686–691. An English translation appears in Basil Chamberlain's *Japanese Things* (Rutland, Vt.: Tuttle, 1971, first edition, 1905), pp. 502–509.

53. *Ekken zenshū*, 3: 216.

54. *Ekken zenshū*, 3: 221–227.

55. *Ekken zenshū*, 3: 218. These originally appeared in the *Elementary Learning*.

56. *Dōji-kyō*, in *Nihon kyōiku bunko*, vol. 9, Kyōkasho, pp. 9–13. A translation of this appears in Basil Chamberlain, "A Translation of the 'Dou-zhi Keu': Teachings for the Young," *TASJ* 9,3 (1881): 223–248.

57. Ronald Dore, *Education in Tokugawa Japan*, p. 279.

58. *Ibid*.

59. The Confucian tone is absent only at the beginning and at the end of the text, in the initial injunction to revere the Buddhist and Shinto gods, and in the closing observation on the pathos of life's brevity.

60. For editions of *Gakusoku* see Yoshikawa Kōjirō, ed., *Ogyū Sorai*, *NST*, vol. 36 (Tokyo: Iwanami shoten, 1973), pp. 188–197. Also in Kanaya Osamu, ed., *Ogyū Sorai shū*, Nihon no shisō, vol. 12 (Tokyo: Chikuma shobō, 1970), pp. 23–46. An English translation appears in Richard Minear, "Ogyū Sorai's *Instructions for Students*: A Translation and Commentary," *HJAS* 36 (1976): 5–81.

61. Richard Minear, "Ogyū Sorai's *Instructions for Students*: A Translation and Commentary," *HJAS* 36 (1976), p. 8.

62. He wrote, for example, "[C]onsider the texts with heart and eye; ponder them and ponder them again, and as if by divine inspiration you will perceive their meaning." *Gakusoku* in Yoshikawa Kōjirō, ed., *Ogyū Sorai, NST*, vol. 36, p. 190. (I have followed Minear's translation, pp. 14–15.) As part of this process of approaching texts directly and intuitively, he rejected the need to rely on commentaries. He noted that "The times change, bearing the words along; the words change, bearing the Way along." (*NST*, vol. 36, p. 190. Minear, p. 16.) Nonetheless, what does not pass away is the written word. Therefore, through study and personal effort one could penetrate the meaning of the classics and "become one with them." (*NST*, vol. 36, p. 191. Minear, p. 18.) For Sorai this meant that, "my words, my tone, my spirit, and my intent all became similar to those found in the old literature." (*NST*, vol. 36, p. 191. Minear, p. 18.)

63. *Ogyū Sorai, NST*, vol. 36, p. 192. Minear, p. 20.

64. *Ogyū Sorai, NST*, vol. 36, p. 193. Minear, p. 24.

65. Ekken's educational ideas are still being invoked as important in contemporary times. See the introduction to *Kaibara Ekken* by Matsuda Michio; and Irizawa Sōju, *Kaibara Ekken*. Both have also reproduced the text of *Wazokudōjikun* in modern Japanese so as to make it easily accessible to modern readers. Similarly, *Kadōkun* has been reproduced in modern Japanese. See Saitō Shigeta, *Jinseikun: Kaibara Ekken 'Kadōkun' o yomu* (Tokyo: Mikasa shoten, 1984).

# CHAPTER 7
# CONCLUSION

1. See *Ekken zenshū, Yamato zokkun*, 3:47b, 49a, and 49b.

2. *Ekken zenshū, Rakkun*, 3:606–607.

3. *Ekken zenshū, Yamato zokkun*, 3:48a.

4. Jean Herbert, *Shinto: The Fountainhead of Japan* (New York: Stein & Day, 1967), p. 65.

5. In the Christian tradition, for example, the following texts might be a useful basis of comparative study: On the Early Church Fathers, see the *Philokolia*; also, Johann Arndt, *True Christianity*; Jacob Boehme, *The Way to Christ*; Francisco de Osuna, *The Third Spiritual Alphabet*.

CHAPTER 8
## NOTES TO TRANSLATION OF YAMATO ZOKKUN

1. The five emperors were Shao Hao, Chuan Hsu, Ti K'u, Yao, and Shun. The three kings were: King Yü of the Hsia, King T'ang of the Shang, and King Wen of the Chou.

2. Woman's characters (*onna moji*) refers to the syllabary system of *hiragana* as distinct from Chinese characters (*kanji*). Women usually were not taught *kanji*. In contrast to other Japanese Confucians who wrote only in Chinese characters, Ekken tried to write in more simplified language so as to make Confucian teachings accessible to a wide range of people, including women and commoners. Here he is expressing his concern that he may be doing an injustice to the Way of the sages by oversimplifying their teachings.

3. *Han shu* (SPTK ed.), 65; 18a.

4. The Asuka River originates in Nara Prefecture where it flows northward to Asukamura and empties into the Yamato River. Its pools and shoals were frequently alluded to in literature to suggest the vicissitudes of life.

5. The title literally means "Japanese Popular Teachings." Yamato is an ancient name for Japan which originally referred to the central mountainous region on the Wakayama peninsula.

6. *Ch'un chiu ching-chuan chi-chieh* (SPPY ed.), 13:30a. *Tso chuan. The Chinese Classics*, vol. 5, trans. by James Legge, p. 407.

7. Small case letters are *komoji*, which indicates the use of *hiragana* rather than *kanji*.

8. *Book of History*, Book of Chou, The Great Declaration, *The Chinese Classics*, vol. 3, trans. by James Legge, p. 283. Legge translates the passage as "Heaven and Earth is the parent of all creatures; and of all creatures man is the most highly endowed."

9. *Jen, I, Li, Chih, Hsin* (Chinese); *Jin, Gi, Rei, Chi, Shin* (Japanese).

10. The five relations are the essential components of the Confucian moral system. They were intended to be models of reciprocal moral responsibilities, not simply one-sided obligations. (See *Book of Ritual*, Li Yun chapter.) Mencius relates how the Sage-Emperor Shun appointed Hsieh as minister of education so as to teach morality to the people by means of human relations (*Mencius*, 3A:4). In the *Book of Ritual*, when the Duke of Ai asks Confucius how government is to be effected, he responds, "Husband and wife have their separate functions; between father and son there should be affection; between ruler and minister there should be a strict adherence to their several parts." (*The Sacred Books of the East*, vol. 28, trans. by James Legge, p. 263). These relations are given a special priority and are

known as the Three Bonds. Chu Hsi stressed the importance of these five relations in the articles of the White Deer Hollow Academy. He, however, put parent and child first, wheras Ekken sometimes put Lord and retainer first, no doubt because of the importance of the latter relationship in Tokugawa Japan. For a comprehensive discussion of the conflict between loyalty to ruler and filiality to parents see I. J. McMullen, "Rulers or Fathers? A Casuistical Problem in Early Modern Japanese Thought," *Past and Present*, (August 1987), 116: 56–97.

11. *The Book of Changes*, Appended Remarks, pt. 1 ch. 4, *The Sacred Books of the East*, vol. 16, p. 356. The full passage is translated by James Legge as follows: "The successive movement of the inactive and active operations constitutes what is called the course (of things). That which ensues as the result (of their movement) is goodness; that which shows its completeness is the natures (of men and things). The benevolent see it and call it benevolence. The wise see it and call it wisdom. The common people act daily according to it, yet have no knowledge of it. Thus it is that the course (of things), as seen by the superior man, is seen by few."

12. This is adapted by Ekken from the *Book of Ritual*. Questions of Duke Ai. *The Sacred Books of the East*, vol. 28, trans. by James Legge, p. 269.

13. Note in the *Classic of Filial Piety*, Ch. 9: "Of all (creatures with their different) natures produced by Heaven and Earth, man is the noblest." *Sacred Books of the East*, vol. 3 (Oxford: Clarendon Press, 1879), p. 476.

14. See the *Book of Ritual*, Li Yun. *The Sacred Books of the East*, vol. 27, trans. by James Legge, p. 382. The five colors are: blue, red, yellow, white, and black. The five tastes are: sweet, sour, acrid, bitter, salty. The five sounds are the five tones of the scale. The five smells are: musty, burning, fragrant, raw, rotten. To see how these were utlized in the Han Confucian synthesis, consult Wm. T. de Bary, ed., *Sources of Chinese Tradition*, p. 199.

15. *Yen shih chia-hsün* (SPPY ed.), 5:19a. Yen Chih-t'ui (531–591) was a Chinese Confucian at the end of the Northern and Southern dynasties. His family was well versed in the *Chou li* and *Tso chuan*. He himself was familiar with the texts of *Lao Tzu* and *Chuang Tzu*. He wrote *The Family Instructions of Mr. Yen*.

16. The Five Classics include the early texts of the *Book of Changes*, the *Book of History*, the *Book of Odes*, the *Book of Ritual*, and the *Spring and Autumn Annals*. The Four Books include the *Analects*, the *Great Learning*, the *Doctrine of the Mean*, and *Mencius*. The Four Books were selected by Chu Hsi as the most essential texts for Confucian learning and they became the basis for the civil service examination system, which lasted from 1313 to 1905.

17. *Mencius*, 3A:4.

18. *Hou Han-shu* (Later Han History) (SPTK ed.), 19:12a.

19. Source unidentified.

20. *Book of History*, Book of Chou, The Hounds of Lu, *The Chinese Classics*, vol. 3, p. 348. Ekken is referring to a fuller passage which is translated by Legge in this manner, "By trifling with men he ruins his virtue, by finding his amusement in things he ruins his aims." Ch'eng Hao quoted this passage to warn against memorization, recitation, and acquiring extensive information. See Wing-tsit Chan, trans., *Reflections on Things at Hand*, p. 52. Hereafter this work will be referred to as *Reflections*.

21. *I-shu* (SPPY ed.), 11:9A in *Erh-Ch'eng ch'üan'shu*.

22. *Mencius*, 2A:6. In this passage Mencius illustrates the essential goodness of human nature with the example of a person rescuing a child who is about to fall into a well. Mencius also discusses the four seeds, which are the potential virtues of humaneness, righteousness, decorum, and wisdom. This optimistic view of human nature was the foundation of the Confucian belief in the importance of education to evoke and develop the innate morality of individuals.

23. *Mencius*, 6A:10.

24. This example refers to a poem from the *Book of Odes*. See *The Chinese Classics*, vol. 4, trans. by James Legge, p. 240. The contemporary poet Gary Snyder uses this same allusion in a book of poems titled *Axe Handles*. He cites its use by Lu Chi (261–303). See *Lu Shih-heng chi* (SPPY ed.), 1:1a, Wen fu.

25. All Confucian thinkers warn against learning that is not concerned with the significant goal of moral rectification. Note *Reflections*, Essentials of Learning, #56 and #57, pp. 63–64.

26. See *Analects*, 7:16. The Sage here refers to Confucius.

27. For a discussion of the importance of knowledge and action see *Chu Tzu ch'üan-shu* (3:8a; 3:8b; 3:12b; 3:26a), translated by Chan in *Source Book of Chinese Philosophy*, pp. 609–610. (Hereafter referred to as *Source Book.*) See also *Chu Tzu yü-lei ta-ch'üan* (Kyoto: Chūbun shuppansha, 1973), ch. 9, p. 441.

28. *Chung yung* (*Doctrine of the Mean*), 20:19. For Chu Hsi's discussion of these methods see his comments in *Reflections*, Essentials of Learning, #72, p. 69.

29. *Wei-shu* (Peking: Chung-hua shu-chü, 1974), p. 789.

30. *Analects*, 15:5.

31. The seven emotions are discussed in the Li Yun chapter of the *Book of Ritual*, *Sacred Books of the East*, vol. 27, trans. by James Legge, p. 379.

32. *Wai-shu* (SPPY ed.), 6:2b; 25:2b in *Erh-Ch'eng ch'üan-shu*.

33. Correcting mistakes is an essential component of learning for moral reflection. See Chu Hsi's two chapters on "Correcting Mistakes" in *Reflections*, ch. 5, pp. 154–170 and ch. 12, pp. 268–278.

34. *Tso chuan, The Chinese Classics*, vol. 5, trans. by James Legge, p. 288.

35. This progression of extending knowledge is from the *Great Learning*. See Chu Hsi's chapters on these subjects in *Reflections*, ch. 6, "The Way to Regulate the Family," pp. 171–182 and ch. 7, "On the Principles of Governing the State and Bringing Peace to the World," pp. 202–217.

36. *Kung Tzu chia-yü* (SPPY ed.), 2:6b.

37. *Book of History*, Book of Shang, The Charge to Yüeh, *The Chinese Classics*, vol. 3, p. 257. The passage to which Ekken is referring is translated by Legge as, "The indulged consciousness of goodness is the way to lose that goodness. Boasting of ability is the way to lose the merit it might produce."

38. See *Chu Tzu yü-lei*, 15:4b. Translated by Wing-tsit Chan in *Reflections*, p. 92: "After we understand one layer, there is another layer under it, and after that, another layer. From simple to complex affairs, we must try to understand one after another. From difficult to easy principles, we must try to understand one level after another."

39. *Analects*, 14:25. Note de Bary's discussion of this phrase in his book, *The Liberal Tradition in China*, pp. 21–23.

40. *Analects*, 6:11.

41. *Great Learning*, 6:1.

42. *Analects*, 1:7. In this passage Tzu-hsia describes the qualities of the learned person.

43. *Hsün Tzu*, Encouraging Learning. Translated by Burton Watson, p. 20.

44. The Four Books were designated by Chu Hsi as central to the process of moral education. These, along with Chu's commentaries, became the basis of the civil service examinations. The *Questions Concerning the Great Learning and Questions Concerning the Mean* were Chu Hsi's *Ta-hsüeh huo-wen* and *Chung-yung huo-wen*, respectively.

45. *Elementary Learning* (Ch. *Hsiao hsüeh*, Jp. *Shogaku*) was compiled by Chu Hsi and was intended to precede the *Great Learning*. Its contents are discussed by Ekken in chapter 2. See translation at 65a.

46. These histories are the *Tso chuan*, the *Shih chi*, and the *T'ung-chien kang-mu*. The *Tso chuan* is Tso's commentary on the *Ch'un-ch'iu*. The *Shih chi*

is Ssu-ma Ch'ien's compilation of 130 chapters covering Chinese history from the Yellow Emperor to the second century B.C. The divisions followed in this work became a model for most official histories. *T'ung-chien kang-mu* was said to have been planned by Chu Hsi and executed by his followers. It selected the most important sections of Ssu-ma Kuang's work, *The General Mirror for the Aid of Government*, and arranged them so as to express the moral implications of historical events. The title of Chu's work literally means, "The Structural Principles and Selected Details of the General Mirror."

47. Hsün Tzu (298–238 B.C.). For his biography see *Shih chi*, chapter 75. His writings are compiled in some thirty-two essays which are models of logical coherency and rational persuasiveness. They range from such topics as learning and self-cultivation to government and military affairs, and they emphasize the importance of music and ritual in education.

48. Yang Tzu (Yang Hsiung, 53-18 B.C.). For his biography see *Han shu*, chapter 87. Yang held the doctrine that human nature was a mixture of good and evil. His thought combined Taoist and Confucian elements reflecting the syncretic tendencies of the Han. He was an official in the Han capital and later served under Wang Mang. His two extant works are *Fa-yen* (Model Sayings) which was modeled on the *Analects*, and *T'ai-hsuan ching* (Classic of the Supremely Profound Principle), which imitated the *Book of Changes*. Ch'eng I said of Yang, "His ability was small; his mistakes were few." (*Reflections*, p. 293.)

49. Huai-nan Tzu (d. 122 B.C.) was a prominent Taoist philosopher whose given name was Liu An. As Prince of Huai-nan, he compiled a lengthy manual of some twenty-one chapters outlining such topics as cosmogony, principles of government, military strategy, and human affairs.

50. *Wen-chung Tzu*. This is a compilation of the conversations of the Sui Confucian scholar Wang T'ung (584–617) and his disciples. It was also known as the *Chung-shuo* and consisted of ten chapters with such headings as "The Kingly Way," "Heaven and Earth," "The Duke of Chou," and "The Book of Ritual." Wang T'ung is considered by Wing-tsit Chan to be the greatest Confucian between the third and seventh centuries. Both Ch'eng I and Chu Hsi seemed to feel that Wen-chung Tzu's book was composed by other people and that it is difficult to determine which are authentic passages and which are not (See *Reflections*, pp. 99 and 297).

51. *Shuo-yüan* (Collection of Discourses). This was a compilation of Liu Hsiang (77–76 B.C.). who was a prominent government official and author. The work was divided into sections such as Honoring Virtue, Repaying Obligations, and the Way of the Lord. It was brought to Japan in the Heian period.

52. Note discussion in *Mencius*, 4B:15, "Learn widely and go into what you have learned in detail so that in the end you can return to the essential." Translation by D. C. Lau (Baltimore: Penguin Books, 1970), p. 130.

53. *Wai-shu* (SPPY ed.), 6:9a; 34:16b in *Erh-Ch'eng ch'üan-shu.*

54. On daily renewal see the *Great Learning*, ch. 2. See also Chu Hsi's discussion of daily renewal in *Reflections*, Essentials of Learning #67, p. 68.

55. This echoes *Mencius*, 4A:27.

56. Note Ch'eng I's similar advice: "When we read, we must first of all understand the meanings of the words. Only then can we find out the ideas of the text. It has never been possible to understand the ideas without knowing the meanings of the words." (*Reflections*, p. 97.)

57. *Chin shu* (SPTK ed.), 66:7a–b. Attributed to T'ao Kan (259–334).

58. *Shi nō kō shō;* these were the four classes of Tokugawa society.

59. Source unidentified.

60. *Hsün Tzu* (SPPY ed.), 1:11b.

61. *Tso chuan. The Chinese Classics*, vol. 5, trans. by James Legge, p. 313.

62. *Huai-nan Tzu*, (SPPY ed.), 1:9b. Yuan-tao hsün (Instructions on the Origin of the Tao).

63. T'ao Yüan-ming, Miscellaneous Poems. For English translations of this poem see: *The Poetry of T'ao Ch'ien*, translated by James R. Hightower (Oxford: Clarendon Press, 1970), p. 185; and *Sunflower Splendor*, co-edited by Wu-chi Liu and Irving Yucheng Lo (Bloomington: Indiana University Press, 1975), pp. 55–56.

64. *Ku-shih yüan* (SPPY ed.), 3:9b. Poem by anonymous author titled, "Ch'ang-ko hsing."

65. *Hsün Tzu*, Encouraging Learning. Trans. by Burton Watson, pp. 14 and 19.

66. For a discussion of the uses of the *Elementary Learning* in Confucian education see Wm. T. de Bary, *The Unfolding of Neo-Confucianism*, pp. 9 and 10; also see de Bary, *The Learning of the Mind-and-Heart*, pp. 136, 145, and 146.

67. In the *Analects*, 19:12 these are described as the branches of learning. They were used in Chu Hsi's *Hsiao hsüeh* (Elementary Learning) as a method of beginning to study. For further discussion of this topic see de Bary, *The Learning of the Mind-and-Heart*, p. 136.

68. Ch'eng I taught that the character *ch'in (to love)* should be read *hsin* (to renew or renovate). See his revision of the text of the *Great Learning* in *Ching-shuo* in *Erh-Ch'eng ch'üan-shu* (SPPY ed.), 5:3a. Chu Hsi followed this reading of the passage while Wang Yang-ming emphasized the reading of "loving the people." See Wang's discussion in his "Inquiry on the Great

Learning," translated by W. T. Chan in *Instructions for Practical Living and Other Neo-Confucian Writings by Wang Yang-ming* (New York: Columbia University Press, 1963), p. 276.

69. *Kuo-yü (Conversations of the States)* (SPPY ed.), 5:9a. This is a book which records the history of the Spring and Autumn period as related by Tso Ch'iu-ming.

70. The traditional position of the emperor was facing south (see *Analects*, 6:1 and 15:4), while retainers would sit below him. However, because a teacher was held in higher esteem than a retainer, he would sit to the side of the emperor.

71. *Kung Tzu chia-yü* (SPPY ed.), 9:3b.

72. *Analects*, 17:2.

73. *Wai-shu* (SPPY ed.), 2A:3b, 2B:4a in *Erh-Ch'eng ch'üan-shu*.

74. The *I-wei* recorded predictions of good and evil, fortune and misfortune. It contains sections on the stars, on the heavens, on heaven and earth, and on the spirits. It is considered to be an apocryphal text.

75. *Lao Tzu*, chapter 64.

76. The distinction between true knowledge and small knowledge has been an important one in Confucian studies. Note Chang Tsai's observations in Chapter 6 of *Cheng-meng*, (Correcting Youthful Ignorance): "Knowledge gained through enlightenment which is the result of sincerity is the innate knowledge of one's natural character. It is not the small knowledge of what is heard or what is seen." (Chan, *Source Book*, p. 507.)

77. *Analects*, 14:25. See discussion in de Bary, *The Liberal Tradition in China*, pp. 21–23.

78. *Analects*, 6:11.

79. *Yang Tzu Fa-yen* (SPTK ed.), 1:3a.

80. *Chou-i cheng-i* (Correct Meaning of the Book of Changes). This is a commentary on the *Book of Changes* compiled primarily by K'ung Ying-ta of the T'ang who lived from 574–648. He was commissioned to write commentaries on each of the five classics.

81. *Hou-Han shu*, (Later Han History), (SPTK ed.), 19:12a.

82. Source unidentified.

83. Source unidentified.

84. Source unidentified.

85. *Wei shu* (Peking: Chung-hua shu-chü, 1974), p. 789.

86. *Analects*, 4:8.

87. *Book of History*, Announcement of Chung Hui. *The Chinese Classics*, vol. 3, trans. by James Legge, p. 182.

88. Ch'en Chi-ju (1558–1639) was a Ming literary figure who wrote compositions from his youth. He was considered a superior poet, writer, calligrapher, and artist. He built a house on Tung Yu mountain in the Shanghai region and was engaged principally in writing. However, his fame spread, and people came from various regions to receive his instructions. A collection of his writings remains.

89. *Book of History*, Counsels of Great Yü, *The Chinese Classics*, vol. 3, trans. by James Legge, pp. 61–62. In this section the character for mind-and-heart is translated as "mind" or "heart" respectively for smoothness of style as well as to emphasize different aspects of a single reality.

90. *Book of Poetry*, Odes to the Temple and Altar, Sacrificial Odes of Chou, The Decade of Ch'ing Miao, Wo Chien. *The Chinese Classics*, vol. 4, trans. by James Legge, p. 576.

91. *Mencius*, 2A:6. This whole paragraph is adapted from this section of *Mencius*.

92. *Mencius*, 6A:11.

93. *Book of Changes*, Hsi-tz'u chuan. *Sacred Books of the East*, vol. 16, p. 381. James Legge translates this passage as follows: "The great attribute of heaven and earth is the giving and maintaining of life."

94. This important Neo-Confucian phrase appears in the complete works of the two Ch'engs, *Erh Ch'eng ch'üan-shu, I-shu* (SPPY ed.), 2A:3a. Translated in Wing-tsit Chan, *Source Book*, p. 523.

95. *Book of Ritual*, The Meaning of Sacrifices. *Sacred Books of the East*, vol. 28, trans. by James Legge, pp. 227–228.

96. Mo Tzu was a philosopher of the Spring and Autumn period who advocated universal love in contrast to the Confucians, who advocated a doctrine of love with distinctions such as is expressed in the five relations.

97. *Analects*, 5:11; *Doctrine of the Mean*, ch. 13.

98. *Analects*, 6:28.

99. *Chu Tzu ta-ch'üan* (SPPY ed.), 37:5b. From Chu Hsi's letter to Fan Chih-ko.

100. Source unidentified.

101. In *Tso chuan*, *The Chinese Classics*, vol. 5, trans. by James Legge, p. 288.

102. Source unidentified.

103. Source unidentified.

104. *Sun-chih chai chi* (SPPY ed.), 1:33b. Fang Hsiao-ju (1368–1444) was a Neo-Confucian scholar and statesman of the early Ming period. He was an advisor to Emperor Chu Yun-wen, the grandson of the Ming founder, who was eventually overthrown by his uncle, Chu Ti. This usurper failed to persuade Fang to write a rescript proclaiming his legitimate succession. Fang denounced Chu Ti and was sentenced to be tortured. Fang achieved something of a martyr's status for his courageous moral stance. For further details see *Dictionary of Ming Biography*, Carrington Goodrich and Chaoying Fang, eds., (New York: Columbia University Press, 1976), pp. 423–433.

105. *Ts'ai-ken t'an* (*Saikontan*) by Hung Tzu-ch'eng (fl. 1596) in Imai Usaburō, ed., *Chūgoku koten shinshō* (Tokyo: Meitoku shuppansha, 1967), vol. 6, p. 302. See the English translation by William Scott Wilson, *The Roots of Wisdom* (Tokyo: Kōdansha International, 1985), p. 143.

106. The *Shan-yu wen* (TSCC ed.), by Ch'en Lu (fl. 1221), p. 1.

107. See *Mencius*, 1A:2; 1B:1; 1B:4 for discussions of the importance of the ruler sharing his enjoyments with the people.

108. This doctrine of universal brotherhood and its expression in compassionate activity for others is a cornerstone of Confucian thought, which found one of its highest expressions in Chang Tsai's "Western Inscription." See Wing-tsit Chan, *Source Book*, pp. 497–500. See also *Book of Ritual*, Li Yun chapter, which says that when a public spirit ruled, then the people "showed kindness and compassion to widows, orphans, childless men, and those who were disabled by disease, so that they were all sufficiently maintained." In *Sacred Books of the East*, vol. 27, trans. by James Legge, p. 365.

109. From the *Ku-chin shih-wen lei-chu* (Compilation of Affairs and Culture) by Chu Mu of the Sung, a disciple of Chu Hsi. The text is divided into sections on the Way of Heaven, on the Seasons, on Geography, and on Imperial Lineage. (*Wen-yüan ko ssu-k'u ch'üan-shu* ed.) pieh-chi, 32:14a.

110. Source unidentified.

111. *Chung yung* (The Doctrine of the Mean), 20:18.

112. *Analects*, 1:8, 2.

113. *I-shu* (SPPY ed.), 11:8a, in *Erh Ch'eng ch'üan-shu*.

114. *Doctrine of the Mean*, ch. 25.

115. *Tsurezuregusa* (Essays in Idleness) by Yoshida Kenko, chapter 85, Commentary on the Ancients. See *Tsurezuregusa kaishakutaisei* (Tokyo: Iwasaki shoten, 1967), p. 562.

116. Wang Mang (45 B.C.–23 A.D.) was a ruler of the Hsin dynasty (9–23 A.D.). He was enamored of certain apocryphal Confucian literature which had developed in the Former Han period and he used these works to support his position of divine election following his overthrow of the Former Han dynasty. He also created a genealogy to trace his roots back to the Yellow Emperor and legitimize his rule. Wang instituted a land reform based on the well-field system. However, this failed, as did most of his other attempted reforms in the area of economics.

Wang Ching-kung (Wang An-shih, 1021–1086) also promoted economic reforms based on ancient practices, including the well-field system. When he retired from government office and taught at his own home, he practiced the well-field system himself.

117. From *San-kuo chih* (History of the Three Kingdoms), compiled by Ch'en Shou. (SPTK ed.), 8:14a.

118. The *Great Learning*, ch. 6.

119. *Book of Changes*, Appendices, Section 2, Hexagram 41. *Sacred Books of the East*, vol. 16, p. 317.

120. For a similar discussion see *Chu Tzu yü-lei*, 52:76-8a. Translated by Wing-tsit Chan in *Reflections*, p. 149.

121. This is a gloss on a passage in *Shih ching hsü* (Preface to the *Book of Odes*), *The Chinese Classics*, vol. 4, appendix 1, trans. by James Legge, p. 36.

122. Source unidentified.

123. *Mencius*, 6A:15, 2.

124. *Analects*, 12:22.

125. *Analects*, 12:1. This phrase is frequently quoted by Neo-Confucians. See de Bary's discussion in *The Liberal Tradition in China*, pp. 24–27.

126. *Book of History*, Book of Chou, Chun Ch'in. *The Chinese Classics*, vol. 3, trans. by James Legge, p. 542.

127. *Ibid*.

128. Tu Mu, *Fan-Ch'uan shih-chi* (SPPY ed.), 4:21b.

129. *Shih-hua tsung-kuei* (SPTK ed.), 30:2b.

130. *The Book of Odes*, The Sacrificial Odes of Chou, The Decade of Shu Kung, *The Chinese Classics*, vol. 4, trans. by James Legge, p. 585.

131. *The Book of Odes*, Lessons from the States, Odes of P'ei, Mao Ch'iu. *The Chinese Classics*, vol. 4, trans. by James Legge, p. 60.

132. *Analects*, 7:30.

133. Actually the original intention of this saying was to imply that combining caution and discretion leads to being overly careful or even foolishly fastidious. See *Rigen Daijiten*, Nakano Kichihei, ed. (Tokyo: Tōhō shoin, 1933), p. 994.

134. There is a mistake in the text here, as it should read King Wu and not *bushi* (samurai). This inscription of King Wu can be found in *Ta Tai li-chi* (SPTK ed.), 6:2b. I am grateful to Ron-Guey Chu for discovering this discrepancy and for locationg the source of the quotation.

135. *Hsün Tzu*, A Discussion of Heaven. Trans. by Burton Watson, p. 81.

136. *Shih-chi* (SPTK ed.), 68: 14b.

137. See *Book of History*, Book of Shang, Announcement of Chung Hui, *The Chinese Classics*, vol. 3, trans. by James Legge, p. 182.

138. Source unidentified.

139. Liu I-chih (1078–1160). Hsing-chien was his *hao* (honorific name). *T'iao-hsi chi* (Ssu-k'u ch'üan-shu chen-pen), 11:9b.

140. Chia I was a scholar and literary figure of the former Han who lived from 200 to 168 B.C. *Hsin-shu* (SPTK ed.), 1:7a.

141. *Book of Ritual*, Record of Music, *Sacred Books of the East*, vol. 28, trans. by James Legge, p. 125.

142. *Lao Tzu*, chapter 33.

143. This is a gloss on a passage in the *Book of Changes*. See *Sacred Books of the East*, vol. 16, trans. by James Legge, p. 153.

144. Hsi-men Pao served the Lord of Wei at the beginning of the Warring States period. He stopped a custom of sacrificing a young woman to the river god which the local shamans had encouraged and he instituted a program for digging canals and irrigating the fields.

145. An allusion to *Analects*, 15:26.

146. *Han-shih wai chuan* was a compilation of the Han scholar, Han Ying, and consisted of sayings selected from the *Book of Poetry*. This quote

is from chapter 1, section 13. See translation by James R. Hightower, *Han-Shih Wai Chuan* (Cambridge: Harvard University Press, 1952), p. 23.

147. *Analects*, 1:16.

148. The *Pao-p'u Tzu* was compiled in the Chin dynasty by Ko Hung and was said to be completed around 317 A.D. It contains two major sections: one is concerned with Taoism and contains descriptions of the alchemical techniques of the Taoist hermits; the other section deals with Confucianism and discusses correct government and moral behavior. *Pao-p'u Tzu* (SPTK ed.), wai-p'ien, 39:11a.

149. *Book of Ritual*, Record of Music, Section 2, 19. *Sacred Books of the East*, vol. 28, trans. by James Legge, p. 112.

150. Yen Hui was Confucius' favorite disciple.

151. In a modern version of *Yamato zokkun* edited by Matsuda Michio in *Kaibara Ekken* (Tokyo, 1969), Hsü Hsiao-chieh is identified as a scholar of the Six dynasties period. (p. 121) For a biography of Hsü Hsiao-chieh see *Ch'en-shu* (Peking: Chung-hua shu-chu, 1972), pp. 188–190. There is no reference in the biography to the passage quoted here. Apparently this scholar's name has been mistakenly reversed in the text. His name was Hsü Chi (1028–1103), and his posthumous title was Chieh-hsiao. A reference to this passage can be found in *San-ch'ao ming-ch'en yen-hsing lu* (SPTK ed.), 14D:5b. I am grateful to Ron-Guey Chu for discovering this discrepancy and for locating the source of the quotation.

152. This is based on a similar saying from the *Ho-kuan Tzu* (SPPY ed.), 1:9b. "If you can cover your eye with one leaf you cannot see a large mountain."

153. Shan-ku was a Sung poet. *Shan-ku shih chi-chu* (SPPY ed.), 4:1a.

154. Source unidentified.

155. *Book of History*, Book of Chou, Chun Ch'in. *The Chinese Classics*, vol. 3, trans. by James Legge, p. 542.

156. An allusion to *Tso chuan*. *The Chinese Classics*, vol. 5, trans. by James Legge, p. 562.

157. *Analects*, 15:20. James Legge translated this passage, "What the superior man seeks is in himself; what the mean man seeks is in others." *The Chinese Classics*, vol. 1, p. 300.

158. *Book of History*, Book of Shang, Announcement of Chung Hui. *The Chinese Classics*, vol. 3, trans. by James Legge, p. 182.

159. Source unidentified.

160. *Analects*, 20:3, 1.

# Glossary of Names, Terms, and Titles Cited in Part I

| | |
|---|---|
| Abe Yoshio | 阿部吉雄 |
| Andō Seian | 安藤省庵 |
| Arai Hakuseki | 新井白石 |
| bakufu | 幕府 |
| bakuhan | 幕藩 |
| banbutsu no rei | 萬物の靈 |
| bu; bun | 武；文 |
| bushidō | 武士道 |
| Chang Tsai | 張載 |
| Ch'en Chien | 陳建 |
| Ch'en Pai-sha (Ch' en Hsien-chang) | 陳白沙 |
| Chen Te-hsiu | 眞德秀 |
| ch'eng (Ch.) makoto (Jp.) | 誠 |
| Ch'eng I-ch'uan (Ch'eng I) | 程伊川 |
| ch'eng i (Ch.) seii (Jp.) | 誠意 |
| Ch'eng Ming-tao (Ch'eng Hao) | 程明道 |
| ch'i (Ch.) ki (Jp.) | 気 |
| chih (Ch.) kokorozashi (Jp.) | 志 |
| chih chih (Ch.) shichi (Jp.) | 致知 |
| Chikamatsu Monzaemon | 近松門左衛門 |

| | |
|---|---|
| Chikuzen | 筑前 |
| *Chin-ssu lu* (Ch.) *Kinshiroku* (Jp.) | 近思録 |
| ching (Ch.) kei (Jp.) | 敬 |
| Ch'iu Chün | 邱濬 |
| ch'iung li (Cho) kyūri (Jp.) | 究理 |
| chōnin | 町人 |
| Chou Tun-i | 周敦頤 |
| chu ching (Ch.) kyo kei (Jp.) | 居敬 |
| Chu Hsi (Ch.) Shushi (Jp.) | 朱熹 |
| chun tzu (Ch.) kunshi (Jp.) | 君子 |
| chung (Ch.) chū, naka (Jp.) | 中 |
| chung (Ch.) chū (Jp.) | 忠 |
| *Chung-yung* (Ch.) *Chūyō* (Jp.) | 中庸 |
| daimyō | 大名 |
| *Dōji-kyō* | 童子教 |
| fudai | 譜代 |
| Fujiwara Seika | 藤原惺窩 |
| Fukuoka | 福岡 |
| genpuku | 元服 |
| Genroku | 元禄 |
| *Hagakure* | 葉隠 |
| Hakata | 博多 |
| han | 藩 |
| hankō | 藩校 |
| *Han shu* | 漢書 |
| hatamoto | 旗本 |
| Hayashi Gahō | 林鵞峰 |
| Hayashi Razan | 林羅山 |

| | |
|---|---|
| *Heiji monogatari* | 平治物語 |
| *Heike monogatari* | 平家物語 |
| heinō bunri | 兵農分離 |
| *Hōgen monogatari* | 保元物語 |
| Hoshino Sanenobu | 星野實宣 |
| hōtoku | 報德 |
| Hsiao-hsüeh (Ch.) Shōgaku (Jp.) | 小學 |
| hsiao-jen (Ch.) shōjin (Jp.) | 小人 |
| hsin (Ch.) shin, kokoro (Jp.) | 心 |
| *Hsin ching* (Ch.) *Shinkyō* (Jp.) | 心經 |
| *Hsin-ching fu-chu* | 心經附註 |
| hsin hsüeh (Ch.) shingaku (Jp.) | 心學 |
| hsin min (Ch.) shin min (Jp.) | 親民 |
| hsing (Ch.) sei (Jp.) | 性 |
| Hsü Heng | 許衡 |
| *Hsüeh p'u t'ung-pien* | 學蔀通辯 |
| *Hua-Yen fa-chieh kuan* | 華嚴法界觀 |
| i (Ch.) gi (Jp.) | 義 |
| i (Ch.) i (Jp.) | 意 |
| *I Ching* (Ch.) *Ekikyō* (Jp.) | 易經 |
| Inao Jakusui | 稻生若水 |
| Inoue Tadashi | 井上忠 |
| Inoue Tetsujirō | 井上哲次郎 |
| Ise Teijō | 伊勢貞丈 |
| Ishida Baigan | 石田梅岩 |
| Ishida Ichirō | 石田一郎 |
| Ishikawa Jōzan | 石川丈山 |
| Itō Jinsai | 伊藤仁齊 |

| | |
|---|---|
| jen (Ch.) jin (Jp.) | 仁 |
| jen hsin (Ch.) jin shin (Jp.) | 人心 |
| jitsugaku | 實學 |
| jugakusha; jusha | 儒學者；儒者 |
| juyō no gaku | 受用の學 |
| Kaibara Atsunobu | 貝原篤信 |
| *also*      Sonken | 損軒 |
| Ekken | 益軒 |
| Jūsai | 柔齊 |
| Kaibara Ichibei (Ekken's grandfather) | 貝原市兵衛 |
| *also*  Kyūbei | 久兵衛 |
| Sōgi | 宗喜 |
| Kaibara Mototada (Ekken's brother) | 貝原元端 |
| *also*  Sonzai | 存齊 |
| Kaibara Toshisada (Ekken's father) | 貝原利貞 |
| *also*  Kansai | 寬齊 |
| Kaibara Yoshitada (Ekken's brother) | 貝原義質 |
| *also*  Rakken | 楽軒 |
| kakun | 家訓 |
| kana | 仮名 |
| kanbun | 漢文 |
| kigaku | 気學 |
| kinoshisō | 気の思想 |
| Kinoshita Jun'an | 木下順庵 |
| Kogaku | 古學 |
| koku | 石 |
| kokudaka | 石高 |
| Kokugaku | 國學 |

| | |
|---|---|
| ko wu (Ch.) kakubutsu (Jp.) | 格物 |
| kuge | 公卿 |
| Kumazawa Banzan | 熊沢番山 |
| *K'un-chih chi* | 困知記 |
| kunmono | 訓もの |
| Kuroda Josui | 黒田如水 |
| Kuroda Mitsuyuki | 黒田光久 |
| Kuroda Tadayuki | 黒田忠久 |
| Kuroda Tsunamasa | 黒田綱正 |
| Kurokawa Dōyū | 黒川道祐 |
| Kusunoki Masashige | 楠木正成 |
| li (Ch.) ri (Jp.) | 理 |
| li-i fen-shu (Ch.) riichi bunshu (Jp.) | 理一分殊 |
| Li Shih-chen | 李時珍 |
| liang chih (Ch.) ryōchi (Jp.) | 良知 |
| Lo Ch'in-shun | 羅欽順 |
| Lu Hsiang-shan | 陸象山 |
| *Lun-yü* (Ch.) *Rongō* (Jp.) | 論語 |
| Maruyama Masao | 丸山眞男 |
| Matsunaga Sekigo | 松永五尺 |
| Matsuo Bashō | 松尾芭蕉 |
| Matsushita Kenrin | 松下見林 |
| Meng Tzu (Ch.) Mōshi (Jp.) [Mencius] | 孟子 |
| Minamoto Ryōen | 源了園 |
| ming ming-te (Ch.) mei mei toku (Jp.) | 明明徳 |
| Miyazaki Yasusada | 宮崎安貞 |
| Mukai Genshō | 向井元升 |
| Nagasaki | 長崎 |

| | |
|---|---|
| Nakae Tōju | 中江藤樹 |
| *Nōgyō zensho* | 農業全書 |
| Oda Nobunaga | 織田信長 |
| Ogyū Sorai | 荻生徂徠 |
| Okada Takehiko | 岡田武彦 |
| *Onna daigaku* | 女大學 |
| Ōno Hokkai | 大野北海 |
| pen-hsin (Ch.) honshin (Jp.) | 本心 |
| *Pen-ts'ao kang-mu* (Ch.) *Honzō komoku* (Jp.) | 本草綱目 |
| rigaku | 理學 |
| ri no jōhen | 理の常変 |
| rōnin | 浪人 |
| sakoku | 鎖国 |
| samurai | 士；侍 |
| sankin kōtai | 参勤交代 |
| seidō | 聖堂 |
| seigaku | 性學 |
| seiri | 性理 |
| Sekigahara | 関ヶ原 |
| *Setsuyōshū* | 節用集 |
| sheng sheng (Ch.) sei sei (Jp.) | 生生 |
| *Shih chi* | 史記 |
| shijuku | 私塾 |
| shikai dōhō | 四海同胞 |
| Shimabara | 島原 |
| shimpan | 親藩 |
| shingaku | 心學 |
| shinjutsu | 心術 |

| | |
|---|---|
| shinōkōshō | 士農工商 |
| Shōheikō | 昌平黌 |
| Tachibana Kanzaemon | 立花勘左衛門 |
| t'ai-chi (Ch.) daikyoku (Jp.) | 太極 |
| *T'ai-chi-t'u shuo* | 太極圖説 |
| *Taigiroku* | 大疑録 |
| *Taiheiki* | 太平記 |
| *Ta-hsüeh* (Ch.) *Daigaku* (Jp.) | 大學 |
| *Ta-hsüeh yen-i* | 大學衍義 |
| Takeda Shun'an | 竹田春庵 |
| T'ang Chün-i | 唐君毅 |
| tao-hsüeh (Ch.) dōgaku (Jp.) | 道學 |
| tao-hsin (Ch.) dōshin (Jp.) | 道心 |
| tenchi | 天地 |
| terakoya | 寺小屋 |
| t'i-yung (Ch.) taiyō (Jp.) | 體用 |
| t'ien chi (Ch.) tenki (Jp.) | 天機 |
| t'ien li (Ch.) tenri (Jp.) | 天理 |
| t'ien ming (Ch.) tenmei (Jp.) | 天命 |
| Tōkaidō | 東海道 |
| Tōken | 東軒 |
| Tokugawa | 徳川 |
| Tokugawa Iemitsu | 徳川家光 |
| Tokugawa Ieyasu | 徳川家康 |
| Tokugawa Mitsukuni | 徳川光圀 |
| Tokugawa Tsunayoshi | 徳川綱吉 |
| Toyotomi Hideyoshi | 豊臣秀吉 |
| tozama | 外様 |

| | |
|---|---|
| *Tso chuan* | 左傳 |
| *T'ung-chien kang-mu* | 通鑑綱目 |
| *T'ung-shu* | 通書 |
| Tu Shun | 杜順 |
| tzu-te (Ch.) jitoku (Jp.) | 自得 |
| wan wu i- t'i (Ch.) banbutsu ittai (Jp.) | 萬物一體 |
| Wang T'ing-hsiang | 王廷相 |
| Wang Yang-ming | 王陽明 |
| wu chi (Ch.) mukyoku (Jp.) | 無極 |
| Yamaga Sokō | 山鹿素行 |
| *Yamato zokkun* | 大和俗訓 |
| Yamazaki Ansai | 山崎闇齊 |
| Yasui Shunkai | 保井春海 |
| Yen Chih-tu'i | 彥久推 |
| yin; yang | 陰;陽 |
| Yi T'oegye | 李退溪 |
| *Yōjōkun* | 養生訓 |
| yōjō no jutsu | 養生の術 |
| yu (Ch.) yoku (Jp.) | 欲 |
| yuan ch'i (Ch.) genki (Jp.) | 元気 |
| Yushima Seidō | 湯島聖堂 |

# Glossary of Terms Cited
## in the Translation

| | |
|---|---|
| art of learning (gakujutsu) | 學術 |
| art of the mind-and-heart (shinjutsu) | 心術 |
| assimilating (juyō) | 受用 |
| being rigorous in practice (rikkō) | 力行 |
| biases of one's disposition (kishitsu no hen) | 気質の偏 |
| conscience (ryōshin) | 良心 |
| contentment; enjoyment (raku; tanoshii) | 楽 |
| controlling desires (yoku o shinobu) | 慾を忍ぶ |
| daily renewal (nisshin) | 日新 |
| decorum (rei) | 礼 |
| desires (yoku) | 慾 |
| disciplining oneself (shūshin) | 修身 |
| establishing one's resolve or establishing a goal (risshi) | 立志 |
| evil thoughts (janen) | 邪念 |
| exegesis (kunko no gaku) | 訓詁の學 |
| extension of knowledge (chichi) | 致知 |
| faults (ayamachi) | 過 |
| five constant virtues (gojō) | 五常 |

| | |
|---|---|
| forming one body with all things (banbutsu o ittai to su) | 萬物を一體とす |
| getting it for oneself; self-attainment (jitoku) | 自得 |
| having reverent control; being mindful (tsutsushimu) | 慎む |
| heaven's mandate (tenmei) | 天命 |
| hidden virtue (intoku) | 陰徳 |
| hold fast to the Mean (inshū ketsuchū) | 允執厥中 |
| human desires (jinyoku) | 人欲 |
| humaneness (jin) | 仁 |
| human mind is precarious (jinshin iki) | 人心惟危 |
| human relations; morality (jinrin) | 人倫 |
| human Way; Way to be Human (jindō) | 人道 |
| impartial; public-minded (kō) | 公 |
| inferring from ourselves and extending it to others (suiki kyūnin) | 推己及人 |
| innate knowledge of the good (ryōchi) | 良知 |
| investigation of things (kakubutsu) | 格物 |
| learning of the mind-and-heart (shingaku) | 心學 |
| life-giving (sei) | 生 |
| love and respect (aikei) | 愛敬 |
| making clear one's luminous virtue; manifesting illustrious virtue (meimeitoku) | 明明德 |
| make loyalty and faithfulness the master (shuchūshin) | 主忠信 |
| making one's intention sincere (seii) | 誠意 |
| making peace under heaven (heitenka) | 平天下 |
| mandate of heaven (tenmei) | 天命 |
| the mean (chū; naka) | 中 |

| | |
|---|---|
| memorization (kisho no gaku) | 記誦の學 |
| method of the mind-and-heart (shinhō) | 心法 |
| moral principles; duty (giri) | 義理 |
| moral sense (zenshin) | 善心 |
| Noble Person (kunshi) | 君子 |
| original heart (honshin) | 本心 |
| passion(s); desires (yoku) | 慾 |
| petty person (shōjin) | 小人 |
| principle (ri; kotowari) | 理 |
| prohibitions (kinkai) | 禁戒 |
| psycho-physical disposition (kishitsu) | 気質 |
| pursuit of learning (igaku) | 為學 |
| reason, truth; the Way and its principles (dōri) | 道理 |
| reciprocity (jo) | 恕 |
| rectifying the mind-and-heart (seishin) | 正心 |
| regulating the family (seika) | 齊家 |
| remorse (kōkai) | 後悔 |
| renewing the people (shinmin) | 新民 |
| resting in the highest good (shizen) | 至善 |
| reverence (kei) | 敬 |
| reverent mindfulness (tsutsushimu) | 慎む |
| reverence and harmony; peace of mind (kyōkei waraku) | 恭敬和楽 |
| righteousness (gi) | 義 |
| ruling the country (chikoku) | 治國 |
| School of the Way (Dōgaku) | 道學 |
| selfish desires (shiyoku) | 私慾 |
| selfish; private (shi) | 私 |

| | |
|---|---|
| sincere resolution (makoto no kokorozashi) | 誠の志 |
| sincerity (makoto) | 誠 |
| single-minded (senitsu) | 專 |
| singleness of mind (yuitsu) | 惟 |
| spirit of the universe; soul of all things (banbutsu no rei) | 萬物の靈 |
| study of poetry and prose (shishō no gaku) | 詞章の學 |
| subduing the self; self-control (kokki) | 克己 |
| universal love (kenai) | 兼愛 |
| useful learning (yūyō no gaku) | 有用の學 |
| useless learning (muyō no gaku) | 無用の學 |
| utmost refinement (isei) | 惟精 |
| virtue (dōtoku) | 道德 |
| Way of Heaven (ten no michi) | 天の道 |
| Way of learning (gakumon no michi) | 學門の道 |
| Way mind is barely perceptible (dōshin icho) | 道心惟微 |
| wisdom (chi) | 知 |
| without excess or deficiency (kafukyū naku) | 過不及なく |
| workings of heaven (tenki) | 天機 |

# Bibliography

## BOOKS AND ARTICLES IN JAPANESE

Abe Yoshio. *Jukyō no hensen to genkyō* (The development and the present situation of Confucianism). Tokyo: Kazankai, 1977.

————. *Nihon Shushigaku to Chōsen* (The Japanese Chu Hsi School and Korea). Tokyo: Tokyo Daigaku shuppankai, 1971, first published in 1965.

Aoki Yoshinori. "Kaibara Ekken no 'Shinju heikō fusō hairon' " (A discussion of similarities and differences between Shinto and Confucianism). *Shigaku zasshi*. 50, 1 (Jan. 1939): 223–239.

Bitō Masahide. *Nihon hōken shisōshi kenkyū* (Studies in the history of thought in Japanese feudalism). Tokyo: Aoki shoten, 1961.

Fukuoka ken kyōiku hyakunen shi hensan iinkai. *Fukuoka ken kyōiku hyakunen shi* (Hundred year history of education in Fukuoka Prefecture). Vol. 5. Fukuoka: Fukuoka ken kyōiku iinkai, 1980.

Hongō Takamori and Fukaya Katsumi, eds. *Kinsei shisōron* (Discussions of pre-modern Japanese thought). Tokyo: Yūhikaku, 1981.

Inoue Tadashi. *Kaibara Ekken*. Tokyo: Yoshikawa kōbunkan, 1963.

————. "Kaibara Ekken no 'Dōjimon higo' ni tsuite" (Concerning Kaibara Ekken's critique of 'Boy's questions'). *Kyushu Daigaku kenkyū hōkoku*. (1977): 121–177.

Inoue Tadashi and Araki Kengo, eds. *Kaibara Ekken, Muro Kyūsō. Nihon shisō taikei*. Vol. 34. Tokyo: Iwanami shoten, 1970.

Inoue Tetsujirō. *Nihon Shushigakuha no tetsugaku*. (The philosophy of the Chu Hsi school in Japan). Tokyo: Fuzanbō, 1926.

Inoue Tetsujirō, et al. *Nihon tetsugaku zensho* (Collected works in Japanese philosophy). *Jukyōhen*. Vol. 3; *Jukyōka no shizenkan*. Vol. 9. Tokyo: Daiichi shobō, 1937.

Irizawa Sōju. *Kaibara Ekken. Nihon kyōiku sentetsu sōsho*. Tokyo: Bunkyō shoin, 1954.

Ishii Shirō. *Kinsei buke shisō* (Pre-modern samurai thought) *Nihon shisō taikei*. Vol. 27. Tokyo: Iwanami shoten, 1974.

427

Ishikawa Matsutarō, ed. *Kaibara Ekken, Muro Kyūsō shū. Sekai kyōiku hōten, Nihon kyōiku hen*. Vol. 3. Tokyo: Tamagawa Daigaku shuppanbu, 1968.

Iwabashi Junsei. *Dainihon rinri shisō hattatsushi* (A history of the development of ethical thought in Japan). Vol. 1. Tokyo: Meguro shoten, 1915.

Iwao Seiichi. *Sakoku* (Seclusion policy). *Nihon no rekishi*. Vol. 14. Tokyo: Chūō kōronsha, 1966.

Kaibara Ekken. *Ekken jikkun* (Ekken's ten moral treatises). 2 Vols. ed. by Tsukamoto Tetsuzō. Tokyo: Yūhōdō shoten, 1927.

————. *Ekken zenshū* (The collected works of Kaibara Ekken). 8 Vols. Tokyo: Ekken zenshū kankōbu, 1910–1911.

————. *Yamato zokkun* (Precepts for daily life in Japan). Tokyo: Kiyomizu Kakujirō, 1967.

Kanaya Osamu, ed. *Ogyū Sorai shū* (A collection of Ogyū Sorai's writings). *Nihon no shisō*. Vol. 12. Tokyo: Chikuma shobō, 1970.

Kinugasa Yasuki. *Kinsei Jugaku shisōshi no kenkyū* (Studies in the history of pre-modern Confucian thought). Tokyo: Hōsei Daigaku shuppankyoku, 1976.

Komoguchi Isao and Okada Takehiko. *Andō Seian; Kaibara Ekken*. Tokyo: Meitoku shuppansha, 1985.

Kondō Hitoshi, ed. *Sengoku jidai buke kakun no kenkyū* (Studies in family codes of the samurai from the Warring States period). Tokyo: Kazama shobō, 1978.

Kōsaka Masaaki, et al. *Tokugawa jidai ni okeru ningen sonchō shisō no keifu* (Lineage of the thought of human respect in the Tokugawa period). 2 Vols. Tokyo: Fukumura shoten, 1961.

Kumida Yoshio. "Kaibara Ekken no yōjōkan no tokushitsu" (Special characteristics of Kaibara Ekken's views on health care). *Shisō* 528 (June 1968): 82–94.

Kyushu shiryō kankōkai, ed. *Kyushu shiryō sōsho*. 1964. [Includes: Sonken nikkiryaku, Kanbun nikki, Enpō shichinen nikki, Nikki (5 & 6), Kyoka nikki, Zakki, Shokanshū, Kaibara Ekken ate shokan, Ganko mokuroku, Atsunobu isei yōzaiki.]

Maki Katsumi. "Kaibara Ekken no ichigenki ni tsuite" (Concerning Kaibara Ekken's monism of *ch'i*). *Shinagaku kenkyū* (Oct. 1960): 217–222.

————. "Kaibara Ekken no uchūkan ni tsuite" (Concerning Kaibara Ekken's view of the universe." *Shinagaku kenkyū* (Nov. 1966): 42–49.

Matsuda Michio, ed. *Kaibara Ekken. Nihon no meicho*. Vol. 14. Tokyo: Chūō kōronsha, 1969.

Minamoto Ryōen. *Kinsei shoki jitsugaku shisō no kenkyū* (Studies in practical learning at the beginning of the pre-modern era). Tokyo: Sōbunsha, 1980.

————. *Tokugawa gōri shisō no keifu* (The lineage of rational thought in the Tokugawa period). Tokyo: Chūō kōronsha, 1972.

————. *Tokugawa shisō shōshi* (A short history of Tokugawa thought). Tokyo: Chūō kōronsha, 1973.

Morimoto Kakuzō. *Gokyō sakuin* (An index to the Five Classics). 4 Vols. To-kyo: Rinsen shoten, 1970.

—. *Shisho sakuin* (An index to the Four Books). Tokyo: Keisho sakuin kankōjo, 1921.

Morishita Sanao. "Kaibara Ekken no tendō shisō." (The idea of the heavenly Way of Kaibara Ekken). *Rekishi to chiri* 17, 5 (May 1925): 412–420.

Morohashi Tetsuji. *Chūgoku koten meigen jiten* (A dictionary of phrases in the Chinese classics). 13 Vols. Tokyo: Kōdansha, 1972.

—. *Dai Kanwa jiten* (The great Chinese-Japanese dictionary). 12 Vols. Tokyo: Taishūkan shoten, 1955–1960.

Naramoto Tatsuya and Kinugasa Yasuki. *Edo jidai no shisō* (Edo period thought). Tokyo: Tokuma shoten, 1966.

—. *Nihon kyōiku bunko* (A collection of Japanese educational works). Tokyo: Dōbunkan henshūkyoku, 1910–1911.

Nishioka Toranosuke. *Nihon shisōshi no kenkyū* (Studies in the history of Japanese thought). Tokyo: Shōkasha, 1936.

Ogawa Kandō, ed. *Kangakusha denki oyobi chojutsu shūran* (Bio-bibliography of Japanese scholars of the Chinese classics). Tokyo: Seki shoin, 1935.

Saegusa Hiroto, ed. *Nihon tetsugaku shisō zensho* (Collected works in Japanese philosophical thought). Vol. 7, Gakumon hen; Vol. 14, Jukyōhen. Tokyo: Heibonsha, 1957.

Sagara Tōru, et al. *Edo no shisōkatachi* (Thinkers in the Edo period). Tokyo: Kenkyūsha, 1979.

Sagara Tōru. *Kinsei Nihon ni okeru Jukyō undō no keifu* (The lineage of the movement of Confucianism in pre-modern Japan). Tokyo: Risōsha, 1965.

Saitō Tokutarō. *Kinsei Jurin hennen shi* (Chronological account of Japanese Confucianists of pre-modern times). Osaka: Zenkoku shobō, 1943.

Saitō Shigeta, ed. *Jinseikun: Kaibara Ekken 'Kadōkun' o yomu* (A reading of Kaibara Ekken's 'Precepts for the Way of the family'). Tokyo: Mikasa shoten, 1984.

Seki Giichirō, Seki Yoshinao, ed. *Kinsei Kangakusha chojutsu mokuroku taisei* (General index to the works of scholars of Chinese classics in the pre-modern period). Tokyo: Tōyō tosho kankōkai, 1941.

Seki Giichirō, Seki Yoshinao, ed. *Kinsei Kangakusha denki chosaku daijiten* (A dictionary of the bio-bibliographies of pre-modern Japanese scholars of the Chinese classics). Tokyo: Rinrōkaku shoten, 1966, first printed in 1943.

Tada Akira. "Kaibara Ekken no keizai shisō ni tsuite" (Concerning Kaibara Ekken's economic thought). *Chiba Daigaku kyōeibu kenkyū hōkoku* A-3 (1970): 43–74.

Takasu Yoshijirō, ed. *Mitogaku zenshū* (Collected works of the Mito school). 6 Vols. Tokyo: Nittō shoin, 1933.

Takada Shinji. *Nihon Jugakushi* (A history of Japanese Confucianism). Tokyo: Chinin shokan, 1941.

Takebayashi Kan'ichi, ed. *Kangakusha denki shūsei* (Biographies of Japanese scholars of the Chinese classics). Tokyo: Seki shoin, 1928.

Takeuchi Makoto, et al. *Nihon rekishi.* Vol. 12, *Kinsei* (Japanese history: premodern period). Tokyo: Iwanami shoten, 1976.

Takigawa Masajirō, ed. *Kaibara Ekken shū* (Collection of Kaibara Ekken's works). *Kinsei shakai keizai gakusetsu taikei.* Vol. 10. Tokyo: Seibundō shinkōsha, 1939.

Tsuboi Hideo. *Nihon no dōtoku shisō* (Japanese moral thought). Tokyo:Bunka sōgō shuppansha, 1981)

Tsuda Sōkichi. *Jukyō no kenkyū* (Studies in Confucianism). Tokyo: Iwanami shoten, 1956.

Tsuji Tetsuo. "Kaibara Ekken no gakumon to hōhō" (Kaibara Ekken's learning and methodology). *Shisō* 11, 605 (Nov. 1974): 57–71.

Tsukamoto Tetsuzō, ed. *Kaibara Ekken.* Tokyo: Yūhōdō shoten, 1927.

Watanabe Shōichi. *Nihon kinsei dōtoku shisōshi* (A history of moral thought in the pre-modern era in Japan). Tokyo: Sōbunsha, 1961.

Yajima Genryō, ed. *Kangakusha denki sakuin* (An index to biographies of Japanese scholars of the Chinese classics). Sendai: Tohoku Daigaku fuzoku toshokan, 1970.

——, ed. *Tokugawa jidai shuppansha shuppanbutsu shūran* (A record of publications during the Tokugawa period). Sendai: Tōhoku Daigaku fuzoku toshokan, 1968.

Yamamoto Tsunetomo. *Hagakure.* Ed. by Kamiko Tadashi and Nabeshima Naotsugu. Tokyo: Tokuma shoten, 1967.

Yoshikawa Kōjirō, ed. *Ogyū Sorai. Nihon shisō taikei.* Vol. 36. Tokyo: Iwanami shoten, 1973.

# BOOKS IN WESTERN LANGUAGES

Ackroyd, Joyce, trans. *Told Round A Brushwood Fire: The Autobiography of Arai Hakuseki.* Princeton and Tokyo: Princeton University Press and University of Tokyo Press, 1979.

Anesaki Masaboru. *History of Japanese Religion.* Rutland, Vt.: Charles E. Tuttle, 1968.

Armstrong, Robert C. *Just Before the Dawn, The Life and Work of Ninomiya Sontoku.* New York: Macmillan, 1912.

——. *Light From the East. Studies in Japanese Confucianism.* Toronto: University of Toronto Press, 1914.

Bellah, Robert. *Tokugawa Religion: The Values of Pre-Industrial Japan.* Boston: Beacon Press, 1957.

Bix, Herbert. *Peasant Protest in Japan 1590–1884.* New Haven: Yale University Press, 1986.

Bloom, Irene T., trans. *Knowledge Painfully Acquired: The K'un-chih chi by Lo Ch'in-shun.* New York: Columbia University Press, 1987.

Boas, Mary. *The Scientific Renaissance 1450–1630*. New York: Harper and Row, 1962.

Bolitho, Harold. *Treasures Among Men: The Fudai Daimyo in Tokugawa Japan*. New Haven: Yale University Press, 1974.

Boot, Willem Jan. *The Adoption and Adaptation of Neo-Confucianism in Japan: The Role of Fujiwara Seika and Hayashi Razan*. Ph.D. dissertation, University of Leiden, 1982.

Borton, Hugh. *Peasant Uprising in Japan of the Tokugawa Period*. New York: Paragon, 1968, reprint ed. Originally in *Transactions of the Asiatic Society of Japan* 16, 2 (1938): 1–220.

Bowers, John Z. *Western Medical Pioneers in Feudal Japan*. Baltimore: Johns Hopkins University, 1970.

———. *Medical Education in Japan*. New York: Harper and Row, 1965.

Boxer, Charles R. *The Christian Century in Japan 1549–1650*. Berkeley: University of California Press, 1951; revised edition, 1967.

Bresler, Laurence. *Origins of Popular Travel and Travel Literature in Japan*. Ph.D. dissertation, Columbia University, 1975.

Bruce, J. Percy. *Chu Hsi and His Masters*. London: Probasthain, 1923.

Caron, Francois and Joost Schouten. *A True Description of the Mighty Kingdoms of Japan and Siam*. Reprinted from the English edition of 1663. Ed. by C. R. Boxer. London: The Argonaut Press, 1935.

Chan, Wing-tsit, ed. *Chu Hsi and Neo-Confucianism*. Honolulu: University of Hawaii Press, 1986.

———, trans. *Instructions for Practical Living and Other Neo-Confucian Writings by Wang Yang-ming*. New York: Columbia University Press, 1963.

———. *Neo-Confucianism, Etc.* Hanover, New Hampshire: Oriental Society, 1969.

———, trans. *Neo-Confucian Terms Explained: The Pei-hsi tzu-i by Ch'en Ch'un, 1159–1223*. New York: Columbia University Press, 1986.

———, trans. *Reflections on Things at Hand: The Neo-Confucian Anthology Compiled by Chu Hsi and Lu Tsu-chien*. New York: Columbia University Press, 1967.

———, trans. *A Source Book in Chinese Philosophy*. Princeton: Princeton University Press, 1963.

Chang, Carson. *The Development of Neo-Confucian Thought*. 2 vols. New York: Bookman Associates, 1957 and 1962.

Cheng Chung-ying, trans. *Tai Chen's Inquiry Into Goodness*. Honolulu: East-West Center Press, 1971.

Ching, Julia. *Confucianism and Christianity*. Tokyo: Kodansha International, 1977.

———. *To Acquire Wisdom: The Way of Wang Yang-ming*. New York: Columbia University Press, 1976.

Cooper, Michael, ed. *They Came to Japan: An Anthology of European Reports on Japan, 1543–1640*. Berkeley: University of California Press, 1965; paperback edition, 1981.

Craig, Albert and Donald Shively, eds. *Personality in Japanese History*. Berkeley: University of California Press, 1970.

Creel, Herrlee G. *Chinese Thought from Confucius to Mao Tse-tung*. Chicago: University of Chicago Press, 1953.

de Bary, Wm. Theodore. *East Asia: The Great Dialogue*. Cambridge: Harvard University Press, 1988.

———. *The Liberal Tradition in China*. New York: Columbia University Press, 1983.

———. *The Message of the Mind in Neo-Confucian Thought, 1200–1850*. New York: Columbia University Press, 1988.

——— and John W. Chaffee, eds. *Neo-Confucian Education: The Formative Stage*. Berkeley: University of California Press, 1989.

———. *Neo-Confucian Orthodoxy and the Learning of the Mind-and-Heart*. New York: Columbia University Press, 1981.

——— and Irene T. Bloom, eds. *Principle and Practicality*. New York: Columbia University Press, 1979.

de Bary, Wm. Theodore, ed. *Self and Society in Ming Thought*. New York: Columbia University Press, 1970.

———, Wing-tsit Chan, and Burton Watson, eds. *Sources of Chinese Tradition*. New York: Columbia University Press, 1960.

———, ed. *The Unfolding of Neo-Confucianism*. New York: Columbia University Press, 1975.

Dore, Ronald P. *Education in Tokugawa Japan*. Berkeley: University of California Press, 1965.

Dunn, C. J. *Everyday Life in Traditional Japan*. New York: Putnam and Sons, 1969.

Earhart, H. Byron. *Japanese Religion: Unity and Diversity*. Belmont, Cal.: Dickenson Pub. Co., 1974.

Earl, David M. *Emperor and Nation in Japan: Political Thinkers of the Tokugawa Period*. Seattle: University of Washington Press, 1964.

Elison, George. *Deus Destroyed: The Image of Christianity in Early Modern Japan*. Cambridge: Harvard University Press, 1973.

Fingarette, Herbert. *Confucius—The Secular as Sacred*. New York: Harper and Row, 1972.

Fung Yu-lan. *History of Chinese Philosophy*. Trans. by Derk Bodde. 2 vols. Princeton: Princeton University Press, 1953.

Graf, Olaf. *Kaibara Ekiken*. Leiden: E. J. Brill, 1942.

Graham, A. C. *Two Chinese Philosophers: Ch'eng Ming-tao and Ch'eng Yi-ch'uan*. London: Lund Humphries, 1958.

Hall, John W., Nagahara Keiji, Kozo Yamamura, eds. *Japan Before Tokugawa: Political Consolidation and Economic Growth, 1500–1650*. Princeton: Princeton University Press, 1981.

Hall, John W. and Marius B. Jansen, eds. *Studies in the Institutional History of Early Modern Japan*. Princeton: Princeton University Press, 1968.

Haskel, Peter, trans. and Yoshito Hakeda, ed. *Bankei Zen: Translations from the Record of Bankei*. New York: Grove Press, 1984.

BIBLIOGRAPHY 433

Herbert, Jean. *Shinto: At the Fountainhead of Japan.* New York: Stein & Day, 1967.

Honjō Eijirō. *Economic Theory and History of Japan in the Tokugawa Period.* New York: Russell & Russell, 1965.

Jansen, Marius B., ed. *Changing Japanese Attitudes Toward Modernization.* Princeton: Princeton University Press, 1965.

Jiang, Paul Yun-ming. *The Search for Mind: Ch'en Pai-sha, Philosopher-Poet.* Singapore: Singapore University Press, 1980.

Kaempfer, Engelbert. *The History of Japan Together with a Description of the Kingdom of Siam 1690–1692.* Trans. by J. G. Scheuchver, 3 vols. Glasgow: James MacLehose and Sons, 1906.

Kaibara Ekken. *Onna Daigaku.* Trans. by Basil Chamberlain in *Japanese Things.* Rutland, Vt.: Tuttle, 1971, first published in 1905.

———. *The Way of Contentment.* Trans. by Ken Hoshino. London: John Murray, 1913.

———. *Yōjōkun. Japanese Secret of Good Health.* Trans. by Masao Kunihiro. Tokyo: Tokuma Shoten, 1974.

Kang, Thomas. *The Making of Confucian Societies in Tokugawa Japan and Yi Korea.* Ph.D. dissertation, American University, 1971.

Kasoff, Ira E. *The Thought of Chang Tsai (1020–1077)* Cambridge: Cambridge University Press, 1984.

Kearney, Hugh. *Science and Change 1500–1700.* New York: McGraw Hill, 1971.

Keene, Donald. *World Within Walls: Japanese Literature of the Pre-Modern Era (1600–1867).* New York: Holt, Rinehart and Winston, 1976.

Keenleyside, Hugh and A. F. Thomas. *History of Japanese Education.* Tokyo: Hokuseidō Press, 1937.

Kirkwood, Kenneth B. *Renaissance in Japan: A Cultural Survey of the Seventeenth Century.* Rutland, Vt.: Charles E. Tuttle, 1970, reprint of 1938 edition.

Kobayashi Tetsuya. *Society, Schools and Progress in Japan.* Oxford: Pergamon Press, 1976.

La Fleur, William R. *The Karma of Words: Buddhism and the Literary Arts in Medieval Japan.* Berkeley: University of California Press, 1983; paperback, 1986.

Legge, James, trans. *The Ch'un Ts'ew with the Tso Chuen. The Chinese Classics.* Vol. 5, London: Oxford University Press, 1895.

———, trans. *The Confucian Analects, the Great Learning, and the Doctrine of the Mean. The Chinese Classics.* Vol. 1, Oxford: Clarendon Press, 1893.

———, trans. *The She King (Shi-ching). The Chinese Classics.* Vol. 4, Oxford: Clarendon Press, 1871.

———, trans. *The Shou King (Shu-ching). The Chinese Classics.* Vol. 3, Oxford: Clarendon Press, 1865.

———, trans. *Li Chi: Book of Rites.* 2 vols., reprinted by New Hyde Park, New York: University Books, 1967.

————, trans. *The Works of Mencius*. *The Chinese Classics*. Vol. 2, Oxford: Clarendon Press, 1895.

Lidin, Olof, *The Life of Ogyū Sorai, A Tokugawa Confucian Philosopher*. Lund: Scandinavian Institute of Asian Studies, 1973.

————. trans. *Ogyū Sorai's Distinguishing the Way*. Tokyo: Sophia University Press, 1970.

Maruyama Masao. Trans. by Mikiso Hane. *Studies in the Intellectual History of Tokugawa Japan*. Princeton and Tokyo: Princeton University Press and University of Tokyo Press, 1974.

Masao Kunihirō, trans. *Yōjōkun: Japanese Secret of Good Health*. Tokyo: Tokuma Shoten, 1974.

McEwan, J. R., trans. *The Political Writings of Ogyū Sorai*. Cambridge: University of Cambridge Press, 1969.

McMullen, Ian James. *Kumazawa Banzan: The Life and Thought of a Seventeenth-Century Japanese Confucian*. Ph.D. dissertation, Cambridge University, 1968.

Morris, Ivan. *The Nobility of Failure: Tragic Heroes in the History of Japan*. New York: Holt, Rinehart and Winston, 1975.

Munro, Donald, ed. *Individualism and Holism: Studies in Confucian and Taoist Values*. Ann Arbor: Center for Chinese Studies, University of Michigan, 1985.

Najita, Tetsuo and Irwin Scheiner, eds. *Japanese Thought in the Tokugawa Period 1600–1868: Methods and Metaphors*. Chicago: University of Chicago Press, 1978.

Najita, Tetsuo. *Visions of Virtue in Tokugawa Japan: The Kaitokudō Merchant Academy of Osaka*. Chicago: University of Chicago Press, 1987.

Nakamura Hajime. *A History of the Development of Japanese Thought from A.D. 592 to 1868*. Tokyo: Kokusai Bunka Shinkokai, 1969.

Needham, Joseph. *Clerks and Craftsmen in China and the West*. Cambridge: Cambridge University Press, 1970.

————. *Science in Traditional China*. Cambridge: Harvard University Press, 1981.

Norman, E. Herbert. *Origins of the Modern Japanese State*. Ed. by John W. Dower. New York: Random House, 1975.

Nosco, Peter, ed. *Confucianism and Tokugawa Culture*. Princeton: Princeton University Press, 1984.

Ooms, Herman. *Tokugawa Ideology: Early Constructs, 1570–1680*. Princeton: Princeton University Press, 1985.

Passin, Herbert. *Society and Education in Japan*. New York: Teachers College and East Asian Institute with Columbia University Press, 1965.

Peterson, Willard J. *Bitter Gourd. Fang I-chih and the Impetus for Intellectual Change*. New Haven: Yale University Press, 1979.

Pollack, David. *The Fracture of Meaning: Japan's Synthesis of China from the Eighth through the Eighteenth Centuries*. Princeton: Princeton University Press, 1986.

Ro, Young-chan. *Korean Neo-Confucianism of Yi Yulgok.* Albany: State University of New York Press, 1988.

Ronan, Colin A. *The Shorter Science and Civilization in China.* An Abridgement of Joseph Needham's Original Text. Cambridge: Cambridge University Press, 1978.

Rozman, Gilbert. *Urban Networks in Ch'ing China and Tokugawa Japan.* Princeton: Princeton University Press, 1973.

Rubinger, Richard. *Private Academies of Tokugawa Japan.* Princeton: Princeton University Press, 1982.

Sadler, Arthur L. *The Maker of Modern Japan: The Life of Shogun Tokugawa Ieyasu.* London: George Allen and Unwin Ltd., 1932. Reprint ed., Rutland Vt.: Charles E. Tuttle, 1978.

Sansom, George. *A History of Japan.* 3 vols. Stanford: Stanford University Press, 1958–1963.

———. *Japan, A Short Cultural History.* New York: Appleton-Century-Crofts, 1962.

———. *The Western World and Japan.* London: The Cresset Press, 1950.

Sargent, G. W., trans. *The Japanese Family Storehouse.* Cambridge: Cambridge University Press, 1959.

Satow, Ernest. *The Jesuit Mission Press in Japan 1591–1610.* London: (Private Printing), 1888.

Sheldon, Charles D. *The Rise of the Merchant Class in Tokugawa Japan 1600–1868.* Locust Valley, New York: J. J. Augustin, 1958.

Smith, Thomas C. *The Agrarian Origins of Modern Japan.* Stanford: Stanford University Press, 1959.

Smith, Warren W. *Confucianism in Modern Japan: A Study of Conservatism in Japanese Intellectual History.* Tokyo: Hokuseidō Press, 1959.

Song, Whi-chil. *Yomeigaku as a Philosophy of Action in Tokugawa Japan: Ōshio Heihachirō (1793–1837) and his Rebellion in 1837.* Ph.D. dissertation, University of Southern California, 1982.

Spae, Joseph. *Itō Jinsai: A Philosopher, Educator and Sinologist of the Tokugawa Period.* New York: Paragon, 1967.

Sparling, Kathryn. *The Way of the Samurai. Yukio Mishima on 'Hagakure' in Modern Life.* New York: Basic Books, 1977.

Steenstrup, Carl. *Hōjō Shigetoki 1198–1261: and his Role in the History of Political and Ethical Ideas in Japan.* London: Curzon Press, 1979.

Sugimoto Masayoshi and David Swain. *Science and Culture in Traditional Japan A.D. 600–1854.* Cambridge: Massachusetts Institute of Technology Press, 1978.

Sugita Genpaku. *Dawn of Western Science in Japan: Rangaku Kotohajime.* Trans. by Ryozo Matsumoto and Eiichi Kiyooka. Tokyo: Hokuseidō Press, 1969.

Taylor, Rodney L. *The Confucian Way of Contemplation. Okada Takehiko and the Tradition of Quiet Sitting.* Columbia: University of South Carolina Press, 1988.

————. *The Cultivation of Sagehood as a Religious Goal in Neo-Confucianism: A Study of Selected Writings of Kao P'an-lung, 1562–1626.* Missoula, Mont.: Scholars Press, 1978.

Tiedemann, Arthur. *An Introduction to Japanese Civilization.* New York: Columbia University Press, 1974.

Tillman, Hoyt C. *Utilitarian Confucianism: Ch'en Liang's Challenge to Chu Hsi.* Cambridge: Council on East Asian Studies, Harvard University Press, 1982.

Toby, Ronald. *State and Diplomacy in Early Modern Japan: Asia in the Development of the Tokugawa Bakufu.* Princeton: Princeton University Press, 1984.

Totman, Conrad D. *Politics in the Tokugawa Bakufu, 1600–1843.* Cambridge: Harvard University Press, 1967.

————. *Tokugawa Ieyasu, Shogun: A Biography.* San Francisco: Heian, 1983.

Tsuda, Sōkichi. *An Inquiry into the Japanese Mind as Mirrored in Literature: The Flowering Period of Common People Literature.* Trans. by Fukamatsu Matsuda. Tokyo: Japan Society for the Promotion of Science, 1970.

Tsukahira, Toshio G. *Feudal Control in Japan: The Sankin Kōtai System.* Cambridge: East Asian Research Center, Harvard, 1966.

Tsunoda, Ryusaku, Wm. Theodore de Bary and Donald Keene, eds. *Sources of Japanese Tradition.* New York: Columbia University Press, 1958.

Tu Wei-ming. *Centrality and Commonality: An Essay on Chung-yung,* Monograph no. 3 of the Society for Asian and Comparative Philosophy. Honolulu: The University Press of Hawaii, 1976.

————. *Confucian Thought: Selfhood as Creative Transformation.* Albany: SUNY Press, 1985.

————. *Neo-Confucian Thought in Action: Wang Yang-ming's Youth (1472–1509).* Berkeley and Los Angeles: University of California Press, 1976.

Tyler, Royall. *Suzuki Shōsan: A Fighting Man of Zen.* Ph.D. dissertation, Columbia University, 1977.

Varley, H. Paul. *Japanese Culture. A Short History.* New York: Praeger, 1973.

Vlastos, Stephen. *Peasant Protests and Uprising in Tokugawa Japan.* Berkeley: University of California Press, 1986.

Watson, William, ed. *The Great Japan Exhibition: Art of the Edo Period 1600–1868.* London: Royal Academy of Art, 1981.

Watt, Paul. *Jiun Sonja (1718–1804) Life and Thought.* Ph.D. dissertation, Columbia University, 1982.

Webb, Herschel. *The Japanese Imperial Institution in the Tokugawa Period.* New York: Columbia University Press, 1968.

Wilhelm, Richard. *Heaven, Earth and Man in the Book of Changes.* Seattle: University of Washington Press, 1979.

Wilhelm, Richard, trans. *The I Ching, or Book of Changes.* Trans. from German to English by Cary F. Baynes. Princeton: Princeton University Press, Bollingen Series 19, 1969.

Yamamoto Tsunetomo. *Hagakure: The Book of the Samurai.* Trans. by William Scott Wilson. Tokyo: Kōdansha, 1979.

————. *Hagakure: A Code to the Way of the Samurai.* Trans. by Takako Mukoh. Tokyo: Hokuseidō, 1980.

Yamamura Kozo. *A Study of Samurai Income and Entrepreneurship.* Cambridge: Harvard University Press, 1974.

Yamashita, Samuel H. *Compasses and Carpenter's Squares: A Study of Itō Jinsai (1627–1705) and Ogyū Sorai (1666–1728).* Ph.D. thesis, University of Michigan, 1981.

Yampolsky, Philip B., trans. *The Zen Master Hakuin: Selected Writings.* New York: Columbia University Press, 1971.

Yazaki Takeo. *Social Change and the City in Japan, from Earliest Times Through the Industrial Revolution.* Tokyo: Japan Publications Inc., 1968.

Yoshikawa Kojirō. *Jinsai, Sorai, Norinaga: Three Classical Philologists of Mid-Tokugawa Japan.* Tokyo: Tōhō Gakkai, 1983.

Yoshimoto Tadasu. *A Peasant Sage of Japan: The Life and Work of Sontoku Ninomiya.* Trans. from the *Hōtokuki.* New York: Longmans Green and Co., 1912.

## ARTICLES IN WESTERN LANGUAGES

Abe Yoshio. "Development of Neo-Confucianism in Japan, Korea and China: A Comparative Study." *Acta Asiatica* 19 (1970): 16–39.

————. "The Characteristics of Japanese Confucianism." *Acta Asiatica* 25 (1973): 1–21.

————. "Influence of Lo Ch'in-shun's *K'un-chih chi* in the Early Edo Period and the State of Practical Learning among the Students of Kinoshita Jun'an and Yamazaki Ansai." Draft paper for the June 1974 ACLS conference on Neo-Confucianism and Practical Learning in the Ming and Early Tokugawa Periods.

————. "The Unique Confucian Development of Japan: A Brief Survey and a Few Suggestions." *Asian Culture Quarterly* 4, 1 (Spring 1976): 8–13.

Ackroyd, Joyce. "Women in Feudal Japan." *Transactions of the Asiatic Society of Japan* 7 (1959): 31–68.

Aoki, M. Y. and Dardess, M. B. "The Popularization of Samurai Values: A Sermon by Hosoi Heishū." *Monumenta Nipponica* 31, 4 (1976): 393–413.

Asakawa, K. "Notes on Village Government in Japan after 1600." *Journal of the American Oriental Society* 30–31 (1910–11): 259–300, 151–216.

————. "Some Aspects of Japanese Feudal Institutions." *Transactions of the Asiatic Society of Japan* 46 (1918): 76–102.

Asao Naohiro and Marius B. Jansen. "Shogun and *Tennō.*" In John W. Hall et al., eds. *Japan Before Tokugawa.* Princeton: Princeton University Press, 1981. pp. 248–270.

Backus, Robert L. "The Kansei Prohibition of Heterodoxy." *Harvard Journal of Asiatic Studies* 39, 1 (1979): 55–106.

————. "The Motivation of Confucian Orthodoxy in Tokugawa Japan." *Harvard Journal of Asiatic Studies* 39, 2 (1979): 275–338.

——— . "The Relationship of Confucianism to the Tokugawa Bakufu as Revealed in the Kansei Educational Reform." *Harvard Journal of Asiatic Studies* 34 (1974): 97–162.

Bailey, Beatrice Bodart. "The Laws of Compassion." *Monumenta Nipponica* 40, 2 (1985): 163–189.

Beasley, W. G. and Carmen Blacker. "Japanese Historical Writing in the Tokugawa Period (1603–1863)." In W. G. Beasley and E. G. Pulleyblank, eds. *Historians of China and Japan.* London: Oxford University Press, 1961, pp. 245–263.

Bellah, Robert N. "Baigan and Sorai: Continuities and Discontinuities in Eighteenth-Century Japanese Thought." In Tetsuo Najita and Irwin Scheiner, eds. *Japanese Thought in the Tokugawa Period.* Chicago: University of Chicago Press, 1978, pp. 137–151.

Bitō Masahide. "Confucian Thought During the Tokugawa Period." In George A. De Vos and Takao Sofue, eds. *Religion and the Family in East Asia.* Berkeley: University of California Press, 1986, pp. 127–138.

——— . "Society and Social Thought in the Tokugawa Period." In *The Japan Foundation Newsletter* 9, 2–3 (June, Sept. 1981): 1–9.

Bocking, Brian. "Neo-Confucian Spirituality and the Samurai Ethic." *Religion* 10, 1 (Spring 1980): 1–15.

Boxer, C. R. "Hosokawa Tadaoki and the Jesuits 1587–1645." *Transactions and Proceedings of the Japan Society, London* 32 (1935): 79–119.

——— . "Some Aspects of Portuguese Influence in Japan, 1542–1640." *Transactions and Proceedings of the Japan Society, London* 33 (1936): 13–64.

Chamberlain, Basil H. "A Translation of the *Dou-zhi keu* 'Teachings for the Young.' " *Transactions of the Asiatic Society of Japan* 9 (1881): 223–248.

Chan Wing-tsit. "Chinese and Western Interpretations of *Jen* (Humanity)." *Journal of Chinese Philosophy* 2 (March 1975): 107–129.

——— . "Chu Hsi's Completion of Neo-Confucianism." In Francoise Aubin, ed. *Etudes Song—Sung Studies in Memoriam Etienne Balazs.* 2, 1 (1973): 59–90.

——— . "The Evolution of the Confucian Concept *Jen.*" *Philosophy East and West* 4, 4 (1955): 295–319.

——— . "Neo-Confucianism and Chinese Scientific Thought." *Philosophy East and West* 6, 4 (1957): 309–332.

Cheng Chung-ying. "Reason, Substance, and Human Desires in Seventeenth-Century Neo-Confucianism." In Wm. T. de Bary, ed. *The Unfolding of Neo-Confucianism.* New York: Columbia University Press, 1975, pp. 469–509.

——— . "Religious Reality and Religious Understanding in Confucianism and Neo-Confucianism." *International Philosophical Quarterly.* 13, 1 (March 1973): 33–61.

Ching, Julia. "Confucianism: Ethical Humanism as Religion?" Paper delivered to the Regional Seminar in Neo-Confucian Studies, Columbia University, October 2, 1987.

———. "The Idea of God in Nakae Tōju." *Japanese Journal of Religious Studies* 11, 4 (Dec. 1984): 293–311.

———. "What is Confucian Spirituality?" Irene Eber, ed., *Confucianism: The Dynamics of Tradition.* New York: Macmillan, 1986, pp. 63–80.

Chu Ron-Guey. "Chu Hsi and Public Instruction." In Wm. T. de Bary and J. Chaffee, eds. *Neo-Confucian Education: The Formative Stage.* Berkeley: University of California Press, 1989.

Clement, Ernest W. "Instructions of a Mito Prince to His Retainers." *Transactions of the Asiatic Society of Japan* 26 (1898): 115–153.

Coulborn, Rushton. "The Origin and Early Development of Feudalism in Japan and Western Europe." In R. Coulborn, ed. *Feudalism in History.* Princeton: Princeton University Press, 1956, pp. 188–214.

Craig, Albert M. "Science and Confucianism in Tokugawa Japan." In Marius B. Jansen, ed. *Changing Japanese Attitudes Toward Modernization.* Princeton: Princeton University Press, 1965, pp. 133–166.

Crawcour, E. S. "Changes in Japanese Commerce in the Tokugawa Period." *Journal of Asian Studies* 22, 4 (1963): 387–400.

———. "The Development of a Credit System in Seventeenth-Century Japan." *Journal of Economic History* 21, 3 (1961): 342–360.

———. "Documentary Sources of Tokugawa Economic and Social History." *Journal of Asian Studies* 20, 3 (1961): 343–351.

de Bary, Wm. Theodore. "A Reappraisal of Neo-Confucianism." In Arthur Wright, ed. *Studies in Chinese Thought.* Chicago: University of Chicago Press, 1953, pp. 81–111.

———. "Some Common Tendencies in Neo-Confucianism." In David Nivison and Arthur Wright, eds. *Confucianism in Action.* Stanford: Stanford University Press, 1959, pp. 25–49.

Dening, Walter. "Confucian Philosophy in Japan: Reviews of Dr. Tetsujirō Inoue's Three Volumes on This Philosophy." *Transactions of the Asiatic Society of Japan* 36 (1908): 101–151.

Dilworth, David A. "*Jitsugaku* as an Ontological Conception: Continuities and Discontinuities in Early and Mid-Tokugawa Thought," in Wm. T. de Bary and I. Bloom, eds. *Principle and Practicality.* New York: Columbia University Press, 1979, pp. 471–514.

Dore, Ronald P. "The Legacy of Tokugawa Education." In Marius B. Jansen, ed. *Changing Japanese Attitudes Toward Modernization.* Princeton: Princeton University Press, 1965, pp. 99–131.

———. "Talent and the Social Order in Tokugawa Japan." In John W. Hall and Marius B. Jansen, eds. *Studies in the Institutional History of Early Modern Japan.* Princeton: Princeton University Press, 1968, pp. 349–361.

Droppers, Garret. "The Population of Japan in the Tokugawa Period." *Transactions of the Asiatic Society of Japan* 22 (1894): 253–284.

Ebisawa Arimichi. "Relation Between the Ethics of *Bushidō* and Christianity." *Cultural Nippon* 7, 3 (November 1939): 1–32; and 7, 4 (December 1939): 9–42.

Fisher, Galen, trans. "*Daigaku Wakumon*. A discussion of 'Public Questions in the Light of the Great Learning,' by Kumazawa Banzan." *Transactions of the Asiatic Society of Japan* 16 (1938): 259–356.

———. "Kumazawa Banzan: His Life and Ideas." *Transactions of the Asiatic Society of Japan* 16 (1938): 221–258.

———. "The Life and Teaching of Nakae Tōju, the Sage of Ōmi." *Transactions of the Asiatic Society of Japan* 36 (1908): 24–94.

Flershem, Robert G. "Some Aspects of Japan Sea Trade in the Tokugawa Period." *Journal of Asian Studies* 23, 3 (1964): 405–416.

Furukawa Tesshi. "The Individual in Japanese Ethics." In Charles A. Moore, ed. *The Japanese Mind*. Honolulu: East-West Center Press, 1967, pp. 228–244.

Gedalecia, David. "Excursion into Substance and Function: The Development of the *T'i-Yung* Paradigm in Chu Hsi." *Philosophy East and West* 24, 4 (1974): 444–451.

Gubbins, J. H. "Laws of the Tokugawa Period." *Transactions of the Asiatic Society of Japan* 26 (1898): 154–162.

———. "A Samurai Manual." *Transactions and Proceedings of the Japan Society, London* 9 (1910): 140–156.

Haga T. "Notes of Japanese Schools of Philosophy." *Transactions of the Asiatic Society of Japan* 20 (1892): 134–147.

Hall, J. Carey. "Dazai on Buddhism." *Transactions of the Asiatic Society of Japan* 38 (1910): 23–35.

———. "Japanese Feudal Laws III—the Tokugawa Legislation Parts I-III." *Transactions of the Asiatic Society of Japan* 38 (1911): 269–331; Part 4 in *TASJ* 41 (1913): 683–803.

———. "Teijō's Family Instruction: A Samurai's Ethical Bequest to His Posterity (1763)." *Transactions and Proceedings of the Japan Society, London* 14 (1915–1916): 128–157.

Hall, John W. "The Castle Town and Japan's Modern Urbanization." *Far Eastern Quarterly* 15, 1 (1955): 37–56. Reprinted in J. W. Hall and M. B. Jansen, eds., *Studies in the Institutional History of Early Modern Japan*. Princeton: Princeton University Press, 1968.

———. "The Confucian Teacher in Tokugawa Japan." In David Nivison and Arthur Wright, eds. *Confucianism in Action*. Stanford: Stanford University Press, 1959, pp. 268–301.

———. "E. H. Norman on Tokugawa Japan." *Journal of Japanese Studies* 3, 2 (1977): 365–374.

———. "Feudalism in Japan—A Reassessment." *Comparative Studies in Society and History* 5 (October 1962): 15–51.

———. "Foundations of the Modern Japanese Daimyo." *Journal of Asian Studies* 20, 3 (1961): 317–329.

———. "Ikeda Mitsumasa and the Bizen Flood of 1654." In Arthur Craig and Donald Shively, eds. *Personality in Japanese History*. Berkeley: University of California Press, 1970, pp. 57–80.

Harootunian, Harry D. "The Functions of China in Tokugawa Thought." In Iriye Akira, ed. *The Chinese and the Japanese*. Princeton: Princeton University Press, 1980, pp. 9–36.

Hatton, Russell. "Ch'i's Role Within the Psychology of Chu Hsi." *Journal of Chinese Philosophy* 9, 4 (1982): 441–469.

Hocking, William E. "Chu Hsi's Theory of Knowledge." *Harvard Journal of Asiatic Studies* 1 (1936): 109–127.

Huang Siu-chi. "Chang Tsai's Concept of *Ch'i*." *Philosophy East and West* 18, 4 (1968): 247–259.

Hu Shih. "The Scientific Spirit and Method in Chinese Philosophy." In Charles A. Moore, ed. *The Chinese Mind*. Honolulu: East-West Center Press, 1967. Since 1971 published by the University Press of Hawaii. pp. 104–131.

Iki Hiroyuki. "Wang Yang-ming's Doctrine of Innate Knowledge of the Good." *Philosophy East and West* 11, 1 & 2 (1961): 27–47.

Ishida Ichirō. "Tokugawa Feudal Society and Neo-Confucian Thought." *Philosophical Studies of Japan* 5 (1964): 1–37.

Ishikawa Ken. "On Kaibara Ekiken's Thought and Reasoning as Expressed in his *Yamato Zokukun*." *Cultural Nippon* 7, 1 (April 1939): 23–35.

Itō Tasaburō. "The Book Banning Policy of the Tokugawa Shogunate." *Acta Asiatica* 22 (1972): 36–61.

Iwadō Tamotsu. "*Hagakure Bushidō* or the Book of the Warrior." (I & II) *Cultural Nippon* 11, 3 (November 1939): 33–55; *Cultural Nippon* 11, 4 (December 1939): 57–78.

Katō Eiichi. "Development of Japanese Studies on *Sakoku* (Closing the Country): A Survey." *Acta Asiatica* 22 (1972): 84–103.

Katō Hidetoshi. "The Significance of the Period of National Seclusion Reconsidered." *Journal of Japanese Studies* 7, 1 (1981): 85–109.

Kim, Ha Tai. "The Religious Dimension of Neo-Confucianism." *Philosophy East and West* 27, 3 (1977): 337–348.

Kirby, R. J. "Food and Wealth. An Essay by Dazai Jun." *Transactions of the Asiatic Society of Japan* 35 (1908): 115–190.

———. "Translations of Dazai Jun's Economic Essay upon 'Doing Nothing' and 'Divination.' " *Transactions of the Asiatic Society of Japan* 41 (1913): 195–213.

———. "Translations of Dazai Jun's Essay on *Gakusei* (Educational Control)." *Transactions of the Asiatic Society of Japan* 34 (1907): 133–144.

Keene, Donald. "Individuality and Pattern in Japanese Literature." In *Landscapes and Portraits*. London: Secker and Warburg, 1972: 40–51.

Kline, Carol. *Early Tokugawa Education and Ethics: An Annotated Translation of 'The General Introduction' to the Five Constants by Kaibara Ekken*. Master's Thesis, Columbia University, 1970.

Knox, G. William, trans. "Autobiography of Arai Hakuseki." *Transactions of the Asiatic Society of Japan* 30 (1903): 89–238.

———. "A Japanese Philosopher." *Transactions of the Asiatic Society of Japan* 20 (1892): 1–133.

Lane, Richard. "The Beginnings of the Modern Japanese Novel: *Kanazōshi,* 1600–1682." *Harvard Journal of Asian Studies* 20 (1957): 644–701.

Laures, Johannes. "Takayana Ukon, A Critical Essay." *Monumenta Nipponica* 5, 1 (1942): 86–112.

Lloyd, Arthur. "Historical Development of the *Shushi* Philosophy in Japan." *Transactions of the Asiatic Society of Japan* 34 (1907): 5–80.

Marti, Jeffrey. "Intellectual and Moral Foundations of Empirical Agronomy in Eighteenth-Century Japan." *Select Papers from the Center for Far Eastern Studies, University of Chicago.* No. 2 (1977–1978).

McClatchie, Thomas. "The Castle of Yedo." *Transactions of the Asiatic Society of Japan* 6 (1878): 119–150.

———. "The Feudal Mansions of Yedo." *Transactions of the Asiatic Society of Japan* 7 (1879): 157–182.

McCune, George M. "The Exchange of Envoys Between Korea and Japan during the Tokugawa Period." *Far Eastern Quarterly* 5, no. 3 (1946): 308–325.

McMullen, Ian James. "Kumazawa Banzan and *Jitsugaku:* Toward Pragmatic Action." In Wm. T. de Bary and Irene Bloom, eds. *Principle and Practicality.* New York: Columbia University Press, 1979, pp. 337–373.

———. "Non-Agnatic Adoption: A Confucian Controversy in Seventeenth-Century and Eighteenth-Century Japan." *Harvard Journal of Asiatic Studies* 35 (1975): 133–189.

———. "Rulers or Fathers? A Casuistical Problem in Early Modern Japanese Thought." *Past and Present: A Journal of Historical Studies* 116 (August 1987): 56–97.

Meriwether, C. "The Life of Date Masamune." *Transactions of the Asiatic Society of Japan* 21 (1893): 3–105.

Minamoto Ryōen. "The Development of the *Jitsugaku* Concept in the Tokugawa Period." *Philosophical Studies of Japan* 11 (1975): 61–93.

———. "*Jitsugaku* and Empirical Rationalism in the First Half of the Tokugawa Period," in Wm. T. de Bary and I. Bloom, eds. *Principle and Practicality.* New York: Columbia University Press, 1979, pp. 375–469.

Minear, Richard H. "Ogyū Sorai's 'Instructions for Students': A Translation and Commentary." *Harvard Journal of Asiatic Studies* 36 (1976): 5–81.

Mitsui Takaharu. "Travel in the Tokugawa Era." *Cultural Nippon* 7, 3 (November 1939): 69–80.

Moore, Ray A. "Adoption and Samurai Mobility in Tokugawa Japan." *Journal of Asian Studies* 29, 3 (1970): 617–632.

Mou Tsang-san. "Confucianism as Religion." Douglas Lancashire, trans. *Chinese Essays on Religion and Faith.* San Francisco: Chinese Materials Center, 1981, pp. 22–43.

Nagazumi Yoko. "Japan's Isolationist Policy as Seen through Dutch Source Materials." *Acta Asiatica* 22 (1972): 18–35.

Najita, Tetsuo. "Intellectual Change in Early Eighteenth-Century Tokugawa Confucianism." *Journal of Asian Studies* 34, 4 (1975): 932–944.

————. "Political Economism in the Thought of Dazai Shundai (1680–1747)." *Journal of Asian Studies* 31, 4 (1972): 821–839.

Nakai, Kate Wildman. "The Naturalization of Confucianism in Tokugawa Japan: The Problem of Sinocentrism." *Harvard Journal of Asian Studies* 40 (1980): 157–199.

Nakamura Hajime. "Suzuki Shōsan, 1579–1655, and the Spirit of Capitalism in Japanese Buddhism." Trans. by Wm. Johnston. *Monumenta Nipponica* 22, 1–2 (1967): 1–14.

Nivison, David S. "The Problem of 'Knowledge' and 'Action' in Chinese Thought Since Wang Yang-ming." In Arthur Wright, ed. *Studies in Chinese Thought*. Chicago: University of Chicago Press, 1953, pp. 112–145.

Norman, E. Herbert. "Andō Shoeki and the Anatomy of Japanese Feudalism." *Transactions of the Asiatic Society of Japan* 2 (1949).

Okada Takehiko. "The Chu Hsi and Wang Yang-ming Schools at the End of the Ming and Tokugawa Periods." *Philosophy East and West* 23, 1–2 (1973): 139–162.

————. "Practical Learning in the Chu Hsi School: Yamazaki Ansai and Kaibara Ekken." In Wm. T. de Bary and Irene Bloom, eds. *Principle and Practicality*. New York: Columbia University Press, 1979, pp. 231–305.

Purnell, C. J. "The Log Book of William Adams, 1614–1619 and Related Documents." *Transactions and Proceedings of the Japan Society, London* 13 (1915): 156–302.

Ramseyer, J. Mark. "Thrift and Diligence: House Codes of Tokugawa Merchant Families." *Monumenta Nipponica* 34 (1979): 209–230.

Riess, Ludwig. "History of the English Factory at Hirado (1613–1622)." *Transactions of the Asiatic Society of Japan* 26 (1898): 1–114.

Robertson, Jennifer. "Rooting the Pine: *Shingaku* Methods of Organization." *Monumenta Nipponica* 34, 3 (1979): 311–332.

Rozman, Gilbert. "Edo's Importance in the Changing Tokugawa Society." *Journal of Japanese Studies* 1, 1 (1974): 91–112.

Sagara Tōru. "The Spiritual Strength and Independence in *Bushidō*." *Acta Asiatica* 25 (1973): 91–106.

Sakai Atsuharu. "Kaibara Ekiken and *Onna-Daigaku*." *Cultural Nippon* 7, 4 (December 1939): 43–56.

Scheiner, Irwin. "Benevolent Lords and Honorable Peasants: Rebellion and Peasant Consciousness in Tokugawa Japan." In Tetsuo Najita and Irwin Scheiner, ed. *Japanese Thought in the Tokugawa Period*. Chicago: University of Chicago Press, 1978, pp. 39–62.

————. "The Mindful Peasant: Sketches for a Study of Rebellion." *Journal of Asian Studies* 32, 4 (1973): 579–591.

Shirai Mitsutarō. "A Brief History of Botany in Old Japan." In *Scientific Japan: Past and Present*. Tokyo: National Research Council of Japan, 1926, pp. 213–227.

Shively, Donald H. "Sumptuary Regulation and Status in Early Tokugawa Japan." *Harvard Journal of Asiatic Studies* 25 (1964–1965): 123–164.

———. "Tokugawa Tsunayoshi, the Genroku Shogun." In Albert Craig and Donald Shively, eds. *Personality in Japanese History.* Berkeley: University of California Press, 1970, pp. 85–126.

Smith, Neil S. "An Introduction to Some Japanese Economic Writings of the Eighteenth Century." *Transactions of the Asiatic Society of Japan* 11 (1934): 32–105.

Smith, Robert J. "Small Families, Small Households, and Residential Instability: Town and City in 'Pre-Modern' Japan." In Peter Laslett, ed. *Household and Family in Past Times.* Cambridge: Cambridge University Press, 1972, pp. 429–471.

Smith, Thomas C. "The Japanese Village in the Seventeenth-Century." *Journal of Economic History* 12, 1 (1952): 1–20.

———. "Old Values and New Techniques in the Modernization of Japan." *Far Eastern Quarterly* 14, 3 (May 1955): 355–363.

Steenstrup, Carl. "The Gokurakuji Letter." *Monumenta Nipponica* 32, 1 (1977): 1–34.

———. "The Imagawa Letter: A Muromachi Warrior's Code of Conduct which Became a Tokugawa Schoolbook." *Monumenta Nipponica* 28, 3 (1973): 295–316.

Strayer, Joseph R. "The Tokugawa Period and Japanese Feudalism." In J. W. Hall and M. Jansen, eds. *Studies in the Institutional History of Early Modern Japan.* Princeton: Princeton University Press, 1968, pp. 3–14.

T'ang Chün-i. "Chang Tsai's Theory of Mind and its Metaphysical Basis." *Philosophy East and West* 6, 2 (1956): 113–136.

———. "The Criticisms of Wang Yang-ming's teachings as raised by his contemporaries." *Philosophy East and West* 23, 1–2 (1973): 163–186.

———. "The Development of the Concept of Moral Mind from Wang Yang-ming to Wang Chi." In Wm. T. de Bary, ed. *Self and Society in Ming Thought.* New York: Columbia University Press, 1970, pp. 93–119.

———. "The Spirit of Religion and Modern Man." Douglas Lancashire, trans. *Chinese Essays on Religion and Faith.* San Francisco: Chinese Materials Center, 1981, pp. 48–52.

Tashirō Kazui. "Foreign Relations During the Edo Period: *Sakoku* Reexamined." Trans. by Susan D. Videen. *Journal of Japanese Studies* 8, 2 (1982): 283–306.

Taylor, Rodney L. "The Centered Self: Religious Autobiography in the Neo-Confucian Tradition." *History of Religions,* 1978: 266–281.

———. "Confucianism: Scripture and the Sage." In Frederick M. Denny and Rodney L. Taylor, eds. *The Holy Book in Comparative Perspective.* Columbia: University of South Carolina Press, 1985, pp. 181–203.

———. "Neo-Confucianism, Sagehood and the Religious Dimension." *Journal of Chinese Philosophy* 2 (1975): 389–415.

———. "Of Animals and Man: The Confucian Perspective," in Tom Regan, ed. *Animal Sacrifices: Religious Perspectives on the Use of Animals in Science.* Philadelphia: Temple University Press, 1986, pp. 237–263.

———. "Proposition and Praxis: The Dilemma of Neo-Confucian Syncretism." *Philosophy East and West* 32, 2 (1982): 187–199.

———. "The Sudden/Gradual Paradigm and Neo-Confucian Mind-Cultivation." *Philosophy East and West* 33, 1 (1983): 17–34.

Toby, Ronald P. "Carnival of the Aliens: Korean Embassies in Edo-Period Art and Popular Culture." *Monumenta Nipponica* 41, 4 (1986): 415–456.

———. "Reopening the Question of *Sakoku:* Diplomacy in the Legitimation of the Tokugawa Bakufu." *Journal of Japanese Studies* 3, 2 (1977): 323–363.

Tomoeda Ryūtarō. "The Characteristics of Chu Hsi's Thought." *Acta Asiatica* 21 (October 1971): 52–72.

Totman, Conrad. "Tokugawa Peasants: Win, Lose, or Draw?" *Monumenta Nipponica* 41, 4 (1986): 457–476.

Tu Wei-ming. "The Creative Tension Between *Jen* and *Li.*" *Philosophy East and West* 18, 1–2 (1968): 29–39.

———. "*Li* as a Process of Humanization." *Philosophy East and West* 22, 2 (1972): 187–201.

———. "The 'moral universal' from the perspectives of East Asian Thought." *Philosophy East and West* 31, 3 (1981): 259–267.

———. "The Neo-Confucian Concept of Man." *Philosophy East and West* 21, 1 (1971): 79–87.

———. "On Neo-Confucianism and Human Relatedness." *Religion and the Family.* Ed. by George A. De Vos and Takao Sofue. Berkeley: University of California Press, 1986, pp. 111–125.

———. "Subjectivity and Ontological Reality—An Interpretation of Wang Yang-ming's Mode of Thinking." *Philosophy East and West* 23, 1–2 (1973): 187–205.

———. "Wang Yang-ming's Four Sentence Teaching." *Eastern Buddhist* 7, no. 2 (October 1974): 32–48.

Uenaka Shuzo. "Last Testament in Exile: Yamaga Sokō's *Haisho Zampitsu.*" *Monumenta Nipponica* 32, 2 (1977): 125–152.

Vaporis, Constantine N. "Post Stations and Assisting Villages: Corvée Labor and Peasant Contention." *Monumenta Nipponica* 41, 4 (1986): 377–414.

# Index

447